[WRITING NOW]

[WRITING NOW]
Shaping Words and Images

Lee Odell
Rensselaer Polytechnic Institute

Susan M. Katz
North Carolina State University

Bedford/St. Martin's
Boston • New York

For Bedford/St. Martin's

Senior Developmental Editor: Kristin Bowen
Senior Production Supervisor: Nancy Myers
Marketing Manager: Molly Parke
Editorial Assistant: Stacey Gawronski
Art Director: Lucy Krikorian
Copy Editor: Lisa Wehrle
Text Design, Production Management, and Composition: Nesbitt Graphics, Inc.
Photo Research: Susan McDermott Barlow
Cover Design: Kristin Bowen and Billy Boardman
Cover Art: Bridge. © Sigmund M/plainpicture/Veer
Printing and Binding: RR Donnelley and Sons

President: Joan E. Feinberg
Editorial Director: Denise B. Wydra
Editor in Chief: Karen S. Henry
Director of Development: Erica T. Appel
Director of Marketing: Karen R. Soeltz
Director of Editing, Design, and Production: Marcia Cohen
Assistant Director of Editing, Design, and Production: Elise S. Kaiser
Managing Editor: Elizabeth M. Schaaf

Writing Now: Shaping Words and Images was formerly titled *Writing in a Visual Age*.

Library of Congress Control Number: 2008933122

Manufactured in the United States of America.

4   3   2   1   0   9
f   e   d   c   b   a

For information, write: Bedford/St. Martin's, 75 Arlington Street, Boston, MA 02116
(617-399-4000)

ISBN-10: 0-312-47347-8
ISBN-13: 978-0-312-47347-1

Acknowledgments

Preface

Writing isn't magic, but then magic isn't magic either.
Magicians know their craft, and writers must also know their craft.

—Donald Murray

Some years ago, a colleague told us this story:

> One of my students asked me what he needed to do in order to get an A in my writing course. When I told him I couldn't give him a very precise answer to that question, he looked at me as though I were either a fool or a knave—a fool because I couldn't answer what seemed to him a straightforward question about my discipline or a knave because I knew the answer but wouldn't tell him.

We know our colleague is right. There is no "magic" formula that will turn students into superb writers. But Don Murray is also right: Writing entails craft, and insofar as writing is a craft, it can be learned. We created *Writing Now* to guide students as they learn and improve in this essential craft.

As we have worked on this book and experimented with our ideas in the laboratory of our own classrooms, we have been guided by two basic assumptions. The first is that "writing now" is no longer just about words. It is, rather, a process of shaping words and images into a coherent message. Perhaps, as a number of scholars have suggested, we should replace the term *writing* with the term *composing*. But whichever term we use, we have come to recognize that it is increasingly important for students to integrate visual and verbal information, whether they are writing an evaluative essay for their composition class, reporting results of some research in a biology class, or creating a Web site for an upper-division marketing course.

Our second assumption is that no matter what sort of composing students are doing, they need help with improving their writing skills. More specifically, they need strategies or techniques that will help them communicate effectively in a wide range of media for a range of writing situations. Granted, the process of composing is not neat or predictable. But when we look at the work of highly successful writers—whether students or professionals—we can see habits of mind, or ways of perceiving and reflecting on a topic and formulating and expressing ideas. If we introduce students to these strategies and habits of mind we can help them adapt or apply them to achieve a given rhetorical purpose. We present the strategies within each genre chapter of *Writing Now* to increase students' chances of finding something worthwhile to say and saying it effectively. We've seen these strategies help our own students, and we are confident they can help yours as well. Our purpose in teaching these strategies is also to accomplish goals articulated by the Council of Writing Program Administrators. Our writing courses must help students do the following.

▶ **Understand the rhetorical context** within which they are working, addressing the needs of different audiences, creating a voice that is appropriate for a given audience, understanding the conceptual and stylistic demands of various genres, and making everything in a text work toward their purpose in writing

▶ **Read critically**, identifying the strengths and weaknesses of any text (verbal or visual), whether it's one they have composed or a text created by their classmates or professional writers

▶ **Work through the processes** of developing their ideas and creating and revising a draft

▶ **Communicate through a variety of genres**, such as memoirs, reports, position papers, and proposals

Writing Now helps students accomplish these goals in a variety of ways. For a guide to the WPA Outcomes Statement and more on how *Writing Now* addresses these outcomes for students, see page xvii.

▷ How to Use This Book

The structure of *Writing Now* offers flexibility for instructors choosing a genre approach, with assignment chapters that cover six of the key genres students encounter in their college work. These assignment chapters are organized around practical how-to strategy boxes for the basic elements of the composing process (such as developing and organizing ideas, creating an appropriate voice, and integrating visual and verbal information). These chapters offer all students complete support as they work through their assignments. More accomplished writers can choose the strategies that work best for them, while those who may need help with a particular step find plenty of encouragement and explanation. After a chapter on how to read actively and critically, the book is divided into three main parts:

▶ **Writing Assignments:** The genre chapters include Memoirs, Profiles, Reports, Position Papers, Evaluations, and Proposals

▶ **Strategies for Design and Research:** Reading and Writing about Visual Images, Designing Pages and Screens, Starting Research and Finding Sources, Conducting Field Research, Evaluating Sources and Taking Notes, and Documenting Sources: MLA and APA Style

▶ **Strategies for Special Writing Situations:** Writing for Essay Exams, Writing Portfolios, Writing for the Community, Writing in Online Environments, and Making Oral Presentations

The book concludes with a Glossary of Visual and Rhetorical Terms. In addition to writing-related terms, the glossary includes definitions, examples, and cross-references for many terms related to visuals and design.

Any decision about how to use a textbook depends on a particular instructor's teaching style. We have designed *Writing Now* to be flexible, to suit a variety of teaching strategies. As do many writing teachers, we often use selections in the "Reading to Write" section of each chapter to stimulate class discussion. But we also use those selections to help students read like writers, identifying rhetorical strategies they might incorporate into their own writing.

Although we occasionally require students to read all the selections in a "Reading to Write" section, we never have students read all of a given chapter at one sitting. Instead our decision about what we will have students read depends on the sort of help students need at any one point of the composing process or any one point of the students' development over the course of a semester.

Our own experience persuades us that our students are likely to need help accomplishing at least some—more likely all—of the following tasks. All the genre chapters in *Writing Now* offer help with each of these tasks within the guides.

▶ **Understanding audience and purpose** by first determining what readers are likely to know and care about and then deciding what goals the writing is intended to accomplish

▶ **Exploring a topic and developing ideas** in order to have something worthwhile to say

▶ **Engaging the audience**, especially by creating introductions that will give readers a reason to begin (and continue) reading

▶ **Creating a voice** (a set of attitudes, a personality) that will let readers like and/or trust the writer

▶ **Organizing**, helping readers follow a train of thought or find the information they are looking for

▶ **Concluding effectively**, usually by reiterating the main point or saying something that will prompt readers to think or act in a particular way

▶ **Integrating visual information**, using images, charts, graphs, and other visual elements to enhance readers' understanding of the topic

Early in the semester, we work through these tasks more or less in this sequence, although we show students that this is not a neat, linear process. As students' understanding increases and they become accustomed to these tasks, the flexibility of the genre chapters will allow us to focus on tasks with which students need more help.

▷ Special Features of *Writing Now*

Writing Now is a radical revision that simplifies and streamlines our earlier work, *Writing in a Visual Age. Writing Now* reflects our extensive teaching and research on composing with both words and images. We rethought and redesigned the book with an eye on the demands of today's writing courses, giving students clearly laid out steps for reading and writing in a format that will engage and help students through each assignment. Some highlights are listed here.

Genre-Specific Advice

We know that genres overlap, that any two genres may have some of the same features. But we also know that different genres make somewhat different demands on writers. *Writing Now*'s genre-specific advice helps students negotiate these demands by giving them concrete strategies that address the needs of each genre. To write about personal experiences in a memoir, for example, students learn the importance of telling a good story. To create an effective proposal, on the other hand, students need strategies to identify a problem, explain how the problem can be solved, and respond to counterarguments.

Genre-specific reading strategies open each assignment chapter and help students connect their reading with the assignment at hand.

Guides to writing for six genres—memoirs, profiles, reports, position papers, evaluations, and proposals—are presented within each assignment chapter. These are streamlined yet thorough guides to writing with clearly laid out steps for writing each assignment. Advice is presented in unique how-to boxes that offer a choice of strategies, illustrated with examples from that chapter's readings. With a consistent focus on important rhetorical concerns, the guides help students through the challenges of understanding the rhetorical context for their own work and following a clear process for their writing.

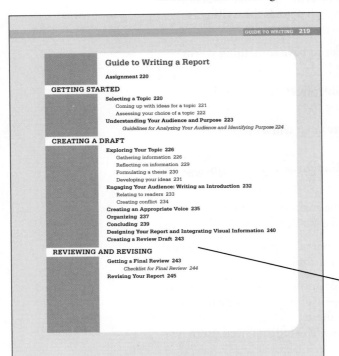

GUIDE TO WRITING   219

Guide to Writing a Report

Assignment 220

GETTING STARTED

Selecting a Topic 220
    Coming up with ideas for a topic 221
    Assessing your choice of a topic 222
Understanding Your Audience and Purpose 223
    Guidelines for Analyzing Your Audience and Identifying Purpose 224

CREATING A DRAFT

Exploring Your Topic 226
    Gathering information 226
    Reflecting on information 229
    Formulating a thesis 230
    Developing your ideas 231
Engaging Your Audience: Writing an Introduction 232
    Relating to readers 233
    Creating conflict 234
Creating an Appropriate Voice 235
Organizing 237
Concluding 239
Designing Your Report and Integrating Visual Information 240
Creating a Review Draft 243

REVIEWING AND REVISING

Getting a Final Review 243
    Checklist for Final Review 244
Revising Your Report 245

Each Guide to Writing opens with a directory to highlight the steps of each assignment.

A Visual Presentation of Key Information

The illustrations and visual explanations in *Writing Now*—incorporating charts, photographs, and icons—highlight key information to help students work through the steps for each assignment.

Designed for clear, easy reference, *Writing Now* offers complete support for the writing process in an inviting, easy-to-navigate layout.

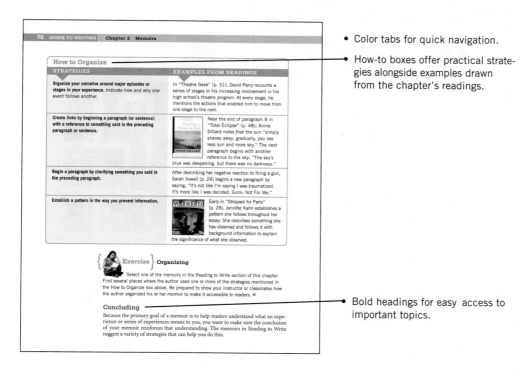

- Color tabs for quick navigation.

- How-to boxes offer practical strategies alongside examples drawn from the chapter's readings.

- Bold headings for easy access to important topics.

Icons help highlight student voices throughout, appearing alongside student essays that provide practical models for all assignments and in unique Q & A boxes that interview students on the choices they made during the writing process.

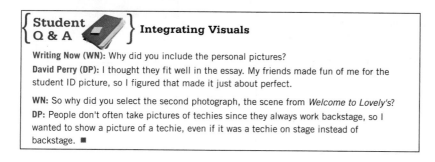

Student Q & A **Integrating Visuals**

Writing Now (WN): Why did you include the personal pictures?

David Perry (DP): I thought they fit well in the essay. My friends made fun of me for the student ID picture, so I figured that made it just about perfect.

WN: So why did you select the second photograph, the scene from *Welcome to Lovely's*?

DP: People don't often take pictures of techies since they always work backstage, so I wanted to show a picture of a techie, even if it was a techie on stage instead of backstage. ■

Readings for Students at Home in the Modern World

Thirty-nine engaging, contemporary readings provide models from a variety of genres and media—books, magazines, newspapers, and journals. Substantive readings—many from well-known sources and writers (Malcolm Gladwell, Sarah Vowell, Al Gore)—are presented much as they were in the original publication.

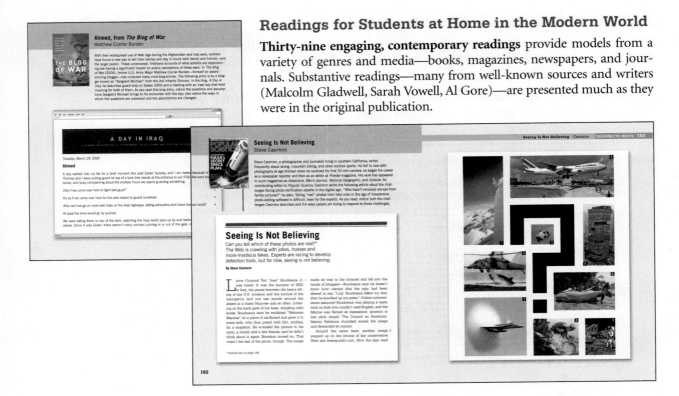

Practical advice on critical reading in Chapter 1 helps students develop a process for reading, with instructions for reading analytically, taking notes, and annotating, including annotated examples.

Chapter 1, Reading: Words and Images, helps students read critically and connect their reading and writing.

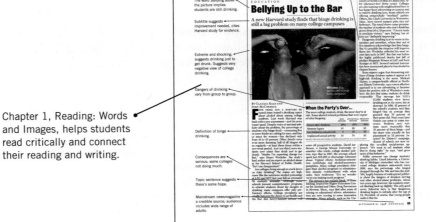

Complete Coverage of Research and Documentation

Annotated sample sources give step-by-step guidelines to help students effectively cite print and electronic materials in MLA and APA styles.

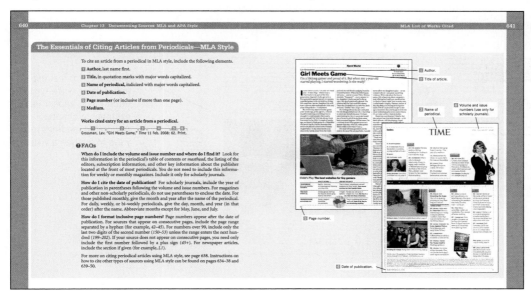

A complete chapter on field research enables students to take their research projects into the real world.

Extensive Help with Analyzing and Producing Visual Texts

Coverage of analyzing and integrating visuals is comprehensive, with genre-specific strategies for design in each of the assignment chapters, in Chapter 9, Designing Pages and Screens, and in strategies throughout the book.

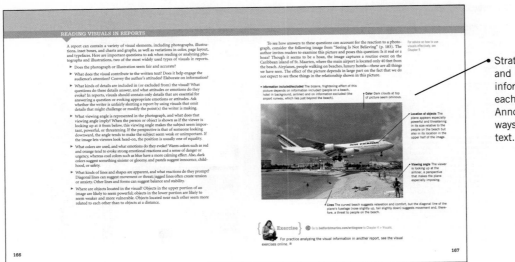

Strategies for reading—and writing with—visual information appear in each genre chapter. Annotated readings model ways to analyze a visual text.

A complete chapter on analyzing visuals, Chapter 8, Reading and Writing about Visual Images, offers help for writing a close analysis of a visual image, including three student essays analyzing a public service ad, posters, and a painting.

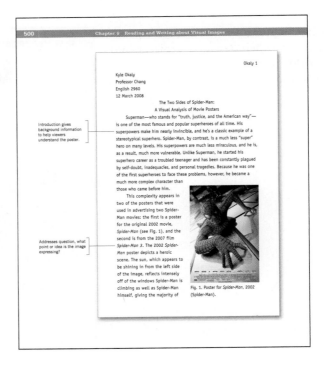

An album of sample images in Chapter 8 offers opportunities for analysis.

Chapter 9, Designing Pages and Screens, offers coverage of basic design principles, guidelines for formatting documents effectively, lots of samples, and advice for incorporating or manipulating images carefully and ethically.

Sample visuals guide students to use graphics and images successfully.

▷ A Complete Package for Writing Courses

CompClass for Writing Now at **yourcompclass.com** is an easy-to-use online course space that integrates all the innovative media supporting *Writing Now,* including the *Writing Now* online student center, *Re:Writing Plus,* and more. In *CompClass,* students can read assignments, do their work and peer review, and see their grades all in one place; and instructors can easily monitor student progress and give feedback right away. To order *CompClass* packaged with *Writing Now,* use ISBN-10: 0-312-55690-X or ISBN-13: 978-0-312-55690-7.

Writing Now e-book at **bedfordstmartins.com/writingnow** is available online, all the time. Easy to search and use, the e-book is integrated with all the free resources available on the Student Center site. The e-book allows students to bookmark the sections they use most often, add their own examples and notes, and print material they might need when not online. The e-book is available as a stand-alone with a value price or packaged for free with the print book. To order the *Writing Now e-Book* packaged with the print book, use ISBN-10: 0-312-60920-5 or ISBN-13: 978-0-312-60920-7.

Student Center for *Writing Now* at **bedfordstmartins.com/writingnow.** This free companion Web site complements and extends the coverage of *Writing Now.* It includes a wealth of resources, including interactive visual exercises, checklists for working in each genre, help with research, tutorials, sample student essays, and more.

Re:Writing Plus at **bedfordstmartins.com/rewritingplus** neatly gathers our collections of premium digital content into one online library for composition, including hundreds of model documents; *i·cite visualizing sources,* which brings research to life through animation, tutorials, and hands-on source practice; and *Peer Factor,* the first-ever peer review game. New in 2009 is *VideoCentral,* a growing collection of over fifty brief videos for the writing classroom, in which real writers talk about what it means to write at work, at school, and to change the world. *Re:Writing Plus* is available stand-alone or packaged at a discount with the print book. To order *Re:Writing Plus* packaged with *Writing Now,* use ISBN-10: 0-312-60945-0 or ISBN-13: 978-0-312-60945-0.

Instructor's Resource Manual for Writing Now by Susan M. Katz (ISBN-10: 0-312-53940-1 or ISBN-13: 978-0-312-53940-5). Available on the book's Web site, this handy manual provides a comprehensive guide to teaching writing with *Writing Now.* It features thorough advice on working with each of the genres covered in Part 1, special help for teachers new to working with visual texts, and more.

▷ Acknowledgments

Many people have helped us make this book a reality. We are especially indebted to students who have allowed us to use their work as sample papers in this book: Jenna Gatsch, Stephanie Guzik, Melanie Markham, Kyle Okaly, Michelle Pelersi, David Perry, Jonathan Quimby, Ashley B. Roberts, Lauren Spinelli, Samantha Sterner, Margaret Tomeo, and Zane Van Dusen. We are also grateful to the other students who have contributed materials to the book and the Web site: Holly Adams, Ryan Balzer, Laura Beyer, Matthew Blake, Joshua Patrick Brien, Nathan Burstein, Michelle Williams Chipley, Jonathan Dance, Justin Ferrazzano, Crystal L. Gilson, Ivan Hall, Diane Kalendra, Joshua Khoury, Aaron Kline, JoyceLynn Lagula, Michael Laurino, Carolyn Leverett, Adam Lowry, Kristy Megill, Jenny Ming, David Nicolai, Tiffany Beth Peters, Donna Phillips, John David Roberts, Shirl Rogers, Raghav Sachdev, Kevin Sichler, Natasha Sim, David Stepp, and Patrick Vitarius.

We are grateful to colleagues whose ideas and discussion have helped us with this book: Gabriele Bechtel, Simone Billings, Ken Denberg, Sandrine Dincki, Kim Duckett, Andreas Karatsolis, Jennifer King, Barbara J. Lewis, Donna Phillips, Jason Pickavance, Shaun Slattery, and Jason Waite.

We also want to thank the following reviewers for their valuable insights and suggestions over the course of the book's development: Josh Adair, Northern Illinois University; Michelle Allred, University of Missouri–Kansas City; Maria Assif, Truman College; Martha K. Bailie, Iowa Central Community College; Michelle Buchanan, Arizona State University; Annmarie Chiarini, The Community College of Baltimore County, Essex; Ron Christiansen, Salt Lake Community College; Avon Crisimore, Indiana University–Purdue University; Stephanie L. Dowdle, Salt Lake Community College; Clark Draney, College of Southern Idaho; Justin Everett, University of the Sciences in Philadelphia; Blaise Farina, Rensselaer Polytechnic Institute; Rebecca Flannagan, Francis Marion University; Vivian Foss, University of Wisconsin Oshkosh; Callae Frazier, Iowa State University; John Gides, California State University, Northridge; Jennifer Golz, Tennessee Technological University; Letizia Guglielmo, Kennesaw State University; Amy Hawkins, Columbia College Chicago; Cynthia Haynes, Clemson University; Brenda Helmbrecht, California Polytechnic State University; Damla Isik, University of Arizona; Melanie Jenkins, Snow College; Beth Ann Jones, Azusa Pacific University; Andreas Karatsolis, Albany College of Pharmacy; Julie Kearney, Penn State, Harrisburg; Darci Kellen, Iowa State University; Peggy Kilgore, Tennessee Technological University; Dana Kinnison, University of Missouri–Columbia; Eric Lane, The University of Tennessee at Chattanooga; Barbara J. Lewis, Rensselaer Polytechnic Institute; Patricia Lynne, Framingham State College; Molly Magestro, Iowa State University; Rita Malenczyk, Eastern Connecticut State University; Ann M. McGill, Merrimack College; Billy McGowan, Worcester Polytechnic Institute; Jim McKeown, McLennan Community College; Pat McQueeney, Johnson County Community College; Erica Messenger, Bowling Green State University; Nicole Montoya, University of Texas at El Paso; Donna

Niday, Iowa State University; Leanora Olivia, University of Colorado at Boulder; Sandra Olmstead, St. Louis University; Colleen Page, Rockford College; Laura Palmer, Texas Tech University; Carole Papper, Hofstra University; Jason Pickavance, Salt Lake Community College; Kelly Ritter, Southern Connecticut State University; Larry Roderer, J. Sargeant Reynolds Community College; Michael John Schofield, California State University, Northridge; Ingrid Schreck, College of Marin; Andrew Scott, Ball State University; Erica L. Scott, Slippery Rock University; Eileen Seifert, DePaul University; Dee Seligman, Foothill College; Mark Smith, Valdosta State University; Lynn Sykes, College of DuPage; Grace Talusan, Tufts University; Alice L. Trupe, Bridgewater College; Jason Waite, Western Oregon University; Stacia Watkins, Middle Tennessee State University; Patricia Webb, Arizona State University; and Stephanie Zerkel-Humbert, Metropolitan Community College, Maple Woods. We think that their comments have done much to make our work more useful to students and instructors alike.

We are deeply grateful to a number of people at Bedford/St. Martin's: Joan Feinberg, who supported this project from the very outset, and Denise Wydra, who kept the big picture in focus; Genevieve Hamilton, who guided us through initial stages; Kristin Bowen, who helped us make major improvements to the manuscript and who helped us with finishing touches; Laura Arcari, who helped with Parts 2 and 3; Anne Noonan and Mary Sanger, who saw us through the production process; Erica Appel and Karen Henry, who guided the book toward publication; and Brielle Matson and Nancy Myers, who gave painstaking attention to every detail. We also want to thank Harriet Wald and Victoria Sandbrook for their work on the book's Web site and media; Jerilyn Bockorick for her innovative book design; Billy Boardman for our cover; and Sandy Schechter, Sue McDermott Barlow, and Sue Brekka for securing permissions for all of the text and art. We are also grateful to all of the other editors and in-house people who made contributions large and small: Lisa Wehrle, Karita dos Santos, Molly Parke, Mary Ellen Smith, Nick Carbone, Melissa Cooke, and Stacey Gawronski. Susan wishes to thank Paul for his love and support when she was working on yet another revision. Lee wishes to thank Geraldine Anderson, Arthur Bushing, and Richard Young—whose influence continues to this day—and, of course, Linda, whose love and patience have made so much possible. Finally, both of us acknowledge our indebtedness to students we have worked with over the years. We think we have helped our students become better writers; we know they have helped us become better teachers.

Lee Odell
Susan M. Katz

▷ Features of *Writing Now* Correlated to the WPA Outcomes Statement

Note: Page references in this chart point to Chapter 4, Reports, for examples when describing features common to all chapters in Part 1 of *Writing Now*.

Rhetorical Knowledge

Desired Outcomes	Relevant Features in *Writing Now*
Focus on a purpose	Each assignment chapter (Chapters 2–7) opens with a discussion of purposes for that genre (see p. 163 in Chapter 4, for example). Each Guide to Writing gives extensive advice on analyzing purpose and the rhetorical context, with questions to ask and a sample student analysis (see pp. 223–26 in Chapter 4).
	Each guide also has a full section for "Getting a Final Review" of a draft that encourages peer review for the draft's purposes (see pp. 243–44).
Respond to the needs of different audiences	▷ **READING REPORTS** In the following section, you will find reports on a variety of topics ranging from the untrustworthiness of digital photography to the search for the science behind moral decision making. Following each report are questions that pertain specifically to the report you have just read. In addition to these specific questions, there are several basic questions you should ask in reading any report. [Questions for Reading Reports] ▶ **Who is the intended audience?** Consider the language, visuals, and information included in (and excluded from) the report. What does the writer appear to be assuming about the following? • Readers' background knowledge of the subject • The audience's values, beliefs, attitudes, or preconceptions regarding the subject • The questions the audience will want to have answered
	Each assignment chapter opens with questions to ask about the audience for that particular genre (see "Reading Reports," p. 164, for example). Each assignment chapter gives extensive advice and guidelines for analyzing audience (see "Understanding Your Audience and Purpose," pp. 223–26 in Chapter 4).
	Each assignment chapter has a full section of strategies for "Engaging Your Audience: Writing an Introduction" (see pp. 232–35).
	Writing Now also focuses on audience when covering such special writing tasks as research projects, oral presentations, and writing for the community, among others (throughout Parts 2 and 3).

continued on next page ▶

Rhetorical Knowledge (continued)

Desired Outcomes	Relevant Features in *Writing Now*
Identify and respond appropriately to different kinds of rhetorical situations	Each of the assignment chapters (Chapters 2–7) opens with brief overviews of rhetorical situations and gives guidelines for analyzing the readings rhetorically (see pp. 163–65, for example). Specific advice on responding to a variety of rhetorical situations appears throughout each chapter's Guide to Writing. Detailed help for analyzing rhetorical situations appears in each guide under the heading "Understanding Your Audience and Purpose" (see pp. 223–26 in Chapter 4). Within this section is a sample student analysis, written by the author of the student essay in the "Reading to Write" section (see pp. 225–26). Student Q & A boxes throughout the guides reveal more about a particular student writer's choices (see pp. 223, 229, and 234, for examples).
Write in multiple genres and use genre conventions appropriate to the rhetorical situation	 The readings represent many genres and have been designed to look much as they did when originally published to highlight important genre conventions and visual elements. Each Guide to Writing in Part 1 points out features of effectively structured writing and helps students develop their own effective structures. See the "Organizing" section (pp. 237–39), for example. Genre-specific design advice appears in each assignment chapter: see "Designing Your Report and Integrating Visual Information," pp. 240–42. Document format is covered in Chapter 9, Designing Pages and Screens.
Adopt appropriate tone	In each assignment chapter, a section on "Creating an Appropriate Voice" (pp. 235–37 in Chapter 4) discusses using appropriate language, details, evidence, quotations, and photographs, among other means, to create an effective, appropriate tone.

Desired Outcomes	Relevant Features in *Writing Now*
Understand how genres shape reading and writing	The readings are designed to look much as they did when originally published—in magazines, journals, online, and so on. "Reading Visuals" sections of all assignment chapters (see pp. 168–218) give students questions and a model for analyzing the visual information and design of various genres and texts. Part 1 chapters also offer readings and writing advice for a variety of rhetorical situations, from writing a report to proposing a solution to evaluating. Reading and working through a chapter, students learn strategies to help them produce appropriate, relevant texts in any setting. (See also Chapter 1, pp. 10–11, for a brief overview of a writer's objectives.)
Understand the nature and development of literacies	{Student Q & A} Selecting Secondary Sources Writing Now (WN): How did you decide which sources to use in your report? Margaret Tomeo (MT): I tried to use information that I kept finding in more than one source. And if I found something in only one source, I tried to find something to back it up. I was looking for sources that matched, that had facts that were agreed on. WN: How did you know you were asking the right questions? MT: I was a member of the audience, and those were the questions I would ask. I just figured that since I was a female athlete, those were the right questions. ■ Student voices are highlighted throughout Part 1. Sample student essays in each chapter offer accessible examples, and Student Q & A boxes feature interviews that highlight the choices students made. The section at the end of each Part 1 chapter, "Taking Stock of Where You Are" (pp. 245–46 in Chapter 4), offers help students can use to assess their own development as writers. Chapter 1, Reading: Words and Images, helps students become reflective readers and helps them understand the importance of reading actively and critically.

Critical Thinking, Reading, and Writing

Desired Outcomes	Relevant Features in *Writing Now*
Use writing and reading for inquiry, learning, thinking, and communicating	The introduction to reading (Chapter 1) includes an overview on critical reading and tips for how to read like a writer.
	In each genre, students learn strategies to develop their own ideas (see "Exploring Your Topic," pp. 226–32 in Chapter 4). And throughout each Guide to Writing, examples taken from the chapter's readings illustrate strategies students use in their own drafting (see the how-to boxes throughout Chapters 2–7).
	Additionally, the apparatus that accompanies the readings in Chapters 2–7 encourages close, critical reading and helps students engage with readings to write effectively.
Understand a writing assignment as a series of tasks, including finding, evaluating, analyzing, and synthesizing appropriate primary and secondary sources	Each chapter in Part 1 breaks down writing assignments, giving students just the advice they need for each part of the writing process (see overview, "Guide to Writing a Report," p. 219).
	Each guide includes genre-specific strategies for gathering information and working with sources (see pp. 226–29).
	Additionally, coverage of research (Chapters 10–13) includes detailed coverage of finding, evaluating, and synthesizing sources.
Integrate their own ideas with those of others	See Chapter 12's advice on "Quoting" (p. 615), "Paraphrasing" (pp. 616–19), and "Summarizing" (pp. 619–20). Advice on "Synthesizing Your Research" (pp. 621–23) and on "Avoiding Plagiarism" (pp. 623–24) helps students work with sources effectively and thoughtfully.
	Chapter 13, Documenting Sources: MLA and APA Style, provides complete guidelines for citing sources.
Understand the relationships among language, knowledge, and power	Although there is no dedicated coverage of this issue, this goal is implicit throughout the book. (See, for example, advice about "Analyzing the Verbs" and "Examining the Nouns" in essay questions, pp. 683–90.)

Processes

Desired Outcomes	Relevant Features in *Writing Now*
Be aware that it usually takes multiple drafts to create and complete a successful text	Each assignment in Part 1 assumes students work through drafts and then revise. Advice on revising and getting feedback appears in "Reviewing and Revising" sections (see pp. 243–45).
Develop flexible strategies for generating ideas, revising, editing, and proofreading	See the coverage of "Getting Started," "Creating a Draft," and "Reviewing and Revising" in each Guide to Writing (beginning p. 219 in Chapter 4, for example). Strategies are presented in orange how-to boxes, which also point to examples within the readings that implement these strategies. The how-to boxes make it easy for students to choose the most appropriate strategies for their purposes and audience.
Understand writing as an open process that permits writers to use later invention and rethinking to revise their work	See the genre-specific coverage of "Creating a Draft" (pp. 226–43) and "Reviewing and Revising" in Part 1 chapters (pp. 243–45).
Understand the collaborative and social aspects of writing processes	See the "For Collaboration" exercises throughout the book (for example, pp. 78 and 165).
Learn to critique their own and others' works	See the peer-editing advice at the end of each Part 1 chapter (pp. 243–44). See also the "For Collaboration" exercises throughout the book.
Learn to balance the advantages of relying on others with the responsibility of doing their part	This goal is implicit in the group learning coverage throughout the book.
Use a variety of technologies to address a range of audiences	Chapter 17, Writing in Online Environments, offers rhetorical advice for using technology effectively. Chapter 9, Designing Pages and Screens, includes specific tips for creating both print and online documents that work for a number of different purposes. Advice on using technology effectively also appears in Part 2's coverage of research, Chapter 10, Starting Research and Finding Sources, and Chapter 11, Conducting Field Research. Support for using technology is extended with the book's ancillaries, including the online student center, the e-book, and *CompClass*.

Knowledge of Conventions

Desired Outcomes	Relevant Features in *Writing Now*
Learn common formats for different kinds of texts	See comprehensive advice for designing and formatting various pages and screens in Chapter 9. Advice for presenting specific kinds of writing is also included within each of the assignment chapters in Part 1. Examples of specific formats appear on • pp. 529, 549 Web sites • p. 532 outline • p. 528 magazine article • pp. 544–45 tables, graphs, charts • p. 602 survey • pp. 650–56, 676 research essays • p. 726 e-mail • p. 705 portfolio introduction • pp. 714–15 brochure • p. 712 newsletter • pp. 735, 737 PowerPoint slides
Develop knowledge of genre conventions ranging from structure and form to tone and mechanics	Genre-specific advice on "Organizing" appears in each assignment chapter (see pp. 237–39). Tone is covered within advice on "Creating an Appropriate Voice" in each Guide to Writing (see pp. 235–37). Mechanics are not covered in *Writing Now*.
Practice appropriate means of documenting their work	MLA and APA documentation are covered in Chapter 13. A complete MLA sample student essay appears on pp. 650–56.
Control such surface features as syntax, grammar, punctuation, and spelling	No handbook is included within *Writing Now*.

Contents in Brief

Contents

3 PROFILES   85

4 REPORTS   163

5 POSITION PAPERS 249

6 EVALUATIONS 341

7 PROPOSALS 415

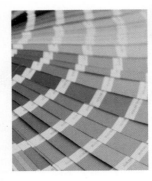

9 DESIGNING PAGES AND SCREENS   521

10 STARTING RESEARCH AND FINDING SOURCES   557

11 CONDUCTING FIELD RESEARCH   589

12 EVALUATING SOURCES AND TAKING NOTES 609

13 DOCUMENTING SOURCES: MLA AND APA STYLE 627

PART THREE — Strategies for Special Writing Situations

14 WRITING FOR ESSAY EXAMS   679

15 WRITING PORTFOLIOS   699

16 WRITING FOR THE COMMUNITY   709

17 WRITING IN ONLINE ENVIRONMENTS   723

18 MAKING ORAL PRESENTATIONS 733

[WRITING NOW]

Reading: Words and Images

Although this is a book about writing, you'll find that reading figures prominently in the work you are asked to do. And some of this reading will entail understanding visual as well as written information. In many instances, you will be working as a critic, assessing the strengths and weaknesses of an argument, for example, or determining whether a report seems credible. But you will also be reading as a writer, trying to learn things that will help you improve the way you incorporate written and visual information not only in the assignments you do for this course and other college courses but also in the writing you do for your work outside school.

To help you read both as a critic and a writer, the remainder of this chapter will introduce you to some questions that can guide your reading of a wide variety of texts. Later in the chapter, you'll see how several students answered these questions as they read both written texts and visual images.

▷ BECOMING A REFLECTIVE READER

To a certain extent, your reading process depends on the kind of text you're reading and your purposes for reading. You'll learn more about that in each of the next six chapters. But whatever the text and your purposes may be, there are two things you can always do: understand yourself as a reader and get an overview of a text before you begin reading that text closely.

It may seem strange to be asked to think about yourself as a reader. People often assume that the meaning of a text comes from the words, images, and details in the text itself. Because that assumption is partially true, this chapter will show you how to look closely and critically at texts. But you never approach a text—or any other experience—as a blank slate. In some cases you may know more than you do in other cases, and your assumptions (feelings, beliefs, attitudes) may be more valid or appropriate. In any event when you begin reading any text, you always bring with you any number of prior experiences, all of which shape the meaning you derive from a text. To understand what you are contributing to the meaning of a text, consider such questions as the following.

Questions for
Reflecting on
Yourself as a
Reader

► What do you already know about the subject of the text? What have you personally experienced? What have you heard from other people? What have you learned from other texts on the same subject?

► What attitudes, values, and feelings do you have concerning the subject?

► Why are you reading this text?

► What assumptions do you make about the subject? What assumptions do you make about the medium (textbook, magazine article, brochure, Web site) in which the text appears?

► What questions do you hope the text will answer?

Student Reflection Notes

Here is how one student, Lauren Spinelli, answered these questions before she began reading "Bellying Up to the Bar," a report on binge drinking among college students (p. 6).

What do you already know about the subject of the text? What have you personally experienced? What have you heard from other people? What have you learned from other texts on the same subject?

I've heard lectures and seminars given in high school showing the dangers of drinking, but don't know any statistics about the problem. I've been to parties where excessive drinking has occurred. But I've never seen these parties as a major problem or danger. Also I know that some experts say you shouldn't have more than one drink per hour.

What attitudes, values, and feelings do you have concerning the subject?

I think that the amount of consumption is probably slightly higher than it should be and that individual situations can become dangerous.

Why are you reading this text?

I am reading to see if there are dangers of drinking that I may be unaware of simply because I was always told "don't drink" and not what would happen if I did drink. In addition, I am reading this to find out if situations I have witnessed are abnormal or particularly dangerous. Finally, I want to see how drinking at other schools compares to what I see here on campus.

What assumptions do you make about the subject? What assumptions do you make about the medium (textbook, magazine article, brochure, Web site) in which the text appears?

College students are going to drink no matter what the situation. So I am hesitant to believe that an article that simply shines a light on a situation can actually change the current problem. However, I respect the source of the article, *Newsweek*. I read it often; the stories seem credible, factual, and quote worthy.

What questions do you hope the text will answer?

1. Is the situation all that serious? Has it caused any real problems?
2. Who's doing the drinking? Here at my school there's a lot of drinking at fraternity parties. Are these the main places where students drink too much?
3. What are schools doing to reduce students' drinking? Is it working?

Previewing and Annotating a Text

In addition to reflecting on yourself as a reader, you should also get a quick overview of a text before you read it in detail. You can do this by scanning the text fairly quickly, noticing your first impressions and making notes that answer some of the following questions.

▶ What do you know about the author or creator of the text? What can you learn about the author's purpose? Possible bias? Expertise or use of evidence?

▶ Where was the text published? When?

▶ What ideas and attitudes are expressed in the title or subtitle?

▶ When you look at the final sentence(s) of the introductory section, what can you learn about the main point (thesis) the author is making or the main question the author is raising?

▶ If paragraphs begin with topic sentences, what do they tell you about the main points the author wants to make?

▶ Does the text include headings? If so, what topics do they lead you to expect the writer to talk about?

▶ Are portions of the text highlighted—in bulleted lists, for example, or large, colored type? If so, what do they tell you about details the author considers especially important?

▶ Are there visual elements such as pictures, graphs, or charts? What information do they contain and what attitudes do they imply?

> [**Questions for Previewing a Text**]

Answers to these questions will help you decide whether a particular text is likely to be useful enough to read carefully. And if you are reading an article or a book for a class assignment, the answers to these questions can help you follow the detailed information in the article or chapter.

As you answer these questions, you don't need to write out lengthy answers; just put them on note cards or in a computer file, along with information about where you found the text—title of article or book, page number, date of publication. Or if—and *only* if—you own the article or book or if you have a printout of the text, you might want to make notes in the margins of the text itself, as Lauren did in making notes on the article "Bellying Up to the Bar."

For more information on doing library research, especially skimming, taking notes, and paraphrasing, see Chapter 12.

Lauren Spinelli's Annotated Text

Big problem in fraternities/sororities; positive way to change drinking.

The word Bellying *above the picture implies students are still drinking.*

Subtitle suggests improvement needed, cites Harvard study for evidence.

Extreme and shocking; suggests drinking just to get drunk. Suggests very negative view of college drinking.

Dangers of drinking vary from group to group.

Definition of binge drinking.

Consequences are serious; some colleges not doing much.

Topic sentence suggests there's some hope.

Mainstream newsmagazine a credible source; audience includes wide range of adults.

EDUCATION

Bellying Up to the Bar

A new Harvard study finds that binge drinking is still a big problem on many college campuses

Wild ones: *Keg parties still rule on many campuses*

ANDREW LICHTENSTEIN

BY CLAUDIA KALB AND JOHN MCCORMICK

FOUR YEARS AGO A HARVARD RE search team issued a shocking report about alcohol abuse among college students. Last week Harvard was back with a new assessment—and the news wasn't good. Despite years of national publicity about the problem, the percentage of students who binge-drink—consuming five or more drinks in a sitting for men, and four or more for women—has declined only from 44 to 43 percent. Other details were even more damning: half of all bingers do so regularly—at least three times within a two-week period. And one-third *more* students now admit they drink just to get drunk. "Maybe I'm expecting change too fast," says Henry Wechsler, the study's lead author and an expert on alcohol abuse at the Harvard School of Public Health, "but I am disappointed."

Are colleges doing enough to crack down on risky drinking? The stakes are high: cases like the notorious alcohol poisonings at LSU and MIT last year kill an estimated 50 students annually. Although some schools present comprehensive programs to educate students about the dangers of drinking, many campuses offer only perfunctory efforts. College presidents are caught between the desire to act boldly and the fear that heavy-handed actions will

When the Party's Over...

The more college students drink, the more they're at risk. Some alcohol-related problems that were reported after bingeing:

	NON-BINGERS	OCCASIONAL BINGERS	FREQUENT BINGERS
Drove after drinking	20%	43%	59%
Memory lapses	10	29	56
Got behind in schoolwork	9	25	48
Unplanned sexual activity	10	24	45

SOURCE: THE HARVARD SCHOOL OF PUBLIC HEALTH COLLEGE ALCOHOL STUDY

scare off prospective students. David Anderson, a George Mason University researcher who tracks college alcohol policies, says that in 1997, the average school spent just $13,300 to discourage substance abuse. Typical efforts: freshman-orientation workshops and alcohol-awareness pamphlets. Many college presidents delegate their alcohol programs to administrators already overburdened with other tasks. Says Anderson: "It's no wonder we're not making much progress."

The picture's not entirely bleak. William DeJong, head of the Higher Education Center for Alcohol and Other Drug Prevention in Newton, Mass., says that after years of relying on educational efforts, administrators are now turning to more innovative strategies. Many schools, such as the Uni-

versity of North Carolina at Chapel Hill, offer substance-free dorm rooms. Colleges are also teaming with neighborhood bars to ban happy-hour advertising on campus and to enforce drinking laws. Some schools are offering nonalcoholic "mocktail" parties. Others, like Clark University in Worcester, Mass., have turned campus pubs into coffeehouses. The trend shows some promise: the number of students who don't drink has grown from 16 to 19 percent. "I'm not ready to proclaim victory," says DeJong, but efforts are "definitely improving."

Dangerous drinking is at its worst in fraternities and sororities, where four out of five members acknowledge that they binge. But it's possible the situation will improve there, too. Wechsler collected his most recent data early in 1997. But that was before the highly publicized deaths last fall of pledges Benjamin Wynne at LSU and Scott Krueger at MIT. Several national fraternities have announced plans to ban alcohol in chapter houses.

Some experts argue that demonizing millions of binge drinkers makes it appear as if high-risk drinking is the norm. Michael Haines, a campus-health official at Northern Illinois University, says a more effective approach is to use advertising to hammer home the positive side of Wechsler's numbers: the fact that many students do drink responsibly. That message lets NIU's 22,000 students view heavy drinking not as the norm, but as aberrant. In 1989, 45 percent of the school's students said they binged—but on average they guessed that 70 percent of their peers did. Nine years later Haines can point to some successes. Students now estimate more reasonably that 33 percent of them binge—and the share who actually do has plummeted to 25 percent. Inspired by Haines's campaign, dozens of schools are now exploring this so-called social-norms approach. "We want to tell students what they're doing right," he says, "and grow more of that behavior."

Public pressure can change students' drinking habits. Lloyd Johnston, a University of Michigan researcher who has surveyed college drinkers nationwide since 1980, says the percentage who binged dropped through the '80s and into the mid-'90s, largely because of widespread publicity about the dangers of drunken driving and other alcohol-abuse problems. About two years ago, however, the numbers started climbing back up slightly. The only good news, Johnston says, is that dangerous drinking begins to subside after the age of 22. Provided, of course, that young people make it that far. ∎

► Identify any key terms and ideas. Mark definitions and examples that seem important.

► What main ideas or questions does the author raise? What passages seem especially important?

► What sources does the text rely on? Are there any sources, evidence, or examples that you question?

► Ask questions about the text. Highlight questions that the text presents or anything you need further information on. Are there things you find confusing? Things you need to look up?

► Consider making an outline, a map, or a numbered list of the text's main points. These quick notes can help you understand the text's organization and overall approach to the topic.

Guidelines for Annotating

{ Exercise } **Taking Notes about a Reading**

Look ahead to the report "The Record Industry's Slow Fade" (p. 176). Read the essay and then, using the questions on page 5, write a paragraph or two of your first impressions about this article. What have you learned from what you have written? ■

▷ READING CRITICALLY

As mentioned earlier, different kinds of texts require different kinds of critical reading. When you read an evaluation (a review of a new car, for example), you'll find yourself asking whether the writer's criteria are clear and whether the author's judgments make sense, given the criteria used and the evidence presented. When you read a proposal, you'll need to decide whether the writer's recommendations are practical and whether those recommendations are likely to have the benefits the writer thinks they will. But in all cases, the goal of critical reading is the same: deciding how seriously you can take what a writer says. In making this decision, you can ask several basic questions.

► What kinds of information does the author include? For example, does the author cite statistics, personal observations, or comments from authorities? Are there important kinds of information the author is omitting?

Guidelines for Analyzing a Text

► Is the information drawn from credible sources? Are there other sources the author should have drawn on?

► What questions is the author answering? Are there any questions that the author seems to be avoiding? Are there questions you wish the author had answered?

▶ Go to
bedfordstmartins.com/
writingnow to download
these questions from
Chapter 1 > Worksheets.

▶ If the text contains images, charts, graphs, or tables, what questions do they answer? What attitudes do the images imply? What emotions or reactions are they likely to evoke?

▶ Does the author acknowledge other points of view? Does the author explain and respond to them fairly?

Student Critical Reading Notes

When Lauren Spinelli analyzed "Bellying Up to the Bar," she jotted down these notes.

What kinds of information does the author include? For example, does the author cite statistics, personal observations, or comments from authorities? Are there kinds of information the author is omitting?

The authors give lots of statistical information to emphasize severity of situation. (Example: Forty-three percent of students admitted to binge drinking, and schools spent only $13,300 to discourage substance abuse.) Authors also use statistics to show some hope things will improve: The amount of students who don't drink has increased from 16 to 19 percent (and one school has reduced its binge drinking community from 45 percent to 25 percent). Authors also mention accounts from various schools to show what is or is not working in different places.

Is the information drawn from credible sources? Are there other sources the author should have drawn on?

Information comes from credible sources, including researchers at Harvard and other schools, as well as administrators who work with the problem.

I'd like to see testimony or argument from a student's point of view. But I would find it difficult to see such statements as valid and credible because of the lack of noteworthiness of a no-name student.

What questions is the author answering? Are there any questions that the author seems to be avoiding? Are there questions you wish the author had answered?

The authors answer many of the questions I anticipated before reading the article.

However, the dangers of drinking were not elaborated on as much as I had expected to truly paint a picture of how badly change is needed. Also, they did not answer several important questions. How do students perceive the drinking situation on campus? How do they define binge drinking—is it four to five drinks in a single hour or is it four to five drinks in a single evening? How many students drink that allotted number of drinks (five for men and four for women) more quickly than one drink per hour? Answering would truly show how many students were drinking irresponsibly.

If the text contains images, charts, graphs, or tables, what questions do they answer? What attitudes do the images imply? What emotions or reactions are they likely to evoke?

The table answers questions about who does the most drinking and what the consequences are. Picture seems sort of extreme—sort of gross. Suggests that all college students are drinking too much.

Does the author acknowledge other points of view? Does the author explain and respond to them fairly?

I do not believe that many people would have different points of view on this topic, arguing that excessive drinking on campuses is a good thing. However, the right of students all over the nation to defend themselves has been rejected. Nowhere in this article could I find the testimony of students arguing that they technically binge drink while still being responsible. In this aspect, the other point of view failed to be mentioned. But the authors do mention two attitudes toward the problem—it's alarming but "picture's not entirely bleak."

Student Summary of Reading

Bearing in mind her answers to all these questions, Lauren made the following overall assessment of "Bellying Up to the Bar."

Overall, I feel that "Bellying Up to the Bar" is a respectable piece that uses noteworthy pieces of information, persuasive visuals, and credible sources. The authors know that the use of statistics will better their arguments that (1) college students are drinking in extremely high numbers and that (2) college administrators are not doing nearly as much as they should to improve the situation. The visual aids help the reader in two ways. First, the authors present a recognizable but disturbing image that will draw the reader into the article, creating expectations pertaining to the elaboration of the issue going on with college students and drinking. Second, the authors provide the chart of useful information that further embellishes their argument and the dangers of drinking in a clear and concise way. In addition, the authors use credible sources such as statistics from a study conducted by Harvard University and testimonies from experts and researchers at established institutions.

It bothers me a little bit that the authors leave several important questions unanswered. Exactly who counts as a "binge drinker"? Is it someone who drinks four or five drinks in one hour or four or five drinks over several hours, like people sometimes do at a party? Since we don't know the answers, the problem could be more (or less) serious than the authors say it is. Also, how do students see this problem? Do they think the problem is serious? And if their school has set up a program to reduce binge drinking, how effective do they think the program has been? (Credible answers about the students' perspective would have to come from a variety of specific students.)

Margin notes:
Notes emotions picture evokes.

Chart answers questions about dangers.

Cites different, credible sources of information.

Points to unanswered questions.

Even though the authors do not answer these questions, they have used sources that are reliable, and they have done a good job of making the numbers and statistics work entirely in their favor. Basically, this seems like a credible, informative report.

▷ READING LIKE A WRITER

One of the best ways to become a better writer is to become a better reader—that is, to learn to read like a writer—especially when you find work that is widely considered excellent. Of course, what counts as excellent in one context might not rank so highly in some other context. To use an obvious example, an autobiographical essay will go over better in an assignment for a writing class than for a biology laboratory report assignment. But when you find some excellent writing, it is always useful to ask two questions: *What* did that writer do? And *how* did he or she (or they) do it? As you will see in all the chapters in the next section of this book, there are certain things good writers almost always do. They always find something worthwhile (informative, persuasive, moving) to say. Lauren's analysis of "Bellying Up to the Bar" shows some useful strategies for doing this: draw on different sources of information, use different types of information, and—above all—answer readers' questions.

In addition to finding something to say, good writers set objectives they want to meet when drafting a text. The following objectives help writers produce an appropriate, effective text.

Engage the audience. Show how the topic relates to what they know or care about, create a question (problem, conflict) that will motivate them to begin and continue reading, and assert a point (or raising a question) that will let readers see what to expect in the remainder of the article (book chapter, speech, essay). For example, the authors of "Bellying Up to the Bar" include a disturbing visual image, and the first paragraph engages readers by establishing a problem many readers should care about.

Provide structure. Make it easy for readers to see what point the writer is getting at, give cues that help readers find the information they are looking for, or indicate how one fact or idea is related to others. In the third paragraph of "Bellying Up to the Bar," for example, the topic sentence at the beginning makes it easy for readers to see the point the writers are getting at.

Create an appropriate voice. Writers should reveal their attitude toward the subject and establish a relationship with their readers. The second paragraph of "Bellying Up to the Bar" includes a question that suggests a fairly casual, conversational relationship with readers, while the photo reveals a negative attitude toward college drinking.

Conclude the text effectively. For example, writers should summarize their main points or pose questions or provide information that will lead readers to continue being concerned about the topic. The conclusion of "Bellying Up to the Bar" provides information that should prompt continued concern.

Include visuals. These visuals should do some or all of the preceding—answer questions, create a voice, or meet other goals for the text. In "Bellying Up to the Bar," the chart makes it easy for readers to find information that will answer certain questions.

[PART ONE]

Writing Assignments ▷

2 ▷

Memoirs

In many of the writing assignments in subsequent chapters of this book, you will occasionally have the opportunity to write about your personal experiences. But in your assignment for this chapter, the primary focus is on you and your experiences—what you've done, what you've observed, what you've thought. Writing that focuses on these types of personal experiences is called memoir writing. In writing a memoir, you may want to describe what it was like to begin a new job, what you observed and how you felt when you were in an unusual situation, or what you learned from a family member, mentor, or teacher. Even though memoirs describe real experiences, they very often read like stories.

Whatever topic you choose, your primary goal in writing a memoir is to help readers share your experiences. It's very likely that your work will take the form of a story, but in any case, you will select details that have special meaning for you and write about them in ways that convey that significance. As you do so, you may help readers gain insight into their own experiences.

You may be asked to write memoirs in several different contexts. For a course in sociology, for example, you may be asked to explore issues (the consequences of discrimination, for example) by recounting ways in which you have experienced the issue. In work or in a community organization, you may be asked to reflect on your experiences in implementing a policy.

▷ READING MEMOIRS

In the following section, you will read memoirs in which authors describe a variety of personal experiences ranging from observing a total eclipse of the sun to meeting needy children in Iraq. Following each reading, you will find questions that pertain specifically to the memoir you have just read. In addition to these specific questions, there are several basic questions you should ask in reading any memoir.

$$\left[\begin{array}{c}\text{Questions for}\\\text{Reading Memoirs}\end{array}\right]$$

► **Who is the intended audience?** Consider the language, visuals, and information included in (and excluded from) the memoir. What does the writer appear to be assuming about the following?

- Readers' background knowledge (Have they, for example, had comparable experiences?)
- Ways readers are likely to react to events the author is recounting
- The extent to which readers are likely to sympathize or empathize with the writer or people the writer talks about
- The extent to which readers share the writer's attitudes and values
- The questions readers want to have answered

► **What specific purpose is the writer trying to accomplish?** In addition to achieving the basic goal of getting the audience to share and understand the writer's experiences and feelings, is the writer trying to accomplish a more specific purpose, such as one or more of the following?

- Shed new light on experiences that compare to readers' experiences
- Help readers see why and how events happened as they did
- Let readers experience what it's like to be in a situation they have never been in
- Reassure readers they are not alone in their experiences, that other people have felt much the same way readers have
- Give new insight into people's characters and values
- Give readers a fresh perspective on something they may have observed but never thought about or understood fully

► **How informative is the memoir?**

- What questions does the memoir answer?
- Are these the kinds of questions readers will want to have answered?
- Are these questions answered with the kinds of specific details and explanations that allow readers to share the writer's experiences, understand who the writer is, and form their own conclusions about the writer and the meaning of the writer's experiences?
- Are there significant questions that the memoir does not answer?

► **How credible is the memoir?**

- Do the facts "ring true"? Do they seem plausible or consistent with what you know or can imagine?
- If the writer explicitly states his or her conclusions about the significance of the facts, do those conclusions seem warranted by the facts that are presented?

▶ **How well organized is the memoir?**

- Can readers follow the train of events the author is describing?
- Even if the event moves from one vignette (short episode) to another, do all the events add up to some coherent theme or overall impression?

▶ **What sort of voice would readers hear in the memoir?**

- What attitudes, values, or emotions are suggested in the text? Does the writer seem likable? Witty? Thoughtful? Sensitive?
- Does the writer seem like someone readers can empathize or sympathize with?

{ For Collaboration } **Reading Memoirs**

Quickly read through the memoirs found on pages 21–58 of this chapter. Find one that you respond to strongly (positively or negatively). Highlight passages that answer one or more of the previous questions and be prepared to explain why those answers lead you to respond as you do. ■

A memoir can contain a variety of visual elements, including photographs, illustrations, and inset boxes, as well as variations in page layout and typefaces. Here are important questions to ask when reading or analyzing photographs, the most widely used type of visuals in memoirs.

▶ Does the photograph help convey the attitudes expressed in the written text?

▶ What kinds of details are included in (or excluded from) the image? How do these details convey the writer's basic attitude toward or understanding of the experiences described in the memoir?

▶ What is the setting? What people or objects surround the person being depicted?

▶ What do nonverbal cues (facial expression, posture, gestures) tell you about the personality or character of the people in the image?

▶ How is the picture composed? How are people, objects, or parts of an object related to one another?

▶ Where are people located within the frame (or edges) of the image?

▶ What viewing angle is represented, and what does that viewing angle imply?

▶ What colors are used, and what emotions do they evoke?

▶ How is the picture captioned? What does the caption add to your understanding?

To see how these questions can guide an analysis of photographs in a memoir, consider the following two photographs from David Perry's memoir "Theatre Geek" (p. 51). In this memoir, David says that when he was in middle school, he preferred to be inconspicuous, "part of the scenery rather than standing out." And the first photograph, on his middle school ID card, is ideal for someone who felt this way; the picture shows only his head and shoulders and gives no indication of personality or attitudes. In the second picture, where David is depicted as a central character in his senior play, personality and attitudes come through clearly.

For advice on how to use photographs effectively in a memoir, see Chapter 9.

{ **Exercise** } ▶ Go to bedfordstmartins.com/writingnow to Chapter 2 > Visuals.

For practice analyzing the visual information in another memoir, see the visual exercises online. ■

Attitude Nothing in this picture makes David seem distinctive or outstanding. His smile and casual clothing are typical of pictures in middle school IDs, and the picture occupies only a small space on the ID card.

Fig. 1. My middle school ID, age 13.

Relative size and location Although the customers are closer to the viewer, David appears larger than they do. He is literally and figuratively looking down at them.

Setting A relatively upscale restaurant where diners wear sport coats and expect courtesy from staff.

Nonverbal language The black pants, slightly rumpled white shirt, and bow tie are typical clothing for a bus boy in a restaurant. His facial expression and slumped posture suggest boredom and mild contempt for diners, who are ignoring him.

Viewing angle The viewer is looking up at David, as is appropriate in viewing someone who has been assigned what David refers to as a "central role" in the play. Clearly, David is no longer someone who, as he puts it in his memoir, "never had the confidence to put myself on display."

Fig. 4. Appearing in *Welcome to Lovely's*. Source: Jim Motes.

Caption Given David's apparent attitudes toward customers in this play, the caption "Welcome to Lovely's" is quite ironic.

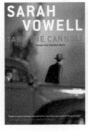

{ Exercise } **Analyzing Visuals in Memoirs**

Bring to class a memoir or reflective essay that contains several striking photographs. Identify the effects these photographs create and, by answering some of the questions discussed above, try to determine how the effect is achieved. Be prepared to show the photographs to your classmates and explain how they create a particular effect and what they add to the impressions conveyed through the written text. ■

▷ READING TO WRITE

The following essays are taken from a range of sources: books, magazines, blogs. Memoir is a genre that is read eagerly and widely—from celebrity and political authors recounting their experiences in blockbuster hardcover books to the postings that appear on many personal and professionally edited blogs. The variety of subjects reflects the different kinds of topics you might consider when you create your own memoir for the major assignment in this chapter.

After each of these essays, you will find two sets of questions. One set, Reflecting on What You Have Read, will help you analyze the essay carefully and help you recognize strategies and techniques you can use in writing about your own experiences. The other, Thinking Ahead, will suggest some of the kinds of topics you might write about.

▶ Go to
bedfordstmartins.com/
writingnow and click on
Chapter 2 > Examples for
additional memoirs.

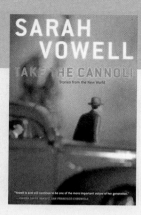

Shooting Dad
Sarah Vowell

Sarah Vowell is a journalist and writer whose humorous essays and radio appearances often draw on autobiographical material. Her work has appeared in numerous magazines and newspapers, including *Time, Esquire, Spin*, and the *New York Times*. In this essay, which originally aired in a different form on public radio's *This American Life* on October 24, 1997, she explores with humor the differences between herself and her conservative family. As you read this essay, notice the ways Vowell selects details that let you see—literally *see*—the relationship she has with her father.

▶ Go to **bedfordstmartins.com/writingnow** and click on Chapter 2 > Examples to hear Sarah Vowell read an audio version of this story.

Shooting Dad

If you were passing by the house where I grew up during my teenage years and it happened to be before Election Day, you wouldn't have needed to come inside to see that it was a house divided. You could have looked at the Democratic campaign poster in the upstairs window and the Republican one in the downstairs window and seen our home for the Civil War battleground it was. I'm not saying who was the Democrat or who was the Republican—my father or I—but I will tell you that I have never subscribed to *Guns & Ammo*, that I did not plaster the family vehicle with National Rifle Association stickers, and that hunter's orange was never my color. 1

About the only thing my father and I agree on is the Constitution, though I'm partial to the First Amendment, while he's always favored the Second. 2

I am a gunsmith's daughter. I like to call my parents' house, located on a quiet residential street in Bozeman, Montana, the United States of Firearms. Guns were everywhere: the so-called pretty ones like the circa 1850 walnut muzzleloader hanging on the wall, Dad's clients' fixer-uppers leaning into corners, an entire rack right next to the TV. I had to move revolvers out of my way to make room for a bowl of Rice Krispies on the kitchen table. 3

I was eleven when we moved into that Bozeman house. We had never lived in town before, and this was a college town at that. We came from Oklahoma—a dusty little Muskogee County nowhere called Braggs. My parents' property there included an orchard, a horse pasture, and a couple of acres of woods. I knew our lives had changed one morning not long after we moved to Montana when, during breakfast, my father 4

21

heard a noise and jumped out of his chair. Grabbing a BB gun, he rushed out the front door. Standing in the yard, he started shooting at crows. My mother sprinted after him screaming, "Pat, you might ought to check, but I don't think they do that up here!" From the look on his face, she might as well have told him that his American citizenship had been revoked. He shook his head, mumbling, "Why, shooting crows is a national pastime, like baseball and apple pie." Personally, I preferred baseball and apple pie. I looked up at those crows flying away and thought, I'm going to like it here.

Dad and I started bickering in earnest when I was fourteen, after the 1984 Demo- 5 cratic National Convention. I was so excited when Walter Mondale chose Geraldine Fer- raro as his running mate that I taped the front page of the newspaper with her picture on it to the refrigerator door. But there was some sort of mysterious gravity surge in the kitchen. Somehow, that picture ended up in the trash all the way across the room.

Nowadays, I giggle when Dad calls me on Election Day to cheerfully inform me that 6 he has once again canceled out my vote, but I was not always so mature. There were times when I found the fact that he was a gunsmith horrifying. And just *weird*. All he ever cared about were guns. All I ever cared about was art. There were years and years when he hid out by himself in the garage making rifle barrels and I holed up in my room reading Allen Ginsberg poems, and we were incapable of having a conversation that didn't end in an argument.

Our house was partitioned off into territories. While the kitchen and the living room 7 were well within the DMZ, the respective work spaces governed by my father and me were jealously guarded totalitarian states in which each of us declared ourselves dictator. Dad's shop was a messy disaster area, a labyrinth of lathes. Its walls were hung with the mounted antlers of deer he'd bagged, forming a makeshift museum of death. The available flat surfaces were buried under a million scraps of paper on which he sketched his mechanical inventions in blue ball-point pen. And the floor, carpeted with spiky metal shavings, was a tetanus shot waiting to happen. My domain was the cramped, cold space known as the music room. It was also a messy disaster area, an obstacle course of musical instruments—piano, trumpet, baritone horn, valve trombone, various percussion doo-dads (bells!), and recorders. A framed portrait of the French composer Claude Debussy was nailed to the wall. The available flat surfaces were buried under piles of staff paper, on which I penciled in the pompous orchestra music given titles like "Prelude to the Green Door" (named after an O. Henry short story by the way, not the watershed porn flick *Behind the Green Door*) I starting writing in junior high.

It has been my experience that in order to impress potential suitors, skip the teen 8 Debussy anecdotes and stick with the always attention-getting line "My dad makes guns." Though it won't cause the guy to like me any better, it will make him handle the inevitable breakup with diplomacy—just in case I happen to have any loaded family heir-looms lying around the house.

But the fact is, I have only shot a gun once and once was plenty. My twin sister, Amy, and 9 I were six years old—six—when Dad decided that it was high time we learned how to shoot. Amy remembers the day he handed us the gun for the first time differently. She liked it.

Amy shared our father's enthusiasm for firearms and the quick-draw cowboy mythol- 10 ogy surrounding them. I tended to daydream through Dad's activities—the car trip to Dodge City's Boot Hill, his beloved John Wayne Westerns on TV. My sister, on the other hand, turned into Rooster Cogburn Jr., devouring Duke movies with Dad. In fact, she named her teddy bear Duke, hung a colossal John Wayne portrait next to her bed, and took to wearing one of those John Wayne shirts that button on the side. So when Dad led us out to the backyard when we were six and, to Amy's delight, put the gun in her hand, she says she felt it meant that Daddy trusted us and that he thought of us as "big girls."

But I remember holding the pistol only made me feel small. It was so heavy in my 11 hand. I stretched out my arm and pointed it away and winced. It was a very long time before I had the nerve to pull the trigger and I was so scared I had to close my eyes. It felt like it just went off by itself, as if I had no say in the matter, as if the gun just had this *need*. The sound it made was as big as God. It kicked little me back to the ground like a bully, like a foe. It hurt. I don't know if I dropped it or just handed it back over to my dad, but I do know that I never wanted to touch another one again. And, because I believed in the devil, I did what my mother told me to do every time I felt an evil presence. I looked at the smoke and whispered under my breath, "Satan, I rebuke thee."

It's not like I'm saying I was traumatized. It's more like I was decided. Guns: Not For 12 Me. Luckily, both my parents grew up in exasperating households where children were considered puppets and/or slaves. My mom and dad were hell-bent on letting my sister and me make our own choices. So if I decided that I didn't want my father's little death sticks to kick me to the ground again, that was fine with him. He would go hunting with my sister, who started calling herself "the loneliest twin in history" because of my reluctance to engage in family activities.

Of course, the fact that I was allowed to voice my opinions did not mean that my 13 father would silence his own. Some things were said during the Reagan administration that cannot be taken back. Let's just say that I blamed Dad for nuclear proliferation and Contra aid. He believed that if I had my way, all the guns would be confiscated and it would take the commies about fifteen minutes to parachute in and assume control.

We're older now, my dad and I. The older I get, the more I'm interested in becoming 14 a better daughter. First on my list: Figure out the whole gun thing.

Not long ago, my dad finished his most elaborate tool of death yet. A cannon. He 15 built a nineteenth-century cannon. From scratch. It took two years.

My father's cannon is a smaller replica of a cannon called the Big Horn Gun in front 16 of Bozeman's Pioneer Museum. The barrel of the original has been filled with concrete ever since some high school kids in the '50s pointed it at the school across the street and shot out its windows one night as a prank. According to Dad's historical source, a man known to scholars as A Guy at the Museum, the cannon was brought to Bozeman around 1870, and was used by local white merchants to fire at the Sioux and Cheyenne Indians who blocked their trade access to the East in 1874.

"Bozeman was founded on greed," Dad says. The courthouse cannon, he continues, 17 "definitely killed Indians. The merchants filled it full of nuts, bolts, and chopped-up horseshoes. Sitting Bull could have been part of these engagements. They definitely ticked off the Indians, because a couple of years later, Custer wanders into them at Little Bighorn. The Bozeman merchants were out to cause trouble. They left fresh baked bread with cyanide in it on the trail to poison a few Indians."

Because my father's sarcastic American history yarns rarely go on for long before he 18 trots out some nefarious ancestor of ours—I come from a long line of moonshiners, Confederate soldiers, murderers, even Democrats—he cracks that the merchants hired some "community-minded Southern soldiers from North Texas." These soldiers had, like my great-great-grandfather John Vowell, fought under pro-slavery guerrilla William C. Quantrill. Quantrill is most famous for riding into Lawrence, Kansas, in 1863 flying a black flag and commanding his men pharaohlike to "kill every male and burn down every house."

"John Vowell," Dad says, "had a little rep for killing people." And since he abandoned 19
my great-grandfather Charles, whose mother died giving birth to him in 1870, and wasn't
seen again until 1912, Dad doesn't rule out the possibility that John Vowell could have
been one of the hired guns on the Bozeman Trail. So the cannon isn't just another gun to
my dad. It's a map of all his obsessions—firearms, certainly, but also American history
and family history, subjects he's never bothered separating from each other.

After tooling a million guns, after inventing and building a rifle barrel boring 20
machine, after setting up that complicated shop filled with lathes and blueing tanks and
outmoded blacksmithing tools, the cannon is the most ambitious project ever. I thought
that if I was ever going to understand the ballistic bee in his bonnet, this was my chance.
It was the biggest gun he ever made and I could experience it and spend time with it with
the added bonus of not having to actually pull a trigger myself.

I called Dad and said that I wanted to come to Montana and watch him shoot off the 21
cannon. He was immediately suspicious. But I had never taken much interest in his work
before and he would take what he could get. He loaded the cannon into the back of his
truck and we drove up into the Bridger Mountains. I was a little worried that the National
Forest Service would object to us lobbing fiery balls of metal onto its property. Dad
laughed, assuring me that "you cannot shoot fireworks, but this is considered a fire*arm.*"

It is a small cannon, about as long as a baseball bat and as wide as a coffee can. But 22
it's heavy—110 pounds. We park near the side of the hill. Dad takes his gunpowder and
other tools out of this adorable wooden box on which he has stenciled "PAT G. VOWELL
CANNONWORKS." Cannonworks: So that's what NRA members call a metal-strewn
garage.

Dad plunges his homemade bullets into the barrel, points it at an embankment just 23
to be safe, and lights the fuse. When the fuse is lit, it resembles a cartoon. So does the
sound, which warrants Ben Day dot words along the lines of *ker-pow!* There's so much
Fourth of July smoke everywhere I feel compelled to sing the national anthem.

I've given this a lot of thought—how to convey the giddiness I felt when the cannon 24
shot off. But there isn't a sophisticated way to say this. It's just really, really cool. My dad
thought so, too.

Sometimes, I put together stories about the more eccentric corners of the American 25
experience for public radio. So I happen to have my tape recorder with me, and I've never
seen levels like these. Every time the cannon goes off, the delicate needles which keep
track of the sound quality lurch into the bad, red zone so fast and so hard I'm surprised
they don't break.

The cannon was so loud and so painful, I had to touch my head to make sure my 26
skull hadn't cracked open. One thing that my dad and I share is that we're both a little
hard of hearing—me from Aerosmith, him from gunsmith.

He lights the fuse again. The bullet knocks over the log he was aiming at. I instantly 27
utter a sentence I never in my entire life thought I would say. I tell him, "Good shot, Dad."

Just as I'm wondering what's coming over me, two hikers walk by. Apparently, they 28
have never seen a man set off a homemade cannon in the middle of the wilderness while his
daughter holds a foot-long microphone up into the air recording its terrorist boom. One
hiker gives me a puzzled look and asks, "So you work for the radio and that's your dad?"

Dad shoots the cannon again so that they can see how it works. The other hiker says, 29
"That's quite the machine you got there." But he isn't talking about the cannon. He's talking
about my tape recorder and my microphone—which is called a *shotgun* mike. I stare back at
him, then I look over at my father's cannon, then down at my microphone, and I think, Oh.
My. God. My dad and I are the same person. We're both smart-alecky loners with goofy
projects and weird equipment. And since this whole target practice outing was my idea, I
was no longer his adversary. I was his accomplice. What's worse, I was liking it.

I haven't changed my mind about guns. I can get behind the cannon because it is a 30
completely ceremonial object. It's unwieldy and impractical, just like everything else I
care about. Try to rob a convenience store with this 110-pound Saturday night special,
you'd still be dragging it in the door Sunday afternoon.

I love noise. As a music fan, I'm always waiting for that moment in a song when 31
something just flies out of it and explodes in the air. My dad is a one-man garage band,
the kind of rock 'n' roller who slaves away at his art for no reason other than to make his
own sound. My dad is an artist—a pretty driven, idiosyncratic one, too. He's got his last
Gesamtkunstwerk all planned out. It's a performance piece. We're all in it—my mom, the
loneliest twin in history, and me.

When my father dies, take a wild guess what he wants done with his ashes. Here's a 32
hint: It requires a cannon.

"You guys are going to love this," he smirks, eyeballing the cannon. "You get to drag 33
this thing up on top of the Gravellies on opening day of hunting season. And looking off
at Sphinx Mountain, you get to put me in little paper bags. I can take my last hunting trip
on opening morning."

I'll do it, too. I will have my father's body burned into ashes. I will pack these ashes 34
into paper bags. I will go to the mountains with my mother, my sister, and the cannon. I
will plunge his remains into the barrel and point it into a hill so that he doesn't take anyone with him. I will light the fuse. But I will not cover my ears. Because when I blow what
used to be my dad into the earth, I want it to hurt.

Reflecting on What You Have Read

1 At the beginning of her essay, in what ways does Vowell establish the relationship she and her father had during her childhood? In what ways does she convey the everyday experiences of growing up in her family home?

2 How does Vowell organize this essay? What are the effects of the anecdotes she uses throughout? How do these anecdotes come together to create an impression about the Vowell family? Do you think she succeeds in creating a memoir that rings true? Why or why not?

3 What impressions do you get from the image that accompanies this essay? What do these images tell you about Vowell, her father, and her book?

4 At the end of this essay, Vowell becomes her father's accomplice in firing the cannon. Were you surprised at this change in her attitudes? Why or why not?

Thinking Ahead

In this essay, Vowell humorously describes her relationship with her father and at the end of the essay shows how that relationship changed. Though her experiences with guns and the cannon may seem unusual to some readers, most people have had the experience of arguing with a parent or other important family member during adolescence. If you can recall crucial points in a relationship in your family, those experiences might serve as a good subject for a memoir. But as you think of a possible topic, think about experiences within important relationships in your life, including those that may have occurred over long periods—an older relative you see only on summer vacations, for example, or a teacher, mentor, or employer who has influenced you in specific ways. What is important is that the remembered experiences have the potential to matter to someone else and allow you to have some distance from the subject.

Stripped for Parts
Jennifer Kahn

Jennifer Kahn is a journalist and a contributing editor to *Wired* magazine and has written for other publications such as *National Geographic, Discover*, and the *New York Times*. In the following essay, she writes about spending twenty-four hours in a hospital at the side of a donor who has undergone brain death, as he is prepared for surgery to remove several organs. While acknowledging that transplant surgeries routinely save the lives of thousands of people every year who would otherwise die, Kahn focuses this essay on the treatment of one donor. Her observations include descriptions of her own reactions to the "dead man's" care. As you read, notice the places where Kahn inserts her own responses— and quotes those of others—to the practices that accompany transplant surgeries.

Stripped for Parts

By Jennifer Kahn

1 The television in the dead man's room stays on all night. Right now the program is *Shipmates*, a reality-dating drama that's barely audible over the hiss of the ventilator. It's 4 am, and I've been here for six hours, sitting in the corner while three nurses fuss intermittently over a set of intravenous drips. They're worried about the dead man's health.

2 To me, he looks fine. His face is slack but flush, he breathes steadily, and his heart beats like a clock, despite the fact that his lungs have recently begun to leak fluid. The nurses roll the body from side to side periodically so that the liquid doesn't pool. At one point, a white plastic vest designed to clear the lungs inflates and begins to vibrate violently—as if some invisible person has seized the dead man by the shoulders and is trying to shake him awake. The rest of the time, the nurses consult monitors and watch for signs of cardiac arrest. When someone scratches the bottom of the dead man's foot, it twitches.

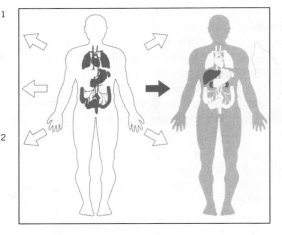

3 None of this is what I expected from an organ transplant. When I arrived last night at this Northern California hospital I was prepared to see a fast-paced surgery culminating in renewal: the mortally ill patient restored to glorious health. In all my preliminary research on transplants, the dead man was rarely mentioned.

Even doctors I spoke with avoided the subject, and popular accounts I came across ducked the matter of provenance altogether. In the movies, for instance, surgeons tended to say it would take time to "find" a heart—as though one had been hidden behind a tree or misplaced along with the car keys. Insofar as corpses came up, it was only in anxious reference to the would-be recipient whose time was running out.

In the dead man's room, a different calculus 4 is unfolding. Here the organ is the patient, and the patient a mere container, the safest place to store body parts until surgeons are ready to use them. It can be more than a day from the time a donor dies until his organs are harvested—the surgery alone takes hours, not to mention the time needed to do blood tests, match tissue, and fly in special surgical teams for the evisceration. And yet, a heart lasts at most six hours outside the body, even after it has been kneaded, flushed with preservatives, and packed in a cooler. Organs left on ice too long tend to perform poorly in their new environment, and doctors are picky about which viscera they're willing to work with. Even an ailing cadaver is a better container than a cooler.

These conditions create a strange medical 5 specialty. Rather than extracting this man's vitals right away, the hospital contacts the California Transplant Donor Network, which dispatches a procurement team to begin "donor maintenance": the process of artificially supporting a dead body until recipients are ready. When the parathyroid gland stops regulating calcium, key to keeping the heart pumping, the team sends the proper amount down an intravenous drip. When blood pressure drops, they add vasoconstrictors, which contract the blood vessels. Normally the brain would compensate for a decrease in blood pressure, but with it out

Organs stored in chemicals or on ice last only a matter of hours. The far more desirable container: a brain-dead body.

of commission, the three-nurse procurement team must take over.

In this case, the eroding balance will have to 6 be sustained for almost 24 hours. The goal is to fool the body into believing that it's alive and well, even as everything is falling apart. As one crew member concedes, "It's unbelievable that all this stuff is being done to a dead person."

Unbelievable and, to me, somehow barbaric. 7 Sustaining a dead body until its organs can be harvested is a tricky process requiring the latest in medical technology. But it's also a distinct anachronism in an era when medicine is becoming less and less invasive. Fixing blocked coronary arteries, which not long ago required prying a patient's chest open with a saw and spreader, can now be accomplished with a tiny stent delivered to the heart on a slender wire threaded up the leg. Exploratory surgery has given way to robot cameras and high-resolution imaging. Already, we are eyeing the tantalizing summit of gene therapy, where diseases are cured even before they do damage. Compared with such microscale cures, transplants—which consist of salvaging entire organs from a heart-beating cadaver and sewing them into a different body—seem crudely mechanical, even medieval.

"To let an organ reach a state where the only solution is to cut it out is not progress; it's a failure of medicine," says pathologist Neil Theise of NYU. Theise, who was the first researcher to demonstrate that stem cells can become liver cells in humans, argues that the future of transplantation lies in regeneration. Within five years, he estimates, we'll be able to instruct the body to send stem cells to the liver from the store that exists in bone marrow, hopefully countering the effects of a disease like hepatitis A or B and letting the body heal itself. And numerous researchers are forging similar paths. One outspoken surgeon, Richard Satava from the University of Washington, says that medicine is only now catching on to the fundamental lesson of modern industry, which is that when our car alternator breaks, we get a brand new one. Transplantation, he argues, is a dying art.

Few researchers predict that human-harvested organs will become obsolete anytime soon, however; one cardiovascular pathologist, Charles Murry, says we'll still be using them a century from now. But it's reasonable to expect—and hope for—an alternative. "I don't think anybody enjoys recovering organs," Murry says frankly. "You tell yourself it's for a good cause, which it is, a very good cause, but you're still butchering a human."

Intensive care is not a good place to spend the evening. Tonight, the ward has perhaps 12 patients, including a woman who moans constantly and a deathly pale man who reportedly jumped out the window of a moving Greyhound bus. The absence of clocks and the always-on lights create a casino-like timelessness. In the staff lounge, which smells of stale pizza, a lone nurse corners me and describes watching a man bleed to death ("He was conscious. He knew what was happening"), and announces, sotto voce, that she knows of South American organ brokers who charge $60,000 for a heart, then swap it for a baboon's.

Although I don't admit it to the procurement team, I've grown attached to the dead man. There's something vulnerable about his rumpled hair and middle-aged body, naked save a waist-high sheet. Under the hospital lights, everything is exposed: the muscular arms gone flabby above the elbow; the legs, wiry and lean, foreshortened under a powerful torso. It's the body of a man in his fifties, simultaneously bullish and elfin. One foot, the right, peeps out from the sheet, and for a brief moment I want to hold it and rub the toes that must be cold—a hopeless gesture of consolation.

Organ support is about staving off entropy. In the moments after death, a cascade of changes sweeps over the body. Potassium diminishes and salt accumulates, drawing fluid into cells. Sugar builds up in the blood. With the pituitary system offline, the heart fills with lactic acid like the muscles of an exhausted runner. Free radicals circulate unchecked and disrupt other cells, in effect causing the body to rust. The process quickly becomes irreversible. As cell membranes grow porous, a "death gene" is activated and damaged cells begin to self-destruct. All this happens in minutes.

When transplant activists talk about an organ shortage, it's usually to lament how few people are willing to donate. This is a valid worry, but it eclipses an important point, which is that the window for retrieving a viable organ is staggeringly small. Because of how fast the body degrades once the heart stops, there's no way to recover an organ from someone who dies at home, in a car, in an ambulance, or even

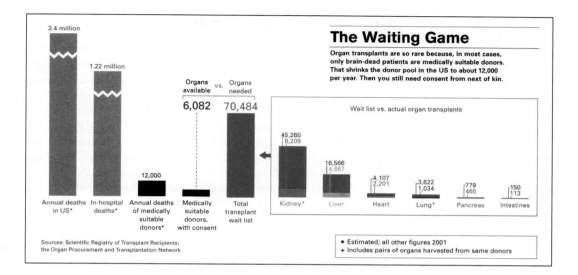

The Waiting Game

Organ transplants are so rare because, in most cases, only brain-dead patients are medically suitable donors. That shrinks the donor pool in the US to about 12,000 per year. Then you still need consent from next of kin.

Organs available vs. Organs needed

6,082   70,484

Wait list vs. actual organ transplants

45,260 / 8,209 — Kidney*
16,566 / 4,667 — Liver
4,107 / 2,201 — Heart
3,622 / 1,034 — Lung*
779 / 465 — Pancreas
150 / 113 — Intestines

2.4 million — Annual deaths in US*
1.22 million — In-hospital deaths*
12,000 — Annual deaths of medically suitable donors*
Medically suitable donors, with consent
Total transplant wait list

Sources: Scientific Registry of Transplant Recipients; the Organ Procurement and Transplantation Network

★ Estimated; all other figures 2001
+ Includes pairs of organs harvested from same donors

while on the operating table. In fact, the only situation that really lends itself to harvest is brain death, which means finding an otherwise healthy patient whose brain activity has ceased but whose heart continues to beat—right up until the moment it's taken out. In short, victims of stroke or severe head injury. These cases are so rare (approximately 0.5 percent of all deaths in the US) that even if everybody in America were to become a donor, they wouldn't clear the organ wait lists.

14 This is partly a scientific problem. Cell death remains poorly understood, and for years now, cadaveric transplants have lingered on a research plateau. While immunosuppressants have improved incrementally, transplants proceed much as they did 20 years ago. Compared with a field like psychopharmacology, the procedure has come to a near-standstill.

15 But there are cultural factors as well. Medicine has always reserved its glory for the living. Even among transplant surgeons, a hierarchy exists: Those who put organs into living patients have a higher status than those who extract them from the dead. One anesthesiologist confesses that his peers don't like to work on cadaveric organ recoveries. (Even brain-dead bodies require sedation, since spinal reflexes can make a corpse "buck" in surgery.) "You spend all this time monitoring the heartbeat, the blood pressure," the anesthesiologist explains. "To just turn everything off when you're done and walk out. It's bizarre."

16 Although the procurement team will stay up all night, I break at 4:30 am for a two-hour nap on an empty bed in the ICU. The nurse removes a wrinkled top sheet but leaves the bottom one. Doctors sleep like this all the time, I know, catnapping on gurneys, but I can't shake the feeling of climbing onto my deathbed. The room is identical to the one I've been sitting in for the past eight hours, and I'd prefer to sleep almost anywhere else—in the nurses' lounge or even on the small outside balcony. Instead, I lie down in my clothes and pull the sheet up under my arms.

For a while I read a magazine, then finally 17 close my eyes, hoping I won't dream.

By morning, little seems to have changed, 18 except that the commotion of chest X rays and ultrasounds has left the dead man's hair more mussed. On both sides of his bed, vital stats scroll across screens: oxygen ratios, pulse, blood volumes.

All of this vigilance is good, of course: After 19 all, transplants save lives. Every year, thousands of people who would otherwise die survive with organs from brain-dead donors; sometimes, doctors say, a patient's color will visibly change on the operating table once a newly attached liver begins to work. Still—and with the possible exception of kidneys—transplants have never quite lived up to their initial promise. In the early 1970s, few who received new organs lasted even a year, and most died within weeks. Even today, 22 percent of heart recipients die in less than four years, and 12 percent reject a new heart within the first few months. Those who survive are usually consigned to a lifetime regime of costly immunosuppressive drugs, some with debilitating side effects. . . . Recipients of artificial hearts traditionally fare the worst, alongside those who receive transplants from animals. Under the circumstances, it took a weird kind of perseverance for doctors operating in 1984 to suggest sewing a walnut-sized baboon heart into a human baby. And there was grief, if not surprise, when the patient died of a morbid immune reaction just 21 days later.

By the time we head into surgery, the patient 20 has been dead for more than 24 hours, but he still looks pink and healthy. In the operating room, all the intravenous drips are still flowing, convincing the body that everything's fine even as it's cleaved in half.

Although multiorgan transfer can involve as 21 many as five teams in the OR at once, this time there is only one: a four-man surgical unit from Southern California. They've flown in to retrieve the liver, but because teams sometimes swap favors, they'll also remove the kidneys for a group of doctors elsewhere—saving them a last-minute, late-night flight. One of the doctors has brought a footstool for me to stand on at the head of the operating table, so that I can see over the sheet that hangs between the patient's head and body. I've been warned that the room will smell bad during the "opening," like flesh and burning bone—an odor that has something in common with a dentist's drill. Behind me, the anesthesiologist checks the dead man's mask and confirms that he's sedated. The surgery will take four hours, and the doctors have arranged for the score of Game Five of the World Series to be phoned in at intervals.

I've heard that transplant doctors are the 22 endurance athletes of medicine, and the longer I stand on the stool, the better I understand the comparison. Below me, the rib cage has been split, and I can see the heart, strangely yellow, beating inside a cave of red muscle. It doesn't beat forward, as I expect, but knocks anxiously back and forth like a small animal trapped in a cage. Farther down, the doctors rummage under the slough of intestines as though through a poorly organized toolbox. When I tell the anesthesiologist that the heart is beautiful, he says that livers are the transplants to watch. "Hearts are slash and burn," he shrugs, adjusting a dial. "No finesse."

Two hours pass, and the surgeons make 23 progress. Despite the procurement team's best efforts, however, most of the organs have already been lost. The pancreas was deemed too old before surgery. One lung was bad at the outset, and the other turned out to be too big for the only matching recipients—a short list given the donor's rare blood type. At 7 this morning, the heart went bust after someone at the receiving hospital suggested a shot of thyroid hormone, shown in some studies to stimulate contractions—but even before then, the surgeon had had second thoughts. A 54-year-old heart can't travel far—and this one was already questionable—but the hospital may have thought this would improve its chances. Instead, the dead man's pulse shot to 140, and his blood began circulating so fast it nearly ruptured his arteries. Now the heart will go to Cryolife, a biosupply company that irradiates and freeze-dries the valves, then packages them for sale to hospitals in screw-top jars. The kidneys have remained healthy enough to be passed on—one to a man who will soon be in line for a pancreas, the other to a 42 year-old woman.

Both kidneys have been packed off in quart- 24 sized plastic jars. Originally, the liver was going to a nearby hospital, but an ultrasound suggested it was hyperechoic, or fatty. On the second pass, it was accepted by a doctor in Southern California and ensconced in a bag of icy slurry.

The liver is enormous—it looks like a pol- 25 ished stone, flat and purplish—and with it gone, the body seems eerily empty, although the heart continues to beat. Watching this pumping vessel makes me oddly anxious. It's sped up slightly, as though sensing what will happen next. Below me, the man's face is still flushed. He's the one I wish would survive, I realize, even though there was never any chance of that. Meanwhile, the head surgeon has walked away. He's busy examining the liver and relaying a description over the phone to the doctor who will perform the attachment. Almost unnoticed, an aide clamps the arteries above and below the heart, and cuts. The patient's face doesn't move, but its pinkness drains to a waxy yellow. After 24 hours, the dead man finally looks dead.

Once all the organs are out, the tempo picks 26 up in the operating room. The heart is packed in a cardboard box also loaded with the kidneys, which are traveling by Learjet to a city a few hundred miles away. Someday, I'm convinced, transporting organs in coolers will seem as strange and outdated as putting a patient in an iron lung. In the meantime, transplants will survive: a vehicle, like the dead man, to get us to a better place. As an assistant closes, sewing up the body so that it will be ready for its funeral, I get on the plane with the heart and the kidneys. They've become a strange, unhealthy orange in their little jars. But no one else seems worried. "A kidney almost always perks up," someone tells me, "once we get it in a happier environment." ■

Reflecting on What You Have Read

1 Kahn opens her essay by describing an unusual scene in the hospital. What words and details does she use to describe what is happening to the patient? In what ways is the scene different from what she expected to observe?

2 Kahn has worked as a journalist and published in a number of sources. What are some ways in which her account seems like something you might find in a newspaper or news magazine?

3 How does Kahn's perspective influence the organization of this essay? What are the effects of her including personal, firsthand observations as she follows this organ donor's case?

4 What impressions do you get from examining the graph that accompanies this essay? What questions does it answer? How does the comparison of data in this graph support the point Kahn makes about organ shortage?

5 By the end of this essay, Kahn concludes that organ donation is necessary as a vehicle "to get us to a better place." How does she reconcile her discomfort with the process of transplant surgeries and the dying of the donor with the end results of transplants?

Thinking Ahead

In this essay, Kahn focuses on a single twenty-four-hour period in the intensive care unit of a Northern California hospital. By limiting the scope of her essay this way, Kahn is able to focus on the details of one patient's care and relate them to larger questions about the future of organ transplants. As you think about topics for your personal experience essay, consider situations in which you would be similarly able to observe and record your experiences with careful, detailed notes and then relate those experiences to some larger question or idea.

Ahmed, from *The Blog of War*
Matthew Currier Burden

With their widespread use of Web logs during the Afghanistan and Iraq wars, soldiers have found a new way to tell their stories and stay in touch with family and friends—and the larger public. These uncensored, firsthand accounts of what soldiers are experiencing are having a significant impact on public perceptions of these wars. In *The Blog of War* (2006), former U.S. Army Major Matthew Currier Burden—himself an award-winning blogger—has collected many vivid blog entries. The following entry is by a blogger known as "Sergeant Michael" from the 3rd Infantry Division. In his blog, *A Day in Iraq*, he describes guard duty on Easter 2005 and a meeting with an Iraqi boy that held meaning for both of them. As you read this blog entry, notice the questions and assumptions Sergeant Michael brings to his encounter with the boy; also notice the ways in which the questions are answered and the assumptions are changed.

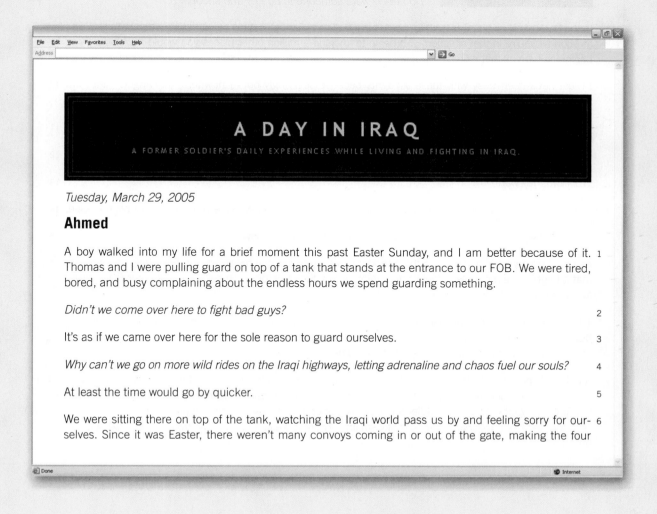

Tuesday, March 29, 2005

Ahmed

A boy walked into my life for a brief moment this past Easter Sunday, and I am better because of it. 1
Thomas and I were pulling guard on top of a tank that stands at the entrance to our FOB. We were tired, bored, and busy complaining about the endless hours we spend guarding something.

Didn't we come over here to fight bad guys? 2

It's as if we came over here for the sole reason to guard ourselves. 3

Why can't we go on more wild rides on the Iraqi highways, letting adrenaline and chaos fuel our souls? 4

At least the time would go by quicker. 5

We were sitting there on top of the tank, watching the Iraqi world pass us by and feeling sorry for our- 6
selves. Since it was Easter, there weren't many convoys coming in or out of the gate, making the four

File Edit View Favorites Tools Help

Address ⌄ → Go

ABOUT ME

**MICHAEL
IRAQ**

adayiniraq@yahoo.com

VIEW MY COMPLETE PROFILE

hours seem endless. I tried hard not to glance at my watch again, knowing that I would be disappointed with what it had to tell me. Thomas and I had run out of things to talk about and were both in a daze of exhaustion.

I was behind the M240, and he was behind the .50 cal. Both of us were secretly wishing for a reason to make these guns talk. The guns sat lifeless, inanimate tools of death, begging to be brought to life. 7

Do I really want someone to ride by and shoot at us? 8

In the back of my mind I was grateful not to have bullets whizzing past my head. I know what that's like, and as soon as you're in that situation, you begin to imagine a million other places you would rather be. I was beginning to think that a firefight would be a welcome intrusion into my otherwise peaceful, boring day. 9

I must have been busy with these thoughts because seemingly out of nowhere, like angels sent from heaven, two young boys appeared at the gates, beckoning us with their voices. 10

Where the hell had they come from? 11

Thomas looked up and wondered the same thing. 12

What did they want? 13

One of them waved a piece of paper in his hand as if he was a messenger, anxious to deliver his message. 14

"I'll go see what they want," Thomas said. "Hopefully they won't blow me up." 15

As I held up my hand to signal for them to wait there, I realized that his comment didn't hold the sarcasm that it might have a couple of weeks ago before a boy their age blew himself up outside our FOB, killing four Iraqi soldiers in the process. 16

Thomas got off the tank and began walking toward the boys, holding up his hand at one point when they began to duck under the gate. They got the message and stood there waiting, leaning against the long arm stretching from one side of the gate to the other. 17

As Thomas got close to the gate, the boy with the message held out the paper for him to take. The boys both smiled and looked at each other with relief, as if their mission had finally been accomplished in handing this young American soldier this piece of paper. I could see Thomas shake his head a little as he read the piece of paper. With the boys still smiling, Thomas walked back to the tank with a bleak look on his face. 18

Done   Internet

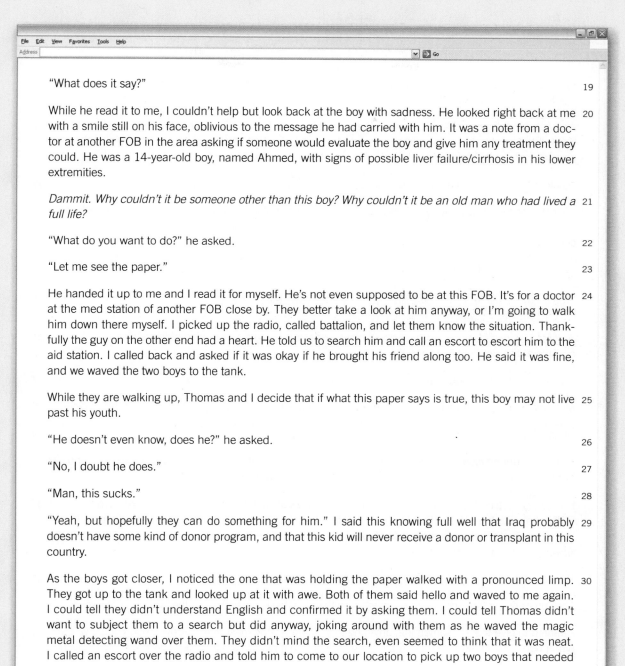

File Edit View Favorites Tools Help

Address ▾ → Go

"What does it say?" 19

While he read it to me, I couldn't help but look back at the boy with sadness. He looked right back at me 20
with a smile still on his face, oblivious to the message he had carried with him. It was a note from a doctor at another FOB in the area asking if someone would evaluate the boy and give him any treatment they
could. He was a 14-year-old boy, named Ahmed, with signs of possible liver failure/cirrhosis in his lower
extremities.

Dammit. Why couldn't it be someone other than this boy? Why couldn't it be an old man who had lived a 21
full life?

"What do you want to do?" he asked. 22

"Let me see the paper." 23

He handed it up to me and I read it for myself. He's not even supposed to be at this FOB. It's for a doctor 24
at the med station of another FOB close by. They better take a look at him anyway, or I'm going to walk
him down there myself. I picked up the radio, called battalion, and let them know the situation. Thankfully the guy on the other end had a heart. He told us to search him and call an escort to escort him to the
aid station. I called back and asked if it was okay if he brought his friend along too. He said it was fine,
and we waved the two boys to the tank.

While they are walking up, Thomas and I decide that if what this paper says is true, this boy may not live 25
past his youth.

"He doesn't even know, does he?" he asked. 26

"No, I doubt he does." 27

"Man, this sucks." 28

"Yeah, but hopefully they can do something for him." I said this knowing full well that Iraq probably 29
doesn't have some kind of donor program, and that this kid will never receive a donor or transplant in this
country.

As the boys got closer, I noticed the one that was holding the paper walked with a pronounced limp. 30
They got up to the tank and looked up at it with awe. Both of them said hello and waved to me again.
I could tell they didn't understand English and confirmed it by asking them. I could tell Thomas didn't
want to subject them to a search but did anyway, joking around with them as he waved the magic
metal detecting wand over them. They didn't mind the search, even seemed to think that it was neat.
I called an escort over the radio and told him to come to our location to pick up two boys that needed

Done   Internet

File Edit View Favorites Tools Help

Address | | Go

to go to the aid station. I knew it would be a few minutes before he arrived, so I got down off the tank to talk to them.

Ahmed's friend's name was Mohamed. They were both wearing long-sleeve t-shirts with sweat pants that were dirty from the knee down. Ahmed and Mohamed, good ol' pals, were having the time of their life just getting to walk into the Americans' camp and talk with some soldiers. 31

"Look at his foot," Thomas said. "It looks pretty bad." 32

His right foot was twice the size of his left, so that it wouldn't fit into his sandal. Ahmed saw me look at his foot, and I tried to hide the surprised look on my face. With the hand signals that became our way of communicating, he asked me if I wanted to see it. 33

"Yeah, let me take a look at it." 34

He slid his pants leg up and pulled his sock down, revealing a hugely swollen foot with a bandage around it that had been stained by blood and pus. 35

At least they can clean it up and put on a new bandage, I thought, as I tried to hide the disgusted look on my face at the sight of his wound. 36

"What happened to your foot?" I asked. 37

Mohamed somehow understood and began moving his arms in an upward motion around his body. 38

"Was it fire, did he get burned?" 39

Mohamed understood the word fire and said yes, it was fire. Ahmed, still smiling, showed me another burn scar on his hand. This poor kid got burned and now it won't heal. 40

Letting my fingers do the walking, I asked them if they had walked all the way over here from the other FOB. They didn't understand until I asked them if they had ridden in a sierra over here. Sierra is Arabic for car, and with that word they understood. I wouldn't have been surprised if Ahmed had limped all the way over here with his bad foot. 41

Where were Ahmed's parents? Why hadn't they come with him? 42

They only answer that I could come up with was that they too knew nothing of the severity of his wound. 43

I wanted to give this kid something, anything that would maybe make him happy. I wish I could've given him a ride in the tank. I wish I had the power to get him a ride on a helicopter. I wish I could've put him 44

Done   Internet

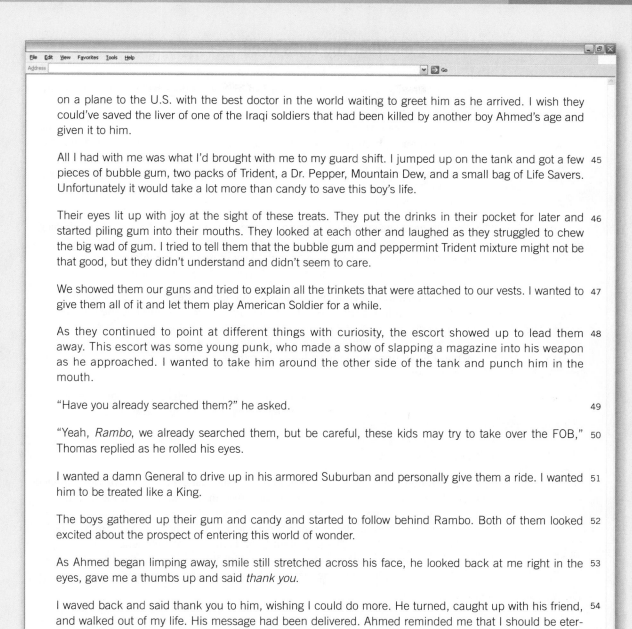

on a plane to the U.S. with the best doctor in the world waiting to greet him as he arrived. I wish they could've saved the liver of one of the Iraqi soldiers that had been killed by another boy Ahmed's age and given it to him.

All I had with me was what I'd brought with me to my guard shift. I jumped up on the tank and got a few pieces of bubble gum, two packs of Trident, a Dr. Pepper, Mountain Dew, and a small bag of Life Savers. Unfortunately it would take a lot more than candy to save this boy's life. 45

Their eyes lit up with joy at the sight of these treats. They put the drinks in their pocket for later and started piling gum into their mouths. They looked at each other and laughed as they struggled to chew the big wad of gum. I tried to tell them that the bubble gum and peppermint Trident mixture might not be that good, but they didn't understand and didn't seem to care. 46

We showed them our guns and tried to explain all the trinkets that were attached to our vests. I wanted to give them all of it and let them play American Soldier for a while. 47

As they continued to point at different things with curiosity, the escort showed up to lead them away. This escort was some young punk, who made a show of slapping a magazine into his weapon as he approached. I wanted to take him around the other side of the tank and punch him in the mouth. 48

"Have you already searched them?" he asked. 49

"Yeah, *Rambo*, we already searched them, but be careful, these kids may try to take over the FOB," Thomas replied as he rolled his eyes. 50

I wanted a damn General to drive up in his armored Suburban and personally give them a ride. I wanted him to be treated like a King. 51

The boys gathered up their gum and candy and started to follow behind Rambo. Both of them looked excited about the prospect of entering this world of wonder. 52

As Ahmed began limping away, smile still stretched across his face, he looked back at me right in the eyes, gave me a thumbs up and said *thank you*. 53

I waved back and said thank you to him, wishing I could do more. He turned, caught up with his friend, and walked out of my life. His message had been delivered. Ahmed reminded me that I should be eternally grateful for all that has been given to me. 54

At this point, guard duty didn't seem like that bad a deal. 55

Reflecting on What You Have Read

1 In what ways does Sergeant Michael establish himself as a typical American soldier at the beginning of this post to his blog? In what ways does he convey his everyday experiences in Iraq?

2 Although Sergeant Michael is on guard duty, he has no expectation of encountering Iraqi children at the beginning of this entry. When the boys appear, he and his partner must analyze and determine the best course of action. How does Sergeant Michael help readers experience what it's like to be in a situation they have likely never been in? What are some of the ways he attempts to do so? Do you think he succeeds? Why or why not?

3 What impressions do you get from the images that anchor and accompany this blog? What do these images—a black, simple heading and a small American flag—tell you about the writer? To what extent does the lack of images and information about "Sergeant Michael" convey an image of a typical American soldier?

4 In the first several paragraphs of his post, Michael relates his thoughts about guard duty and being in a daze. When the Iraqi boys appear, he describes the tension he and his colleague feel about the boys' appearance. What attitudes and emotions does Sergeant Michael go through during the course of his encounter? What does he achieve by writing about his feelings—from boredom to empathy—in the encounter with Ahmed?

5 In editing *The Blog of War*, Burden could choose from literally thousands of blog entries. What reasons do you see for including this particular entry?

Thinking Ahead

In this selection from *The Blog of War*, Sergeant Michael describes wartime experiences most readers would find remote. If you have served in the military or worked abroad, those experiences might serve as a good topic for a profile. But as you think of a possible topic, be careful not to overlook experiences (in school, at work, in a social group) that are less exotic. The important thing is to think of experiences in which you made some assumptions that changed as you went through the experience. Also, look for experiences that invite strong reactions from those who read about it.

Bill Buford lives in New York City and is a journalist and staff writer for *The New Yorker*. He has written two books based on firsthand research: one examining British soccer hooliganism, *Among the Thugs* (1992), and the second, *Heat* (2006), recounting his training to become a cook in an elite New York restaurant. The following reading is an excerpt from a longer article published in *The New Yorker* in 1999. In this excerpt, Buford recounts his experiences working in a sweatshop while he was student at the University of California at Berkeley in the 1970s. As you read this essay, notice the way Buford selects specific details that reflect his attitudes and his relationships with his coworkers.

Sweat Is Good

Remembering his own sweatshop days, the author revisits America's most maligned industry.

By Bill Buford

What is a sweatshop? My understanding was fashioned twenty-five years ago. In 1974, I was a student at the University of California at Berkeley and—determined to pay my own way, looking for a job—found myself below San Pablo Avenue, near the bay, in a factory that had all the design flair of an aircraft hangar: aluminum walls, no windows, floor fans, rows and rows of fluorescent lighting, and an overwhelming sense that the entire operation could be packed up and shipped off overnight. A new clothing manufacturer, Snow Lion, was looking for cutters. In that Sierra Club-friendly town, Snow Lion made outdoor clothes, sleeping bags, and camping jackets, the fat-man kind that, in winter, used to render so many California college students into identical-looking Michelin Men of indeterminate sex and girth. Snow Lion made such bubble clothes, but bubble clothes of a new type, made of a lightweight, quick-drying fabric that was meant to be as warm as goose down—the thing that prefigured the thing that came before Gore-Tex.

There were three whites in the company: the founder, William Simon, with whom I would have one conversation, two years later, when he confessed that his real ambition wasn't to be a millionaire running a factory of immigrant labor but to write a novel about the revolution ("'68 and all that"); the floor manager, a roly-poly figure with a bulldog face and the easy manner of a neighborhood cop; and Steve, the sandy-haired supervisor of the cutters. And now there was a fourth: me. Most of the people in the factory were Chinese, but there were, unusually for the time, a large number of Hindi-speaking Indians.

One was Vikram Singh. (His name and some details about his background have been

I believed the mindless work would allow for an active mind. In fact, small repetitive tasks remove any chance of thought.

changed.) He and I were hired at the same time. Vikram was in his early twenties, although I always thought of him as much older, for no other reason than that our situations were so different. When my work was done, I rejoined a houseful of Berkeley undergraduates. Vikram, a recent immigrant self-consciously embarking on a new life, crossed the bay to the far side of San Francisco, where he lived in one of the subsidized housing projects. He had recently married—I would meet his wife later, a pretty, petite woman, always dressed in a sari, with a shy manner and deep brown eyes—and by his third month on the job she was pregnant. He made the announcement in a manner which suggested he'd be making the same one every year or so for many years to come. Vikram had a lean, mature face, thin feminine arms, a wiry build, and, initially at least, an immigrant's deferential manner. He always wore the same thing: a white cotton shirt and a pair of lightweight dark-brown wool trousers, a uniform attractively at odds both with the informal style of bluejean Berkeley and with what I assumed had been the hot-weather fashion of where he was from. Vikram was from Trinidad, a country I didn't know and pictured only in caricature: a cartoon Caribbean of calypso and rum. I knew nothing about the Indian population there, or the sad history of indentured labor, or what it meant to be a member of a self-contained, self-preserving culture that had been imported across the globe because it was prepared to work cheap. . . .

My job consisted of a simple, relentlessly repeated routine. I began by clamping down my synthetic mountain fabric at one end of my long cutter's table, rolling it out taut, and clamping it down at the other end. I went back to the beginning of the table and marked out patterns on the fabric with chalk—two pieces for a sleeping bag, five pieces for a jacket. Then I returned once again and cut out the pieces with an electric rotary-blade cutter. Finally, I returned to bundle each item up, tucking a perforated tally sheet inside. This sheet was the basis of my paycheck: I'd tear off one perforated tab for each garment I cut—forty cents for a sleeping bag, sixty-five cents for a jacket—and hand over my tabs when my shift was completed. Other tasks in the assembly—trimming, sewing, finishing— also had perforated tabs to be torn off. At first, I couldn't cut more than twenty jackets a shift, fewer than three meticulously, tediously carved parcels an hour.

When I began, I believed that mindless work would actually allow for an active mind: that with nothing to think about, it would be possible to think. In fact, small repetitive tasks, done under pressure, remove any chance of thought, except possibly one or two small thoughts, irritatingly small thoughts, which, like the work itself, are also endlessly repeated. I would often arrive prepared, with a specific subject I wanted to think about—an essay I was meant to write, say—but in the course of my work some small thought would present itself and, locked in by the routine of everything else, would become fixed and never leave. It might be something trivial, the lyrics of a song, invariably a terrible song, and never all of its lyrics ("You're just too good to be true, can't take my eyes off of you . . ."). Or it might be something someone had said or done. I remember repeating: *Why did she have to kiss him?* A girlfriend problem. Clamp it down (look at my watch—twenty seconds gone). Run back. Pick up the patterns (ten seconds). Mark them out with chalk (ninety seconds). *And on the lips, too.* Toss the patterns to one side. Run back. Turn on the rotary blade. Buzz, buzz, buzz (two minutes, five seconds). *Couldn't she have kissed him on the cheek?* Run back. Bundle the first one. *Or maybe a little peck?* Bundle the second one (twenty-five seconds gone, running late). *Especially such a wet kiss!* Bundle the third. Run back, start again. (Shit, twenty seconds behind my target.) *What else did she do?* And that, for eight hours, would be the sum of my mind's activity.

I got faster. My three jackets an hour had long been increased to fifteen when I tried to see just how many I could do. Finally I got to twenty, although I could never sustain the pace. If I had, that would have been an earning of thirteen dollars an hour, a good wage in 1974—not bad now. Vikram Singh was also fast, and we had competitions. When I hit twenty, he got twenty-one. He had such a lithe, effeminate build—how did he do it? When I matched him, he beat me again. And then one night, on my own, having already worked an eleven-hour day, needing the money, late on rent, no one else in the factory, I sliced off the tip of my finger, all of it happening, in the way of these things, in an eerie slow motion: my hand always moving just ahead of the cutter, fingers spread, holding down the fabric while I was carving out the curve of a sleeve, when—*zip!*—for some reason the blade went left by two inches, making a shortcut diagonal, ruining the sleeve, and slicing through the top of my finger. It fell onto the fabric, the fingernail intact. I put it into my pocket, which was already filled with chalk—a souvenir to display to my roommates at breakfast—the rump of my finger now a gushing red spout. When I got to the hospital, I discovered that a doctor could sew the tip back on. ("The cut-off bit? Yes, it's here in my pocket somewhere—hold on a second.")

7 I seemed to have passed through some kind of initiation rite. The roly-poly manager now smiled when he saw me. Vikram, my fellow-cutter (who still had his fingers), actively befriended me. We'd meet on a dock on breezy San Francisco Sunday afternoons, our time off, and he'd have brought fish heads (twenty-five cents a bag), which he'd put into a net and lower off the side. We'd drink a bottle of beer, and then pull up the net, which, miraculously, had filled with crabs. We returned to his home, a Monopoly board of tower-block apartments, where his wife made a crab curry, along with a number of other Indian dishes, more than I could count, which we'd have, sitting on the floor, one dish after another, until I moaned with pain, astonished at how much they'd persuaded me to eat. . . .

8 SNOW LION moved to bigger premises toward the end of my first year. I was spared the task of the move itself (which took most of the workweek, and for which the principal complaint was that everyone was paid an hourly wage), because during the academic term I had a weekend schedule. The Friday before, the floor manager had waited for me so that he could give me the new address, and the news that my friend Vikram Singh had become a supervisor. He also had a piece of information that he knew I'd enjoy learning: in the new place, the tables were going to be longer.

9 Because of the kind of cutting we did—one layer at a time—the length of the table was meaningful. Rolling out the fabric and then having to run back used up more time than any other segment in the cutting process; with a longer table, a cutter could get in two extra units before having to rush back. The company would make more money; I'd make more money, too. The equation is a feature of piecework when it's functioning equitably, and it's one that people outside the business don't always understand. The popular notion of sweatshop workers is that they are ignorant, desperate people exploited by a factory owner getting rich on their slavelike labors, but as I made my way around New York I found myself naturally sympathizing with workers *and* owners, if only because the plights of both parties are so bound together. Translated, the floor manager that evening was saying this: "Great news. I've figured out how you can do even more work for me!" And my reply was "Hip, hip, hurray!"

10 The new place had two unusual features: big windows and, just as important, a parking lot. When I started, most of the sewers were dropped off in the morning by their husbands. Once we'd settled into the new place, they started arriving in their own vehicles. A car had become an expression of achievement, and the parking lot was its display. And, appropriately enough, the biggest, most conspicuous car—something square and flamboyantly impractical—was driven by the fastest sewer, a fleshy, round-faced Chinese woman in her early thirties who, at full speed, was a blurry marvel to witness. She was the factory miracle, known to complete twice as many jackets as anyone else, and the reason my weekend schedule was tolerated, even required: I gave her something to do on Monday mornings.

11 The new place had another novelty: time cards, and we were told that we had to use them—told insistently, because at first no one bothered. Why time cards when you're being paid by the piece? I now suspect that the factory must have had a visit and a warning from labor inspectors. Today, they rarely issue warnings. Their position is that a worker has been cheated of wages, and that money must be paid

back or else the clothing will be seized as "hot goods"—goods made illegally—and held until somebody in the chain (contractor, manufacturer, or retailer) comes up with the cash. You can sometimes spot an inspector, sitting outside a factory, drinking coffee from a paper cup, clocking when people enter and leave, in order to compare the results with the time cards inside: provided there are time cards inside. Factory owners like Wing Ma and David Chan attribute this new, highly moral, highly inflexible approach of the Department of Labor to what they call the Kathie Lee factor: there's public approval to be had in harassing the garment factories. Meanwhile, if the factories themselves can't make a go of it, they say, then far more people will be out of pocket.

12 When Vikram was made supervisor, I felt a reflected pride on his behalf. He hadn't been working that long; he hadn't been in America that long. But the promotion seemed to change him. He seemed to smile less, and he held himself in a new way, more upright, straighter, and with his chin—just so. Almost preening. And there was an impatience in his manner which I hadn't seen before. The promotion had created an awkwardness between us.

13 With the new vigilance about overtime, I worked with only one or two other cutters, sometimes on my own. Working alone was the preference: no distractions, no shoptalk, no cigarettes out back with a friend, only the night, dead quiet late on a Friday, except for the long San Francísco moan of a foghorn when the weather came in. The fact was you didn't want to socialize. You were there to make money. There was an honesty about the task, a bluntness. This is not a task that's meant to pass from one generation to the next. People are there because they have a job that's going to help them get to the next place.

14 Then things went genuinely wrong between Vikram and me—little stuff at first, persnickety things, which came to a head one Friday when I arrived and discovered that I had been accused of cheating. At issue were the perforated tabs, your credits for the pieces you do. More tabs had been turned in than there were garments to match. A lot more, evidently. It had been the crisis of the week. By the time I arrived, Vikram had let the suspicion fall on me. I was taken aside by the manager. Had I cheated, I was asked. No, I said, and that was the end of it. But I remember the icy stare that passed between Vikram and me.

15 Vikram had already become someone I was no longer comfortable with. He had become obsessed with sex—he used to phone to tell me about women he'd persuaded to go off with him, prostitutes from University Avenue, Berkeley hitchhikers. Then the floor manager told me about an incident from earlier in the week. One day, at the end of a shift, Vikram locked a woman in the factory and threatened to beat her with a pipe. The incident was hushed up, but I found myself thinking compulsively about the details. A strong man in a fury. A young woman. A locked garment-factory door. When I asked Vikram about it, he dismissed it as a family matter: the woman was a relative, who was threatening to tell his wife about his sexual escapades. I understand the matter differently now. Sexual abuse is a feature of a business in which lots of women are accountable to what is often one man. And there is the image of the locked door. In the Triangle Shirtwaist Factory fire, in 1911—three floors incinerated in minutes, a hundred and forty-six dead—many of the casualties resulted from women being trapped inside, pressed against locked doors, unable to get out.

16 The next month, I quit. ■

Reflecting on What You Have Read

1 Buford opens his essay by offering a definition of a sweatshop. How does Buford's definition and descriptions of work in a sweatshop fit with your own ideas and what you already know about sweatshops? Buford also introduces his experiences by explaining his background as a student paying his way through college. How does this background information help you understand his experiences?

2 While working at Snow Lion, Buford relates the story of an ongoing competition with Vikram to see who could work fastest. What does this competition tell you about work in the sweatshop? About Buford? What effect does this conflict with a coworker have on his story?

3 Buford describes in detail the "relentlessly repeated routine" of his work. He says that he hoped the mindless job would allow him plenty of time to think. What reason(s) do you see for including so many examples of his more trivial thoughts? What is your reaction to his description of his thoughts as he does this work?

4 At the end of this essay, Buford is extremely uncomfortable with Vikram as his supervisor. He also says that he understands the situation differently now. Does his response to the situation seem appropriate, given the description he presents? Why or why not?

Thinking Ahead

⏵ Go to
bedfordstmartins.com/
writingnow and click on
Chapter 2 > Examples to read
an unabridged version of Bill
Buford's *New Yorker* essay
"Sweat Is Good."

In this essay, Bill Buford uses a minute-by-minute account of events he remembers to convey a vivid sense of what sweatshop labor is like. As you think over events you remember and might like to recount for your memoir, consider whether you can relate similarly detailed descriptions of your thoughts or the events. Think about what you said and did, and what others did in response. Can you report any dialogue or recreate any conversations? Try recalling memorable remarks you or others made, thinking about the language used.

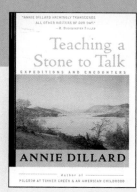

Teaching a
Stone to Talk
EXPEDITIONS AND ENCOUNTERS

ANNIE DILLARD

Author of
PILGRIM AT TINKER CREEK & AN AMERICAN CHILDHOOD

Total Eclipse
Annie Dillard

Annie Dillard is a Pulitzer Prize–winning writer best known for her books of nonfiction. The following excerpt from *Teaching a Stone to Talk* (1982) is part of a larger work that recounts a trip she and her husband Gary took to the Yakima valley in central Washington to witness a total eclipse. The excerpt begins with Dillard's description of the scene immediately prior to the eclipse. As you read, notice Dillard's observations and the passages that succeed in giving a strong impression of the elements of the Washington landscape and the eclipse itself. How does Dillard's writing accomplish this?

Total Eclipse

1 The hill was five hundred feet high. Long winter-killed grass covered it, as high as our knees. We climbed and rested, sweating in the cold; we passed clumps of bundled people on the hillside who were setting up telescopes and fiddling with cameras. The top of the hill stuck up in the middle of the sky. We tightened our scarves and looked around.

2 East of us rose another hill like ours. Between the hills, far below, was the highway which threaded south into the valley. This was the Yakima valley; I had never seen it before. It is justly famous for its beauty, like every planted valley. It extended south into the horizon, a distant dream of a valley, a Shangri-la. All its hundreds of low, golden slopes bore orchards. Among the orchards were towns, and roads, and plowed and fallow fields. Through the valley wandered a thin, shining river; from the river extended fine, frozen irrigation ditches. Distance blurred and blued the sight, so that the whole valley looked like a thickness or sediment at the bottom of the sky. Directly behind us was more sky, and empty lowlands blued by distance, and Mount Adams. Mount Adams was an enormous, snow-covered volcanic cone rising flat, like so much scenery.

3 Now the sun was up. We could not see it; but the sky behind the band of clouds was yellow, and, far down the valley, some hillside orchards had lighted up. More people were parking near the highway and climbing the hills. It was the West. All of us rugged individualists were wearing knit caps and blue nylon parkas. People were climbing the nearby hills and setting up shop in clumps among the dead grasses. It looked as though we had all gathered on hilltops to pray for the world on its last day. It looked as though we had all crawled out of spaceships and were preparing to assault the valley below. It looked as though we were scattered on hilltops at dawn to sacrifice virgins, make rain, set stone stelae in a ring. There was no place out of the wind. The straw grasses banged our legs.

4 Up in the sky where we stood the air was lusterless yellow. To the west the sky was blue. Now the sun cleared the clouds. We cast rough shadows on the blowing grass;

freezing, we waved our arms. Near the sun, the sky was bright and colorless. There was nothing to see.

It began with no ado. It was odd that such a well-advertised public event should have 5 no starting gun, no overture, no introductory speaker. I should have known right then that I was out of my depth. Without pause or preamble, silent as orbits, a piece of the sun went away. We looked at it through welders' goggles. A piece of the sun was missing; in its place we saw empty sky.

I had seen a partial eclipse in 1970. A partial eclipse is very interesting. It bears 6 almost no relation to a total eclipse. Seeing a partial eclipse bears the same relation to see-ing a total eclipse as kissing a man does to marrying him, or as flying in an airplane does to falling out of an airplane. Although the one experience precedes the other, it in no way prepares you for it. During a partial eclipse the sky does not darken—not even when 94 percent of the sun is hidden. Nor does the sun, seen colorless through protective devices, seem terribly strange. We have all seen a sliver of light in the sky; we have all seen the crescent moon by day. However, during a partial eclipse the air does indeed get cold, precisely as if someone were standing between you and the fire. And blackbirds do fly back to their roosts. I had seen a partial eclipse before, and here was another.

What you see in an eclipse is entirely different from what you know. It is especially 7 different for those of us whose grasp of astronomy is so frail that, given a flashlight, a grapefruit, two oranges, and fifteen years, we still could not figure out which way to set the clocks for Daylight Saving Time. Usually it is a bit of a trick to keep your knowledge from blinding you. But during an eclipse it is easy. What you see is much more convinc-ing than any wild-eyed theory you may know.

You may read that the moon has something to do with eclipses. I have never seen the 8 moon yet. You do not see the moon. So near the sun, it is as completely invisible as the stars are by day. What you see before your eyes is the sun going through phases. It gets narrower and narrower, as the waning moon does, and, like the ordinary moon, it travels alone in the simple sky. The sky is of course background. It does not appear to eat the sun; it is far behind the sun. The sun simply shaves away; gradually, you see less sun and more sky.

The sky's blue was deepening, but there was no darkness. The sun was a wide cres- 9 cent, like a segment of tangerine. The wind freshened and blew steadily over the hill. The eastern hill across the highway grew dusky and sharp. The towns and orchards in the valley to the south were dissolving into the blue light. Only the thin river held a trickle of sun.

Now the sky to the west deepened to indigo, a color never seen. A dark sky usually 10 loses color. This was a saturated, deep indigo, up in the air. Stuck up into that unworldly sky was the cone of Mount Adams, and the alpenglow was upon it. The alpenglow is that red light of sunset which holds out on snowy mountaintops long after the valleys and tablelands are dimmed. "Look at Mount Adams," I said, and that was the last sane moment I remember.

I turned back to the sun. It was going. The sun was going, and the world was wrong. 11 The grasses were wrong; they were platinum. Their every detail of stem, head, and blade shone lightless and artificially distinct as an art photographer's platinum print. This color has never been seen on earth. The hues were metallic; their finish was matte. The hillside was a nineteenth-century tinted photograph from which the tints had faded. All the people you see in the photograph, distinct and detailed as their faces look, are now dead. The sky was navy blue. My hands were silver. All the distant hills' grasses were finespun metal which the wind laid down. I was watching a faded color print of a movie filmed in the Middle Ages; I was standing in it, by some mistake. I was standing in a movie of hillside grasses filmed in the Middle Ages. I missed my own century, the people I knew, and the real light of day.

I looked at Gary. He was in the film. Everything was lost. He was a platinum print, a 12 dead artist's version of life. I saw on his skull the darkness of night mixed with the colors of day. My mind was going out; my eyes were receding the way galaxies recede to the rim of space. Gary was light-years away, gesturing inside a circle of darkness, down the wrong end of a telescope. He smiled as if he saw me; the stringy crinkles around his eyes moved. The sight of him, familiar and wrong, was something I was remembering from centuries hence, from the other side of death: yes, *that* is the way he used to look, when we were living. When it was our generation's turn to be alive. I could not hear him; the wind was too loud. Behind him the sun was going. We had all started down a chute of time. At first it was pleasant; now there was no stopping it. Gary was chuting away across space, moving and talking and catching my eye, chuting down the long corridor of separation. The skin on his face moved like thin bronze plating that would peel.

The grass at our feet was wild barley. It was the wild einkorn wheat which grew on 13 the hilly flanks of the Zagros Mountains, above the Euphrates valley, above the valley of the river we called *River*. We harvested the grass with stone sickles, I remember. We found the grasses on the hillsides; we built our shelter beside them and cut them down. That is how he used to look then, that one, moving and living and catching my eye, with the sky so dark behind him, and the wind blowing. God save our life.

From all the hills came screams. A piece of sky beside the crescent sun was detach- 14 ing. It was a loosened circle of evening sky, suddenly lighted from the back. It was an abrupt black body out of nowhere; it was a flat disk; it was almost over the sun. That is when there were screams. At once this disk of sky slid over the sun like a lid. The sky snapped over the sun like a lens cover. The hatch in the brain slammed. Abruptly it was dark night, on the land and in the sky. In the night sky was a tiny ring of light. The hole where the sun belongs is very small. A thin ring of light marked its place. There was no sound. The eyes dried, the arteries drained, the lungs hushed. There was no world. We were the world's dead people rotating and orbiting around and around, embedded in the planet's crust, while the earth rolled down. Our minds were light-years distant, forgetful of almost everything. Only an extraordinary act of will could recall to us our former, living selves and our contexts in matter and time. We had, it seems, loved the planet and loved our lives, but could no longer remember the way of them. We got the light wrong. In the sky was something that should not be there. In the black sky was a ring of light. It was a thin ring, an old, thin silver wedding band, an old, worn ring. It was an old wedding band in the sky, or a morsel of bone. There were stars. It was all over.

Reflecting on What You Have Read

1 Before describing the eclipse, Dillard describes the setting in the Yakima valley. How does the description of the valley compare with what she sees as the eclipse begins? What effect does this contrast have?

2 Throughout "Total Eclipse," Dillard uses comparisons and analogies to relate her experiences. How do these comparisons and analogies contribute to (or detract from) your understanding of the significance of the event she's describing?

3 Toward the end, after the "last sane moment" in the eclipse, she relates feeling as though she were "standing in a movie of hillside grasses filmed in the Middle Ages." What effect does this disorienting description have on your image of the eclipse?

4 Dillard focuses this essay on a single natural event—a total eclipse—that she describes as "a well-advertised public event," but with "no starting gun, no overture, no introductory speaker." What do these descriptions tell you about the assumptions Dillard was making before the eclipse occurred?

Thinking Ahead

Dillard describes in detail the colors and light she saw during the eclipse to convey a vivid sense of what she felt and how the experience differed from what she had expected. Think of comparable experiences in your life—situations in which you found your initial assumptions and expectations challenged. Especially think of times when these challenges have led you to grow intellectually or personally. What were your initial thoughts and feelings? How do you understand the situation now? What happened that led you to your current understanding?

Theatre Geek
David Perry

In the following memoir, undergraduate David Perry talks about one aspect of growing up, specifically his change from a shy, retiring middle-school student to a high-school senior who had the confidence to take a major role in his high school's senior play. This change was important to David. But he doesn't take the experience—or himself—too seriously. As you read, notice ways David is able to laugh (gently) at some of the things he does and thinks, without losing sight of how significantly he had changed.

Theatre Geek

When high school started I was a big, non-athletic kid and I was painfully self-conscious 1 of how these things made me different. In middle school, while most kids would hang out after school or play sports, I could usually be found on my couch watching the Discovery Channel. I always wanted to be recognized for something, but I never had the confidence to put myself on display. This wasn't some crippling fear that kept me from enjoying my life or interacting with my peers, but it did keep me from ever making an effort to stand out. Even in my two favorite grade-school activities, band and Boy Scouts, I preferred to be part of the scenery rather than standing out. Band never put me on the spot; I could always be just another trumpet so long as I didn't play too loud or show off too much. I could sail smoothly through scouting as long as I tied knots, earned badges, and followed the leader. But all this time something was missing. I wasn't being noticed like I secretly wanted. I needed a little boost of self-esteem—something to show me that I could be great. I found this in my school's theatre department, but not before it dealt my ego another blow.

My career in the Gilford High School Performing Arts Department began with middle- 2 school rejection. I was thirteen years old and intent on following in my older sisters' footsteps (Fig. 1). Lauren had been an active member of the drama department, performing in middle-school, high-school, and community productions. Rachel had played clarinet for years in a marching band, pep band, symphonic band and ended high school as first chair for her instrument. My parents would always take me to watch my sisters perform, and I couldn't have been more jealous. I wanted that kind of attention, and one winter day in middle school I saw my window of opportunity.

It was the last class of the day, and I heard on the afternoon announcements that 3 auditions for the middle-school show would begin in one week. I was terribly excited. This

Fig. 1. My middle school ID, age 13 (Guilford).

was my chance to shine; I would put aside any anxiety I felt and prepare for my big debut. No doubt I would be a prodigy on the first go-around. After all, I wasn't actually shy; I had just been temporarily underground all these years, hiding my talent from the world only to unleash it now in a fury of dramatic prowess.

Auditions did not start well for me. I showed up at the stage only to be greeted by strangers with hammers and drills. After some confusion, they told me I wanted to go across the hall to what I knew as the chorus room; they called it the Green Room, which was a lie because the walls were white. By the time I made it to this supposedly green room, people had already chosen monologues to read for the audition; all that was left over for me were lines for someone called Beth. I decided to make the best of things, though, and turn this misfortune to my advantage. I would read my lines with a girl's voice, because nobody had ever thought of that before. Surely they would see how dynamic I could be.   4

For the next week I anxiously awaited role postings. Unfortunately, this much anticipated day did not bring good news. I didn't get the lead role. I didn't get a supporting role. I wasn't even an extra. Apparently there was no place for me in *Little Women*. Discouraged, my continued involvement with middle-school theatre was limited at best.   5

When high school came I gave the theatre department another try, but put off by my snubbing in the years before, I turned from the green room and decided to see what was happening across the hall. There, I entered the realm of the techies: the people with hammers and drills behind all the shows. They did twice as much work as the actors in return for half the recognition . . . perfect for someone who wanted to avoid the spotlight.   6

My first role on tech crew was my role as the Curtain Boy. Scott, our mountain-man technical director with big curly hair like Bob Ross, assured me this task was essential to the show's success. Taking his words to heart, I was careful to pull my ropes hand over hand, making each opening and closing of the curtains smooth and flawless. In my mind,   7 curtains were the center of attention for each and every scene change; I couldn't perform for people myself, but I could live vicariously through my curtains. I was the glue that held each show together and surely it all would have gone to pieces if not for my natural talent. At curtain call each night, I felt as though I should be taking a bow as well. But then who would close the curtains when it was all over? I could not abandon my post.

My next show was in the spring of my freshman year. Spring shows at Gilford were often taken to a drama festival where we competed against other schools for a chance to move on to higher levels of competition. Scott promoted me to props for this show for reasons that I could only assume had to do with my stellar curtain handling. And these weren't just any props—they were Johnny Wright's personal props. A senior at the time, Johnny seemed like a movie star to me. He was the lead in the show, and I had been given the task of creating the tools he would use. Playing the role of an invalid, he needed a wide array of medicines and elixirs. I cleverly crafted these with everything from cinnamon sticks to dish soap in clear vials. Although my props were used only once in the entire show, I felt they played a pivotal role. When he went on to win awards at the festival, I couldn't help but feel partially responsible.

8

My progression through the tech crew ranks really took off after I took a course in computer-aided drafting. When Scott discovered my new skill, I quickly became of greater

9

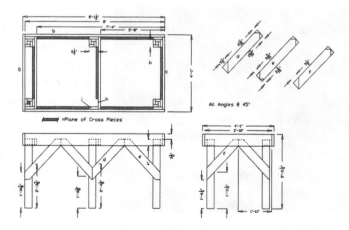

Fig. 2. A computer-aided design (CAD) I created for *The Scarlet Pimpernel* (personal drawing).

value. He recruited me to do set and lighting design, and this was a turning point for me: I had stumbled into something I was actually good at.

My role as a designer started out as a supporting one. My only significance was giving structure to conceptual ideas from more artistically-inclined senior techies. I was still very much in the background. Not only was I not onstage myself, neither was my vision for the world we were creating. Soon enough, all the seniors graduated and the whole design process became my responsibility.   10

Unsure of myself, I started with simple set designs and lighting plots. Even with this modest work, however, I had my first taste of recognition by the end of opening night. People actually came up to me and said things like, "Hey, nice work with the lights." These compliments may have been insignificant and cursory, but they were purely intoxicating to the geeky sophomore that I was. From that point forward, I took on ambitious design projects in the hopes that people would notice my work. I created an elevator for *Little Shop of Horrors* that was completely hidden beneath the stage floor and hoisted a 400-pound antique dentist's chair. For *The Scarlet Pimpernel*, I created a trick guillotine that carried out dramatic French Revolution beheadings, while sparing the actors any undue harm. My lights and set pieces became as much a part of the show as the actors themselves, and with each new project my head grew a little bigger.   11

Fig. 3. A scene from the staging of *The Scarlet Pimpernel,* featuring my guillotine (personal photograph).

This strange new self-esteem soon became apparent in other places. No longer was I just another trumpet in the band. I was the First Chair trumpet player by sophomore year. I played the loudest at pep band performances, and shouted until I was hoarse. My friends and I took the lead in getting the crowd excited; I tried my best to be rousing and obnoxious, and proved to be at least adept at the latter. In   12

Boy Scouts, I took on much more responsibility and became a leader for the entire troop. I served as the Senior Patrol Leader, held meetings that taught the boys how to canoe, and took on a large Eagle Project that I got around to finishing a couple years later. Late or not, done is done.

As my senior year drew to a close, I started to think about my last show with the Gilford Performing Arts department. The last show is where you do your best work—something great that people will remember you for. Every actor hopes to get a lead role for the last show; every techie plans something elaborate and hopes it will fascinate the audience. I decided, instead, to start from the beginning and make my last show the first time I appeared onstage. At least, that's what I told the director I would do. I never actually planned on auditioning, but he didn't take me seriously, so I did.   13

Gilford decided to use an original script for the spring drama festival. AJ, a friend of mine, wrote a play called *Welcome to Lovely's*. In this show, men were the victims, and women were cast as overbearing, manipulative, deceitful, and willfully ignorant. This was a refreshing departure from the norm. I had never acted before, and this show had no place for extras, but seeing as I was a prominent senior and this was my last show, I was guaranteed a central role. Deserved or not, I gladly took it.   14

My role in AJ's play was The Busboy; my job was to eavesdrop and take abuse. These two things come naturally when you have two older sisters and spent most of middle school as a spectator to social interaction. Using my keen powers of observation, I would pick up pieces of conversations on topics that ranged from problems with widespread poverty to "pink and yellow mini skirts," and other items of spirit squad importance. At other points in the evening, I would apply my related life experience and remain silent   15

Fig. 4. Appearing in *Welcome to Lovely's* (Motes).

while I took abuse from the waitress. I did this as she denounced men in general, and again as she dismissed the obvious offense since I was "not really a man anyway." I never really needed to perform for this show, just act natural for a little while.

I have to admit that during my years of tech I had always assumed that actors did 16 hardly any work and yet got all the attention. As an actor, I realized that I couldn't have been more right. Previously, I would be found working at the school with a few fellow techies well past midnight, only stopping when the night custodians wanted to lock up and go home. Across the hall I found that nobody really wanted to stay later than six or so. I did feel a little guilty as I passed the busy techies on my way out, but not quite so guilty that I stuck around to help.

Our show was a great success. The audience actually laughed, and not just out of 17 courtesy; when we finished they even gave us a standing ovation. This all came as a surprise to me—I hadn't actually planned on success. It continued, however, and in the theatre festival we were advanced to the state level of competition. It was here that I was given an award for my acting. I felt pretty clever for that and figured I must have tricked the judges somehow.

It was great to finally be in the spotlight, but I realized that all the work I had done 18 in the years before was far more rewarding and defining. All the recognition and attention in the world can't compare to believing what you did was worthwhile. I didn't follow exactly in either sister's footsteps as planned, but I did find my own way through high school. No longer the big, geeky, non-athletic kid of freshman year, I left for college bigger, geekier, and arguably less athletic. Some people think it's a big deal that they kicked a ball further or ran in circles faster than their friends in high school, but I know better than to buy into that. As I look back now, I can see there were no accomplishments like "Top Soccer Scoring Leader" or "Athletic Hall of Fame" for me; that's kid's stuff. I made chairs rise from beneath the floor, lights dance across the stage, and curtains open flawlessly—now that's something to be proud of. Those are real accomplishments of a true theatre geek.

Works Cited

Guilford Middle School. Guilford Middle/High School ID. 1999. JPEG file.

Motes, Jim. *Scene from* Welcome to Lovely's. 23 May 2007. JPEG file.

Perry, David. Guillotine for *The Scarlet Pimpernel*. Personal drawing. 25 Mar. 2005. PDF file.

Perry, David. Staging of Guillotine for *The Scarlet Pimpernel*. Personal photograph. 15 Apr. 2005. JPEG file.

Reflecting on What You Have Read

1 What is your reaction to the title of this essay, "Theatre Geek"? After reading the title, what impressions did you have of David? Of the topic for his essay? What preconceptions about the author does this title bring to mind?

2 At the beginning of his essay, David provides background information about himself as a middle-school student and describes his participation in bands, scouts, and other activities. He also includes stories about his middle-school activities and early rejections from the performing arts department. How do these stories contribute to your understanding of his work in the play *Welcome to Lovely's*?

3 David relies heavily on his memories of his school days for this essay, as well as photographs and documents. What reasons do you see for David to include the various images in the essay? What impressions do you form of him and his work in the performing arts department?

4 In several places, David uses humor to describe the ups and downs of his participation in the performing arts. How does his use of humor contribute to your understanding of what his life was like? What questions do these humorous stories answer?

Thinking Ahead

David Perry wanted his essay to tell his story about high school, for an audience he believed would be familiar with the concept of the high-school geek. Think of incidents or experiences you had when you were a student in middle and high school. As you reconsider those experiences now from a more mature perspective, think about what those incidents or experiences reveal about you as a person. You might recall more recent experiences that seem significantly different from—or interestingly similar to—the way you see yourself now. If possible, spend time talking to people who knew you or were present at the incident(s) you are recalling, and ask what they remember and how they felt.

Guide to Writing a Memoir

▷ GUIDE TO WRITING A MEMOIR

The next section of this chapter will guide you through the process of recounting a personal experience in ways that allow others to share that experience and understand what it means to you. The first steps are selecting a topic and understanding your audience and purpose. The remainder of this chapter will help you through the process of creating a credible, informative memoir that someone will want to read. Then you will work on creating a draft, using many of the strategies illustrated in the personal experience essays in Reading to Write. These strategies can help you explore your topic (that is, find something to say), write an introduction that will engage readers' interest, create an appropriate voice, organize your work, conclude your account effectively, and integrate visual elements into your account. Finally, in Reviewing and Revising, you will receive guidance in creating a review draft, assessing your work carefully, and using that assessment to revise what you have written.

As you work through the assignment for this chapter, you can read about how undergraduate David Perry wrote his memoir. In the Q & A box on page 62, you will find the first of several brief conversations that David had with the authors of this book.

▷ Assignment

Write an account of one personal experience (or a series of closely related experiences) that allows readers to share that experience and understand what it means to you and why it has that meaning. Your instructor may prefer that you write in some detail about a relatively brief period of time (as in "Stripped for Parts") or recount a series of related anecdotes that occur over a longer period of time but still develop a unified theme (as in "Shooting Dad"). Your instructor may also have specific requirements about how long your essay should be, what sort of topic you should write about, whether you should prepare your account as a print or online document (or as an oral presentation), and whether you should include or exclude any particular visual elements. Be sure you understand those requirements before you start working on the assignment.

GETTING STARTED

Almost all accounts of personal experience are, well, personal. To a greater or lesser degree, they reflect the writer's unique perspective on events or people that matter to the writer, even if other people may be unaware of or indifferent to those events and people. Thus the challenge in this type of writing is to talk about your experiences in ways that will let others understand and appreciate your perspective on them. As you begin doing this, you will select the experience you want to write about, analyze your audience, and identify the purpose(s) you hope to achieve through your writing.

Selecting a Topic

As the readings for this chapter show, topics for personal experience writing vary widely. But whatever you choose to write about, your topic should:

▶ Have the potential to matter to someone else, perhaps because your experiences compare to those of your readers or relate to a theme or issue that concerns your readers

▶ Be fresh and vivid enough in your mind that you can provide the kinds of details that will help readers share your experience

▶ Be relatively limited in scope, either because your topic allows you to focus in detail on a single event or because it allows you to present several vignettes that create a unified impression

▶ Allow you to have some distance from it (If an experience is too recent or too filled with emotion, you may find it difficult to write about or may not be able to describe it in ways that will be meaningful to someone else)

Coming Up with Ideas for a Topic

If you're having trouble coming up with ideas for a topic, you might identify good topics by reading the suggestions in the Thinking Ahead passages that follow each of the selections in Reading to Write. Or you might consider some of the basic kinds of personal experience topics people often write about.

▶ People who mean a great deal to the writer—family members, teachers, mentors, employers, friends, enemies

▶ Experiences in organizations—jobs, clubs, fraternities/sororities, community or religious organizations

▶ Events that have had a strong impact on the writer—concerts, family gatherings, memorable trips

You might also get some ideas for topics by engaging in the following activities.

Brainstorm ideas for topics. Writing as quickly as you can, list every topic you can think of. For the moment, don't worry about how good these topics sound; just list as many potential topics as possible.

Review what you have written with a small group or the entire class. Notice which topics strike your classmates as especially interesting. See if they can suggest related topics. Don't feel you have to accept their suggestions; just see if any sound like good possibilities.

Select a topic that seems like it might have potential, and then brainstorm about that topic. Writing as quickly as you can, answer these questions: What do I already know about this topic? How does it affect me or people I care about? What additional questions might I like to answer concerning this topic?

Student Q & A — Selecting a Topic

Writing Now (WN): There must have been lots of personal experiences you could have written about. Why did you choose to write about your experience as a theatre geek?

David Perry (DP): As much as I talked about theatre, other things such as band and Boy Scouts were equally as important. I could have written a whole paper on each of them, or even claimed that it was these activities that broke me out of my shell. My progression through the theatre department just seemed to lend itself more easily to a story. The plays served as definite benchmarks in my memory and helped me keep everything in some sort of chronological order.

WN: Why did you refer to yourself as a geek?

DP: It's something you'd call somebody when giving them a hard time. And I thought the term *theatre geek* might change people's idea of what a geek could be. ■

Assessing Your Choice of a Topic

Once you have identified one topic that you might like to write about, you need to assess your choice, making sure that you can find plenty of information about it and that it will be as meaningful to someone else as it is to you. Working with a small group or the entire class, try some or all of the following activities.

Summarize what you wrote when you brainstormed about your topic. Ask classmates to help you think of audiences who might be interested in the topic you think you might want to write about. As is true with your choice of topic, your choice of an audience may change. But if you and your classmates can't think of potential audiences, you're probably going to have difficulty in writing a good account of your personal experience.

Think further about your own experience. Write down as much as you can remember about the specific situation, recounting who did what and how you reacted.

List some of the people who shared your experience. Will you be able to talk with them about this experience as you prepare to write?

List some of the additional sources you might draw on. For example, did you keep a diary or write to someone about the experience?

Conduct a brief reality check. Does it seem like you will have access to plenty of specific information about your topic? Have you identified an audience that actually needs or wants to know what you have to say about the topic? Do you see a compelling reason why the audience will want to read about this topic at this particular time? If you can't answer yes to at least two of these questions, consider changing your topic or your audience. Do this now, not the night before the assignment is due.

Understanding Your Audience and Purpose

Up to this point, your main task has been to identify an experience that has particular meaning for you and that might serve as the topic of the assignment you write for this chapter. As you work through the rest of this chapter, you will continue to gain insight into the experience you are recounting. But as you do this, you will need to be guided by an understanding of your audience and purpose. Interesting as your experiences are to you, it is unlikely that everyone will find it as interesting as you do. Consequently, you will need to narrow the audience you hope to appeal to, identifying people who might be especially interested in learning about your experiences.

Also, you will need to think specifically about the purpose(s) you hope to accomplish by writing about your experience. Your basic purpose is to help your readers share your experience and understand the meaning it has for you. But people usually have more specific purposes in mind when they write about their personal experiences. To identify your specific purposes for writing, write out your answers to the following questions.

Audience knowledge, needs, and attitudes

- What do your readers already know about you or the kind of experiences you are describing? For example, have they shared the experiences you describe? Do they know people who have gone through the experiences you describe? Have they read anything about you or people who have had experiences similar to yours? Met you or people who share some of your characteristics?

- Why would your readers want or need to know about your experiences? For example, would they want a better understanding of why and how events happened as they did? Experience what it's like to be in a situation they have never been in? Get a fresh perspective on something they may have observed but never thought about or understood fully?

- What biases or preconceptions do readers have where you are concerned? Are they likely to make any questionable assumptions? For example, have they formed some impressions that aren't really justified? Have they misunderstood your actions or motives?

Audience expectations for content

- What questions are your readers likely to want to have answered?
- What kinds of details will they need in order to understand and appreciate your experiences?

Audience expectations for layout or format

- Are there any visual features (for example, photographs, illustrations, charts, bulleted lists) your readers are likely to expect or appreciate?
- What sort of layout will your audience expect? For example, should you use one column or two? Headings?

> [Guidelines for Analyzing Your Audience and Identifying Purpose]

For more information about layout, see Chapter 9, pages 526–38.

▶ Go to
**bedfordstmartins.com/
writingnow** to download
these questions from
Chapter 2 > Worksheets.

Purpose(s)

- What purpose(s) are you trying to accomplish in writing about your experiences?
- What overall impression do you want to leave with your readers?
- What sort of voice do you want readers to hear when they read your memoir? What image do you want to convey of yourself?
- Are you trying to accomplish any of the specific purposes listed on page 16 of this chapter?

To answer these questions, talk with one or more members of your audience. Describe your experiences and ask how their experiences are similar to or different from your own. Make notes of the details that surprise or particularly interest them. Also draw on your knowledge of yourself, asking, "If I were in my audience's place, what details would most interest me? What questions would I want to have answered?" Then use what you are learning about your audience and topic to decide on the purpose(s) you hope to accomplish by writing your memoir.

As you work on your account of your personal experience, your understanding of your audience and purpose may change. You may, for example, get a clearer idea of what the audience knows or expects, and that may lead you to rethink your purpose. Similarly, you may want to change your ideas about the sort of format that is appropriate. Consequently, you may want to change your answers to the preceding questions as you work on your assignment. But for now, write out answers to the questions on pages 63–64 as specifically as you can. They will help you determine what you want to say and how you want to say it. Then, as you learn more about your topic, look back at these answers and see how you need to revise them.

Student Analysis of Audience and Purpose

Here's how David Perry describes the audience and purpose for his essay on being a "Theatre Geek" (p. 51).

Audience knowledge, needs, and attitudes

I don't think the high school geek is an unfamiliar concept to anybody; either you knew some or you were one.

Perhaps my reader has spent his early years as one of the cool kids and wants a look at how the other side lives. Or, maybe he's the geeky, self-conscious type looking for some comfort in the experiences we share.

The worst thing my audience is likely to do is take this paper, or being a geek, too seriously. The fact that being different is OK emerges as a theme, but we've all heard that before and I'm not trying to get up on a soapbox about it. I just want to share some stories.

Audience expectations for content

If my audience belonged to the cool kids group, they may ask: What's it like to be a geek? If readers were geeks, they may want to know whether it's possible to have some sort of social life in high school. I hope that in the stories and pictures I've included they are left with no doubt.

They'll want to know a lot about my personal experiences, but they'll also want some proof that I have some evidence about what I accomplished and not just my impressions.

Audience expectations for layout or format

They may want to know why I say I was geeky in middle school, so I included my middle school photo. They may not know what a CAD drawing looks like, so I included a piece of a drawing. When I talk about the guillotine and other features of a play, they may be curious as to exactly what things looked like, so I provided pictures.

Other than the pictures, I didn't give much thought to what sort of layout my audience would expect, beyond being pretty and easy to read. I did my best to make my essay easy to read, and I think it is.

Purpose(s)

I wanted to touch on the fact that there is no "right way" through high school, or any other chapter of life for that matter. Mostly though, I just wanted to tell a story, and with any luck entertain my audience a little.

For more information about layout, see Chapter 9, pages 526–38.

CREATING A DRAFT

As you did the earlier work on selecting a topic, analyzing your audience, and identifying your purpose(s) for writing your account of personal experiences, you began to think about what you might want to tell people about those experiences. Now you need to develop your initial ideas into a coherent text that someone else will want to read. The next few sections of this chapter outline a variety of verbal and visual strategies that will help you do this, taking you through the processes of understanding your topic, engaging your audience, and so forth. As in other chapters in this book, you will be working with strategies that appear in readings found in Reading to Write. You can always add to the following lists of strategies by analyzing other accounts of personal experience that you find especially engaging.

Exploring Your Topic

For this assignment, you will be writing about an experience that means a great deal to you and that may have been on your mind for some time. But to make that experience clear and meaningful to others, you will probably need to examine it more carefully and understand it more fully.

Gathering Information

No matter how clear an experience may be in your memory, there is a good chance that you will need to gather additional information. Much of this information will come from personal experiences but you should also consider drawing on secondary sources.

Draw on personal experience. In working on this assignment, you will probably rely heavily on your memory, your recollection of what people did or said, what you observed, and how you and others reacted to a particular situation. But don't rely solely on your memory. If you have kept some sort of written record—diary entries, blog posts, or e-mails, for example—you may find useful information there. Also, look for photographs of yourself and others who were involved in the experience, especially if the photographs show people actually engaged in the experience you are writing about.

Use secondary sources. If you are writing about an experience that involved some larger issue—an experience with technology, for example, or participation in a political campaign—you should look for background information on the topic. Some of this may come from library research: newspaper accounts, magazine articles, or letters and diaries others have written. But some of this information may come from other people who took part in or observed the experience you are writing about. If you can identify such people, talk with them and try to draw them out about what they remember or how they felt. Ask if they have any diary entries, letters, or e-mails they are willing to share. Also see if they have any photographs you might be able to use.

As you look for information to develop your topic, you can use a variety of strategies such as the following.

For more advice on locating and evaluating good sources online, see Chapters 10 and 12. For suggestions about ways to locate useful visuals, see Chapter 9.

How to Gather Information

STRATEGIES	EXAMPLES FROM READINGS
Draw on different sources of information. These include not only your own memories and observations, but also comments from others who are involved in your memoir and information from authorities on the kinds of experiences you are describing.	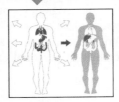 In "Stripped for Parts" (p. 28), Jennifer Kahn does more than just observe the process carefully. She quotes medical specialists involved in the transplant process, investigates lifesaving alternatives to organ transplants, and acquires enough medical information to let her explain what has to happen for organs to be suitable for transplant.

STRATEGIES	EXAMPLES FROM READINGS
Incorporate different types of information. Quotations are often useful, especially if they are drawn from a variety of participants in the experience you are recounting. Visuals such as photographs are also useful in showing specific details you observed.	In "Shooting Dad" (p. 21), Sarah Vowell includes comments from both of her parents and her twin sister. And in "Theatre Geek" (p. 51), David Perry includes not only photographs but also a technical drawing and an image of his school ID.
Look for background information. Include all the people involved in the experience(s) you are describing (including yourself).	 Before describing his experiences working in a sweatshop ("Sweat Is Good," p. 42), Bill Buford mentions that he was a college student living in a "houseful of undergraduates" and was working to "pay my own way" through college. By contrast, his coworker, Vikram Singh, lived in subsidized housing and had experienced "the sad history of indentured labor" in his home country.
Think of specific episodes that stand out in your memory. Explain who did what, how people reacted to what people said, and so on to help readers understand your experiences.	In "Theatre Geek," David Perry uses specific details to help readers understand how naïve he was when he first auditioned for a play: He didn't realize that *green room* referred to any room where actors wait for their cue to go on stage, and it never occurred to him that a male wouldn't have a lead role in the play *Little Women*.

Keeping track of information. When you have gathered a lot of material and are getting ready to write an account of your experience, it can be very frustrating to find that you remember only part of an important quotation or that you aren't sure where you found an interesting detail. To avoid this frustration, you should do two things. First, keep detailed notes based on what you read, remember, or observe. If you find useful secondary sources, record the author's name, the title of the piece (article, book, Web site), and all the information required to locate the piece if you need to come back to it for more information (the URL of the Web site and the date you accessed it, for example, or date and page number of the magazine article). In your note taking, jot down responses to questions such as the following: What did you see or hear? What did people do or say? What was the setting? What are the important details you notice in the visual materials you have gathered? What ideas or emotions are evoked by the information you have gathered?

For advice on taking notes and creating a working bibliography, see Chapter 12.

Reflecting on Information

Now that you have gathered a good bit of information about your topic, begin reflecting on this information, identifying specific experiences you might write about and noting ideas or feelings you associate with those experiences. In doing this, read back over your notes on the information you have gathered and underline passages that seem especially informative or that answer significant questions you or your readers might have about the topic. Then reread your answers to the questions on pages 63–64 about audience and purpose. Are there some questions that aren't answered very well? For example, are you lacking information about your readers' knowledge, needs, and values? Do you have a good sense of what your readers will expect in terms of content, both verbal and visual?

When you have done this, look back over the information you have gathered and highlight key points. Then set aside twenty to thirty minutes and write as rapidly as you can in response to the following prompts, elaborating as much as you can.

One thing I remember/observed is _____.

This is so memorable or meaningful because _____.

One thing I learned from reading or talking with others is _____.

This is so memorable or meaningful because _____.

Another thing I remember/observed is _____.

This is so memorable or meaningful because _____.

Another thing is _____.

Keep doing this until you have used the full twenty to thirty minutes.

After completing this reflective work, read or show what you have written to other students (either to a small group or to the entire class). Describe the intended audience to your classmates, and then ask them to answer the following questions.

▶ Does it seem like my topic would be interesting to the audience I have in mind? If not, can you help me think of other audiences?

▶ Do the details I have recorded seem likely to be especially interesting or meaningful to my audience?

▶ Do you notice any places where readers might want more elaboration?

▶ Can you think of any visuals I might use to make my experience seem clearer or more meaningful?

On the basis of this discussion, list the main experiences you will want to write about.

Formulating a Thesis or Unifying Theme

Once you have identified the main experience you want to cover in your account, you will need to give some overall shape or coherence to it. Sometimes this takes the form of an explicit thesis statement indicating exactly how an experience affected you or asserting the meaning you have drawn from the experience. In other cases, the main point may be only implicit. But whether or not there is a thesis, personal experience writing is likely to have some sort of unifying theme, an attitude or meaning that is implicit in the details of the experience. As you work on your assignment, you may find that your theme or thesis changes. That's fine. But you need to start focusing your work. To do this, complete the following sentence:

> The main conclusion or impression I want to convey through my writing is _____.

Keep this sentence on your computer or in a notebook so that you can review it from time to time. You may find that this changes as you work on your assignment. You may also find that it helps you decide whether you need to gather more information or delete some of the information you have gathered. And if you're thinking well about your topic, you may find that both things happen.

Developing Your Ideas

At this point, you should have at least a tentative idea of the experiences you want to recount and the thesis or theme that will unify your work. Now you need to develop your ideas more thoroughly. You can do this by continuing one or more of the strategies listed earlier for gathering information, but one of the best ways to develop your ideas is to create a compelling narrative, a series of events that tells not only *what* happened but also *when, where, how,* and *why* each event happened. Frequently, narratives take the form of a story. Here are some strategies that will help you create a good story.

 **Student Q & A**   **Developing Your Ideas**

Writing Now: You didn't go into much detail about some of your experiences—being Curtain Boy, for example. Why not?

David Perry: I could have gone on for pages about each one of my experiences, but I had to think hard about how interested my audience would really be, and how much the story actually did to advance the point of the paper. ■

How to Tell a Good Story

STRATEGIES	EXAMPLES FROM READINGS
Describe the scene(s) in which your story takes place. Especially mention details of the scene that will help explain how and why people felt or acted as they did.	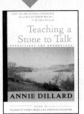 Annie Dillard (p. 47) describes the setting in which she observes a solar eclipse: "This was the Yakima valley . . . justly famous for its beauty. . . . All its hundreds of low, golden slopes bore orchards." But when the eclipse occurs, "the world [became] wrong. The grasses were wrong; they were platinum. Their every detail of stem, head, and blade shone lightless and artificially distinct as an art photographer's platinum print."
Present conflicts people face or problems they try to solve.	In "Stripped for Parts" (p. 28), Jennifer Kahn must reconcile her idealized view of organ transplant surgery with the gruesome reality she encounters. In "Sweat Is Good" (p. 41), Bill Buford tells of a relatively routine conflict—his competition with a fellow sweatshop worker to see who could make more jackets in an hour.
Give a moment-by-moment account of specific events. Tell who did and said what and how people reacted.	 In an excerpt from *The Blog of War* (p. 35), the first third of Sgt. Michael's story takes place in what must have been a two-minute time period: Two boys approach Sgt. Michael and his buddy; one of the boys waves a piece of paper; Sgt. Michael reacts; his buddy "[gets down] off the tank and [begins] walking toward the boys, holding up his hand at one point when [the boys begin] to duck under the gate" to Sgt. Michael's base; then both boys smile, "with relief, as if their mission had finally been accomplished."
Look for telling details that help readers understand your reactions, attitudes, or personality.	Sgt. Michael creates a good bit of sympathy for one of the boys in his blog entry when he mentions an injury that made the boy's right foot "twice the size of his left, so that it wouldn't fit into his sandal." This sympathy becomes tinged with admiration when readers realize that the boy hadn't even mentioned an injury that must have been extremely painful.

STRATEGIES	EXAMPLES FROM READINGS
Mention ways in which other people's words or actions affect you.	In "Theatre Geek" (p. 51), David Perry mentions that when the technical director of his school's plays noticed his skill with computer-aided drafting, "my progression through the tech crew ranks really took off." He was "recruited . . . to do set and lighting design, and this was a turning point for me: I had stumbled into something I was actually good at."
Record your thoughts, perceptions, or reactions to events as they are happening.	Annie Dillard reports what she observes as the eclipse occurs: The sky changed from a light blue to an indigo, "a color never seen"; the grasses became platinum; her hands were silver; her husband seemed "light-years away," even though he was standing near her.
Mention or imply contrasts. For example, you could focus on contrasts between what one might expect (or assume, hope, believe) and what actually is the case.	Sarah Vowell (p. 21) explains that unlike many twins, she and her sister shared so few interests that her sister referred to herself as "the loneliest twin in history." In explaining his first theatre job—the apparently trivial task of pulling the curtain for school plays—David Perry explains that "in my mind, curtains were the center of attention for each and every scene change. . . . At curtain call each night, I felt . . . I should be taking a bow as well. But . . . I could not abandon my post."

Engaging Your Audience: Writing an Introduction

Even if you hope your memoir will be read by people who know you personally, you can't necessarily assume they will want to read it. Readers, after all, have their own feelings, ideas, and experiences to think about. So you will have to give them a reason for expanding their focus, becoming engaged with the details of someone else's life. To do this, you will write an introduction that captures their interest. To accomplish this, you should do two things. First, establish a relationship with readers, showing them how your experience has something to do with things they know or care about. Second, create some sort of conflict—tension, question, uncertainty—that gives your audience a motive for reading what you have to say.

Relating to Readers

The memoirs in the Reading to Write section of this chapter display a variety of strategies for relating to readers. Here are three strategies that will help your writing relate to your readers.

How to Relate to Readers

STRATEGIES	EXAMPLES FROM READINGS
Create a scene or situation readers can recognize and empathize with.	 Sarah Vowell (p. 21) sets the scene for her memoir by referring to the political sentiments suggested by posters that appeared in the windows of her home: One presented one political viewpoint and a second represented quite another point of view. Even if readers don't argue about politics with members of their families, most are familiar with family arguments and know how they can create serious differences between people who are otherwise very close.
Mention a familiar experience.	Bill Buford begins his narrative in "Sweat Is Good" (p. 41) by referring to his situation (a student working in order to pay for college) that many college students (and their parents) will relate to.
Provide background information that enables readers to understand why you acted or reacted as you did.	In "Theatre Geek" (p. 51), David Perry explains that he became interested in theatre because of his older sisters' success as performers, both in theatre and musical groups.

 { Exercise } **Engaging Your Audience**

Using one or some combination of the strategies explained above, write one or more introductory paragraphs that seem likely to engage the attention of your intended audience. Consider using a photograph along with these paragraphs. Bring this introductory material to class, along with your analysis of your audience and purpose (p. 63). Then ask your classmates to tell you whether the introduction you have written (and perhaps the photograph you have included) seems likely to engage the intended audience. Also ask your classmates whether they can think of other strategies to engage your audience. ■

Creating Conflict

In addition to establishing a relationship with your readers, you have to motivate them to begin and continue reading. And the best way to do this is to create a conflict that they want to have resolved. As you'll see in the how-to box that follows, conflict may take several forms—a difference between what people expect or want and what they find, an argument between two or more people, a contrast between what appears to be true and what actually is true. But in all cases, this conflict creates some uncertainty: Are my expectations valid? Who will win the argument? What is really the case in a particular situation? If you create a conflict that makes readers aware of these kinds of questions, they are likely to read until the uncertainty is resolved or they find a satisfactory answer. If they don't find the answer, they will probably quit reading. If the question does not matter to them, they probably will not begin reading in the first place. The following list illustrates strategies for creating conflict that will motivate people to begin—and continue—reading.

How to Create Conflict

STRATEGIES	EXAMPLES FROM READINGS
Mention a difference between what readers might expect and what actually is the case.	In "Stripped for Parts" (p. 28), Jennifer Kahn explains how cadavers have to be treated in order to ensure that their organs do not cease functioning before doctors salvage those organs for transplant into living patients. She mentions that "three nurses fuss intermittently over a set of intravenous drips" that prevent the dead man's organs from deteriorating. Then she remarks, "They're worried about the dead man's health."
Refer to an argument between people.	The basic conflict between Sarah Vowell (p. 21) and her father is established immediately in her reference to the different political posters seen in the windows of her house. This conflict recurs throughout the story.
Mention a difference between what actually is true for a person and what he or she wishes were true.	At the beginning of the entry "Ahmed" (p. 35), Sgt. Michael writes that his guard duty assignment left him and another soldier "tired, bored, and busy complaining about the endless hours we spend guarding something." He was so bored that he "was beginning to think that a firefight would be a welcome intrusion into my otherwise peaceful, boring day."

Creating an Appropriate Voice

Although you may occasionally use a personal voice in other writing assignments in this book, this sort of voice is important—even necessary—in your assignment for this chapter. After all, you are writing *your* memoir, your account of an experience or experiences that mean a great deal to you. So you probably will use personal pronouns—*I, we, us*—and occasionally may write explicitly about your feelings and reactions—*I was angry, I was delighted*, and so forth. However, it can be very effective to convey your reactions in ways that illustrate or dramatize what you felt or thought, letting your readers share in your experience rather than just read what you thought about that experience. Here are several strategies to help you do this.

How to Create an Appropriate Voice

STRATEGIES	EXAMPLES FROM READINGS
Mention details that let readers infer your attitudes.	 In characterizing her differences with her father, Sarah Vowell (p. 21) initially declines to express her attitudes toward guns and hunting, but she notes that "I will tell you that I have never subscribed to *Guns & Ammo*, that I did not plaster the family vehicle with National Rifle Association stickers, and that hunter's orange was never my color."
Let others speak for you. If possible, try to quote dialogue from the people in your story. If you are writing about an event that happened too long ago to accurately quote people, try to remember the language you and others used at the time of the event.	To show how gruesome she finds the whole process of recovering organs from a dead body, Jennifer Kahn (p. 28) quotes a pathologist who works in this medical specialty. "I don't think anybody enjoys recovering organs. . . . You tell yourself it's for a good cause, which it is, a very good cause, but you're still butchering a human."
Mention questions or thoughts that run through your mind and reflect your attitudes or state of mind.	 While Bill Buford (p. 41) is carrying out his routine task of cutting material for jackets, he accompanies each stage of the task with comments to himself regarding a "girlfriend problem": *"Why did she have to kiss him? . . . And on the lips, too. . . . Couldn't she have kissed him on the cheek? . . . Or maybe a little peck? . . . Especially such a wet kiss!"*

STRATEGIES	EXAMPLES FROM READINGS
Mention misperceptions that show your misguided attitudes or limited level of understanding.	Everyone who spends time in the theatre knows that the "green room" is an offstage area where performers wait before they go on stage. But David Perry (p. 52) shows his naïveté in his first audition: "They told me I wanted to go across the hall to what I knew as the chorus room; they called it the Green Room, which was a lie because the walls were white."
Make comparisons that reflect your attitudes, personality, or assumptions.	In "Total Eclipse" (p. 48), Annie Dillard explains the difference between a partial eclipse of the sun and a total eclipse in this analogy: "Seeing a partial eclipse bears the same relation to seeing a total eclipse as kissing a man does to marrying him, or as flying in an airplane does to falling out of an airplane."
Occasionally use understatement or exaggeration. But be careful here. Make sure you are exaggerating or understating in order to reflect your perceptions rather than expecting your readers to take what you say literally.	To parody the exaggerated sense of self-importance he found in his role as Curtain Boy, David Perry remarks, "In my mind, curtains were the center of attention for each and every scene change. . . . I was the glue that held each show together." In describing the fake guillotine he created for a school play, David understates the safety of the device by remarking that it caused actors no "undue harm."

{ Student Q & A }   **Creating an Appropriate Voice**

Writing Now: How would you describe the voice you created?

David Perry: I wanted to sound pretty casual and not like I was taking myself too seriously. ∎

Organizing

Since memoirs rely so heavily on narrative, it's likely that one of your principal strategies for organizing your work will be creating a clear sequence of events, using transition words (*when, then, next, because, consequently*) to indicate when and why events occur. And in recounting this sequence of events, you may want to begin some paragraphs with topic sentences, something Jennifer Kahn does frequently in "Stripped for Parts" (p. 28). In addition, you may find it useful to use one or more of the strategies listed below as you organize your memoir.

How to Organize

STRATEGIES	EXAMPLES FROM READINGS
Organize your narrative around major episodes or stages in your experience. Indicate how and why one event follows another.	In "Theatre Geek" (p. 51), David Perry recounts a series of stages in his increasing involvement in his high school's theatre program. At every stage, he mentions the actions that enabled him to move from one stage to the next.
Create links by beginning a paragraph (or sentence) with a reference to something said in the preceding paragraph or sentence.	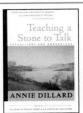 Near the end of paragraph 8 in "Total Eclipse" (p. 48), Annie Dillard notes that the sun "simply shaves away; gradually, you see less sun and more sky." The next paragraph begins with another reference to the sky: "The sky's blue was deepening, but there was no darkness."
Begin a paragraph by clarifying something you said in the preceding paragraph.	After describing her negative reaction to firing a gun, Sarah Vowell (p. 24) begins a new paragraph by saying, "It's not like I'm saying I was traumatized. It's more like I was decided. Guns: Not For Me."
Establish a pattern in the way you present information.	 Early in "Stripped for Parts" (p. 28), Jennifer Kahn establishes a pattern she follows throughout her essay: She describes something she has observed and follows it with background information to explain the significance of what she observed.

{ **Exercise** } **Organizing**

Select one of the memoirs in the Reading to Write section of this chapter. Find several places where the author used one or more of the strategies mentioned in the How to Organize box above. Be prepared to show your instructor or classmates how the author organized his or her memoir to make it accessible to readers. ■

Concluding

Because the primary goal of a memoir is to help readers understand what an experience or series of experiences means to you, you want to make sure the conclusion of your memoir reinforces that understanding. The memoirs in Reading to Write suggest a variety of strategies that can help you do this.

How to Conclude

STRATEGIES	EXAMPLES FROM READINGS
Explain what happened (or may happen) as a result of the story you have told.	Jennifer Kahn concludes "Stripped for Parts" (p. 33) by relating what happens at the conclusion of the surgery: Organs will be placed in coolers and transported to other hospitals. Eventually, she speculates, transplant surgery may be replaced by other treatments. But to convey the short-term prospects for one of the organs—and also to reiterate a matter-of-fact attitude she has commented on earlier in her essay—she concludes with a comment from a member of the surgical team: "'A kidney almost always perks up . . . once we get it in a happier environment.'"
Reflect on the meaning of your experiences.	 David Perry concludes "Theatre Geek" (p. 56) by referring to experiences he considers even more important than his acting in the senior play. "I made chairs rise from beneath the floor, lights dance across the stage, and curtains open flawlessly—now that's something to be proud of. Those are real accomplishments of a true theatre geek."
Tell what you did to resolve a conflict in your story.	Although Bill Buford and Vikram Singh were initially good friends ("Sweat Is Good," p. 41), they gradually became estranged. After Singh received a promotion, Buford worked for him briefly, but Singh proved to be "someone I was no longer comfortable with," in large part because of his treatment of women. Eventually, Singh's conduct became so offensive that Buford took the only course he thought was open to him: "The next month, I quit."
Frame your memoir. Come back to something you mentioned at the beginning, especially if your experience has led you to rethink something you said earlier.	A DAY IN IRAQ At the beginning of "Ahmed" (p. 35), Sgt. Michael complains about being assigned to guard duty. But after coming to understand the difficulties of the boys in his narrative—and the limitations of what he could do to help them—he concludes, "At this point, guard duty didn't seem like that bad a deal."

{ For Collaboration } **Concluding**

Using a strategy identified earlier (or a different strategy from a memoir you have analyzed), write a conclusion for your memoir. Share your draft with some classmates or your instructor, and ask for their response. Can they identify the strategy, and do they think it is appropriate? If not, what strategy would they recommend? Would that conclusion reinforce or extend the dominant impression created throughout your memoir? ■

Designing Your Memoir and Integrating Visual Information

Most memoirs are relatively conventional in design, varying principally in the number of columns of text on each page. But one of the essays in this chapter ("Stripped for Parts") departs dramatically from the norm, using an illustration and a bar graph. Another memoir ("Theatre Geek") includes photographs and a technical drawing. You should check with your instructor about the visual features that are appropriate for the text you are writing; bear in mind the goals of the course and your intended audience. If you decide to include photographs or other images, be sure to observe the following guidelines.

Choose images that connect clearly to the tone and attitude of your text. Visuals should not simply depict people or places mentioned in your memoir; they should also convey the same attitude or tone you create in the written text. See, for example, David Perry's explanation (p. 51) of how the images in his essay help reflect key elements of his personality at different stages of his life.

Use captions for visuals and mention each visual in the body of your text. Occasionally an image is self-explanatory, but as a rule, it should be accompanied by written text that explains what the photograph is and helps the photograph convey the intended effect, as the caption "Appearing in *Welcome to Lovely's*" (p. 55) does.

Cite sources for visuals and cite them in your bibliography. If you use photographs that you have not taken yourself, be sure to give appropriate credit. If possible, indicate who took the photograph. In all cases, indicate the source in which you found the photograph.

As you choose and evaluate appropriate visuals for your memoir, it may be helpful to share them with classmates for feedback. Once you find images that you think convey the attitudes or impressions you hope to communicate through the written text of your memoir, draft the captions and bring the images and captions to class. Show the photographs or drawings to your classmates and ask what messages the images convey to them. Then show both the images and the captions to your classmates. Ask them to tell you whether the captions either (1) explain clearly and succinctly what is going on in the photographs or (2) indicate an attitude that seems consistent with the photographs. If your classmates' reactions differ greatly from your own, you might need to look for other visuals or get additional reactions from people who are as similar as possible to your intended readers.

{ **Student Q & A**  } **Integrating Visuals**

Writing Now (WN): Why did you include the personal pictures?
David Perry (DP): I thought they fit well in the essay. My friends made fun of me for the student ID picture, so I figured that made it just about perfect.

WN: So why did you select the second photograph, the scene from *Welcome to Lovely's*?
DP: People don't often take pictures of techies since they always work backstage, so I wanted to show a picture of a techie, even if it was a techie on stage instead of backstage. ∎

Creating a Review Draft

By now, you should thoroughly understand the significance of events you recounted in your memoir. You are ready to create a draft that will convey that understanding as effectively as possible. This is not a final draft, but neither is it a rough draft. Instead, it is a review draft; it represents the best effort you can make at this point. After completing this draft, you will need to assess it carefully by critiquing it yourself and also by getting others' perspectives. This means that you will subject the review draft to a final review (from one or more of your classmates or from your instructor). Then you will use this assessment to make revisions in content, organization, style, and format.

In preparation for writing the review draft, look back at what you wrote about your audience and purpose. Has your sense of audience and purpose changed? If so, revise what you've said about audience and purpose and keep that in mind as you decide what to say and how to say it in the review draft. Also, look back at what you wrote when you were reflecting on information you gathered (see p. 68). Do you need to modify any of the statements you made there? Are there any places where you need to add information that would make your experiences clearer or more meaningful to your readers?

As you work on your review draft, think carefully about your introduction and conclusion. Does the introductory material establish the voice you want to create? Does it seem likely to engage the intended audience? Does the conclusion reinforce the basic point you want to convey? Do your introduction and conclusion still seem appropriate for your audience? If not, modify them by using one or more of the strategies identified in this chapter. In addition, take some pains to organize your ideas, using one or more of the strategies described on pages 75–76 of this chapter.

REVIEWING AND REVISING

After writing this draft, assess it carefully—not only by critiquing it yourself but also by getting others' perspectives in a final review. Then, use what you learn from this assessment to make revisions in content, organization, style, and/or format.

Getting a Final Review

Once you have made your review draft as complete and polished as possible, have it reviewed by one or more people who understand the principles (analyzing audience, engaging readers, and so on) that you have been working with in this chapter. These reviewers might include your instructor, your classmates, or a tutor in your school's writing center. You will use this review to guide a revision of your review draft before you turn your work in for grading.

Give the reviewer a copy of your draft, one he or she can make notes on. Give the reviewer a copy of your statement of audience and purpose in response to the questions on pages 63–64. If necessary, revise that statement before giving it to the reviewer. Ask the reviewer to adopt the perspective of the audience you have described, and then use the following checklist in commenting on your work.

[Checklist for
Final Review]

1. In my description of my audience, please highlight any statements that give you a good sense of the knowledge, values, and needs of my intended audience. Please indicate any statements that need to be clarified.

2. What is the overall impression you get from reading my memoir? What words would you use to describe the people or events I am writing about? Given what I say about my audience and purpose, how likely does it seem that this impression will come through clearly and be interesting to my intended audience?

3. In what specific passages have I developed my topic thoroughly, helping readers understand what I experienced and why my experience is so meaningful? What are some passages in which I could make that understanding clearer or more effective? What are some strategies (explained on pp. 70–71) I might use to do this? Do the photographs or other visuals I have used contribute to the impression I am trying to create?

4. What portions of my introduction seem likely to engage the interest of my intended audience? What are some strategies (explained on pp. 72–73) that might make the introduction more engaging?

5. How would you describe the voice I have created? At what points does that voice seem appropriate, given my intended audience and the experience I am recounting? What strategies (explained on pp. 74–75) might help me make the voice clearer or more appropriate?

6. How well organized is my memoir? What are some words or phrases that make the organization clear? What strategies (explained on p. 76) might I use to make the organization clearer?

7. Is the conclusion of my memoir effective? What strategies (explained on p. 77) might I use to make it more effective?

8. If the memoir includes photographs or other visual elements, how do they contribute to the overall impression conveyed in the memoir? Do the images have appropriate captions?

▶ Go to **bedfordstmartins.com/ writingnow** to download the checklist from Chapter 2 > Worksheets.

If possible, ask the reviewer to talk with you about your review draft as well as make notes on it. During this conversation, make careful notes about what the reviewer finds to be clear or unclear, interesting or uninteresting; also note any suggestions he or she makes. Sometimes you may have a strong impulse to argue with your reviewers, showing them where they are wrong or where they have missed the point. Resist this impulse, at least at first. Instead, try to find out why they disagree with you. Once you have a good idea of what their concerns or objections are, you might respond to what they have said, asking how persuasive they find your responses.

Revising Your Work

Once you have a good idea of how the reviewer responds to your memoir (after you have listened without explaining, arguing, or making judgments), go back through your notes on your reviewer's comments. Bearing in mind your intended audience and purpose, decide which comments are most valid and use those comments to guide you in revising your memoir.

After resolving all the issues that need attention, proofread carefully and correct any typographical or formatting errors. Then submit this final draft to your instructor.

▷ TAKING STOCK OF WHERE YOU ARE

Although you will find differences among the writing assignments in this book, there are also some important similarities. For example, you always have to analyze the intended audience, write an introduction that will engage that particular audience, and so forth. Each assignment in *Writing Now* will teach you strategies that can help you grow as a writer and improve your work on subsequent assignments. This will be especially true if you make a conscious effort to assess your development as a writer as you go along.

To help with this assessment and growth, continually review what you're learning and try to determine what you need to work harder on in the future. Once your instructor has returned the final draft of your work, think back over all the comments you received—from classmates as well as your instructor—and write out answers to the following questions. (You might want to keep these in a journal or a special section of a notebook.)

Questions for Assessing Your Growth as a Writer

▶ Go to bedfordstmartins.com/ writingnow to download these questions from Chapter 2 > Worksheets.

1. What appears to be my greatest area of strength?
2. Where am I having the greatest difficulty?
3. What am I learning about the process of writing?
4. What am I learning about giving and receiving feedback on writing?
5. What have I learned from writing a memoir that I can use in my next assignment for this course, for another course, or for work?

Here's how David Perry answered these questions for the memoir he wrote on being a theatre geek (p. 51).

1. This answers this question and the next. It's easy for me to come up with all sorts of stories that I want to tell, but I have a hard time fitting them together without just going off on a tangent. All too often I'll get really excited about a certain story and spend all sorts of time telling it, only to realize it doesn't do anything to advance the point of the paper. At this point I will either try to bend its meaning to fit or just get rid of it entirely. The latter is hard to do since I've become somewhat attached, but usually it is the best option.

2. (See above.)

3. The more you read your own work the less you're satisfied with it, and the more you want to change and fix it. It gets to a point where you need to just say it's good enough and move on.

4. It is best to be honest when reviewing somebody's work, and just hope they can take it as constructive criticism. If you try not to hurt the author's feelings, revision becomes a very painful process.

5. Tossing in a vocabulary word every now and then may make you feel smart, but most people just stop listening. If you really want readers to hear you, write to them the same way you'd speak with them.

Profiles

An introduction to a college dropout who is now CEO of his own company (which happens to be Facebook), a photo-essay about one night in a hospital emergency room, a personal account of what makes a friend truly exceptional. Different subjects, different page layouts, different messages. What they have in common, however, is that they are all profiles—efforts to capture in words and images the unique character, quality, or spirit of a remarkable person, place, occupation, or activity. The subject of the profile may be familiar to most readers even before they begin reading, or it may be completely unfamiliar to most readers until they read the profile. Whether famous or obscure, the subjects of the profiles in this chapter will take you into unusual or unfamiliar situations, increasing your understanding of these situations and the people and activities associated with them.

No matter what the topic is, profiles have one basic goal: to provide readers with an insider's view of the topic. That is, profiles try to give readers a sense of experiencing the topic for themselves: hearing someone speak candidly, observing activities that happen spontaneously, or reaching understandings that are not readily apparent to people who are not insiders. In part, creating such an experience entails providing readers with information—verifiable facts about a person, place, occupation, or activity. But it also entails choosing facts that evoke emotions, attitudes, or values, conveying the full richness of an experience.

▷ READING PROFILES

In the following section, you will find profiles of a variety of people in a variety of situations. Following each profile are questions that pertain specifically to the profile you have just read. In addition to these specific questions, there are several basic questions you should ask in reading any profile.

$\begin{bmatrix} \text{Questions for} \\ \text{Reading Profiles} \end{bmatrix}$

▶ **Who is the intended audience?** Consider the language, visuals, and information included in (and excluded from) the profile. What does the writer appear to be assuming about the following characteristics of the intended audience?

- Background knowledge of the person or place being profiled
- Values, beliefs, and attitudes
- Biases or preconceptions regarding the subject
- The kinds of insights they would appreciate having

▶ **What specific purpose(s) is the writer trying to accomplish?** In addition to achieving the basic goal of giving readers an insider's view of the subject, is the writer trying to accomplish a more specific purpose such as one or more of the following?

- Expand or revise readers' knowledge of the person or place being profiled
- Reinforce readers' existing attitudes toward the subject of the profile
- Make readers see the subject in a more (or less) favorable light than they currently do

▶ **How informative is the profile?**

- Does the profile give a clear idea of what's unique about the subject?
- What questions does the profile answer?
- Are these the kinds of questions readers will want to have answered?
- Are these questions answered with the kinds of specific details and explanations that will make sense to readers?
- Are there significant questions that the profile does not answer?

▶ **How credible is the profile?**

- Are the facts accurate and up to date?
- Do the facts justify the overall impression the writer is trying to create?
- Is information drawn from sources readers are likely to trust?
- If it's likely that there are multiple perspectives on the topic, are those perspectives presented fairly? Are any perspectives left out?

▶ **How well organized is the profile?**

- Can you readily identify the overall impression the writer is trying to convey?
- Can you tell how each paragraph or section of the profile contributes to that overall impression?
- Does the profile seem to "flow," giving you a clear sense of how a particular sentence or paragraph leads to the next?

▶ **What sort of voice do you hear in the profile?**

- What attitudes, values, or emotions are suggested in the text? Does the writer seem sympathetic toward the subject of the profile? Unsympathetic? Fair? Biased?

- Does the writer appear to have the experience and knowledge needed to speak authoritatively on the subject?

{ For Collaboration } **Sharing an Insider's View**

Think about situations in which you are an insider. Perhaps you play a sport your classmates don't know much about, or you have an unusual hobby or job. Perhaps you have spent time in a place your classmates haven't been to. Choose one situation you know well and make a list of some of the details that you know as an insider but that would not be apparent to someone who is an outsider to the sport, job, hobby, or place. Using your insider knowledge, get together with several classmates and explain what is distinctive or special about your topic. Give them an insider's view of that topic. ■

{ Exercise } **Analyzing Photographs in Profiles**

Bring to class a profile that contains several striking photographs. Identify the effect these photographs create and, by answering some of the questions discussed above, try to determine how the effect is achieved. Be prepared to show the photographs to your classmates and explain how they create a particular effect and what they add to the impressions conveyed through the written text. ■

Profiles may contain a wide variety of visual elements—charts, graphs, inset boxes, and so forth. But the most widely used visuals in profiles are photographs. Here are important questions to ask when reading or analyzing photographs in a profile.

▶ Does the photograph convey an understanding of the unique qualities of the subject of the profile expressed in the written text?

▶ What kinds of details are included (or excluded)? How do these details convey the overall impression the profile is intended to give? Are the details included in a photograph fair and typical of the subject?

▶ What do nonverbal cues (facial expression, posture, gestures, clothing, relative size) tell you about the personalities or characters of people in a photograph?

▶ What is the setting? What people or objects surround the subject and influence viewers' understanding? Is the setting extreme or unusual?

▶ How is the photograph composed? Where are people, objects, or parts of objects located in relation to one another? Things are likely to seem relatively important or powerful if they are larger than others, are located in the upper half of a photograph, or appear closer to the viewer. The opposite is often true for things that are relatively small, are located in the lower half of a photo-graph, or are located in the background.

▶ Where are people located within the frame—or edges—of the photograph? When something breaks through the frame's boundaries or limits, it is likely to seem especially powerful or important.

▶ What kinds of lines and shapes do you notice? Diagonal lines suggest move-ment or threat; jagged lines create tension or anxiety. Shapes that appear ready to collide, collapse, or crush other shapes can also create tension or anxiety. Curved lines can seem soothing or calming; straight lines suggest stability.

▶ What viewing angle is represented, and what does that viewing angle imply? When a person or object is shown so the viewer is looking up from below, this viewing angle usually makes the subject seem important, powerful, or threatening. If the perspective is that of looking downward, the angle tends to make the subject seem weak or unimportant. If the image lets viewers look head-on, the position is usually one of equality. If the person depicted appears to be making eye contact with the viewer, this person is likely to seem honest or trustworthy, with nothing to hide.

▶ What colors are used? What emotions do they evoke? Warm colors such as red and orange evoke strong emotional reactions and a sense of danger or urgency. Cool colors such as blue have a more calming effect. Dark colors suggest some-thing sinister or gloomy, and pastels suggest innocence, childhood, or safety.

To see how these questions can guide an analysis of photographs in a profile, consider the first page from Ellen McGirt's profile "Hacker. Dropout. CEO." (p. 91). The photograph of Mark Zuckerberg, the college dropout who created Facebook, helps convey a view of the profile's subject that appears in the written text: The overall impression is that he is casual and friendly but also energetic and not easily intimidated.

For advice on how to use visual elements effectively in your own profile, see Chapter 9.

Setting Focus is on Zuckerberg; information about his work setting—the context in which he often appears—is missing.

Position in frame The top of his head breaks the picture frame, suggesting an energy that lets Zuckerberg overcome constraints or limitations.

Photograph by Michael Elins

Color Blue background in the picture suggests calmness, relaxation.

Lines and shapes Every line suggested by Zuckerberg's posture or clothing is slightly rounded. Zuckerberg's left shoulder is slumped, beginning a circle that moves through his bent elbows and ends with the collar of his sweatshirt. These rounded lines make him seem free from anxiety or tension.

Viewing angle Zuckerberg leans toward the viewer, his body appearing to press against the word *hacker*. He looks directly at the viewer, giving the sense that he's someone the viewer can trust.

Details His informal clothing—blue jeans with tattered cuffs, sandals, sweatshirt—is unexpected for the CEO of a successful business, especially one profiled in a national magazine.

{ **Exercise** }   ▷ Go to bedfordstmartins.com/writingnow to Chapter 3 > Visuals.

For practice analyzing the visual information in another profile, see the visual exercises online. ■

▷ READING TO WRITE

As part of your work for other courses, you might write a profile to personalize a trend, issue, or abstract concept. An assignment in a sociology course, for example, might ask you to write a profile of someone who is typical of a larger social trend such as homelessness. In a history course, you might have to write a profile of a historical figure, possibly someone who has played a significant but unrecognized role in shaping events of a particular historical period.

The following essays, which are taken from a range of sources—newspapers, books, and magazines—will help you see some of the strategies you might use to write a profile that provides an insider's view. "E. R. Unscripted" (p. 116), for example, will take you into a location many people know only from television—the emergency room in a big-city hospital. The variety of subjects reflects the different kinds of topics you might consider when you create your profile for the major assignment in this chapter. After each of these essays are two sets of questions. One, titled Reflecting on What You Have Read, will help you analyze the profile carefully and help you recognize strategies and techniques you can use in writing about your own profile subject. The other, Thinking Ahead, will suggest some of the kinds of topics you might write about.

▷ Go to bedfordstmartins.com/ writingnow and click on Chapter 3 > Examples for additional profiles.

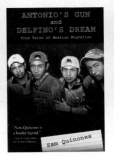

Hacker. Dropout. CEO.

Ellen McGirt

Ellen McGirt is a print, online, and broadcast journalist, and a senior writer for *Fast Company*, in which this article first appeared. In her early work as a financial writer, she founded CassandrasRevenge.com, a site for investor education for women. For the following profile, McGirt meets Facebook CEO Mark Zuckerberg and explores the story of his business—and pressures surrounding it—in the context of Web 2.0, where trends have led to increased interactivity and collaboration for users. The first time she sees Zuckerberg, he is climbing on his bike outside the Facebook offices on his way home. As you read her profile, notice the elements of the article that help you understand the personal characteristics of someone who has a profound impact on business or society.

Photograph by Michael Elins

91

FAST COMPANY

DROPOUT.
CEO.

WHEN MARK ZUCKERBERG SHOWED UP IN PALO ALTO
THREE YEARS AGO, HE HAD NO CAR, NO HOUSE, AND NO JOB.
TODAY, HE'S AT THE HELM OF A SMOKIN'-HOT
SOCIAL-NETWORKING SITE, **FACEBOOK,**
AND TURNING DOWN BILLION-DOLLAR OFFERS.
CAN THIS KID BE FOR REAL?

By Ellen McGirt

LIFE ON THE EDGE

In three years, the Facebook operation has moved from sublet apartments to corporate office space, complete with three catered meals a day, free laundry, and dry-cleaning services. But it still looks a bit like a dorm.

Photographs by Jonathan Sprague

I'm just lucky to be alive." Mark Zuckerberg, the 22-year-old founder and CEO of social-networking site Facebook, is talking about the time he came face-to-face with the barrel of a gun. It was the spring of 2005, and he was driving from Palo Alto to Berkeley.

Just a few hours earlier, he had signed documents that secured a heady $12.7 million in venture capital to finance his fledgling business. It was a coming-of-age moment, and he was on his way to celebrate with friends in the East Bay. But things turned weird when he pulled off the road for gas. As Zuckerberg got out of the car to fill the tank, a man appeared from the shadows, waving a gun and ranting. "He didn't say what he wanted," Zuckerberg says. "I figured he was on drugs." Keeping his eyes down, Zuckerberg said nothing, got back into his car, and drove off, unscathed.

Today, it is an episode that he talks about only reluctantly. (A former employee spilled the beans.) But it fits the road he has taken—an adventure with unexpected, sometimes harrowing, moments that has turned out better than anyone might have predicted.

Zuckerberg's life so far is like a movie script. A supersmart kid invents a tech phenomenon while attending an Ivy League school—let's say, Harvard—and launches it to rave reviews. Big shots circle his dorm to make his acquaintance; he drops out of college to grow his baby and Change The World As We Know It. Just three years in, what started as a networking site for college students has become a go-to tool for 19 million registered users, including employees of government agencies and *Fortune* 500 companies. More than half of the users visit every day. When a poorly explained new feature brought howls of protests from users—some 700,000—the media old and new jumped to cover the backlash. But Facebook emerged stronger than ever. According to comScore Media Metrix, which tracks Web activity, it is now the sixth most-trafficked site in the United Stages—1% of all Internet time is spent on Facebook. ComScore also rates it the number-one photo-sharing site on the Web, with 6 million pictures uploaded daily. And it is starting to compete with Google and other tech titans as a destination for top young engineering talent in Silicon Valley. Debra Aho Williamson, a senior analyst at eMarketer, says it is on track to bring in $100 million in revenue this year—serious money indeed.

Yet there is an undercurrent of controversy about whether Mark Zuckerberg is making the right decisions about the juggernaut he has created. Late last year, a blog called TechCrunch posted documents said to be a part of an internal valuation of Facebook by Yahoo. The documents projected that Facebook would generate $969 million in revenue, with 48 million users, by 2010. *The New York Times* and others reported that Yahoo had made a $1 billion offer to buy Facebook—and Zuckerberg and his partners had turned it down. This followed an earlier rumor of a $750 million offer from Viacom. Yahoo, Viacom, and Facebook would not comment on the deal talk (and they still won't). But Silicon Valley has been abuzz ever since.

"It's all been very interesting," deadpans Zuckerberg, sitting in a conference room in Facebook's Palo Alto headquarters. He looks every bit the geek in his zippered brown sweatshirt, baggy khakis, and Adidas sandals. He came into the room eating breakfast cereal from a paper bowl with a plastic spoon. He still lives in a rented apartment, with a mattress on the floor and only two chairs and a table for furniture. ("I cooked dinner for a girlfriend once," he admits at one point. "It didn't work well.") He walks or bikes to the office every day.

Zuckerberg's college-kid style reinforces the 7 doubts of those who see the decision to keep Facebook independent as a lapse in judgment. In less than two years, the two reigning Web 2.0 titans have sold out to major corporations: MySpace accepted $580 million to join News Corp., and YouTube took $1.5 billion from Google. Surely any smart entrepreneur would jump at a chance to piggyback on those deals.

Looming over the Facebook talk is the 8 specter of Friendster, the first significant social-networking site. It reportedly turned down a chance to sell out to Google in 2002 for $30 million, which if paid in stock, would be worth about $1 billion today. Now Friendster is struggling in the Web-o-sphere, having been swiftly eclipsed by the next generation of sites. The same thing could happen to Facebook. New social-networking sites are popping up every day. Cisco bought Five Across, which sells a software platform for social networking to corporate clients. Microsoft is beta-testing a site named Wallop. Even Reuters is planning to launch its own online face book, targeting fund managers and traders.

So is Zuckerberg being greedy—holding out 9 for a bigger money buyout? If so, will that come back to haunt him? If not, what exactly is his game plan?

Zuckerberg's answer is that he's playing a 10 different kind of game. "I'm here to build something for the long term," he says. "Anything else is a distraction." He and his compatriots at the helm of the company—cofounder and VP of engineering Dustin Moskovitz, 22, his roommate at Harvard, and chief technology officer Adam D'Angelo, 23, whom he met in prep school—are true believers. Their faith: that the openness, collaboration, and sharing of information epitomized by social networking can make the world work better. You might think they

"I'm here to build something for the long term. Anything else is a distraction."

—MARK ZUCKERBERG

YOUTH PATROL
Zuckerberg's brain trust is populated mostly by twenty-somethings. Here, he shares a moment with Moskovitz, 22, and Cohler—an old hand at 30.

were naive, except that they're so damn smart and have succeeded in a way most people never do. From a ragtag operation run out of sublet crash pads in Palo Alto, they now have two buildings (soon to be three) of cool gray offices and employ 200 people who enjoy competitive salaries and grown-up benefit packages—not to mention three catered meals a day with free laundry and dry cleaning thrown in. And they continue to crank out improvements to a Web site that is in every meaningful way a technological marvel.

Right now, the folks who fronted Zuckerberg 11 that $12.7 million back in the spring of 2005 and the other venture investors whose money and connections have helped juice Facebook's growth describe themselves as content. After all, since news of the Yahoo deal surfaced, the user base has continued to boom, arguably increasing Facebook's value. But when those money guys start agitating to realize a gain on their investment, can a sale—or more likely an IPO—be far behind?

"What most people think when they hear the 12 word 'hacker' is breaking into things." Zuckerberg admits to being a hacker—but only if he's sure you understand that the word means something different to him. To him, hacker culture is about using shared effort and knowledge to make something bigger, better, and faster than an individual can do alone. "There's an intense focus on openness, sharing information, as both an ideal and a practical strategy to get things done," he explains. He has even instituted what he calls "hackathons" at Facebook— what others might call brainstorming sessions for engineers.

But it was old-fashioned breaking-and- 13 entering hacking that spawned Facebook—and Zuckerberg was the culprit. Zuckerberg grew up in the well-to-do New York suburb of Dobbs Ferry, the second of four kids and the only son of a dentist (he has no cavities) and a psychiatrist (insert your own mental-health joke here). He began messing around with computers early on, teaching himself how to program. As a high school senior, at Phillips Exeter Academy, he and D'Angelo built a plug-in for the MP3 player Winamp that would learn your music listening habits, then create a playlist to meet your taste. They posted it as a free download and major companies, including AOL and Microsoft, came calling. "It was basically, like, 'You can come work for us, and, oh, we'll also take this thing that you made,'" Zuckerberg recalls. The two decided to go to college instead, D'Angelo to Caltech and Zuckerberg to Harvard.

That's where the hacking episode occurred. 14 Harvard didn't offer a student directory with photos and basic information, known at most schools as a face book. Zuckerberg wanted to build an online version for Harvard, but the school "kept on saying that there were all these reasons why they couldn't aggregate this information," he says. "I just wanted to show that it could be done." So one night early in his sophomore year, he hacked into Harvard's student records. He then threw up a basic site called Facemash, which randomly paired photos of undergraduates and invited visitors to determine which one was "hotter" (not unlike the Web site Hot or Not). Four hours, 450 visitors, and 22,000 photo views later, Harvard yanked Zuckerberg's Internet connection. After a dressing-down from the administration and an uproar on campus chronicled by *The Harvard Crimson*, Zuckerberg politely apologized to his fellow students. But he remained convinced he'd done the right thing: "I thought that the information should be available." (Harvard declined to comment on the episode.)

Ultimately, Zuckerberg did an end run around the administration. He set up the Facebook template and let students fill in their own information. The new project consumed so much of his time that by the end of the first semester, with just two days to go before his art-history final, he was in a serious jam: He needed to be able to discuss 500 images from the Augustan period. "This isn't the kind of thing where you can just go in and figure out how to do it, like calculus or math," he says, without a trace of irony. "You actually have to learn these things ahead of time." So he pulled a Tom Sawyer: He built a Web site with one image per page and a place for comments. Then he emailed members of his class and invited them to share their notes, like a study group on cybersteroids. "Within two hours, all the images were populated with notes," he says. "I did very well in that class. We all did."

Thefacebook.com, as it was originally called, launched on February 4, 2004. Within two weeks, half the Harvard student body had signed up. Before long, it was up to two-thirds. Zuckerberg's roommates, Moskovitz and Chris Hughes, joined in, helping to add features and run the site using a shared hosting service that cost $85 a month. Students from other colleges began approaching them, asking for online face books of their own. So the trio carved out new areas on the site for places like Stanford and Yale. By May, 30 schools were included, and banner-type ads for student events and college-oriented businesses had brought in a few thousand dollars.

"We just wanted to go to California for the summer." That's how Zuckerberg describes his decision, at the end of sophomore year, to head out to Palo Alto with Moskovitz and Hughes. They sublet a house not far from the Stanford campus. And then fortune intervened.

15

16

17

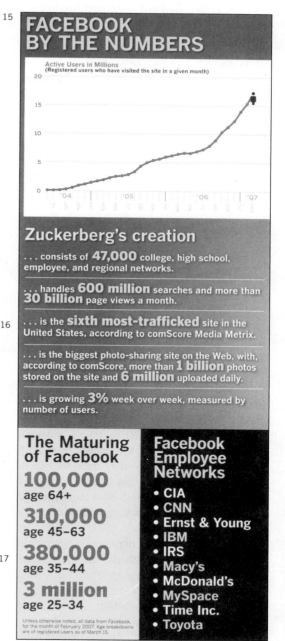

FACEBOOK BY THE NUMBERS

Active Users in Millions
(Registered users who have visited the site in a given month)

Zuckerberg's creation

. . . consists of **47,000** college, high school, employee, and regional networks.

. . . handles **600 million** searches and more than **30 billion** page views a month.

. . . is the **sixth most-trafficked** site in the United States, according to comScore Media Metrix.

. . . is the biggest photo-sharing site on the Web, with, according to comScore, more than **1 billion** photos stored on the site and **6 million** uploaded daily.

. . . is growing **3%** week over week, measured by number of users.

The Maturing of Facebook

100,000
age 64+

310,000
age 45–63

380,000
age 35–44

3 million
age 25–34

Unless otherwise noted, all data from Facebook, for the month of February 2007. Age breakdowns are of registered users as of March 15.

Facebook Employee Networks

- **CIA**
- **CNN**
- **Ernst & Young**
- **IBM**
- **IRS**
- **Macy's**
- **McDonald's**
- **MySpace**
- **Time Inc.**
- **Toyota**

Out on the street one evening, Zuckerberg 18 bumped into Sean Parker, a cofounder of the file-sharing program Napster. The two had met briefly back East. It turned out Parker was moving to Palo Alto but didn't yet have an apartment. "Basically we just let him crash with us," Zuckerberg says.

Parker moved in, bringing with him an irrepressible spirit, lots of ideas, a killer Rolodex— 19 and a car. Parker was also a walking, talking cautionary tale for what can happen to young entrepreneurs. After Napster was derailed by legal challenges from the music and movie industries, Parker had helped launch Plaxo, a site that updates contacts. But he told everyone he'd been pushed out by venture heavyweight Michael Moritz of Sequoia Capital, an early backer of Yahoo, Google, and YouTube. (Sequoia declined to comment.) Zuckerberg took it all in.

Within a few weeks, Parker introduced 20 Zuckerberg to his first major investor, Peter Thiel, cofounder of PayPal, president of hedge fund Clarium Capital, and managing partner of the Founders Fund. After Zuckerberg's 15-minute pitch on Facebook, Thiel was clearly interested. "Peter is a fast-talking, sort of intimidating guy," says Matt Cohler, then a colleague of Thiel's who was in the room. "But Mark stayed calm and got the information he needed." By the end of the talk, he also got a commitment for $500,000 in seed money and an entrée into the exclusive social network of Silicon Valley.

Zuckerberg and his friends had caught the 21 entrepreneurial bug. With the end of summer approaching, Zuckerberg thought back to a presentation he'd heard at Harvard from a well-known dropout. While taking a computer-science class, he recalls, "Bill Gates came and talked." Gates encouraged the students to leave and go make something, since Harvard lets students take as much time off as they want. "If Microsoft ever falls through, I'm going back to Harvard," he joked. With Thiel's money to sustain them, Zuckerberg and Moskovitz decided to follow Gates's advice.

Zuckerberg and a growing cadre of engi- 22 neers managed the Facebook site from a series of sublets around Palo Alto, coding together in endless sessions on rickety furniture. "We never had any money," he recalls with a laugh. "We actually bought a car on Craigslist. You didn't need a key. You just had to turn the ignition." In November 2004, Facebook passed the 1 million-users mark. Six months later, with the help of Thiel, Zuckerberg signed the papers for that $12.7 million in financing from Accel Partners. He hired a new fleet of engineers (including Steve Chen, who would leave a few months later to cofound YouTube). And he moved the company into real office space, on Palo Alto's University Avenue. By the fall of 2005, there were 5 million active users, those who visit the site at least once a month.

Ask anyone who works there what Facebook 23 is, and you will get pretty much the same answer: a social utility that lets people share information with the people in their world quickly and efficiently. Unlike MySpace, where anyone can trawl the site or take on a different persona, Facebook is based on real-world networks of people who share the same email domain and actually want to know more about one another. What you share—vacation photos, contact information, favorite movies, current whereabouts, upcoming events, whatever—is entirely up to you. This all made perfect sense for the college crowd, who show up at school hungry to meet the people around them. But Web 2.0 watchers wondered how Facebook could grow into something that would work for

A CAUTIONARY TALE

Rumors of Facebook's refusal to sell to Yahoo set off a chorus of predictions that it would repeat Friendster's fall from grace.

JONATHAN ABRAMS
Friendster founder

"PEOPLE SAID I STARTED THE SITE JUST TO MEET GIRLS," says Jonathan Abrams, founder of Friendster, one of the earliest social-networking companies. "But if I wanted to do that, I'd have opened a bar or started a rock group." Now the poster child for missed opportunities, he was the belle of the ball for a while: The site went live in March 2003 and with virtually no marketing had more than 3 million users by the fall. Every publication from *Time* to *Vanity Fair* was writing about him; he even made an appearance on late-night talk show *Jimmy Kimmel Live*. Google reportedly came calling, offering some $30 million for the site. Instead, Abrams went the venture route, taking $13 million from Kleiner Perkins Caulfield & Byers and Benchmark Capital—and that, he says, is where his troubles began. "I had basically made a prototype which worked fine for a couple of million users," he says. "But we needed to really rebuild things if we were going to scale." He says his board and investors "didn't get Friendster and wouldn't focus on something boring like fixing the technology." He was replaced as CEO and watched as a succession of marketing deals failed and a parade of CEOs followed—three in one 12-month period. By fall of 2005, Abrams was gone, "I'm never going to make a ton of money off of Friendster like Mark [Zuckerberg] will probably make from Facebook," he says. "But I've learned a lot."

Today, Abrams, 37, owns a bar (but has a girlfriend) and is starting a new networking site, Socializr, which will be a cross between a networking site like Friendster and an events-management site like Evite. He has raised about $1 million, some from former Friendster investors. And he's keeping things small until he knows the technology works. "I plan to make it scalable and well designed from the get-go." As for Facebook, he says, "Clearly, Mark has already done a lot of smart things." Keeping control and having a board he can work with are the critical issues. "Everyone hopes for a story like Facebook," Abrams says, but most stories are about entrepreneurs persistently failing before they find success. What's happened to Facebook is "like winning the lottery."

the rest of us. And it needed to do that, if for no other reason than that the original audience was growing up and getting jobs.

In September of 2005, Facebook was opened up to high school students, many of whom had older siblings already on the site. The following month, the site added a photo feature, and technical demands skyrocketed. "We're one of the largest MySQL Web sites in production," says chief operating officer Owen Van Natta, 37. MySQL, a popular open-source software, "has been a revolution for young entrepreneurs,"

Van Natta explains, partly because it frees them from paying the licensing fees of, say, an Oracle. But with sophistication comes heat. Literally. "In computing, as things get smaller, they run hotter," Van Natta says. When he first joined the company in late 2005, he recalls, it was growing so rapidly there was almost a meltdown. "We were trying to predict how many new users we'd get, how they would use the site, and what we'd need to serve that," he says. There weren't enough people to do all the analysis. "We were just trying to keep the wheels on the wagon." When he went to check the data center, he was horrified. "There were little fans like this big—holding up his hands to indicate the size of a grapefruit—"tucked between the servers. It was over 110 degrees in some aisles." And the data-center guys were plugging in more servers and screwing them into racks, trying to keep up with the rapidly scaling site. The Plexiglas sides of the server racks were warping from the heat. "I was, like, *Mayday!*" he recalls. "We need to get on top of this!"

Growth continued. In June 2006, the site 25 was opened to work networks. There are more than 20,000 networks of employees, from the Central Intelligence Agency and the Internal Revenue Service to Macy's, McDonald's, Time Inc., and the U.S. Marine Corps. Even MySpace, considered by many to be a Facebook rival, has a corporate network of 22 employees.

Then in September, Facebook announced 26 what it called "open registration": Anyone with a valid email address could join a regional network. It was an auspicious moment—until the Facebook community rose up and almost destroyed its creator. The problem was a new option called News Feed, which creates regular reports about the activity within a network or group of friends. It may have seemed like a good idea at the time, but it set off a revolt in the Facebook community. Users felt that their personal information was being broadcast all over the Web without their permission. Never mind that they had posted it all publicly themselves. Or that it went only to people who were friends or already in their networks. Facebook is a fast-moving, throw-it-up-and-see-if-it-works sort of place that typically adds a feature, watches how people use it, and, based on feedback, adds things such as extra privacy controls. But this time, Zuckerberg and his crew

had made a mistake by not putting privacy features in place first.

Taking advantage of another new feature, 27 which allowed individuals to start their own issue-oriented "global groups," disgruntled users set up a group they called Students Against Facebook News Feed (Official Petition to Facebook). Ironically, the News Feed service itself then spread the campaign ("Your friend has just joined this group!"). In less than 48 hours, 700,000 people had joined the protest, and the blogosphere declared it the end of Facebook. News crews camped outside the Facebook offices, as if a bald Britney Spears were being held captive inside. "There was a hilarious email thread as we discussed what to do," says Zuckerberg, who was stuck in New York fending off his own onslaught from the media. "Someone writes, 'Okay, it's like midnight, and we want to leave. But we can't even look through the blinds because they're videotaping us. I'll pay someone $50 to go streaking.'"

From his New York hotel, Zuckerberg posted 28 an open letter to users via the blog on the site. "We really messed this one up," he wrote. "When we launched News Feed and Mini-Feed we were trying to provide you with a stream of information about your social world. Instead, we did a bad job of explaining what the new features were and an even worse job of giving you control of them." His engineers worked around the clock for three days to add better privacy features.

The storm eventually passed, and Zucker- 29 berg now claims News Feed has actually been a hit. "Once people had the controls and knew how to use them, they loved News Feed," he says, launching into some uncharacteristic hyperbole. "We're actually producing more news in a single day for our 19 million users than every other media outlet has in their entire existence." (Facebook has also been snared in a more lingering dispute: When the site first launched, four other Harvard students sued, claiming that Zuckerberg stole their idea. The Facebook defendants filed a countersuit. At press time, litigation is continuing.)

"We're private, and we just don't talk publicly 30 about these types of things." We're in the Facebook conference room at the end of the day, and Zuckerberg is politely ducking questions about the company's financials. Last spring, Facebook received another infusion of VC funding—$25 million led by Greylock Partners and Meritech Capital; Accel and Thiel also reinvested. But conversations with the executive team make it clear that Facebook isn't living on VC cash, at least not anymore. When I met with Cohler, who joined Facebook as the vice president of strategy and business operations, I asked bluntly whether a report in *The New York Times* that said the company was profitable was correct. At first, he hemmed and hawed. "It depends on how you look at GAAP accounting." But then he allowed: "We're growing very fast, and we're funding the growth of the company through revenue and the operations of the business as opposed to financing."

And the scale of those operations is signifi- 31 cant. Beyond the 200 staffers and prime Valley office space, explains cofounder and chief of engineering Moskovitz, Facebook has multiple server facilities. The company is also about to invest what COO Van Natta says is "many millions of dollars" on more infrastructure.

So how does Facebook make its money? 32 Advertising and sponsorships, mostly. Apple was an early backer, sponsoring a site for iTunes enthusiasts. JPMorgan Chase and Southwest, among others, pay for similar programs. "Flyers,"

"Okay," Zuckerberg says, "you have a Viacom, News Corp., and Yahoo. So you compare and think, This is social, but we're a technology company. What's in it for us? How will it work?"

the online version of the paper ads that students use to publicize events, also provide a very modest source of revenue. And there is a nascent-but-growing local advertising business. The big money, though, comes from an ad-placement alliance with Microsoft in which the software giant will place banner ads on the site through 2011. It mirrors a deal MySpace inked with Google last year. (MySpace reportedly got $900 million over three years. Facebook hasn't released the value of its program, and neither party will comment on the terms.) Facebook also just inked a deal with Comcast to create and Webcast an episodic show based on user-generated video content. Called "Facebook Diaries," the series will be shown on both Facebook and Ziddio .com, Comcast's video-uploading site, as well as through Comcast's video-on-demand service.

As everyone remembers from the heady 33 sock-puppet days of Web 1.0, you hatch an idea, build it into a company, and concoct an exit strategy—that's the key to taking the business to the next level and rewarding early-stage investors for their money and employees for their hard work. And there are two basic formulas: Sell to a bigger company, or file an initial public offering. With all the talk about valuations and acquisitions, not to mention the pressure of investors and employees with stock options, exit has to be on Zuckerberg's mind, right?

"The word—it applies a certain frame to 34 thinking about things," he says, decompressing after a long day of meetings. "If you sell your company, that is the exit. That's just not how we think about it."

He pauses, then says with a sigh, "Okay, you 35 have a Viacom, News Corp., and Yahoo. So you compare and think, This [site] is social, sure, but we're a technology company. What's in it for us? How will this work?" The companywide focus is on innovation and engineering, and the commitment to optimizing the user experience, he says. The goal is not to create a media company. It is not about selling movies. "There are ways that you could do it, but right now, we're focused on building this. And if you look at the stats we have, it's been a good decision so far." But eventually? "At some point, it probably makes sense to do something. But we're in no rush."

One clue to the company's future plans 36 comes from early investor Thiel, who has mentored Zuckerberg through the last year's swirl of acquisition talks and rumors. Bottom line, Thiel asserts, "it's much more valuable than anybody on the outside thinks." He points to the growing user base and page views as evidence. "The people who understand the power are the users. The people who wanted the company don't understand the power and don't want to pay enough for it. So we're not going to sell." He adds, "I think the MySpace sale was a giant mistake. The Flickr sale to Yahoo—a giant mistake." A better idea, he believes, is to focus on the technology, which he says is the Facebook team's great strength, and continue to grow the company. He points to a laundry list of benchmarks that they'd all like to see. "Can we get to 35 million users this year?" Dominating another sector beyond the college crowd would be key. "If we were to see that in the high school space, that would be very significant."

But Thiel is aware of a ticking clock of sorts, 37 determined by a Securities and Exchange Commission rule. "Once we get to 500 shareholders, we'll be forced into a situation where you have to give full financial disclosure," he says. (Facebook employees have shares as part of their compensation packages.) Most companies go public at that point. "But our current bias is not to do it any sooner."

What seems most likely is some version of a 38 publicly traded Facebook, one that might emulate the quirky Dutch-auction IPO that Google filed in 2004. It seems like a natural fit; Facebook admires the minimalist sensibilities of Google's design, its focus on engineering, and the "do no evil" philosophy that, theoretically, at least, informs its business. Best of all, if handled properly, an IPO keeps the founders firmly at the helm, just like Sergey Brin and Larry Page at Google.

And an IPO would seem to be a good fit for 39 Meritech Capital Partners, which participated in the last round of financing for Facebook a year ago. "Certainly most of our companies go through liquidity in the public markets," says Meritech founder Paul Madera. "Public markets seem to want to pay more than acquirers these days." If Facebook got a very large offer, they'd have to consider it, he says. "But today, any offer around a billion would be way low."

But Zuckerberg maintains that nothing is 40 happening quickly. "It's a really big change if you go public—all the regulations and stuff, so it's not something that you do lightly."

For now, the company is on track to double 41 its engineering team of 50 this year (check out the first step in the application process at facebook.com/jobs_puzzles) as well as its 50-person customer-service group, headed by Tom LeNoble, who ran global service operations for Palm and customer service for walmart.com and MCI. His reps are mostly from top-shelf universities. (By my estimate, there's $5 million worth of tuition handling customer service at Facebook.)

New users keep flooding on board— 42 100,000 signed on in a single day this past February. The college markets in Canada and the UK have been growing almost 30 percent a month (Prince Harry and his girlfriend are Facebook users, according to breathless reports in the British tabloids), and nearly 28 percent of all users are now outside the United States. And slowly but surely, the site is adding older folks: 3 million users are age 25 to 34, 380,000 are 35 to 44, and a pioneering 100,000 users are currently eligible for Medicare. With stats like that, you can certainly see public-market investors getting excited.

Thirty-six months ago, Zuckerberg was a 43 college sophomore cruising out to California on summer break. Now he approves everything from new hires to the activities of every advertising partner and runs the board meetings of a very-much-established company. Zuckerberg was even invited to speak at Davos this year. How did it go? "It was great," he says, leaning forward conspiratorially. "I wore shoes." ■

Reflecting on What You Have Read

1 It would come as no surprise to most readers to learn that a computer programmer— even the CEO of a valuable company like Facebook—cultivates a public image that does not reflect traditional corporate standards of dress and behavior. McGirt describes Mark Zuckerberg as a hacker and "geek" with "college-kid style." In what ways does the author of this profile try to convince you that Zuckerberg's youthful, noncorporate image actually fits him? Does she succeed in convincing you? Why or why not?

2 To what extent do the photographs of Zuckerberg and the offices of Facebook convey an image of a company that is going to "Change the World As We Know It"? What aspects of the photographs convey this image?

3 For the audience of *Fast Company*, a business newsmagazine, McGirt highlights statistics and explanations about Facebook's growth and business plans and ends the profile with information that has investors "getting excited" about Facebook. How does the final paragraph—revisiting Zuckerberg's brief professional timeline—contrast with the information about Facebook's business? What reasons do you see for McGirt's concluding the profile with Zuckerberg's comment about wearing shoes when he spoke at a major conference?

4 Consider the graph and sets of lists in the sidebar "Facebook by the Numbers" (p. 97). What do these tell you about Facebook? What reason(s) do you see for including this data in this format?

Thinking Ahead

The author of this profile tries to give readers a sense not only of what the founder of this famous company is like but also of why he does some of the things he does. Think about people in public life such as politicians, athletes, and historical figures. Are there any about whom you wonder, What makes this person tick? What background influences and motivations cause this person to act a certain way or attain certain achievements? Could you give readers an insider's view of this person's character and motivations?

Timothy Egan is a journalist, novelist, and third-generation westerner who lives in Seattle. He was a reporter for the *New York Times* for eighteen years covering "national enterprise" and now writes an online column, "Outposts," on politics and the American West. In 2001, he was one of a team of reporters for the *New York Times* who won the Pulitzer Prize for a series of articles on experiences with and attitudes about race in the United States. For his book, *The Worst Hard Time: The Untold Story of Those Who Survived the Great American Dust Bowl*, Egan won the National Book Award in 2006. The following essay appeared in *Class Matters* (2007), a collection that looks at the future of the American dream by exploring how social class is a powerful force that affects the way we live our lives. In this profile of two former factory workers, Egan tells the story of men whose foothold in the middle class may be slipping away. As you read, notice the different kinds of details the author includes in order to help you understand the predicaments these men face.

No Degree, and
No Way Back to the Middle

Over the course of his adult life, Jeff Martinelli married three women and buried 1 one of them, a cancer victim. He had a son and has watched him raise a child of his own. Through it all, one thing was constant: a factory job that was his ticket to the middle class.

It was not until that job disappeared, and he tried to find something—anything—to 2 keep him close to the security of his former life that Martinelli came to an abrupt realization about the fate of a workingman with no college degree in twenty-first-century America.

He has skills developed operating heavy machinery, laboring over a stew of molten 3 bauxite at Kaiser Aluminum, once one of the best jobs in Spokane, Washington, a city of 200,000. His health is fine. He has no shortage of ambition. But the world has changed for people like him.

"For a guy like me, with no college, it's become pretty bleak out there," said Mar- 4 tinelli, who is fifty years old and deals with life's curves with a resigned shrug.

His son Caleb already knows what it is like out there. Since high school, Caleb has had 5 six jobs, none very promising. Now twenty-eight, he may never reach the middle class, he said. But for his father and others of a generation that could count on a comfortable life

Jeff Martinelli began working in pest control after he lost a job that had established him in the middle class. (Jim Wilson/*The New York Times*)

without a degree, the fall out of the middle class has come as a shock. They had been frozen in another age, a time when Kaiser factory workers could buy new cars, take decent vacations, and enjoy full health care benefits.

The have seen factory gates close and not reopen. They have taken retraining classes 6 for jobs that pay half their old wages. And as they hustle around for work, they have been constantly reminded of the one thing that stands out on their résumés: the education that ended with a high school diploma.

It is not just that the American economy has shed six million manufacturing jobs 7 over the last three decades; it is that the market value of those put out of work, people like Jeff Martinelli, has declined considerably over their lifetimes, opening a gap that has left millions of blue-collar workers at the margins of the middle class.

And the changes go beyond the factory floor. Mark McClellan worked his way up 8 from the Kaiser furnaces to management. He did it by taking extra shifts and learning everything he could about the aluminum business.

Still, in 2001, when Kaiser closed, McClellan discovered that the job market did not 9 value his factory skills nearly as much as it did four years of college. He had the experience, built over a lifetime, but no degree. And for that, he said, he was marked.

He still lives in a grand house in one of the nicest parts of town, and he drives a big 10
white Jeep. But they are a facade.

"I may look middle class," said McClellan, who is forty-five, with a square, honest 11
face and a barrel chest. "But I'm not. My boat is sinking fast."

By the time these two Kaiser men were forced out of work, a man in his fifties with a 12
college degree could expect to earn 81 percent more than a man of the same age with just
a high school diploma. When they started work, the gap was only 52 percent. Other studies show different numbers, but the same trend—a big disparity that opened over their
lifetimes.

Martinelli refuses to feel sorry for himself. He has a job in pest control now, killing 13
ants and spiders at people's homes, making barely half the money he made at the Kaiser
smelter, where a worker with his experience would make about $60,000 a year in wages
and benefits.

"At least I have a job," he said. "Some of the guys I worked with have still not found 14
anything. A couple of guys lost their houses."

Martinelli and other former factory workers say that, over time, they have come to 15
fear that the fall out of the middle class could be permanent. Their new lives—the frustrating job interviews, the bills that arrive with red warning letters on the outside—are
consequences of a decision made at age eighteen.

The management veteran McClellan was a doctor's son, just out of high school, when 16
he decided he did not need to go much farther than the big factory at the edge of town. He
thought about going to college. But when he got on at Kaiser, he felt he had arrived.

His father, a general practitioner, now dead, gave him his blessing, even encouraged 17
him in the choice, McClellan said.

At the time, the decision to skip college was not that unusual, even for a child of the 18
middle class. Despite McClellan's lack of skills or education beyond the twelfth grade,
there was good reason to believe that the aluminum factory could get him into middle-
class security quicker than a bachelor's degree could, he said.

By twenty-two, he was a group foreman. By twenty-eight, a supervisor. By thirty- 19
two, he was in management. Before his fortieth birthday, McClellan hit his earnings peak,
making $100,000 with bonuses.

Friends of his, people with college degrees, were not earning close to that, he said. 20

"I had a house with a swimming pool, new cars," he said. "My wife never had to 21
work. I was right in the middle of middle-class America and I knew it and I loved it."

If anything, the union man, Martinelli, appreciated the middle-class life even more, 22
because of the distance he had traveled to get there. He remembers his stomach growling
at night as a child, the humiliation of welfare, hauling groceries home through the snow
on a little cart because the family had no car.

"I was ashamed," he said. 23

He was a C student without much of a future, just out of high school, when he got 24 his break: the job on the Kaiser factory floor. Inside, it was long shifts around hot furnaces. Outside, he was a prince of Spokane.

College students worked inside the factory in the summer, and some never went 25 back to school.

"You knew people leaving here for college would sometimes get better jobs, but you 26 had a good job, so it was fine," said Mike Lacy, a close friend of Martinelli and a coworker at Kaiser.

The job lasted just short of thirty years. Kaiser, debt-ridden after a series of failed 27 management initiatives and a long strike, closed the plant in 2001 and sold the factory carcass for salvage.

McClellan has yet to find work, living off his dwindling savings and investments 28 from his years at Kaiser, though he continues with plans to opens his own car wash. He pays $900 a month for a basic health insurance policy—vital to keep his wife, Vicky, who has a rare brain disease, alive. He pays an additional $500 a month for her medications. He is both husband and nurse.

"Am I scared just a little bit?" he said. "Yeah, I am."   29

He has vowed that his son David will never do the kind of second-guessing that he 30 does. Even at sixteen, David knows what he wants to do: go to college and study medicine. He said his father, whom he has seen struggle to balance the tasks of home nurse with trying to pay the bills, had grown heroic in his eyes.

He said he would not make the same choice his father did twenty-seven years earlier. 31 "There's nothing like the Kaiser plant around here anymore," he said.

McClellan agrees. He is firm in one conclusion, having risen from the factory floor 32 only to be knocked down: "There is no working up anymore."

Reflecting on What You Have Read

1 The first two paragraphs of Egan's profile introduce Jeff Martinelli and give a clear, brief overview of the problems he faces. What effect is achieved by beginning the profile with these short paragraphs?

2 In the course of this profile, Egan quotes Martinelli, Mark McClellan, and others talking about their work choices and histories. What is the effect of including these quotations?

3 Egan's profile does not use his firsthand impressions or the words *I* or *we*. Although he does not use the first-person voice in this essay, in what ways does he make clear his impressions about the work situation for his subjects?

4 Look at the photo of Martinelli that begins this profile. What effect is achieved by beginning the profile with this image of Martinelli in his job in pest control? Notice the caption that accompanies the photograph. What does this caption add to your understanding of or attitudes toward Martinelli?

5 Most profiles focus on a single individual, place, or activity. But this profile tells the story of two different men who once worked for the same employer. What reasons do you see for including both men in the same profile? Would it change the effect of the profile if the author wrote about only one of the men? Why or why not?

Thinking Ahead

Think of someone you know who has experienced a significant challenge—a personal or professional loss or triumph, a big move, or another major life event. Consider your impressions of this person: How well did he or she cope with this challenge? What qualities were most important in dealing with it? Did this person deal with the challenge in ways that surprised you? Spend some time talking with, observing, and—if possible—reading about this person or his or her experiences. In what ways are your impressions of the person different from what you first thought or expected?

My Cancer Year
Jim McLauchlin

Jim McLauchlin is a writer and editor, the former editor-in-chief for Top Cow, a comic book publisher, and currently the director of content for a fantasy sports Web site. As president of the Hero Initiative, a nonprofit organization for comic book creators in need, he also oversees financial and other support for comic book artists. He wrote the following profile of artist Michael Turner for *Wizard: The Comics Magazine*, a magazine read primarily by young adult males who collect comic books and are very familiar with the artists whose work appears in these comic books. Turner, who died about a year after this profile was written, was a successful cover artist and publisher of comic books whose best known work has been on the comics *Witchblade* and *Fathom*. As you read the profile, notice ways McLauchlin reveals his attitude toward Turner. Also note passages that help explain why Turner's colleagues would remember him as "one of those rare individuals who come around once, maybe twice in a lifetime, a cut above the rest of us, special in every way, undeniably touched by God or whatever higher power you believe in."

My Cancer Year

Living with Chemotherapy and Intense Pain, Artist Michael Turner
Finds Strength by Meeting His Fans as He Continues to Battle Cancer

By Jim McLauchlin

1 Conventional wisdom tells you that "the numbers don't lie." Try this math on for size:

2 On Jan. 1, 2007, Michael Turner weighed 140 pounds and was taking 12 painkillers a day, three of them just to get *some* sleep. Since then, he's taken 96 hours of chemotherapy, and he hasn't done a single comic book page, zero.

3 This math is the sum of the last seven years of Turner's life. In 2000, Turner was riding high with a dream career and a nice income as a comic artist. Then a small pain in his right hip led to tests, followed by more tests, followed

by the chilling diagnosis—bone cancer. Turner went under the knife, and lost 8 *pounds* of flesh and bone to the surgeon's scalpel. It was absolutely necessary, to excise what Turner termed "this alien inside me."

4 Since then, Michael Turner's life has been a bizarre crossroads of booming shouts and hushed whispers. He's fought through pain, nausea, and the spectre of his own mortality to launch a new publishing company, all the while remaining perhaps the most in-demand cover artist in comics. Walk the halls at Marvel Comics, and editors will tell you that a

Turner cover on their book can spike sales by 40,000 copies.

And oh, yeah—those whispers. At the same 5 time that Turner remains highly visible on top-selling comics at Marvel, DC and his own Aspen Comics, people are . . . afraid. No one likes to talk about bad things, and cancer is near as bad as it gets. Even some of Turner's friends and past collaborators will ask, "Hey, is Mike doing okay? I heard he might have had a relapse. Is he all right? If you see him, please pass along my best. . . ."

People are afraid of the unknown. They're 6 afraid of what the answer *might* be. Well, there are answers. But first, you'll have to know what Michael Turner knows.

And believe us, he *knows* things. He knows 7 things about pain you pray you'll never know. "A broken bone? That's not pain," he says. Or maybe he doesn't so much say it as half-laugh it, a nervous laugh. "You can actually get comfortable with a broken bone, just sit there so it doesn't move. But nerve pain? It always hurts. There's nowhere you can hide. And just *try* getting some sleep when that hits."

Turner relays this information as he sits in a 8 high-backed chair in his home in Los Angeles. Even while sitting, Turner is a blur of activity.

He shuffles pillows around. One underneath, another propping up his right leg. One positioned at the lower back, another up high on the back. Another is under the arm, at the ready just in case he needs another. The shuffle and movement are constant.

The shuffle and movement are also neces- 9 sary, as yes, the cancer came back. For two whole years, from June 2001 to June 2003, things were fine. Then the most unwelcome of guests returned.

"It came back, little bits here and there in the 10 lungs or wherever," Turner relays. "Little things would pop up again, and for the last year and a half, it's been . . . pretty aggressive, especially in my back."

The aggressive nature of the new outbreak 11 necessitated new rounds of chemo. Other small operations were also required, including one that made a pair of crutches Turner's new companion. "The right leg has gotten weak to the point where it sometimes gives out," he says. "I can actually walk on it, but it's risky. One nerve had to be cut in half during a surgery, and a couple other nerves pressed off by a tumor have gotten weaker."

The leg is slowly starting to work again. "But 12 you never know," Turner cautions.

"Never knowing" is the status quo in 13 Turner's life. And he's fine with it. "My expectations are sort of MRI to MRI," he says. "It changes based on the results. I've got one tomorrow. I'm looking forward to seeing the results. I'm usually a *wreck* the day before, just because I want to see what's happening. But there are so many of them, I'm a little desensitized to the nerve wracking-ness."

Please make no mistake: Turner doesn't 14 seek pity. And he's always looking forward to what's next. "It's as simple as your choice," he says. "You can choose to go on living, or you

Michael Turner offered this take on Prince Namor for the cover of *Sub-Mariner* #1.

can sit and do nothing. I definitely choose living. I've *never* thought I was going to lose my life over this. It's always just been a thing where I knew I was going to be less able to do certain things."

Some of Turner's "things" were of the very active variety. He's an avid skier and snowboarder, and championship water skier. He even looks at that philosophically. "Maybe it slowed me down a bit, and that's good in a roundabout way," he laughs. "I was always the extreme sports guy. Maybe it stopped me from going off the wrong cliff or something."

In the here-and-now, Michael Turner *is* doing better, getting stronger every day. "I'm feeling good," he says. "I'm working in the pool, doing exercise, getting healthy. I swim laps in the pool to get the cardio up, and I have a basketball setup in the pool, so I can shoot some hoop."

Every cloud has its silver lining for Turner. The weakness in his leg makes driving a clutch dangerous, so he had to sell his beloved old Toyota Supra, a white-knuckle ride for anyone who had the "privilege" of riding in it. "But it's now a collector's item, 10 years old!" he exclaims. Turner now has a Range Rover, an automatic. "My seat is just a little higher up now," he remarks. "But I'm still hell on wheels. It goes fast. . . ."

Yes, the crutches are there, but they're a fallback. He pads around the house just fine. Turner had his mother, Grace, over for Mother's Day dinner, and he cooked steaks, even enjoying two glasses of wine with mom. "That's a lot of drinking for me these days," he says. "My tolerance isn't quite what it used to be."

Turner's tolerance is waning in another way as well. Marvel and DC covers are great, but they're the side order to the main course he wants. "That's the one thing I miss—actually drawing a story," Turner laments. "But so much of life has just been catching up on health issues. I've had a blast doing the covers, and they've also been a good vehicle to keep me in the public eye. But I wanna get back to where I'm creating new stuff, and drawing it myself."

Turner's *Soulfire* from his own company, 20 Aspen Comics, has remained unfinished for two-plus years. He bites his lip when he speaks of Aspen, and his good friends there. "I've been wanting to finish *Soulfire* for, like, forever," he says. "But I find myself doing two, three covers a week. And two or three covers can *be* a week in work-time. I just want to be healthy so I can do more *work*," he says, clenching his fists. Turner knows how to do it. In the first 18 months after his initial 2000 surgery and recovery, he penciled 14 full issues and a staggering 80 covers.

In his current recovery, Turner has been 21 doing most of his work from home. "It's been tough," he says. "But we've got a good group of guys, a small, cohesive family. I went into the studio a couple days last week to do some work there, and it was nice just to see everyone and have some hang time. But we're now doing some things that don't require me to be there. The 'Heroes' web [comics] have been a very good addition to the company's profile. We've been strategizing to not put the focus on me, so the company can survive in my absence."

Turner has, somehow and miraculously, kept 22 up a rigorous convention schedule, even in the face of surgeries and chemotherapy. To him, it's therapy.

"More than anything, I enjoy going out and 23 seeing the people that you do the work for," he says. "So much of any creative process is done by yourself. [At cons], you see all these people who are just as into this thing as you were when you were drawing it. It's extremely rewarding. And I always come back full of *that*, ready to get back to work. It fuels me."

Peter Dixon of Paradise Comics, a store 24 owner and convention promoter from Toronto, is awed at Turner's give-and-take with the crowds. "He'll have an autograph line longer than anyone else, and he won't leave until everyone is satisfied. You can tell maybe he's not too comfortable. But he's got a smile for everyone. He's more than just 'there' physically for the fans. It's like he's there spiritually for them as well. And they're definitely there for him."

The conventions are a peak. Chemotherapy 25 is a deep valley. And Turner has remained the consummate professional throughout. Novelist and comic book writer Brad Meltzer sees that. "In this day and age, superstar artists are always late," he remarks. "And Mike has every reason to be late. He's got cancer. But on *Justice League of America* and *Identity Crisis*, he's *never* been late. And every image we get is better than the last, from Red Tornado to Batman to all the group shots. He's the reason so many people pick up the book. Every month, he makes 75-year-old characters look brand new, and never once complains or stalls."

"Mike has hit every deadline with beautiful work. Frankly, he functions a lot more professionally than other artists who aren't doing constant battle with a life-threatening illness."
—Marvel Editor Tom Brevoort

On the Marvel side of the aisle, Executive 26 Editor Tom Brevoort agrees. "Regardless of whatever life circumstances he's been dealing with over the years, Michael Turner—and his Aspen teammates—has been among the most professional, most reliable artists I've worked with. He has hit every cover deadline, and turned in beautiful work on a clockwork basis. Frankly, he functions a lot more professionally than any number of other artists who aren't doing constant battle with a life-threatening illness."

Those words ring true with massive gravity. 27 Constant battle. Life-threatening illness. "I've always been positive, but as I face facts, it's been a rough run for the last six months," Turner reflects as he waits for results of his latest MRI. "It's been trying, both mentally and physically, especially when it feels like things just keep getting worse. But now things feel like they're getting better. And I'm hoping this could be the last time. You hope that on every single one. But I'm prepared to do anything I have to do."

If passing through any struggle gives one 28 wisdom, "Then I'm like an old man by now," Turner laughs. "I actually feel strangely rewarded in the things I've learned from this experience. Some people talk about how they're a 'grateful recovering alcoholic,' because of the friends they made and the experiences they had while in AA. I don't think I needed this experience to have appreciated life, but I have learned about people, and generated deeper friendships."

No matter what the outcome, Turner's 29 appreciation of life *has* grown. "I want everybody to know how much I appreciate their support through all this. DC's always been great, Marvel's been great, and all the fans have been great. They've seen me bald and in pain, but they're always so nice. They're always saying, 'We feel for you, we're praying for you.' I just want everyone to know how much that means to me. It's nice to know it's not just strangers out there I'm drawing for. I consider these people *friends*."

A day later, the phone rings, and it's the 30 results of the most recent full-body MRI scan. Turner has his answer. You have your answer.

"It's very good news. Everything has stabi- 31 lized, or is getting *smaller*," he says in a breathy voice punctuated with genuine relief. Some tumors are still there, but they've been beaten back. There is no new surgery on the horizon. The tide has turned.

So "conventional wisdom" be damned. 32 Michael Turner will tell you that the numbers *do* lie. And he'll be happy to tell you his weight is up to 172 pounds, oh-so-close to his norm of 175 to 180. He's taking *zero* painkillers, and sleeps just fine. Chemotherapy is in the past, at least for now. He's drawn an astonishing 30 covers since Jan. 1, and is looking to get back into finishing *Soulfire*, or start the much-anticipated *Ultimate Wolverine* at Marvel.

"In my mind, I've killed this," Turner says. 33 "We'll see. I'm not sure, but I feel great. My leg is getting stronger. My body is getting stronger. And I'm starting to feel like 'me' again."

Reflecting on What You Have Read

1 At several points, McLauchlin includes quotations from Michael Turner. What do those quotations tell you about Turner? What do they imply about McLauchlin's attitude toward Turner?

2 Look at the visuals that accompany this profile, examining the composition—how they are put together—and the details in each. To what extent do the photographs of Turner convey an image of someone who is strong while battling cancer? What aspects of the photographs help create this image? What is your reaction to the drawing of "Prince Namor" (p. 112)? What reasons do you see for including this drawing?

3 What is your reaction to the concluding two paragraphs of McLauchlin's profile? How does he use Turner's words? How does he come back to the ideas mentioned in the introduction to the profile?

4 McLauchlin talks directly to readers of this profile, using the word *you* and directing the reader to "Try this math on for size" in the first paragraph and later to "Please make no mistake." He also uses a lot of colloquial language and sentence fragments. For example, after a paragraph in which he refers to the "hushed whispers" in which people often talk about Turner, McLauchlin begins a new paragraph with the words, "And oh, yeah—those whispers." Does this style seem appropriate for McLauchlin's readers? Why or why not?

Thinking Ahead

In "My Cancer Year," McLauchlin profiles a person—a leading cover artist and publisher of comics—whom most readers of *Wizard* magazine would find interesting. Think of someone you know (or have read about) who has special talents, especially if that person has had to overcome serious obstacles. As you do this, be careful not to overlook people who, although very talented, may be less famous than Turner—a teacher, coworker, or mentor. What is important is that the person has a distinct personality or is admirable in some way.

E.R. Unscripted

Robert Mackey and Naomi Harris

The New York Times

Many people know about hospital emergency rooms through the television program *ER*, but relatively few people have spent much time in one. In the following *New York Times Magazine* piece, "E.R. Unscripted," author Robert Mackey and photographer Naomi Harris introduce readers to Sandra Scott, a physician in an inner-city hospital emergency room. In addition to his career as a print journalist, Mackey has also worked as a video journalist and a Web producer. Harris's photography appears in a variety of publications, ranging from *Entertainment Weekly* to *ESPN Magazine* to *Fortune Magazine*. As you read, notice the attitudes Dr. Scott's patients express—toward her and toward their injuries. How do these attitudes help shape your impressions of Dr. Scott and what it must be like to work as an emergency room doctor?

E.R. Unscripted

ROBERT MACKEY
NAOMI HARRIS

Sandra Scott's night begins with a resuscitation 1 and ends, after dawn, with a pile of paperwork. In between is a 12-hour shift at Kings County Hospital Center in Brooklyn. Scott, a 34-year-old specialist in emergency medicine, has worked at Kings County since 1998. Because Kings County is a publicly financed hospital in a low-income neighborhood, many who come in are uninsured, but the hospital is obliged to treat them. Which means that Scott sees a wider range of cases than doctors in most E.R.'s. In addition to dealing with cuts and bullet wounds, on any given night Scott will treat everything from miscarriages and S.T.D.'s to dental problems and what one patient believed was sleep disturbance caused by a spell.

The work is exhausting, but Scott has turned 2 down cushier offers outside the city. "I like taking care of uninsured patients," she says. "My experience in more private settings is that the patients are maybe overeducated. They pick up a *Cosmo* magazine and it tells them that Xanax is good for them, and then you have to explain to them why you don't want to give them Xanax. Patients here, they're pretty grateful." Scott, who grew up in Louisiana, also recently started a rape crisis center at the hospital and spends part of her vacation each year in Haiti, teaching medicine in Port-au-Prince and treating patients in the countryside. She came to Kings County, she says, "because New York City emergency medicine sounded glamorous at the time." When I ask her if it still seems glamorous after four years, she looks at the popping flashbulbs and smiles. "Well," she says, "you're here."

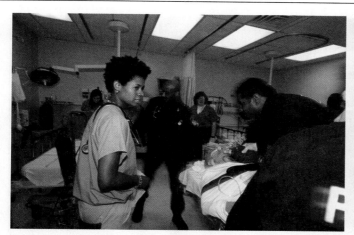

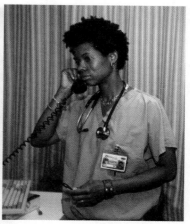

7:42 p.m. Early in the shift, Eli D'Attilo, an 84-year-old man with advanced Alzheimer's, is brought in by paramedics and E.M.T.s, who began resuscitating him at his nursing home. D'Attilo had signed a living will asking that "heroic measures" not be taken to keep him alive, but until they get clearance from the hospital to honor this, Scott and her colleagues must do everything they can to keep D'Attilo from dying.

8:20 p.m. While resuscitation continues on D'Attilo, Scott calls the hospital administration. "What can we do to stop this?" she asks. She is told to keep D'Attilo on a respirator, but they can stop treating aggressively. "We developed a relationship with the family," Scott says. "We told them we were hoping he would die while in our care."

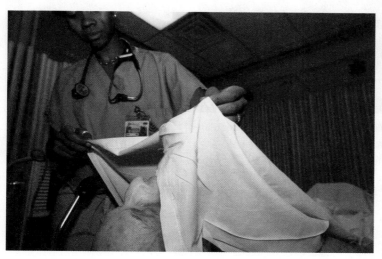

12:40 a.m. As expected, Eli D'Attilo dies on Scott's shift. She pronounces the death, then goes to call his son. "My father didn't just fall asleep," Joseph says. "It took him three and a half years to die." Thankfully, the care in his father's final hours was "very, very excellent," he says. "You'd think Kings County would be the pits, but it was the Cadillac."

12:43 a.m. Diobenton Delmas, 25, comes in after being slashed during an attempted carjacking. Delmas, whose wound stretches from his collarbone to his armpit, seems unshaken by it all. "That's what happens when you're driving those Navigators," he says. "They want those Navigators."

1:02 a.m. Scott examines Roman Mantachev, a Russian tennis instructor who has arrived with a deep wound in his leg. Mantachev claims that he was attacked in the street by people he didn't know. "He was saying they took a stick and poked it through his skin," Scott says, "but it turned out it was from a nice big, fat kitchen knife."

7:25 a.m. By the end of Scott's 12-hour shift, Delmas and Mantachev have been discharged. Scott leaves with a bag packed for a few days in Miami. "It's always nice to finish a shift," she says. "The best thing is just stepping outside."

Reflecting on What You Have Read

1 After reading and viewing this profile, what impressions do you have of Dr. Sandra Scott? What aspects of the written text and the photographs lead you to form this impression?

2 Notice the quotations in the captions that accompany the photographs. What reasons do you see for including these quotations?

3 Consider the composition of the photograph that accompanies the caption beginning "1:02 a.m." What is the detail you notice first? Why do you notice that detail? In this photograph you don't see the face or body of the patient; you see only the people standing around the patient. What details do you notice about the facial expressions and body language of these people? What effect does the photographer create by showing you these details and not showing the face or body language of the patient?

4 Most of the activities that take place in the emergency room are shocking or sad. But the author expresses no reactions to any of them; he just records what people do and say. Would this profile be more effective if it included his personal reactions? Why or why not?

5 What is your reaction to the final image of Dr. Scott? How do the composition and details of the picture help create this reaction? What does the caption contribute to your reaction?

Thinking Ahead

In "E.R. Unscripted," Robert Mackey and Naomi Harris profile an unfamiliar but important workplace, conveying a sense not only of the activities that go on there but also of the people who work there. Think about places where you have worked, places that have a distinct atmosphere or that employ people with interesting personalities or life stories. Looking ahead to your own writing, consider using both photographs and written text to help readers appreciate the unique qualities of an activity that goes on in one of those special places.

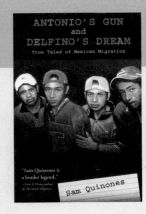

Diez in the Desert

Sam Quinones

Sam Quinones is a journalist who grew up in California and attended the University of California, Berkeley. Early in his career he lived in Mexico for ten years, writing as a freelancer for a variety of U.S. publications on aspects of Mexican culture. He returned in 2004 to become a staff writer for the *Los Angeles Times*. He writes frequently about the lives of Mexican immigrants to the United States. His first book, *True Tales from Another Mexico: The Lynch Mob, the Popsicle Kings, Chalino, and the Bronx* (2001), grew out of his reporting in Mexico. The following profile is another story about real people, from *Antonio's Gun and Delfino's Dream: True Tales of Mexican Migration* (2007). In this excerpt, Diez, a sixteen-year-old "coyote" (a person paid to smuggle immigrants across the border) leads eleven Mexican immigrants through the Arizona desert in a desperate effort to reach Los Angeles. As you read this profile, notice ways in which people's characters are revealed in the ways they respond to obstacles presented by the hostile environment in which they find themselves.

Diez in the Desert

The boy wasn't happy with his line of work, and in his short life he had never imag- 1
ined that it was work he'd do. But by taking people illegally into the United States, he'd seen Ohio, Kentucky, and snakes in the desert, and he was proud of that. He was sure that he'd seen more of the world than men in his village who were twice his age. He had shepherded his first crew of people across the desert and into the United States before he could have legally driven in that country. Fear accompanied him always, but he'd seen that he could control it. One night, driving a group of illegals into Birmingham, Alabama, his car broke down, he calmly walked them all night along the highway into town. This kind of accomplishment was liberating and left him trusting his own abilities. Almost eighty people were in the United States because of him. He studied the awesome highways of America in a large book that contained maps of each state. He boasted that he knew some parts of the United States better than he knew Mexico City. He'd been to Georgia, California, and Colorado, and he was most impressed with the casinos that he thought were near Indianapolis.

His mother had named him Daniel, but everyone called him Diez—Ten—a nick- 2
name that was for his having been born on May 10, this in 1987. So he'd been sixteen for less than a month when, on June 7, 2003, he led a raggedy group of ten folks from Veracruz through the Arizona desert. . . .

June is the desert's hottest month. In July, the summer rains begin. The saguaros 3 produce their fruit, the ocotillo's bare branches grow a green fur and red berry, and the Tohono O'odham calendar begins. But the desert's denizens can only hunker down and endure June. Moisture vanishes from the air. The sun is at its highest point. In June, the National Weather Service often reports temperatures well over 100 degrees. But even when they are only 98 to 101 degrees, as they were on June 7, 2003, temperatures on the unprotected desert floor can rise to 130 degrees or more.

As it happened, Diez was aware of none of this. This was only the second group he'd 4 led, though he had walked the desert with his partner many times and felt he knew the routine. Walking steadily, they would need ten to twelve hours to arrive at the Indian village of Santa Cruz, where Diez had a contact who would take them to Tucson. From there they would connect with the legion of private drivers that has emerged in Tucson and Phoenix. Diez could hire them to take each immigrant where he wanted to go in the United States.

Together, his group carried six limes, cans of corn and sardines, a sheet, a blanket, and 5 twenty-two five-liter bottles of water. He'd told his charges to wear dark clothing—nothing white or red or yellow that might stand out. He wore tennis shoes, black jeans, a gray basketball jersey, and his lucky black baseball cap emblazoned with the letters *SA*. He had no idea what they referred to. He'd been given the cap about the time he took his first trip. It was tattered, and his friends had told him to get rid of it, but he always used it when he was taking people across. No one had sunglasses, and, other than Diez, no one had a hat. Diez, Delfino, Guadalupe, and the chubby woman wore tennis shoes. Others wore the cheap formal shoes that serve as all-purpose footwear for Mexico's poor. The group had eaten little on the bus trip, and nothing that morning, conserving their money for what lay ahead.

During the first few hours, the trek proceeded as planned. The group walked single 6 file behind Diez. Guadalupe thought they were almost done when they crossed the border an hour after dawn. Delfino was filled with bravado. Walking a couple hours in the early morning, he felt nothing and didn't know what all the fuss was about, this desert and its heat. He figured he was just tough.

Within a few hours, though, the sun was high in the sky, and its intensity unnerved 7 the tenderfoots. Diez kept walking and walking. Each walker quickly learned to concentrate on what was before him. The rocks could twist an ankle. Cactus spines pierced shoe soles and even slightly grazing a cholla could lacerate skin. Talking ceased. All their mental energy focused on avoiding the dangers the desert presented with every step.

Four hours into the walk, they passed Federal Route 21. And a half hour after that, 8 things began to fall apart. The heavyset woman had been doing poorly. The group was walking fast, and she couldn't keep up. Guadalupe saw the blood again coming from her nose. She asked how far they had to go. They weren't even a quarter of the way, Diez told her. He tried to encourage her, but she had to stop.

They made her a shade hut by placing the sheet over some plants, while the rest of 9 the group stood around her in the sun. She was scared and bleeding, and they joked with her to cheer her up. After a while, they asked if she could go on. She said she could. They began walking with her, pulling her along at times. But as she walked, she grew delirious. She hallucinated. She recognized no one, and finally she foamed at the mouth. She collapsed. The group stopped. Guadalupe saw she was going to die. He kept this to himself. The flow of blood from her nose increased and drenched her shirt. It terrified him.

Diez said they should turn back, put a quick end to the trip, and give up to the Bor- 10 der Patrol. The highway wasn't that far away. So they laid her on the blanket and began to carry her back the way they'd come. After a few dozen agonizing yards, they stopped to rest. The woman lurched her head to the side, threw up, and died.

"I don't think she's breathing anymore," said her sister-in-law.   11

Diez stood over her, stunned and panicked. They gravity of what had occurred set 12 in. He began to cry. The others gathered around. Looking down at her, the sun above, their shadows fell over her corpse. They were terrified in the silent desert. She'd been talking, hoping. Now she lay dead. No matter what they'd seen on television about people dying in this desert, they were too flush with the dreams of dollars to believe they'd see it.

The looked at each other and stared down at her body. Quickly, what to do? Pulling 13 himself together, Diez said they should reach the highway and give up. But now that the woman was dead, no one wanted to do that. Maybe we should bury her, suggested Delfino. Diez thought he should stay with the body, but realized that no one else knew the way to the Indian settlement ahead, and he didn't want to answer police questions about how they got where they were.

Finally, the woman's friends and Tavo, the coyote trainee, decided to stay with the 14 body. Diez and the others would head on. Wait till we've been gone for three hours, he told the three who stayed with the corpse, then go back to the highway and wave down the Border Patrol.

Diez's group was now down to six men. They would have to make time. To lighten 15 their load, he buried the cans of sardines and corn near where the woman died. . . .

Just twenty-four hours earlier they were watching *Scooby-Doo* and imagining their 16 new lives in the United States. Now the trek had become a grim march. The woman's ordeal had slowed them irreparably. This terrified Diez. He calculated that they had spent two or three hours with her. Another seven or eight hours of walking remained. He didn't like walking at night. It was too easy to break a leg or walk face first into a cactus. They would have to spend the night in the desert.

All this coursed through his mind as he and his group walked on, each man alone 17 with his thoughts. After three hours, shadows lengthened across the desert floor. They found a ravine and the six of them crumbled into its shade. Diez told them that the Indian's house was a couple hours away and they could do it easily in the morning. It was a lie, but he didn't want to upset them. It was ten miles to Santa Cruz. In their condition, that distance would take at least five hours of walking.

The others were quickly asleep. For Diez, though, the night seemed endless. He tried 18 to sleep but could not. He smoked cigarettes and tried to drink, but he threw up whatever went down. His mind churned over the day's events. The death of the woman whose name he didn't know weighed upon him. Out there alone, through the night, he thought of her dying on the desert floor. He'd go to jail. His mother would die of anguish. What would people say of him? Several times during the night, he closed his eyes. But the wind made a high cooing sound that Diez, in his panic, took for police radios. He'd start awake with a charge of adrenalin.

Through the night, he thought of what lay ahead. They had packed only enough 19 water for a ten-hour trip. They were down to a few gulps of water apiece and the six limes. He didn't know if they'd make it.

None of this did he tell his charges as he woke them at first light. They trudged off 20 into the desert again. They walked for one hour, then another, and another. They found nothing. The sun was high in the sky, and its rays drenched them in inescapable heat.

By 8:00 a.m., they were out of water. They turned to the limes and sucked them fero- 21 ciously. Diez's skin burned and was stuck with cactus spines. His face was lacerated from the brush. It was so hot, he felt, that if you had put a plate of beans on his head, it would have cooked. He wilted quickly, and now knew he wouldn't make it.

His charges, who had slept well, carried him on. They were terrified. He alone knew 22 the trail to the Indian settlement. It was now they who gave him the pep talk. Come on, Diez, they told him, you can do it. How many times have you made this trip before? His arms slung around their shoulders, Diez slipped in and out of consciousness.

By midmorning, the limes were gone. They were oblivious to the tanks of water 23 standing in the mighty saguaros around them. Only one source of liquid remained. To survive, Diez told them, they would now have to drink their own urine. They began to urinate in plastic baggies, but the liquid was too hot to drink. So they dug down beneath the topsoil and found cool earth and mixed this with the liquid. Diez was so dehydrated that his body could produce no urine at all. He drank the urine of one of the men from Tijan.

This, however, was not enough to sustain him. He sagged as they carried him along, 24 his arms draped across their shoulders. Finally, be told them, "I can't go on." Far off in the distance, he knew, was a white water tank and the Indians' houses. They couldn't see it, but he knew it was there.

"Go that way," he told them.   25

Some of the men wanted to stay and wait for the temperature to drop. Privately,   26
Guadalupe said to Delfino, "Let's go. If we stay here, we're going to die." So the group left
Diez lying there and walked on in the direction he had pointed them.

Diez's mother had always told him to think of happy moments when in a hard spot.   27
He was now going to die. So he remembered his girlfriends. Rosanna, Silvia, Iris. He
remembered diving in the river with Diana and drinking beer with his friends on the
street corner back in Chocarnán.

People who are dying in the desert often jettison money, gold, anything of great tem-   28
poral value, as, without water, these become absurdly unimportant. One desert wanderer
once told how he began to imagine an entire monetary system based on drops of water,
so valuable does the liquid become to those lost in the desert.

From his pocket, Diez took a wad of three thousand dollars and threw it in the air.   29
What good was money to him now? The bills fluttered and settled around him. Diez
wanted the people who found his corpse to put the money to good use. He lay down and
placed his cap over his face and passed out. He lay there for a long time.

The six men, meanwhile, stumbled on. They'd been on the desert floor now for a day   30
and a half of sun. The woman was dead. Diez, with whom they trusted with their lives, was
dying. They were out of water and had drunk their own urine. Their skin boiled, and they
were near tears. Waves of chills swept over them and made them shudder. Their lips were torn
and no one could talk. No one cared anymore about the dollars he was going to make. . . .

Believing someone had seen something, one of them scaled a paloverde and, finally,   31
spotted a house in the distance.

"Casa," he yelled and pointed.   32

They made for it.   33

The house belonged to an Indian couple, who were startled to see five ragged   34
Mexicans stumble out of the desert.

"Agua," they said. "Agua."   35

Then they collapsed in the shade under the enormous salt cedar tree in front of the   36
couple's house. For one hundred dollars, the Indian couple filled their jugs with water and
gave them bread and a few sodas. The kid who'd spotted the house broke down and sobbed.

As this was going on, Diez lay under the sun a couple hundred yards back. At one   37
point he picked himself up and tried to walk but could not go far and collapsed again,
facedown in the dirt. He passed out.

He woke to voices calling, "Diez, Diez." He raised his lucky *SA* hat and waved it list-   38
lessly, then his arm fell to the ground. The next thing he knew, they were over him, pouring water on him and plying him with soda. His skin was green, and his eyes were deep in
their sockets. He had soiled himself and he was crying and couldn't talk.

Two months later, on the Tohono O'odham reservation in the dead heat of August, a 39 thin boy with a black baseball cap sat on a rock not far from where the woman died. He dug up the cans of corn and sardines he had buried and discovered they hadn't spoiled. Around him sat another group of seven would-be immigrants, heading to Los Angeles and counting the dollars they would make. This time none were women. As they ate, in his crackly voice and dry laugh, he told them the story of how the heavyset woman he'd known only as "Señora" had died, and how he'd had to drink another man's urine, thrown his money in the air, and almost expired himself.

"She died," he said, "right over there," pointing to the spot. 40

Reflecting on What You Have Read

1 Diez's experiences as a coyote in this profile have deadly consequences for one woman and almost lead to Diez's own death. How do these experiences and the ways Diez reacts to them help you understand what life is like for a "coyote"?

2 Quinones talks about the physical setting—the Arizona desert—throughout the profile. How do his descriptions of the desert help you visualize the scene Diez experienced?

3 Quinones recounts how Diez felt and what he thought as he led the trip through the desert. He reports conversations Diez had, but does not quote them. Why do you think Quinones does this? What effect does he create by reporting what the travelers said (and did) this way?

4 Quinones ends the profile by briefly describing a scene in which "a thin boy with a black baseball cap" is talking to a group of illegal immigrants he is leading across the Arizona desert. The boy is obviously Diez, but Quinones doesn't refer to him by name. Why not? And what reasons do you see for ending the profile with this scene?

Thinking Ahead

In this profile, Quinones gives an insider's view of one person's effort to lead a group through an incredibly difficult situation, even though the leader was ill equipped to do so. Think of other efforts (those you have experienced or those you have read about) to lead people through difficult situations. As you think about a possible topic for your profile, note the ways people respond to those situations, and give readers a sense of how the experiences changed the leader or those he or she was leading.

Behind a Plain White Lab Coat
Stephanie Guzik

It may seem that the most interesting subjects for a profile would be people who are extremely well known. That is not necessarily the case, as Stephanie Guzik shows in the following profile of Diane Turcotte, a fellow college student whose life is not limited to the time she spends working in the lab. As you read this profile, notice the different ways Guzik helps readers see how remarkable Diane is.

Behind a Plain White Lab Coat

After an exhausting day of classes one Monday afternoon early in the semester, I decided to walk across campus to the cell culture lab to feed my fibroblast cells. As I lazily walked up the three flights of stairs to the biology floor and wandered slowly into room 309, I saw Diane Turcotte's smiling face peer up from her computer screen. According to our instructor, George, Diane was the pride of our Cancer Cell Group. He often told me, "You could learn a lot from that girl. She's a wonderful, dedicated member of this group," and I always had to hold back from asking, "What could this senior possibly teach me about this program that you couldn't?" I always seemed to run into Diane whenever I went to the lab; in fact, it often made me wonder if she ever left.

On this particular Monday afternoon, Diane was waiting for the components of a reagent solution to dissolve in a beaker of distilled water and writing a paper for one of her classes in the meantime. "Hey Steph!" she called out cheerfully. "How was your day?" I looked at her, feeling somewhat dazed, and replied, "How in the world can you be so extremely perky after classes on a Monday?" She just smiled and went back to her paper. I put down my bag, grabbed my lab notebook, and went across the hall into the sterile culture lab, closing the door behind me.

I prepared myself in the lab, setting up all my equipment, washing my hands, and putting on my plain white lab coat. I logged into the lab in the notebook that we keep on top of the refrigerator and went to open up the incubator. I took my two large culture flasks off the second shelf and looked at them under the microscope. One appeared very clear, with a good growth of cells, while the other had black blotches floating in the bright orange growth medium. I wasn't sure what to do, but I fed my cells anyway, cleaned up the lab, and left, saying goodbye to a still-perky Diane as I walked out.

Fig. 1. Diane at work in the lab.

Thursday rolled around and it was once again time to feed my cells. After class, I   4
wandered over to the lab, trudged up the stairs, and walked slowly down the hall. Once
again, Diane was in room 309, this time waiting for proteins to run through her
polyacrilamide gel. "Is today any better?" she asked. "Well, it's not a Monday; we'll put it
that way," I replied as I put my things down and went back into the sterile lab across the
hall. I prepared everything again and went to open up the incubator in the lab. As I
swung the door open, I immediately noticed a flask on the second shelf with bright yellow
growth medium: a clear sign of contamination. My stomach dropped as I saw the letters
SG on the bottom of the flask. I took out both of my cultures and saw that one was bright
yellow and the other was cloudy orange, which meant I had killed all the cells I had been
growing for almost three weeks. I closed the incubator, took off my plain white lab coat,
and went back into room 309 with both of my flasks.

Diane was hunched over her gel, waiting patiently for the proteins to be pulled to   5
the bottom by the current running through the apparatus. She saw me as I walked in,
somewhat frustrated. I quietly asked, "Does this happen to you?" Diane took one look at
the flasks I held outstretched and understood. She smiled and replied, "Actually, this is
perfect timing. I've been growing roller bottles of cells for about a month now and had
finally gotten a culture to grow, but today I came in and they had all 'jumped off.' So I get

to start all over too. Come on, let's go." She turned off the current running through her gel, took the apparatus apart, and walked past me into the sterile lab. I put down my contaminated flasks long enough to put on my lab coat again. Still frustrated, I squirted bleach into my two flasks to kill off all the bacteria and remaining cells, while Diane washed her hands and put on her plain white lab coat. We sat there together in that lab, passaging new cells from one flask into another, for a little under an hour. In that hour, I began to understand what our instructor had been talking about.

As we sat down at the sterile hoods to begin working, Diane said, "Stephanie, you 6 can't give up. That's what I've learned in this place. I've spent three years in this room, and no matter how many flasks and roller bottles I've gone through, no matter how many cells I've stained incorrectly, no matter how many gels I've run, I finally realized that getting frustrated over this stuff is completely pointless. Cell culture is not your whole life. There's so much beyond this one little room that is much more important than passaging these cells into a new flask."

It struck me as funny that this woman who I had seen so many times in the lab was 7 talking about everything outside of the lab. But one hour in the lab talking with Diane convinced me that she is not only the amazing and dedicated cell culturist George told me about, but also such an active participant in so many campus activities that she far outshines every other student I have met in my time here. I came to realize that behind Diane's plain white lab coat is a woman who has had a full life at college, who has experienced everything, and who has made her time on campus one to remember and cherish. Behind it was someone I wanted to be like.

Whereas I simply go to class, go to the lab, go back to my dorm, and occasionally go 8 out with my friends (and to this point thought that I was doing pretty well!), I discovered that Diane has an entire spectrum of things to do once she walks down that staircase out of the lab. Our college is known to have students who struggle to do well in their classes and struggle even more to have a good time while at school because classes outweigh the rest of their activities. Diane has certainly overcome that challenge.

Diane told me she's taking a Senior Advanced Lab course based in Molecular Biology, 9 a Statistical Analysis course, and Immunology and Human Physiology. In all, she said, it adds up to seventeen hours of class time each week, not including the several hours of homework required by each class. It was clear to me that even though she is a senior, Diane had chosen courses that are quite difficult and time-consuming—unlike other

Fig. 2. Sorority sisters after a formal. Diane is the third from the left in the middle row.

seniors, who coast through their last two semesters with less intellectually challenging courses like Introduction to Sculpture. The only response I could manage was, "That's amazing." "It's not too bad," Diane replied. "I just go to class, do all of my work after class either here or in the library, and then I have time to do everything else I want to do." *Everything else? What else could there be,* I wondered. *I'm having enough of a hard time balancing school, the lab, and my sorority.*

Diane belongs to the same sorority I do on campus, so I know how much time she 10 spends at the house. She has been a member since her freshman year and is so kind and enthusiastic that all the sisters adore her. I have yet to find a sister who has anything bad to say about Diane, and I believe Melissa put it best when she told me, "Diane is just your average, run-of-the-mill amazing person."

Until I started working in the Cancer Cell Group, I never would have guessed that 11 Diane was so involved in academics, simply because the majority of people on our campus who are extremely involved in their courses don't seem very happy or relaxed. However, Diane is an exception. During recruitment periods for our sorority, she is constantly at the house, socializing with the sisters and the potential members. She is so relaxed that no one could guess that she'd be heading back to the lab afterwards.

When recruitment is over, Diane can still be found hanging out at the house a few times during the week or getting ice cream at the local Friendly's with some of the other senior sisters.

Although I knew about Diane's sorority involvement, before this afternoon in the lab   12 I had no idea that she cared about any activities beyond that and her coursework. But she told me about several other groups on campus that are important to her. First, there's CASA—the Chinese American Student Association. When Diane came to college, she initially wanted to be a member of the Vietnamese Student Association, but since our campus didn't have one, she decided to join CASA instead to "embrace her Asian ethnicity." "It's really nice to be able to associate with people that have a similar background to me," Diane said. "I grew up in a house that embraced Vietnamese culture, and I wanted to continue that feeling once I got to campus."

Second, she told me about TriBeta, which is a national Biology Honor Society. Our   13 campus has not established a definite chapter of TriBeta, but Diane, along with some other biology students, is working very hard to get the campus TriBeta group recognized nationally. For the past year she has acted as the secretary of the campus TriBeta group, and she is currently in the process of contacting the representative who will come examine our facilities to make sure that we have met the national society's requirements. She is also actively recruiting students to become a part of the group she helped establish. "Right now, TriBeta is a lot of work just because we don't have our chapter established yet, but once the menial labor is done, it should be a lot of fun," she said enthusiastically.

After she told me about her involvement in CASA and TriBeta, I was expecting Diane   14 to say something along the lines of "Between those groups and my coursework, I'm fairly busy." Instead, she continued, "I'm also part of the Order of Omega for being a sorority sister and for meeting the requirements." Although Diane said this modestly, I personally know that being a member of this, the national Greek Honor Society, is much more than "meeting requirements"; it has to do with being a leader, being active—basically being amazing in one way or another.

Finally, Diane added that she lives at home, which is close to campus, and spends as   15 much time as she can with her family and her two nephews. She usually goes home for dinner and spends a little time with her parents, then goes back to the lab to work for most of the night. *I have trouble seeing my friends on a weekly basis, I thought, but she makes sure she spends time with her family every night. How does she do it? How can she be so active on campus, so wonderful in her coursework, and yet so involved at home?* I just didn't get it. While I sat there absorbing what Diane had told me, she decided to add that she also does work-study for our instructor, spending some time testing new products that George is considering for purchase, purifying reagents that the group uses on a regular basis, and organizing and cleaning the lab. Was I sitting next to some sort of machine? "Oh, and I also had to study for my GRE's all semester because I wasn't sure if I wanted to go to graduate school or go directly into a lab to work." After Diane took the exam and thought about it a lot, she decided to look for a research position and work for a few years. *Yes, indeed, there is a machine behind that plain white lab coat,* I decided. *There has to be. No one could possibly be so active and yet seem so relaxed at the same time.*

There was an awkward silence after Diane told me about everything she did. I didn't   16
know what to say. All I could think of was "wow," but somehow I didn't feel that would do any justice to what I had just heard.

As we were doing our final steps for the passaging, I decided to ask, "So what about   17
sleep? Do you ever sleep?" Diane just smiled, like she always does, and said, "Of course I sleep. It's not always as much as I'd like, and it's not as much as some of the other students on campus, but I get my rest. Sometimes I'm in the lab for anywhere from 5 to 24 hours in a day doing protocols, so when it's a busy night with work and with the lab, I get anywhere from no sleep to 3 hours. On nights when I'm not quite so busy, I get around 6 hours. It's not so bad once you get used to it." No sleep? Who does that? That's all I could think as we capped up our flasks and labeled them with the date and our initials.

By that time, it was around 7 o'clock. I was completely exhausted and still trying to   18
absorb everything Diane had just told me. We put our flasks in the incubator--mine on the second shelf and hers on the top shelf. We cleaned up the hoods and all our materials. We washed our hands. We took off our plain white lab coats.

Then I followed Diane out of the sterile lab and into room 309. She went back over   19
to her gel as I put away my lab notebook. As she sat there preparing her gel for a Western blot protocol, which would take about another five hours or so, I thought to myself, The poor thing is going to be stuck in the lab all night again. But then I realized that whereas I would be "stuck" in the lab, she would simply "be" in the lab, enjoying just one of the many tasks in the busy life that she leads.

As I put my bag on my back, Diane said with a smile, "Are you going out tomorrow   20
night?" This time, I smiled back. "I know a couple of the sisters are going out, and
Vanessa and I definitely are. Would you like to come with us?" As always, Diane smiled,
looked at her gel, and said, "If all goes well with this thing, I'm with you. Just let me
know what time."

"Of course," I said, and turned to walk out the door. "Have a good night," I added. As I 21
walked to the door I heard Diane say, "You too. Don't forget, there's a whole different place
outside of that door. Take advantage of it while you can." I smiled and slowly walked out of
room 309, down the hallway, and down the stairs in a better mood than I had been at any
other time during the past few weeks. I felt inspired, still touched by my conversation with
the amazing woman I had discovered hidden behind a plain white lab coat.

Reflecting on What You Have Read

1 When Stephanie's instructor tells her that "you could learn a lot from that girl,"
Stephanie is at first doubtful, as she reveals in the first paragraph of her profile. Why
do you think Stephanie decided to express her doubts so early in the profile?

2 What are some of the ways in which Stephanie contrasts her actions and reactions
with Diane's? What do those contrasts tell you about Diane?

3 Notice the questions Stephanie asks—of herself and of Diane. How do they add to
your understanding of Diane?

4 Look closely at the pictures Stephanie includes in her profile, considering both
composition and details. In what ways do these pictures succeed (or fail) in
reinforcing the attitudes Stephanie conveys in her written text?

Thinking Ahead

Think about someone you know well—a classmate, coworker, or family member, for
example. What qualities set this person apart? For example, how does he or she confront
problems that seem overwhelming to most other people? What is distinctive about
this person's daily routines? How do other people react to this person? Can you get
photographs that show what this person is like? It may be that someone you see every
day would be a good subject for a profile.

Guide to Writing a Profile

▷ GUIDE TO WRITING A PROFILE

The remainder of this chapter will guide you through the process of creating a profile that reveals an insider's view of an interesting subject. The first step is covered in Getting Started—selecting a topic and analyzing the context in which your profile will be read. Then you will work on creating a draft, using many of the strategies or techniques illustrated in profiles you were introduced to in Reading to Write. These strategies can guide you through the entire process of writing a profile, beginning with your early efforts to identify a good topic and continuing through revising your work and submitting a final draft.

As you work through the assignment for this chapter, you can also read a little bit about how undergraduate Stephanie Guzik wrote her profile. In the Student Q & A box on page 137, you will find the first of several brief conversations that Stephanie had with the authors of this text.

▷ Assignment

Write a profile that provides an insider's view on either a topic of your choice or one selected by your instructor. You will draw on various sources such as readings, personal experiences, and interviews in order to satisfy your readers' curiosity about what a particular person, place, or activity is like. Your instructor may have specific requirements about how long the profile should be, what sort of topic to write about, whether you should prepare the profile as a print or online document (or as an oral presentation), and whether you should include or exclude any particular visual elements. Be sure you understand those requirements before you start working on the assignment.

GETTING STARTED

When you begin thinking of topics for this assignment, it will probably make sense to think of people, places, or activities that you already know something about and that have personal meaning for you—people you admire greatly, for example, or places for which you have very positive associations. But ultimately, you will have to create a profile that will have as much meaning for others as it does for you. Consequently, you will need to begin by selecting an appropriate topic, analyzing your audience, and deciding on the specific purpose(s) you want your profile to achieve.

Selecting a Topic

Once you have thought of several people, places, or activities that might be good as the focus for a profile, narrow that list by choosing a topic that will allow you to:

▶ draw on your own observations or experiences, at least in part.

▶ be attractive to others, either because they have some prior experience with it or because the subject somehow relates to other things they know and care about.

▶ be fair, making it possible to convey your own feelings and reactions without ignoring information that might challenge your initial view of the subject.

Even if you are writing a profile of a historical character or a famous person you have never met, make sure you can find what is referred to as "primary source" material—for example, photographs, letters, diary entries, or film or video clips. Also, avoid topics that either (1) matter only to you or (2) evoke such strong emotions (whether positive or negative) that you can't assess your subject fairly.

For more on primary sources, see Chapter 10, pages 564–67.

Coming Up with Ideas for a Topic

If you are having trouble thinking of a good topic, you might review suggestions in the Thinking Ahead passages that follow each of the profiles in the Reading to Write section of this chapter. Or you might consider some of the topics that often appear in profiles.

▶ Well-known figures in fields such as sports, entertainment, or government (especially those you have been able to observe in action)

▶ Mentors such as teachers, family members, or leaders of an organization to which you belong

▶ Friends who embody admirable qualities (other than or in addition to their friendship with you)

▶ People you have come to admire through your contact with them in a job or a social, charitable, or religious organization

▶ Places and activities (a work site, for example), especially those that help you understand the feelings, ideas, or motivations of people who live in a specific place or participate in a particular activity

You might also get some ideas for topics by engaging in the following activities.

Brainstorm ideas for topics. Write as quickly as you can, listing people, places, or activities that particularly interest you. It may help to complete sentences such as the following.

One person I really admire among my family or friends is _____.

One historical figure I admire is _____.

One intriguing person in sports/music/politics is _____.

One place that has special meaning for me is _____.

An event or experience that had a profound impact on me (or someone else) is _____.

For the moment, do not worry about how good your answers sound. In brainstorming, the primary goal is quantity, so just list as many ideas as you can.

Review what you have written with a small group or the entire class. Explain what is remarkable or distinctive about the subjects you have identified. Notice which ones strike them as most interesting. Ask them if the topics you have come up with suggest any other topics. Don't worry about how good these topics sound. Just see what people come up with.

Select a topic that seems like it might have potential and then brainstorm about that topic. Writing as quickly as you can, answer the following questions.

▶ What makes the subject of your profile so special to you?

▶ What are the impressions it has left on you? Why did it leave those impressions?

▶ What did you learn from it?

▶ How has it affected other people?

If you can answer at least some of these questions, you probably have a topic with good potential. If not, you may need to go back and engage in some of the activities listed above.

Assessing Your Choice of a Topic

Once you have identified a subject, you need to assess how well it will work as the topic for your profile, making sure that you can find plenty of information and that it will mean as much to others as it does to you. To do this, try the following activities, making notes about what you learn.

Summarize what you have written and share with a group. Ask them to help you think of audiences who might be interested in the person, place, or activity you are considering writing a profile about. As is true with your choice of topic, your choice of an audience may change. But if you and your classmates can't think of someone who would want to read about the topic of your profile, you're probably going to have difficulty in writing a good profile.

Think further about your own experience. Have you had any personal contact with the person, place, or activity you think you might want to write about? If so, do you have any anecdotes that help explain what is so special about it?

Talk with others who may know something about your subject. What are their experiences? Can they tell you any good stories about the person, place, or activity you are interested in? Can they provide any factual information that surprises you or adds to your understanding of your topic?

Do some reading. Do a preliminary survey of your library's databases and look on the Internet. Can you find primary source materials? Does it seem likely that you'll be able to find good stories that illustrate the distinctive qualities of your topic? Without too much digging, can you find background information on those qualities?

Look for good photographs. Can you find or take any photographs that will help readers appreciate how significant your topic is?

Conduct a brief reality check after doing a fair amount of reading and talking. Are you finding plenty of interesting material? Have you identified an audience that actually needs or wants to know what you have to say about your topic? Do you see a compelling reason why the audience will want to read about this topic at this particular time? If you can't answer yes to at least two of these questions, consider changing your topic or your audience. Do this now, not the night before the assignment is due.

{ **Student Q & A** } **Selecting a Topic**

Writing Now: You give the impression that you decided almost immediately that you wanted to write your profile about Diane. Is that true? If so, how did you decide to write about her?

Stephanie Guzik: I had toyed with other ideas for the profile, about famous people or a vacation spot I know of, but I also thought of Diane initially for the profile. She is such a great role model and I admire her so much that I figured it would be easy to give a firsthand view of what a great person she really is. Also, when I first started thinking about the paper, I looked into the other topic ideas and didn't come up with much information that would be useful. I decided it would be better to write about someone I know directly so I could give my perspective as well as input from other people she's close with (our instructor, other sorority sisters, and so on). After I thought about it, Diane just seemed like the obvious choice for my topic. ■

Understanding Your Audience and Purpose

As you began the process of getting started on your assignment for this chapter, you focused on one basic question: Can I find information that interests me and gives me a sense of the distinctive character of a certain person, place, or activity? The other part of getting started is thinking about the audience you hope to reach and the purpose(s) you hope to accomplish by writing the profile. It will be easiest to do this by thinking in terms of one or two individual readers who are typical of the larger group you hope to reach. Not everyone has the same knowledge of, experiences with, or attitudes toward the subject of your profile. If you are to give an insider's view to the audience you hope to reach, you will have to think carefully about what they know and care about.

As we suggested earlier, your basic purpose is to give readers an insider's view of your topic, leaving your readers with a dominant impression, a strong sense of what a person, place, or activity is really like. But beyond that, the purposes profile writers try to achieve may vary widely. Consider the profiles found in this chapter. In one, the author invites readers to appreciate the courage with which a cancer patient confronts his illness. In another, a student explains why and how one of her classmates had a profound personal influence on her.

Given the importance of understanding your audience and purpose, and given that you have begun gathering a good bit of information about the subject of your profile, you should be ready to start answering questions about the audience's knowledge, values, and needs as well as their expectations for content, layout, and format and the purposes you hope your profile will achieve.

If you hope to give readers an insider's view of your topic, you need to understand those readers as fully as possible. And you need to think carefully about the purpose(s) you hope to accomplish. To do this, you need to write out answers to the following questions.

| Guidelines for Analyzing Your Audience and Identifying Purpose |

Audience knowledge, needs, and attitudes

- What does your audience already know about the subject of your profile? Have they met the subject of your profile? If so, what impressions have they formed? What have they heard or read regarding your subject?

- Why would your readers want or need to know about your topic? Are there any recent events that might motivate your audience to read your profile? If not, what sort of background information should you provide?

- What biases or preconceptions do readers have concerning the subject of your profile? Are they making any questionable assumptions?

Audience expectations for content

- What questions are your readers likely to want to have answered?

- What kinds of information are your readers likely to see as especially interesting or informative?

Audience expectations for layout or format

- What sort of layout will your audience expect? For example, should you use one column or two? Should you use inset boxes or pull quotes, lines of text "pulled out" and set off for emphasis?

- Are there any visual features (for example, photographs, charts, bulleted lists) your readers are likely to expect or appreciate?

Purpose(s)

- What overall impression do you want to leave your readers with? In addition to giving readers an insider's view of your topic, what else do you hope to accomplish by writing your profile? For example, do you want to expand or revise readers' knowledge of the person or place being profiled?

For more information about layout, see Chapter 9, page 526.

▶ Go to
bedfordstmartins.com/
writingnow to download these guidelines from Chapter 3 > Worksheets.

Reinforce readers' existing attitudes toward the subject of the profile? Make readers see the subject in a more (or less) favorable light than they currently do?

- What sort of voice do you want readers to hear when they read your profile? What attitude are you trying to convey?

To answer these questions about audience and purpose, you should talk with one or more members of your audience. Ask them what they already know. Mention some of the facts you are discovering and see whether these facts surprise them. Ask what questions they may have. Also, draw on your knowledge of yourself, asking such questions as these: If I were in my audience's place, what questions would I want to have answered? What aspects of my topic would I find most interesting? Then use what you are learning about your audience and topic to decide on the purpose(s) you hope to accomplish by writing your profile.

As you work on the profile, your understanding of your audience and purpose may change. For example, you may get a clearer idea of what the audience knows or expects, and that may lead you to rethink your purpose. You might discover, for example, that they have a more positive (or negative) attitude than you expected. Or they might know a lot more than you anticipated. Consequently, you may want to revise your responses to the Guidelines for Analyzing Your Audience and Identifying Purpose as you work on the profile. But for now, be as clear and specific as possible.

Student Analysis of Audience and Purpose

Here's how Stephanie Guzik described her audience and purpose for the profile she wrote, "Behind a Plain White Lab Coat" (p. 126).

Audience knowledge, needs, and attitudes

The students who read this wouldn't necessarily know Diane, but they would have an idea of how much work is involved in college and the time commitment required for participating in college-level extracurricular activities.

The college students I know (including myself) would all love to be able to do well in class but still have a life outside of class.

A common misconception is that there's no way to accomplish that goal. Either you're tied up with work and never have a social life, or your life is simply social and not much else. This profile exemplifies how a college student has gotten the best of both worlds. She works when she needs to and does extremely well in class because of it, but she's also involved in several groups on campus as well as a sorority.

Audience expectations for content

What is so special about this student? How much does she actually do in class and on campus? How is she able to balance so many things during college? Why do I have such a high opinion of her?

Students are intrigued by other students and what they do. They like to compare themselves to others. By including personal anecdotes in this paper, I make sure that the audience is more likely to relate to the paper as if they knew Diane.

Audience expectations for layout or format

I don't think they would necessarily expect this profile to look like a magazine, and I wanted it to seem more like a page of a book rather than a magazine article, so I just used one column and didn't use any inset boxes.

I chose photographs to highlight what I wrote about Diane. Readers will appreciate them because they put a face with the story. The pictures of Diane in the lab show where she spends most of her time and show her in action while working with her cells. The picture of Diane at the formal shows her having fun with her sisters and provides an image of her as more than just a student—she's also involved in many activities and enjoys having fun with her friends.

Purpose(s)

Overall, I want my readers to admire Diane as much as I do, but I don't want to sound like she's too good to be true. She is what most college students consider successful, but unlikely. Most college students focus on either work or fun, but most don't balance the two. Diane has established a strong academic life with a balanced social life and several on-campus activities. I think my profile will inspire some readers to become more active on campus and to strive to have a fuller life while in college.

CREATING A DRAFT

As you did the earlier work on selecting a topic, analyzing your audience, and identifying your purpose(s) for writing your profile, you began to think about the things you might want to say about the subject of your profile. Now you need to develop your initial ideas into a coherent document that someone else will want or need to read. The next few sections outline a variety of strategies that will help you explore your topic, engage your audience, and so forth. You will be working with strategies that appear in profiles found in Reading to Write. The following discussions include how-to lists of strategies and examples that will help you see how specific passages in the readings reflect strategies that you can apply to your own writing. These strategies are not recipes or formulas that will guarantee success. But they do suggest ways you can go about exploring your topic, engaging your audience, and so forth. If one strategy doesn't help in a particular situation, try one or more other strategies. And you can always add to these lists of strategies by analyzing other profiles to help you get an insider's view of a particular topic.

Exploring Your Topic

To give your readers an insider's view of the topic of your profile, you will need to explore your topic thoroughly, gathering information that will give your readers new insight into your topic and reflecting on that information to articulate a thesis or the dominant impression you want to create.

Gathering Information

Many profiles draw on secondary sources, things others have written or said about the subject of the profile. They may also draw on materials (diaries or blog entries, for example) created by people you are writing about. But much of what you say will likely come from your own experiences with or observations of the subject of your profile.

Draw on personal experiences. If you are writing about a person or place known only to you and a few other people, you will have to draw heavily on your own experiences. But even if you are writing about a well-known person or place, you should look for opportunities to tell what you have heard or observed. You might also want to draw on primary sources (photographs, blogs, diary entries, letters written by the person you are writing about, and so on). As is the case with materials you have read, be careful not to rely entirely on your memory. Keep notes, quoting and summarizing what people say and recording what you observe.

> For more advice on conducting interviews and recording observations, see Chapter 11.

Use secondary sources. If you have chosen to write about a well-known person or place, you should have little trouble finding information from other writers. You might check the library for biographies or databases, using an electronic database service such as Wilson Select or LexisNexis. You might also do an Internet search using search engines such as Google, Yahoo!, and AltaVista. If you are writing a profile of a person, look for interviews or news stories that contain little-known facts or quotations (from the person or from others who know the person well) that give some special insights into his or her character. If you are writing a profile of a place, try to find stories others have written about the place, newspaper articles, or information from sources such as guidebooks or a local Chamber of Commerce. And whether you are profiling a person, place, or activity, be on the lookout for photographs or other images that will help give readers an insider's view of your topic. If you plan to reproduce visuals from secondary sources, be sure to record the photographer's name and the date the picture was taken, as well as any other information about it (along with source information for the print source or Web site that included the image). Credit the sources in a caption, include a reference in your text, and put an entry in your list of references or works cited.

> For more advice on taking notes, see Chapter 12. For more advice on integrating images, see Chapter 9. For more advice on documenting sources, see Chapter 13.

As you continue looking for information on your topic, you can use a variety of strategies such as the following.

How to Gather Information

STRATEGIES	EXAMPLES FROM READINGS
Look for images your readers know, can recognize, or care about. People understand new information by relating it to what they already know. Consequently, the more remote your topic is from your readers' personal experience, the more important it is to show how your subject is similar to or different from things they already know or care about.	 Although Mark Zuckerberg is the head of a successful business, his photograph in "Hacker. Dropout. CEO." (p. 91) shows him dressed like any college student—sandals, blue jeans, T-shirt, hooded sweat shirt. He is seated and leaning forward with elbows on his legs as if he might be having a conversation with a college friend.
Find out about some of your subject's more impressive accomplishments or distinctive characteristics. If you do a thorough job of gathering this sort of information, you will probably have more information than you can include. This is a good problem to have; it allows you to select only those accomplishments or characteristics that are especially meaningful to your readers.	Dr. Sandra Scott ("E.R. Unscripted," p. 116) has an exhausting job at "one of New York City's busiest trauma centers." The fact that she rejected "cushier offers" at other hospitals gives some insight into her unusual dedication to helping people who have little access to other medical care.
Look for background information that helps readers understand what the subject is currently thinking or doing. Is there anything in your subject's past that will help readers understand your subject's current situation? Are there any unique accomplishments? For example, are there any obstacles your subject has had to overcome? Is your subject part of a trend? Does your subject have any distinctive or especially interesting hobbies?	 In "No Degree, and No Way Back to the Middle" (p. 105), Timothy Egan helps readers understand the irony of one worker's current predicament—unemployed, in debt, barely able to afford health insurance for his wife who is seriously ill—by telling about how he had worked his way up to a well-paying managerial position, only to lose his job when the corporation went out of business.
Find out whether your subject is part of a larger social or economic trend. Find out whether your subject helped to create the trend or is among the people affected by it. Also, notice ways they respond to that trend.	In "No Degree," Egan explains how his subjects are just two examples of people caught up in a serious economic trend, the disappearance of high-paying jobs for people who do not have college degrees.

STRATEGIES	EXAMPLES FROM READINGS
Look for different types of information—stories, comments from people who know your subject well, your personal observations.	 In "My Cancer Year" (p. 110), Jim McLauchlin gives readers an insider's perspective on the life of a cancer survivor by talking with his subject's colleagues, presenting statistics that show his subject's accomplishments, and observing his subject in different situations.
Watch your subject in action. Follow him or her through a typical day or observe them in a typical activity—working on a project, planning a party, and so on. See if your subject (and anyone else involved in the activity) is willing to let you take pictures.	"E.R. Unscripted" follows Dr. Scott through a typical night's work, showing her interacting with the different patients she treats during her shift.
Look for revealing details about the setting in which actions take place. Notice the unique features of the setting as well as ways people affect or are affected by the setting.	 The setting for "Diez in the Desert" (p. 120) is the Arizona desert during the hottest time of the year. It is a treacherous place, one with "rocks [that] could twist an ankle" and cactus needles that pierce shoe leather. It's a setting that drives people to despair, death, and even—in the case of those who rescue Diez—acts of great kindness.

{ **Student Q & A** } **Gathering Visuals**

Writing Now: One of the photographs you included was a group picture of Diane and some of her sorority sisters at a formal dance. Where did you find this photograph, and why did you include it?

Stephanie Guzik: I got the picture of the sisters off of one of the senior members' Web sites. It was taken at a formal that I had attended last fall, where I got my first glimpse into the sorority. I had found a few other photographs of Diane with some sorority sisters, but this one seemed like the perfect fit. It shows Diane right in the middle of a group of girls having a great time together. In the profile, I wanted to make sure that Diane was seen in many lights: academic, extracurricular, family, and friends. This picture showed exactly what I wanted to portray by her being a sister in the sorority, having fun with friends, and being able to hold a balanced life socially and academically. ■

Keep track of information. When you have done a lot of research and are getting ready to write a draft of your profile, it can be very frustrating to find that you remember only part of an important quotation or that you aren't sure where you found an interesting statistic. To avoid this frustration, do two things. First, keep detailed notes of any personal experiences you want to include in the profile. Jot down responses to questions such as the following: What did you see or hear? What did people do or say? What was the setting?

For advice on taking notes, see Chapter 12.

Second, create a working bibliography. At the very least, keep complete bibliographic information for each source you read. Record the author's name, the title of the piece (whether from a periodical or newspaper, book, Web site, or other source), and all the information required to locate the piece if you need to come back to it for more information (the URL of the Web site and the date you accessed it, for example, or date and page number of the magazine article). You need not record all this information according to the precise guidelines of the documentation style you are using, but noting all this information will save you time later. Also note the main point of each source and how it relates to your topic. It can be especially useful to list the main questions the source poses and summarize the answers it gives.

Reflecting on Information

At this point, you should be about ready to reflect on the information you have gathered, trying to identify and explain the main characteristics that make your subject unique and interesting. But before you begin this work, reread the way you answered questions about audience and purpose from the list of guidelines on page 138. Are there some questions in your statement that are not answered very well? For example, are you lacking information about your readers' knowledge, needs, and attitudes? Do you have a good sense of what your readers will expect in terms of content, both verbal and visual? At this point, complete your responses to the best of your ability.

Once you have reviewed what you wrote about your audience and purpose, reread the information you gathered to get a good sense of what you found. Underline passages that seem especially informative or that answer significant questions you or your readers might have about the topic. After doing this, don't try to write a formal essay right away; don't even worry about paragraphing or organization. Just set aside twenty to thirty minutes and write as rapidly as you can in response to the following prompts, trying to elaborate on the impressions you want to convey.

The main impression I want to give my readers concerning my topic is _____ .

One thing that makes my topic so unique/remarkable/impressive is _____ .

Without stopping to look back at the information you gathered, elaborate on that statement as much as you can.

> Something else that makes my topic so unique/remarkable/ impressive is _____.

Continue to elaborate as much as possible from memory. Keep stating and elaborating on your impressions until you have used up your allotted time.

After you have done this reflective work, read or show what you have written to other students (either a small group or the entire class). Describe your intended audience, and then ask your classmates to answer the following questions.

▶ What details give a particularly clear impression of the person, place, or activity that is the subject of my profile?

▶ Are any passages unclear or confusing? If so, which ones are they, and what makes them unclear or confusing?

▶ Are there passages in which my intended readers would appreciate more details? If so, where are these passages, and what details might be helpful? Would a photograph be useful at any of these points?

After considering your classmates' responses, determine whether there are places where you might use some of the strategies explained in How to Gather Information (pp. 142–43) to give readers more insight into your profile topic.

Formulating a Thesis or Dominant Impression

As is the case with memoirs (Chapter 2), profiles do not always state an explicit thesis. But they do convey a *dominant impression*—a basic attitude toward the subject or a sense of what the subject is like. So after discussing your work with your classmates, complete the following sentence.

> The basic point I want to make—or impression I want to convey—about my subject is _____.

This sentence will become your tentative thesis, the principal attitude or impression you want to convey concerning the subject of your profile. As you continue to develop your topic, you may want to revise this sentence. But it will serve as the starting point from which you can look for ways to give readers an insider's view of your topic.

Developing Your Ideas

Once you have at least tentatively decided on the basic point you want to make in your profile, you still need to develop your topic in ways that will let readers have an insider's view of that topic. One way you can do this is by using strategies described on pages 142–43 to gather further information. Another good way is to create narratives that will further reveal unique qualities of your subject. These narratives may be vignettes (brief episodes recounting what happened at a given moment), or, as in "E.R. Unscripted" (p. 116), they may comprise the entire profile, taking readers through an extended series of events that show what is distinctive about your subject.

    Use narratives. Almost all profiles use some narrative. After all, it's hard to talk about a person without telling what he or she does or says. Usually stories or anecdotes about people reveal something significant—not only what happens but also when, where, and why something happens. Narratives also entail some sort of conflict—within a character or person in the story, between characters, or between a character and his or her environment. As you look for stories to use in your profile, remember that not all stories are equally useful. Choose stories that provide some original insight into the unique qualities of the subject you are profiling.

    The following chart introduces some of the strategies you can use in telling stories about your subject. However, because a good story is always richer and more engaging than any summary provided here, you might want to reread the profiles in Reading to Write.

How to Use Narratives

STRATEGIES	EXAMPLES FROM READINGS
Locate your subject in a setting. The context in which you see people—and the way they act in that context—can tell you a lot about their characters or personalities.	 "Hacker. Dropout. CEO." (p. 93) presents a collage of photographs taken in the offices at Mark Zuckerberg's company—pizza boxes, backpacks, and guitars lie casually around, and a coworker reclines while talking on the phone. All of these photographs suggest Zuckerberg's informal, unpretentious character.
Mention specific actions that show personality or character. In some cases, actions really do speak louder than words—or at least louder than generalizations like "he was very friendly," "she was extremely smart," and so on.	When Stephanie Guzik describes her friend Diane in "Behind a Plain White Lab Coat" (p. 126), she doesn't simply say that Diane is helpful or generous. Instead, Stephanie explains how Diane helps her solve a complicated problem she encounters while doing a biology experiment.

STRATEGIES	EXAMPLES FROM READINGS

Mention obstacles your subject faces and the ways he or she reacts to them. One of the best ways to learn about a person is to see how he or she deals with adversity. Tell your readers what your profile subject says and does in solving problems, overcoming difficulties, or dealing with unpleasant people.

When Diez began leading would-be immigrants across the Arizona desert ("Diez in the Desert," p. 120), he felt confident in his ability as a guide and optimistic about the chances for crossing the desert successfully. But difficulties increasingly weigh on him, first keeping him from sleeping and eventually leading to a state of despair in which he assumed he would die. As a result, Diez threw away the money he had been paid for leading the trip across the desert. "No Degree" (p. 107) describes how Jeff Martinelli loses a high-paying job that he can't replace. Instead of complaining or giving up, he accepts a much lower-paying job, commenting, "At least I have a job. . . . Some of the guys I worked with have still not found anything."

Note ways other people react to your subject. What do people say to and about him or her? What sort of actions does this person seem to inspire in others?

"My Cancer Year" (p. 111) shows how serious Michael Turner's illness is by mentioning that "people are . . . afraid. No one likes to talk about bad things, and cancer is near as bad as it gets."

Listen to your subject. Record comments that reflect character or personality.

According to "Hacker. Dropout. CEO.," Zuckerberg received several offers—some reportedly as high as $1 billion—from other firms that wanted to buy his company. (p. 94). Although "Silicon Valley [had] been abuzz" about these reports, Zuckerberg's only comment was, "It's all been very interesting."

{ Student Q & A }   Using Narrative

Writing Now: In the fourth paragraph of your profile, you narrate a brief incident in which you discover that something went wrong with your experiment. Why did you include both your reaction and Diane's?

Stephanie Guzik: I included both of our reactions to the dying culture as a means of contrast. Whereas I was upset about the dead culture, Diane took it in stride and convinced me that it wasn't the end of the world. I carried that thought throughout the paper, focusing on the difference between Diane and myself (representing most college students who are just trying to make it through). That situation in the lab also brought up the idea of how caring Diane is and how much of a mentor she is. ■

{ Exercise }   Using Narrative

Find or write a narrative that reveals something significant about the person or place that is the subject of your profile. Bring this narrative to class, and be prepared to answer the following questions.

- What does this narrative reveal about the subject of my profile?
- Does the narrative offer my readers an insider's view of the subject of my profile?
- What strategies were used in developing this narrative?
- Are there additional strategies that might make the narrative more effective? ■

Engaging Your Audience: Writing an Introduction

Why would you read a profile? Because you are interested in the person who is the subject of the profile? Well, maybe. If you are a fan of, say, a particular movie star, you might be drawn to anything that gives you new information about the movie star. But notice that none of the profiles in this chapter count on this sort of automatic attraction. Most likely, neither would any profile you might choose to read on your own. Instead, profile writers have to engage their readers, giving them strong incentives to stop and read rather than skip on to the next article.

The key to motivating readers lies in observing two basic principles. First, you have to establish a relationship with readers, showing them how your subject has something to do with things they know or care about. Second, you have to create some sort of conflict—tension, question, uncertainty—that will give your audience a motive for reading what you have written.

Relating to Readers

Readers of profiles—or any other kind of writing, for that matter—are likely to become interested in the subject of your profile when they see how it relates to what they know or care about. Thus your introduction needs to establish some common ground with readers, mentioning events, people, or attitudes that are likely to matter to your readers. To do this, consider using one or more of the following strategies illustrated by profiles in the Reading to Write section of this chapter.

How to Relate to Readers

STRATEGIES	EXAMPLES FROM READINGS
Begin by referring to something readers know about, appreciate, or recognize. Such references can take the form of both written text and visual images.	"Hacker. Dropout. CEO." (p. 91) begins by identifying Mark Zuckerberg as the founder of Facebook and showing a photograph that would fit most readers' preconceptions about what a hacker might look like.
Create a scene the reader can visualize.	 In "Behind a Plain White Lab Coat" (p. 126), undergraduate Stephanie Guzik locates the subject of her profile in a setting that most college students should recognize or at least be able to imagine: her subject, Diane Turcotte, is seated at a computer in a biology laboratory.
Provide background information that enables readers to understand and empathize with your subject. Such information can take the form of written text or visuals such as photographs.	"My Cancer Year" (p. 110) begins by explaining how Michael Turner has gone from being a highly successful comic artist to a cancer patient who has undergone ninety-six hours of chemotherapy and takes twelve pills a day to relieve pain. This background enables readers to appreciate subsequent information about how Turner continues to remain active, adapting so as to enjoy as many of his pre-cancer activities as possible.
Begin with an anecdote that reveals traits or attitudes readers can appreciate.	 "Hacker. Dropout. CEO." begins by telling how Mark Zuckerberg responded with enviable calm to a threatening situation that might cause others to panic. Perhaps even more significant, author Ellen McGirt notes that Zuckerberg would not have even mentioned the experience if one of Zuckerberg's coworkers had not told her about it.

Creating Conflict

In addition to establishing a relationship with your readers, your introduction should present or suggest a conflict—a problem your profile will solve, an uncertainty your profile will clarify, a question your profile will answer. This conflict should be one readers will want to resolve in order to develop an insider's view of your subject. If common ground leads readers to begin reading your work, the desire to resolve a conflict—or at least find out where it will lead—will greatly increase people's motivation to continue to read what you have written.

A word of caution: If the conflict is too strong, it may offend or alienate readers. But the right amount of the right sort of conflict will make them aware of questions or problems, which will prompt them to read the rest of your profile in search of answers or solutions. The right amount or type of conflict depends on your purpose(s) in writing and your analysis of the intended audience. What works for one audience might be inappropriate for a different audience.

The following chart illustrates strategies for creating effective conflicts.

How to Create Conflict

STRATEGIES	EXAMPLES FROM READINGS
Juxtapose two very different things.	 "E.R. Unscripted" (p. 116) refers to two extremes of Dr. Scott's nightly work, which "begins with a resuscitation and ends, after dawn, with a pile of paperwork."
Present information that shows a difference from what one might hope or expect. Understanding such a difference—or perhaps finding out that it does not actually exist—can be a powerful motive for continuing to read what someone has written.	Jeff Martinelli, the subject of "No Degree, and No Way Back to the Middle" (p. 105), had assumed that whatever other difficulties he experienced, he would continue to have "a factory job that was his ticket to the middle class." With the closing of the company where he had worked for most of his adult life, both Martinelli and the reader understand that he no longer has a chance of living a relatively comfortable middle-class life.
Suggest a contrast between what the reader knows and what the writer is going to say. One main reason people read profiles is to gain insight they wouldn't otherwise have. By making readers aware that your information will take them beyond what they already know, you appeal to your readers' desire to be insiders.	 The word *unscripted* in the title "E.R. Unscripted" (p. 116) implies that the writer will take the reader beyond the impressions created by televised hospital dramas—where problems are under the control of writers and are usually resolved within one or two hour-long episodes.

{ **Exercise** } **Writing an Introduction**

Using one or more of the strategies explained for relating to readers and creating conflict, write one or more introductory paragraphs that seem likely to engage the attention of the audience you have described. Consider using a photograph along with these paragraphs. Bring this introductory material to class, along with your analysis of audience and purpose (p. 138). Ask your classmates to tell you whether the introduction you have written (and perhaps the photograph you have included) seems likely to engage the intended audience. Also ask your classmates whether they can think of other strategies to engage your audience. ■

Creating an Appropriate Voice

In providing readers with an insider's view of your topic, you will need to make it clear that you yourself are an insider, someone whose attitudes and perceptions can be trusted because you have access to information that is not widely known. In doing this, you may or may not need to state your attitudes explicitly. In "Hacker. Dropout. CEO.," Ellen McGirt's attitudes are very explicit: Her subject is leading a life that "is like a movie script." By contrast, Timothy Egan never directly states that the people in "No Degree" are in a terrible predicament, but the details he includes leave no doubt that he feels this way. But in all cases, you want to sound like an insider, someone whose attitudes and perceptions are based on information that is not readily accessible to those who are not insiders.

Some authors decide to create a personal voice when telling stories about a subject, using words such as *I* and *we*, while conveying personal reactions and feelings. When authors have personal experiences with their subjects, those experiences can sometimes give readers unique insights. Will your readers need to understand your personal experiences with and reactions to the person, place, or activity of your profile? For the author of "Behind a Plain White Lab Coat," the answer is clearly yes. Stephanie Guzik was aware that most members of her audience would need to know about her personal experiences with the subject of her profile—a fellow student at her college—to understand her purpose in writing the piece.

As you decide whether to use a personal voice, keep in mind that you have a couple of basic options.

▶ **Using (or avoiding) first-person pronouns (*I, me, we*).** Stephanie Guzik uses these pronouns since her understanding of her subject derives from her personal experience. Writers of other profiles in Reading to Write avoid first-person pronouns—not because they are necessarily a bad idea, but rather because these writers' understanding of their topics does not stem directly from their personal experiences.

▶ **Talking *with* your readers or talking *to* them.** "My Cancer Year" establishes the feeling of talking directly with readers, using personal pronouns *you* and *he* when the author quotes the people who are subjects of his profile. McLauchlin also deliberately uses sentence fragments, that is, sentences that lack a subject or verb or both. ("And oh, yeah—those whispers.")

Whichever options you choose, there are several strategies you can use to give readers the sense that you are an insider.

How to Create an Appropriate Voice

STRATEGIES	EXAMPLES FROM READINGS
Choose details that exemplify the attitudes you want to convey, especially the kinds of details that are known by insiders. There may be times when you need to directly state your attitude toward your subject. But more important, choose details that will let readers see for themselves the emotions or attitudes your subject inspires.	Robert Mackey, the author of "E.R. Unscripted" (p. 116), clearly admires Dr. Sandra Scott and presents her as dedicated to practicing medicine in a chaotic environment. But he never explicitly says these things. Instead, he chooses details that illustrate the chaos and stress. He notes, for example, that "in addition to dealing with cuts and bullet wounds, on any given night Scott will treat everything from miscarriages and S.T.D.'s to dental problems and what one patient believed was sleep disturbance caused by a spell."
Allow your subject to speak for himself or herself, displaying the attributes you admire. Be selective; listen for comments that in just a few words convey some important attitude or character trait.	Michael Turner, the subject of "My Cancer Year" (p. 111), frequently displays a stoic courage in matter-of-fact comments such as this remark about living with cancer: "It's as simple as your choice. . . . You can choose to go on living, or you can sit and do nothing. I definitely choose living."
Let others convey your attitudes. Especially look for comments from people who can speak authoritatively about your subject. Again, be selective. Choose only those comments that express your point more succinctly or effectively than you can.	Ellen McGirt is not the only person who admires her subject in "Hacker. Dropout. CEO." (p. 102). A partner in an organization that finances Facebook testifies to Mark Zuckerberg's success in commenting, "Today, any offer [to buy Facebook] around a billion [dollars] would be way low."
Choose photographs that imply your impressions of or attitudes toward the subject of your profile. Pay special attention to the composition of these photographs and to the details they include (and exclude).	 "Behind a Plain White Lab Coat" (p. 129) includes a photograph that shows Diane in a different setting (in Figure 2), reinforcing the point that her life is not limited to a science lab.

{ Exercise } **Creating an Appropriate Voice**

If you have not already begun to do so, think about the voice you want to convey in your profile. What are your attitudes toward your subject? How personal do you want your voice to be? To find answers to these questions, try the following activities.

- Review what you have previously written about your purpose and audience (and revise this information if you need to).
- List some of the words and phrases you hope readers would use to describe the voice in your profile.
- Show both the statement of audience and the list of words and phrases to someone else (a classmate or your instructor). Ask this person to tell you whether the voice you hope to create makes sense, given what you have said about your intended audience and purpose.
- Using what you learn, revise the list of words that describe the voice you want to create. ■

{ Student Q & A } **Creating an Appropriate Voice**

Writing Now: In several places, you interject questions in italics that run through your mind as you talk with Diane. What was your purpose in including these questions? What do they say about you and your attitudes toward Diane?

Stephanie Guzik: The highlighted thoughts italicized in the text continue to add contrast between myself and Diane. Whereas I often struggle to balance my work, sorority, and friends, Diane somehow finds time to do that and much more without much stress. In writing the essay, I could imagine several questions that readers might raise about how Diane actually manages to do everything. So I interjected these italicized thoughts, which the reader could most likely relate to while reading the essay. ■

Organizing

Profiles should always convey a coherent overall impression of the profile subject. And the details of the profile must be organized in such a way as to convey that impression. You can convey an insider's perspective on a particular topic by giving readers cues that make it easy to understand what you're getting at and that help readers find the information they need. You may already be familiar with some of the best ways of providing this structure: using thesis statements, beginning paragraphs with topic sentences, and using words that forecast the content of a paragraph or series of paragraphs. Not all profiles have thesis statements, nor do all paragraphs have topic sentences. Nevertheless, it is part of your responsibility as a writer to make it easy for readers to find what they are looking for. The following list describes a variety of strategies you can use to organize and make your work accessible.

How to Organize

STRATEGIES	EXAMPLES FROM READINGS
Consider using thesis statements and topic sentences. If used in a profile, the thesis statement usually appears near the end of the introductory paragraph(s). Topic sentences appear at or near the beginning of a paragraph, to state the main idea of that paragraph and to show readers what the rest of the paragraph will say.	In "No Degree, and No Way Back to the Middle" (p. 105), Timothy Egan states his thesis at the end of the third paragraph. After explaining that Jeff Martinelli is healthy, ambitious, and skilled, Egan asserts: "But the world has changed for people like him." Egan goes on to explain what those changes are and how they affect Martinelli and Mark McClellan. Later in the profile, after he has explained some of the changes in Martinelli's "market value," Egan begins a paragraph with this assertion: "And the changes go well beyond the factory floor." Egan then provides details for readers that justify his assertion.
Tell a story, using transitional words or phrases to indicate when, where, and why events happened.	 "E.R. Unscripted" (p. 116) consists of a single narrative, with time cues indicating precisely when events took place. And within each event, there are further cues as to when and why specific events occurred. At 12:43 a.m., for example, a patient comes in explaining exactly when he was wounded ("during an attempted carjacking") and why ("'That's what happens when you're driving those Navigators. . . . They want those Navigators.'"
Group details around related areas of your subject's life. Think of ways to "chunk" information, grouping closely related facts to make a point or create an impression.	Stephanie Guzik in "Behind a Plain White Lab Coat" (p. 126) gives information about her subject's life in the laboratory, in campus organizations, in a sorority, and in her family life.

STRATEGIES	EXAMPLES FROM READINGS
Establish a pattern: Talk about actions and reactions or problems and solutions. Repeat the pattern in your profile as needed.	 In "Hacker. Dropout. CEO." (p. 91), Ellen McGirt describes her subject's solutions to a series of problems: Harvard provided Mark Zuckerberg with no way to create an online facebook, so he created one by hacking into Harvard's student records. When Harvard cut off Zuckerberg's Internet connection, he apologized and then created an alternative site. When his time working on the Web site interfered with his studying for an art history final exam, he created a site to which members of his art history class could post their notes, thereby providing him with the information he needed.
Link passages by beginning a new passage with information that refers to information from the passage that immediately precedes it. This will create a "flow" that leads your readers from one point or idea to the next.	In "My Cancer Year" (p. 111), McLauchlin reports the difficult, uncertain progress of treating the cancer that has developed in Michael Turner's leg. This passage concludes, "The leg is slowly starting to work again. 'But you never know,' Turner cautions." The next passage begins, "'Never knowing' is the status quo in Turner's life." This new passage goes on to explain how Turner copes with the fact of never knowing.
Use visuals to reinforce the point or overall impression you want to convey. Not all profiles use this organizational strategy. But photographs, illustrations, inset boxes, and pull quotes (text "pulled out" and set off for emphasis) can provide a way to echo an attitude or illustrate a statement expressed in the written text.	 "Hacker. Dropout. CEO." includes photographs of Zuckerberg's work environment (boxes of pizza, guitars lying about on the office floor, an employee wearing a large sombrero), all of which reflect a relaxed, casual atmosphere that is consistent with Zuckerberg's unconventional approach to his work. The success of Zuckerberg's business is indicated not only in the text of the profile but also in the inset box that contains a graph showing a dramatic increase in the number of people who use Facebook.

{ Exercise } **Considering Organization**

Bring to class a copy of a profile that does a good job of making its structure very clear. Be prepared to show your instructor and/or classmates how the author(s) enabled you to see the structure of the profile. After identifying strategies other writers have used, review your exploratory draft, looking for ways you might use some of these strategies to make the structure of your own profile clear. ■

Concluding

Because the goal of a profile is to reveal an insider's view of an interesting topic, your conclusion should reinforce the overall impression of your subject and solidify the attitude you have expressed directly or indirectly about it. The profiles in Reading to Write suggest a variety of strategies that can help you end with something memorable that reinforces or extends the message you have sought to convey.

How to Conclude

STRATEGIES	EXAMPLES FROM READINGS
Create an evocative image. Using words and/or visual images, leave the reader with the overall impression you have sought to create throughout the profile.	"E.R. Unscripted" (p. 118) concludes with a photograph of Dr. Sandra Scott leaving the hospital alone, in a seemingly endless hospital corridor.
Refer to a detail you mentioned earlier, adding new information about it.	When Diez and his group ("Diez in the Desert," p. 120) are crossing the Arizona desert, one member of the group dies. At that point, Diez was so "stunned and panicked" that he began to cry. But at the end of the profile when Diez tells another group of would-be immigrants of her death, he seems to have grown hardened; he simply tells about her death with a "dry laugh."
End with a quotation from the person you are profiling. Don't use just any quotation. Use a comment that reveals something important about the subject's personality or character.	At the end of "No Degree, and No Way Back to the Middle" (p. 108), Timothy Egan concludes by having Mark McClellan reiterate the point Egan has made throughout the profile: "There is no working up anymore."

STRATEGIES	EXAMPLES FROM READINGS
Frame your profile. Come back to an image or idea you mention at the beginning of the profile, but expand on that image, giving it additional meaning.	The conclusion of "Behind a Plain White Lab Coat" (p. 131) returns to Diane in the setting where readers first saw her—in the lab. But at this point, Stephanie Guzik provides the details that let readers take Diane seriously when she says: "Don't forget, there's a whole different place outside of that door [to the lab]. Take advantage of it while you can."

{ Exercise } **Concluding Your Profile**

Using a strategy identified here (or a different strategy from a profile you have analyzed), write a conclusion for your profile. Share your draft with some class-mates or your instructor, and ask for their responses. Can they identify the strategy, and do they think it is appropriate? If not, what strategy would they recommend and why? Would that conclusion reinforce or extend the dominant impression created throughout your profile? ■

Designing Your Profile and Integrating Visual Information

As you have seen, profiles can make effective use of different kinds of design and visuals—pull quotes, inset boxes, and two-column layout. But many profiles consist solely or primarily of written text. Check with your instructor about the visual features that are appropriate for the profile you are writing: bear in mind the goals of the course and your intended audience. If you decide to include photographs, be sure to observe the following guidelines.

▶ Photographs should not simply depict the subject of your profile; they should also convey the same attitude or tone you create in the written text. See, for example, the explanation (p. 89) of how the photograph of Mark Zuckerberg reflects key elements of his personality.

▶ On some occasions, photographs will be self-explanatory, but as a rule you should use captions with photographs that either indicate what is going on (as in "E.R. Unscripted") or what the photographs depict. For example, the photo-graph in "No Degree" (p. 106) introduces one subject of the profile and briefly explains what he is doing and why he is doing it.

▶ If you use photographs that you have not taken yourself, be sure to give appropriate credit, following the guidelines from your instructor or those on page 141.

▶ If you are considering whether to include particular photos in your text, bring the photographs and captions to class. Show the photographs to your classmates and ask what messages the photographs convey to them. Then show both the photographs and the captions to your classmates. Ask them to tell you whether the captions either (1) explain clearly and succinctly what is going on in the photographs or (2) indicate an attitude that seems consistent with the photographs. If your classmates' reactions differ greatly from your own, you might need to look for other photographs or get additional reactions from people who are as similar as possible to your intended readers.

Creating a Review Draft

By now, you should have some strong impressions and views of the subject of your profile, so you should be ready to create a draft that will convey those impressions as effectively as possible. This is not a final draft, but neither is it a rough draft. Instead, it is a review draft; it represents the best effort you can make at this point. After completing this draft, you will need to assess it carefully not only by critiquing it yourself but also by getting others' perspectives. This means that you will subject the review draft to a final review (from one or more of your classmates or from your instructor). Then you will use this assessment to make revisions in content, organization, style, and format.

For more on creating working bibliographies, see Chapter 10. For advice on documenting sources, see Chapter 13.

In preparation for writing the review draft, look back at what you wrote about your audience and purpose (p. 138). Has your sense of audience and purpose changed? If so, revise what you said about audience and purpose and keep that in mind as you decide what to say and how to say it in the review draft. Also, look back at what you wrote when you were reflecting on information you had gathered (p. 144). Do you need to modify any of the points expressed there? Are there any places where you need to add information that would make your points clearer or answer questions the audience is likely to ask? Finally, review your notes and working bibliography. Make sure that quotes and other references are accurate. Also make sure that each source is appropriately cited.

As you work on your review draft, think carefully about your introduction and conclusion. Does the introductory material establish the voice you want to create? Does it seem likely to engage the intended audience? Does the conclusion reinforce the overall impression you want to convey? Do your introduction and conclusion still seem appropriate for your audience? If not, modify them by using one or more of the strategies identified in this chapter.

In addition, take some pains to make sure your structure is clear and your ideas are well organized. It might help to make an informal outline indicating your main points. You should also use one or more of the strategies described on pages 154–55.

REVIEWING AND REVISING

After creating your review draft, assess it carefully—not only by critiquing it yourself but also by getting others' perspectives in a final review. Most writers find it very helpful to have others read and comment on their drafts, and the advice in this section will help you gather feedback that will be useful as you revise.

Getting a Final Review

Once you have made your review draft as complete and polished as possible, have it reviewed by one or more people who understand the principles (analyzing audience and purpose, engaging readers, and so on) that you have been working with in this chapter. These reviewers might include your instructor, your classmates, or a tutor in your school's writing center. You will use this review to guide a revision of your review draft before you turn your work in for grading.

Give the reviewer a copy of your draft, one he or she can make notes on. Also give the reviewer a copy of your statement of audience and purpose (see p. 138). If necessary, revise that analysis before giving it to the reviewer. Ask the reviewer to adopt the perspective of the audience you have described, and then use the following checklist in commenting on your work.

[**Checklist for Final Review**]

1. In my explanation of audience and purpose, please highlight any statements that give you a good sense of the knowledge, needs, and attitudes of my intended audience. (For an example of one student's analysis of audience and purpose, see page 139.) Please indicate any statements that need to be clarified.

2. What is the overall impression you get from reading my profile? What words would you use to describe the person, place, or activity I am writing about? Given what I say in my statement of audience and purpose, how likely does it seem that this impression will come through clearly and be interesting to my intended audience?

3. In what specific passages have I developed my topic thoroughly, creating a clear, dominant impression of my subject? What are some passages in which I could make that impression clearer or more effective? What are some strategies (explained on pp. 145–47) I might use to do this? Do the photographs I have used contribute to the impression I am trying to create?

4. What portions of my introduction seem likely to engage the interest of my intended audience? What are some strategies (explained on pp. 149–50) that might make the introduction more engaging?

5. How would you describe the voice I have created? At what points does that voice seem appropriate, given my intended audience and profile topic? What strategies (explained on p. 152) might help me make the voice clearer or more appropriate?

6. What are some words or phrases that help make the organization of my profile clear? What strategies (explained on pp. 154–55) might I use to make the organization of my profile clearer?

7. How does the conclusion of my profile reinforce or extend the dominant impression I am trying to create? What strategies (explained on pp. 156-57) might I use to make my conclusion more effective?

8. If the profile includes photographs or other visual elements, what do they contribute to the overall impression conveyed in the profile? Do the images have appropriate captions?

Go to bedfordstmartins.com/ writingnow to download these questions from Chapter 3 > Worksheets.

If possible, ask the reviewer to talk with you about your review draft as well as make notes on it. During this conversation, make careful notes about what the reviewer finds to be clear or unclear, interesting or uninteresting; also note any suggestions he or she makes. Sometimes you may have a strong impulse to argue with your reviewers, showing them where they are wrong or have missed the point. Resist this impulse, at least at first. Instead, try to find out why they disagree with you. Once you have a good idea of what their concerns or objections are, you might respond to what they have said, asking how persuasive they find your responses.

Revising Your Profile

Once you have a good idea of how the reviewer responds to your profile (after you have listened without explaining, arguing, or making judgments), go back through your notes on your reviewer's comments. Bearing in mind your intended audience and purpose, decide which comments are most valid. Then use the strategies referred to in the Checklist for Final Review.

After resolving all the issues that need attention, proofread carefully and correct any typographical or formatting errors. Then submit this final draft to your instructor.

▷ TAKING STOCK OF WHERE YOU ARE

Although you will find differences among the writing assignments in this book, there are also some important similarities. For example, you always have to analyze the intended audience, write an introduction that will engage that particular audience, and so forth. Each assignment in *Writing Now* will teach you strategies that can help you grow as a writer and improve your work on subsequent assignments. This will be especially true if you make a conscious effort to assess your development as a writer as you go along.

To help with this assessment and growth, continually review what you're learning and try to determine what you need to work harder on in the future. Once your instructor has returned the final draft of your work, think back over all the comments you received—from classmates as well as your instructor—and write out answers to the following questions. (You might want to keep these in a journal or a special section of a notebook.)

Questions for Assessing Your Growth as a Writer

1. What appears to be my greatest area of strength?
2. Where am I having the greatest difficulty?
3. What am I learning about the process of writing?
4. What am I learning about giving and receiving feedback on writing?
5. What have I learned from writing a profile that I can use in my next assignment for this course, for another course, or for work?

Following are Stephanie Guzik's answers to these questions for the profile she wrote on Diane Turcotte (p. 126).

1. I feel that my strength is (other than meeting a deadline) providing a personal look into the subject by using personal experiences, thoughts, and feelings.

2. My greatest difficulty (other than evaluating my writing like this) is wanting to add too much information in too short a time. After I initially wrote the paper, there were several sections that I had to take out; they had information that originally seemed pertinent but when I reviewed it, didn't seem as important as I had thought.

3. In writing this paper, I learned how to add personal touches to my writing. Whereas other papers I've written are devoid of emotion or personal thoughts, I was able to incorporate what I thought of Diane into this paper.

4. While I was writing this paper, I talked several times with people about what I should change and what I should do with what I had written. It was a little harder with this paper to accept criticism without thinking about it, simply because my own personal thoughts and feelings were involved in writing the paper. However, I learned to take the criticism and rather than completely change what I had written, I simply altered what I had already written to compensate for whatever comments had been made.

5. Writing the profile was definitely a breath of fresh air compared to other pieces of writing. However, I feel that from writing this paper, I will be able to incorporate more feeling into my other papers, although indirectly. I can use my thoughts to guide my writing rather than just providing facts about the topic.

▶ Go to **bedfordstmartins.com/ writingnow** to download these questions from Chapter 3 > Worksheets.

Reports

At this point in your education, you have probably written any number of reports—research papers, lab reports, book reports. And in college and in your career, you are certain to write still more: summaries of developments in a particular area of research, explanations of trends in an organization or society at large, descriptions of problems (or solutions) that affect a group or organization. As you will see later in the chapter, the information you report may take different forms—written texts as well as visuals (charts, graphs, pictures). It may also come from different sources—perhaps from your own personal experiences and observations as well as secondary sources such as statements from recognized authorities, results of surveys or experiments, or firsthand accounts of observers who are in good positions to report accurately and fairly.

In spite of all these differences, all reports share one basic purpose: to convey a factual, reasonably comprehensive account of a topic. However, simply providing information is not enough. Usually a report will attempt to do one or more of the following.

- ► Make readers aware that a serious problem exists

- ► Inform readers of a solution to a problem they are concerned about

- ► Provide readers with facts they can use in making a decision

- ► Challenge readers' preconceptions

- ► Make readers aware of a situation or trend that is likely to affect them

- ► Reassure readers who are concerned about a particular topic

You may be able to think of other purposes you want to accomplish in writing a report. But whatever the purpose, the report will have to answer this fundamental question any reader is likely to raise: How does this matter to me or people or organizations I care about? In other words, a report will have to provide readers with factual information they will see as meaningful.

▷ READING REPORTS

In the following section, you will find reports on a variety of topics ranging from the untrustworthiness of digital photography to the search for the science behind moral decision making. Following each report are questions that pertain specifically to the report you have just read. In addition to these specific questions, there are several basic questions you should ask in reading any report.

<table>
<tr><td>[Questions for
Reading Reports]</td><td>

▶ **Who is the intended audience?** Consider the language, visuals, and information included in (and excluded from) the report. What does the writer appear to be assuming about the following?

- Readers' background knowledge of the subject
- The audience's values, beliefs, attitudes, or preconceptions regarding the subject
- The questions the audience will want to have answered

▶ **What specific purpose(s) is the writer trying to accomplish?** In addition to achieving the basic goal of providing a thorough, factual account of information, is the writer trying to accomplish a more specific purpose, such as one or more of the following?

- Make readers aware that a serious problem exists
- Inform readers of a solution to a problem about which they are concerned
- Challenge readers' preconceptions
- Make readers aware of a situation or trend that is likely to affect them or their organization
- Reassure readers who may be concerned about the topic of the report
- Provide readers with a credible basis for making a decision

▶ **How informative is the report?**

- What questions does the report answer?
- Are these the kinds of questions readers want to have answered?
- Are these questions answered with the kinds of details and explanations that will make sense to readers?
- Are there significant questions that the report does not answer?

▶ **How believable is the report?**

- Are the facts accurate and up to date?
- Do the author's claims seem justified by the facts?
- Is information drawn from sources the audience is likely to trust?
- If it's likely that there are multiple perspectives on the topic, are those perspectives presented fairly? Are any perspectives left out?

</td></tr>
</table>

▶ **How well organized is the report?**

- Is it easy for readers to find the information they are looking for?
- Can readers readily identify the main point (or thesis) of the report?
- Can readers identify the main point of each paragraph? Of each visual?
- Does the report seem to "flow," giving readers a clear sense of how a particular sentence or paragraph leads to the next?

▶ **What sort of voice would readers hear in the report?**

- What attitudes, values, or emotions are suggested in the text? Does the writer seem fair? Alarmed? Calm and reasonable? Angry? Biased? Sympathetic toward the audience or toward the people or organizations mentioned in the report?
- Does the writer appear to have the experience and knowledge needed to speak authoritatively on the subject?

{ For Collaboration } **Reading Reports**

The bulleted list of specific purposes for reports above is by no means complete. Try adding to it. Read (or listen to or watch on TV) several different reports. Ask yourself whether the authors of these reports are trying to accomplish one or more of the purposes mentioned in this list. What other purposes might they be trying to accomplish? Then, working with one or two classmates, list the purposes for the reports you found. ■

A report can contain a variety of visual elements, including photographs, illustrations, inset boxes, and charts and graphs, as well as variations in color, page layout, and typefaces. Here are important questions to ask when reading or analyzing photographs and illustrations, two of the most widely used types of visuals in reports.

▶ Does the photograph or illustration seem fair and accurate?

▶ What does the visual contribute to the written text? Does it help engage the audience's attention? Convey the author's attitudes? Elaborate on information?

▶ What kinds of details are included in (or excluded from) the visual? What questions do these details answer, and what attitudes or emotions do they evoke? In reports, visuals should contain only details that are essential for answering a question or evoking appropriate emotions or attitudes. Ask whether the writer is unfairly slanting a report by using visuals that omit details that might challenge or modify the point(s) the writer is making.

▶ What viewing angle is represented in the photograph, and what does that viewing angle imply? When the person or object is shown as if the viewer is looking up at it from below, this viewing angle makes the subject seem important, powerful, or threatening. If the perspective is that of someone looking downward, the angle tends to make the subject seem weak or unimportant. If the image lets viewers look head-on, the position is usually one of equality.

▶ What colors are used, and what emotions do they evoke? Warm colors such as red and orange tend to evoke strong emotional reactions and a sense of danger or urgency, whereas cool colors such as blue have a more calming effect. Also, dark colors suggest something sinister or gloomy, and pastels suggest innocence, childhood, or safety.

▶ What kinds of lines and shapes are apparent, and what reactions do they prompt? Diagonal lines can suggest movement or threat; jagged lines often create tension or anxiety. Other lines and forms can suggest balance and stability.

▶ Where are objects located in the visual? Objects in the upper portion of an image are likely to seem powerful; objects in the lower portion are likely to seem weaker and more vulnerable. Objects located near each other seem more related to each other than to objects at a distance.

To see how answers to these questions can account for the reaction to a photograph, consider the following image from "Seeing Is Not Believing" (p. 183). The author invites readers to examine this picture and poses this question: Is it real or a hoax? Though it seems to be a hoax, the image captures a routine event on the Caribbean island of St. Maarten, where the main airport is located only 40 feet from the beach. Airplanes, people walking on beaches, luxury hotels—these are all things we have seen. The effect of the picture depends in large part on the fact that we do not expect to see these things in the relationship shown in this picture.

For advice on how to use visuals effectively, see Chapter 9.

- **Information included/excluded** The bizarre, frightening effect of this picture depends on information included (people on a beach, hotel in background, airliner) and on information excluded (the airport runway, which lies just beyond the beach).

Color Dark clouds at top of picture seem ominous.

Location of objects The plane appears especially powerful and threatening in its size relative to the people on the beach but also in its location in the upper half of the image.

Viewing angle The viewer is looking up at the airliner, a perspective that makes the plane especially imposing.

Lines The curved beach suggests relaxation and comfort, but the diagonal line of the plane's fuselage (nose slightly up, tail slightly down) suggests movement and, therefore, a threat to people on the beach.

{ **Exercise** } ▶ Go to bedfordstmartins.com/writingnow to Chapter 4 > Visuals.

For practice analyzing the visual information in another report, see the visual exercises online. ■

{ Exercise } **Analyzing Visuals in Reports**

Bring to class a piece of writing that you find very informative—not only in the written text but in the visual elements it contains. These visuals may take the form of images (photographs or drawings), graphs, diagrams, maps, or tables. Or the visual elements may make special use of written text, setting it off with columns, color, sidebars (inset boxes of text), or pull quotes (highlighted quotations from the text). In all cases, be able to explain what there is about the visual elements that help make the text informative. ■

▷ READING TO WRITE

In the following section of this chapter, you will find six reports covering a variety of subjects, ranging from current technologies to trends in society and processes by which people make ethical choices. People read reports because they are seeking factual answers to questions such as these: What events have recently occurred? Why have these events occurred? What problems are people currently facing? What is being done to solve these problems? What are significant trends in business, society, technology, or religion?

The following reports address these and other questions. They also reflect the different kinds of topics you might consider when you create your own report for the major assignment in this chapter. After each of these essays, you will find a set of questions, titled Reflecting on What You Have Read, that will help you not only assess the content of the report but also recognize strategies and techniques you can use in your own writing. You will also find suggestions for Thinking Ahead, which will help you think of topics you might write about.

▶ Go to
bedfordstmartins.com/
writingnow and click on
Chapter 4 > Examples for
additional examples
of reports.

The Perils of Higher Education

Steven Kotler

Steven Kotler is a freelance journalist who lives in Los Angeles and has written for such publications as *National Geographic,* the *New York Times Magazine, Details,* and *Wired.* His book, *West of Jesus: Surfing, Science, and the Origins of Belief* (2006), is an account of his own spiritual quest through surfing. The following article, from *Psychology Today*, questions the effect of the learning environment for many college students.

THE PERILS OF HIGHER EDUCATION

Can't remember the difference between declensions and derivatives? Blame college. The undergrad life is a blast, but it may lead you to forget everything you learn.

BY STEVEN KOTLER
PHOTOGRAPHS BY KARJEAN LEVINE

We go to college to learn, to soak ¹ up a dazzling array of information intended to prepare us for adult life. But college is not simply a data dump; it is also the end of parental supervision. For many students, that translates into four years of late nights, pizza banquets and boozy weekends that start on Wednesday. And while we know that bad habits are detrimental to cognition in general—think drunk driving—new studies show that the undergrad urges to eat, drink and be merry have devastating effects on learning and memory. It turns out that the exact place we go to get an education may in fact be one of the worst possible environments in which to retain anything we've learned.

Dude, I Haven't Slept in Three Days!

Normal human beings spend one-third of their ² lives asleep, but today's college students aren't normal. A recent survey of undergraduates and medical students at Stanford University found 80 percent of them qualified as sleep-deprived, and a poll taken by the National Sleep Foundation found that most young adults get only 6.8 hours a night.

All-night cramfests may seem to be the only ³ option when the end of the semester looms, but in fact getting sleep—and a full dose of it— might be a better way to ace exams. Sleep is crucial to declarative memory, the hard, factual kind that helps us remember which year World War I began, or what room the French Lit class is in. It's also essential for procedural memory, the "know-how" memory we use when learning to drive a car or write a five-paragraph essay. "Practice makes perfect," says Harvard Medical School psychologist Matt Walker, "but having a night's rest after practicing might make you even better."

Walker taught 100 people to ⁴ bang out a series of nonsense sequences on a keyboard—a standard procedural memory task. When asked to replay the sequence 12 hours later, they hadn't improved. But when one group of subjects was allowed to sleep overnight before being retested, their speed and accuracy improved by 20 to 30 percent. "It was bizarre," says Walker. "We were seeing people's skills improve just by sleeping."

For procedural memory, the ⁵ deep slow-wave stages of sleep

were the most important for improvement—particularly during the last two hours of the night. Declarative memory, by contrast, gets processed during the slow-wave stages that come in the first two hours of sleep. "This means that memory requires a full eight hours of sleep," says Walker. He also found that if someone goes without sleep for 24 hours after acquiring a new skill, a week later they will have lost it completely. So college students who pull all-nighters during exam week might do fine on their tests but may not remember any of the material by next semester.

Walker believes that the common practice of 6 back-loading semesters with a blizzard of papers

and exams needs a rethink. "Educators are just encouraging sleeplessness," says Walker. "This is just not an effective way to force information into the brain."

Who's Up for Pizza?

Walk into any college cafeteria and you'll find 7 a smorgasbord of French fries, greasy pizza, burgers, potato chips and the like. On top of that, McDonald's, Burger King, Wendy's and other fast-food chains have been gobbling up campus real estate in recent years. With hectic schedules and skinny budgets, students find fast food an easy alternative. A recent Tufts University survey found that 50 percent of students eat too much fat, and 70 to 80 percent eat too much saturated fat.

But students who fuel their 8 studies with fast food have something more serious than the "freshman 15" to worry about: They may literally be eating themselves stupid. Researchers have known since the late 1980s that bad eating habits contribute to the kind of cognitive decline found in diseases like Alzheimer's. Since then, they've been trying to find out exactly how a bad diet might be hard on the brain. Ann-Charlotte Granholm, director of the Center for Aging at the Medical University of South Carolina, has recently focused on trans fat, widely used in fast-food cooking because it extends the shelf life of foods. Trans fat is made by bubbling hydrogen through unsaturated fat, with copper or zinc added to speed the chemical reaction along.

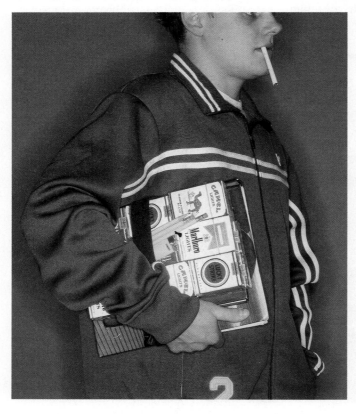

These metals are frequently found in the brains of people with Alzheimer's, which sparked Granholm's concern.

To investigate, she fed one group of rats a diet high in trans fat and compared them with another group fed a diet that was just as greasy but low in trans fat. Six weeks later, she tested the animals in a water maze, the rodent equivalent of a final exam in organic chemistry. "The trans-fat group made many more errors," says Granholm, especially when she used more difficult mazes. 9

When she examined the rats' brains, she found that trans-fat eaters had fewer proteins critical to healthy neurological function. She also saw inflammation in and around the hippocampus, the part of the brain responsible for learning and memory. "It was alarming," says Granholm. "These are the exact types of changes we normally see at the onset of Alzheimer's, but we saw them after six weeks," even though the rats were still young. 10

Her work corresponds to a broader inquiry conducted by Veerendra Kumar Madala Halagaapa and Mark Mattson of the National Institute on Aging. The researchers fed four groups of mice different diets— normal, high-fat, high-sugar and high-fat/high-sugar. Each diet had the same caloric value, so that one group of mice wouldn't end up heavier. Four months later, the mice on the high-fat diets performed significantly worse than the other groups on a water maze test. 11

Students who fuel their studies with fast food have something serious to worry about: They may literally be eating themselves stupid.

The researchers then exposed the animals to a neurotoxin that targets the hippocampus, to assess whether a high-fat diet made the mice less able to cope with brain damage. Back in the maze, all the animals performed worse than before, but the mice who had eaten the high-fat diets were most seriously compromised. "Based on our work," says Mattson, "we'd predict that people who eat high-fat diets and high-fat/high-sugar diets are not only damaging their ability to learn and remember new information, but also putting themselves at much greater risk for all sorts of neurodegenerative disorders like Alzheimer's." 12

Welcome to Margaritaville State University

It's widely recognized that heavy drinking doesn't exactly boost your intellect. But most people figure that their booze-induced foolishness wears off once the hangover is gone. Instead, it turns out that even limited stints of overindulgence may have long-term effects. 13

Less than 20 years ago, researchers began to realize that the adult brain wasn't just a static lump of cells. They found that stem cells in the brain are constantly churning out new neurons, particularly in the hippocampus. Alcoholism researchers, in turn, began to wonder if chronic alcoholics' memory problems had something to do with nerve cell birth and growth. 14

In 2000, Kimberly Nixon and Fulton Crews at the University of North Carolina's Bowles Center for Alcohol Studies subjected lab rats to four days of heavy alcohol intoxication. They gave the rats a week to shake off their hangovers, then tested them on and off during the next month in a water maze. "We didn't find anything at first," says Nixon. But on the 19th day, the rats who had been on the binge performed much worse. In 19 days, the cells born during the binge had grown to maturity—and clearly, the neurons 15 born during the boozy period didn't work properly once they reached maturity. "The timing was almost too perfect," says Nixon.

While normal rats generated about 2,500 new brain cells in three weeks, the drinking rats produced only 1,400. A month later, the sober rats had lost about half of those new cells through normal die-off. But all of the new cells died in the brains of the binge drinkers. "This was startling," says Nixon. "It was the first time anyone had found that alcohol not only inhibits the birth of new cells but also inhibits the ones that survive." In further study, they found that a week's abstinence produced a twofold burst of neurogenesis, and a month off the sauce brought cognitive function back to normal.

What does this have to do with a weekend keg party? A number of recent studies show that college students consume far more alcohol than anyone previously suspected. Forty-four percent of today's collegiates drink enough to be classified as binge drinkers, according to a nationwide survey of 10,000 students done at Harvard University. The amount of alcohol consumed by Nixon's binging rats far exceeded intake at a typical keg party—but other research shows that the effects of alcohol work on a sliding scale. Students who follow a weekend of heavy drinking with a week of heavy studying might not forget everything they learn. They just may struggle come test time.

Can I Bum a Smoke?

If this ledger of campus menaces worries you, here's something you really won't like: Smoking cigarettes may actually have some cognitive benefits, thanks to the power of nicotine. The chemical improves mental focus, as scientists have known since the 1950s. Nicotine also aids concentration in people who have ADHD and may protect against Alzheimer's disease. Back in 2000, a nicotine-like drug under development by the pharmaceutical company Astra Arcus USA was shown to restore the ability to learn and remember in rats with brain lesions similar to those found in Alzheimer's patients. More recently Granholm, the scientist investigating trans fats and memory, found that nicotine enhances spatial memory in healthy rats. Other researchers have found that nicotine also boosts both emotional memory (the kind that helps us *not* put our hands back in the fire after we've been burned) and auditory memory.

There's a catch: Other studies show that nicotine encourages state-dependent learning. The idea is that if, for example, you study in blue sweats, it helps to take the exam in blue sweats. In other words, what you learn while smoking is best recalled while smoking. Since lighting up in an exam room might cause problems, cigarettes probably aren't the key to getting on the dean's list.

Nonetheless, while the number of cigarette smokers continues to drop nationwide, college students are still lighting up: As many as 30 percent smoke during their years of higher education. The smoking rate for young adults between the ages of 18 and 24 has actually risen in the past decade.

All this news makes you wonder how anyone's ever managed to get an education. Or what would happen to GPAs at a vegetarian university with a 10 P.M. curfew. But you might not need to go to such extremes. While Granholm agrees that the excesses of college can be "a perfect example of what you shouldn't do to yourself if you are trying to learn," she doesn't recommend abstinence. "Moderation," she counsels," just like in everything else. Moderation is the key to collegiate success." ■

Reflecting on What You Have Read

1 What questions does this report answer? Does it neglect to answer any questions that you think are important? If so, what would those questions be, and why do you think they are important?

2 Some of the information in this report comes from laboratory studies of rats, but none of it comes from interviews with college students or people who work in college health centers. Would such interviews make the report seem more (or less) credible? Why or why not?

3 What is your reaction to the photographs of the students that accompany this article? How is your reaction influenced by the details included in (and excluded from) the photographs? How is your reaction influenced by the viewing angle? The colors? What reasons might *Psychology Today* have had for including these pictures?

4 Do you agree that information in this report should "make you wonder how anyone's ever managed to get an education"? Why or why not?

Thinking Ahead

The report on the effects of little sleep, fast food, and binge drinking on college learning discusses a social trend that is likely to matter to a great many readers. As you think of topics for your own report, consider reporting on such a trend. You might, for example, follow up on the topic of binge drinking. The report in Chapter 1, "Bellying Up to the Bar" (p. 6), suggests that binge drinking has been a serious problem on college campuses, although some efforts have been made to solve that problem. Have college students' drinking patterns changed since this article appeared several years ago? Have schools developed new ways of responding to this trend? Or you might consider investigating other trends—voting patterns of young people, for example, or incidents of road rage on highways in the United States—that are likely to interest a specific group of readers.

The Record Industry's Slow Fade
Brian Hiatt and Evan Serpick

Brian Hiatt and Evan Serpick, both associate editors for *Rolling Stone*, wrote the following report in June 2007 as the first of two articles on the continuing decline of the music industry. The second article featured interviews with record industry executives offering predictions on the future of the music business. The following report includes graphs, sidebars, and illustrations that offer specific data and comparisons. As you read the article, consider ways these visual elements contribute to your understanding of the topic.

The Record Industry's Slow Fade

Sales are tanking, and there's no hope in sight:
How it all went wrong

By Brian Hiatt and Evan Serpick

1 FOR THE MUSIC INDUSTRY, it was a rare bit of good news: Linkin Park's new album sold 623,000 copies in its first week this May—the strongest debut of the year. But it wasn't nearly enough. That same month, the band's record company, Warner Music Group, announced that it would lay off 400 people, and its stock price lingered at fifty-eight percent of its peak from last June.

> **"We have a business that's dying. There won't be any major labels pretty soon."**

2 Overall CD sales have plummeted sixteen percent for the year so far—and that's after seven years of near-constant erosion. In the face of widespread piracy, consumers' growing preference for low-profit-margin digital singles over albums, and other woes, the record business has plunged into a historic decline.

3 The major labels are struggling to reinvent their business models, even as some wonder whether it's too late. "The record business is over," says music attorney Peter Paterno, who represents Metallica and Dr. Dre. "The labels have wonderful assets—they just can't make any money off them." One senior music-industry source who requested anonymity went further: "Here we have a business that's dying. There won't be any major labels pretty soon."

4 In 2000, U.S. consumers bought 785.1 million albums; last year, they bought 588.2 million (a figure that includes both CDs and downloaded albums), according to Nielsen Sound-Scan. In 2000, the ten top-selling albums in the U.S. sold a combined 60 million copies; in 2006, the top ten sold just 25 million. Digital sales are growing—fans bought 582 million digital singles last year, up sixty-five percent from 2005, and purchased $600 million worth of ringtones—but the new revenue sources aren't making up for the shortfall.

5 More than 5,000 record-company employees have been laid off since 2000. The number of

major labels dropped from five to four when Sony Music Entertainment and BMG Entertainment merged in 2004—and two of the remaining companies, EMI and Warner, have flirted with their own merger for years.

About 2,700 record stores have closed across the country since 2003, according to the research group Almighty Institute of Music Retail. Last year the eighty-nine-store Tower Records chain, which represented 2.5 percent of overall retail sales, went out of business, and Musicland, which operated more than 800 stores under the Sam Goody brand, among others, filed for bankruptcy. Around sixty-five percent of all music sales now take place in big-box stores such as Wal-Mart and Best Buy, which carry fewer titles than specialty stores and put less effort behind promoting new artists.

Just a few years ago, many industry executives thought their problems could be solved by bigger hits. "There wasn't anything a good hit couldn't fix for these guys," says a source who worked closely with top executives earlier this decade. "They felt like things were bad and getting worse, but I'm not sure they had the bandwidth to figure out how to fix it. Now, very few of those people are still heads of the companies."

More record executives now seem to understand that their problems are structural: The Internet appears to be the most consequential technological shift for the business of selling music since the 1920s, when phonograph records replaced sheet music as the industry's profit center. "We have to collectively understand that times have changed," says Lyor Cohen, CEO of Warner Music Group USA. In June, Warner announced a deal with the Web site Lala.com that will allow consumers to stream much of its catalog for free, in hopes

Last year's hit *High School Musical* soundtrack sold a fraction of 2000's chart-toppers, 'NSync and Eminem.

The Story of the Decline

The record business has been shrinking since the beginning of the decade. U.S. album sales have fallen twenty-five percent since 2000, the biggest year on record – and the year Napster went mainstream. Sales of digital singles – which are up 2,930 percent since 2003 – haven't come close to making up the difference, driving revenue down sharply.

U.S. TOTAL ALBUM SALES
Year-end figures show sales erosion

Year	Sales
2006	588.2
2005	618.9
2004	666.7
2003	635.8
2002	649.5
2001	762.8
2000	785.1

0 Million | 250 Million | 500 Million | 750 Million | 1 Billion

DIGITAL-SINGLE SALES
Online tunes are hot, but not so profitable

Year	Sales
2006	581.9
2005	352.7
2004	140.9
2003	19.2

0 Million | 250 Million | 500 Million | 750 Million | 1 Billion

Global Music Revenue

The major labels are global companies – and business is bad all over. Total revenue is down fourteen percent since 2000.

▼ **2006**
31.8 BILLION

▼ **2000**
36.9 BILLION

Sales data courtesy Nielsen SoundScan. Revenue figures courtesy IFPI.

that they will then pay for downloads. It's the latest of recent major-label moves that would have been unthinkable a few years back:

■ In May, one of the four majors, EMI, began allowing the iTunes Music Store to sell its catalog without the copy protection that labels have insisted upon for years.

■ When YouTube started showing music videos without permission, all four of the labels made licensing deals instead of suing for copyright violations.

■ To the dismay of some artists and managers, labels are insisting on deals for many artists in which the companies get a portion of touring, merchandising, product sponsorships and other non-recorded-music sources of income.

So who killed the record industry as we knew it? "The record companies have created this situation themselves," says Simon Wright, CEO of Virgin Entertainment Group, which operates Virgin Megastores. While there are factors outside of the labels' control—from the rise of the Internet to the popularity of video games and DVDs—many in the industry see the last seven years as a series of botched opportunities. And among the biggest, they say, was the labels' failure to address online piracy at the beginning by making peace with the first file-sharing service, Napster. "They left billions and billions of dollars on the table by suing Napster—that was the moment that the labels killed themselves," says Jeff Kwatinetz, CEO of management company the Firm. "The record business had an unbelievable opportunity there. They were all using the same service. It was as if everybody was listening to the same radio station. Then Napster shut down, and all those 30 or 40 million people went to other [file-sharing services]."

It all could have been different: Seven years ago, the music industry's top executives gathered for secret talks with Napster CEO Hank Barry. At a July 15th, 2000, meeting, the execs—including the CEO of Universal's parent company, Edgar Bronfman Jr.; Sony Corp. head Nobuyuki Idei; and Bertelsmann chief Thomas Middelhof—sat in a hotel in Sun Valley, Idaho, with Barry and told him that they wanted to strike licensing deals with Napster. "Mr. Idei started the meeting," recalls Barry, now a director in the law firm Howard Rice. "He was talking about how Napster was something the customers wanted."

The idea was to let Napster's 38 million users keep downloading for a monthly subscription fee—roughly $10—with revenues split between the service and the labels. But ultimately, despite a public offer of $1 billion from Napster, the companies never reached a settlement. "The record companies needed to jump off a cliff, and they couldn't bring themselves to jump," says Hilary Rosen, who was then CEO of the Recording Industry Association of America. "A lot of people say, 'The labels were dinosaurs and idiots, and what was the matter with them?' But they had retailers telling them, 'You better not sell anything online cheaper than in a store,' and they had artists saying, 'Don't screw up my Wal-Mart sales.'" Adds Jim Guerinot, who manages Nine Inch Nails and Gwen Stefani, "Innovation meant cannibalizing their core business."

Even worse, the record companies waited almost two years after Napster's July 2nd, 2001, shutdown before licensing a user-friendly legal alternative to unauthorized file-sharing services: Apple's iTunes Music Store, which launched in the spring of 2003. Before that, labels started their own subscription services: PressPlay, which initially offered only Sony, Universal and EMI music and MusicNet, which had only EMI, Warner and BMG music. The services failed. They were expensive, allowed little or no CD burning and didn't work with many MP3 players then on the market.

Rosen and others see that 2001–03 period as disastrous for the business. "That's when we lost the users," Rosen says. "Peer-to-peer took hold. That's when we went from music having real value in people's minds to music having no economic value, just emotional value."

R&R

The Growth of File-Sharing
Since 2002, the average number of people sharing files has nearly doubled

▼ 2006	▼ 2002
9.4 MILLION	**4.9** MILLION

Where Record Stores Went
Around thirty-six percent of American record stores have closed since 2003

▼ 2007	▼ 2003
4,850 STORES	**7,550** STORES

TOWER RECORDS
ITS THE END OF THE WORLD AS WE KNOW IT

THANKS FOR YOUR LOYALTY

TOP TEN ALBUMS, NOW AND THEN
It's a stark comparison: The Number Ten disc of 2000 (Destiny's Child's *Writing's on the Wall*) sold more copies than last year's Number One

	2006	UNITS SOLD		2000	UNITS SOLD
1	SOUNDTRACK **High School Musical**	3,719,071	1	'NSYNC **No Strings Attached**	9,936,104
2	RASCAL FLATTS **Me and My Gang**	3,479,994	2	EMINEM **Marshall Mathers LP**	7,921,107
3	CARRIE UNDERWOOD **Some Hearts**	3,015,950	3	BRITNEY SPEARS **Oops! ... I Did It Again**	7,893,544
4	NICKELBACK **All the Right Reasons**	2,688,166	4	CREED **Human Clay**	6,587,834
5	JUSTIN TIMBERLAKE **FutureSex/LoveSounds**	2,377,127	5	SANTANA **Supernatural**	5,857,824
6	JAMES BLUNT **Back to Bedlam**	2,137,142	6	THE BEATLES **The Beatles 1**	5,068,300
7	BEYONCÉ **B'day**	2,010,311	7	NELLY **Country Grammar**	5,067,529
8	SOUNDTRACK **Hannah Montana**	1,987,681	8	BACKSTREET BOYS **Black & Blue**	4,289,865
9	DIXIE CHICKS **Taking the Long Way**	1,856,284	9	DR. DRE **Dr. Dre 2001**	3,992,311
10	HINDER **Extreme Behavior**	1,817,350	10	DESTINY'S CHILD **Writing's on the Wall**	3,802,165

Beyoncé went Top Ten in both 2000 and 2006.

File-sharing figures courtesy BigChampagne. Store figures courtesy Almighty Institute of Music Retail. Top Ten charts courtesy Nielsen SoundScan.

14 In the fall of 2003, the RIAA filed its first copyright-infringement lawsuits against file sharers. They've since sued more than 20,000 music fans. The RIAA maintains that the lawsuits are meant to spread the word that unauthorized downloading can have consequences. "It isn't being done on a punitive basis," says RIAA CEO Mitch Bainwol. But file-sharing isn't going away—there was a 4.4 percent increase in the number of peer-to-peer users in 2006, with about a billion tracks downloaded illegally per month, according to research group BigChampagne.

15 Despite the industry's woes, people are listening to at least as much music as ever. Consumers have bought more than 100 million iPods since their November 2001 introduction, and the touring business is thriving, earning a record $437 million last year. And according to research organization NPD Group, listenership to recorded music—whether from CDs, downloads, video games, satellite radio, terrestrial radio, online streams or other sources—has increased since 2002. The problem the business faces is how to turn that interest into money. "How is it that the people that make the product

of music are going bankrupt, while the use of the product is skyrocketing?" asks the Firm's Kwatinetz. "The model is wrong."

16   Kwatinetz sees other leaner kinds of companies—from management firms like his own, which now doubles as a record label, to outsiders such as Starbucks—stepping in. Paul McCartney recently abandoned his longtime relationship with EMI Records to sign with Starbucks' fledgling Hear Music. Video-game giant Electronic Arts also started a label, exploiting the promotional value of its games, and the newly revived CBS Records will sell music featured in CBS TV shows.

17   Licensing music to video games, movies, TV shows and online subscription services is becoming an increasing source of revenue. "We expect to be a brand licensing organization," says Cohen of Warner, which in May started a new division, Den of Thieves, devoted to producing TV shows and other video content from its music properties. And the record companies are looking to increase their takes in the booming music publishing business, which collects songwriting royalties from radio play and other sources. The performance-rights organization ASCAP reported a record $785 million in revenue in 2006, a five percent increase from 2005. Revenues are up "across the board," according to Martin Bandier, CEO of Sony/ATV Music Publishing, which controls the Beatles' publishing. "Music publishing will become a more important part of the business," he says. "If I worked for a record company, I'd be pulling my hair out. The recorded-music business is in total confusion, looking for a way out."

18   Nearly every corner of the record industry is feeling the pain. "A great American sector has been damaged enormously," says the RIAA's Bainwol, who blames piracy, "from songwriters to backup musicians to people who work at labels. The number of bands signed to labels has been compromised in a pretty severe fashion, roughly a third."

19   Times are hard for record-company employees. "People feel threatened," says Rosen. "Their friends are getting laid off left and right." Adam Shore, general manager of the then-Atlantic Records-affiliated Vice Records, told ROLLING STONE in January that his colleagues are having an "existential crisis." "We have great records, but we're less sure than ever that people are going to buy them," he says. "There's a sense around here of losing faith." ■

Reflecting on What You Have Read

1 The report begins with an example of a particular record company's ups and downs, followed by an overview of the problems of the music industry and a quotation from one source: "Here we have a business that's dying. There won't be any major labels pretty soon." What effect is achieved by starting the report with the example, overview, and quotation?

2 The authors of this report predict a very bleak future for the record industry. Given your experience, does this prediction seem justified?

3 This report contains a number of graphs, lists, and comparisons. What purposes might the authors have been trying to accomplish through the presentation of the information in this way? Also notice the captions that accompany the photographs and charts in this report. In what ways do the captions add to or detract from the effect of the visuals?

4 This report contains a lot of statistical information about the recording industry. But it concludes not with statistics but with comments from two people who know the industry well. What reasons do you see for concluding the report with these comments?

Thinking Ahead

One of the main reasons people write reports is to make readers aware of a problem, especially one that readers assume pertains only to other people. Consider areas of your life (health, sports, social organizations, jobs) in which you are encountering problems that may affect other people too, even if they do not fully appreciate that this is true. Consider writing a report that will make readers realize what the problems are and why they are significant.

Steve Casimiro, a photographer and journalist living in southern California, writes frequently about skiing, mountain biking, and other outdoor sports. He fell in love with photography at age thirteen when he received his first 35 mm camera; he began his career as a newspaper reporter and then as an editor at *Powder* magazine. His work has appeared in such magazines as *Adventure, Men's Journal, National Geographic,* and *Outside.* As contributing editor to *Popular Science*, Casimiro wrote the following article about the challenges facing photo-verification experts in the digital age. "Who hasn't removed red-eye from family pictures?" he asks. Telling "real" photos from fake ones in the age of inexpensive photo-editing software is difficult, even for the experts. As you read, notice both the challenges Casimiro describes and the ways people are trying to respond to those challenges.

Seeing Is Not Believing

Can you tell which of these photos are real?*
The Web is crawling with jokes, hoaxes and
more-insidious fakes. Experts are racing to develop
detection tools, but for now, seeing is not believing.

By Steve Casimiro

Lance Corporal Ted "Joey" Boudreaux Jr. 1 was bored. It was the summer of 2003 in Iraq, the pause between the heavy lifting of the U.S. invasion and the turmoil of the insurgency, and you can joyride around the desert in a dusty Humvee only so often. Loitering at the back gate of his base, mingling with locals, Boudreaux says he scribbled "Welcome Marines" on a piece of cardboard and gave it to some kids, who then posed with him, smiling, for a snapshot. He e-mailed the picture to his mom, a cousin and a few friends, and he didn't think about it again. Boredom moved on. That wasn't the last of the photo, though. The image

made its way to the Internet and fell into the hands of bloggers—Boudreaux says he doesn't know how—except that the sign had been altered to say, "Lcpl. Boudreaux killed my dad, then he knocked up my sister." Online commentators assumed Boudreaux was playing a nasty trick on kids who couldn't read English, and the Marine was flamed as insensitive, ignorant or just plain stupid. The Council on American-Islamic Relations stumbled across the image and demanded an inquiry.

Around the same time, another image 2 popped up on the forums of the conservative Web site *freerepublic.com.* Now the sign read

*Answer key on page 184.

HOW WELL DID YOU SPOT THE PHONIES?

[1] FAKE From *worth 1000.com*, which hosts Photoshop contests **[2] REAL** Plane landing at the St. Maarten airport, located about 40 feet from the beach **[3] FAKE** *worth 1000.com* **[4] FAKE** A skyscraper—Jenga game merger, from *worth 1000.com* **[5] FAKE** A composite that hit the Internet as a purported *National Geographic* photo **[6] REAL** Nine-foot, 646-pound catfish recently caught in Thailand **[7] REAL** An F/A-18's sonic boom. Experts are unsure what creates the cloud; it may be caused by water-droplet condensation **[8] FAKE** *worth 1000.com* **[9] FAKE**

"Lcpl. Boudreaux saved my dad, then he rescued my sister," and a debate raged. Other versions of the sign appeared—one was completely blank, apparently to show how easily a photo can be doctored, and another said "My dad blew himself up on a suicide bombing and all I got was this lousy sign." By this point, Boudreaux, 25, was back in his hometown of Houma, Louisiana, after his Iraq tour, and he found out about the tempest only when a fledgling Marine brought a printout of the "killed my dad" picture to the local recruiters' office where Boudreaux was serving. Soon after, he learned he was being investigated by the Pentagon. He feared court-martial. It would be months before he would learn his fate.

Falling victim to a digital prank and having it 3 propagate over the Internet may seem about as likely as getting struck by lightning, but in the digital age, anyone can use inexpensive software to touch up photos, and their handiwork is becoming increasingly difficult to detect. Most of these fakes tend to be harmless—90-pound housecats, sharks attacking helicopters, that sort of thing. But hoaxes, when convincing, can do harm. During the 2004 presidential election campaign, a potentially damning image proliferated on the Internet of a young John Kerry sharing a speaker's platform with Jane Fonda during her "Hanoi Jane" period. The photo was eventually revealed to be a deft composite of two images, but who knows how many minds had turned against Kerry by then. Meanwhile, politicians have begun to engage in photo tampering for their own ends: This July it emerged that a New York City mayoral candidate, C. Virginia Fields, had added two Asian faces to a promotional photograph to make a group of her supporters seem more diverse.

As fakes proliferate, real evidence, such as the photos of abuse at Abu Ghraib prison, could be discounted as unreliable.

"Everyone is buying low-cost, high-quality 4 digital cameras, everyone has a Web site, everyone has e-mail, Photoshop is easier to use; 2004 was the first year sales of digital cameras outpaced traditional film cameras," says Hany Farid, a Dartmouth College computer scientist and a leading researcher in the nascent realm of digital forensics. "Consequently, there are more and more cases of high-profile digital tampering. Seeing is no longer believing. Actually, what you see is largely irrelevant."

That's a problem when you consider that 5 driver's licenses, security cameras, employee

IDs, and other digital images are a linchpin of communication and a foundation of proof. The fact that they can be easily altered is a big deal—but even more troubling, perhaps, is the fact that few people are aware of the problem and fewer still are addressing it.

It won't be long—if it hasn't happened 6 already—before every image becomes potentially suspect. False images have the potential to linger in the public's consciousness, even if they are ultimately discredited. And just as disturbingly, as fakes proliferate, real evidence, such as the photos of abuse at Abu Ghraib prison in Iraq, could be discounted as unreliable.

And then there's the judicial system, in which 7 altered photos could harm the innocent, free the guilty, or simply cause havoc. People arrested for possession of child pornography now sometimes claim that the images are not of real children but of computer-generated ones—and thus that no kids were harmed in the making of the pornography (reality check: authorities say CG child porn does not exist). In a recent civil case in Pennsylvania, plaintiff Mike Soncini tussled with his insurance company over a wrecked vehicle, claiming that the company had altered digital photos to imply that the car was damaged before the accident so as to avoid paying the full amount due. In Connecticut, a convicted murderer appealed to the state supreme court that computer-enhanced images of bite marks on the victim that were used to match his teeth were inadmissible (his appeal was rejected). And in a Massachusetts case, a police officer has been accused of stealing drugs and money from his department's evidence room and stashing them at home. His wife, who has accused him of spousal abuse, photographed the evidence and then confronted the cop, who allegedly destroyed the stolen goods. Now the only evidence that exists are digital pictures shot by someone

Signs of Trouble Both these photos of a U.S. soldier with an Iraqi boy circulated on the Internet. The Marine, Ted Boudreaux Jr., says both are fake and that the original sign was a bland "Welcome Marines." A military investigation was inconclusive.

who might have a motive for revenge. "This is an issue that's waiting to explode," says Richard Sherwin, a professor at New York Law School, "and it hasn't gotten the visibility in the legal community that it deserves."

So far, only a handful of researchers have 8 devoted themselves to the science of digital forensics. Nevertheless, effective, if not foolproof, techniques to spot hoaxes are emerging—and advances are on the horizon. Scientists are developing software, secure cameras and embedded watermarks to thwart image manipulation and sniff out tampering. Adobe and Microsoft are among the private funders, but much of the work is seeded by law-enforcement agencies and the military, which face situations in which more than just reputations are at risk. (Maintaining the integrity of the chain of evidence is of utmost importance to law enforcement, and the military is concerned about the veracity of images arriving from, say, Iraq or Afghanistan. Does that picture really portray Osama bin Laden? Are those hostages in the grainy video really American solders?)

But Farid and other experts are concerned 9 that they'll never win. The technologies that enable photo manipulation will grow as fast as the attempts to foil them—as will forgers' skills. The only realistic goal, Farid believes, is to keep prevention and detection techniques sophisticated enough to stop all but the most determined and skillful. "We're going to make it so the average schmo can't do it," he says.

Faked photography has a long and inglorious 10 history. In the 1870s, "spirit photographs" were the rage—images of dead loved ones were combined with shots of living kin taken during séances and passed off by charlatans as proof of the spirit world. During the Cold War, the Russian and Chinese governments were notorious for their propaganda fakes; discredited officials were routinely removed from state photographs. But the human eye isn't easily fooled: Hardwired for pattern recognition, people can readily spot subtle inconsistencies.

Verification experts look for these anomalies— differences in light, shadow and shading; perspective that's out of whack; and incorrect proportions, such as one person's head being unnaturally larger than another's. Thanks to the digital nature of today's photos, though, never has it been so easy to fool the eye with high-quality forgeries, reshaping reality with a few clicks of a mouse. A digital camera contains a light-sensitive plate covered with tiny sensors called cells, which receive photons of light when the shutter opens. The cells collect photons like raindrops in buckets, then convert them into electrical charges, which are amplified and themselves converted from analog to digital form. In every digital image format—JPEG, TIFF, RAW—a photograph is really just a data file consisting of strings of zeros and ones. A program is required to translate that binary code into pictures, much the way your TV converts digital cable or satellite signals into moving images.

CHINA LANDS ON MOON!
NOT REALLY. BUT MAKING IT LOOK AUTHENTIC IS EASY, FOR A FORGER

We asked Hany Farid, a Dartmouth digital-forensics expert, to make a fake image of a Chinese lunar landing. Whereas forgery detection is a mathematical process, creating a forgery is a more artistic one. Farid imported three images into Photoshop: a generic Chinese flag [1]; Chinese astronaut Yang Liwei waving outside his *Shenzhou 5* spacecraft after orbiting the Earth in 2003 [2]; and a Shenzhou recovery photo [3]. Farid began with a classic image of *Apollo 17* commander Eugene Cernan from 1972 [A]. Using a Photoshop tool that isolates similarly

Such programs abound. Five million copies of Adobe Photoshop have been licensed, iPhoto is bundled with all new Apple computers, and Picasa 2 is available free from Google. This software not only interprets the original data; it's capable of altering it—to remove unwanted background elements, zoom in on the desired part of an image, adjust color, and more. And the capabilities are increasing. The latest version of Photoshop, CS2, includes a "vanishing point" tool, for example, that drastically simplifies the specialized art of correcting perspective when combining images, to make composites look more realistic. Nor are these programs difficult to master. Just as word-processing programs like Microsoft Word have made the production of professional-looking documents a cakewalk, photo-editing tools make us all accomplished photo manipulators fairly quickly. Who hasn't removed red-eye from family pictures?

Before the digital age, photo-verification experts sought to examine the negative—the single source of all existing prints. Today's equivalent of a negative is the RAW file. RAWs are output from a camera before any automatic adjustments have corrected hue and tone. They fix the image in its purest, unaltered state. But RAW files are unwieldy—they don't look very good and are memory hogs—hence only professional photographers tend to use them. Nor are they utterly trustworthy: Hackers have shown themselves capable of making a fake RAW file based on an existing photo, creating an apparent original.

But digital technology does provide clues that experts can exploit to identify the fakery. In most cameras, each cell registers just one color—red, green or blue—so the camera's microprocessor has to estimate the proper color based on the colors of neighboring cells, filling in the blanks through a process called interpolation. Interpolation creates a predictable pattern, a correlation among data points that is potentially recognizable, not by the naked eye but by pattern-recognition software programs.

colored pixels, he removed the Chinese flag from its background, flipped it, and swapped it in [B]. Isolating Yang from his background to place him over Cernan was dicier—he magnified the image by 400 percent and pared away with a digital "eraser" [C]. Next he turned the suit's stripes red, added Chinese characters [see photo 3], applied a lighting gradient to put Yang's right side in shadow, and added dirt under Yang's right foot. Then he removed all traces of Cernan (except his backpack, which holds the breathing apparatus essential for a moonwalk) with a "cloning" tool that copies parts of background—sky, lunar surface, shadow [D]. The finishing touch: a helmet taken from another Apollo photo [not shown]. Grafted onto it is Cernan's visor with its realistic reflection, which was resized to fit [E].

Farid has developed algorithms that are remarkably adept at recognizing the telltale signs of forgeries. His software scans patterns in a data file's binary code, looking for the disruptions that indicate that an image has been altered. Farid, who has become the go-to guy in digital forensics, spends a great deal of time using Photoshop to create forgeries and composites and then studying their underlying data. What he's found is that most manipulations leave a statistical trial. 14

Consider what happens when you double the size of an image in Photoshop. You start with a 100-by-100-pixel image and enlarge it to 200 by 200. Photoshop must create new pixels to make the image bigger; it does this through interpolation (this is the second interpolation, after the one done by the camera's processor when the photo was originally shot). Photoshop will "look" at a white pixel and an adjoining black pixel and decide that the best option for the new pixel that's being inserted between them is gray. 15

Digital watermarks are the modern equivalent of dripping sealing wax on a letter.

Each type of alteration done in Photoshop or iPhoto creates a specific statistical relic in the file that will show up again and again. Resizing an image, as described above, creates one kind of data pattern. Cutting parts of one picture and placing them into another picture creates another. Rotating a photo leaves a unique footprint, as does "cloning" one part of a picture and reproducing it elsewhere in the image. And computer-generated images, which can look strikingly realistic, have their own statistical patterns that are entirely different from those of images created by a camera. 16

None of these patterns is visible to the naked eye or even easily described, but after studying thousands of manipulated images, Farid and his students have made a Rosetta stone for their recognition, a single software package consisting of algorithms that search for seven types of photo alteration, each with its own data pattern.

If you employed just one of these algorithms, a fake would be relatively easy to miss, says digital-forensic scientist Jessica Fridrich of the State University of New York at Binghamton. But the combination is powerful. "It would be very difficult to have a forgery that gets through all those tests," she says. 17

The weakness of Farid's software, through— and it's a big one—is that it works best with high-quality, uncompressed images. Most nonprofessional cameras output data files known as JPEGs. JPEGs are digitally compressed so that they will be easy to e-mail and won't take up too much space on people's hard drives. But compression, which throws away less-important image data to reduce size at the expense of visual quality, removes or damages the statistical patterns that Farid's algorithms seek. So at least for now, until Farid's next-generation software is finished, his tool is relatively powerless to provide information about the compressed and lower-quality photos typically found on the Internet. 18

Given those rather large blind spots, some scientists are taking a completely different tack. Rather than try to discern after the fact whether a picture has been altered, they want to invisibly mark photos in the moment of their creation so that any subsequent tampering will be obvious. 19

Jessica Fridrich of SUNY Binghamton works on making digital watermarks. Watermarked data are patterns of zeros and ones that are 20 created when an image is shot and embedded in its pixels, invisible unless you look for them with special software. Watermarks are the modern equivalent of dripping sealing wax on a letter—if an image is altered, the watermark will be "broken" digitally, and your software will tell you.

Watermarking is currently available in one consumer product, Canon's DVK-E2 data-verification kit. This $700 system uses proprietary software and a small USB plug-in application to authenticate images shot with Canon's pro-level cameras. It would seem ideal for news organizations: Photo editors (or anyone needing to authenticate) plug in the device, click on an image, and the software alerts them when a photo has been altered. Most digital news photos will be tweaked, of course, to adjust hue, saturation, contrast and brightness—editing procedures that were traditionally conducted in the darkroom—and then saved as a new file, but if the editor suspects funny business, he can compare the unaltered original with the altered copy and find out exactly how much it deviates.

The Canon kit won't prevent self-made controversies, such as *National Geographic*'s digitally relocating an Egyptian pyramid to fit better on its February 1982 cover, or *Newsweek*'s grafting Martha Stewart's head onto a model's body on its March 7, 2005, cover, but it would have caught, and thus averted, another journalism scandal: In 2003 photographer Brian Walski was fired from the *Los Angeles Times* for melding two photographs to create what he felt was a more powerful composition of a British soldier directing Iraqis to take cover. Still, many media outlets remain dismissive of verification technology, putting their faith in the integrity of trusted contributors and their own ability to sniff out fraud. "If we tried to verify every picture, we'd never get anything done," says Stokes Young, managing editor at Corbis, which licenses stock photos. As damaging mistakes pile up, though, wire services and newspapers may change their attitude.

Meanwhile, work is progressing at Fridrich's lab to endow photos with an additional level of security. Fridrich, whose accomplishments include winning the 1982 Czechoslovakian Rubik's Cube speed-solving championship, is developing a camera that not only watermarks a photograph but adds key identifying information about the photographer as well. Her team has modified a commercially available Canon camera, converting the infrared focusing sensor built into its viewfinder to a biometric sensor that captures an image of the photographer's iris at the instant a photo is shot. This image is converted to digital data that is stored invisibly in the image file, along with the time and date and other watermark data.

Just as bullets are traced to a specific gun, photos might reveal the camera that made them.

The application for a police photographer is obvious: If challenged in court, the image, camera and shoot are verifiable, the entire system secure. Unfortunately, the world of justice is the Dark Ages to academia's Renaisssance. The FBI has a special Digital Evidence Section and is funding authentication research, but federal rules of evidence don't require verification of digital images other than by the photographer or someone else at the scene, let alone a secure photography system, and there's been little effort to change them. "Most criminal courts are technically illiterate," says Grant Fredericks, a forensic-video analyst with forensic-systems maker Avid Technology. "They don't have the tools and experience to deal with advanced technology."

Lawyers are just beginning to grasp the technology and its ramifications, but the bench is especially ignorant. "Trial judges have not been adequately apprised of the risks and technology," says New York Law School's Sherwin. "I can recount one example where in order to test an animation that was being offered in evidence, the judge asked the attorney to print it out. What we really have is a generation gap in the knowledge base. Courts are going to have to learn about these risks themselves and find ways to address them." 25

One bright spot is that for now, at least, we only have to worry about still images. Fredericks says that to modify video convincingly remains an incredibly painstaking business. "When you're dealing with videotape, you're dealing with 30 frames per second, and a frame is two individual pictures. The forger would have to make 60 image corrections for each second. It's an almost impossible task." There's no Photoshop for movies, and even video altered with high-end equipment, such as commercials employing reanimated dead actors, isn't especially believable. 26

Digital-forensics experts say they're in an evolutionary race not unlike the battle between spammers and anti-spammers—you can create all the filters you want, but determined spammers will figure out how to get through. Then it's time to create new filters. Farid expects the same of forgers. With enough resources and determination, a forger will break a watermark, reverse-engineer a RAW file, and create a seamless fake that eludes the software. The trick, Farid says, is continuing to raise the bar high enough that most forgers are daunted. 27

WORLD EVENTS GET BLURRY

IF YOU FELL FOR ANY OF THESE, YOU WEREN'T ALONE. REALITY IS INCREASINGLY UP FOR GRABS.

There have always been people who question historical fact—like the fringe types who insist that U.S. astronauts never reached the moon. But now that anyone can whip up a falsified photo, documentary truth is becoming a mushy notion. Fake photos—like a composite showing a British soldier addressing civilians in Iraq that ran on the front page of the *L.A. Times*—have appeared in major news sources, only to be withdrawn amid embarrassment. So when word goes out on the Internet that, say, the Pentagon was never attacked on September 11, 2001, reasonable people increasingly have cause to doubt. The images below circulated widely, further eroding the public's ability to judge with confidence what in world events is really real. —SPENCER ROBINS

GOTCHA Doctored photos that made the Internet rounds, clockwise from top left: A modified satellite photo purporting to show the August 2003 blackout; after the December 2004 tsunami, a Chilean coastal city with a fake wave added; a so-called "last photo" of a tourist atop the World Trade Center, with plane added.

CUT AND PASTE One photo shows John Kerry at a peace rally in Mineola, N.Y. in 1971. The other shows Jane Fonda at a Miami Beach peace rally in 1972. Their melding in 2004 created a damaging political association between a presidential candidate and a celebrity known for her divisive stance on Vietnam.

The near future of detection technology is more of the same, only (knock wood) better: more-secure photographer-verification systems, more tightly calibrated algorithms, more-robust watermarks. The future, though, promises something more innovative: digital ballistics. Just as bullets can be traced to the gun that fired them, digital photos might reveal the camera that made them. No light sensor is flawless; all have tiny imperfections that can be read in the image data. Study those glitches enough, and you recognize patterns—patterns that can be detected with software. 28

Still, no matter what technologies are in place, it's likely that top-quality fakes will always elude the system. Poor-quality ones, too. The big fish learn how to avoid the net; the smallest ones slip through it. Low-resolution fakes are more detectable by Farid's latest algorithm, which analyzes the direction of light falling on the scene, but if a photo is compressed enough, forget about it. It becomes a mighty small fish. 29

Which brings us back to Joey Boudreaux, the Marine who found himself denounced by his local paper, the New Orleans *Times-Picayune*, as having embarrassed "himself, the Marine Corps and, unfortunately, his home 30

state." The Marines conducted two investigations last year, both of which were inconclusive. Even experts with the Naval Criminal Investigative Services couldn't find evidence to support or refute claims of manipulation.

Boudreaux has taken the incident in stride. "My first reaction, I thought it was funny," he said in a telephone interview. "I didn't have a second reaction until they called and said, 'You're getting investigated.'" He insists that he never gave the Iraqi boy a sign with any words but "Welcome Marines," but he has no way to prove it. Neither he nor anyone he knows still possesses a version of the image the way he says he created it, and no amount of Internet searching has turned it up. All that exists are the low-quality clones on the Web. Farid's software can't assess Boudreaux's claim because the existing images are too compressed for his algorithms. And even Farid's trained eye can't tell if either of the two existing images—the "good" sign or the "bad" one—are real or if, as Boudreaux claims, both are fakes. 31

An unsatisfactory conclusion, but a fitting one. Today's authentication technology is such that even after scrutiny by software and expert eyes, all you may have on your side is your word. You'd better hope it's good enough. ■ 32

Reflecting on What You Have Read

1 This report begins with a very dramatic collection of images that asks readers to determine which are real and which are hoaxes. (The answers appear in the box "How Well Did You Spot the Phonies?") Checking your responses against the answers on page 184, how many images did you identify correctly? What is accomplished by asking readers to participate in the subject of the report in this way?

2 Look carefully at the images on page 190 under the heading "World Events Get Blurry." What do you notice about the doctored photos that "made the Internet rounds" as Casimiro describes? What purpose do you think the authors of these doctored photos had in mind when creating them?

3 Casimiro relies on sources that include both researchers into digital forensics and one person, Joey Boudreaux, who is directly affected by a digital photography hoax. How does each of these kinds of sources add credibility to the report?

4 Casimiro mentions that some experts on photo manipulation are very pessimistic about the prospects of detecting all digital hoaxes. Given your experience, does this pessimism seem justified? Casimiro also cites one expert who hopes that it will be possible to become "sophisticated enough to stop all but the most determined and skillful." Again, given your experience, does this seem like a realistic hope?

Thinking Ahead

The author of this report draws on interviews with experts and on close analysis of specific examples of digital photography fraud to give insight into a problem that faces many readers of images today. You might review recent issues of popular science magazines (*Scientific American, Wired,* or *Popular Science*, for example) to identify topics that relate to other challenges technology presents our culture.

Whose Life Would You Save?

Carl Zimmer

Carl Zimmer is an award-winning science writer and the author of many articles and books about evolution and biology. His books include *Evolution: The Triumph of an Idea* (2001), and *Soul Made Flesh* (2004), a history of the brain. He writes frequently for the *New York Times* and such magazines as *National Geographic* and *Scientific American*. In his blog, *The Loom*, he writes about thought-provoking research into life and evolution. He is also a frequent radio guest and lecturer. As a contributing editor to *Discover*, he wrote the following essay about the biology and evolutionary history behind our ability to make moral judgments. As you read, consider ways you would respond to some of the moral dilemmas he describes.

Whose Life Would You Save?

Scientists say morality may be hardwired
into our brains by evolution.

By Carl Zimmer, Illustrations by Jeff West

Dinner with a philosopher is never just 1 dinner, even when it's at an obscure Indian restaurant on a quiet side street in Princeton with a 30-year-old postdoctoral researcher. Joshua Greene is a man who spends his days thinking about right and wrong and how we separate the two. He has a particular fondness for moral paradoxes, which he collects the way some people collect snow globes.

"Let's say you're walking by a pond and 2 there's a drowning baby," Greene says, over chicken tikka masala. "If you said, 'I've just paid $200 for these shoes and the water would ruin them, so I won't save the baby,' you'd be an awful, horrible person. But there are millions of children around the world in the same situation, where just a little money for medicine or food could save their lives. And yet we don't consider ourselves monsters for having this dinner rather than giving the money to Oxfam. Why is that?"

Philosophers pose this sort of puzzle over 3 dinner every day. What's unusual here is what Greene does next to sort out the conundrum. He leaves the restaurant, walks down Nassau Street to the building that houses Princeton University's psychology department, and says hello to graduate student volunteer Nishant Patel. (Greene's volunteers take part in his study anonymously; Patel is not his real name.) They walk downstairs to the basement, where Patel dumps his keys and wallet and shoes in a basket. Greene waves an airport metal-detector paddle up and down Patel's legs, then guides him into an adjoining room dominated by a magnetic resonance imaging scanner. The student lies down on a slab, and Greene closes a cagelike device over his head. Pressing a button, Greene maneuvers Patel's head into a massive doughnut-shaped magnet.

How Moral Are You?

You are checking in for a flight when the person at the counter accidentally gives you a boarding pass for a first-class seat. Your ticket is for coach.

Do you point out the mistake?

Greene goes back to the control room to cali- 4 brate the MRI, then begins to send Patel messages. They are beamed into the scanner by a video projector and bounce off a mirror just above Patel's nose. Among the messages that Greene sends is the following dilemma, cribbed from the final episode of the TV series *M*A*S*H*: A group of villagers is hiding in a basement while enemy soldiers search the rooms above. Suddenly, a baby among them starts to cry. The villagers know that if the soldiers hear it they will come in and kill everyone. "Is it appropriate," the message reads, "for you to smother your child in order to save yourself and the other villagers?"

As Patel ponders this question—and oth- 5 ers like it—the MRI scans his brain, revealing crackling clusters of neurons. Over the past four years, Greene has scanned dozens of people making these kinds of moral judgments. What he

has found can be unsettling. Most of us would like to believe that when we say something is right or wrong, we are using our powers of reason alone. But Greene argues that our emotions also play a powerful role in our moral judgments, triggering instinctive responses that are the product of millions of years of evolution. "A lot of our deeply felt moral convictions may be quirks of our evolutionary history," he says.

Greene's research has put him at the leading 6 edge of a field so young it still lacks an official name. Moral neuroscience? Neuroethics? Whatever you call it, the promise is profound. "Some people in these experiments think we're putting their soul under the microscope," Greene says, "and in a sense, that is what we're doing."

The puzzle of moral judgments grabbed 7 Greene's attention when he was a philosophy major at Harvard University. Most modern theories of moral reasoning, he learned, were powerfully shaped by one of two great philosophers: Immanuel Kant and John Stuart Mill. Kant believed that pure reason alone could lead us to moral truths. Based on his own pure reasoning, for instance, he declared that it was wrong to use someone for your own ends and that it was right to act only according to principles that everyone could follow.

John Stuart Mill, by contrast, argued that the 8 rules of right and wrong should above all else achieve the greatest good for the greatest number of people, even though particular individuals might be worse off as a result. (This approach became known as utilitarianism, based on the "utility" of a moral rule.) "Kant puts what's right before what's good," says Greene. "Mill puts what's good before what's right."

By the time Greene came to Princeton for gradu- 9 ate school in 1997, however, he had become dissatisfied with utilitarians and Kantians alike.

You are running down a crowded corridor in the airport, trying to catch a flight that's about to leave. Suddenly, an old woman in front of you slips and falls hard.

Do you stop to help, knowing that you'll miss your plane?

None of them could explain how moral judgments work in the real world. Consider, for example, this thought experiment concocted by the philosophers Judith Jarvis Thompson and Philippa Foot: Imagine you're at the wheel of a trolley and the brakes have failed. You're approaching a fork in the track at top speed. On the left side, five rail workers are fixing the track. On the right side, there is a single worker. If you do nothing, the trolley will bear left and kill the five workers. The only way to save five lives is to take the responsibility for changing the trolley's path by hitting a switch. Then you will kill one worker. What would you do?

Now imagine that you are watching the runaway trolley from a footbridge. This time there is no fork in the track. Instead, five workers are on it, facing certain death. But you happen to be standing next to a big man. If you sneak up on him and push him off the footbridge, he will fall to his death. Because he is so big, he will stop the trolley. Do you willfully kill one man, or do you allow five people to die?

Logically, the questions have similar answers. Yet if you poll your friends, you'll probably find that many more are willing to throw a switch than push someone off a bridge. It is hard to explain why what seems right in one case can seem wrong in another. Sometimes we act more like Kant and sometimes more like Mill. "The trolley problem seemed to boil that conflict down to its essence," Greene says. "If I could figure out how to make sense of that particular problem, I could make sense of the whole Kant-versus-Mill problem in ethics."

The crux of the matter, Greene decided, lay not in the logic of moral judgments but in the role our emotions play in forming them. He began to explore the psychological studies of the 18th-century Scottish philosopher David Hume. Hume argued that people call an act good not because they rationally determine it to be so but because it makes them feel good. They call an act bad because it fills them with disgust. Moral knowledge, Hume wrote, comes partly from an "immediate feeling and finer internal sense."

Moral instincts have deep roots, primatologists have found. Last September, for instance, Sarah Brosnan and Frans de Waal of Emory University reported that monkeys have a sense of fairness. Brosnan and De Waal trained capuchin monkeys to take a pebble from them; if the monkeys gave the pebble back, they got a cucumber. Then they ran the same experiment with two monkeys sitting in adjacent cages so that each could see the other. One monkey still got a cucumber, but the other one got a grape—a tastier reward. More than half the monkeys who got cucumbers balked at the exchange. Sometimes they threw the cucumber at the researchers; sometimes they refused to give the pebble back. Apparently, De Waal says, they realized that they weren't being treated fairly.

In an earlier study, De Waal observed a 14 colony of chimpanzees that got fed by their zookeeper only after they had all gathered in an enclosure. One day, a few young chimps dallied outside for hours, leaving the rest to go hungry. The next day, the other chimps attacked the stragglers, apparently to punish them for their selfishness. The primates seemed capable of moral judgment without benefit of human reasoning. "Chimps may be smart," Greene says. "But they don't read Kant."

The evolutionary origins of morality are easy 15 to imagine in a social species. A sense of fairness would have helped early primates cooperate. A sense of disgust and anger at cheaters would have helped them avoid falling into squabbling. As our ancestors became more self-aware and acquired language, they would transform those feelings into moral codes that they then taught their children.

This idea made a lot of sense to Greene. For 16 one thing, it showed how moral judgments can feel so real. "We make moral judgments so automatically that we don't really understand how they're formed," he says. It also offered a potential solution to the trolley problem: Although the two scenarios have similar outcomes, they trigger different circuits in the brain. Killing someone with your bare hands would most likely have been recognized as immoral millions of years ago. It summons ancient and overwhelm-

ingly negative emotions—despite any good that may come of the killing. It simply *feels* wrong.

Throwing a switch for a trolley, on the other 17 hand, is not the sort of thing our ancestors confronted. Cause and effect, in this case, are separated by a chain of machines and electrons, so they do not trigger a snap moral judgment. Instead, we rely more on abstract reasoning—weighing costs and benefits, for example—to choose between right and wrong. Or so Greene hypothesized. When he arrived at Princeton, he had no way to look inside people's brains. Then in 1999, Greene learned that the university was building a brain-imaging center.

The heart of the Center for the Study of Brain, 18 Mind, and Behavior is an MRI scanner in the basement of Green Hall. The scanner creates images of the brain by generating an intense magnetic field. Some of the molecules in the brain line up with the field, and the scanner wiggles the field back and forth a few degrees.

Your plane has been taken over by a terrorist. He has taken a passenger's baby hostage and is holding a knife to his throat.

Do you rush the terrorist to subdue him, knowing that the baby will die before you get there?

As the molecules wiggle, they release radio waves. By detecting the waves, the scanner can reconstruct the brain as well as detect where neurons are consuming oxygen—a sign of mental activity. In two seconds, the center's scanner can pinpoint such activity down to a cubic millimeter—about the size of a peppercorn.

When neuroscientists first started scanning 19 brains in the early 1990s, they studied the basic building blocks of thought, such as language, vision, and attention. But in recent years, they've also tried to understand how the brain works when people interact. Humans turn out to have special neural networks that give them what many cognitive neuroscientists call social intelligence. Some regions can respond to smiles, frowns, and other expressions in a tenth of a second. Others help us get inside a person's head and figure out intentions. When neuroscientist Jonathan Cohen came to Princeton to head the center, he hoped he could dedicate some time with the scanner to study the interaction between cognition and emotion. Greene's morality study was a perfect fit.

Working with Cohen and other scientists at 20 the center, Greene decided to compare how the brain responds to different questions. He took the trolley problem as his starting point, then invented questions designed to place volunteers on a spectrum of moral judgment. Some questions involved personal moral choices; some were impersonal but no less moral. Others were utterly innocuous, such as deciding whether to take a train or a bus to work. Greene would then peel away the brain's general decision-making circuits and focus in on the neural patterns that differentiate personal from impersonal thought.

Some scenarios were awful, but Greene sus- 21 pected people would make quick decisions about them. Should you kill a friend's sick father so he can collect on the insurance policy? Of course not. But other questions—like the one about the smothered baby—were as agonizing as they were gruesome. Greene calls these doozies. "If they weren't creepy, we wouldn't be doing our job," he says.

As Greene's subjects mulled over his ques- 22 tions, the scanner measured the activity in their brains. When all the questions had flashed before the volunteers, Greene was left with gigabytes of data, which then had to be mapped onto a picture of the brain. "It's not hard, like philosophy hard, but there are so many details to keep track of," he says. When he was done, he experienced a "pitter-patter heartbeat moment." Just as he had predicted, personal moral decisions tended to stimulate certain parts of the brain more than impersonal moral decisions.

The more people Greene scanned, the 23 clearer the pattern became: Impersonal moral decisions (like whether to throw a switch on a trolley) triggered many of the same parts of the brain as nonmoral questions do (such as whether you should take the train or the bus to work). Among the regions that became active was a patch on the surface of the brain near the temples. This region, known as the dorsolateral prefrontal cortex, is vital for logical thinking. Neuroscientists believe it helps keep track of several pieces of information at once so that they can be compared. "We're using our brains to make decisions about things that evolution hasn't wired us up for," Greene says.

Personal moral questions lit up other areas. 24 One, located in the cleft of the brain behind the center of the forehead, plays a crucial role in understanding what other people are thinking or feeling. A second, known as the superior temporal sulcus, is located just above the ear; it gathers information about people from the way they move their lips, eyes, and hands. A third, made up of parts of two adjacent regions known as the posterior cingulate and the precuneus, become active when people feel strong emotions.

Greene suspects these regions are part of a neural network that produces the emotional instincts behind many of our moral judgments. The superior temporal sulcus may help make us aware of others who would be harmed. Mind reading lets us appreciate their suffering. The precuneus may help trigger a negative feeling—an inarticulate sense, for example, that killing someone is plain wrong. 25

When Greene and his coworkers first began their study, not a single scan of the brain's moral decision-making process had been published. Now a number of other scientists are investigating the neural basis of morality, and their results are converging on some of the same ideas. "The neuroanatomy seems to be coming together," Greene says. 26

Another team of neuroscientists at Princeton, for instance, has pinpointed neural circuits that govern the sense of fairness. Economists have known for a long time that humans, like capuchin monkeys, get annoyed to an irrational degree when they feel they're getting short-changed. A classic example of this phenomenon crops up during the "ultimatum game," in which two players are given a chance to split some money. One player proposes the split, and the other can accept or reject it—but if he rejects it, neither player gets anything. 27

If both players act in a purely rational way, as most economists assume people act, the game should have a predictable result. The first player will offer the second the worst possible split, and the second will be obliged to accept it. A little money, after all, is better than none. But in experiment after experiment, players tend to offer something close to a 50-50 split. Even more remarkably, when they offer significantly less than half, they're often rejected. 28

The Princeton team (led by Alan Sanfey, now at the University of Arizona) sought to explain that rejection by having people play the ultimatum game while in the MRI scanner. Their subjects always played the part of the responder. In some cases the proposer was another person; in others it was a computer. Sanfey found that unfair offers from human players—more than those from the computer—triggered pronounced reactions in a strip of the brain called the anterior insula. Previous studies had shown that this area produces feelings of anger and disgust. The stronger the response, Sanfey and his colleagues found, the more likely the subject would reject the offer. 29

Another way to study moral intuition is to look at brains that lack it. James Blair at the National Institute of Mental Health has spent years performing psychological tests on criminal psychopaths. He has found that they have some puzzling gaps in perception. They can put themselves inside the heads of other people, for example, acknowledging that others feel fear or sadness. But they have a hard time *recognizing* fear or sadness, either on people's faces or in their voices. 30

Blair says that the roots of criminal psychopathy can first be seen in childhood. An abnormal level of neurotransmitters might make children less empathetic. When most children see others get sad or angry, it disturbs them and makes them want to avoid acting in ways that provoke such reactions. But budding psychopaths don't perceive other people's pain, so they don't learn to rein in their violent outbreaks. 31

As Greene's database grows, he can see more clearly how the brain's intuitive and reasoning networks are activated. In most cases, one dominates the other. Sometimes, though, they produce opposite responses of equal 32

Your plane has made an emergency landing on the ocean. All but one lifeboat has been destroyed, and it's so full it's beginning to sink.

Should you throw people overboard, beginning with the elderly who are too weak to resist, to save yourself and the others?

strength, and the brain has difficulty choosing between them. Part of the evidence for this lies in the time it takes for Greene's volunteers to answer his questions. Impersonal moral ones and nonmoral ones tend to take about the same time to answer. But when people decide that personally hurting or killing someone is appropriate, it takes them a long time to say yes—twice as long as saying no to these particular kinds of questions. The brain's emotional network says no, Greene's brain scans show, and its reasoning network says yes.

When two areas of the brain come into con- 33 flict, researchers have found, an area known as the anterior cingulate cortex, or ACC, switches on to mediate between them. Psychologists can trigger the ACC with a simple game called the Stroop test, in which people have to name the color of a word. If subjects are shown the word blue in red letters, for instance, their responses slow down and the ACC lights up. "It's the area of the brain that says, 'Hey, we've got a problem here,'" Greene says.

Greene's questions, it turns out, pose a sort 34 of moral Stroop test. In cases where people take a long time to answer agonizing personal moral questions, the ACC becomes active. "We predicted that we'd see this, and that's what we got," he says. Greene, in other words, may be exposing the biology of moral anguish.

Of course, not all people feel the same sort of 35 moral anguish. Nor do they all answer Greene's questions the same way. Some aren't willing to push a man over a bridge, but others are. Greene nicknames these two types the Kantians and the utilitarians. As he takes more scans, he hopes to find patterns of brain activity that are unique to each group. "This is what I've wanted to get at from the beginning," Greene says, "to understand what makes some people do some things and other people do other things."

Greene knows that his results can be disturbing: "People sometimes say to me, 'If everyone 36 believed what you say, the whole world would fall apart.'" If right and wrong are nothing more than the instinctive firing of neurons, why bother being good? But Greene insists the evidence coming from neuroimaging can't be ignored. "Once you understand someone's behavior on a sufficiently mechanical level, it's very hard to look at them as evil," he says. "You can look at them as dangerous; you can pity them. But evil doesn't exist on a neuronal level."

By the time Patel emerges from the scanner, 37 rubbing his eyes, it's past 11 p.m. "I can try to print a copy of your brain now or e-mail it to you later," Greene says. Patel looks at the image on the computer screen and decides to pass. "This doesn't feel like you?" Greene says with a sly smile. "You're not going to send this to your mom?"

Soon Greene and Patel, who is Indian, are talking about whether Indians and Americans might answer some moral questions differently. All human societies share certain moral universals, such as fairness and sympathy. But Greene argues that different cultures produce different kinds of moral intuition and different kinds of brains. Indian morality, for instance, focuses more on matters of purity, whereas American morality focuses on individual autonomy. Researchers such as Jonathan Haidt, a psychologist at the University of Virginia, suggest that such differences shape a child's brain at a relatively early age. By the time we become adults, we're wired with emotional responses that guide our judgments for the rest of our lives. 38

Many of the world's great conflicts may be rooted in such neuronal differences, Greene says, which may explain why the conflicts seem so intractable. "We have people who are talking past each other, thinking the other 39

people are either incredibly dumb or willfully blind to what's right in front of them," Greene says. "It's not just that people disagree; it's that they have a hard time imagining how anyone could disagree on this point that seems so obvious." Some people wonder how anyone could possibly tolerate abortion. Others wonder how women could possibly go out in public without covering their faces. The answer may be that their brains simply don't work the same: Genes, culture, and personal experience have wired their moral circuitry in different patterns.

Greene hopes that research on the brain's moral circuitry may ultimately help resolve some of these seemingly irresolvable disputes. "When you have this understanding, you have a bit of distance between yourself and your gut reaction," he says. "You may not abandon your core values, but it makes you a more reasonable person. Instead of saying, 'I am right, and you are just nuts,' you say, 'This is what I care about, and we have a conflict of interest we have to work around.'" 40

Greene could go on—that's what philosophers do—but he needs to switch back to being a neuroscientist. It's already late, and Patel's brain will take hours to decode. ■ 41

Reflecting on What You Have Read

1 Although Joshua Greene is a scientist, he also has training in philosophy. Consequently, Zimmer is concerned with showing both ways Greene thinks about his research when presenting information in this report. What are some of the ways he attempts to create this balance? Do you think he succeeds? Why or why not?

2 Throughout his report, Zimmer relates stories about the scientists and other people responding to their work. Why do you think Zimmer chose to include so much information about the scientists, rather than focusing solely on the content of their studies? What effect does Zimmer achieve by quoting Greene?

3 What purpose do the cartoons that accompany this report serve? What effect do they have on you as you read? How would you describe the tone of these visuals? What is accomplished by using cartoons to illustrate ethical questions?

4 Zimmer notes that "when we say something is right or wrong, we are using our powers of reason alone," but then he cites a researcher who says that emotion plays a large role in decisions about right and wrong. How would you describe your own way of making difficult moral decisions? To what extent are these decisions guided by reason, and to what extent are they guided by emotion?

Thinking Ahead

Scientists produce new research all the time that offers new insights about the relationship between biology and human behavior. Often this research challenges conventional assumptions. Zimmer draws on a close look at the work of one neuroscientist to give insight into a current question about the origins and evolution of morality in human beings. As you think about topics for your own report, you might look for ways that work in other disciplines (biology, sociology, or psychology, for example) helps explain why people act as they do.

The Art of Failure: Why Some People Choke and Others Panic
Malcolm Gladwell

Malcolm Gladwell is a staff writer for *The New Yorker* magazine and the author of the bestselling books *The Tipping Point: How Little Things Make a Difference* (2000), and *Blink: The Power of Thinking without Thinking* (2005). His work often focuses on social issues and popular culture while drawing on research and academic work in the social sciences. He was born in England, grew up in rural Ontario, Canada, started his career as a reporter for the *Washington Post*, and is now also a frequent public speaker. In the following essay written in 2000 for *The New Yorker*, Gladwell describes ways people respond to intense pressure and explains two different reasons this pressure can cause them to fail, even in activities they are very good at. As you read, think about how you or others have responded to intense pressure and how well Gladwell's explanations account for what you have seen or experienced.

The Art of Failure

Why Some People Choke and Others Panic

By Malcolm Gladwell

There was a moment, in the third and deciding set of the 1993 Wimbledon final, when Jana Novotna seemed invincible. She was leading 4–1 and serving at 40–30, meaning that she was one point from winning the game, and just five points from the most coveted championship in tennis. She had just hit a backhand to her opponent, Steffi Graf, that skimmed the net and landed so abruptly on the far side of the court that Graf could only watch, in flatfooted frustration. The stands at Center Court were packed. The Duke and Duchess of Kent were in their customary place in the royal box. Novotna was in white, poised and confident, her blond hair held back with a headband—and then something happened. She served the ball straight into the net. She stopped and steadied herself for the second serve—the toss, the arch of the back—but this time it was worse. Her swing seemed halfhearted, all arm and no legs and torso. Double fault. On the next point, she was slow to react to a high shot by Graf, and badly missed on a forehand volley. At game point, she hit an overhead straight into the net. Instead of 5–1, it was now 4–2. Graf to serve: an easy victory, 4–3. Novotna to serve. She wasn't tossing the ball high enough. Her head was down. Her movements had slowed markedly. She doublefaulted once, twice, three times. Pulled wide by a Graf forehand, Novotna inexplicably hit a low, flat shot directly at Graf, instead of a high crosscourt forehand that would have given her time to get back into position: 4–4. Did she suddenly realize how terrifyingly close she was to victory? Did she remember that she had never won a major tournament before? Did she look across the net and see Steffi Graf—Steffi Graf!—the greatest player of her generation?

Jana Novotna's collapse at Wimbledon was as baffling to her as it was to onlookers.

On the baseline, awaiting Graf's serve, Novotna was now visibly agitated, rocking back and forth, jumping up and down. She talked to herself under her breath. Her eyes darted around the court. Graf took the game at love; Novotna, moving as if in slow motion, did not win a single point: 5–4, Graf. On the sidelines, Novotna wiped her racquet and her face with a towel, and then each finger individually. It was her turn to serve. She missed a routine volley wide, shook her head, talked to herself. She missed her first serve, made the second, then, in the resulting rally, mishit a backhand so badly that it sailed off her racquet as if launched into flight. Novotna was unrecognizable, not an élite tennis player but a beginner again. She was crumbling under pressure, but exactly why was as baffling to her as it was to all those looking on. Isn't pressure supposed to bring out the best in us? We try harder. We concentrate harder. We get a boost of adrenaline. We care more about how well we perform. So what was happening to her? 2

At championship point, Novotna hit a low, cautious, and shallow lob to Graf. Graf answered with an unreturnable overhead smash, and, mercifully, it was over. Stunned, Novotna moved to the net. Graf kissed her twice. At the awards ceremony, the Duchess of Kent handed Novotna the runner-up's trophy, a small silver plate, and whispered something in her ear, and what Novotna had done finally caught up with her. There she was, sweaty and exhausted, looming over the delicate white-haired Duchess in her pearl necklace. The Duchess reached up and pulled her head down onto her shoulder, and Novotna started to sob. 3

Human beings sometimes falter under pressure. Pilots crash and divers drown. Under the glare of competition, basketball players cannot find the basket and golfers cannot find the pin. When that happens, we say variously that people have "panicked" or, to use the sports colloquialism, "choked." But what do those words mean? Both 4 are pejoratives. To choke or panic is considered to be as bad as to quit. But are all forms of failure equal? And what do the forms in which we fail say about who we are and how we think? We live in an age obsessed with success, with documenting the myriad ways by which talented people overcome challenges and obstacles. There is as much to be learned, though, from documenting the myriad ways in which talented people sometimes fail.

"Choking" sounds like a vague and all-encompassing term, yet it describes a very specific kind of failure. For example, psychologists often use a primitive video game to test motor skills. They'll sit you in front of a computer with a screen that shows four boxes in a row, and a keyboard that has four corresponding buttons in a row. One at a time, x's start to appear in the boxes on the screen, and you are told that every time this happens you are to push the key corresponding to the box. According to Daniel Willingham, a psychologist at the University of Virginia, if you're told ahead of time about the pattern in which those x's will appear, your reaction time in hitting the right key will improve dramatically. You'll play the game very carefully for a few rounds, until you've learned the sequence, and then you'll get faster and faster. Willingham calls this "explicit learning." But suppose you're not told that the x's appear in a regular sequence, and even after playing the game for a while you're not aware that there is a pattern. You'll *still* get faster: you'll learn the sequence unconsciously. Willingham calls that "implicit learning"—learning that takes place outside of awareness. These two learning systems are quite separate, based in different parts of the brain. Willingham says that when you are first taught something—say, how to hit a backhand or an overhead forehand—you think it through in a very deliberate, mechanical manner. But as you get better the implicit system takes

over: you start to hit a backhand fluidly, without thinking. The basal ganglia, where implicit learning partially resides, are concerned with force and timing, and when that system kicks in you begin to develop touch and accuracy, the ability to hit a drop shot or place a serve at a hundred miles per hour. "This is something that is going to happen gradually," Willingham says. "You hit several thousand forehands, after a while you may still be attending to it. But not very much. In the end, you don't really notice what your hand is doing at all."

Under conditions of stress, however, the explicit system sometimes takes over. That's what it means to choke. When Jana Novotna faltered at Wimbledon, it was because she began thinking about her shots again. She lost her fluidity, her touch. She double-faulted on her serves and mis-hit her overheads, the shots that demand the greatest sensitivity in force and timing. She seemed like a different person—playing with the slow, cautious deliberation of a beginner—because, in a sense, she *was* a beginner again: she was relying on a learning system that she hadn't used to hit serves and overhead forehands and volleys since she was first taught tennis, as a child. The same thing has happened to Chuck Knoblauch, the New York Yankees' second baseman, who inexplicably has had trouble throwing the ball to first base. Under the stress of playing in front of forty thousand fans at Yankee Stadium, Knoblauch finds himself reverting to explicit mode, throwing like a Little Leaguer again.

Panic is something else altogether. Consider the following account of a scuba-diving accident, recounted to me by Ephimia Morphew, a human-factors specialist at NASA: "It was an open-water certification dive, Monterey Bay, California, about ten years ago. I was nineteen. I'd been diving for two weeks. This was my first time in the open ocean without the instructor. Just my buddy and I. We had to go about forty feet down, to the bottom of the ocean, and do an exercise where we took our regulators out of our mouth, picked up a spare one that we had on our vest, and practiced breathing out of the spare. My buddy did hers. Then it was my turn. I removed my regulator. I lifted up my secondary regulator. I put it in my mouth, exhaled, to clear the lines, and then I inhaled, and, to my surprise, it was water. I inhaled water. Then the hose that connected that mouthpiece to my tank, my air source, came unlatched and air from the hose came exploding into my face.

"Right away, my hand reached out for my 8 partner's air supply, as if I was going to rip it out. It was without thought. It was a physiological response. My eyes are seeing my hand do something irresponsible. I'm fighting with myself. *Don't do it*. Then I searched my mind for what I could do. And nothing came to mind. All I could remember was one thing: If you can't take care of yourself, let your buddy take care of you. I let my hand fall back to my side, and I just stood there."

This is a textbook example of panic. In that 9 moment, Morphew stopped thinking. She forgot that she had another source of air, one that worked perfectly well and that, moments before, she had taken out of her mouth. She forgot that her partner had a working air supply as well, which could easily be shared, and she forgot that grabbing her partner's regulator would imperil both of them. All she had was her most basic instinct: *get air*. Stress wipes out short-term memory. People with lots of experience tend not to panic, because when the stress suppresses their short-term memory they still have some residue of experience to draw on. But what did a novice like Morphew have? *I searched my mind for what I could do. And nothing came to mind*.

Panic also causes what psychologists call per- 10 ceptual narrowing. In one study, from the early seventies, a group of subjects were asked to perform a visual-acuity task while undergoing what they thought was a sixty-foot dive in a pressure chamber. At the same time, they were asked to push a button whenever they saw a small light flash on and off in their peripheral vision. The subjects in the pressure chamber had much higher heart rates than the control group, indicating that they were under stress. That stress didn't affect their accuracy at the visual-acuity task, but they were only half as good as the control group at picking up the peripheral light. "You tend to focus or obsess on one thing," Morphew says. "There's a famous airplane example, where the landing light went off, and the pilots had no way of knowing if the landing gear was down. The pilots were so focused on that light that no one noticed the autopilot had been disengaged, and they crashed the plane." Morphew reached for her buddy's air supply because it was the only air supply she could see.

Panic, in this sense, is the opposite of chok- 11 ing. Choking is about thinking too much. Panic is about thinking too little. Choking is about loss of instinct. Panic is reversion to instinct. They may look the same, but they are worlds apart.

Why does this distinction matter? In some 12 instances, it doesn't much. If you lose a close tennis match, it's of little moment whether you choked or panicked; either way, you lost. But there are clearly cases when *how* failure happens is central to understanding *why* failure happens.

Take the plane crash in which John F. 13 Kennedy, Jr., was killed last summer. The details of the flight are well known. On a Friday evening last July, Kennedy took off with his wife and sister-in-law for Martha's Vineyard. The night was hazy, and Kennedy flew along the Connecticut coastline, using the trail of lights below him as a guide. At Westerly, Rhode Island, he left the shoreline, heading straight out over Rhode Island Sound, and at that point, apparently disoriented by the darkness and haze, he began a series of curious maneuvers: He banked his plane to the right, farther out into the ocean, and then to the left. He climbed and descended. He sped up and slowed down. Just a few miles from his destination, Kennedy lost control of the plane, and it crashed into the ocean.

Kennedy's mistake, in technical terms, was 14 that he failed to keep his wings level. That was critical, because when a plane banks to one side it begins to turn and its wings lose some of their vertical lift. Left unchecked, this process accelerates. The angle of the bank increases, the turn gets sharper and sharper, and the plane starts to dive toward the ground in an ever-narrowing corkscrew. Pilots call this the grave-yard spiral. And why didn't Kennedy stop the dive? Because, in times of low visibility and high stress, keeping your wings level—indeed, even knowing whether you are in a graveyard spiral—turns out to be surprisingly difficult. Kennedy failed under pressure.

Had Kennedy been flying during the day or 15 with a clear moon, he would have been fine. If you are the pilot, looking straight ahead from the cockpit, the angle of your wings will be obvious from the straight line of the horizon in front of you. But when it's dark outside the horizon dis-appears. There is no external measure of the plane's bank. On the ground, we know whether we are level even when it's dark, because of the motion-sensing mechanisms in the inner ear. In a spiral dive, though, the effect of the plane's G-force on the inner ear means that the pilot *feels* perfectly level even if his plane is not. Simi-larly, when you are in a jetliner that is banking at thirty degrees after takeoff, the book on your neighbor's lap does not slide into your lap, nor will a pen on the floor roll toward the "down" side of the plane. The physics of flying is such that an airplane in the midst of a turn always feels per-fectly level to someone inside the cabin. . . .

This inability to sense, experientially, what 16 your plane is doing is what makes night flying so stressful. And this was the stress that Kennedy must have felt when he turned out across the water at Westerly, leaving the guiding lights of the Connecticut coastline behind him. A pilot who flew into Nantucket that night told the National Transportation Safety Board that when he descended over Martha's Vineyard he looked down and there was "nothing to see. There was no horizon and no light. . . . I thought the island might [have] suffered a power failure." Kennedy was now blind, in every sense, and he must have known the danger he was in. He had very little experience in flying strictly by instru-ments. Most of the time when he had flown up to the Vineyard the horizon or lights had still been visible. That strange, final sequence of maneuvers was Kennedy's frantic search for a clearing in the haze. He was trying to pick up the lights of Martha's Vineyard, to restore the lost horizon. Between the lines of the National Transportation Safety Board's report on the crash, you can almost feel his desperation:

> About 2138 the target began a right turn in a southerly direction. About 30 seconds later, the target stopped its descent at 2200 feet and began a climb that lasted another 30 seconds. During this period of time, the target stopped the turn, and the airspeed decreased to about 153 KIAS. About 2139, the target leveled off at 2500 feet and flew in a southeasterly direction. About 50 sec-onds later, the target entered a left turn and climbed to 2600 feet. As the target continued in the left turn, it began a descent that reached a rate of about 900 fpm.

But was he choking or panicking? Here the distinction between those two states is critical. Had he choked, he would have reverted to the mode of explicit learning. His movements in the cockpit would have become markedly slower and less fluid. He would have gone back to the mechanical, self-conscious application of the lessons he had first received as a pilot—and that might have been a good thing. Kennedy *needed* to think, to concentrate on his instruments, to break away from the instinctive flying that served him when he had a visible horizon.   17

But instead, from all appearances, he panicked. At the moment when he needed to remember the lessons he had been taught about instrument flying, his mind—like Morphew's when she was underwater—must have gone blank. Instead of reviewing the instruments, he seems to have been focussed on one question: Where are the lights of Martha's Vineyard? His gyroscope and his other instruments may well have become as invisible as the peripheral lights in the underwater-panic experiments. He had fallen back on his instincts—on the way the plane *felt*—and in the dark, of course, instinct can tell you nothing. The N.T.S.B. report says that the last time the Piper's wings were level was seven seconds past 9:40, and the plane hit the water at about 9:41, so the critical period here was less than sixty seconds. At twenty-five seconds past the minute, the plane was tilted at an angle greater than forty-five degrees. Inside the cockpit it would have felt normal. At some point, Kennedy must have heard the rising wind outside, or the roar of the engine as it picked up speed. Again, relying on instinct, he might have pulled back on the stick, trying to raise the nose of the plane. But pulling back on the stick without first levelling the wings only makes the spiral tighter and the problem worse. It's also possible that Kennedy did nothing at all, and that he was frozen at the controls, still frantically   18

searching for the lights of the Vineyard, when his plane hit the water. . . .

What happened to Kennedy that night illustrates a second major difference between panicking and choking. Panicking is conventional failure, of the sort we tacitly understand. Kennedy panicked because he didn't know enough about instrument flying. If he'd had another year in the air, he might not have panicked, and that fits with what we believe—that performance ought to improve with experience, and that pressure is an obstacle that the diligent can overcome. But choking makes little intuitive sense. Novotna's problem wasn't lack of diligence; she was as superbly conditioned and schooled as anyone on the tennis tour. And what did experience do for her? In 1995, in the third round of the French Open, Novotna choked even more spectacularly than she had against Graf, losing to Chanda Rubin after surrendering a 5–0 lead in the third set. There seems little doubt that part of the reason for her collapse against Rubin was her collapse against Graf—that the second failure built on the first, making it possible for her to be up 5–0 in the third set and yet entertain the thought *I can still lose*. If panicking is conventional failure, choking is paradoxical failure.   19

Claude Steele, a psychologist at Stanford University, and his colleagues have done a number of experiments in recent years looking at how certain groups perform under pressure, and their findings go to the heart of what is so strange about choking. Steele and Joshua Aronson found that when they gave a group of Stanford undergraduates a standardized test and told them that it was a measure of their intellectual ability, the white students did much better than their black counterparts. But when the same test was presented simply as an abstract laboratory tool, with   20 no relevance to ability, the scores of blacks and whites were virtually identical. Steele and Aronson attribute this disparity to what they call "stereotype threat": when black students are put into a situation where they are directly confronted with a stereotype about their group—in this case, one having to do with intelligence—the resulting pressure causes their performance to suffer.

Steele and others have found stereotype threat 21 at work in any situation where groups are depicted in negative ways. Give a group of qualified women a math test and tell them it will measure their quantitative ability and they'll do much worse than equally skilled men will; present the same test simply as a research tool and they'll do just as well as the men. Or consider a handful of experiments conducted by one of Steele's former graduate students, Julio Garcia, a professor at Tufts University. Garcia gathered together a group of white, athletic students and had a white instructor lead them through a series of physical tests: to jump as high as they could, to do a standing broad jump, and to see how many pushups they could do in twenty seconds. The instructor then asked them to do the tests a second time, and, as you'd expect, Garcia found that the students did a little better on each of the tasks the second time around. Then Garcia ran a second group of students through the tests, this time replacing the instructor between the first and second trials with an African-American. Now the white students ceased to improve on their vertical leaps. He did the experiment again, only this time he replaced the white instructor with a black instructor who was much taller and heavier than the previous black instructor. In this trial, the white students actually jumped less high than they had the first time around. Their performance on the pushups, though, was unchanged in each of the conditions. There is no stereotype, after all,

that suggests that whites can't do as many pushups as blacks. The task that was affected was the vertical leap, because of what our culture says: *white men can't jump*.

It doesn't come as news, of course, that 22 black students aren't as good at test-taking as white students, or that white students aren't as good at jumping as black students. The problem is that we've always assumed that this kind of failure under pressure is panic. What is it we tell underperforming athletes and students? The same thing we tell novice pilots or scuba divers: to work harder, to buckle down, to take the tests of their ability more seriously. But Steele says that when you look at the way black or female students perform under stereotype threat you don't see the wild guessing of a panicked test taker. "What you tend to see is carefulness and second-guessing," he explains. "When you go and interview them, you have the sense that when they are in the stereotype-threat condition they say to themselves, 'Look, I'm going to be careful here. I'm not going to mess things up.' Then, after having decided to take that strategy, they calm down and go through the test. But that's not the way to succeed on a standardized test. The more you do that, the more you will get away from the intuitions that help you, the quick processing. They think they did well, and they are trying to do well. But they are not." This is choking, not panicking. Garcia's athletes and Steele's students are like Novotna, not Kennedy. They failed because they were good at what they did: only those who care about how well they perform ever feel the pressure of stereotype threat. The usual prescription for failure—to work harder and take the test more seriously—would only make their problems worse.

That is a hard lesson to grasp, but harder still 23 is the fact that choking requires us to concern ourselves less with the performer and more with the situation in which the performance occurs. Novotna herself could do nothing to prevent her collapse against Graf. The only thing that could have saved her is if—at that critical moment in the third set—the television cameras had been turned off, the Duke and Duchess had gone home, and the spectators had been told to wait outside. In sports, of course, you can't do that. Choking is a central part of the drama of athletic competition, because the spectators *have* to be there—and the ability to overcome the pressure of the spectators is part of what it means to be a champion. But the same ruthless inflexibility need not govern the rest of our lives. We have to learn that sometimes a poor performance reflects not the innate ability of the performer but the complexion of the audience; and that sometimes a poor test score is the sign not of a poor student but of a good one.

24 Through the first three rounds of the 1996 Masters golf tournament, Greg Norman held a seemingly insurmountable lead over his nearest rival, the Englishman Nick Faldo. He was the best player in the world. His nickname was the Shark. He didn't saunter down the fairways; he stalked the course, blond and broad-shouldered, his caddy behind him, struggling to keep up. But then came the ninth hole on the tournament's final day. Norman was paired with Faldo, and the two hit their first shots well. They were now facing the green. In front of the pin, there was a steep slope, so that any ball hit short would come rolling back down the hill into oblivion. Faldo shot first, and the ball landed safely long, well past the cup.

25 Norman was next. He stood over the ball. "The one thing you guard against here is short," the announcer said, stating the obvious. Norman swung and then froze, his club in midair, following the ball in flight. It was short. Norman watched, stone-faced, as the ball rolled thirty yards back down the hill, and with that error something inside of him broke.

26 At the tenth hole, he hooked the ball to the left, hit his third shot well past the cup, and missed a makable putt. At eleven, Norman had a three-and-a-half-foot putt for par—the kind he had been making all week. He shook out his hands and legs before grasping the club, trying to relax. He missed: his third straight bogey. At twelve, Norman hit the ball straight into the water. At thirteen, he hit it into a patch of pine needles. At sixteen, his movements were so mechanical and out of synch that, when he swung, his hips spun out ahead of his body and the ball sailed into another pond. At that, he took his club and made a frustrated scythe-like motion through the grass, because what had been obvious for twenty minutes was now official: he had fumbled away the chance of a lifetime.

27 Faldo had begun the day six strokes behind Norman. By the time the two started their slow walk to the eighteenth hole, through the throng of spectators, Faldo had a four-stroke lead. But he took those final steps quietly, giving only the smallest of nods, keeping his head low. He understood what had happened on the greens and fairways that day. And he was bound by the particular etiquette of choking, the understanding that what he had earned was something less than a victory and what Norman had suffered was something less than a defeat.

28 When it was all over, Faldo wrapped his arms around Norman. "I don't know what to say—I just want to give you a hug," he whispered, and then he said the only thing you can say to a choker: "I feel horrible about what happened. I'm so sorry." With that, the two men began to cry. ∎

Reflecting on What You Have Read

1 How does Gladwell distinguish between choking and panicking? What different sources does he draw on for his explanation? How well does his explanation of each phenomenon help you understand why you or others have caved in under pressure?

2 Gladwell begins and ends his report with stories about ways famous athletes have lost a competition because they choked in the face of intense pressure. Presumably these athletes have lost other competitions without crying. But in both of these stories, the athletes cry. And in the final story, both the winner and loser cry. Does this crying seem justified? Why or why not? And what reasons do you see for Gladwell's including these stories?

3 What is your reaction to the cartoon that appears near the beginning of this essay? How is your reaction shaped by the details the artist included in the drawing? By the caption? What reasons might *The New Yorker* have had for including this image near the beginning of this essay?

4 Gladwell argues that it is important to understand not only the different ways in which people fail but also the reasons they fail. Do you agree with him? Why or why not?

5 Gladwell makes some claims about what must have caused John F. Kennedy Jr.'s plane to crash, even though he had no way to know what actually went through Kennedy's mind before he crashed. How does he justify (or fail to justify) those claims?

Thinking Ahead

Gladwell draws on several sources of information—events he has observed, interviews with experts, research studies—to explain why people don't respond well to a particular difficulty—intense pressure. Think of other difficult situations in which you or others have not responded well under pressure. Consider drawing on the same kinds of sources Gladwell uses to explain why you or others responded as you did.

ACL: The Curse of Women Athletes
Margaret Tomeo

In recent years, there has been a dramatic increase in the popularity of women's sports. Unfortunately, there has been an equally dramatic increase in the number of sports injuries to which women are especially vulnerable. Margaret Tomeo reports on one of the most serious of these injuries: damage in the knee to the anterior cruciate ligament, or ACL. A varsity soccer player at her university, Margaret wrote this piece with herself and her teammates in mind. On a bus trip to a soccer game, Margaret asked one of her teammates to read the report. This prompted a general discussion of ACL injuries, and several other teammates read the draft without being asked. As you read, try to determine what aspects of Margaret's report led her teammates to read the entire piece carefully.

ACL: The Curse of Women Athletes

"I knew right away exactly what I did" (McCallum and Gelin 44). 1

After hearing a rip in her right knee, Tiffany Woosley, a shooting guard for the 2
University of Tennessee Lady Vols, knew she had torn her ACL, or anterior cruciate

Fig. 1. Monique Currie and her knee brace (Wass D1).

ligament. She was performing a simple jump shot and landed incorrectly—and her injury caused her to miss the rest of the season. This has become the story for too many women athletes, including Woosley's teammate Nikki McCray, an All-American forward who tore her ACL in a pickup game (McCallum and Gelin). Duke University's Monique Currie tore her ACL in a preseason game, possibly ruining their hopes for a big season. (See Fig. 1.) And Brandi Chastain missed her 1987 and 1988 college soccer seasons after having surgery for the ACL in both knees (Patrick). ACL tears are turning into an epidemic among women athletes at all levels of sports,

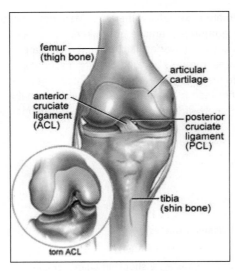

Fig. 2. Diagram of the ACL (What Is the ACL?).

especially among high school and college players. As the number of women competing in sports continues to increase, understanding the causes of this common injury will enable us to help these athletes reduce their risk.

What Is the ACL?

The anterior cruciate ligament, ACL for short, is a ligament in the knee to which much of the stress of physical activity is transmitted. The knee depends so much on the ACL that it is one of the most vulnerable parts of the human body. When people run or walk, the knee bears the entire weight of the body, continually flexing and absorbing the shock of every step. Central to all this activity and stress is the ACL, which runs through the knee to form a cross connecting the thigh bone (femur) with the shin bone (tibia) (Wilkinson 68). (See Fig. 2.) The ACL keeps the femur aligned with the tibia when the knee is bent and prevents the tibia from sliding forward too much (Hawaleshka). It also stabilizes the knee while an athlete is running and changing directions. When an ACL tear occurs, the knee gives out and becomes unstable. This instability does not go away until the injury is treated through surgery and rehabilitation. Even after all this, athletes with torn ACLs may have problems with recurrent instability, further joint damage, and early arthritis.

When Are ACL Injuries Most Common?

ACL injuries can happen at almost any time, but the majority of ACL injuries are non-contact, resulting from "planting" on one foot or making lateral movements such as changing direction suddenly. Other movements, such as straight-knee landings and one-step stopping while the knee is hyperextended, cause tears in the anterior cruciate ligament as well (Moeller and Lamb). The ligaments in the knee become extremely prone to injury when an athlete has exercised her quadriceps (muscles in the front of the thigh) and hamstrings (muscles in the back of the thigh) to fatigue. The muscular fatigue causes increased tibia movement at the knee and allows the knee to bend in ways in which it should not. When the ACL gives way, a player may feel and hear a pop in her knee as she collapses to the ground, unable to support her own weight.

As a player's muscles become fatigued, the player also becomes mentally fatigued. 5
When this happens, a player can lose sight of what her body can handle. As this occurs, the athlete often attempts maneuvers that her body cannot withstand. The combination of muscular and mental fatigue makes knee injuries most common in sports that involve frequent jumps, landings, rapid changes in direction, and abrupt deceleration and acceleration. Tears are most common in high-risk sports such as soccer, basketball, volleyball, field hockey, gymnastics, and skiing (Hawaleshka). Although this sort of injury can happen to both males and females, it is especially common among female athletes.

Why Are Women at a Greater Risk?

The discrepancy in the numbers of women and men suffering from ACL tears is due 6
partly to biological factors and partly to social factors. Anatomically, women are more prone to an ACL tear for several reasons. One is that women have a decreased hamstring-to-quadriceps strength ratio compared to that of men. Women's hamstring muscles are usually about half as strong as their quadriceps, whereas men's hamstrings are two-thirds as strong as their quadriceps. This muscle imbalance creates a stress on a woman's ACL because the quadriceps can overpower the hamstring, causing the tibia to be pulled too far forward (Wilkinson 69). The body depends on the hamstring to stabilize the knee, so there is greater risk of strain and injury when the hamstring is much weaker than the quadriceps.

Another anatomical difficulty is that women have wider hips than men, and 7
a woman's femur, the bone connecting hip and knee, is shorter than a man's. Consequently, women's legs slope inward at the knees, placing additional stress on the anterior cruciate ligament (McCallum and Gelin 46). In women, the angle from hip to knee (the quadriceps angle, or Q-angle) is greater than the Q-angle in

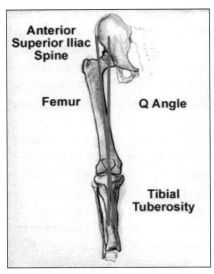

Fig. 3. Diagram of the Q-angle (Pribut).

men. (See Fig. 3.) Men's Q-angles usually range from 11 to 13 degrees, whereas women's Q-angles can be up to 17 degrees (Moeller and Lamb). This means that in women's knees, the force of the body is not transmitted directly downward, but instead is directed at a greater angle than in men's knees. The greater the angle, the more strain on the knee and the greater risk for ACL injury. Tears can also occur when a woman's femur acts as a guillotine, shearing the anterior cruciate ligament if the knee is hyperextended (Hawaleshka). This occurs in women because of the size and shape of the femoral notch, the point through which the ACL passes in order to connect the femur to the tibia. In women, the femoral notch is narrower than the femoral notch in men. It also tends to be in the shape of an "A" whereas a man's femoral notch is shaped more like a "U." When the knee is overextended, more pressure is put on the ACL. The narrower arch, combined with its sharper angle, increases the risk that a woman's femoral arch will cut into the ACL, resulting in a tear of that ligament (McCallum and Gelin 46).

Female hormones can also have a significant effect on the anterior cruciate ligament. A 1998 University of Michigan study showed that most ACL tears occurred when estrogen levels in women were the highest (Harden and Spurgeon). Estrogen weakens the ACL cells by altering their metabolism and increasing the laxity of the muscular tissue so the ligament is easily stretched and torn (Simonian). Another study, done at UCLA, found that the anterior cruciate ligament has receptors that react to estrogen and weaken in its presence (Harden and Spurgeon). In addition, females are at a greater risk because their joints tend to be looser than those of males (Hawaleshka).

8

Not only does the female anatomy contribute to the high risk of ACL injury, but   9
societal factors affecting body movement and muscle strength also make women more
susceptible. For one thing, women generally have less exposure to physical activities and,
on average, their conditioning is at a lower starting point than men's. Furthermore, many
women are not taught simple motor skills early in their development and consequently
maneuver the wrong way. For instance, males typically land using both legs, so that both
knees absorb the impact, while females favor one-legged landings. "I'm not saying that a
man would never make the same move the same way, but it's much more likely that he
would've learned the right way to do it," states Iowa trainer Alex Kane. "Either because of
budgetary constraints or philosophical reasons, that teaching is not going on in the
physical education system. Therefore you have impaired neuromuscular coordination. The
foundation is simply not there. Girls aren't taught it, and they aren't encouraged to learn
it" (McCallum and Gelin 47).

How Can These Injuries Be Reduced?

Currently, it is still unclear how to prevent anterior cruciate ligament injuries. But   10
female athletes can reduce the risk of ACL tears by learning proper motor skills, wearing
the right equipment, and undertaking a program of strength training. Mary Lloyd Ireland,
MD, director of the Kentucky Sports Medicine Clinic, suggests that women should be
encouraged to play sports as young girls and should be taught the proper athletic
techniques for actions such as jumping and pivoting (Schnirring). Young women athletes
also need to take advantage of programs that provide special training through local sports
clinics, physical therapists, and athletic trainers.

The right equipment can also decrease the number of ACL tears. Recently,   11
manufacturers have begun trying to create a shoe that reduces friction without
eliminating grip. According to Dr. Bill Youmans, an orthopedic consultant for the
University of Tennessee, wearing such shoes would reduce the number of ACL injuries for
men and women alike (McCallum and Gelin 48). Shoe manufacturers are also trying to
accommodate a woman's foot so that shoes fit better and provide ankle support that helps
reduce excess tension on the knee. Finally, arch supports, known as orthotics, can help
keep the foot balanced, reducing the strain on the knee.

The most important element in preventing ACL tears is appropriate strength training.   12
Female athletes should be encouraged to begin weight training to establish a proper

relationship between muscle groups, especially the hamstring and quadriceps. To establish this relationship, women should consider activities such as squats and lunges, which increase muscle strength while reducing the stress on the knee. Similarly, using the leg press machine, pushing the weight away from the body while lying down, is beneficial, strengthening the lower body while not placing any strain on the ACL. In addition, women can benefit from balancing exercises and Plyometrics, exercises that involve training for power and explosiveness using rapid muscle contraction.

Paying close attention to preventative measures can reduce the number of women   13
suffering from ACL injuries and prolong their careers. If we start now, we can greatly reduce the number of anterior cruciate tears that plague so many of our female players, players such as the outstanding Tennessee shooting guard, Tiffany Woosley.

Works Cited

Harden, Blaine, and Devon Spurgeon. "Knee Injuries Abound for Female Athletes." *Washington Post* 29 Mar. 1998, final ed.: A1. *LexisNexis Academic*. Web. 18 Mar. 2004.

Hawaleshka, Danylo. "ACL: A Real Pain in the Knee." *Maclean's* 7 Apr. 1997: 66. Print.

McCallum, Jack, and Dana Gelin. "Out of Joint." *Sports Illustrated* 13 Feb. 1995: 44–48. Print.

Moeller, James L., and Mary M. Lamb. "Anterior Cruciate Ligament Injuries in Female Athletes: Why Are Women More Susceptible?" *The Physician and Sportsmedicine* 25.4 (1997): 31. *LexisNexis Academic*. Web. 3 Mar. 2004.

Patrick, Dick. "Plant, Pop, then Pain." *USA Today* 25 June 2003: 1c. *Newspaper Source*. Web. 15 Mar. 2004.

Pribut, Stephen M. Q Angle. 22 Jan. 2004. *Dr. Stephen M. Pribut's Sport Pages*. Web. 10 Mar. 2004.

Schnirring, Lisa. "What's New in Treating Active Women." *The Physician and Sportsmedicine* 25.7 (1997): 91. *LexisNexis Academic*. Web. 19 Mar. 2004.

Simonian, Peter. "Knee Injuries Stepped up among Women." *Health Beat*. 4 May 1999: 3. Print.

Wass, Nick. *Monique Currie*. "No. 1 Blue Devils Counting on Currie." By Jim Reedy. *Washington Post* 16 Mar. 2004: D1. Print.

What Is the ACL? 2001. *ACL Solutions.com*. Web. 10 Mar. 2004.

Wilkinson, Todd. "Pop, Crackle, Snap." *Women's Sports & Fitness* Apr. 1998: 68–69. Print.

Reflecting on What You Have Read

1 Why do you think some of Margaret's teammates read her report carefully without being asked to? Can you identify certain aspects of the text that would draw them in? If so, what are they?

2 Although Margaret is an athlete, she has no training in sports medicine. Consequently, she was especially concerned about establishing her credibility in talking about this topic. What are some of the ways she attempts to do so? Do you think she succeeds? Why or why not?

3 What differences do you see between the first photograph in this report and the subsequent images? What do these differences tell you about the visuals' different functions?

4 In the third paragraph of her report, Margaret explains what the ACL does and what happens when it is damaged. But before discussing the ACL specifically, Margaret writes more generally about the knee. What does she achieve by writing about the knee before the ACL?

Thinking Ahead

As you will see on page 223, Margaret considered several topics before deciding to write about injuries to the anterior cruciate ligament. She chose this topic because she knew it was a problem that concerned her and some of her friends. As you try to think of topics for your own report, you might try Margaret's approach: Think of problems that concern you and your friends, teammates, or family. Would any of these people find it helpful to understand the cause of a particular problem and steps that could be taken to avoid or minimize it?

Guide to Writing a Report

▷ GUIDE TO WRITING A REPORT

This chapter will guide you through the process of creating a credible, informative report that someone will actually want or need to read. The first steps are selecting a topic, analyzing your audience, and identifying the specific purpose you hope to achieve in your report. Then you will work on creating a draft, using many of the strategies or techniques illustrated in reports included in Reading to Write. These strategies can help you explore your topic, write an introduction that will engage readers' interest, create an appropriate voice, organize your work, conclude your report effectively, and use visual elements (photographs, charts, page layout) to convey the message(s) you want to convey. Finally, in Reviewing and Revising, you will receive guidance in creating a review draft, assessing your work carefully, and using that assessment to revise your report.

As you work through the assignment for this chapter, you can also read a little bit about how undergraduate Margaret Tomeo wrote her profile. In the Student Q & A box on page 223, you will find the first of several brief conversations that Margaret had with the authors of this text.

▷ Assignment

Write a report, either on a topic of your choice or on one selected by your instructor, that answers questions that matter to the members of your intended audience. The topic should be significant—that is, it should matter to someone else (an individual, a group, or an organization) as much as it matters to you. Your instructor may have specific requirements about how long the report should be, what sort of topic you should write about, whether you should prepare the report as a print or online document (or as an oral presentation), and whether you should include or exclude any particular visual elements or use a particular documentation style to formally cite sources. Be sure you understand those requirements before you start working on the assignment.

GETTING STARTED

You could, of course, start working on your report by just gathering a lot of information that seems interesting to you and then beginning to type. But, in fact, the writing process begins much earlier than that, as you select a topic to write about. If you want to create a report that will be genuinely informative, one that an audience will want to read and will learn from, you'll need to begin by giving some very careful thought to selecting your topic and understanding your audience and purpose.

Selecting a Topic

You may not always have a lot of choice as to the topics you write about. Your instructor (or, eventually, an employer or a client) may say, in effect, "I want you to do a report on . . ." In many situations, however, you will have some freedom in selecting a topic for your report. Consequently, you will have to make some choices.

► Choose a topic that is not too broad to cover in the assigned number of pages or in the number of weeks you have to work on your assignment.

► Choose a topic you care about and know something about.

► Make sure your topic is one about which you can get plenty of information.

► Choose a topic that matters not just to you but also to someone else—an individual, a group of people, a business, or some other organization.

► Make sure your topic will let you achieve some purpose in addition to gathering and presenting factual information.

These last two recommendations will have a lot to do with the ultimate success of your report. How do you carry them out? One approach is to think of topics that directly affect you and people you know. Then think about what those people might hope to gain by reading your report. Another approach is to immerse yourself in a topic that interests you, gathering as much information as possible. As your understanding of the topic grows, you will need to clarify the purpose(s) you hope to achieve. Are you, for example, becoming aware of a serious problem? If so, identify a specific individual or group that is likely to be affected by it, even though they are currently unaware of it. Then write a report that alerts this audience to the problem. Alternatively, if your reading and observations lead you to conclude that some people have serious and potentially harmful misconceptions about the topic, you might write a report that informs them of those misconceptions and the potential harm they may cause. As you read (or watch) other reports, ask yourself what purposes and audiences they address. Perhaps you will decide to set a comparable goal for a comparable audience. (For a list of other purposes reports are often intended to achieve, see page 164.)

If you cannot think of someone who would need or want to read a report on a given topic, find another topic. Your sense of audience and purpose will affect what you say and how you express your ideas. The more specifically you can define your audience and purpose, the greater chance you will have of creating an interesting, useful report.

Coming Up with Ideas for a Topic

If you are having trouble coming up with possible topics, you might identify good topics by reading the suggestions in the Thinking Ahead passages that follow each of the reports in Reading to Write. Or you might consider some of the basic kinds of topics that often prompt a report of information. For example, reports are often written about the following.

► Problems that either currently affect people (or organizations) or have the potential to affect them

► Solutions to problems

▶ Recent discoveries or breakthroughs in medicine, technology, and similar areas

▶ Trends that have the potential to affect readers, especially trends that relate to social customs, organizations, or values

▶ Widespread practices (road rage, for example) that are likely to affect your audience

You might also get some ideas for topics by engaging in the following activities.

Brainstorm ideas for topics. Writing as quickly as you can, list every topic you can think of that might have some potential as a topic for this report. It may help to complete the following sentences.

One topic that really interests me is _____.

Another is _____.

For the moment, don't try to elaborate on any of these ideas or worry about how good these topics sound; just list as many potential topics as possible.

Review what you have written with a small group or the entire class. Notice the potential topics that strike your classmates as especially interesting. See if they can suggest related topics. Don't feel you have to accept their suggestions; just see if any sound like good possibilities.

Select a topic that seems like it might have potential and then brainstorm about that topic. Writing as quickly as you can, answer these questions: What do you already know about this topic? How does it affect you or people you care about? What are some questions you might like to answer concerning this topic? If you can answer at least some of these questions, you probably have a topic with good potential. If not, you may need to go back and engage in some of the activities listed above.

Assessing Your Choice of a Topic

Once you have identified a topic for your report, you need to assess that topic, making sure that you can find plenty of information and that it will mean as much to others as it does to you. To do this, try the following activities, making notes about what you learn.

Summarize what you have written and share with a group. Ask your classmates to help you think of audiences who might be interested in the topic you're considering. As is true with your choice of topic, your choice of an audience may change. But if you and your classmates can't think of audiences who would need to read a report on your topic, you should consider writing on a different topic.

Think further about your own experience. Have you had any personal contact with the topic of your report? Have you taken part in activities associated with your topic or observed it yourself? If so, do you have any anecdotes or facts that seem relevant?

Talk with others who may know something about your topic. What are their experiences? Can they tell you any good stories about your topic? Can they provide any factual information that surprises you or adds to your understanding of the topic?

Do some reading. Do a preliminary search in your library's databases or the Internet, but remember that information on the Web is not always reliable or complete. Don't try to read everything carefully at this point. Just read enough to confirm that your proposed topic is interesting and worthwhile and that there is plenty of credible material available on it.

For help in evaluating the credibility of sources, see Chapter 12.

Look for visual information—images, charts, graphs, and so forth—that provides insight into the topic for your report.

Conduct a brief reality check. After doing a fair amount of reading and talking, are you finding plenty of interesting material that will let you speak authoritatively on your topic? Have you identified an audience that actually needs or wants to know what you have to say about the topic? Do you see a compelling reason why the audience will want to read a report on this topic at this particular time? If you can't answer yes to at least two of these questions, consider changing your topic or your audience. Do this now, not the night before the assignment is due.

Student Q & A   **Selecting a Topic**

Writing Now (WN): What topics did you consider writing about?

Margaret Tomeo (MT): Pollution, recycling, endangered species.

WN: How did you come to choose ACL injuries as your topic?

MT: I was playing soccer at the time, and there were a couple of times ACL injuries happened to people I knew. So it was a recurring thing I kept hearing about.

WN: At what point were you certain you had a good topic to write about?

MT: I passed my draft around on the bus on the way to a soccer game. And the girls on the team all had personal stories about ACL, but my draft had a lot of information they didn't know. They found it helpful. It appealed to them. So that showed me it was a popular topic. ■

Understanding Your Audience and Purpose

Up to this point, you have primarily been concentrating on selecting a topic, asking in effect whether you can find plenty of interesting information about that topic. As you work through the rest of this chapter, you will continue to learn about your topic. But as you do this, you will need to be guided by an understanding of your audience and purpose. Who am I writing this for? Why am I writing this—other than to fulfill an assignment? And what do I hope to accomplish by writing about my topic?

Sometimes a piece of informative writing may be read by a wide variety of people simply because they happen to be interested in the topic. But don't count on it. Typically, you will write for a relatively limited group of readers, none of whom will be required to read what you have written. And even if you hope your work will be attractive to a larger group of readers, you can better understand your audience by focusing on a small group of people or even on an individual who is typical of the larger audience you hope to reach. You will also need to think specifically about the purpose(s) you hope to accomplish by writing the report. To identify your audience and your specific purposes for writing, write out your answers to the following questions.

[
Guidelines for Analyzing Your Audience and Identifying Purpose
]

▶ Go to
bedfordstmartins.com/ writingnow to download these guidelines from Chapter 4 > Worksheets.

Audience knowledge, needs, and attitudes

- What do your readers already know about your topic? For example, what have they read or heard about your topic? What personal experiences have they had with it?
- Why would your readers want or need to know about your topic? For example, how does your topic affect them or people they care about? Does it address a concern they feel? Are they in a situation where they need to know about your topic?
- What biases or preconceptions do your readers have concerning your topic? Are they making any questionable assumptions?

Audience expectations for content

- What questions are your readers likely to want to have answered?
- What kinds of information are your readers likely to see as credible?
- Are there authorities or other sources of information they would find especially credible?

Audience expectations for layout or format

- Are there any visual features (for example, photographs, charts, bulleted lists) your readers are likely to expect or appreciate?
- What sort of layout will your audience expect? For example, should you use one column or two? Do you need to cite sources? To use pull quotes or inset boxes?

For more information about layout, see Chapter 9, page 526.

Purpose(s)

- In addition to providing credible, meaningful information about your topic, what else do you hope to accomplish by writing your report? For example, do you hope to make readers aware of a serious problem, trend, or situation? Inform them of a solution? Challenge their preconceptions? Reassure them? Provide readers with a credible basis for making a decision?
- What sort of voice do you want readers to hear when they read your report? What image do you want to convey of yourself?

To answer these questions about audience and purpose, talk with one or more members of your audience, asking them what they already know. Mention some of the facts you are discovering, see whether these facts surprise them, and ask what questions they have. Also, draw on your knowledge of yourself, asking such questions as these: If I were in my audience's place, what questions would I want to have answered? What biases and preconceptions might I have concerning the topic of my report? Then use what you are learning about your audience and topic to decide on the purpose(s) you hope to accomplish by writing your report.

As you work on the report, your understanding of your audience and purpose may change. You may, for example, get a clearer idea of what the audience knows or expects, and that may lead you to rethink your purpose. You might, for example, discover that they are already aware of the problem you are concerned with and that your purpose should be to help them understand possible solutions. Consequently, you may want to revise your responses to questions posed in the Guidelines for Analyzing Your Audience and Identifying Purpose as you work on the report. But for now, be as clear and specific as possible.

Student Analysis of Audience and Purpose

Margaret Tomeo's report "ACL: The Curse of Women Athletes" could be read by women athletes in any number of sports. But when she wrote her report, she had one particular group of women in mind: teammates on her women's college soccer team. Here is how Margaret describes her audience and explains her purpose.

Audience knowledge, needs, and attitudes

They are not very knowledgeable on the topic but want to learn more because they know how common the injury is.

Most of them know of someone who has experienced an ACL tear. They know it has happened to many professional female athletes, especially basketball players (Rebecca Lobo) and soccer players (Brandi Chastain), and even Michelle Yeoh, a movie actress.

They know the injury could happen to them or to a teammate. They want to learn how to be safe and prevent injuries throughout their careers. They are in the middle of a soccer season, and soccer is a sport where the injury is likely to happen to women.

They may believe that the injury occurs only in younger and weaker athletes. They may feel that most people are not at risk—want to know risk factors. Also, they may think that these injuries cannot be prevented.

Audience's expectations for content

Questions my readers will most likely want to have answered.
- What is the ACL? What does it do?
- Why is the ACL so important?
- Can these injuries be prevented? How?
- Why and when do ACL tears commonly occur?
- How many people are affected? How common is this injury?
- Why are ACL injuries more common in women than in men?

The information will have to be based on medical research.

Audience expectations for layout or format

They are used to reading reports with headings and visuals, especially visuals that are more technical than human interest.

Purpose

I'm trying to make my readers aware of this common problem so that they can help themselves and others reduce the risk of the injury. I hope my readers will incorporate my advice into their sports and/or workouts.

I want to sound concerned about this topic, but not too emotional. I want to sound like someone who really understands the physiology involved in this injury.

CREATING A DRAFT

As you did the earlier work on selecting a topic, analyzing your audience, and identifying your purpose(s) for writing your report, you began to think about the things you might want to say in your report. Now you need to develop your initial ideas into a coherent report that someone else will want or need to read. The next few sections of this chapter outline a variety of verbal and visual strategies that will help you explore your topic, engage your audience, and so forth. As in other chapters in this book, you will be working with strategies that appear in readings found in Reading to Write. The following discussions, along with the lists of strategies and examples, will help you see how specific passages reflect strategies that you can apply to your own writing. You can always add to these lists of strategies by analyzing other reports you find interesting and credible.

Exploring Your Topic

To add significantly to your reader's understanding of your topic, you will probably have to understand that topic a lot better than you currently do—unless, of course, you're already an expert on your topic. This will require you to explore your topic thoroughly, gathering a good bit of information, reflecting on it in ways that will help you come to new insights, and articulating a thesis and developing your ideas.

Gathering Information

For certain topics and audiences, you may be able to base your report on personal experience. But in almost all cases, you will also need to gather additional information from secondary sources such as magazine articles, government reports, surveys, and Web sites.

Draw on personal experience. You will need to be selective in drawing on personal experience because it is not appropriate for all reports. However, references to personal experience (your own or the experience[s] of others) often can give readers a sense of how an abstract topic affects individuals. Or personal experience can establish your credentials as someone who has observed the topic firsthand. Here are two strategies that can help you draw on personal experience.

How to Draw on Personal Experience

STRATEGIES	EXAMPLES FROM READINGS
Record your observations. Note what people say and do as well as the setting in which your experiences took place.	 "Whose Life Would You Save?" (p. 193), begins with Carl Zimmer's conversation with a philosopher who studies the ways people make moral decisions. When he accompanies the philosopher into the research laboratory, Zimmer notes key features of the setting (video projector, a slab on which research subjects lie, the MRI machine), all of which suggest that this philosopher takes a unique approach to studying philosophical problems.
Talk with others. Include experts or people who went through an experience with you. Especially listen for stories they can tell you about their experiences with your topic. Pay attention not only to the events they recount but also how their experiences affected them and what meanings those experiences had for them.	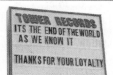 Although we can't be certain, it appears that Brian Hiatt and Evan Serpick in "The Record Industry's Slow Fade" (p. 176) report comments they heard in conversations with industry insiders. In "The Art of Failure" (p. 204) Malcolm Gladwell explains what he means by panicking by telling a story he heard from a woman who was involved in a scuba-diving accident. Her account explains not only why she panicked but what it felt like to experience the emotional state Gladwell refers to as panic.

Use secondary sources. Secondary sources include magazine articles, government reports, surveys, and Web sites. From a technological perspective, perhaps the simplest way to find these sources is to do a keyword search on the Internet. But remember: Although the Internet can be a useful source, it can also be problematic. Anyone can say almost anything on the Web. Somewhat more reliable sources of information can be found in your school library's online catalog and databases. Listings in databases are usually taken from well-known, reputable sources—government or scientific reports, newspapers, and magazines. Though none of these sources is infallible, the materials your library has chosen to subscribe to are likely to be reliable. These databases will let you search for information on specific topics, and some of them (Academic Search Premier, for example) may let you print out copies of articles free of charge. Many campus libraries offer access to these resources via their Web sites, so much of the information is available to browse and print from your own computer.

For additional information about primary and secondary sources, see Chapter 10. For more advice on locating and evaluating good sources online, see Chapter 12.

For advice on locating useful visuals, see Chapter 9.

While consulting secondary sources, be on the lookout for pictures or other graphics that will help you understand and elaborate on your topic. Also, look for written information you might be able to incorporate into a chart, table, or graph.

As you continue looking for information on your topic, you can use a variety of strategies such as the following.

How to Use Secondary Sources

STRATEGIES	EXAMPLES FROM READINGS
Draw on different sources of information. Many reports draw on the work of authorities, people who have invested a great deal of time in thinking about or investigating a particular topic. But you should also consider drawing on your own experiences and on comments from people who are involved in or concerned about your topic.	The author of "Whose Life Would You Save?" (p. 193) reports his observations of work in one particular laboratory as well as information from other experiments and the theories of three philosophers.
Incorporate different types of information. Quotations are often useful, especially if they are drawn from a variety of sources; so are statistics, narratives, case histories, eyewitness accounts, and your personal observations and experiences.	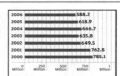 "The Record Industry's Slow Fade" (p. 176) includes statistics showing declining sales of record albums, quotations from record producers and their attorneys, and historical information that explains how the current "slow fade" could have been prevented.
Look for stories that help explain the ideas you want to convey. Stories by themselves don't always tell everything one needs to know about a topic, but they can help make abstract ideas more concrete.	"The Art of Failure" (p. 202) includes several stories to illustrate the difference between choking (anecdotes about famous athletes) and panicking (a scuba diver's reaction to a disconnected air hose).
Look for ways to represent information visually. Photographs can convey both information and attitudes; graphs, charts, and tables can present a lot of information succinctly and dramatically.	 "Seeing Is Not Believing" (p. 182) relies heavily on photographs, both authentic and altered. "The Record Industry's Slow Fade" documents changes in the recording industry through graphs.
Explore the history of your topic. Don't include history just because you happen to think it is interesting, but do look for information about prior events that will help readers understand the current situation.	"Seeing Is Not Believing" briefly explains "the long and inglorious history" of altered photographs. This history is important because it helps readers appreciate the significance of recent advances in the technology that enable people to alter photographs in ways that are difficult to detect.

{ Student Q & A }   Selecting Secondary Sources

Writing Now (WN): How did you decide which sources to use in your report?

Margaret Tomeo (MT): I tried to use information that I kept finding in more than one source. And if I found something in only one source, I tried to find something to back it up. I was looking for sources that matched, that had facts that were agreed on.

WN: How did you know you were asking the right questions?

MT: I was a member of the audience, and those were the questions I would ask. I just figured that since I was a female athlete, those were the right questions. ■

Keep track of information. When you've done a lot of research and are getting ready to write a draft of your report, it can be very frustrating to find that you remember only part of an important quotation or that you aren't sure where you found an interesting statistic. To avoid this frustration, you should do two things. First, keep detailed notes of any personal experiences you want to include in the report. Jot down responses to questions such as the following: What did you see or hear? What did people do or say? What was the setting?

Second, create a working bibliography. At the very least, keep complete bibliographic information for each source you read. You should record the author's name, the title of the piece (article, book, Web site), and all the information required to locate the piece if you need to come back to it for more information (the URL of the Web site and the date you accessed it, for example, or date and page number of the magazine article). You need not record all this information according to the precise guidelines of the documentation style you're using, but noting all this information will save you time later. Also note the main point of each source and how it relates to your report topic. It can be especially useful to list the main questions the source poses and summarize the answers it gives.

For advice on taking notes and creating a working bibliography, see Chapter 12.

Reflecting on Information

After you have gathered a good bit of information about your topic, you should begin reflecting on the information you have gathered, trying to identify the main points you want to make. But before you begin this work, reread the way you answered the questions posed in the Guidelines for Analyzing Your Audience and Identifying Purpose on page 224. Are there some questions that are not answered thoroughly or specifically? For example, are you lacking information about your readers' knowledge, needs, and attitudes? Do you have a good sense of what your readers will expect in terms of content, both verbal and visual? At this point, complete your responses to the best of your ability. After doing this, don't try to write a formal essay right away; don't even worry about paragraphing or organization. Just set aside twenty to thirty minutes and write as rapidly as you can in response to the following prompts, stating and elaborating on the points you want to make.

One point I want to make about my topic is _____.

Without stopping to look back at the information you gathered, elaborate on that statement as much as you can. Continue to elaborate as much as possible from memory.

Another point I want to make is _____.

Another point is _____.

Another point is _____.

Keep on making and elaborating on your points until you have used the full twenty to thirty minutes.

After completing this reflective work, read or show what you have written to other students (either to a small group or to the entire class). Describe your intended audience, and then ask your classmates to answer the following questions.

- ▶ Do any of my points seem likely to be especially interesting or informative to my audience? (If so, one of these points may become the thesis of your report, or several of your points may become topic sentences for your paragraphs.)

- ▶ Can you think of additional questions my audience might want to have answered?

- ▶ Can you think of other types of information I might use to elaborate on the points I am trying to make?

- ▶ Can you think of places in the report where some sort of visual (a photograph, for example, or a chart) might make my report more informative or credible?

After considering your classmates' responses, determine whether there are places where you might use some of the strategies explained on pages 227 and 228 to give readers more insight into your topic. Use your classmates' responses to guide you in deciding whether or how to add to, delete, or modify information you have gathered thus far.

Formulating a Thesis

After discussing your work with your classmates, complete the following sentence.

The basic point I want to make is _____.

This sentence will become your tentative thesis, the principal idea you want to convey in your report. As you continue to develop your topic, you may want to revise that thesis. But it will serve as the starting point from which you can look for ways to make your report as clear and informative as possible.

Developing Your Ideas

Once you have a tentative thesis, you need to develop your ideas more in ways that will give readers a comprehensive, credible understanding of the topic on which you are reporting. To do this, begin by reviewing the work you did for the exercise on pages 229–30, where you listed and briefly explained the basic points you thought you would make in your report. Decide whether you need to eliminate or modify some points or add others. Then develop these ideas by using some of the strategies explained below.

How to Develop Ideas

STRATEGIES	EXAMPLES FROM READINGS
Notice problems and solutions. One reason people read reports is to find out what is being done to solve an important problem. Identify problems associated with your topic and find out what is being done to solve them.	"ACL: The Curse of Women Athletes" (p. 211) explains reasons female athletes are susceptible to ACL injuries and then outlines exercise programs to prevent these injuries.
Acknowledge different perspectives on your topic. If you are writing about a complex topic, different people or groups will likely have different perspectives on it. You will need to acknowledge these.	Although the author of "The Perils of Higher Education" (p. 169) believes that smoking is a bad idea, he does note that smoking can help students remember what they read.
Notice comparisons and/or contrasts. One of the ways people understand something is to see how a person, an idea, an action, or a place is similar to or different from something else. It can be especially helpful to compare or contrast something that is new to readers with something they already know or care about.	The most extensive use of contrast appears in "The Art of Failure" (p. 202) where Malcolm Gladwell talks at length about the ways panicking is different from choking. In "the Perils of Higher Education," Steven Kotler notes a similarity between the brain structure of animals that had been fed fast foods and the brain structure of humans with Alzheimer's.
Classify. Although you must avoid stereotyping, an individual entity (a person, an object, an action) is always a member of a larger class of things. It can be useful to notice the qualities the entity shares with a larger group. It can also be useful to break your topic down into subcategories or subtopics.	 In "Whose Life Would You Save?" (p. 193), Carl Zimmer reports on people's responses to three different types of choices: personal moral choices that have significant consequences, impersonal moral choices that have serious consequences but do not affect the person who makes the choices, and "innocuous" or routine choices that have no moral consequences.

continued on next page ▶

How to Develop Ideas (continued)

STRATEGIES	EXAMPLES FROM READINGS
Look for causes and effects. Chances are the question "why?" will occur to your readers. Therefore, notice the reasons people give for their actions, and try to identify their motives. Determine whether cultural, social, or economic forces are at work. Also consider the consequences or implications associated with your topic. If something happens (an action is taken, a law is passed, a discovery is made), what is likely to happen—or what did happen—as a result?	In "The Art of Failure," Gladwell identifies several factors that led to the airplane crash that killed John F. Kennedy Jr.
Notice changes or trends. Technology changes, and so do individuals, social groups, institutions, societies, and people's views of the world. Explore your topic's history to discover trends or significant changes—whether in the topic, the people associated with the topic, or people's view of the topic. Determine how much your readers need to understand about these trends and changes.	**Global Music Revenue** The major labels are global companies – and business is bad all over. Total revenue is down fourteen percent since 2000. ▼2006 **31.8** BILLION ▼2000 **36.9** BILLION / "The Record Industry's Slow Fade" (p. 176) focuses on one major trend—the declining sales of records.

For advice on how to use stories as a way to develop your ideas, see Chapter 2, page 70.

It may help to think of the strategies here as questions to answer as you read or examine your own experience with the topic. For example, how is one person's perspective on your topic different from that of another? If one strategy or question doesn't turn up something interesting, try another one. Also, don't rely entirely on your memory. Use your working bibliography or copies of key materials with important points underlined.

Engaging Your Audience: Writing an Introduction

To make sure your intended audience becomes engaged with the topic of a report, you need to do two things. First, establish a relationship with readers. Almost invariably this entails providing information that will let readers see how the information in the report pertains in some way to them. Sometimes this includes giving readers whatever background information they need to understand the topic. Second, make readers aware of a conflict—an uncertainty, a question, a problem—that they will want to resolve by reading the report. Readings in this chapter illustrate a variety of strategies you might use in establishing a relationship with your readers and creating a conflict that will motivate them to begin (and continue) reading your report.

Relating to Readers

The reports in the Reading to Write section of this chapter display a variety of strategies for establishing a relationship with readers. Here are four that can be especially useful.

How to Relate to Readers

STRATEGIES	EXAMPLES FROM READINGS
Mention (or show images of) people, situations, or events that readers recognize and care about before they begin reading your report.	In the first paragraph of "ACL: The Curse of Women Athletes" (p. 211), Margaret Tomeo cites comments by athletes her audience will recognize, and she provides a photograph of a well-known female athlete wearing a knee brace, which most readers will recognize as symptomatic of knee injury.
Begin with an assertion readers are likely to agree with or at least recognize as a widely shared opinion.	"The Perils of Higher Education" (p. 171) begins with a claim that represents a familiar perspective on why people go to college—or at least why they might be expected to go to college: "We go to college to learn, to soak up a dazzling array of information intended to prepare us for adult life."
Provide background information that will show why the topic is important or that will help readers understand information in the rest of the report.	The second and third paragraphs of "Seeing Is Not Believing" (p. 184) provide examples of the potential kinds of harm caused by photo-editing technology. These examples give a compelling reason for understanding the technology explained in the remainder of the report. The third paragraph of "Whose Life Would You Save?" (p. 193) describes the laboratory procedure underlying many of the experiments that are mentioned later in the report.
Tell a story readers can relate to.	Almost all sports fans can appreciate the story at the beginning of "The Art of Failure" (p. 202), in which a professional athlete inexplicably succumbs to pressure at just the moment victory is within her grasp.

{ Student Q & A }   **Relating to Readers**

Writing Now (WN): Why did you use the picture of the basketball player at the beginning of your report?

Margaret Tomeo (MT): I wanted the audience to know right away that they could relate to it.

WN: Why did you choose this particular picture?

MT: This picture was really clear. In a lot of other pictures, the brace wasn't really the center of attention. Also, you could tell exactly what she was doing. The brace was a focus of the picture. ■

Creating Conflict

In addition to letting readers see how your topic relates to what they know, care about, or need, you should create a conflict that will motivate your audience to read your report. The following chart illustrates several strategies for doing this.

How to Create Conflict

STRATEGIES	EXAMPLES FROM READINGS
Use visuals showing something that conflicts with what readers want, value, or expect. The best way to do this may be through the use of photographs that depict people, actions, or scenes that readers will find startling or disturbing.	 One image in "Seeing Is Not Believing" (p. 183) seems familiar (an airliner and people walking on a beach), but shows them much closer together than readers are likely to expect or think safe.
Tell a story about actions that conflict with what readers expect or that dramatizes a problem about which readers are concerned. This sort of beginning must be filled with specific, credible details; otherwise, readers may dismiss it as too sensationalist.	The story at the beginning of "The Art of Failure" (p. 202) recounts a familiar phenomenon—failing under pressure in a sporting event. But the consequences of the failure—a loss at a point where victory seems almost certain—is, to say the least, disturbing and frustrating.
Introduce a problem or dilemma, especially one that challenges readers' assumptions or values.	The very title "Seeing Is Not Believing" challenges an assumption that is still widely held: Photographs are reliable records of events.

A word of caution: If the conflict is too strong, it may offend or alienate readers. But the right amount of the right sort of conflict will make them aware of questions or problems that will prompt them to read the rest of your report in search of answers or solutions. The right amount or type of conflict depends on your purpose(s) in writing and your analysis of the intended audience. What works for one audience might be inappropriate for a different audience.

{ Exercise } **Writing an Introduction**

Review—and, if necessary, revise—your audience analysis, being especially careful to describe your readers' knowledge, needs, and attitudes. Then, using one or more of the strategies explained above, write one or more introductory paragraphs that seem likely to engage the attention of the audience you have described. Consider using a photograph along with these paragraphs. Bring this introductory material to class, along with your audience analysis and statement of purpose. Ask your classmates to tell you whether the introduction you have written (and perhaps the photograph you have included) seems likely to engage the intended audience and whether they can think of other strategies to engage your audience. ■

Creating an Appropriate Voice

People often assume reports are impersonal, "objective," somehow reporting only the facts that actually happened. Of course, reports should be well grounded in factual information. But they always reflect the conclusions, observations, attitudes, and values of the people who are doing the reporting. Thus creating an appropriate voice in a report often requires a careful balancing act in which writers convey information in ways that their readers will see as credible while simultaneously acknowledging their own attitudes and conclusions. Writers also have to show that they understand readers' level of knowledge as well as their expectations about the level of formality or informality that is appropriate.

You can demonstrate credibility by using strategies for exploring your topic found on pages 226–29. And you can show that you understand readers' expectations about formality and informality by carefully choosing language and sentence structure and by using or avoiding personal pronouns. As a rule, your voice will seem informal if you talk as though you were having a conversation with a close friend—that is, if your language includes personal pronouns, colloquial or slang terms, contractions, or sentence fragments. Your voice will be more formal if you write complete sentences instead of fragments, use few (or no) personal pronouns, and choose more technical or infrequently used terms.

How to Create an Appropriate Voice

STRATEGIES	EXAMPLES FROM READINGS
To demonstrate your credibility, elaborate on your claims with evidence from authoritative sources. This evidence may include your personal experiences and observations, if—but *only* if—you actually witnessed the events you are describing and you have the knowledge and expertise to interpret those events accurately.	In "Whose Life Would You Save?" (p. 193), Carl Zimmer draws on his personal experiences at several points: his dinner with a researcher who studies people's responses to moral dilemmas, his observations of the laboratory in which the researcher works, and conversations in which the researcher explains his work. But Zimmer also draws much of his information from the work of philosophers and from reports of research.
To display your attitudes and conclusions, choose words and details that indicate, implicitly or explicitly, your perspective on the topic.	The author of "Seeing Is Not Believing" (p. 182) chooses words (*fake, damning, hoax*) that indicate a very clear attitude toward the increasing use of altered photographs. In "The Art of Failure" (p. 202), Malcolm Gladwell never directly says that "choking" is a terrible experience. But the stories with which he begins and ends his report leave little question about his view of "choking."
To show that you understand the knowledge and values of your readers, use terminology that will be familiar to most of them.	In "ACL: The Curse of Women Athletes" (p. 211), Margaret Tomeo describes the location of the ACL using familiar terms (*thigh bone, shin bone*) as well as more technical terms (*femur, tibia*).
Let others speak for you, especially those whose information is highly credible and can obviously speak with authority.	 In Steve Casimiro's report, "Seeing Is Not Believing," the key point is asserted not by the author but by a leading researcher: "Seeing is no longer believing. Actually, what you see is largely irrelevant."
Use the kinds of details that will be intuitively meaningful to your audience.	In "The Art of Failure" (p. 205), Malcolm Gladwell uses the technical term *perceptual narrowing*. But then he goes on to illustrate the term by talking about how people acted in a specific situation.

STRATEGIES	EXAMPLES FROM READINGS
Define only those terms that are likely to be unfamiliar or ambiguous to your particular audience.	Although Margaret Tomeo (p. 211) uses terminology that some people may not be familiar with (*Plyometrics, squats, lunges*), she does not define these terms since her audience of athletes already understands them. She does, however, carefully define the term *anterior cruciate ligament*; although her readers have heard of this ligament, they do not understand exactly what it is or how it functions.

{ Exercise } **Creating an Appropriate Voice**

Think about the way you want to sound. Do you want to seem formal or informal? Concerned? Helpful? Do you want readers to have the sense they are listening to you talk, almost as though you were having a conversation with them? Or do you want to seem more impersonal? To clarify and perhaps revise the voice of your report, try the following activities.

- Review your audience analysis and statement of purpose (revise what you have written if you need to).
- List some of the words and phrases you hope readers would use to describe the voice in your report.
- Show this list of words and phrases to a classmate or your instructor; ask this person to tell you whether the voice you hope to create makes sense, given what you have said about your intended audience and purpose.
- Using what you learn from your classmate or instructor, revise the list of words that describe the voice you want to create.
- Write a paragraph or two in which you explain one of the main points you will make in your report.
- Ask someone (a classmate, your instructor, or a friend) to read this passage aloud and listen to the sound of his or her voice. Can you hear the attitude you want to create in the sound of this reader's voice? If you can't, look closely at your draft to see what words and phrases you need to change in order to create the voice you want. ■

Organizing

People rarely read reports just for pleasure, and they are rarely willing to follow along patiently, waiting to see where you are headed or what point you are trying to make. Instead, readers usually try to make predictions about what you are going to say next and about how details or ideas are related to each other. And sometimes they just look for pieces of information that answer their questions, confirm their suspicions, or fill some gap in their understanding of the topic you are writing about. Consequently, you will need to organize your report so that readers will see what to expect you to say next and how sentences or paragraphs are related. You will also have to make information accessible; that is, you will need to make it easy for readers to find the information they are looking for. The following chart explains several ways you can do all this.

How to Organize

STRATEGIES	EXAMPLES FROM READINGS
To create clear expectations, use thesis statements, topic sentences, and forecasting words within paragraphs.	 The *thesis* of "The Record Industry's Slow Fade" (p. 176) appears at the end of the second paragraph: "The record business has plunged into a historic decline." The next paragraph begins with a clear *topic sentence*: "The major labels are struggling to reinvent their business models, even as some wonder whether it's too late." A sentence in the middle of the eighth paragraph includes this *forecasting phrase:* "Major-label moves that would have been unthinkable a few years back." The subsequent sentences list and briefly explain some of those "moves."
To make information accessible, consider using headings. Use wording that announces the topic to be discussed or the question to be answered in a given section of text.	 The headings in "The Perils of Higher Education" (p. 169) are whimsical ("Welcome to Margaritaville State University," for example), but they do announce or strongly imply the topic to be discussed.
Consider using visual elements (boldface type, white space, lists, charts, graphs) to highlight key points.	Many of these elements appear in "The Record Industry's Slow Fade." There is a pull quote set in boldface type ("We have a business that's dying . . ."), a graph showing the "erosion" of sales of record albums, and two numbered lists that enable readers to compare record sales in the year 2000 with record sales in 2006.

STRATEGIES	EXAMPLES FROM READINGS
To show how ideas or details are connected, use *transition words.*	To illustrate a moral dilemma involving a potential accident with a trolley that is running out of control, Carl Zimmer (p. 195) uses the following italicized transition words: "*Now* imagine that you are watching the runaway trolley from a footbridge. *This time* there is no fork in the track. *Instead,* five workers are on it, facing certain death. *But* you happen to be standing next to a big man. *If* you sneak up on him and push him off the footbridge, he will fall to his death. *Because* he is so big, he will stop the trolley. Do you willfully kill one man, or do you allow five people to die?"
Use words or phrases that refer to something mentioned previously.	After two paragraphs describing the desperate actions of a scuba diver whose air supply had been cut off, Malcolm Gladwell in "The Art of Failure" (p. 205) begins the next paragraph, "*This* [the actions recounted in preceding paragraphs] is a textbook example of panic."

Concluding

Although your instructor and some of your classmates will likely read your drafts from beginning to end, readers of other reports may not read your conclusion, especially if they are using your work as a fact sheet or a source for specific information. But even fact sheets can have conclusions, usually titled something like "For Further Reading" or "More to Explore." Other types of reports will require something more, if only to keep readers from assuming you have simply gotten tired of the topic and decided to stop. One way to conclude is to summarize the main ideas you presented and reiterate your basic point. This is a useful strategy, but it is not the only one.

How to Conclude

STRATEGIES	EXAMPLES FROM READINGS
Frame the report. Provide further information or comments about the topic that you mentioned at the beginning.	In the conclusion of "ACL: The Curse of Women Athletes" (p. 216), Margaret Tomeo refers briefly to Tiffany Woosley, the athlete whose injury she mentions in the first paragraph of her report.

continued on next page ▶

How to Conclude (continued)

STRATEGIES	EXAMPLES FROM READINGS
End with a story that dramatizes your main point. People often remember a good story. If you can tell one that reiterates your main point, you increase the chances of readers' remembering the gist of what you said.	 Malcolm Gladwell concludes "The Art of Failure" (p. 209) in much the same way he begins his report—with a story of a famous athlete's losing a major competition because he "choked." To emphasize the emotional consequences of losing in this manner, Gladwell reports that both the athlete and the man to whom he lost were reduced to tears.
Use a compelling quotation.	 After explaining the overwhelming difficulties of the record industry, "The Record Industry's Slow Fade" (p. 180) ends with a quotation from a former executive with the Recording Industry Association of America: "'We have great records, but we're less sure than ever that people are going to buy them. . . . There's a sense around here of losing faith.'"
End with the implications of what you have said. Readers should not come away wondering, "So what? How does all this affect me or things I care about?" It's a good idea to anticipate these questions, explaining how readers can use the information you reported to solve or avoid problems that matter to them.	After explaining what women athletes need to do to avoid injury, "ACL: The Curse of Women Athletes" concludes with the hope that "if we start now, we can greatly reduce the number of anterior cruciate tears that plague so many of our female players."

Designing Your Report and Integrating Visual Information

By this point you should know which major visual elements—headings, images, charts, graphs, or tables—you want to use in your report. Now it's time to think about the overall layout—where these elements will appear on the page (or screen), how many columns you will use, and whether you will include sidebars (also called inset boxes), pull quotes, or bulleted lists. As you do this, be sure to check with your instructor to see what other guidelines he or she has for the design of your report. The guidelines presented below are widely applicable, but they seem especially important for reports, where your basic goal is to convey credible information in ways that add to your audience's understanding of your topic while also reflecting your own perspective and achieving your specific purpose in creating your report. (See the list of purposes on page 164.)

You can find general guidelines on layout and the use of visuals in any type of writing in Chapter 9.

How to Design Your Report and Integrate Visual Information

STRATEGIES	EXAMPLES FROM READINGS
Choose visual elements that have a clear function— for example, helping to engage the audience, making information accessible, or elaborating on a point made in the written text. *Never use visuals just for decoration.*	When combined with the title "Seeing Is Not Believing" (p. 182), the images at the beginning of that report pose a question ("Can you tell which of these photos are real?") that should engage readers.
Locate visuals as close as possible to the passage of written text they relate to.	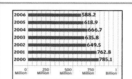 In "The Record Industry's Slow Fade" (p. 177), the inset box labeled "The Story of the Decline" appears alongside the written explanation of changes in the record industry.
Label each visual clearly, providing captions and acknowledging sources as necessary. In reports for technical or academic audiences, adding a caption means giving a visual a number—"Fig. 1," for example. In most captions for reports written in the humanities, you should add a label to the figure number, giving the source of the information, explaining what the visual represents, and indicating why its contents are important.	The first visual in "ACL: The Curse of Women Athletes" (p. 211) not only identifies the player depicted but also briefly connects the visual to the point it supports in the text and acknowledges the source of the image.
Choose photographs when you want to help readers see what you or someone else actually saw. Or use them when you want to give a concrete illustration of a generalization or abstract concept.	"Seeing Is Not Believing" illustrates the general problem of photo manipulation with a series of photographs that show how difficult it can be to detect photo manipulation.
Use line drawings when you want to highlight a few features of a subject. If you use a line drawing, you must be careful that it shows only the features you are concerned with, and those features must be clearly labeled.	The ACL is only one component of the human knee. But when Margaret Tomeo explains how the ACL functions in "ACL: The Curse of Women Athletes," she does not show all the details of the knee. She uses a line drawing that is clearly labeled and that shows only those aspects of the knee she is trying to explain.

continued on next page ▶

How to Design Your Report and Integrate Visual Information (continued)

STRATEGIES	EXAMPLES FROM READINGS
Use charts and bar graphs when you want to help readers make comparisons.	 In "The Record Industry's Slow Fade," the bar graph titled "The Story of the Decline" lets readers quickly compare overall sales figures for the years 2000 to 2006. The chart "Top Ten Albums, Now and Then" lets readers make more specific comparisons, giving the sales figures for the top ten albums in 2006 and in 2000.
Use inset boxes when you want to highlight key pieces of information or concepts.	In "Whose Life Would You Save?" (p. 193), inset boxes include drawings and questions that highlight the kinds of moral dilemmas the article is concerned with.

{ **Exercise** } **Sketching Out a Design**

Review the visuals in the reports in the Reading to Write section and any other reports you may have found as you were working on this assignment. Identify visual features (for example, charts, photographs, page layouts) that you think might be appropriate for your report. Discuss these features with your classmates or your instructor, explaining why you think they might be appropriate for your intended audience.

It can also help to sketch out how each page will look, indicating headings, written text, and rough sketches of the photographs, illustrations, and so forth that will appear on each page. Again, you should be able to explain to your classmates or instructor why you intend to use the visual features in your sketch and why you plan to arrange them in a certain way. Designers call this kind of rough sketch a mock-up. ■

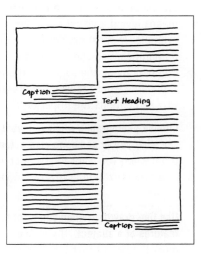

Creating a Review Draft

If you have not already begun to do so, now is the time to create a draft of your report. This is not a final draft, but neither is it a rough draft. Instead, it is a review draft; it represents the best effort you can make at this point. After completing this draft, you will need to assess it carefully not only by critiquing it yourself but also by getting others' perspectives. This means that you will subject the review draft to a final review (from one or more of your classmates or from your instructor). Then you will use this assessment to make revisions in content, organization, style, and format.

In preparation for writing the review draft, look back at what you have said about your audience and purpose. Has your sense of audience and purpose changed? If so, revise what you have said about audience and purpose and keep that in mind as you decide what to say and how to say it in the review draft. Also, look back at what you wrote when you were reflecting on information you had gathered. Do you need to modify any of the points expressed there? Are there any places where you need to add information that would make your points clearer or answer questions the audience is likely to ask? Finally, review your notes and working bibliography. Make sure that quotations and other references are accurate. Also make sure that each source is appropriately cited.

As you work on your review draft, think carefully about the introduction and conclusion. Does the introductory material establish the voice you want to create? Does it seem likely to engage the intended audience? Does the conclusion reinforce the basic point you want to convey? Do your introduction and conclusion still seem appropriate for your audience? If not, modify them by using one or more of the strategies identified in this chapter.

In addition, take some pains to organize your ideas. It might help to make an informal outline indicating your main points. You should also use the strategies described on pages 238–39 to organize your draft.

REVIEWING AND REVISING

Assess your review draft carefully—not only by critiquing it yourself, but also by getting others' perspectives in a final review. Then, use what you learn from this assessment to make revisions in content, organization, style, and format.

Getting a Final Review

Once you have made your review draft as complete and polished as you can, you need to have it reviewed by one or more people who understand the principles (analyzing audience, engaging readers, and so on) that you have been working with in this chapter. You will use this review to guide a revision of your review draft before you turn your work in for grading.

Give the reviewer a copy of your draft, one he or she can make notes on. Give the reviewer a copy of your audience analysis and statement of purpose. If necessary, revise your audience analysis and statement of purpose before giving this information to the reviewer. Ask the reviewer to adopt the perspective of the audience you have described and then use the following checklist in commenting on your work.

[**Checklist for Final Review**   ]

1. In my audience analysis and statement of purpose, please highlight any passages that give you a good sense of the knowledge, needs, and attitudes of my intended audience. Next, highlight phrases that help you understand exactly what purpose(s) I am hoping to achieve. Please indicate any statements that need to be clarified.

2. What are the main points I am making in my report? Given what I say about my audience and purpose, how likely does it seem that this report will be informative and credible to my intended audience?

3. In what specific passages have I developed my topic thoroughly, especially by answering questions my readers are likely to have? What are some passages in which you have questions about what I say, either because my writing seems unclear or because you think my audience would disagree? What are some strategies (explained on pp. 227, 228, and 231–32) I might use to make my report clearer, more complete, or more credible?

4. What portions of my introduction seem likely to engage the interest of my intended audience? What are some strategies (explained on pp. 233 and 234) that might make the introduction more engaging?

5. How would you describe the voice I have created? At what points does that voice seem appropriate, given my intended audience and the subject matter of my report? What strategies (explained on pp. 236–37) might help me make the voice clearer or more appropriate?

6. What are some words or phrases that show how I have organized my report? What strategies (explained on pp. 238–39) might I use to make the organization clearer?

7. Is the conclusion of my report effective? What strategies (explained on pp. 239–40) might I use to make it more effective?

8. If the report includes photographs or other visual elements, how do they help make it informative and credible? Are there any points at which I need to add more visual elements? If so, what should they be—headings, photographs, bulleted lists? At what points do I need to add or revise captions for photographs or legends for charts, graphs, and maps?

▶ Go to
**bedfordstmartins.com/
writingnow** to download these
questions from Chapter 4 >
Worksheets.

If possible, ask the reviewer to talk with you about your review draft as well as make notes on it. Be careful not to argue with the reviewer, especially if he or she raises questions or disagrees with something you have said. When this happens, try to find out why he or she is disagreeing or asking a particular question.

Revising Your Report

Up to this point, you have listened to your reviewer's comments without explaining, arguing, or making judgments about the validity of those comments. Once you have a good idea of how the reviewer responds to your report, however, you should go back through your notes on his or her comments. Bearing in mind your intended audience and purpose, decide which comments are most valid. Then revise your review draft, using strategies referred to in the Checklist for Final Review.

After resolving all the issues that need attention, proofread carefully and correct any typographical or formatting errors. Then submit this final draft to your instructor.

▷ TAKING STOCK OF WHERE YOU ARE

Although you will find differences among the writing assignments in this book, there are also some important similarities. For example, you always have to analyze the intended audience, write an introduction that will engage that particular audience, and so forth. Consequently, there should be a cumulative quality to the writing assignments you do from this book. Each assignment should teach you strategies that can help you grow as a writer and improve your work on subsequent assignments. But this will happen only if you make a conscious effort to assess your development as a writer as you go along.

To help with this assessment and growth, continually review what you're learning and try to determine what you need to work harder on in the future. Once your instructor has returned the final draft of your work, think back over all the comments you received—from classmates as well as your instructor—and write out answers to the following questions. (You might want to keep these in a journal or a special section of a notebook.)

1. What appears to be my greatest area of strength?
2. Where am I having the greatest difficulty?
3. What am I learning about the process of writing?
4. What am I learning about giving and receiving feedback on writing?
5. What have I learned from writing a report that I can use in my next assignment for this course, for another course, or for work?

[**Questions for Assessing Your Growth as a Writer**]

The responses that follow are Margaret Tomeo's answers to these questions for the report she wrote on ACL injuries (p. 211).

1. I think that I'm pretty good at gaining factual information and organizing it in a clear way. I think I also kept my readers in mind when I was writing the report so that the information appealed to them and was also important to them. My audience was very specific, and I think I did a good job focusing the paper on this audience and what questions they would want answered.

▶ Go to bedfordstmartins.com/ writingnow to download these questions from Chapter 4 > Worksheets.

2. Sometimes I had trouble because I knew what certain things meant so I assumed that my readers also knew what they meant. I needed to clarify or describe some points better and not make assumptions. I had trouble with the voice and tone in parts of the report because I'd jump from being personal to being informative. In my first draft, my paragraphs didn't flow together that well, so I needed to improve that. After I added some introductory and concluding sentences, the report flowed a lot better.

3. The process of writing takes a long time and many revisions. The report that you write may seem clear to you, but what is most important is that it is clear to your audience. To make sure of this, it's important to have as much feedback as possible, so get as many people as possible to read the report and state what they feel was done well or what could be improved on.

4. Receiving feedback is important because it allows you to clarify points that may seem clear to you but are vague to others. With the feedback, I was able to learn what points I needed to improve on. For example, I knew what "intrinsic" and "extrinsic" (in my first draft) meant, but my readers did not, so I needed to replace them with terms that were clearer.

5. You have to keep a specific audience in mind so that you know exactly to whom you are writing. Answering questions about the audience helps focus in on what questions the report should answer. This will also help you define the tone and voice of the report. Also, having a specific purpose in mind is important because it helps guide and focus the report. You have to choose a topic that will matter to other people, not just you. When we brainstormed and wrote down topics to write about, some topics didn't have a specific audience, so they weren't easy to write about; the papers about these topics seemed to lose focus.

Position Papers

Should people drive SUVs? Should consumers be worried about where their food comes from? Is the U.S. government doing enough to respond to natural disasters? What's wrong with drinking bottled water? Answers to such questions as these appear in a wide variety of media ranging from newspaper editorials and political cartoons, to television and talk radio shows, to electronic media such as blogs, discussion forums, and Web pages. These answers are produced by a similarly wide range of people, not just nationally known columnists but also organizations or individuals who simply have computer access. When people share positions on issues that matter to them, their goal is to influence an audience in some way. They may try to persuade an audience to change (what they think, how they act, what they believe) or to reinforce the audience's current ideas or ways of acting.

Position papers require writers to assert or strongly imply their opinions. All too often (in the case of many talk radio programs, for example) these assertions resemble shouting matches, with people vehemently claiming that their views are right and attacking people who disagree with them, saying these people are wrong, ill informed, misguided, or just plain stupid. But writing a good position paper is not the same as engaging in a shouting match. Position papers require not only asserting an opinion, but also providing evidence and reasoning that will lead an audience to accept that opinion. In other words, it is not enough just to tell people what you think or how you feel. Instead, you have to give them what they will see as a sound basis for sharing—or at least considering seriously—your thoughts and feelings.

Position papers routinely appear in newspaper editorials, in op-ed pieces, and in the work of columnists writing for newspapers and magazines. But you are also likely to encounter position papers almost any time people confront a topic about which reasonable people may disagree. Managers in a business, for example, may be deciding whether they should lay off workers during an economic slowdown. Some of these managers may point out that layoffs can reduce expenditures, but others may argue that layoffs can harm morale among employees who are not laid off. Or a school board may be deciding whether to implement a new instructional program. Some board members or parents may argue that the program has the potential to raise student scores or help reduce dropout rates. But others may be concerned about the cost of the program or may doubt that the program will have the benefits others claim. Consequently both managers and the school board face such questions as the following. What is the wisest (fairest, most ethical, most effective) course of action? Who will benefit? Who will be harmed? What course of action is most likely to achieve long-term goals? Answers to such questions may take the form of written documents, oral presentations, or even cartoons. But in all cases, a good answer—a good position paper—depends on both the evidence and reasoning that justify a writer's or speaker's position. In the case of cartoons, the reasoning may be implied rather than stated explicitly. But unless readers accept both the evidence and reasoning of any position paper, it is unlikely to influence anyone's opinion.

▷ READING POSITION PAPERS

In the following section, you will find position papers on a variety of topics ranging from why the crime rate in the United States has been decreasing to whether people should drink bottled water. Following each position paper, you will find questions that pertain specifically to what you have just read. In addition to these specific questions, there are several basic questions you should ask any time someone asserts and attempts to justify an opinion.

[Questions for
Reading Position
Papers]

▶ **Who is the intended audience?** Consider the language, visuals, and information included (and excluded) from the position paper. What does the writer appear to be assuming about the following?

- Readers' background knowledge of the subject
- Readers' assumptions about what constitutes credible evidence and valid reasons
- Readers' willingness to challenge the author's claims
- The biases or preconceptions readers have regarding the subject

▶ **What specific purpose(s) is the writer trying to accomplish?** In addition to achieving the basic goal of influencing readers' actions, thoughts, or beliefs, is the writer trying to accomplish a more specific purpose such as one or more of the following?

- Challenge readers' assumptions about an issue
- Refute a point of view the author disagrees with
- Gain respect for his or her opinions
- Alarm (or reassure) readers
- Express views readers may have felt but never articulated very clearly or emphatically

▶ **What claims or main points is the writer making?** Does the writer do one or more of the following?

- Simply repeat information that the readers already know
- Provide new information that either challenges or strengthens readers' positions
- Draw information from sources readers are likely to find credible

▶ **How credible is the argument?**

- Are the facts accurate and up-to-date?
- Is the writer ignoring facts or opinions that might challenge or modify his or her position?
- Does the writer give plausible reasons and evidence for his or her claims?
- Does the writer fairly represent the opinions of people who disagree with him or her?
- Does the writer make assumptions that seem questionable?

▶ **How well organized is the position paper?**

- Can readers readily identify the writer's main point (or thesis)?
- Can readers identify the main point of each paragraph?
- Does the writer stick to the point, or does he or she include extraneous information or jump from one topic to another for no apparent reason?
- Are details (written and visual) consistent with the point(s) the author is making?
- Is it easy to follow the sequence in which ideas and details are presented?
- Does the position paper seem to "flow," giving readers a clear sense of how a particular sentence or paragraph leads to the next?

▶ **What sort of voice would readers hear in the position paper?**

- Does the author make *logical appeals*, citing evidence and plausible reasons, anticipating and answering likely questions?
- Does the author make *emotional appeals*, using language and details that are likely to prompt strong feelings, showing how something will benefit or harm something or someone readers care passionately about?
- Does the author make *ethical appeals*, demonstrating that the writer is someone who is likable, trustworthy, and sympathetic to readers?
- Does the writer appear to have the experience and knowledge needed to speak authoritatively on the subject?

 { For Collaboration }　**Reading Position Papers**

Bring to class a position paper—an editorial, a magazine or newspaper column, a letter, a political cartoon—that you find interesting, either because it is very persuasive or because it presents an argument you find very weak. Then, working with one or two classmates, identify qualities that add to (or detract from) the credibility of the position paper you found. ∎

Many position papers rely principally on written text to argue for a writer's opinion. Although these arguments may include a wide range of visual features—photographs, charts, and distinctive page layouts, for example—visual elements are subordinate to words, serving mainly to highlight or reinforce the written text. But sometimes, especially in the case of editorial cartoons, visual features do most of the work, asserting claims and implying reasons for an opinion. In these situations, words comprise only a small part of the message, usually serving to make sure readers get the point of the cartoon. Since editorial cartoons are so widely read and influential, it is important to read them as carefully as you read written texts.

The questions below can help analyze—that is, read—visual images in any position paper, but they can be especially useful in reading editorial cartoons.

▶ What kinds of details are included in (or excluded from) the image? All visuals require some selection of details; photographs, for example, capture only some of what you might observe in a scene. Cartoons are especially selective, with cartoonists suggesting a specific viewpoint rather than presenting an objective view of objects or people.

▶ What physical attributes of people or objects are emphasized? Which attributes are exaggerated? Most editorial cartoons entail some distortion, emphasizing some physical characteristics while minimizing or excluding others to imply the cartoonist's point of view.

▶ What do those attributes suggest about the attitudes or values of the people represented in the cartoon?

▶ What associations do the details in the cartoon evoke in you? What people, objects, or events do these details bring to mind? What are your attitudes toward these people, objects, or events?

▶ What viewing angle is represented? What does that viewing angle imply? When the person or object is shown as if the viewer is looking up at it from below, this viewing angle makes the subject seem important, powerful, or threatening. If the perspective is that of looking downward, the angle tends to make the subject seem weak or unimportant. If the image lets viewers look head-on, the position is usually one of equality.

▶ If words appear in the cartoon, how do they clarify or emphasize the cartoonist's point of view?

To see how these questions can guide the analysis of a political cartoon that takes a position, consider the following example.

Physical attributes The man's smile looks like a smirk, suggesting complacency, self-satisfaction, or at least indifference to fuel efficiency. Although the word *sport* might be used in connection with his vehicle, it would never apply to the man himself.

Details The vehicle is obviously an SUV, a type of vehicle that typically has low gas mileage. The cartoon excludes details that would enable readers to recognize a specific SUV, suggesting that characteristics of this SUV are typical of vehicles in its class.

Words The license plate (GUZZLER) makes explicit the assertion implicit in the number of gasoline pumps needed to fill the tank of this SUV. And the phrase *fuel efficiency* appears in a cloud of windshield washer, something that has relatively little to do with the overall appearance or performance of the vehicle.

Viewing angle Viewers look down at the man and his vehicle, both literally and figuratively.

{ **Exercise** } ▶ Go to **bedfordstmartins.com/writingnow** to Chapter 5 > Visuals.

For practice analyzing the visual information in another position paper, see the visual exercises online. ■

{ Exercise } **Analyzing Visuals in Position Papers**

Bring to class a position paper that you find especially effective. This position paper may be either a cartoon or an article in which visuals are used effectively to help justify the writer's position. In either case, be able to explain how the visual elements provide evidence and state or imply reasons in support of the position being expressed. ■

▷ READING TO WRITE

People read position papers for any number of reasons. They may be struggling with a difficult decision (about which candidate to support in a hotly contested political race, for example), or they may be seeking a compelling explanation of the causes of a social trend. Or they may simply be looking for additional evidence and reasons to use in supporting a position they already hold. But in all cases, readers are looking for answers to one basic question: Why? That is, what evidence and reasons justify a particular decision, course of action, or interpretation of events in their lives or society at large?

The following position papers address this question with regard to several different topics about which reasonable people might disagree. These readings also reflect the different kinds of topics you might consider when you create your position paper for the major assignment in this chapter. After each of these essays, you will find a set of questions, titled Reflecting on What You Have Read, that will help you not only assess the content of the position paper but also recognize strategies and techniques you can use in your own writing. You will also find suggestions in the Thinking Ahead section, which will help you think of topics you might write about.

Go to
bedfordstmartins.com/
writingnow and click on
Chapter 5 > Examples for
additional position papers.

      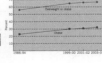

SUVs Belong in Car Ads Only

Ellen Goodman

A winner of the Pulitzer Prize, Ellen Goodman is a syndicated columnist whose work is published in newspapers throughout the United States. She has published six collections of her columns along with two books. Her most recent book, which she coauthored with Patricia O'Brien, is *I Know Just What You Mean: The Power of Friendship in Women's Lives*. As a syndicated columnist, Goodman has to write about topics that are general enough to be interesting to a variety of readers. Here, Goodman focuses on something that almost everyone in the United States is familiar with, Americans' fondness for SUVs. In arguing against SUVs, Goodman relies on her personal experiences. As you read, consider whether you think it is appropriate to talk about an issue of national concern primarily in terms of one's own experiences.

SUVs Belong in Car Ads Only

ELLEN GOODMAN

1   For my second career, I want to write car ads. Or better yet, I want to live in a car ad.

2   In the real world, you and I creep and beep on some misnomered expressway, but in the commercial fantasy land drivers cruise along deserted, tree-lined roads.

3   We stall and crawl on city streets but the man in the Lexus races "in the fast lane"—on an elevated road that curves around skyscrapers. We circle the block looking for a place to park, but the owner of a Toyota Rav4 pulls up onto the sandy beach. We get stuck in the tunnel, but the Escalade man navigates down empty streets because "there are no roadblocks." The world of the car ads bears about as much resemblance to commuter life as the Marlboro ads bear to the cancer ward.

4   All of this is a prelude to a full-boil rant against the archenemy of commuters everywhere: Sport utility vehicles. Yes, those gas-guzzling, parking-space-hogging, bullies of the highway.

5   In this, the last gasp of the 20th century, one out of every five cars sold in America is an SUV. These sport utility vehicles are bought primarily by people whose favorite sport is shopping and whose most rugged athletic event is hauling the kids to soccer practice.

6   The sales and the size of the larger SUVs have grown at a speed that reminds me of the defense budget. In the escalating highway arms race, SUVs are sold

255

for self-defense. Against what? Other SUVs.

As someone who has spent 7 many a traffic-jammed day in the shadow of a behemoth, I am not surprised that the high and weighty are responsible for some 2,000 additional deaths a year. If a 6,000-pound Suburban hits a 1,800-pound Metro, it's going to be bad for the Metro. For that matter, if the Metro hits the Suburban it's still going to be bad for the Metro.

The problem with SUVs is 8 that you can't see over them, you can't see around them, and you have to watch out for them. I am by no means the only driver of a small car who has felt intimidated by the big wheels barreling past me. Their macho reputation prompted even the Automobile Club of Southern California to issue an SUV driver tip: "Avoid a 'road warrior' mentality. Some SUV drivers operate under the false illusion that they can ignore common rules of caution."

But the biggest and burliest of 9 the pack aren't just safety hazards,

they're environmental hazards. Until now, SUVs have been allowed to legally pollute two or three times as much as automobiles. All over suburbia there are people who conscientiously drive their empty bottles to the suburban recycling center in vehicles that get 15 miles to the gallon. There are parents putting big bucks down for a big car so the kids can be safe while the air they breathe is being polluted.

At long last some small con- 10 trols are being promoted. The EPA has proposed for the first time that SUVs be treated like cars. If the agency, and the administration, has its way, a Suburban won't be allowed to emit more than a Taurus. That's an important beginning, but not the whole story.

Consider Ford, for example. The 11 automaker produces relatively clean-burning engines. But this fall it will also introduce the humongous Excursion. It's 7 feet tall, 80 inches wide, weighs four tons and gets 10 miles to the

gallon in the city. No wonder the Sierra Club calls it "the Ford Valdez." This is a nice car for taking the kids to school—if you're afraid you'll run into a tank.

Do I sound hostile? Last 12 week a would-be SUV owner complained to *The New York Times* ethics columnist that his friends were treating him as if he were "some kind of a criminal." The ethicist wrote back: "If you're planning to drive that SUV in New York, pack a suitcase into your roomy cargo area, because you're driving straight to hell."

I wouldn't go that far, though 13 I have wished that hot trip on at least one SUV whose bumper came to eye level with my windshield. It's one thing to have an SUV in the outback, and quite another to drive it around town. In the end, the right place for the big guy is in an ad. There, the skies are always clean, the drivers are always relaxed, and there's never, ever, another car in sight.

Reflecting on What You Have Read

1 What is Goodman's real claim in this article? How far did you have to read before you came to the claim? What do you think her purpose was in writing this column? Do you think she achieved her purpose? Why or why not?

2 In addition to her own driving experiences, what kind of evidence does Goodman use? Do you think this evidence is credible? Why or why not?

3 Although Goodman presents a lot of evidence in support of her position, she doesn't always make her reasons explicit. Look closely at some of her evidence and identify the reasons that enable her to draw her conclusions from this evidence. Would Goodman's argument be stronger if she had made her reasons explicit? Why or why not?

4 What attitudes and personality (or voice—see pp. 326–30) does Goodman convey? Go back through the column and underline or circle the features that give you a sense of her attitudes and personality.

Thinking Ahead

Goodman identifies a fairly routine aspect of daily experience that she thinks constitutes a problem. Reflect on your daily experience—at school, on a job, on a team, or in a club. Is there any aspect of this experience that in your opinion constitutes a significant problem? Is there an audience to whom you might express this opinion—especially an audience that might actually be able to do something to solve the problem?

SUVs
Steve Sack

Steve Sack is a nationally syndicated editorial cartoonist for the *Minneapolis Star Tribune* whose work also appears in such magazines as *Time, Newsweek,* and online in *Slate*. He began his career as a cartoonist with the student newspaper at his alma mater, the University of Minnesota. In 2006, he won the National Press Foundation's award for the best editorial cartoonist of that year. In this cartoon, Sack asserts his position concerning SUVs. As you look closely at the cartoon, notice the ways Sack gives multiple cues regarding his opinion.

Reflecting on What You Have Observed

1 Notice the person cleaning the windshield of the SUV. Is it safe to assume that he is the owner of the vehicle? Why or why not? Look closely at this person's face. What attitudes are suggested by the look on his face?

2 What reasons might Sack have had for drawing the license plate to read "GUZZLER"?

3 How many hoses are going into the gas tank? How does that number compare with the number of gasoline pumps? If you were Sack's editor, would you tell him to make the number of hoses equal to the number of gasoline pumps? Why or why not? Would making such a change alter the type of argument Sack is presenting?

Cheap Food Nation
Eric Schlosser

Eric Schlosser is an investigative journalist who lives in California. His writing has appeared in such magazines as *The Atlantic Monthly, The Nation,* and *Rolling Stone.* He has written two plays—*Americans* and *We the People*—based on American history, and he has won a National Magazine Award and a Sidney Hillman Foundation Award. Schlosser has appeared on a number of television programs such as *60 Minutes, NBC Evening News,* and *CBS Evening News.* He has also testified before Congress on ways bioterrorism can threaten America's food supplies. All three of his books (*Fast Food Nation, Reefer Madness,* and *Chew on This*) have been bestsellers, and in 2006, *Fast Food Nation* was made into a film. He is currently working on a book about prison reform. The following article appeared in *Sierra,* a nature magazine published by the Sierra Club.

Cheap Food Nation

Americans spend a smaller percentage of their income
on food than anyone else, but it costs us dearly.

By Eric Schlosser

1 Whenever a well-known athlete gets caught using anabolic steroids to run faster, pedal harder, or hit a baseball farther, there's a universal chorus of disapproval. Most Americans regard steroid use in sports as an unhealthy form of cheating. Under federal law, all performance-enhancing synthetic hormones are class III controlled substances; obtaining them without a prescription is a felony. Steroid users may suffer from a wide variety of physical and mental ailments, some of them irreversible—and the long-term effects of the drugs are unknown.

2 Meanwhile, for the past two decades, a number of the same steroids abused by athletes have been given to U.S. cattle on a massive scale. Without much publicity or government concern, growth hormones like testosterone are routinely administered to about 80 percent of the nation's feedlot cattle, accelerating their weight gain and making them profitable to slaughter at a younger age. The practice is legal in the United States but banned throughout the European Union, due to concerns about its effect on human health. A recent study by Danish scientists suggested that hormone residues in U.S. beef may be linked to high rates of breast and prostate cancer, as well as to early-onset puberty in girls. Hormone residues excreted in manure also wind up in rivers and streams. A 2003 study of male minnows downstream from one Nebraska feedlot found that many of them had unusually small testes. When female minnows in a laboratory were exposed to trenbolone—

Eric Schlosser: "Changing your eating habits can send ripples far and wide."

a synthetic hormone widely administered to cattle—they developed male sex organs.

The whole idea of bulking up cattle with 3 growth hormones symbolizes how the country's food system has gone wrong. Within a single generation, fundamental changes have occurred not only in how cattle are raised but also in how hogs and chicken are reared, fish are farmed, crops are grown, and most food is processed and distributed. The driving force behind all these changes has been the desire to make food cheaper and produce it faster. The industrialization of agriculture and livestock has made it possible for Americans to spend less of their annual income on food than anyone else in the world. But the true cost of this system can't be measured by the low prices at Wal-Mart and McDonald's. When you consider the harm being done to animals, the land, ranchers, farmers, and our national health, this fast and cheap food is much too expensive.

A narrow and ruthless vision of effi- 4 ciency now extends throughout the U.S. livestock industry, transforming sentient creatures into industrial commodities. Giving steroids to cattle doesn't improve the taste of beef. It doesn't make it more nutritious. It just makes beef cheaper by causing cattle to grow faster. The same pursuit of cheapness also removes livestock from their natural settings. Some feedlots now hold more than 100,000 animals. They live in each other's manure, eating grain from concrete troughs. Poultry houses typically contain tens of thousands of birds that see the outdoors only twice in their lives—on the day they're born and on the day they're taken to the slaughterhouse. Pigs are sensitive, affectionate animals, perhaps more intelligent than dogs. At modern hog farms, they often spend their entire lives crammed into small crates, becoming anxious, hostile, and depressed.

On the prairie, cattle manure serves as a 5 natural fertilizer, scattered intermittently for miles. At U.S. feedlots and factory farms, more than a trillion pounds of manure are deposited every year. On that scale and at such concentrations, a perfectly natural substance can become a toxic one. When the two cattle feedlots outside Greeley, Colorado, operate at full capacity, they produce more excrement than Atlanta, Boston, Denver, and St. Louis combined. But unlike those cities, factory farms don't have elaborate waste-treatment facilities. They either spray the manure on nearby fields or dump it into giant pits, euphemistically known as "lagoons." Runoff from these lagoons and fields is one of the leading causes of water pollution in the United States. The manure also pollutes the air with dangerous chemicals like hydrogen sulfide, causing respiratory and neurological illnesses. And it poisons the land with heavy metals like cadmium, selenium, zinc, copper, and arsenic, which are frequently added to livestock feed. When not fully digested, these mineral additives wind up in manure, then in the soil—and eventually in the animals and people who eat the crops grown in that soil.

6   For years, U.S. farmers and ranchers have been told that the latest chemical and technological advances—hormones, pesticides, genetically modified crops, concentrated animal feeding operations—would increase their income. Instead, farmers and ranchers are steadily being driven off the land. Nine out of ten hog farmers have left the business since 1979. Those who remain are essentially employees of big processors like Smithfield Foods. Poultry growers have lost their independence in much the same way, investing large amounts of their own capital while obeying the directives of Tyson Foods. This concentration has been exacerbated by the lax enforcement of antitrust laws. In 1970s, the top four meatpacking companies controlled 21 percent of the beef market. Today they control nearly 85 percent. The industry is more concentrated than it was in 1906, when Upton Sinclair attacked the unchecked power of the beef trust in *The Jungle*.

7   Such systemic changes might be justifiable if all this fast, cheap food greatly benefited the people who eat it. During the past 30 years, however, industrialized agriculture has posed grave new threats to human health. The incidence of food-borne illness has risen, as gigantic processing facilities serve as an ideal vector for spreading pathogens far and wide. The emergence of mad cow disease and *E. coli* O157:H7 has been linked to changes in how cattle are raised. The indiscriminate use of antibiotics in livestock feed has helped to create new superbugs that can sicken people. And the mass marketing of inexpensive, fatty, high-calorie foods has fueled epidemics of obesity and diabetes. The cost of a 99-cent hamburger doesn't include the dialysis you may need years later.

8   None of this was inevitable. Nor was it the result of the invisible hand or free-market forces. Despite a fondness for free-market rhetoric, the country's large food companies—ConAgra, Archer Daniels Midland, McDonald's, Kraft—have benefited enormously from the absence of real competition. They receive, directly and indirectly, huge subsidies from the federal government. About half of the annual income earned by U.S. corn farmers now comes from government crop-support programs. Cheap corn is turned into cheap fats, oils, sweeteners, and animal feed. Nearly three-quarters of the corn grown in the United States is fed to livestock, providing taxpayer support for inexpensive hamburgers and chicken nuggets. On the other hand, farmers who grow fresh fruits and vegetables receive few direct subsidies. The farm bills Congress enacts every year, with strong backing from agribusiness, help determine what Americans eat, promoting unhealthy foods and making wholesome ones relatively more expensive.

Throughout the European Union, laws have been passed to guarantee food safety and animal welfare, restrict the use of antibiotics among livestock, ban genetically engineered foods, encourage organic production, and begin the deindustrialization of agriculture. These laws do not mean a return to the 19th century. On the contrary, they encourage the wise, careful application of 21st-century technology, along with a sense of humility before nature. U.S. fast-food and agribusiness companies aren't deliberately trying to mistreat animals, poison the land, or sicken their customers. But their relentless pursuit of the fast and the cheap is doing those very things. Like the chemical companies a generation ago that dumped toxic waste in streams without a second thought, they're imposing external costs on the rest of society. And nobody is stopping them—yet.

It would be wonderful if our government cared more about public safety and environmental health than about the profits of a handful of corporations. It would be terrific if the passage of new laws solved every one of these problems. Meaningful change, however, isn't going to come from the top. It's going to come from people who realize that there's a direct link between the food they eat and the society they inhabit. Changing your eating habits can send ripples far and wide in support of agricultural practices that are humane, diverse, and sustainable. "The condition of the passive consumer of food is not a democratic condition," Wendell Berry writes. "One reason to eat responsibly is to live free." ■

Reflecting on What You Have Read

1 Schlosser begins "Cheap Food Nation" by mentioning two apparently contradictory attitudes toward the use of steroids. We ban the use of steroids for purposes of enhancing athletic performance and yet accept it for a different purpose—speeding up the growth of livestock. How concerned are you about this contradiction? Does pointing out this contradiction seem like an effective way to begin this article? Why or why not?

2 Schlosser indicates that the use of steroids may have serious consequences for humans' health. But the key word here is *may*: Steroids may cause "irreversible" mental or physical damage; they may increase the chances of developing various kinds of cancers; they may increase the likelihood people will develop kidney failure and, thus, need to be on dialysis. Does the fact that Schlosser can say only that these consequences *may* happen (rather than *will* happen) weaken his argument? Why or why not?

3 By contrast with what he can say about potential consequences for humans' health, Schlosser can talk about actual consequences to farmers and to the livestock that are fed steroids. How concerned should we be about these consequences? What reasons would justify either concern or lack of concern?

4 Identify a paragraph in which you think Schlosser's argument seems especially strong or weak. Notice the details and the language found in that paragraph. Given his use of details and language, would you say Schlosser is making an emotional appeal, a logical appeal, or both (see pp. 326–30)? What basis do you have for your answers?

5 Schlosser argues (in para. 3) that the low cost of food is offset when we consider the harm being done to animals, ranchers, farmers, farmlands, and our health. Do you find that argument persuasive? Why or why not?

6 Schlosser concludes by saying "meaningful change . . . isn't going to come from the top"—that is, from government regulation. This sort of change, writes Schlosser, will happen only when individuals change their eating habits. Do you accept Schlosser's conclusion? Why or why not?

Thinking Ahead

In "Cheap Food Nation," Schlosser argues by pointing out ways a familiar, widely accepted practice leads to unintended or unanticipated consequences. People don't, for example, buy inexpensive food because they want to harm other people, animals, or the environment. The harm is simply an unintended consequence of their actions. Can you think of other examples of unintended consequences, situations in which people's actions lead to more harm (or good) than they imagined? If so, can you identify evidence and reasons that will lead people to recognize the consequences of their actions and, if necessary, change the way they act?

Drop in the Bucket

Karrie Jacobs

Karrie Jacobs is a journalist and contributing editor to *Metropolis*, a magazine devoted to understanding connections between architecture and the social and natural environments. Before coming to *Metropolis*, Jacobs was architecture critic of *New York Magazine*. She has written about architecture and design for many periodicals including the *New York Times, ID,* and *Fortune*. She was one of the founding editors of *Dwell*, a magazine devoted to modern architecture and design, and she is the author of *The Perfect $100,000 House*, in which she reports on her travels in search of well-built, attractive homes that cost less than $100,000. As you read the essay that follows, consider ways in which Jacobs's understanding of architecture informs her criticism of efforts to provide housing for victims of Hurricane Katrina.

Drop in the Bucket

The number of housing initiatives currently under way in New Orleans is impressive, but without active federal involvement they fall well short of the urgent need.

By Karrie Jacobs

If in late August 2005 you were fortunate 1 enough to be well away from the path of Hurricane Katrina, you were probably watching it on TV. And what you might remember was that frustrating, infuriating sensation of seeing the city of New Orleans, especially its poorest citizens, abandoned by every level of government. There was so much anger afterward, and so many eloquent words spoken—remember President Bush in front of St. Louis Cathedral in his shirt-sleeves—that you would assume that our government was now doing everything possible to make up for that catastrophic failure. As it turns out, that would be a misplaced assumption.

I was in New Orleans 2 in December working on a happy story about Albert Ledner, an 83-year-old Modernist architect who'd brought his one-of-a-kind Katrina-damaged home back to life. Ledner was lucky. His Lakewood South neighborhood was far enough away from the breach in the 17th Street Canal that his house only filled with five feet of water instead of the ten or more farther north. And his insurance company came through.

In Ledner's affluent part of town, it seems as if half the houses are now occupied. That's as good as it gets in the portions of the city that were flooded. After showing me his place, Ledner drove me to Lakewood North and then across town to the Lower Ninth Ward. Closer to where the levee failed, you see more vacant lots where houses have been demolished and more FEMA trailers in front of boarded-up houses. Farther east, in the poorest neighborhoods, especially the Lower Ninth Ward, there are few signs of life. So if you weren't well insured and creditworthy, you're not likely to be back in your New Orleans home. Current estimates put the city's population at about 200,000, less than half the pre-Katrina figure of 485,000. A program called the Road Home, which was supposed to issue grants of up to $150,000 to help the city's residents make their homes habitable again, has as of late December issued grants to 104 out of a total of 91,581 applicants. 3

Initially I believed that rebuilding would be a tremendous opportunity for anyone who cares about innovative approaches to housing. To a limited extent, it has been. Modular-home builders from all over the country are setting up shop in the region, and nonprofits have run architectural competitions to encourage exemplary practices. Global Green USA—an environmental organization with Brad Pitt as one of its celebrity figureheads—held a sustainable-design competition for New Orleans and in August announced a winner, a stylish mixed-use development, by a New York firm called Workshop/apd, featuring modular construction techniques and green roofs. The organization has spent about $100,000 acquiring a site in the Lower Ninth Ward and is now looking for private investors to help it build this model "zero energy" development including a 12-unit multi-family building and six single-family homes. 4

Of the many volunteer organizations working along the Gulf Coast, Habitat for Humanity has been especially energetic. In October 2005, faced with a shortage of volunteers and infrastructure, Habitat began what it calls "Operation Home Delivery," shipping pre-framed houses down the Mississippi River from Minneapolis on barges. Since then, local chapters in Louisiana, Mississippi, and Alabama have stepped in to build a range of modest houses. The church-based organization recently announced the start of its 500th house in the region and plans to have 1,000 completed or under way by midyear. 5

While these efforts (and many more that I haven't cited) will provide roofs for some families, it is nowhere near enough. When you drive through the Lower Ninth Ward of New Orleans or Mississippi towns like Waveland and see the vast empty stretches punctuated by the occasional FEMA trailer, even Habitat's ambitious goal of 1,000 seems like the wrong order of magnitude. 6

You would think that the federal government would be down there, spearheading rebuilding efforts, cutting through red tape, and awarding big contracts to some of those modular-home builders. But the most ambitious initiative from the Feds so far is the Department of Housing and Urban Development's controversial plan to demolish 4,500 units of New Orleans public housing and replace them with mixed-income developments. Parts of the demolition would be done under the auspices of HOPE VI, a Clinton-era program intended to break up the entrenched pockets of poverty in massive Chicago-style housing projects. But here it seems like a perversion of the program's goals—if not flat out criminal—to demolish structurally sound buildings in the midst of a catastrophic housing shortage. It's a decision 7

Louisiana is planning infill development in hard-hit neighborhoods using a version of the Katrina Cottage and something called a Carpet Cottage, designed by Andrés Duany, to answer the need for high-density single-story housing.

that reinforces the widespread belief that the federal government's failure to aid the city's abandoned underclass in the days following the hurricane was due to something worse than incompetence.

And then there's FEMA. On the Friday 8 before Christmas, FEMA announced the recipients of awards from its Alternative Housing Pilot Program. Finally, I thought, the Feds are doing something right. But on closer examination, this oddly structured program is a study in half measures. It was set up so that the states of Alabama, Louisiana, Mississippi, and Texas had to compete against one another for $400 million in funding. Each state proposed pilot programs to test new types of emergency housing, and in the end Mississippi got the lion's share of the money, some $281 million. Louisiana was allocated $74.5 million. (Politically adroit Mississippi governor Haley Barbour, former chairman of the Republican National Committee, has generally proved better than his neighbors at securing and distributing funds. Out of 17,490 applicants for that state's $5 billion federally funded Homeowner's Assistance Grants, about 8,547 have been awarded.)

The real winner here appears to be architect 9 Marianne Cusato and her endearing Katrina Cottage, which featured heavily in the successful Mississippi and Louisiana bids. It was the biggest success story to emerge from the massive Gulf Coast New Urbanist charrette held in Biloxi in October 2005. A small traditional shotgun house designed for rapid, inexpensive construction, it's been picked up for distribution in kit form by Lowe's.

Mississippi plans to use its money to develop 10 improved mobile homes, including a version of Cusato's cottage renamed the Mississippi Cottage, which can be delivered on wheels. Louisiana is planning infill development in hard-hit New Orleans neighborhoods using a version of the Katrina Cottage and something called a Carpet Cottage, designed by Andrés Duany, to answer the need for high-density single-story housing.

According to Cusato, "Both the Katrina and 11 the Carpet Cottages that we will be building with FEMA in the state of Louisiana are permanent buildings." Technically, FEMA doesn't fund permanent housing, so these programs are actually intended to develop new forms of temporary housing. "This pilot program is aimed at exploring options for future disasters," Cusato explains. "It is really a blueprint for how we react in the future." So while some people who were made homeless by Katrina and Rita will get permanent houses out of this exercise, the goal is to find a cost-effective replacement for the ubiquitous FEMA trailer. According to Duany, Louisiana governor Kathleen Blanco believes the funding will build 600 units at $125,000 each.

Duany, who has set up shop in New Orleans, 12 argues that what is needed for the city to be properly rebuilt is a work-around. He says the city's distinct culture is a product of its low cost of living. Eliminate the mortgage-free way of life, and you eliminate the culture. "No way," he contends, "are government grants going to put people in houses without debt." Rather than having the government dictate guidelines to rebuild houses that were in many cases cobbled together generations ago, he suggests suspending building codes in certain parts of the city so that people can rebuild cheaply, in the same improvisatory manner as their grandparents.

Duany's suggestion is brilliant, but his 13 limited-zoning plan can also be read as complete lack of faith in the government to do anything useful or right. And that's the really bad news: the Bush administration has performed so miserably that no one any longer expects anything from it. The biggest thing destroyed by Katrina was not the city of New Orleans but the notion that government exists in part to help those who can't help themselves. ■

Reflecting on What You Have Read

1 In "Drop in the Bucket," Jacobs is concerned with government policies that affect large numbers of the citizens of New Orleans. Although she is not one of those people, Jacobs begins her position paper by talking about her personal experiences in two different parts of the city. What reasons do you see for Jacobs beginning in this way?

2 Although Jacobs is extremely critical of efforts to rebuild New Orleans, she devotes much of her article to pointing out the good work done by such groups as Habitat for Humanity, Global Green USA, and other volunteer organizations. What justifications do you see for her doing this? Does it enhance or undermine her credibility as a critic of rebuilding efforts?

3 In paragraph 7, Jacobs claims that "the federal government's failure to aid the city's abandoned underclass . . . was due to something worse than incompetence." What is that *something*? That is, what is Jacobs implying about the reasons New Orleans's underclass did not receive more assistance? Does her implication seem justified? Why or why not?

4 Notice the different passages in which Jacobs criticizes governmental efforts to rebuild New Orleans. Given the evidence and reasons Jacobs presents in those passages, do her criticisms seem justified? Why or why not?

Thinking Ahead

When individuals, organizations, or governmental agencies respond to a significant problem, there's often a question as to whether their response is adequate or whether they have done everything possible. Can you think of significant problems (at school, at work, or in a social organization) that people have attempted to solve? Were those solutions adequate? What kinds of evidence and reasons might you give to show how adequate or inadequate the solutions were?

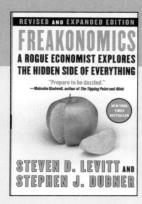

Where Have All the Criminals Gone?
Steven D. Levitt and Stephen J. Dubner

Steven D. Levitt is a professor of economics at the University of Chicago whose well-known writings address a wide audience on subjects that are not usually considered by economists. He has written, for example, about ways the structure of juvenile gangs parallels the structure of large corporations. In 2006, his work on connections between economics and popular culture led *Time* magazine to name him one of the "100 People Who Shape Our World." Stephen J. Dubner, coauthor of *Freakonomics* (2005), is a journalist and author of three other books, including the bestseller *Choosing My Religion* (2006). His articles have appeared in *Time* and *Slate* magazines, and he publishes frequently in the *New York Times* and the *New York Times Magazine*. As you read the following excerpt from *Freakonomics*, consider whether evidence and reasons in this excerpt challenge some widely held assumptions about why the crime rate decreased from 1991 to 2001. Can the decrease be explained by changes in the economy or in the system of justice—the reinstatement of the death penalty, for example, or increases in the number of criminals sent to prison? In the first of two readings on these questions, Steven D. Levitt and Stephen J. Dubner reject all of these explanations.

Where Have All the Criminals Gone?

1   When the crime rate began falling in the early 1990s, it did so with such speed and suddenness that it surprised everyone. It took some experts many years to even recognize that crime was falling, so confident had they been of its continuing rise. Long after crime had peaked, in fact, some of them continued to predict ever darker scenarios. But the evidence was irrefutable: the long and brutal spike in crime was moving in the opposite direction, and it wouldn't stop until the crime rate had fallen back to the levels of forty years earlier.

2   Now the experts hustled to explain their faulty forecasting. The criminologist James Alan Fox explained that his warning of a "bloodbath" was in fact an intentional overstatement. "I never said there would be blood flowing in the streets," he said, "but I used strong terms like 'bloodbath' to get people's attention. And it did. I don't apologize for using alarmist terms." (If Fox seems to be offering a distinction without a difference—"bloodbath" versus "blood flowing in the streets"—we should remember that even in retreat mode, experts can be self-serving.)

3   After the relief had settled in, after people remembered how to go about their lives without the pressing fear of crime, there arose a natural question: just where did all those criminals go?

4   At one level, the answer seemed puzzling. After all, if none of the criminologists, police officials, economists, politicians, or others who traffic in such matters had foreseen the crime decline, how could they suddenly identify its causes?

But this diverse army of experts now marched out a phalanx of hypotheses to explain the 5 drop in crime. A great many newspaper articles would be written on the subject. Their conclusions often hinged on which expert had most recently spoken to which reporter. Here, ranked by frequency of mention, are the crime-drop explanations cited in articles published from 1991 to 2001 in the ten largest-circulation papers in the LexisNexis database:

CRIME-DROP EXPLANATION	NUMBER OF CITATIONS
1. Innovative policing strategies	52
2. Increased reliance on prisons	47
3. Changes in crack and other drug markets	33
4. Aging of the population	32
5. Tougher gun-control laws	32
6. Strong economy	28
7. Increased number of police	26
8. All other explanations (increased use of capital punishment, concealed-weapons laws, gun buybacks, and others)	34

If you are the sort of person who likes guessing games, you may wish to spend the next few 6 moments pondering which of the preceding explanations seem to have merit and which don't. Hint: of the seven major explanations on the list, only three can be shown to have contributed to the drop in crime. The others are, for the most part, figments of someone's imagination, self-interest, or wishful thinking. Further hint: one of the greatest measurable causes of the crime drop does not appear on the list at all, for it didn't receive a single newspaper mention.

Let's begin with a fairly uncontroversial one: *the strong economy*. The decline in crime that 7 began in the early 1990s was accompanied by a blistering national economy and a significant drop in unemployment. It might seem to follow that the economy was a hammer that helped beat down crime. But a closer look at the data destroys this theory. It is true that a stronger job market may make certain crimes relatively less attractive. But that is only the case for crimes with a direct financial motivation—burglary, robbery, and auto theft—as opposed to violent crimes like homicide, assault, and rape. Moreover, studies have shown that an unemployment decline of 1 percentage point accounts for a 1 percent drop in nonviolent crime. During the 1990s, the unemployment rate fell by 2 percentage points; nonviolent crime, meanwhile, fell by roughly *40* percent. But an even bigger flaw in the strong-economy theory concerns violent crime. Homicide fell at a greater rate during the 1990s than any other sort of crime, and a number of reliable studies have shown virtually *no* link between the economy and violent crime. This weak link is made even weaker by glancing back to a recent decade, the 1960s, when the economy went on a wild growth spurt—as did violent crime. So while a strong

1990s economy might have seemed, on the surface, a likely explanation for the drop in crime, it almost certainly didn't affect criminal behavior in any significant way.

Unless, that is, "the economy" is construed in a broader sense—as a means to build and maintain hundreds of prisons. Let's now consider another crime-drop explanation: *increased reliance on prisons*. It might help to start by flipping the crime question around. Instead of wondering what made crime fall, think about this: why had it risen so dramatically in the first place? 8

During the first half of the twentieth century, the incidence of violent crime in the United States was, for the most part, fairly steady. But in the early 1960s, it began to climb. In retrospect, it is clear that one of the major factors pushing this trend was a more lenient justice system. Conviction rates declined during the 1960s, and criminals who were convicted served shorter sentences. This trend was driven in part by an expansion in the rights of people accused of crimes—a long overdue expansion, some would argue. (Others would argue that the expansion went too far.) At the same time, politicians were growing increasingly softer on crime—"for fear of sounding racist," as the economist Gary Becker has written, "since African-Americans and Hispanics commit a disproportionate share of felonies." So if you were the kind of person who might want to commit a crime, the incentives were lining up in your favor: a slimmer likelihood of being convicted and, if convicted, a shorter prison term. Because criminals respond to incentives as readily as anyone, the result was a surge in crime. 9

It took some time, and a great deal of political turmoil, but these incentives were eventually curtailed. Criminals who would have previously been set free—for drug-related offenses and parole revocation in particular—were instead locked up. Between 1980 and 2000, there was a fifteenfold increase in the number of people sent to prison on drug charges. Many other sentences, especially for violent crime, were lengthened. The total effect was dramatic. By 2000, more than two million people were in prison, roughly four times the number as of 1972. Fully half of that increase took place during the 1990s. 10

The evidence linking increased punishment with lower crime rates is very strong. Harsh prison terms have been shown to act as both deterrent (for the would-be criminal on the street) and prophylactic (for the would-be criminal who is already locked up). Logical as this may sound, some criminologists have fought the logic. A 1977 academic study called "On Behalf of a Moratorium on Prison Construction" noted that crime rates tend to be high when imprisonment rates are high, and concluded that crime would fall if imprisonment rates could only be lowered. (Fortunately, jailers did not suddenly turn loose their wards and sit back waiting for crime to fall. As the political scientist John J. DiIulio Jr. later commented, "Apparently, it takes a Ph.D. in criminology to doubt that keeping dangerous criminals incarcerated cuts crime.") 11

The "Moratorium" argument rests on a fundamental confusion of correlation and causality. Consider a parallel argument. The mayor of a city sees that his citizens celebrate wildly when their team wins the World Series. He is intrigued by this correlation but, like the "Moratorium" author, fails to see the direction in which the correlation runs. So the 12 following year, the mayor decrees that his citizens start celebrating the World Series *before the first pitch is thrown*—an act that, in his confused mind, will ensure a victory.

There are certainly plenty of reasons to dislike the huge surge in the prison population. Not everyone is pleased that such a significant fraction of Americans, especially black Americans, live behind bars. Nor does prison even begin to address the root causes of crime, which are diverse and complex. Lastly, prison is hardly a cheap solution: it costs about $25,000 a year to keep someone incarcerated. But if the goal here is to explain the drop in crime in the 1990s, imprisonment is certainly one of the key answers. It accounts for roughly one-third of the drop in crime.   13

Another crime-drop explanation is often cited in tandem with imprisonment: *the increased use of capital punishment.* The number of executions in the United States quadrupled between the 1980s and the 1990s, leading many people to conclude—in the context of a debate that has been going on for decades—that capital punishment helped drive down crime. Lost in the debate, however, are two important facts.   14

First, given the rarity with which executions are carried out in this country and the long delays in doing so, no reasonable criminal should be deterred by the threat of execution. Even though capital punishment quadrupled within a decade, there were still only 478 executions in the entire United States during the 1990s. Any parent who has ever said to a recalcitrant child, "Okay, I'm going to count to ten and this time I'm *really* going to punish you," knows the difference between deterrent and empty threat. New York State, for instance, has not as of this writing executed a single criminal since reinstituting its death penalty in 1995. Even among prisoners on death row, the annual execution rate is only 2 percent—compared with the 7 percent annual chance of dying faced by a member of the Black Gangster Disciple Nation crack gang. If life on death row is safer than life on the streets, it's hard to believe that the fear of execution is a driving force in a criminal's calculus. Like the $3 fine for late-arriving parents at the Israeli day-care centers, the negative incentive of capital punishment simply isn't serious enough for a criminal to change his behavior.   15

The second flaw in the capital punishment argument is even more obvious. Assume for a moment that the death penalty *is* a deterrent. How much crime does it actually deter? The economist Isaac Ehrlich, in an oft-cited 1975 paper, put forth an estimate that is generally considered optimistic: executing 1 criminal translates into 7 fewer homicides that the criminal might have committed. Now to the math. In 1991, there were 14 executions in the United States; in 2001, there were 66. According to Ehrlich's calculation, those 52 additional executions would have accounted for 364 fewer homicides in 2001—not a small drop, to be sure, but less than 4 percent of the actual decrease in homicides that year. So even in a death penalty advocate's best-case scenario, capital punishment could explain only one twenty-fifth of the drop in homicides in the 1990s. And because the death penalty is rarely given for crimes other than homicide, its deterrent effect cannot account for a speck of decline in other violent crimes.   16

It is extremely unlikely, therefore, that the death penalty, as currently practiced in the   17
United States, exerts any real influence on crime rates. Even many of its onetime supporters
have come to this conclusion. "I feel morally and intellectually obligated simply to concede
that the death penalty experiment has failed," said U.S. Supreme Court Justice Harry A.
Blackmun in 1994, nearly twenty years after he had voted for its reinstatement. "I no longer
shall tinker with the machinery of death."

Reflecting on What You Have Read

1 At the beginning of the passage you have just read, Levitt and Dubner mention a number
of authorities who had predicted that crime rates would increase. How would you
describe Levitt and Dubner's attitudes toward these authorities? What specific words,
phrases, or details reflect those attitudes? Given the information Levitt and Dubner
present, do those attitudes seem justified? Why or why not?

2 Levitt and Dubner use rather strong language in rejecting several widely accepted
theories as to why the crime rate decreased. For example, in (paragraph 7) they write, "a
closer look at the data destroys this theory." Instead of *destroys*, they could have used a
more neutral term—*refutes* or *challenges*, for example. Does their use of *destroys* seem
justified? Does their use of such language influence your reaction to their arguments? If
so, how and why? If not, why not?

3 Levitt and Dubner present a good bit of statistical information, but they don't always
explain exactly where they found the data. For example, in paragraph 11, they assert,
"the evidence linking increased punishment with lower crime rates is very strong." But
they don't indicate where this evidence comes from. Does this weaken their argument?
Why or why not?

4 Although one might assume that sentencing people to death would account for at least
some of the decrease in crime, Levitt and Dubner reject this assumption, claiming that
"no reasonable criminal should be deterred by the threat of execution." As part of their
argument, Levitt and Dubner draw a parallel between the threat of execution and a
parent's threat to punish a child. Does this parallel seem persuasive? Why or why not?

Thinking Ahead

Levitt and Dubner identify and argue against several well-known theories for recent drops in
crime rates. Identify some situations in which seemingly obvious causes for a problem might
not be the most significant causes. What reasons and evidence can you find that might
persuade readers to change their minds about the causes for a problem that concerns them?

What Decreased Crime?

John R. Lott Jr.

John R. Lott Jr. is an economist and a senior research scientist at the University of Maryland, College Park. Before coming to the University of Maryland, he taught at several universities including the University of Chicago, Yale University, and Stanford University. In his books and articles, Lott challenges conventional assumptions on many topics, including the reasons for increases in gasoline prices, the forces that help keep politicians honest, problems caused by government intervention in business and politics, and the failure of gun control laws to decrease the crime rate in America. The following reading is an excerpt from his book *Freedomnomics: Why the Free Market Works and Other Half-Baked Theories Don't* (2007), where Lott challenges many of the arguments presented in Steven D. Levitt and Stephen J. Dubner's book *Freakonomics* (2005). As you read this excerpt, consider ways in which Lott's evidence and reasoning differ from the evidence and reasoning presented in the excerpt preceding this one from Levitt and Dubner's book.

What Decreased Crime?

What Decreased Crime? Part I

The Death Penalty

If abortion and affirmative action policies actually increased crime, then what caused the huge fall in crime in the 1990s? Although it would be nice and neat if we could identify a single element as *the* solution, the truth is that numerous factors combined to drive down crime. One of the most important of these was the Supreme Court's 1976 decision to rescind the ban on the death penalty. Three-quarters of the states soon re-imposed the death penalty, though it wasn't until the early 1990s that significant numbers of executions began occurring again. 1

Capital punishment clearly increases the risk to criminals of engaging in various crimes, especially murder. Does this increased risk affect criminals' behavior? Before trying to answer this question, let's first consider how another group that faces similar dangers reacts to the risk of death. 2

Academics classify being a police officer as an "extremely dangerous" job.[1] In 2005, fifty-five police officers were murdered on the job, while another sixty-seven were accidentally killed.[2] With nearly 700,000 full-time, sworn law enforcement officers in the United States, the murder rate of police officers comes to one in 12,500,[3] a ratio that jumps to one in 5,600 when we include accidental deaths. 3

Although the risks of policing cannot be eliminated, police officers undertake a vari- 4
ety of measures to reduce the dangers: they wear bullet-proof vests, develop special procedures for approaching stopped cars, and in some situations officers wait for backup
even when this increases the probability that a suspect will escape.

Officers undertake all these measures as a natural human reaction to the risk of 5
death—the riskier an activity, the more a person will usually avoid it or take steps to
make the activity safer. This rule applies to violent criminals just like anyone else. And the
risk that a violent criminal faces from execution is much greater than the risk of a police
officer being killed. In 2005, there were almost 16,700 murders in the United States and
sixty executions.[4] That translates to one execution for every 278 murders. In other words,
a murderer is twenty times more likely to be executed than a police officer is to be deliberately or accidentally killed on duty.[5]

Those who argue that the death penalty has no effect on violent crime assume that 6
the risk of execution in no way deters criminals from committing capital crimes. "It is
hard to believe that fear of execution would be a driving force in a rational criminal's calculus in modern America," writes Steven Levitt.[6] While criminals, just like police officers,
are naturally less adverse to danger than, say, school teachers or accountants, the notion
that it is irrational for them to take into account such an enormous additional risk runs
contrary to human nature.[7]

There is widespread public debate over the effectiveness of the death penalty. Sadly, 7
this has included some misleading reporting in the popular press. Take a widely publicized *New York Times* study that compared murder rates in 1998 in states with and without the death penalty.[8] The *Times* concluded that capital punishment was ineffective in
reducing crime, noting that "10 of the 12 states without capital punishment have homicide rates below the national average . . . while half the states with the death penalty have
homicide rates above the national average."

This simple comparison really doesn't prove anything. The twelve states without the 8
death penalty have long enjoyed relatively low murder rates due to factors unrelated to
capital punishment.[9] When the death penalty was suspended nationwide from 1968 to
1976, the murder rate in these twelve states was still lower than in most other states. What
is much more important is that the states that reinstituted the death penalty had about a
38 percent larger drop in murder rates by 1998.[10]

There were no executions in the United States between 1968 and 1976, a time when 9
murder rates skyrocketed.[11] Various theories were put forward in the 1970s to explain the
jump in violent crime. Some claimed that the Supreme Court's Miranda decision—
mandating that suspects be read their rights during arrest—reduced criminal confessions
and otherwise hindered convictions. Other blamed softer criminal penalties or lower
arrest rates.[12] Back in the 1970s these studies were generally inconclusive, however, due to
the lack of data available at the time.[13]

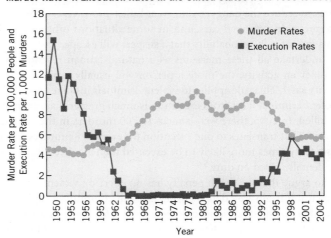

Murder Rates v. Execution Rates in the United States from 1950 to 2005

Economists began to study the death penalty intently after its re-imposition in 1976. 10 Isaac Ehrlich, then a young assistant professor at the University of Chicago, conducted path-breaking research showing that each execution deterred as many as twenty to twenty-four murders.[14] His findings, however, were anathema in liberal academia. His conclusions were roundly condemned, and Ehrlich was denied tenure at the University of Chicago. He even became too controversial to find work at most universities. However, his contentious findings sparked a good deal of new research into the effectiveness of capital punishment, including a special panel convened by the National Academy of Sciences. The panel came to the curious conclusion that greater penalties generally fail to deter criminals.[15]

Although many states immediately re-approved the death penalty after the Supreme 11 Court lifted the ban in 1976, executions were relatively rare until the 1990s, when execution rates spiked dramatically. This elicited a flood of new research on capital punishment. Moreover, the new studies drew upon much more extensive data than had previously been available, allowing researchers to study crime rates over many years and across every state.

This research was conducted as violent crime rates were plummeting while execu- 12 tions were rising sharply. Between 1991 and 2000, there were 9,114 fewer murders per year, while the number of executions per year rose by seventy-one. The fresh studies resurrected Ehrlich's earlier conclusions that the death penalty greatly deters murder. The vast majority of recent scholarly research confirms this deterrent effect.[16] Generally, the studies found that each execution saved the lives of roughly fifteen to eighteen potential murder victims.[17] Overall, the rise in executions during the 1990s accounts for about 12 to 14 percent of the overall drop in murders.

Research by Economists since the Mid-1990s on the Death Penalty

	Reduced Murder Rate	No Discernible Effect on Murder Rate	Increased Murder Rate
Refereed Publications	1) Ehrlich and Liu, *Journal of Law and Economics*, 1999. 2) Lott, *More Guns, Less Crime*, University of Chicago Press, 2000. 3) Cloninger and Marchesini, *Applied Economics*, 2001. 4) Dezhbakhsh, Rubin, and Shepherd, *American Law and Economics Review*, 2003. 5) Mocan and Gittings, *Journal of Law and Economics*, 2003. 6) Shepherd, *Journal of Legal Studies*, 2004. 7) Zimmerman, *Journal of Applied Economics*, 2004. 8) Zimmerman, *American Journal of Economics and Sociology*, 2006. 9) Liu, *Eastern Economics Journal*, forthcoming.	1) Katz, Levitt, and Shustorovich, *American Law and Economics Review*, 2003 2) Berk, *Journal of Empirical Legal Studies*, 2005 3) Narayan and Smyth, *Applied Economics*, 2006	None
Non Refereed Publications	1) Lott and Landes, *Bias Against Guns*, 2003. 2) Shepherd, *Michigan Law Review*, 2005.	1) Fagan, Zimring, and Geller, *Texas Law Review*, 2006 2) Donohue and Wolfers, *Stanford Law Review*, 2005.	None

Despite the generally beneficial effect of capital punishment on crime, there are 13 exceptions. One particular kind of crime where the death penalty shows no significant deterrent effect is multiple victim public shootings. This was the conclusion of a study I performed with Bill Landes at the University of Chicago.[18] This exception stems from the unique circumstances of these kinds of crimes: the vast majority of these killers either commit suicide or are killed at the scene of the crime. The threat of legal punishment, including the death penalty, doesn't really affect their actions since so many of these criminals expect to die in the course of their crime.

The death penalty has a beneficial effect even beyond deterring murders. Because 14 capital punishment can be imposed if a victim dies in the commission of a rape, robbery, or aggravated assault, statistics show the death penalty also acts as a deterrent to these crimes as well.[19] This, however, doesn't mean that the death penalty should be applied directly to these crimes. There is such a thing as "too much" deterrence. For example, utilizing the death penalty too broadly can create some perverse incentives. Suppose the death penalty is used against robbers and rapists. These criminals would then become more determined to kill their victims and any potential witnesses since they would already be facing the death penalty. There would likely be fewer robberies and rapes, but those crimes would probably result in much higher numbers of dead victims.[20]

Polls consistently show that the vast majority of Americans support the death 15 penalty. A 2006 ABC News/*Washington Post* poll found that 65 percent of Americans favor the death penalty for convicted murderers, with 32 percent opposed.[21] There is even majority support for the death penalty in such unlikely places as Brazil, Eastern Europe, Japan, and South Africa.[22] A plurality in Britain also supports it.[23] This should not be too surprising; as Supreme Court Justice Antonin Scalia noted, the death penalty was abolished in many countries by judicial fiat, despite widespread support for it among the general populations.[24]

A lot of people grasp intuitively an idea that economists only now are building a 16 consensus toward: that the death penalty helps deter violent crimes and saves lives.

What Decreased Crime? Part II

Law Enforcement

The nation's prison population grew 2.6 percent last year, the largest increase since 1999, according to a study by the Justice Department. The jump came *despite* a small decline in serious crime in 2002.... Alfred Blumstein, a leading criminologist at Carnegie Mellon University, said it was not illogical for the prison population to go up even when the crime rate goes down.... Professor Blumstein said ... that it has become increasingly clear from statistical research that "there is no reason that the prison count and the crime rate have to be consistent." The crime rate measures the amount of crime people are suffering from, he said, while the prison count is a measure of how severely society chooses to deal with crime, which varies from time to time [emphasis added].

—Fox Butterfield, *New York Times*[25]

Is it really surprising that the number of prisoners increased while crime rates fell?[26] Apparently it is to those who disregard incentives, a group that includes many criminologists as well as writers for the *New York Times*. Although these observers somehow doubt that locking up more criminals can deter crime, a large number of studies indicate that the more certain the punishment, the fewer the crimes committed.[27] Arrest rates of criminals are usually the single most important factor in reducing every type of crime. Sensational topics like the death penalty may get the most media attention, but it is everyday police work that really makes a neighborhood safer. Changes in the arrest rate account for around 16 to 18 percent of the drop in the murder rate.[28] Conviction rates explain another 12 percent. Arrest and conviction rates have an even larger effect on other types of violent crime. And their effect on property crimes is still greater, often two or three times larger than for violent crime overall. 17

While boosting arrest rates indisputably increases deterrence, the evidence on longer prison sentences is less clear. The reason is simple: methodologically, it's surprisingly difficult to measure how long criminals expect to be in prison. The actual time served is often much shorter than the official length of a criminal's sentence. Furthermore, the time that is served varies widely, even for a single type of crime, and depends on such factors as a suspect's criminal history and the severity of the offense. Unfortunately, this kind of data is not readily available to researchers. 18

Arrest and conviction rates and expected prison sentence lengths all deal with deterrence—the cost to the criminal of committing a crime. But some people commit crimes despite those threats. Obviously, locking up the most crime-prone individuals will further decrease crime by keeping habitual criminals off the streets. Indeed, putting more people in prison explains another 10 to 12 percent of the drop in crime rates.[29] 19

Simply being arrested or convicted, even without a prison sentence, carries its own substantial penalties. . . . [T]hese reputational penalties are the worst penalties that many criminals face. 20

Notes

1. Bryan Hubbell and Randall Kramer, "An Empirical Bayes Approach to Combining Estimates of the Value of a Statistical Life for Environmental Policy Analysis," U.S.

Environmental Protection Agency National Center for Environmental Economics working paper, November, 2001. W. Kip Viscusi, *Fatal Tradeoffs: Public and Private Responsibilities for Risk* (New York: Oxford University Press, 1992).

2. Uniform Crime Report, "Law Enforcement Officers Killed and Assaulted, 2005," FBI, Department of Justice, October 2006 (http://www.fbi.gov/ucr/killed/2005/downloaddocs/feloniouslykilled.pdf). For information on accidental deaths of police see http://www.fbi.gov/ucr/killed/2005/table46.htm.

3. This is a fairly typical year. Over the ten years from 1993 to 2002, there were on average 64 law enforcement officers murdered on the job each year (though the number of police officers rose over time). Source: "Law Enforcement Officers Killed and Assaulted, 2002," FBI, U.S. Department of Justice.

4. Obtained via Bureau of Justice Statistics, Capital Punishment, 1985–2005, (http://www.ojp.usdoj.gov/bjs/pubalp2.htm#cp) and from FBI Uniform Crime Reports, 1976–2005, (http://www.ojp.usdoj.gov/bjs/homicide/tables/totalstab.htm).

5. Not all murderers are eligible for the death penalty. To qualify, murderers must have either killed multiple victims, children, or law enforcement officers, or committed murder while committing another felony. The smaller group of criminals that meet this criterion face a 1 in 70 chance of being executed. From 1977 to 2003, about 25 percent of murderers were eligible for the death penalty. This assumes that that ratio holds for 2005. See Jeffrey Fagan, Franklin E. Zimring, and Amanda Geller, "Capital Punishment and Capital Murder: Market Share and the Deterrent Effects of the Death Penalty," *Texas Law Review* (June 2006): 1819.

6. Steven Levitt, "Understanding Why Crime Fell in the 1990s: Four Factors that Explain the Decline and Six that Do Not," *Journal of Economics Perspectives* (2004): 175.

7. For more on the role played by risk in criminal behavior, see W. Kip Viscusi, "The Risks and Rewards of Criminal Activity: A Comprehensive Test of Criminal Deterrence," *Journal of Labor Economics* (1986): 317–340, and Michael K. Block and Vernon E. Gerety, "Some Experimental Evidence on Differences Between Student and Prisoner Reactions to Monetary Penalties and Risk," *Journal of Legal Studies* (January 1995): 123–138.

8. Raymond Bonner and Ford Fessenden, "States With No Death Penalty Share Lower Homicide Rates," *New York Times*, September 22, 2000, A1.

9. These were Alaska, Hawaii, Iowa, Maine, Massachusetts, Michigan, Minnesota, North Dakota, Rhode Island, West Virginia, Wisconsin, and Vermont.

10. From 1977 to 1998, the population-weighted drop in murder rates for the 12 states that never instituted the death penalty fell by 21 percent. For the 38 other states, their murder rate fell by 29 percent. Http://www.disaster-center.com/crime/uscrime.htm.

11. Some analysts inexplicably date the end of capital punishment to the 1972 Furman decision by the Supreme Court, even though executions had stopped in 1968. See

John Donohue and Justin Wolfers, "Uses and abuses of empirical evidence in the death penalty debate," *Stanford Law Review* (2006): 791–845. The graph I show uses the execution rate because it gives readers the best indication of the execution risk that criminals face by committing murder.

12. Paul G. Cassell and Richard Fowles, "Handcuffing the Cops? A Thirty-Year Perspective on Miranda's Harmful Effects on Law Enforcement," *Stanford Law Review* (April 1998): 1055–1144. The Miranda decision may have affected crime rates, but it's precise effect is difficult to evaluate; since it was a Supreme Court decision, we can only evaluate it through time-series data for the entire United States. Furthermore, there were so many other Supreme Court decisions as well as other possible explanatory factors that it is simply impossible to disentangle all of them.

13. The first serious cross-sectional tests using census data were in Isaac Ehrlich, "Capital Punishment and Deterrence: Some Further Thoughts and Additional Evidence," *Journal of Political Economy* (August 1977). The first time-series estimates were in Isaac Ehrlich, "The Deterrent Effect of Capital Punishment," *American Economic Review* (August 1975).

14. Isaac Ehrlich, "Capital Punishment and Deterrence: Some Further Thoughts and Additional Evidence," *Journal of Political Economy* (August 1977): 779.

15. Committee on Research on Law Enforcement and Criminal Justice, Understanding Crime—An Evaluation of the National Institute of Law Enforcement and Criminal Justice (National Academy of Sciences, Susan White, and Samuel Krislow, editors, 1977). See also Alfred Blumstein, Jacqueline Cohen, and Daniel Nagin, *Deterrence and Incapacitation: Estimating the Effects of Criminal Sanctions on Crime Rates* (Washington, D.C.: National Academy of Sciences, 1978). Ehrlich co-authored another study responding to the National Academy of Sciences report. See Isaac Ehrlich and Mark Randall, "Fear of Deterrence," *Journal of Legal Studies* (1977): 293–316.

16. The few studies that fail to find any deterrence from the death penalty either don't use all the data or measure the execution rate in strange ways. For example, ignoring data from individual states, Narayan and Smyth look only at national statistics through a data set that has only thirty-seven observations. Richard Berk, for his part, achieved his result by discarding data for entire states such as Texas. See Paresh Kumar Narayan and Russell Smyth, "Dead Man Walking: An Empirical Reassessment of the Deterrent Effect of Capital Punishment Using the Bounds Testing Approach to Cointegration," *Applied Economics* (2006), and Richard Berk, "New Claims about Executions and General Deterrence," *Journal of Empirical Legal Studies* (2005). Rather than analyzing the percent of murders that result in execution, some researchers measure the number of executions per prisoner. It is not clear why anyone would believe that if jails are filled up with additional prisoners convicted of crimes like drug possession or car theft, the risk murderers face from execution would decline. Comparing two

unrelated statistics, it is hardly surprising that this research cannot identify any benefit from the death penalty. See Lawrence Katz, Steven Levitt, and Ellen Shustorovish, "Prison Conditions, Capital Punishment, and Deterrence," *American Law and Economics Review* (2003): 318–343. Another paper by Donohue and Wolfers has used this approach uncritically. See Donohue and Wolfers, "Uses and abuses of empirical evidence in the death penalty debate," *Stanford Law Review* (2006): 791–845.

17. My work with Bill Landes finds a much larger benefit—implying that each execution saves hundreds of lives. We found that each one percentage point in execution rates lowered the murder rate by at least four percent. Lott, *The Bias Against Guns* (2003), Chapter 6.

18. Lott and Landes in Lott, *The Bias Against Guns* (Regnery, 2003), Chapter 6.

19. Lott, *More Guns, Less Crime* (University of Chicago Press, 2000), Chapter 9.

20. Prison wardens face a similar problem. If a prisoner is sentenced to death, it's hard to find an additional penalty that you can impose on him in order to control his behavior. You can take away some privileges, but without some additional penalty it is difficult for the warden to control the prisoner.

21. ABC News/*Washington Post* Poll. June 22–25, 2006 (http://www.pollingreport.com/crime.htm). A 2006 Gallup poll further found that 51 percent of respondents believed the death penalty is not used enough, compared to 25 percent who think it is used "about right" and 21 percent believing it is used "too often." Gallup Poll May 8–11, 2006 (http://www.pollingreport.com/crime.htm).

22. Polls have found support for the death penalty at 60 percent among Eastern Europeans, 72 percent of South Africans, and 51 percent among Brazilians. See Craig Smith, "In Europe, It's East vs. West on the Death Penalty," *New York Times*, November 19, 2006, p. 4; David W. Moore, "Death Penalty Gets Less Support From Britons, Canadians Than Americans," Gallup Poll News Service, February 20, 2006; Datafolha / Folha de Sao Paulo, http://www.angus-reid.com/polls/index.cfm/fuseaction/viewItem/itemID/12893. See also http://www.angus-reid.com/polls/index.cfrn/fuseaction/viewItem/itemID/11872, http://www.angus-reid.com/polls/index.cfm/fuseaction/viewItem/itemID/9970, http://www.angus-reid.com/polls/index.cfm/fuseaction/viewItem/itemID/11639.

23. 49 percent of Britons support the death penalty (David W. Moore, "Death Penalty Gets Less Support From Britons, Canadians Than Americans," Gallup Poll News Service, February 20, 2006). For somewhat lower percentages, see http://www.angus-reid.com/polls/index.cfm/fuseaction/viewItem/itemID/10758.

24. In a recent debate over the death penalty, Scalia declared:

> What nations are you talking about? You know, public opinion polls in both England and France, at least until very recently, showed that if they had as responsive a democracy as we do, they would still have the death penalty.

> I find it so hypocritical, not that the Europeans don't have the death penalty—fine; although its abolition was imposed by the Court of Human Rights, which said, "You cannot have the death penalty." So it's not as though all the Europeans voted to abolish it. It was judicially imposed, and that doesn't impress me very much.

Source: "ACLU Membership Conference Debate," *Federal News Service*, October 15, 2006.

25. "Study Finds 2.6% Increase In U.S. Prison Population," *New York Times*, July 28, 2003.

26. The *Washington Post* makes a similar argument: "It is one of the least-told stories in American crime-fighting. New York, the safest big city in the nation, achieved its now-legendary 70-percent drop in homicides even as it locked up fewer and fewer of its citizens during the past decade. The number of prisoners in the city has dropped from 21,449 in 1993 to 14,129 this past week. That runs counter to the national trend, in which prison admissions have jumped 72 percent during that time" (Michael Powell, "Despite Fewer Lockups, NYC Has Seen Big Drop in Crime," *Washington Post*, November 24, 2006.) There is a simple explanation for why both prison population and crime can fall in New York. When murders fall by 70 percent, can you really keep on expanding the prison population? Note that the prison population has fallen by a third, but violent crime in the city has fallen by much more than that. The number of prisoners per crime has still gone up dramatically. Or take their example for Idaho. "Perhaps as intriguing is the experience in states where officials spent billions of dollars to build prisons. From 1992 to 2002, Idaho's prison population grew by 174 percent, the largest percentage increase in the nation. Yet violent crime in that state rose by 14 percent." It would have been helpful if they had put the numbers in per capita rates, rather than comparing numbers 10 years apart. Idaho's population grew by more than 14 percent, though less than 174 percent. Thus their crime rate did fall as the prison population grew. Among the academic papers that find an increase in imprisonment leads to less crime, see Thomas Marvell and Carlisle Moody, "Prison Population Growth and Crime Reduction," *Journal of Quantitative Criminology* (1994): 109-140.

27. Gordon Tullock, "Does Punishment Deter Crime?" *The Public Interest 36* (Summer 1974): 103-11. James Q. Wilson, *Thinking About Crime* (New York: Random House, 1985). See a more recent summary in my book, *More Guns, Less Crime* (2000).

28. David B. Mustard, "Re-examining Criminal Behavior: The Importance of Omitted Variable Bias," *Review of Economics and Statistics*, vol. 84, no. 1 (2002).

29. John R. Lott, Jr. and John Whitley, "Abortion and Crime: Unwanted Children and Out-of-Wedlock Births," *Economic Inquiry* (April 2001).

Reflecting on What You Have Read

1 Unlike Levitt and Dubner in "Where Have All the Criminals Gone?" Lott argues that the prospect of capital punishment does deter criminals who might otherwise commit serious crimes. In support of this argument, Lott contends that the greater the risk involved in any activity, the greater measures people will take to reduce this risk. In explaining this point, Lott cites the measures police officers take to reduce their chances of being killed. Lott claim that criminals are as likely to reduce their risk of death as police officers are. Does this claim seem valid? Why or why not?

2 Another way in which Lott's argument differs from Levitt and Dubner's is that he frequently cites studies on which his conclusions are based. Does this add to Lott's credibility? Why or why not?

3 One of Lott's arguments in favor of the death penalty is that, at least in the case of convicted murderers, Americans favor the death penalty by a ratio of two to one. How persuasive do you find this argument?

4 Lott includes a graph showing the relationship between murder rates and execution rates between 1950 and 2005. To what extent do the data in this graph confirm Lott's point of view? To what extent do the data call his view into question?

Thinking Ahead

As is the case in "Where Have All the Criminals Gone?" and "What Decreased Crime?," people often disagree about the causes of significant trends in society. What are some trends you have noticed or read about? How do people explain what causes these trends? How do you explain them? What kinds of evidence and reasons can you find to support your point of view? What evidence and reasons can you find to refute other points of view? As you consider evidence and reasons for other points of view, do you find your own point of view changing?

Message in a Bottle

Charles Fishman

Charles Fishman is an investigative journalist and senior writer for the business magazine *Fast Company*. Throughout his career, Fishman has been able to gather and write about inside information about highly secretive organizations, including America's only bomb factory. His book *The Wal-Mart Effect: How the World's Most Powerful Company Really Works—and How It's Transforming the American Economy* (2006) takes a close look at Wal-Mart's history and growth. He acknowledges ways Wal-Mart's prices have benefited consumers, but he also explains problems caused by Wal-Mart's dominance among retail marketers. The book is based on an article for which Fishman received the New York Press Club's award for the best business magazine article in 2004. In "Message in a Bottle," Fishman explains problems caused by Americans' fondness for bottled water. As you read, consider whether the information he presents justifies the view that Americans live in "a culture of indulgence."

{MESSAGE IN A BOTTLE}

AMERICANS SPENT MORE MONEY LAST YEAR ON BOTTLED WATER THAN ON IPODS OR MOVIE TICKETS: $15 BILLION.

**A JOURNEY INTO THE ECONOMICS—
AND PSYCHOLOGY—OF AN UNLIKELY BUSINESS BOOM.
AND WHAT IT SAYS ABOUT
OUR CULTURE OF INDULGENCE.**

By Charles Fishman

Photographs by Nigel Cox

The largest bottled-water factory in North America is located on the outskirts of Hollis, Maine. In the back of the plant stretches the staging area for finished product: 24 million bottles of Poland Spring water. As far as the eye can see, there are double-stacked pallets packed with half-pint bottles, half-liters, liters, "Aquapods" for school lunches, and 2.5-gallon jugs for the refrigerator.

Really, it is a lake of Poland Spring water, conveniently celled off in plastic, extending across 6 acres, 8 feet high. A week ago, the lake was still underground; within five days, it will all be gone, to supermarkets and convenience stores

24%
of the bottled water we buy is tap water repackaged by Coke and Pepsi.

across the Northeast, replaced by another lake's worth of bottles.

Looking at the piles of water, you can have only one thought: Americans sure are thirsty.

Bottled water has become the indispensable prop in our lives and our culture. It starts the day in lunch boxes; it goes to every meeting, lecture hall, and soccer match; it's in our cubicles at work; in the cup holder of the treadmill at the gym; and it's rattling around half-finished on the floor of every minivan in America. Fiji Water shows up on the ABC show *Brothers & Sisters*; Poland Spring cameos routinely on NBC's *The Office*. Every hotel room offers bottled water for sale, alongside the increasingly ignored ice bucket and drinking glasses. At Whole Foods, the upscale emporium of the organic and exotic, bottled water is the number-one item by units sold.

Thirty years ago, bottled water barely existed as a business in the United States. Last year, we spent more on Poland Spring, Fiji Water, Evian, Aquafina, and Dasani than we spent on iPods or movie tickets—$15 billion. It will be $16 billion this year.

Bottled water is the food phenomenon of our times. We—a generation raised on tap water and water fountains—drink a billion bottles of water a week, and we're raising a generation that views tap water with disdain and water fountains with suspicion. We've come to pay good money—two or three or four times the cost of gasoline—for a product we have always gotten, and can still get, for free, from taps in our homes.

When we buy a bottle of water, what we're often buying is the bottle itself, as much as the water. We're buying the convenience—a bottle at the 7-Eleven isn't the same product as tap water, any more than a cup of coffee at Starbucks is the same as a cup of coffee from the

Krups machine on your kitchen counter. And we're buying the artful story the water companies tell us about the water: where it comes from, how healthy it is, what it says about us. Surely among the choices we can make, bottled water isn't just good, it's positively virtuous.

8 Except for this: Bottled water is often simply an indulgence, and despite the stories we tell ourselves, it is not a benign indulgence. We're moving 1 billion bottles of water around a week in ships, trains, and trucks in the United States alone. That's a weekly convoy equivalent to 37,800 18-wheelers delivering water. (Water weighs 8⅓ pounds a gallon. It's so heavy you can't fill an 18-wheeler with bottled water—you have to leave empty space.)

9 Meanwhile, one out of six people in the world has no dependable, safe drinking water. The global economy has contrived to deny the most fundamental element of life to 1 billion people, while delivering to us an array of water "varieties" from around the globe, not one of which we actually need. That tension is only complicated by the fact that if we suddenly decided not to purchase the lake of Poland Spring water in Hollis, Maine, none of that water would find its way to people who really are thirsty.

10 A chilled plastic bottle of water in the convenience-store cooler is the perfect symbol of this moment in American commerce and culture. It acknowledges our demand for instant gratification, our vanity, our token concern for health. Its packaging and transport depend entirely on cheap fossil fuel. Yes, it's just a bottle of water—modest compared with the indulgence of driving a Hummer. But when a whole industry grows up around supplying us with something we don't need—when a whole industry is built on the packaging and the presentation—it's worth asking how that

happened, and what the impact is. And if you do ask, if you trace both the water and the business back to where they come from, you find a story more complicated, more bemusing, and ultimately more sobering than the bottles we tote everywhere suggest.

11 In the town of San Pellegrino Terme, Italy, for example, is a spigot that runs all the time, providing San Pellegrino water free to the local citizens—except the free Pellegrino has no bubbles. Pellegrino trucks in the bubbles for the bottling plant. The man who first brought bottled water to the United States famously failed an impromptu taste test involving his own product. In Maine, there is a marble temple to honor our passion for bottled water.

12 And in Fiji, a state-of-the-art factory spins out more than a million bottles a day of the hippest bottled water on the U.S. market today, while more than half the people in Fiji do not have safe, reliable drinking water. Which means it is easier for the typical American in Beverly Hills or Baltimore to get a drink of safe, pure, refreshing Fiji water than it is for most people in Fiji.

13 At the Peninsula Hotel in Beverly Hills, where the rooms start at $500 a night and the guest next door might well be an Oscar winner, the minibar in all 196 rooms contains six bottles of Fiji Water. Before Fiji Water displaced Evian, Diet Coke was the number-one-selling minibar item. Now, says Christian Boyens, the Peninsula's elegant director of food and beverage, "the 1 liter of Fiji Water is number one. Diet Coke is number two. And the 500-milliliter bottle of Fiji is number three."

14 Being the water in the Peninsula minibar is so desirable—not just for the money to be made, but for the exposure with the Peninsula's clientele—that Boyens gets a sales call a week from a company trying to dislodge Fiji.

Boyens, who has an MBA 15
from Cornell, used to be indifferent to water. Not anymore. His
restaurants and bars carry 20
different waters. "Sometimes a
guest will ask for Poland Spring,
and you can't get Poland Spring
in California," he says. So what
does he do? "We'll call the Peninsula in New York and have them
FedEx out a case.

"I thought water was water. 16
But our customers know what
they want."

The marketing of bottled 17
water is subtle compared with
the marketing of, say, soft drinks
or beer. The point of Fiji Water in
the minibar at the Peninsula, or
at the center of the table in a
white-tablecloth restaurant, is
that guests will try it, love it, and
buy it at a store the next time
they see it.

Which isn't difficult, because 18
the water aisle in a suburban
supermarket typically stocks a
dozen brands of water—not
including those enhanced with
flavors or vitamins or, yes, oxygen.
In 1976, the average American
drank 1.6 gallons of bottled water
a year, according to Beverage
Marketing Corp. Last year, we
each drank 28.3 gallons of bottled
water—18 half-liter bottles a
month. We drink more bottled
water than milk, or coffee, or beer.
Only carbonated soft drinks are
more popular than bottled water,
at 52.9 gallons annually.

From the islands of

**FIJI WATER
PRODUCES
MORE THAN
A MILLION
BOTTLES
A DAY,**
WHILE MORE THAN
HALF
THE PEOPLE IN FIJI
**DO NOT
HAVE
RELIABLE
DRINKING
WATER**

500 mL (1.05 PT)

No one has experienced this 19
transformation more profoundly
than Kim Jeffery. Jeffery began
his career in the water business
in the Midwest in 1978, selling
Perrier ("People didn't know
whether to put it in their lawn
mower or drink it," he says.) Now
he's the CEO of Nestlé Waters
North America, in charge of U.S.
sales of Perrier, San Pellegrino,
Poland Spring, and a portfolio of
other regional natural springwaters. Combined, his brands
will sell some $4.5 billion worth
of water this year (generating
roughly $500 million in pretax
profit). Jeffery insists that unlike
the soda business, which is
stoked by imaginative TV and
marketing campaigns, the mainstream water business is, quite
simply, "a force of nature."

"The entire bottled-water busi- 20
ness today is half the size of the
carbonated beverage industry,"
says Jeffery, "but our marketing
budget is 15% of what they spend.
When you put a bottle of water in
that cold box, it's the most thirst-
quenching beverage there is.
There's nothing in it that's not
good for you. People just know
that intuitively.

"A lot of people tell me, you 21
guys have done some great marketing to get customers to pay
for water," Jeffery says. "But we
aren't that smart. We had to have
a hell of a lot of help from the
consumer."

Still, we needed help learning to drink bottled water. For that, we can thank the French.

Gustave Leven was the chairman of Source Perrier when he approached an American named Bruce Nevins in 1976. Nevins was working for the athletic-wear company Pony. Leven was a major Pony investor. "He wanted me to consider the water business in the U.S.," Nevins says. "I was a bit reluctant." Back then, the American water industry was small and fusty, built on home and office delivery of big bottles and grocery sales of gallon jugs.

Nevins looked out across 1970s America, though, and had an epiphany: Perrier wasn't just water. It was a beverage. The opportunity was in persuading people to drink Perrier when they would otherwise have had a cocktail or a Coke. Americans were already drinking 30 gallons of soft drinks each a year, and the three-martini lunch was increasingly viewed as a problem. Nevins saw a niche.

From the start, Nevins pioneered a three-part strategy. First, he connected bottled water to exclusivity: In 1977, just before Perrier's U.S. launch, he flew 60 journalists to France to visit "the source" where Perrier bubbled out of the ground. He connected Perrier to health, sponsoring the New York City Marathon, just as long-distance running was exploding as a fad across America. And he associated Perrier with celebrity, launching with $4 million in TV commercials featuring Orson Welles. It worked. In 1978, its first full year in the United States, Perrier sold $20 million of water. The next year, sales tripled to $60 million.

What made Perrier distinctive was that it was a sparkling water, served in a signature glass bottle. But that's also what left the door open for Evian, which came to the United States in 1984. Evian's U.S. marketing was built around images of toned young men and women in tight clothes sweating at the gym. Madonna drank Evian—often onstage at concerts. "If you were cool, you were drinking bottled water," says Ed Slade, who became Evian's vice president of marketing in 1990. "It was a status symbol."

Evian was also a still water, which Americans prefer; and it was the first to offer a plastic bottle nationwide. The clear bottle allowed us to see the water—how clean and refreshing it looked on the shelf. Americans have never wanted water in cans, which suggest a tinny aftertaste before you take a sip. The plastic bottle, in fact, did for water what the pop-top can had done for soda: It turned water into an anywhere, anytime beverage, at just the moment when we decided we wanted a beverage, everywhere, all the time.

Perrier and Evian launched the bottled-water business just as it would prove irresistible. Convenience and virtue aligned. Two-career families, over-programmed children, prepared foods in place of home-cooked meals, the constant urging to eat more healthfully and drink less alcohol—all reinforce the value of bottled water. But those trends also reinforce the mythology.

We buy bottled water because we think it's healthy. Which it is, of course: Every 12-year-old

We pitch into landfills 38 billion water bottles a year— in excess of $1 billion worth of plastic.

If the water we use at home cost what even cheap bottled water costs, our monthly water bills would run $9,000.

who buys a bottle of water from a vending machine instead of a 16-ounce Coke is inarguably making a healthier choice. But bottled water isn't healthier, or safer, than tap water. Indeed, while the United States is the single biggest consumer in the world's $50 billion bottled-water market, it is the only one of the top four—the others are Brazil, China, and Mexico—that has universally reliable tap water. Tap water in this country, with rare exceptions, is impressively safe. It is monitored constantly, and the test results made public. Mineral water has a long association with medicinal benefits—and it can provide minerals that people need—but there are no scientific studies establishing that routinely consuming mineral water improves your health. The FDA, in fact, forbids mineral waters in the United States from making any health claims.

And for this healthy convenience, we're 30 paying what amounts to an unbelievable premium. You can buy a half-liter Evian for $1.35—17 ounces of water imported from France for pocket change. That water seems cheap, but only because we aren't paying attention.

In San Francisco, the municipal water comes 31 from inside Yosemite National Park. It's so good the EPA doesn't require San Francisco to filter it. If you bought and drank a bottle of Evian, you could refill that bottle once a day for 10 years, 5 months, and 21 days with San Francisco tap water before that water would cost $1.35. Put another way, if the water we use at home cost what even cheap bottled water costs, our monthly water bills would run $9,000.

Taste, of course, is highly personal. New 32 Yorkers excepted, Americans love to belittle the quality of their tap water. But in blind taste tests, with waters at equal temperatures, presented in identical glasses, ordinary people can rarely distinguish between tap water, springwater, and luxury waters. At the height of Perrier's popularity, Bruce Nevins was asked on a live network radio show one morning to pick Perrier from a lineup of seven carbonated waters served in paper cups. It took him five tries.

We are actually in the midst of a second love 33 affair with bottled water. In the United States, many of the earliest, still-familiar brands of springwater—Poland Spring, Saratoga Springs, Deer Park, Arrowhead—were originally associated with resort and spa complexes. The water itself, pure at a time when cities struggled to provide safe water, was the source of the enterprise.

In the late 1800s, Poland Spring was already 34 a renowned brand of healthful drinking water that you could get home-delivered in Boston, New York, Philadelphia, or Chicago. It was also a sprawling summer resort complex, with thousands of guests and three Victorian hotels, some of which had bathtubs with spigots that allowed guests to bathe in Poland Spring water. The resort burned in 1976, but at the crest of a hill in Poland Spring, Maine, you can still visit a

marble-and-granite temple built in 1906 to house the original spring.

The car, the Depression, World War II, and perhaps most important, clean, safe municipal water, unwound the resorts and the first wave of water as business. We had to wait two generations for the second, which would turn out to be much different—and much larger. 35

Today, for all the apparent variety on the shelf, bottled water is dominated in the United States and worldwide by four huge companies. Pepsi has the nation's number-one-selling bottled water, Aquafina, with 13% of the market. Coke's Dasani is number two, with 11% of the market. Both are simply purified municipal water—so 24% of the bottled water we buy is tap water repackaged by Coke and Pepsi for our convenience. Evian is owned by Danone, the French food giant, and distributed in the United States by Coke. 36

The really big water company in the United States is Nestlé, which gradually bought up the nation's heritage brands, and expanded them. The waters are slightly different—springwater must come from actual springs, identified specifically on the label—but together, they add up to 26% of the market, according to Beverage Marketing, surpassing Coke and Pepsi's brands combined. 37

Since most water brands are owned by larger companies, it's hard to get directly at the economics. But according to those inside the business, half the price of a typical $1.29 bottle goes to the retailer. As much as a third goes to the distributor and transport. Another 12 to 15 cents is the cost of the water itself, the bottle and the cap. That leaves roughly a dime of profit. On multipacks, that profit is more like 2 cents a bottle. 38

As the abundance in the supermarket water aisle shows, that business is now trying to help us find new waters to drink and new occasions 39

for drinking them—trying to get more mouth share, as it were. Aquafina marketing vice president Ahad Afridi says his team has done the research to understand what kind of water drinkers we are. They've found six types, including the "water pure-fectionist"; the "water explorer"; the "image seeker"; and the "struggler" ("they don't really like water that much . . . these are the people who have a cheese burger with a diet soda").

It's a startling level of thought and analysis—until you realize that within a decade, our consumption of bottled water is expected to surpass soda. That kind of market can't be left to chance. Aquafina's fine segmentation is all about the newest explosion of waters that aren't really water—flavored waters, enhanced waters, colored waters, water drinks branded after everything from Special K breakfast cereal to Tropicana juice. 40

Afridi is a true believer. He talks about water as if it were more than a drink, more than a product—as if it were a character all its own, a superhero ready to take the pure-fectionist, the water explorer, and the struggler by the hand and carry them to new water adventures. "Water as a beverage has more right to extend and enter into more territories than any other beverage," Afridi says. "Water has a right to travel where others can't." 41

Uh, meaning what? 42

"Water that's got vitamins in it. Water that's got some immunity-type benefit to it. Water that helps keep skin younger. Water that gives you energy." 43

Water: It's pure, it's healthy, it's perfect—and we've made it better. The future of water sounds distinctly unlike water. 44

The label on a bottle of Fiji Water says "from the islands of Fiji." Journey to the source of that 45

In 1976 the average American drank 1.6 gallons of bottled water a year. Last year we drank 28.3 gallons.

is shipped to Fiji first, the bottles' journey is even longer. Half the wholesale cost of Fiji Water is transportation—which is to say, it costs as much to ship Fiji Water across the oceans and truck it to warehouses in the United States as it does to extract the water and bottle it.

That is not the only environmental cost 47 embedded in each bottle of Fiji Water. The Fiji Water plant is a state-of-the-art facility that runs 24 hours a day. That means it requires an uninterrupted supply of electricity— something the local utility structure cannot support. So the factory supplies its own electricity, with three big generators running on diesel fuel. The water may come from "one of the last pristine ecosystems on earth," as some of the labels say, but out back of the bottling plant is a less pristine ecosystem veiled with a diesel haze.

water, and you realize just how extraordinary that promise is. From New York, for instance, it is an 18-hour plane ride west and south (via Los Angeles) almost to Australia, and then a four-hour drive along Fiji's two-lane King's Highway.

Every bottle of Fiji Water goes on its own ver- 46 sion of this trip, in reverse, although by truck and ship. In fact, since the plastic for the bottles

Each water bottler has its own version of this 48 oxymoron: that something as pure and clean as water leaves a contrail.

WATERWORKS
An anecdotal journey through the ancient origins and fantastical growth of the bottled water phenomenon
by Alex Pasquariello

5000 B.C.	500 B.C.	218 B.C.	1509	1820	1845	1863	1907	1912
The first water-storing vessels of fired pottery are made in the Middle East.	**Cyrus the Great,** King of Persia, carts boiled drinking water in silver flagons to war.	After crossing the Alps on his way to invade Rome, Carthaginian general **Hannibal** rests his troops and elephants at Les Bouillens, France, where they drink water from what would become the Perrier spring.	Leonardo da Vinci, on a break from painting, declares San Pellegrino water "miraculous."	The Rev. D.O. Griswold begins bottling the springwaters of Saratoga Springs, New York, and selling it under the name "Doctor Clark" as a cure for stomach ailments.	Hiram Ricker begins bottling and selling the springwater on his property in Poland Spring, Maine, as a cure for kidney ailments. Poland Spring is born. The first shipments are 3-gallon jugs that sell for 15 cents at a local grocer.	Perrier water is bottled by decree of **Napoleon III** "for the good of France."	A plant with an underground conveyor system opens at Poland Spring. Bottling room walls are lined with Carrera glass for ease of cleaning; employees must shower and change into white linen uniforms before work.	**Halsey Taylor** invents a water fountain for drinking, founding an eponymous company to market it. The water-cooler office-gossip phenomenon is born.

San Pellegrino's 1-liter glass bottles—so much a part of the mystique of the water itself—weigh five times what plastic bottles weigh, dramatically adding to freight costs and energy consumption. The bottles are washed and rinsed with mineral water, before being filled with sparkling Pellegrino—it uses up 2 liters of water to prepare the bottle for the liter we buy. The bubbles in San Pellegrino come naturally from the ground, as the label says, but not at the San Pellegrino source. Pellegrino chooses its CO_2 carefully—it is extracted from supercarbonated volcanic springwaters in Tuscany, then trucked north and bubbled into Pellegrino.

Poland Spring may not have any oceans to traverse, but it still must be trucked hundreds of miles from Maine to markets and convenience stores across its territory in the northeast—it is 312 miles from the Hollis plant to midtown Manhattan. Our desire for Poland Spring has outgrown the springs at Poland Spring's two Maine plants; the company runs a fleet of 80 silver tanker trucks that continuously crisscross the state of Maine, delivering water from other springs to keep its bottling plants humming.

In transportation terms, perhaps the waters with the least environmental impact are Pepsi's Aquafina and Coke's Dasani. Both start with municipal water. That allows the companies to use dozens of bottling plants across the nation, reducing how far bottles must be shipped.

Yet Coke and Pepsi add in a new step. They put the local water through an energy-intensive reverse-osmosis filtration process more potent than that used to turn seawater into drinking water. The water they are purifying is ready to drink—they are recleaning perfectly clean tap water. They do it so marketing can brag about the purity, and to provide consistency: So a bottle of Aquafina in Austin and a bottle in Seattle taste the same, regardless of the municipal source.

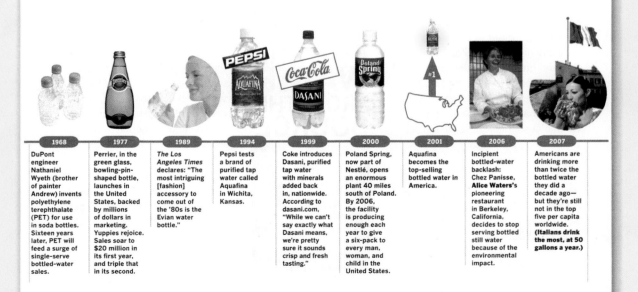

1968
DuPont engineer Nathaniel Wyeth (brother of painter Andrew) invents polyethylene terephthalate (PET) for use in soda bottles. Sixteen years later, PET will feed a surge of single-serve bottled-water sales.

1977
Perrier, in the green glass, bowling-pin-shaped bottle, launches in the United States, backed by millions of dollars in marketing. Yuppies rejoice. Sales soar to $20 million in its first year, and triple that in its second.

1989
The Los Angeles Times declares: "The most intriguing [fashion] accessory to come out of the '80s is the Evian water bottle."

1994
Pepsi tests a brand of purified tap water called Aquafina in Wichita, Kansas.

1999
Coke introduces Dasani, purified tap water with minerals added back in, nationwide. According to dasani.com, "While we can't say exactly what Dasani means, we're pretty sure it sounds crisp and fresh tasting."

2000
Poland Spring, now part of Nestlé, opens an enormous plant 40 miles south of Poland. By 2006, the facility is producing enough each year to give a six-pack to every man, woman, and child in the United States.

2001
Aquafina becomes the top-selling bottled water in America.

2006
Incipient bottled-water backlash: Chez Panisse, **Alice Waters's** pioneering restaurant in Berkeley, California, decides to stop serving bottled still water because of the environmental impact.

2007
Americans are drinking more than twice the bottled water they did a decade ago—but they're still not in the top five per capita worldwide. **(Italians drink the most, at 50 gallons a year.)**

There is one more item in 53 bottled water's environmental ledger: the bottles themselves. The big springwater companies tend to make their own bottles in their plants, just moments before they are filled with water—12, 19, 30 grams of molded plastic each. Americans went through about 50 billion plastic water bottles last year, 167 for each person. Durable, lightweight containers manufactured just to be discarded. Water bottles are made of totally recyclable polyethylene terephthalate (PET) plastic, so we share responsibility for their impact: Our recycling rate for PET is only 23%, which means we pitch into landfills 38 billion water bottles a year—more than $1 billion worth of plastic.

Some of the water companies 54 are acutely aware that every business, every product, every activity is under environmental scrutiny like never before. Nestlé Waters has just redesigned its half-liter bottle, the most popular size among the 18 billion bottles the company will mold this year, to use less plastic. The lighter bottle and cap require 15 grams of plastic instead of 19 grams, a reduction of 20%. The bottle feels flimsy—it uses half the plastic of Fiji Water's half-liter bottle—and CEO Jeffery says that crushable feeling should be the new standard for bottled-water cachet.

THE BUBBLES IN **SAN** PELLEGRINO ARE EXTRACTED **FROM** VOLCANIC SPRINGS IN TUSCANY, **THEN TRUCKED NORTH AND INJECTED INTO THE WATER FROM THE SOURCE**

"As we've rolled out the light- 55 weight bottle, people have said, 'Well, that feels cheap,'" says Jeffery. "And that's good. If it feels solid like a Gatorade bottle or a Fiji bottle, that's not so good." Of course, lighter bottles are also cheaper for Nestlé to produce and ship. Good environmentalism equals good business.

John Mackey is the CEO and 56 cofounder of Whole Foods Market, the national organic-and-natural grocery chain. No one thinks about the environmental and social impacts and the larger context of food more incisively than Mackey—so he's a good person to help frame the ethical questions around bottled water.

Mackey and his wife have a 57 water filter at home, and don't typically drink bottled water there. "If I go to a movie," he says, "I'll smuggle in a bottle of filtered water from home. I don't want to buy a Coke there, and why buy another bottle of water—$3 for 16 ounces?" But he does drink bottled water at work: Whole Food's house brand, 365 Water.

"You can compare bottled 58 water to tap water and reach one set of conclusions," says Mackey, referring both to environmental and social ramifications. "But if you compare it with other packaged beverages, you reach another set of conclusions.

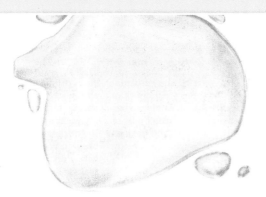

"It's unfair to say bottled water is causing 59 extra plastic in landfills, and it's using energy transporting it," he says. "There's a substitution effect—it's substituting for juices and Coke and Pepsi." Indeed, we still drink almost twice the amount of soda as water—which is, in fact, 90% water and also in containers made to be discarded. If bottled water raises environmental and social issues, don't soft drinks raise all those issues, plus obesity concerns?

What's different about water, of course, is 60 that it runs from taps in our homes, or from fountains in public spaces. Soda does not.

As for the energy used to transport water 61 from overseas, Mackey says it is no more or less wasteful than the energy used to bring merlot from France or coffee from Ethiopia, raspberries from Chile or iPods from China. "Have we now decided that the use of any fossil fuel is somehow unethical?" Mackey asks. "I don't think water should be picked on. Why is the iPod okay and the water is not?"

Mackey's is a merchant's approach to the 62 issue of bottled water—it's a choice for people to make in the market. Princeton University philosopher Peter Singer takes an ethicist's approach. Singer has coauthored two books that grapple specifically with the question of what it means to eat ethically—how responsible are we for the negative impact, even unknowing, of our food choices on the world?

"Where the drinking water is safe, bottled 63 water is simply a superfluous luxury that we should do without," he says. "How is it different than French merlot? One difference is the value of the product, in comparison to the value of transporting and packaging it. It's far lower in the bottled water than in the wine.

"And buying the merlot may help sustain a 64 tradition in the French countryside that we value—a community, a way of life, a set of values that would disappear if we stopped buying French wines. I doubt if you travel to Fiji you would find a tradition of cultivation of Fiji water.

"We're completely thoughtless about hand- 65 ing out $1 for this bottle of water, when there are virtually identical alternatives for free. It's a level of affluence that we just take for granted. What could you do? Put that dollar in a jar on the counter instead, carry a water bottle, and at the end of the month, send all the money to Oxfam or CARE and help someone who has real needs. And you're no worse off."

Beyond culture and the product's value, 66 Singer makes one exception. "You know, they do import Kenyan vegetables by air into London. Fresh peas from Kenya, sent by airplane to London. That provides employment for people who have few opportunities to get themselves out of poverty. So despite the fuel consumption, we're supporting a developing country, we're working against poverty, we're working for global equity.

"Those issues are relevant. Presumably, for 67 instance, bottling water in Fiji is fairly automated. But if there were 10,000 Fijians carefully filtering the water through coconut fiber—well, that would be a better argument for drinking it."

Marika, an elder from the Fijian village of Drauniivi, 68 is sitting cross-legged on a hand-woven mat before a wooden bowl, where his weathered hands are filtering Fiji Water through a long bag of ground kava root. Marika is making a bowl of grog, a lightly narcotic beverage that is an anchor of traditional Fiji society. People with business to conduct sit wearing the traditional Fijian skirt, and drink round after round of grog, served in half a coconut shell, as they discuss the matters at hand.

69 Marika is using Fiji Water—the same Fiji Water in the minibars of the Peninsula Hotel—because Drauniivi is one of the five rural villages near the Fiji Water bottling plant where the plant's workers live. Drauniivi and Beverly Hills are part of the same bottled-water supply chain.

70 Jim Siplon, an American who manages Fiji Water's 10-year-old bottling plant in Fiji, has arranged the grog ceremony. "This is the soul of Fiji Water," he says. The ceremony lasts 45 minutes and goes through four rounds of grog, which tastes a little furry. Marika is interrupted twice by his cell phone, which he pulls from a pocket in his skirt. It is shift change at the plant, and Marika coordinates the minibus network that transports villagers to and from work.

71 Fiji Water is the product of these villages, a South Pacific aquifer, and a state-of-the-art bottling plant in a part of Fiji even the locals consider remote. The plant, on the northeast coast of Fiji's main island of Viti Levu, is a white two-story building that looks like a 1970s-era junior high school. The entrance faces the interior of Viti Levu and a cloud-shrouded ridge of volcanic mountains.

72 Inside, the plant is in almost every way indistinguishable from Pellegrino's plant in Italy, or Poland Spring's in Hollis, filled with computer-controlled bottle-making and bottle-filling equipment. Line number two can spin out 1 million bottles of Fiji Water a day, enough to load 40 20-foot shipping containers; the factory has three lines.

73 The plant employs 200 islanders—set to increase to 250 this year—most with just a sixth- or eighth-grade education. Even the entry-level jobs pay twice the informal minimum wage. But these are more than simply jobs—they are jobs in a modern factory, in a place where there aren't jobs of any sort beyond the villages. And the jobs are just part of an ecosystem emerging around the plant—water-based trickle-down economics, as it were.

74 Siplon, a veteran telecom manager from MCI, wants Fiji Water to feel like a local company in Fiji. (It was purchased in 2004 by privately owned Roll International, which also owns POM Wonderful and is one of the largest producers of nuts in the United States.) He uses a nearby company to print the carrying handles for Fiji Water six-packs and buys engineering services and cardboard boxes on the island. By long-standing arrangement, the plant has seeded a small business in the villages that contracts with the plant to provide landscaping and security, and runs the bus system that Marika helps manage.

75 In 2007, Fiji Water will mark a milestone. "Even though you can drive for hours and hours on this island past cane fields," says Siplon, "sometime this year, Fiji Water will eclipse sugarcane as the number-one export." That is, the amount of sugar harvested and processed for export by some 40,000 seasonal sugar workers will equal in dollar value the amount of water bottled and shipped by 200 water bottlers.

76 However we regard Fiji Water in the United States—essential accessory, harmless treat, or frivolous excess—the closer you get to the source of its water, the more significant the enterprise looks.

No, no coconut-fiber filtering, but rather, a 77 toehold in the global economy. Are 10,000 Fijians benefiting? Not directly. Perhaps 2,000. But Fiji Water is providing something else to a tiny nation of 850,000 people, which has been buffeted by two coups in seven years, and the collapse of its gold-mining and textiles industries: inspiration, a vision of what the country might have to offer the rest of the world. Developed countries are keen for myriad variations on just what Fiji Water is—a pure, unadulterated, organic, and natural product. Fiji has whole vistas of untouched, organic-ready farmland. Indeed, the hottest topic this spring (beyond politics) was how to jump-start an organic-sugar industry.

Of course, the irony of shipping a precious 78 product from a country without reliable water service is hard to avoid. This spring, typhoid from contaminated drinking water swept one of Fiji's islands, sickening dozens of villagers and killing at least one. Fiji Water often quietly supplies emergency drinking water in such cases. The reality is, if Fiji Water weren't tapping its aquifer, the underground water would slide into the Pacific Ocean, somewhere just off the coast. But the corresponding reality is, someone else—the Fijian government, an NGO—could be tapping that supply and sending it through a pipe to villagers who need it. Fiji Water has, in fact, done just that, to some degree—20 water projects in the five nearby villages. Indeed, Roll has reinvested every dollar of profit since 2004 back into the business and the island.

Siplon acknowledges the risk of shipping 79 into capitalistic neo-colonialism. "Does the world need Fiji Water?" he asks. "I'm not sure I agree with the critics on that. This company has the potential of delivering great value—or the results a cynic might have expected."

Water is, in fact, often the perfect beverage— 80 healthy, refreshing, and satisfying in a way soda or juice aren't. A good choice.

Nestlé Waters' Kim Jeffery may be defending 81 his industry when he calls bottled water "a force of nature," but he's also not wrong. Our consumption of bottled water has outstripped any marketer's dreams or talent: If you break out the single-serve plastic bottle as its own category, our consumption of bottled water grew a thousandfold between 1984 and 2005.

In the array of styles, choices, moods, and 82 messages available today, water has come to signify how we think of ourselves. We want to brand ourselves—as Madonna did—even with something as ordinary as a drink of water. We imagine there is a difference between showing up at the weekly staff meeting with Aquafina, or Fiji, or a small glass bottle of Pellegrino. Which is, of course, a little silly.

Bottled water is not a sin. But it is a choice. 83

Packing bottled water in lunch boxes, grabbing a half-liter from the fridge as we dash out the door, piling up half-finished bottles in the car cup holders—that happens because of a fundamental

Worldwide, 1 billion people have no reliable source of drinking water; 3,000 children a day die from diseases caught from tainted water.

thoughtlessness. It's only marginally more trouble to have reusable water bottles, cleaned and filled and tucked in the lunch box or the fridge. We just can't be bothered. And in a world in which 1 billion people have no reliable source of drinking water, and 3,000 children a day die from diseases caught from tainted water, that conspicuous consumption of bottled water that we don't need seems wasteful, and perhaps cavalier.

That is the sense in which Mackey, the CEO 84 of Whole Foods, and Singer, the Princeton philosopher, are both right. Mackey is right that buying bottled water is a choice, and Singer is right that given the impact it has, the easy substitutes, and the thoughtless spending involved, it's fair to ask whether it's always a good choice.

The most common question the U.S. em- 85 ployees of Fiji Water still get is, "Does it really come from Fiji?" We're choosing Fiji Water because of the hibiscus blossom on the beautiful square bottle, we're choosing it because of the silky taste. We're seduced by the *idea* of a bottle of water from Fiji. We just don't believe it really comes from Fiji. What kind of a choice is that?

Once you understand the resources mus- 86 tered to deliver the bottle of water, it's reasonable to ask as you reach for the next bottle, not just "Does the value to me equal the 99 cents I'm about to spend?" but "Does the value equal the impact I'm about to leave behind?"

Simply asking the question takes the care- 87 lessness out of the transaction. And once you understand where the water comes from, and how it got here, it's hard to look at that bottle in the same way again. ∎

Reflecting on What You Have Read

1 Fishman begins his position paper by briefly describing a scene in the warehouse of the Poland Spring water plant. In beginning this way, what assumptions does Fishman seem to be making about his audience? In what ways do those assumptions seem reasonable? Unreasonable?

2 Throughout his article, Fishman includes a number of very startling facts. For example, he mentions that we spend more for a bottle of water than for a comparable amount of gasoline. What other details in this article strike you as especially surprising? Do these details influence your attitudes toward drinking bottled water? Why or why not?

3 What explanations does Fishman give for why people drink bottled water rather than tap water? To what extent do these explanations seem plausible? For example, are they consistent with reasons you or other people you know give for drinking bottled water?

4 "Message in a Bottle" includes a timeline, "an anecdotal journey" through the history of "the bottled water phenomenon." What reasons do you see for including this timeline? Does it add to or detract from your understanding of Fishman's argument? Why or why not?

5 In paragraph 12, Fishman notes that the island of Fiji exports huge amounts of bottled water, even though more than 50 percent of the residents of Fiji have no access to clean drinking water. What point is Fishman making with this reference to Fiji? What assumptions does he expect his readers to make? In what ways does his argument here seem persuasive or unpersuasive?

6 Find a passage in which Fishman makes his strongest (or weakest) argument against drinking bottled water. What evidence and reasons does he give in support of his claim? Do his evidence and reasons seem persuasive to you? Why or why not?

7 Page 289 shows an inset box in the shape of a water bottle to make a point that "Fiji water produces more than a million bottles a day, while more than half the people in Fiji do not have reliable drinking water." How would you characterize the appeal made by this visual? Is it an appeal to emotions? To logic? What basis do you have for your answer?

Thinking Ahead

In "Message in a Bottle," Fishman identifies an apparently harmless, trivial activity that benefits one group (people who want the convenience of buying bottled water) and yet harms the very people (in this case, citizens of Fiji) who make those benefits possible. Can you think of other situations in which one group benefits at the expense of another? What evidence and reasons can you find to persuade people to change a practice that benefits them but harms others?

Considered Living Car-Free?
Ashley B. Roberts

Ashley B. Roberts was an English major with minors in history and philosophy. As an undergraduate, she was a freelance writer for a local paper and was awarded second place for general news reporting for the year 2007 by the North Carolina Press Association. She enjoys riding her bike, reading, and dancing. She now lives in Brooklyn, New York, where she plans to continue her writing career.

Considered Living Car-Free?

If you're like many college students, you look forward to the day when you can move 1
out of your dorm and get your own apartment. It's an exciting transition, but one that requires some lifestyle readjustments. After all, living on campus provides easy access to all your basic necessities: dining hall, Laundromat, library, and so on. You can walk, or take the campus bus, to almost all of your destinations. So before you move you will want a clear idea of how exactly you will get around. The first questions you ask might be "What sort of car should I buy? New or used? Hybrid or gas powered?" A better question, however, is "Do I really need a car?" Initially, the answer may seem obvious: of course you need a car. After all, not living in a "walkable" environment like a college campus means getting to destinations that are not grouped together in one easily accessed package. The grocery store is on one side of town, while your bank is on the other. How could someone live without a car? Amazingly, the answer is quite simple. Not only can most students easily attend to duties outside of their home without a vehicle, but they also will reap massive benefits from living car-free—benefits ranging from improving their health to helping curb pollution and saving money.

Reports in the nightly news and in daily newspapers emphasize that one of the greatest 2
threats to Americans' health is obesity, and one of the biggest causes of obesity is a lack of physical exercise. With busy lifestyles and high-stress vocations, some people assume that setting aside a portion of their day for exercising is not a realistic option. With little available time for keeping fit, it should not be shocking that more than half of U.S. adults are overweight, as shown in Figure 1.

Unfortunately, college students are not exempt from this trend. Although one study 3
finds that the "freshman fifteen" is a "myth," college students on average gain seven pounds during their freshman year ("Freshman Fifteen"). What's worse, they tend to continue gaining weight. Since 1980, the incidence of obesity among people between 18 and 29 has doubled. A survey of 160 college students found that "almost half" of the students surveyed were

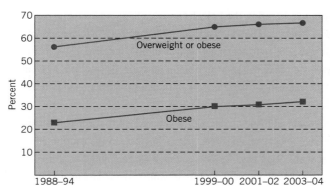

Note: Age adjusted by the direct method to the year 2000 U.S. Bureau of the Census estimates using the age groups 20–39, 40–59, and 60 years and over. Overweight defined as BMI≥25, Obesity defined as BMI≥30.

Fig. 1. Trends in Adult Overweight and Obesity, Ages 20 Years and Over (United States. Dept. of Health and Human Services. Centers for Disease Control and Prevention).

either overweight or obese. Authors of this study concluded that "unless this group of college students make changes in their lifestyle, they will probably experience an increase in overweight and obesity" (Adderly-Kelly). Another study points out that these increases are associated with "type 2 diabetes, stroke, congestive heart failure, coronary heart disease, various cancers, osteoarthritis, and sleep apnea" ("Clinical Guidelines" vii).

Ironically, college students can easily avoid much of this simply by adopting a car-free transportation routine. Over time, walking or biking to their destinations will help students not only avoid gaining weight but also improve their cardiovascular health, muscle strength, and flexibility. The benefits of making such a simple change in lifestyle may sound too good to be true. But a recent study conducted by Lawrence Frank, a professor at the University of British Columbia, found that people who live in suburbs are more prone to drive to destinations than are their city-dwelling counterparts and consequently are more at risk of being overweight or obese. According to the study, "for every extra 30 minutes of commuting time per day, participants had a 3% greater likelihood of obesity than peers who drove less" (Schmidt A624).

4

In addition to lowering the risk of obesity, biking and walking can lead to other   5
positive health benefits. The Thunderhead Alliance's 2007 benchmarking report found
that states in the U.S. that averaged highest in biking and walking had a population with
the lowest levels of diabetes and high-blood pressure (Steele 97). Not only can you avoid
bad health, but you can promote good health as well with a change in the way you
commute.

Another benefit of living car-less is the satisfaction that comes with knowing you are   6
affecting the environment in a positive way. In addition to the concern about an increase in
obesity, national attention has been focused on a concern about pollution. The world faces a
steady rise in the release of greenhouse gases which are directly related to global warming. At
the present rate of warming, global temperatures could increase by as much as seven degrees
by the end of the twenty-first century. And that increase will lead to rising sea levels and
changes in precipitation and storm patterns ("Future Climate Change"). In the United States,
transportation (cars, buses, trucks) contributes about 27% of these gases. Worldwide, the
situation is even worse. Almost one-third of all atmospheric pollution comes from people's
travels ("On the Road").

The problem of global warming might seem out of control, or at least too great for   7
any one individual to solve. Yet every person has the chance to help. According to the
EPA, an average of 1,600 pounds of greenhouse gas emissions can be reduced annually by
one person going car-less two days a week ("On the Road"). Imagine the impact on gas
emissions that living a lifetime car-free can produce. When a single college student lives
car-less for two years, the possible greenhouse gas emission for the time period may be
reduced by 160,000 pounds.

Besides contributing to health problems and pollution, a car is not a very good   8
investment. A reliable vehicle will cost at least $5,000, and the value of that vehicle will begin
to decrease the moment it leaves the dealer's lot. Even if you keep a car for only a few months,
you probably won't be able to sell it for a price anywhere near what you paid for it. And the
longer you keep the car, the less it will be worth. To add to this problem, it's almost certain
that gasoline prices will continue to rise, insurance costs will be high (the younger the driver,
the higher the premium), and even a well-maintained car can have mechanical difficulties.
Beyond the initial investment, there is the expense of taxes, insurance, and annual
maintenance—in all, a huge financial investment that does not yield a financial return.   9

Walking and cycling, by contrast, are much more cost-effective. A pair of good walking
shoes costs approximately $70. Even if the shoes wear out every six months or so, the annual

cost will be less than what many people pay each month for gasoline. Cycling is a little more expensive. A comfortable road bike, proper safety equipment (such as a helmet), and bike accessories cost about $700. Though the financial commitment to own a bike is significantly more than owning a pair of sneakers, the whole cost is merely a fraction of the financial obligation the car owner must face.

Given all of this, it's worth asking yourself if you really do need a car, even if you move off campus. Since you have accustomed to dorm life, you have already learned to live without a personal vehicle, and thus are more acclimated to the car-free lifestyle. Granted, the farther away from campus you live, the more you may need to modify your schedule in order to adjust to the increase in time spent traveling. But there are some real compensations—better health, a better environment, and better finances—all in all, not a bad deal for people who are willing to do without a car for a couple of years. 10

Some Frequently Asked Questions about Living Car-Free

Q: What happens when you're car-free in extremely bad weather?

A: If the weather is really bad, take the bus or carpool with a friend. Otherwise, just dress appropriately for the weather. You can even ride your bike comfortably if you have a poncho and rain boots.

Q: Is it safe to be a pedestrian? What about cycling?

A: Let's face it: even the best drivers can be distracted briefly. So make sure drivers can see you easily. If you're biking, use attachable blinking lights. At night, wear jackets and backpacks made with light-reflective materials. And follow safety rules: If you're biking, do not run red lights. If you're walking, stay on the sidewalk or, if you have to walk on the shoulder of the road, walk facing oncoming traffic.

Q: I don't really like to exercise. And what if I get tired?

A: At first, biking or walking may seem like exercise, but within a couple of weeks, they will become just another part of your daily routine.

Q: What will my friends think? What about social pressure?

A: This article should help to answer some of your friends' questions about why you walk or bike. But if they think you are uncool for not driving, they may might not be the friends you thought they were. Also, riding or walking communicates that you care about your health. This is a very appealing attitude and it attracts others who feel the same way about their well-being.

Works Cited

Adderly-Kelly, Beatrice. "The Prevalence of Overweight and Obesity among College Students." *Virginia Henderson International Nursing Library* Sigma Theta Tau Intl, 2005. Web. 10 Sept. 2007.

"'Freshman Fifteen' Is a Myth, but Weight Gain Is Still a Problem." *Medical News Today* 11 Feb. 2006. Web. 10 Sept. 2007.

Schmidt, Charles W. "Sprawl: The New Manifest Destiny?" *Environmental Health Perspectives* 112.11 (2004): A620–27. JSTOR. Web. 9 Sept. 2007.

Steele, Kristen. *Benchmarking Report: Bicycling and Walking in the U.S.* Washington: Thunderhead Alliance, 2007. Web. 10 Sept. 2007.

United States. Dept. of Health and Human Services. Natl. Inst. of Health. Natl. Heart, Lung, and Blood Inst. *Clinical Guidelines on the Identification, Evaluation, and Treatment of Overweight and Obesity in Adults: The Evidence Report*. Natl. Heart, Lung, and Blood Inst., 2000. Web. 10 Sept. 2007.

United States. Dept. of Health and Human Services. Centers for Disease Control and Prevention. Natl. Center for Health Statistics. "Prevalence of Overweight and Obesity Among Adults: United States, 2003–2004." *NCHS Health E-Stats*. Natl. Center for Health Statistics, 14 July 2007. Web. 9 Sept. 2007.

United States. Environmental Protection Agency. "Future Climate Change." *Climate Change*. US Environmental Protection Agency, 20 Aug. 2007. Web. 9 Sept. 2007.

United States. Environmental Protection Agency. "On the Road." *Climate Change*. US Environmental Protection Agency, 7 May 2007. Web. 9 Sept. 2007.

Reflecting on What You Have Read

1 Ashley begins her essay by mentioning several questions that may cross students' minds when they are considering moving off campus. What reasons do you see for her mentioning these questions before she gets to the question she thinks is most important? ("Do I really need a car?") Do you agree that this is the most important question? Why or why not?

2 Students often comment on the "freshman fifteen"—the tendency to gain weight during the first year at college. But students often assume that this is not a serious problem. Do you share this assumption? How effectively does Ashley challenge this assumption?

3 Does Ashley persuade you that going car-less is something you should do—or something you might even want and be able to do? Why or why not?

4 To what extent does Ashley succeed (or fail) in using ethical appeals in her argument? That is, does she succeed in showing readers that she understands their situation and is someone whose facts and reasons they can trust? In what passages do you find that she is or is not especially successful in making an ethical appeal? Why do you think she succeeds or fails in these passages?

For a more complete discussion of ethical appeals, see pages 328–29.

5 Lists of Frequently Asked Questions don't often appear in academic essays. Given her audience, topic, and purpose, do you think Ashley should have included these questions and answers on page 305? Why or why not?

Thinking Ahead

In her essay, Ashley takes a position on a decision her readers are likely to have to make. What other decisions (at school, at home, at work) do you find yourself or others having to make? What evidence and reasons can you find for arguing that people should choose one course of action rather than some other?

Guide to Writing a Position Paper

▷ GUIDE TO WRITING A POSITION PAPER

The remainder of this chapter will guide you through the process of creating a persuasive position paper that makes clear claims supported by good reasons and credible evidence. The first steps are selecting a topic, analyzing your audience, and identifying the specific purpose you hope to achieve in your position paper. Then you will work on creating a draft, using many of the strategies illustrated by position papers in Reading to Write. These strategies can help you explore your topic, write an introduction that will engage readers' interest, create an appropriate voice, organize your work, conclude your position paper effectively, design and integrate visual elements (photographs, charts, page layout) to convey your messages. Finally, the section Reviewing and Revising will guide you in creating a review draft, assessing your work carefully, and using that assessment to revise and proofread your position paper.

As you work through the assignment for this chapter, you can also read a little bit about how undergraduate Ashley Roberts wrote her position paper. In the Student Q & A box on page 312, you will find the first of several brief conversations that Ashley had with the authors of this text.

▷ Assignment

Write a position paper either on a topic of your choice or on one selected by your instructor. The topic should be an issue—that is, a question about which people disagree—that matters to others (an individual, a group, or an organization) as much as it matters to you. Your instructor may have specific requirements about how long your position paper should be, whether you should prepare the position paper as a print or online document (or as an oral presentation), and whether you should include or exclude any particular visual elements or use a particular documentation style to formally cite sources. Be sure you understand those requirements before you start working on the assignment.

GETTING STARTED

When you begin thinking of topics for this assignment, it will probably make sense to think of issues that matter a great deal to you, perhaps because they affect you or others you care about or perhaps because they relate to some of your fundamental beliefs. But ultimately, you will have to write about an issue that will have as much meaning for others as it does for you. Consequently, the next section of this chapter will help you select an appropriate topic and become very clear about your audience and purpose.

Selecting a Topic

You may not always have a lot of choice as to the topics you write about. Your instructor (or, eventually, an employer or a client) may say, in effect, "I want you to do a position paper on . . ." In many situations, however, you will have some freedom in selecting a topic for your position paper. If you do, think of a topic that has the following characteristics.

▶ The topic should encompass multiple perspectives or have aspects that make it difficult for people to agree on what should be done or how they should feel.

▶ The topic should be one on which reasonable people may reasonably disagree.

▶ The topic should not be one on which viewpoints (your own and your readers') are so highly emotional and strongly entrenched that you have little realistic chance of influencing your readers' thoughts, values, feelings, and actions.

If you feel so strongly about a topic that you can't imagine rational readers having a perspective that differs from yours, it will be difficult to think of evidence and reasons that will influence your readers. If your topic is one on which readers already think exactly as you do, there may be little point in writing a position paper at all—unless you can think of facts and reasons that extend readers' understanding of your topic.

The basic goal of a position paper is to influence another person's thoughts and actions. See page 250 for a list of some more specific purposes writers often try to achieve in writing a position paper. If your topic does not allow you to accomplish such purposes—that is, if it is one on which you have no reasonable chance of influencing a particular reader—you should consider writing on a different topic.

Coming Up with Ideas for a Topic

If you're having trouble coming up with good topics, review suggestions in the Thinking Ahead passages that follow each of the position papers in Reading to Write. Or you might consider some of the kinds of topics about which people write position papers.

▶ Decisions people confront (Should people, for example, support or oppose a particular candidate for political office?)

▶ Policies that affect you or people or organizations you care about (Is it a good idea for government to provide vouchers to support students who attend private schools? Should freshmen be allowed to have cars on campus?)

▶ Trends or issues frequently discussed in news media (Should people be concerned about alcohol or drug use on college campuses?)

You might also get some ideas for topics by engaging in the following activities.

Brainstorm ideas for topics. Writing as quickly as you can, list issues you care about, issues other people care about, or issues you already know something about. Focus on issues that you know people could argue or debate about. It may help to complete sentences such as the following.

One thing I've heard people argue about is _____.

One issue that concerns me is _____.

One really controversial topic is _____.

For now, don't worry about explaining or justifying your ideas. Just write as fast as you can, getting down as many ideas as possible.

Review what you have written with a small group or the entire class. Notice the topics classmates respond to most strongly. Explain your views on some of these topics and notice which topics prompt strong agreement or disagreement. See if classmates can suggest related topics. Don't feel you have to accept their suggestions; just see if any sound like good possibilities.

Select a topic that seems like it might have potential and then brainstorm about that topic. Writing as quickly as you can, answer the following questions.

What's my current position on this topic?

Why does it matter to me or people I care about?

What evidence and reasons can I think of to support my position?

How and where might others agree or disagree with me?

If you can answer at least two of these questions, you probably have a topic with good potential. If not, you may need to go back and engage in some of the activities listed above.

Assessing Your Choice of a Topic

Once you have identified a topic on which you might like to write a position paper, you need to assess that topic, making sure that (1) you can find plenty of factual information to support your opinion, and (2) you have a topic on which reasonable people disagree. To help with this, try the following activities, making notes about what you learn.

Summarize what you have written and share with a group. Ask the group to help you think of audiences whose attitudes or actions you might be able to influence with regard to your topic. If you can't identify an audience that you might have a chance of influencing—either because their minds are already firmly made up or because the topic just doesn't matter to them—you should consider writing on another topic.

Think further about your own experience. How has your opinion been shaped by events that you have witnessed or that have happened to you? List some details about those events: Who did what? When? Why? How did you or others react to those events? What have you done, seen, or heard that influences your opinion?

Find out what others are saying about your topic. Discuss your topic with friends and family. Tune in to a radio or television talk show or a community channel. What opinions do people express? What evidence and reasons do they give to support their opinions?

Do some reading. Do a preliminary search in your library's databases. Check out the Internet, but remember that information online is not always reliable or complete. Do not try to read everything carefully at this point. Just read enough to confirm that your proposed topic is interesting and worthwhile and that there is plenty of credible material available on it.

Look for visual information—images, charts, graphs, and so forth—that you can use to reinforce the position you defend in your written text.

Conduct a brief reality check after doing a fair amount of reading, watching, and listening. Do you have a topic that matters to you? Can you find plenty of credible reasons and evidence to present your opinion? Can you think of an audience that would at least seriously consider the position you are arguing for? If you can't answer yes to at least two of these questions, consider changing your topic or your audience. Do this now, not the night before the assignment is due.

 **Student Q & A   Selecting a Topic**

Writing Now (WN): What were some of the topics you considered writing about?
Ashley Roberts (AR): I thought about plagiarism or the benefits and harms of Division I athletics. But then I decided to write about doing without a car while in college.

WN: Why did you choose that topic?
AR: I like riding my bike a lot. I own a car, but I mainly use it to drive home. Other than that I've pretty much gone car-less since I've been in college. I probably use my bike or walk 90 percent of the time. I can get to the grocery store and do most of my chores on foot or on my bike. So I decided to see if I could persuade other people living off campus to do without a car. ∎

Understanding Your Audience and Purpose

When writing a position paper, you can assume that not all of your readers necessarily share your opinion, either because they have not clearly articulated their opinions on the topic or they have positions that differ from yours. (If everybody in your audience already knows what you know and thinks and feels exactly as you do, there's little point in writing a position paper.) But what else can you assume about what the audience knows, believes, or feels about your topic? And what sort of impact do you want to have on the audience? Do you want to alarm (or reassure) them? Do you want to change the way they think? Do you simply want them to acknowledge the validity of your ideas? Or do you want to achieve one of the other purposes listed on page 250?

There may be times when you try to influence the attitudes or actions of people you don't know very well—your local school board members, for example, or a state legislator. But for this assignment, write to someone whom you actually know and whose opinion you have a good chance of influencing. If you know a member of your school board or have worked directly with a legislator in your work for his or her campaign, go ahead and write to this person. Otherwise, choose an audience who you believe will consider what you have to say about your topic.

If you hope to have a significant impact on your audience, you need to understand that audience as fully as possible. And you need to think carefully about the purpose(s) you hope to accomplish. As you work on your position paper, your understanding of your audience and your specific purpose(s) may change. But at this point, you should be as clear and specific as you can, so you should write out answers to the following questions, and then revise your answers as necessary.

Audience knowledge, needs, and attitudes

- What do your readers already know about your topic? What have they heard or read concerning your topic? What sort of personal experiences have they had concerning your topic?

- Why would your readers want or need to read a position paper on your topic? How does your topic affect them or people they care about? Does it address a concern they feel? Are they in a situation where they need to know about your topic?

- What biases or preconceptions do readers have concerning your topic? Are they making any questionable assumptions?

Audience expectations for content

- What questions or objections are your readers likely to want to have answered?

- What kinds of appeals are your readers likely to respond well to? (Are they, for example, more likely to respond well to logical appeals or to emotional appeals?)

- What kinds of information will your readers see as credible?

- Are there any visual features (for example, photographs, charts, bulleted lists) your readers are likely to appreciate?

Audience expectations for layout or format

- What sort of layout will readers expect? For example, should you use one column or two? Should you use charts, graphs, or illustrations? Should you use pull quotes or inset boxes?

Purpose(s)

- In addition to arguing persuasively for your position on your topic, what else do you hope to accomplish by writing your position paper? For example, do you want to challenge readers' assumptions about an issue? Refute a point of view you disagree with? Gain respect for—if not acceptance of—your opinion? Alarm (or reassure) readers? Express views your readers may hold but have never articulated very clearly or emphatically?

> **Guidelines for Analyzing Your Audience and Identifying Purpose**

For more information about layout, see Chapter 9.

▶ Go to **bedfordstmartins.com/ writingnow** to download these questions from Chapter 5 > Worksheets.

- What sort of voice do you want readers to hear when they read your position paper? What image do you want to convey of yourself? For example, do you want to sound like someone who is extremely logical? Do you want to allow your emotions to come through in your writing? Do you want to seem like someone who is very sympathetic with your audience's situation? Or do you want to create a voice that contains elements of logic, emotion, or sympathy?

To answer these questions about audience and purpose, talk with one or more members of your audience. Ask them what their views are on your topic and what they have heard or read recently that has influenced their positions. Identify points about which you are most likely to disagree with your audience, and determine whether you and your audience share any of the same values, experiences, or attitudes. Also, draw on your knowledge of yourself, asking such questions as the following: If I were in my audience's place, what kinds of evidence and reasoning would I find especially persuasive? How would I react to the arguments I want to make in this position paper? Where would I raise objections? What questions would I ask? As you answer these questions, use what you are learning about your audience and topic to decide on the purpose(s) you hope to accomplish by writing your position paper. Also decide what sort of voice you want to convey.

While you are working on your position paper, your understanding of your audience and purpose may change. You may even find that your views change. That's fine. If you hope to be able to change someone else's opinion, you should also be open to changing your own opinion. But for now, be as clear and specific as possible.

Student Analysis of Audience and Purpose

Here's how Ashley Roberts described the audience and purpose for her position paper, "Considered Living Car-Free?" (p. 302). Ashley's audience consists of college students who may be moving off campus and considering purchasing an automobile. They are aware of global warming, rising national obesity rates, and personal finances, but they have not considered these issues as relating to owning a vehicle.

Audience knowledge, needs, and attitudes

My audience has heard reports about problems caused by obesity and climate change. They have never lived off campus, but everyone they know who lives off campus drives a car.

They are a little bit concerned about gaining weight and causing harm to the environment. And they're really concerned about saving money. They will be moving into off-campus apartments, and they will have some very practical concerns about how they will get around.

They assume that having a car is essential for students who are living off campus. They assume that there are no other convenient, practical ways to get to campus, the bank, etc.

Audience's expectations for content

Questions my readers will likely want to have answered.

• What are the benefits of choosing to live car-free?

- What are some of the difficulties associated with a car-less lifestyle?
- How can people get around town without a personal vehicle? They may think walking and biking aren't good ideas when the weather is bad.

This is a serious, practical matter, so they are most likely to be influenced by facts from authoritative sources. They will also appreciate information from someone who's actually lived off campus without driving a car.

Audience expectations for layout or format

I don't know that they would expect pull quotes or inset boxes. The graphs I wanted to use didn't seem to fit well into a two-column format.

Since they are looking for serious, authoritative information, they will probably want graphs to show exactly how serious the problems are.

Purpose

My purpose is to introduce my audience to the idea of living car-less and not only make it seem like a good idea but also make it seem a little less impossible.

I want to make it clear that I have some solid, authoritative knowledge, but I also want to sound fairly personal, like someone my readers can relate to and not some impersonal authority lecturing readers about what they should do.

CREATING A DRAFT

By now you have identified the issue you want to write about, and you are beginning to get a good idea of what your readers think about that issue and of the purpose(s) you hope to accomplish in writing your position paper. The next few sections of this chapter outline a variety of visual and verbal strategies that will help you create a persuasive position paper by exploring your topic thoroughly, devising ways to engage your audience, and so forth. As in other chapters in this book, you will be working with strategies that appear in position papers found in Reading to Write. The following discussions, along with the strategies in the how-to charts, will help you see how specific passages reflect more general strategies that you can apply to your own writing. You can always add to these lists of strategies by analyzing other position papers you find especially persuasive.

Exploring Your Topic

If you are to have a chance of influencing readers (or at least getting them to consider your point seriously), you will have to explore your topic thoroughly, not only gathering information but identifying reasons that readers will find plausible and compelling.

Gathering Information

As you may have noticed from the position papers in the Reading to Write section of this chapter, position papers can be based on information from a variety of sources—personal experiences (your own or other people's) as well as secondary sources ranging from the opinions of experts to data from a survey.

Draw on personal experiences. In some situations, accounts of personal experiences can be very effective ways to support the position you want to take. These experiences can help establish your credibility, demonstrating that your position is grounded on firsthand knowledge. But you have to be careful here. A single, isolated experience is rarely persuasive. You will need to show that your experiences are typical, that they happen to others and in more than one situation. And it will help greatly if you select experiences that compare directly to those of your specific readers.

Use secondary sources. As a rule, you shouldn't try to develop your argument in a vacuum. Look for other people's opinions and additional information, and consider these carefully. Consider not only your own experiences (always a primary source of information) but also secondary sources: the evidence and reasons found in articles in databases and on the Web, speeches, television or radio reports, and books. Especially try to find data or position papers from people your readers are likely to see as authorities—people whose knowledge or expertise gives them special insight into your topic. You should also be on the lookout for visual information that will help you argue your point— photographs, charts, graphs, tables, and statistics that you might incorporate into a chart or graph.

For more advice on evaluating the credibility of a source, see Chapter 12.

The following chart illustrates strategies for drawing on personal experiences as well as using secondary sources.

How to Gather Information

STRATEGIES

Examine your own experiences. Look for multiple examples of things that have happened to you or people you care about. Especially look for experiences your audience will relate to. But remember: A single, isolated experience is unlikely to be persuasive unless it is very dramatic and obviously typical of other experiences readers have had.

EXAMPLES FROM READINGS

In "SUVs Belong in Car Ads Only" (p. 255), Ellen Goodman explains her position by referring to something her readers have almost certainly experienced—the difference between ads for cars and the actual experience of driving on crowded streets and highways.

STRATEGIES	EXAMPLES FROM READINGS
Find out what others are saying about your topic. This might include comments from an authority, data from a research report, or a survey (either one you create or one conducted by a reputable source).	In "Where Have All the Criminals Gone?" (p. 269), Steven Levitt and Stephen Dubner support their view of the death penalty by citing a Supreme Court justice. In "What Decreased Crime?" (p. 274) John Lott articulates a different view by citing studies done by a variety of researchers.
Look for information that challenges your opinion as well as information that supports your point of view. This information may help you understand and respond to readers who are critical of what you write. It may also help you come to a new understanding of your subject, perhaps changing your opinion altogether.	 In "Drop in the Bucket" (p. 266), Karrie Jacobs clearly believes that people in New Orleans have not received enough help after Hurricane Katrina. But in the fourth and fifth paragraphs of her position paper, she describes some of the successful work that is currently going on in New Orleans.
Look for different types of information.	In addition to providing details about companies that produce bottled water, Charles Fishman in "Message in a Bottle" (p. 294) includes historical information about "the ancient origins and fantastical growth of the bottled water phenomenon."

Keep track of information. As you begin drafting, it can be very frustrating to find that you remember only part of an important quotation or that you aren't sure where you found an interesting statistic. To avoid this frustration, you should do two things. First, keep detailed notes of any personal experiences you want to include in your position paper. Jot down responses to questions such as the following.

▶ What did I see or hear?

▶ What did people do or say?

▶ What was the setting?

Second, create a working bibliography. In a notebook or separate computer file, keep complete bibliographic information for each source you read. Record the author's name, the title of the piece (article, book, Web site), and all the information required to locate the piece if you need to come back to it (the URL of the Web site and the date you accessed it, for example, or date and page numbers of the magazine article). You need not record all this information according to the precise

For advice on taking notes and creating a working bibliography, see Chapter 12.

guidelines of the documentation style you're using, but noting all this information will save you time later. Also note the main point of each source and how it relates to the issue you are discussing. It can be especially useful to list the main questions the source poses and summarize the answers it gives.

{ Student Q & A } Gathering Information

Writing Now (WN): You referred to a lot of research studies. How did you find them?

Ashley Roberts (AR): I went to the library on campus and got one of the librarians to show me how to use JSTOR, a database with refereed scholarly articles.

WN: But how did you know what to look for? You couldn't just look for articles about living off campus without a car.

AR: When I moved off campus, I started walking and riding my bike just about everywhere and realized that I was losing weight and getting into better shape. Also, I knew that obesity was a big issue. So I started looking for articles on obesity and the value of exercise. Some of those articles referred to other articles I could use. ∎

{ Exercise } Evaluating Sources

As you consult secondary sources about your topic, keep a working bibliography, recording the author, title, and other publication information you will need later. Review the entries in your working bibliography, and then evaluate them with the following questions in mind: Are there entries by writers who disagree with you? With each other? Then create a list of the key points made in each source. Write a paragraph summarizing the evidence (and occasionally quoting key phrases) your sources present in support of these points. ∎

Reflecting on Information

After you have identified several personal experiences and read at least a half-dozen sources, you should begin reflecting on the information you have gathered, trying to justify the position you want to take on your topic. But before you begin this work, reread the way you responded to questions about audience and purpose on pages 313–14. Are there some questions that are not answered thoroughly or specifically? For example, are you lacking information about your readers' knowledge, needs, and attitudes? Do you have a good sense of what your readers will expect in terms of content, both verbal and visual? At this point, finish completing your responses to the best of your ability.

Also review the notes you took for your working bibliography. Underline or mark key facts or reasons. After doing this, don't try to write a formal essay right away; don't even worry about paragraphing or organization. Just set aside twenty to thirty minutes and write as rapidly as you can in response to the following prompts.

One claim (or point) I want to make is _____.

I believe this claim is justified because _____.

Without stopping to look back at the information you gathered, continue to elaborate on the position you want to take.

Another claim I want to make is _____.

I believe this claim is justified because _____.

Another claim is _____.

Continue to elaborate as much as possible from memory. Keep on making and justifying claims until you have used up your allotted time.

After completing this reflective work, read or show one or more classmates what you have written. Describe the intended audience and then ask your classmates to answer the following questions.

▶ Do any of my claims seem likely to be especially persuasive to my audience? (If so, one of these claims may become your thesis, or several of your claims may become the topic sentences of supporting paragraphs.)

▶ Can you think of questions or objections my audience might raise in response to the points I am making?

▶ Can you think of other facts or reasons I might use to elaborate on the claims I am making?

▶ Can you think of places in my position paper where a visual (a photograph, for example, or a chart) might make my work more persuasive?

After considering your classmates' responses, determine whether there are places where you might use one or more of the strategies explained in How to Gather Information to find additional support for your claims.

Formulating a Thesis

After discussing your work with your classmates, complete the following sentence.

The basic point I want to make is _____.

This sentence will become your tentative thesis, the principal claim you think you want to make in your position paper. As you continue to develop your topic, you may want to revise that thesis. But it will serve as the starting point from which you can look for ways to make your views as clear and persuasive as possible.

{ Exercise }   **Exploring a Topic**

Choose one or more of the position papers in Reading to Write or work with another piece your instructor assigns, and then answer this question: In what passages does the author use one or more of the strategies explained under Exploring Your Topic (pp. 315–22)? Make notes on the position paper and be prepared to explain your answer to your classmates. ■

Developing Your Ideas

Once you have a tentative thesis, you need to develop your ideas more fully, providing sound arguments in support of your position. To do this, begin by reviewing the work you did with the prompts on page 319, where you listed and briefly explained the basic claims you thought you would make in your position paper. Decide whether you need to eliminate or modify some claims or add others. Then develop these ideas by giving compelling reasons and elaborating with credible evidence.

Give reasons. As is the case with other kinds of writing in this book, a persuasive argument requires evidence—details, statistics, quotations—that supports the claims you make. But a good argument requires something more—reasons that your audience will see as valid and that will show why the evidence you present justifies your claims. Here's an example.

Imagine that you have received a ticket for parking illegally on campus, and you want to avoid paying a fine. Imagine further that the evidence in your case is clear: The time on your parking meter had expired. Even so, you do not believe that you should have to pay the fine. How could you justify that opinion? Here are some reasons you might be tempted to give.

▶ "Other cars were parked illegally, and mine is the only car that was ticketed."

▶ "I did not see the sign."

▶ "I was there for only five (or ten, or whatever) minutes."

These reasons might sound good, but they probably will not work—at least, not if those in charge of parking regulations at your school assume that all people who park on campus are responsible for their actions. In that case, it is irrelevant that other people parked illegally, that you did not see a sign clearly posted, or that you ignored its instructions for only a short time. None of these are acceptable reasons that will excuse you from paying the fine.

Now consider an alternative approach. Suppose your school's parking regulations state that motorists may not be responsible for parking violations caused by circumstances beyond their control. Now you have the basis for a very different argument.

Claim: "I should not have to pay the fine."

Reason: The Parking Office assumes that people should not be held responsible for actions that are genuinely beyond their control.

Evidence: My car's battery was dead, a fact over which I had no control. Here's a receipt showing that shortly after my car was ticketed, I had to pay a mechanic to come give the battery a jump start.

Putting together claim, reasons, and evidence, an argument against paying the fine might go something like this: "Campus parking regulations state that motorists should not be penalized for parking violations caused by circumstances over which they have no control. I had no control over a dead battery. Therefore, I ask that the fine be waived."

So will you have to pay the fine? Probably not. Not if the Parking Office really believes motorists should not be penalized for actions over which they had no control. Of course, the key word here—as in any argument—is *probably*. You can never be absolutely certain what an audience will decide. But if you have come up with reasons the audience accepts, the odds are in your favor. So how do you identify such reasons? You have already seen one example: Refer to a rule or procedure your audience accepts—or, better yet, a rule or procedure your audience has established. The following chart explains other ways to provide good reasons.

How to Give Good Reasons

STRATEGIES	EXAMPLES FROM READINGS
Refer to principles, attitudes, or values your audience accepts.	In "Considered Living Car-Free?" (p. 302), Ashley Roberts explicitly bases her argument on her readers' desire for health, a clean environment, and financial advantage.
Show how something (people's actions, government policies, etc.) violates these principles, attitudes, or values.	In "Cheap Food Nation" (p. 260), Eric Schlosser notes that "most Americans regard steroid use in sports as an unhealthy form of cheating." Then he points out that, ironically, we do not question this unhealthy practice when it comes to raising much of the food we eat.

Provide evidence. The evidence you use may come from a variety of sources: statistics, survey results, comments by authorities, or firsthand observations. But no matter the source, evidence should consist of facts that can be verified—either by reference to an authoritative, reasonably impartial source or by firsthand observation of the facts. For example, you should probably place more value on results of a poll conducted by a major national newspaper than a poll conducted by the staff of a candidate for political office. If you cannot observe the facts directly, find someone who did and who also has the knowledge and integrity to report those facts credibly. Once you have such facts, there are several ways you can use them to provide evidence.

How to Provide Evidence

STRATEGIES	EXAMPLES FROM READINGS
Cite consequences (also known as establishing causes and effects). Set up an if-then situation. Show that one event is the cause or effect of the other, especially noting effects or consequences that readers may not have anticipated.	In "Message in a Bottle" (p. 285), Charles Fishman's argument rests principally on the facts he uses to show that the consumption of bottled water will harm both the environment and the people in some of the areas from which bottled water is obtained.
Point out a difference between what people hope, claim, assume, or expect and what is actually the case.	In "Cheap Food Nation" (p. 262), Eric Schlosser notes that "for years, U.S. farmers and ranchers have been told that the latest chemical and technological advances . . . would increase their income." However, Schlosser points out, "farmers and ranchers are steadily being driven off the land."
Show that your topic is part of a larger trend.	In arguing that college students need to adopt a healthier lifestyle, Ashley Roberts, in "Considered Living Car-Free?" (p. 302), notes that college students have a relatively high probability of becoming obese.
Give multiple examples to prove a point.	In arguing that consumption of bottled water is part of a "culture of indulgence," Fishman (p. 285) notes that the sale of water from the island of Fiji has more than one "environmental cost."
Provide facts that challenge readers' assumptions in ways they might not expect.	In "Message in a Bottle," Fishman recounts an incident in which the person responsible for marketing Perrier was unable to distinguish between it and six other sparkling waters.

 **Engaging an Audience**

Writing Now: You used an inset box titled "Frequently Asked Questions." Why did you do that? Why didn't you just incorporate answers to those questions into the main body of your text?

Ashley Roberts: The questions weren't really necessary to prove my thesis, but I thought answering them might engage my readers better. Also, it shows I was taking their concerns into consideration. ■

Engaging Your Audience: Writing an Introduction

In writing your assignment for this chapter, you are addressing readers who do not necessarily share your point of view. Some readers may be skeptical about your argument because they have already formed their own positions on your topic. Others might have no opinion whatever, especially if they have never thought your topic was important enough to consider seriously. In either case, you will have to create a relationship with your readers. For the skeptical readers, this may entail showing that you and they share some of the same values or concerns. For readers who have never given your topic much thought, establishing a relationship may require showing exactly how your topic relates to them and people they care about.

In addition to establishing a relationship with your readers, you will also need to make them aware of a conflict that will motivate them to read the position you are taking. For readers who have already formed a position that differs from yours, you probably won't have to do much to create a conflict. Indeed, it will probably be more important to establish some kind of common ground with these readers, enabling them to see you as a reasonable person who might have something valuable to say. For readers who have not already formed an opinion, you should develop a conflict that makes them see why they need to begin forming a position on your topic.

Relating to Readers

The position papers in the Reading to Write section display a variety of ways to engage readers. Here are several strategies that will help you relate to your readers.

How to Relate to Readers

STRATEGIES	EXAMPLES FROM READINGS
Create a scene readers can easily visualize.	At the beginning of "Message in a Bottle" (p. 287), Charles Fishman creates a visual image of one plant that bottles water: "As far as the eye can see, there are double-stacked pallets packed with half-pint bottles, half-liters, liters, 'Aquapods' for school lunches, and 2.5-gallon jugs for the refrigerator."

continued on next page ▶

How to Relate to Readers (continued)

STRATEGIES	EXAMPLES FROM READINGS
Mention a situation in which readers have found themselves.	In the first paragraph of "Considered Living Car-Free?" (p. 302), Ashley Roberts mentions some of the "lifestyle readjustments" college students face when they consider living off campus.
Refer to an experience or event your audience will recognize.	 "Drop in the Bucket" (p. 265) begins by reminding readers not only of the experience of watching Hurricane Katrina on television, but also of the "frustrating, infuriating sensation of seeing the city of New Orleans, especially its poorest citizens, abandoned by every level of government."
Provide background information that establishes the importance of your topic.	In "Message in a Bottle," Fishman establishes the importance of his topic by providing background information on the bottled water industry. He points out, for example, that Americans spend more money on bottled water than on movies and popular technology.

{ Student Q & A } Relating to Readers

Writing Now: You begin your essay using the pronoun *you* and talking about the concerns "you" might have. Why did you begin this way?

Ashley Roberts: I didn't want to just jump into a lot of research. I thought that addressing readers directly would let me talk about the concerns they probably had on their minds. ■

{ Exercise } Writing an Introduction

Review—and, if necessary, revise—your statement analyzing your audience and purpose, being careful to describe your readers' knowledge, needs, and attitudes. Then, using one or some combination of the strategies listed here for establishing conflict or relating to readers, write one or more introductory paragraphs that seem likely to engage the attention of the audience you have described. Consider including a photograph or other visual element (such as a chart or graph). Bring this introductory material to class, along with your analysis of audience and purpose. Ask your classmates to tell you whether the introduction seems likely to engage the intended audience and whether they can think of other strategies to engage your audience. ■

Creating Conflict

A conflict lies at the heart of every position paper; there's no need to take a position unless there is a disagreement, a disparity between the way things are and the way they should be, or a difference among competing ideas, attitudes, or courses of action. To engage readers, to push them to read beyond the title of your position paper, you must make them aware of that conflict. Even more important, you must make them see how that conflict affects them directly or relates to what they know, care about, and need. Here are some strategies to help you do this.

For more examples of establishing conflict, see Chapter 3, page 150.

How to Create Conflict

STRATEGIES	EXAMPLES FROM READINGS
Follow good news with bad news.	Karrie Jacobs begins "Drop in the Bucket" (p. 265) with some relatively good news—she mentions a New Orleans resident who is able to rebuild his house in part because it was located some distance from the worst of the flooding. But then, noting "that's as good as it gets," she goes on to describe devastated neighborhoods where floods left "few signs of life."
Mention an incongruity or a paradox.	In the beginning of "Message in a Bottle" (p. 285), Charles Fishman points out that a bottle of water costs at least twice as much as a comparable amount of gasoline, even though water is something "we have always gotten, and can still get, for free, from taps in our homes."
Point out contradictions or inconsistencies.	At the beginning of "Cheap Food Nation" (p. 260), Eric Schlosser notes that Americans' view of steroid use in athletics does not seem to apply to the use of steroids in raising animals for food.
Point out a difference between what readers assume or believe and what is actually true.	In "Where Have All the Criminals Gone?" (p. 270), Steven Levitt and Stephen Dubner note that people often think that a decrease in the crime rate is the result of a "strong economy." The authors then assert, "a closer look at the data destroys this theory."

Creating an Appropriate Voice

Assuming that you have chosen to write about a topic that matters greatly to you, there is a good chance it has evoked some very definite feelings in you, and you may passionately want others to share your views. But you have to express those views in a voice that will make sense given your audience and your topic. If you feel strongly about a topic, you may want to make an *emotional appeal*, using the sort of language and information that will lead your audience to share your feelings of enthusiasm, anger, joy, frustration, optimism, and so forth. In other cases, you may want to make a *logical appeal*, showing your audience that you are someone who is calm, well informed, and thoughtful, someone less moved by emotion than by careful reasoning. Or you may want to make an *ethical appeal*, presenting yourself as a person of good character, someone the readers can identify with and trust, someone who understands their values and concerns. Quite frequently, position papers make all three types of appeals. But as a rule, one or two types will come through most strongly.

Emotional Appeals

Emotional appeals are those that speak directly to people's feelings, referring to fundamental values and attitudes that underlie strong, often highly personal reactions to a topic. Here are several strategies that can help you do this.

How to Make Emotional Appeals

STRATEGIES	EXAMPLES FROM READINGS
Use language and details that are likely to evoke strong emotional reactions in your audience. Different people may have very different reactions to a given word or piece of information. So before you use words and details that create strong emotional reactions, refer to the section of your audience analysis in which you explain what your audience knows, values, and needs. Use that explanation to anticipate your audience's likely reaction to the specific words and details you include.	**The Boston Globe** In "SUVs Belong in Car Ads Only" (p. 255), Ellen Goodman refers to SUVs as "those gas-guzzling, parking-space-hogging, bullies of the highway." She goes on to point out that SUVs pose a threat not only to the safety of drivers of small cars but also to the environment. Drivers of small cars are likely to appreciate this language since it may reflect their own views. Drivers of SUVs, however, are unlikely to have the same reaction.
Describe the actions of a person or group your readers are likely to react to strongly. This reaction can be either positive or negative. It is especially effective if you can let readers see that you join them in a negative reaction.	In "What Decreased Crime?" (p. 274), John R. Lott Jr. points out that one group of his critics were "liberal academics" who denied tenure and promotion to a professor simply because he did not accept their political views. Some conservative readers may react negatively to this group's action, believing it confirms their worst impressions of liberal academics. "Liberal academics," however, are not likely to have the same negative reaction.

STRATEGIES	EXAMPLES FROM READINGS
Identify consequences that are likely to inspire or alarm your readers. Help your readers see what is likely to happen if they act or speak in a certain way; help them see the potential or actual effects of an action, a comment, or a belief.	 In "Cheap Food Nation" (p. 260), Eric Schlosser contends that water runoff from cattle feedlots and large-scale "factory farms" pollutes both air and water with toxic chemicals that eventually wind up in consumers' food.
Make comparisons that are likely to evoke strong feelings in your readers. The key phrase here is *in your readers*. A comparison that means one thing to you might mean something quite different to your readers—or it might mean nothing at all. Consider your readers' knowledge, needs, and attitudes so that you can make comparisons that are valid from your readers' perspective.	In "Where Have All the Criminals Gone?" (p. 272), Steven Levitt and Stephen Dubner claim that current death penalty laws so rarely lead to executions that these laws are comparable to "any parent who has ever said to a recalcitrant child, 'Okay, I'm going to count to ten and this time I'm *really* going to punish you.'"

Logical Appeals

A logical appeal is one that meets a high standard of evidence and reasoning. Such an appeal may also try to stir emotions, and even very emotional arguments may have a kind of logic: Because we have certain feelings, we should act in certain ways. But a logical appeal rests primarily on references to widely shared principles and factual evidence derived from impartial sources. In making this sort of appeal, you can use some of the strategies identified earlier in this chapter for giving good reasons and developing your ideas, especially citing information from sources your audience will see as credible. But one of the main ways to create a logical voice is to avoid oversimplifying complex topics. You will also need to respond thoughtfully to questions or objections your audience is likely to raise, and you may need to limit the claims you make. Here are some specific strategies to use in creating a logical appeal.

How to Create a Logical Appeal

STRATEGIES	EXAMPLES FROM READINGS
Acknowledge and refute opposing points of view. Refute counterarguments clearly, especially by mentioning a principle readers are likely to agree with, providing factual information, or citing authorities that support your point of view.	In "Where Have All the Criminals Gone?" (p. 270), Steven Levitt and Stephen Dubner acknowledge that one cause of the decrease in crime is a "strong economy." However, they point out that this explains only the decrease in crimes "with a direct financial motivation," not in "violent crimes like homicide, assault, and rape."

continued on next page ▶

How to Create a Logical Appeal (continued)

STRATEGIES	EXAMPLES FROM READINGS
Qualify or acknowledge limitations of the claims you want to make.	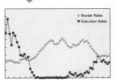 As do Levitt and Dubner, John R. Lott Jr. in "What Decreased Crime?" (p. 278) acknowledges that he can't completely account for the decrease in crime in the 1980s and 1990s. Lott notes that increased imprisonment does not account for one type of violent crime—"multiple victim public shootings." And although Levitt and Dubner basically disagree with Lott on the effect of imprisonment, they acknowledge that "imprisonment is certainly one of the key answers. It accounts for roughly one-third of the drop in crime."
Anticipate and respond to questions readers are likely to raise.	Although she argues strongly that college students should walk or ride bicycles rather than drive a car, Ashley Roberts ("Considered Living Car-Free?" p. 302) anticipates questions such as *Is it safe?* She then uses her own experiences to provide answers.
Be careful about using the personal pronouns *I, me, my.* In some situations, references to your own thoughts or experiences can be very persuasive. But as a rule, logical arguments are based on facts that can be verified by others and information from others whom your readers will see as authorities.	 In "Drop in the Bucket" (p. 267), Karrie Jacobs uses the pronoun *I*, but she usually does so to introduce feelings her readers are likely to share, as when she writes, "Finally, I thought, the Feds are doing something right." But when Jacobs goes on to criticize government actions, she does so not by referring to her ideas or actions, but by citing authorities and verifiable facts.

Ethical Appeals

It is relatively easy to characterize the voices associated with emotional and logical appeals: An appeal to readers' feelings is likely to be expressed with language and details that will evoke a strong emotional reaction; an appeal to logic is likely to be expressed in a rational, unemotional voice. But it is harder to associate any one type of voice with an ethical appeal, since this sort of appeal can vary according to the audience you are addressing. If your audience feels strongly about a given subject, you may need to show them that you feel strongly about it, too. If members of your audience see themselves as logical and unemotional, you may need to create a voice that displays some of these characteristics. If you are writing to a group of researchers in a particular academic discipline, you will want to use the technical language they use and the kinds of evidence they value. (Some disciplines value statistical results of experiments; others value careful observation of people's behavior.)

In all cases, your goal in making an ethical appeal is to get your audience to trust you, to see you as one of them. To do this, you may need to choose judiciously from among the strategies mentioned above for making emotional and logical appeals. There are, however, two other strategies that can be useful in making ethical appeals.

How to Make Ethical Appeals

STRATEGIES	EXAMPLES FROM READINGS
Indicate that you and your audience share the same attitudes and experiences.	Before launching into "a full-boil rant" against SUVs, Ellen Goodman (p. 255) mentions an experience she and her readers have almost certainly shared: They know what it is to "creep and beep on some misnomered expressway."
Avoid insulting your readers. Don't describe them in negative, unflattering terms. (Nobody likes being told they are foolish.)	In "Message in a Bottle" (p. 285), Charles Fishman is very critical of people (including his readers) who drink bottled water. But he never includes the pronoun *you* in his criticisms. For example, he does not say "you" put bottled water in lunch boxes or take bottled water along whether at work or at play. Instead he says, "It [bottled water] starts the day in lunch boxes, it goes to every meeting, lecture hall, and soccer match." Obviously, the water bottles don't put themselves into lunch boxes, but Fishman never explicitly blames his readers.

{ Student Q & A } Creating an Appropriate Voice

Writing Now (WN): How would you describe the voice you were trying to create?

Ashley Roberts (AR): I wanted to seem welcoming and friendly—like someone readers could trust. I wanted to make it clear that I was taking their questions into consideration, not just a voice with an agenda.

WN: How did you try to create that voice?

AR: I did that a little bit by talking directly to my readers at the beginning. Also, I tried not to use a lot of technical language, even though I was using some fairly technical information. ■

{ Exercise } **Creating an Appropriate Voice**

Decide how you want members of your audience to see you. Do you want them to regard you as someone who is passionately committed to a particular point of view? As someone who shares their concerns and values? As someone who takes a cool, rational approach? What are some of the words you would like your readers to use in describing the voice you create in your position paper? Frustrated? Enthusiastic? Thoughtful? Courteous? Angry? Critical? These, of course, are not the only choices—you have the whole range of human emotion and experience to choose from. As part of making these choices, you should do the following.

- Review your answers to the questions for analyzing audience and identifying purpose (pp. 313–14), and revise them if you need to.

- List some of the words and phrases you hope readers would use to describe the voice in your position paper.

- Show both your statement of audience and purpose and the list of words and phrases to someone else (a classmate or your instructor); ask this person to tell you whether the voice you hope to create makes sense, given what your context analysis says about your intended audience and purpose.

- Using what you learn from your classmate or instructor, revise the list of words that describe the voice you want to create.

- Write a brief passage—perhaps a paragraph or two—in which you assert and explain one of the main points you want to make in your position paper.

- Ask someone (a classmate, your instructor, or a friend) to read this passage aloud and listen to the sound of his or her voice. Can you hear the attitude you want to create in the sound of this reader's voice? If you can, good. If you can't, look closely at your draft to see what words and phrases you need to change in order to create the voice you want. ■

Organizing

People who read your position paper want to find out what your opinion is and how plausible your reasons and evidence are. And some of your readers will probably want to argue with you. Consequently, you will need to organize your position paper so readers can easily find the claims you are making and follow the logic of your argument. Two good ways to do this are to (1) assert or strongly imply your main claim (or thesis) at the end of your introductory section and (2) put topic sentences at or near the beginning of each paragraph. Here are several other strategies you can use in organizing your position paper.

How to Organize

STRATEGIES	EXAMPLES FROM READINGS
Pose a question and immediately begin answering it.	In "Where Have All the Criminals Gone?" (p. 271), Steven Levitt and Stephen Dubner end paragraph 8 this way: "Instead of wondering what made crime fall, think about this: why had it risen so dramatically in the first place?" In the following paragraph, they go on to give several reasons that crime had increased so dramatically.
Establish a clear logical sequence by using transition words or phrases. Use words such *as consequently, therefore, thus, because, if . . . then, so forth*, or other words that imply a cause and effect.	Levitt and Dubner argue that one reason crime rates increased in the 1960s was that the justice system had become more lenient. They use the following italicized words to suggest cause and effect. "So *if* you were the kind of person who might want to commit a crime, the *incentives were lining up in your favor:* a slimmer likelihood of being convicted and, if convicted, a shorter prison term. *Because* criminals respond to incentives as readily as anyone, *the result* was a surge in crime."
Establish a clear pattern of the sequence in which you present information. For example, move from cause to effect, mention something you hope or expect and then tell how you were pleased or disappointed by what happened, mention an opposing view and then immediately refute it.	In each paragraph in "Cheap Food Nation" (p. 260), Eric Schlosser sets up a series of causes and effects: One fact (the water runoff from large farms, for example) leads to polluted water, which eventually leads to Americans' consuming toxic chemicals. In three instances, Karrie Jacobs (p. 266) mentions something she had expected ("Initially I believed that rebuilding would be a tremendous opportunity . . .") and then shows how her expectations were not fulfilled. And Levitt and Dubner often mention a point of view others hold and then go on to refute it.

Concluding

The most important thing to do in concluding an argument is to leave readers with something they can remember easily—perhaps something that will make them think about this topic more or that will get them to take action. To get some ideas for writing conclusions, consider the following strategies.

How to Conclude

STRATEGIES	EXAMPLES FROM READINGS
Reiterate your basic point, either in your own words or those of an authority.	Near the end of his argument about the deterrent value of the death penalty, John R. Lott Jr. (p. 278) lists economists who accept his point of view and refers to results of a public opinion poll. Then he concludes by asserting, "A lot of people grasp intuitively an idea that economists only now are building a consensus toward: that the death penalty helps deter violent crimes and saves lives." To conclude their argument that the death penalty does not deter crime, Steven Levitt and Stephen Dubner (p. 273) cite a comment from a Supreme Court justice who had once favored the death penalty: "'I feel morally and intellectually obligated simply to concede that the death penalty experiment has failed. . . . I no longer shall tinker with the machinery of death."
Assert an implication that follows logically from your argument.	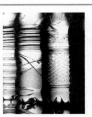 After talking about all the ways the U.S. government failed to respond adequately to victims of Hurricane Katrina, Karrie Jacobs concludes "Drop in the Bucket" (p. 268) by asserting, "The biggest thing destroyed by Katrina was not the city of New Orleans but the notion that government exists in part to help those who can't help themselves." Charles Fishman concludes "Message in a Bottle" (p. 300) with this statement: "once you understand where the [bottled] water comes from, and how it got here, it's hard to look at that bottle the same way again."
Frame your argument, returning to an idea you mentioned in the introduction.	In the first two paragraphs of "SUVs Belong in Car Ads Only" (p. 255), Ellen Goodman talks about the "commercial fantasy land" of car ads. In the last paragraph of her essay, she refers again to this fantasy world, where "the skies are always clean, the drivers are always relaxed, and there's never, ever, another car in sight."

Designing Your Position Paper and Integrating Visual Information

In many cases, position papers make rather limited use of visual cues. Opinion pieces in news magazines, for example, are usually set off from news reports in only two ways: They are printed in two relatively wide columns, as opposed to the three or four narrower columns in which news is reported; and they are often accompanied by a columnist's photograph. As the readings in this chapter suggest, however, position papers can display a wide range of visual features. The chart below shows several ways you can integrate visual features into your position papers. But your instructor may have specific requirements for formatting your position paper. Make sure to check with your teacher before adopting special formatting for your essay.

How to Design and Integrate Visuals

STRATEGIES	EXAMPLES FROM READINGS
Use a graph to illustrate a trend you describe in your written text.	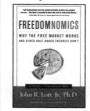 When John R. Lott Jr. talks about the relationship between changes in murder rates and changes in execution rates (p. 276), he illustrates these changes in a graph showing how this relationship changes over a period of more than fifty years.
Use a numbered or bulleted list to emphasize a point.	To reiterate his point that the death penalty deters murder, Lott lists in a table format a number of scholars who share his point of view and a much smaller number of scholars who do not (p. 277).
Highlight key points either by changing the size and shape of type or by including key points in inset boxes (or other shapes).	 "Message in a Bottle" (p. 289) uses the outline of a bottle to highlight the claim that while the island of Fiji produces enormous amounts of bottled water, "more than half the people in Fiji do not have reliable drinking water." Ashley Roberts uses an inset box in "Considered Living Car-Free?" in which she answers frequently asked questions. The questions and answers aren't necessary for proving her thesis, but they engage readers by anticipating their questions and providing answers.

continued on next page ▶

How to Design and Integrate Visuals (continued)

STRATEGIES	EXAMPLES FROM READINGS
Use a photograph that implies attitudes expressed in the written text. Make sure the photograph is placed close to the text it pertains to.	The author of "Cheap Food Nation," (p. 261) Eric Schlosser, is shown standing outside a McDonald's, one of the companies that uses huge amounts of meat from the "factory farms" the author criticizes. To highlight the author's perspective on such companies, the author is holding what appears to be a shopping bag filled with fresh produce.

For advice on selecting images, see pages 539–40 in Chapter 9; for guidance in creating tables, charts, and graphs, see pages 543–47.

If you use a photograph or other visual taken from another source (a newspaper, for example), you should identify that source underneath the visual in a caption. And in all cases, you must make sure that the visual is appropriately labeled and captioned. These captions might take the form of a title and perhaps a sentence that encapsulates the point of the visual.

{ **Student Q & A**  } **Designing and Integrating Visual Information**

Writing Now: You said you wanted to create a friendly voice, so why didn't you include photographs to make your position paper seem more friendly or personal?

Ashley Roberts: I have a lot of photographs of people biking, but about the only caption I could think of was something like, "Here are pictures of people on bikes having fun." So instead I used graphs since they seemed more likely to bolster my argument. ■

{ **Exercise** } **Designing Your Position Paper**

Look back over the selections in Reading to Write, and make a list of visual features you might want to incorporate into your position paper. As you think about the design of your position paper, check with your instructor about the kinds of visual elements that may be appropriate for the assignment. Keeping your instructor's comments in mind, make notes about the visual features you want to create or find for your position paper. ■

Creating a Review Draft

After all the reading and thinking you have been doing, you should have developed a clear position on the topic you have chosen to discuss. You should now be ready to create a review draft that argues your position as clearly and persuasively as possible. Once you have created this draft, you will need to assess it carefully, not only by critiquing it yourself but also by getting others' opinions. In this process, you subject your draft to a final review and then use these assessments to make any needed revisions in content, organization, style, or format.

In preparation for writing the review draft, look back at what you have said about your audience and purpose. Has your sense of audience and purpose changed? If so, revise what you have said about audience and purpose, and keep that revision in mind as you decide what to say and how to say it in the review draft. Also, look back at what you wrote when you reflected on the information you were gathering (pp. 318–19). Do you need to modify any of the claims or points expressed there? Are there any places where you need to add information that would make your points clearer or answer questions the audience is likely to ask? Finally, review your notes and working bibliography. Make sure that quotations and other references are accurate. Also make sure that each source is appropriately cited.

As you work on your review draft, think carefully about the introduction and conclusion. Does the introductory material establish the voice you want to create? Does it seem likely to engage the intended audience? Does the conclusion reinforce the basic point you want to convey? Do your introduction and conclusion still seem appropriate for your audience? If not, modify them by using one or more of the strategies identified in this chapter.

In addition, take some pains to organize your ideas. It might help to make an informal outline indicating your main points. You should also use some of the strategies described on page 331.

REVIEWING AND REVISING

Once you have revised your review draft to make it as complete and polished as you can, you need to have it reviewed, preferably by one or more people who understand the principles (analyzing context, engaging readers, and so on) that you have been working with in this chapter. You will use this review to guide a revision of your review draft before you turn your work in for grading.

Getting a Final Review

Give the reviewer a copy of your draft, one he or she can make notes on. Also give the reviewer a copy of your statement of audience and purpose. If necessary, revise that statement before giving it to the reviewer. Ask the reviewer to adopt the perspective of the audience you have described, and then use the following checklist in commenting on your work.

**Checklist for
Final Review**

1. In my statement of audience and purpose, please highlight any statements that give you a good sense of the knowledge, needs, and attitudes of my intended audience. Also highlight statements that help you understand exactly what purpose(s) I am hoping to achieve. If necessary, point out ways my audience analysis or statement of purpose could be made clearer.

2. Given what I say in my statement of audience and purpose, how likely does it seem that my arguments will be persuasive to the audience I am trying to reach?

3. In what specific passages have I developed my topic thoroughly, especially by (a) providing reasons and evidence that my audience will see as persuasive, (b) anticipating and responding to objections or questions my audience is likely to raise, and (c) making appropriate appeals? (For examples, see pp. 320–21.) What strategies (explained on pp. 321 and 322) might I use to make my work even more persuasive?

4. What portions of my introduction seem likely to engage the interest of my intended audience? What are some strategies (explained on pp. 323–24 and p. 325) that might make the introduction more engaging?

5. How would you describe the voice I have created? At what points does that voice seem appropriate, given my intended audience and topic? What strategies (explained on pp. 326–29) might help me make the voice clearer or more appropriate?

6. What are some words or phrases that show how I have organized my position paper? What strategies (explained on p. 331) might I use to make the organization clearer?

7. Is the conclusion of my position paper effective? What strategies (explained on p. 332) might I use to make it more effective?

8. If the position paper includes photographs or other visual elements, how do they help make it informative and credible? Are there any points at which I need to add more visual elements? If so, what should they be—headings, photographs, bulleted lists? Are there points at which I need to add or revise captions for pictures or legends for charts, graphs, and maps? What strategies (explained on pp. 333–34) might help make the design more effective?

If possible, ask the reviewer to talk with you about your review draft as well as make notes on it. Since position papers invite controversy, it is possible that your reviewer will disagree with one or more claims you make. If this happens, be careful not to argue with your reviewer. Instead, try to find out why he or she disagrees with you. Once you have a good idea of what the concerns or objections are, you might respond to what he or she has said, asking the reviewer how persuasive your responses are.

▶ Go to
bedfordstmartins.com/
writingnow to download these
questions from Chapter 5 >
Worksheets.

Revising Your Position Paper

Once you have a good idea of your reviewer's response, it is time to go back through your notes on those comments. Bearing in mind your intended audience and purpose, decide which comments are most valid. Then use the strategies referred to in the Checklist for Final Review.

After resolving all the issues that need attention, proofread carefully and correct any typographical or formatting errors. Then submit this final draft to your instructor.

▷ TAKING STOCK OF WHERE YOU ARE

Once your instructor has returned the final draft of your work, think back over all the comments you received—from classmates as well as your instructor—and write out answers to the following questions. (You might want to keep these in a journal or in a special section of a notebook.)

1. What appears to be my greatest area of strength?
2. Where am I having the greatest difficulty?
3. What am I learning about the process of writing?
4. What am I learning about giving and receiving feedback on writing?
5. What have I learned from writing a position paper that I can use in my next assignment for this course, for another course, or for work?

[**Questions for Assessing Your Growth as a Writer**]

The responses that follow are Ashley Roberts's answers to these questions for the position paper she wrote about living off campus without a car (p. 302).

1. I feel like my organization of factual data is my greatest strength. I introduce an idea about the topic and then demonstrate the validity of my statement with statistics taken from legitimate sources. The material I collected from peer-reviewed journals was instrumental in building my line of reasoning in the paper. I had a basic idea of my thesis before I started researching, but only after I read journal articles concerning my topic was I able to have a clear vision of how I wanted to structure my argument.

2. My greatest difficulty seemed to come from presenting my thesis without writing too much of my own personal opinions. I had to constantly remember that though my views helped shape my idea for the paper, the argument in the essay had to be based on research and not my own beliefs.

3. I am learning that the process of writing takes constant revisions. A basic outline is necessary, but it must not be limiting. As I began to write the paper, I realized that some of the arguments I thought I might employ should be left out while others I had not considered

▶ Go to
bedfordstmartins.com/
writingnow to download these
questions from Chapter 5 >
Worksheets.

should be included. A basic blueprint of the paper is a solid springboard for the process of writing a research essay, but you must allow the paper to develop as you learn more about your subject. Also, being prepared to rewrite the paper, experimenting with different writing tones and techniques, as well as being open to questioning the success of the paper were necessary for me to feel confident with my work in the final copy.

4. Feedback was essential. Sometimes, I just needed a fresh set of eyes on the paper so I could ask: Where is my argument weak? What are the strongest parts of my paper? Where do you think I have done something particularly well? Getting a perspective on my work from someone who does not hold the same attitude as me was instrumental to understanding my paper's successes and failures. I also found it helpful to walk away from the paper for a day or two, and then return to the computer with a rested mind. I found that sitting in front of the screen for hours affected my ability to discover the weaknesses in my writing.

5. The most important thing I learned from writing this paper is the benefit of utilizing the "why" question. I constantly asked myself "Why would someone choose to live car-free?" I will use this technique for other papers in the future, because it streamlined my thoughts. I would ask myself the question, get an answer, and write a page. Then I would repeat the same process for the next aspect of my argument.

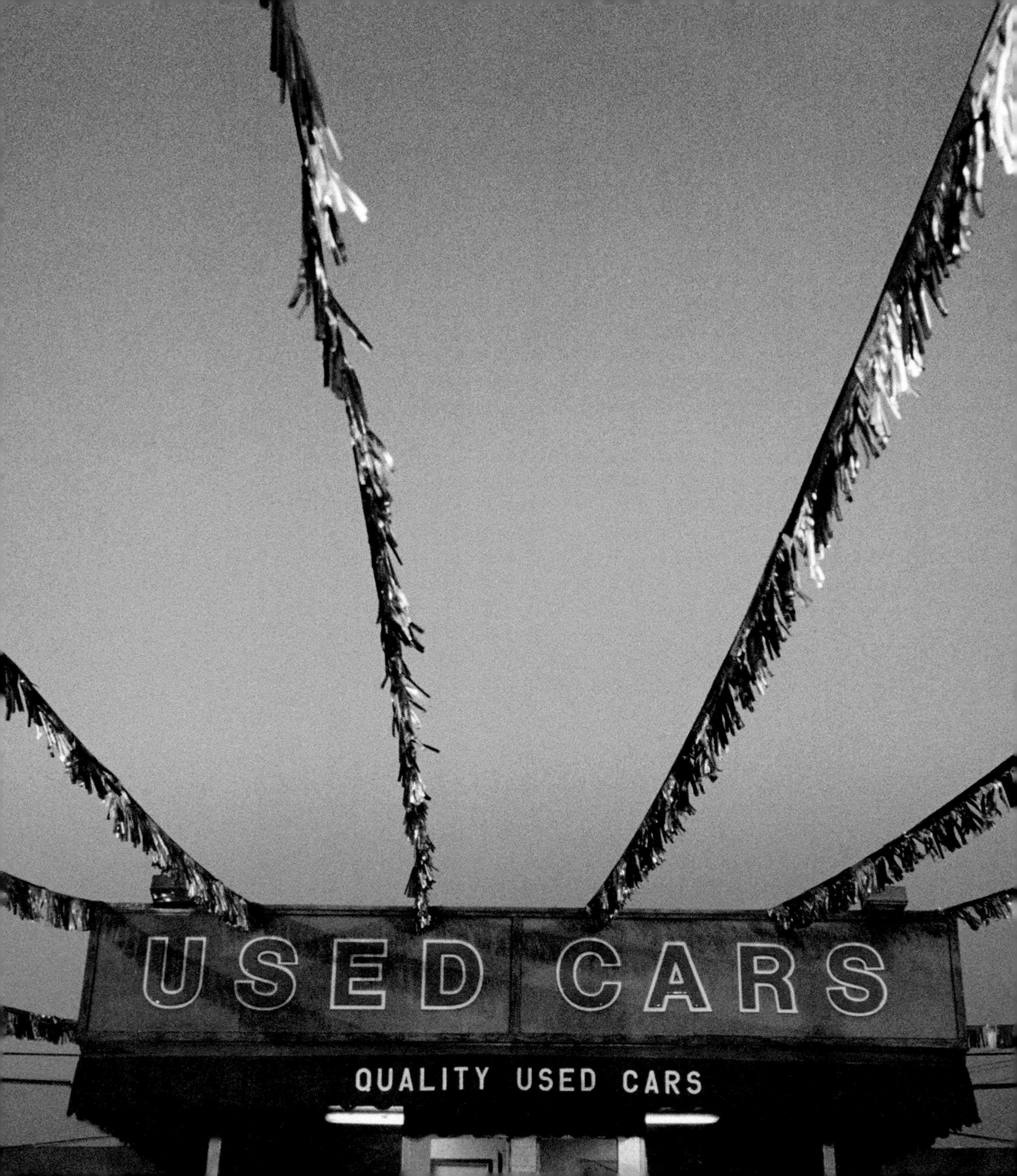
USED CARS
QUALITY USED CARS

6 ▷

Evaluations

Every day, in almost every aspect of our lives, we make value judgments: "Professor X is a good teacher," "That movie is not worth seeing," or "Our organization's plan for raising money is a smart idea." Sometimes these evaluations are little more than efforts to blow off steam: "That test was ridiculously unfair!" Was the test really unfair? Maybe it was. But maybe the speaker is just asking for a little sympathy or expressing frustration that was actually caused by failure to study for the test. In other situations, however, evaluations are taken much more seriously. They may keep someone from getting a job, or a potentially successful plan might be unfairly rejected. They can also have implications for the person who does the evaluating. A habit of making careless or thoughtless value judgments can cost people credibility, friendships, status, promotions, or jobs. Consequently, value judgments must be fair and carefully reasoned, based on criteria that readers will see as valid and documented with credible details.

People may evaluate any number of things, including products, people, policies, situations, literary works, works of art, films, and musical or dramatic performances. But all evaluations come down to one basic question of value: Is the thing—a product, for example, or an idea, a movie, or a policy—good or bad, worthy or worthless, desirable or undesirable, fair or unfair? To answer basic questions about something's value, writers of evaluations give clear, appropriate reasons or *criteria*—the reasons that underlie a judgment about whether something is good or bad, and so forth.

Sources of Criteria

The criteria you use as a basis for your evaluation may come from several different sources, and their persuasiveness may vary from one audience to another. As you choose from the following general sources, consider the kinds of sources your particular audience will be most likely to find convincing.

▶ **The evaluator's own needs and values.** A novice computer user might evaluate a piece of software on the basis of one criterion: ease of use. A more experienced computer user might rely on multiple criteria, such as excellent graphics capability and compatibility with other sophisticated technology.

▶ **A moral or legal code.** Most legal and ethical systems frown on such acts as lying, cheating, and stealing. So in evaluating, say, a course of action, someone might ask whether that course of action violates a particular legal or ethical code. If so, that course of action is wrong or at least questionable.

▶ **The goals or practical needs of an organization.** If a fraternity places high value on winning at intramural sports, any plan for recruiting new members will probably be judged in terms of how likely the plan is to attract members with exceptional athletic ability. If the fraternity is currently facing academic probation, any plan for increasing membership will almost certainly be judged in terms of how likely the plan is to attract members with strong academic records.

▶ **The culture—the shared assumptions and practices—of a group or a larger society.** Some businesses, for example, assume that they must continually change if they are to stay competitive in their fields. Consequently, when it comes time to evaluate employees, these companies may value risk-taking and innovation. Employee evaluations are likely to focus on whether employees propose new projects or more innovative ways to carry out existing projects, even if these proposals entail some degree of risk. Other companies, however, are conservative, placing more value on avoiding risk and maintaining an established routine. When these companies evaluate employees, they may ask how well a particular employee follows established procedures or whether the employee's proposals minimize risks to the company.

{ Exercise } **Thinking about Evaluations**

Think about one type of evaluation that all students routinely encounter: grading. List some of the criteria usually used in grading. What, for example, are some reasons the instructor might have for saying that someone's work is good or bad, acceptable or unacceptable, or better or worse than another student's work? How are those criteria similar to or different from those you and your classmates accept? ■

▷ READING EVALUATIONS

In the following section, you will find evaluations on a variety of topics ranging from an Internet encyclopedia to an imported car. Following each evaluation, you will find questions that pertain specifically to the evaluation you have just read. In addition to these specific questions, there are several basic questions you should ask in reading any evaluation.

[Questions for Reading Evaluations]

▶ **Who is the intended audience?** Consider the language, visuals, and information included in (and excluded from) the evaluation. What does the writer appear to be assuming about the following?

- Readers' prior experience with the subject (Have they used the product or service being evaluated? Have they been affected by the policy or trend being evaluated?)
- The criteria that are likely to matter to readers
- Readers' biases or preconceptions concerning the subject
- The questions readers want to have answered

▶ **What specific purpose(s) is the writer trying to accomplish?** In addition to achieving the basic goal of making a credible value judgment, is the writer trying to accomplish a more specific purpose, such as one or more of the following?

• Persuade readers to accept or reject the subject

• Articulate a feeling or belief that readers may accept but have not explored in any detail

• Give readers a new perspective on a familiar topic, perhaps challenging their preconceptions, perhaps showing them more good (or bad) qualities than they had previously recognized

• Give readers a sound basis for making a decision

▶ **How informative is the evaluation?**

• What questions does the evaluation answer?

• Are these the kinds of questions that intended readers will want to have answered? Are they the kinds of questions *you* would want to have answered?

• Are there significant questions that the evaluation does not answer?

• Does the writer provide specific details that show how the topic does or does not meet his or her criteria?

• Does the author provide the kinds of details and explanations that will make sense to intended readers? Do the details and explanations make sense to you?

▶ **How credible is the evaluation?**

• Are the facts accurate and up to date?

• Is information drawn from sources readers are likely to trust?

• Is the evaluation based on criteria readers are likely to see as valid and appropriate? Do the criteria seem valid and appropriate to you?

• If it's likely that there are multiple perspectives on the topic, are those perspectives presented fairly? Are any perspectives left out?

▶ **How well organized is the evaluation?**

• Is it easy for readers to find the information they are looking for?

• Can readers readily identify the main point (or thesis) of the evaluation?

• Can readers identify the main point of each paragraph? Of each visual?

• Does the evaluation seem to "flow," giving readers a clear sense of how a particular sentence or paragraph leads to the next?

▶ **What sort of voice would readers hear in the evaluation?**

• What attitudes, values, or emotions are suggested in the text? For example, does the writer seem fair? Alarmed? Calm and reasonable? Angry? Biased?

• Does the writer appear to have the experience and knowledge needed to speak authoritatively on the subject?

For more advice on reading photographs, see pages 489–92 in Chapter 8.

Visuals in evaluations may take several forms: photographs (intended either to convey an overall impression of a product or to focus in on specific features the audience is interested in), bulleted lists highlighting key features of the subject being evaluated, or tables that compare one subject (usually a product) with other subjects. Analyzing bulleted lists is fairly straightforward, requiring answers to one basic question: Do items in the list answer questions readers are likely to be most concerned about? Analysis of tables is somewhat more complex. Here are important questions to ask when reading and analyzing tables, one of the most widely used types of visuals evaluations.

▶ Are data taken from credible sources?

▶ Does the table present data that answer questions readers are most interested in?

▶ Does the table help readers make comparisons? If there are several criteria by which the subject is being judged, are details about each criterion presented in clearly labeled columns?

▶ If colors are used, do they highlight key differences between subjects or between types of information?

▶ Is the table well organized? Is each column in the table clearly and succinctly labeled? Is there a clear sequence in which items are listed—for example, is the most highly rated item placed first in a column that lists the subjects that were evaluated?

▶ If there are comments about each subject being evaluated, are those comments relatively brief, and do they convey the gist of what the author wants to say?

▶ Is the table complete? Does the table include the criteria and types of details the readers are most interested in?

▶ Does the table omit relevant information that might influence readers' understanding?

To see how these questions can guide an analysis of a table in an evaluation, consider this section from "Popcorn: Which Kernels Are King?" (p. 354). This table is typical of the kinds of information presented in *Consumer Reports* magazine, a widely read source of evaluations of a wide range of consumer products and services.

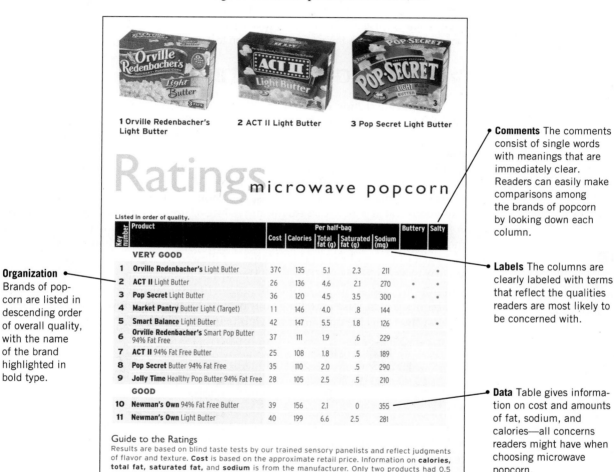

1 Orville Redenbacher's Light Butter

2 ACT II Light Butter

3 Pop Secret Light Butter

Comments The comments consist of single words with meanings that are immediately clear. Readers can easily make comparisons among the brands of popcorn by looking down each column.

Ratings microwave popcorn

Listed in order of quality.

Key number	Product	Cost	Calories	Total fat (g)	Saturated fat (g)	Sodium (mg)	Buttery	Salty
	VERY GOOD							
1	**Orville Redenbacher's** Light Butter	37¢	135	5.1	2.3	211		•
2	**ACT II** Light Butter	26	136	4.6	2.1	270	•	•
3	**Pop Secret** Light Butter	36	120	4.5	3.5	300	•	•
4	**Market Pantry** Butter Light (Target)	11	146	4.0	.8	144		
5	**Smart Balance** Light Butter	42	147	5.5	1.8	126		•
6	**Orville Redenbacher's** Smart Pop Butter 94% Fat Free	37	111	1.9	.6	229		
7	**ACT II** 94% Fat Free Butter	25	108	1.8	.5	189		
8	**Pop Secret** Butter 94% Fat Free	35	110	2.0	.5	290		
9	**Jolly Time** Healthy Pop Butter 94% Fat Free	28	105	2.5	.5	210		
	GOOD							
10	**Newman's Own** 94% Fat Free Butter	39	156	2.1	0	355		
11	**Newman's Own** Light Butter	40	199	6.6	2.5	281		

Organization Brands of popcorn are listed in descending order of overall quality, with the name of the brand highlighted in bold type.

Labels The columns are clearly labeled with terms that reflect the qualities readers are most likely to be concerned with.

Data Table gives information on cost and amounts of fat, sodium, and calories—all concerns readers might have when choosing microwave popcorn.

Guide to the Ratings
Results are based on blind taste tests by our trained sensory panelists and reflect judgments of flavor and texture. **Cost** is based on the approximate retail price. Information on **calories, total fat, saturated fat,** and **sodium** is from the manufacturer. Only two products had 0.5 grams or more of trans fat per half-bag: Market Pantry had 1.4 grams; Jolly Time, 0.5. The popcorns had 3.5 grams to 7.5 grams of fiber per half-bag.

{ Exercise } ▶ Go to bedfordstmartins.com/writingnow to Chapter 6 > Visuals.

For practice analyzing the visual information in another evaluation, see the visual exercises online. ▪

{ **Exercise** } **Analyzing Visuals in Evaluations**

Bring to class an evaluation that presents information in a visually interesting way. It might contain images, graphs, or tables. Or it might make special use of text by setting it off with columns, with color, as pull quotes, or in boxed sidebars. Consider the effects these visual elements create by answering the questions listed on page 344. Be prepared to explain how the visual elements create a particular effect and how they add to the impressions conveyed through the evaluation's written text. ■

▷ READING TO WRITE

In the following section of this chapter, you will find evaluations taken from several different sources—popular magazines, the scientific journal *Nature*, a college's student newspaper, and the online version of a nationally distributed newspaper. People read evaluations for any number of reasons. They may read an evaluation of a new sports car, for example, just because they want to imagine owning one, even though they may not be able to afford it. But as a rule, people read an evaluation when they are trying to make some sort of decision—about whether they should see a movie, buy a book, eat at a particular restaurant, or hire or fire an employee. In all cases, readers are seeking answers to such questions as these: How good is something? Does it measure up to a particular set of standards? Is it better or worse than something else?

Each of the readings in this chapter is followed by sections titled Reflecting on What You Have Read and Thinking Ahead. The questions in "Reflecting" will help you not only assess the content of the evaluation but also recognize strategies and techniques you can use in writing your own evaluation. In Thinking Ahead are suggested ways to decide on a topic for your own evaluation.

▷ Go to
**bedfordstmartins.com/
writingnow** and click on
Chapter 6 > Examples for
additional examples of
evaluations.

{ **For
Collaboration** } **Reading Evaluations**

Bring to class an evaluation of a topic (a movie, a product, a restaurant, a college policy) that interests you. Think about whether the author seems to be trying to persuade readers, evoke an emotional response in them, or produce some other reaction. Share your evaluation with one or two classmates and, working together, identify the purpose(s) of the evaluation each of you brought in. ■

Internet Encyclopedias Go Head to Head
Jim Giles

Currently a reporter for the journal *New Scientist*, Jim Giles was a writer for the journal *Nature* when he published "Internet Encyclopedias Go Head to Head." (Additional research for this article was contributed by Declan Butler, Jenny Hogan, Michael Hopkin, Mark Peplow, and Tom Simonite.) Giles has also worked as a freelance writer, having published articles in such major newspapers as the *New York Times*. Giles has an undergraduate degree in physics and a master's degree in computational neuroscience from Oxford University. He writes on a wide range of subjects (such as mental health, climate change, and relationships between doctors and drug manufacturers) that allow him to draw surprising connections among science, politics, and social issues. As you read this evaluation, consider how successful he is in challenging the authority of one of the world's most highly regarded encyclopedias.

Internet Encyclopedias Go Head to Head

Jimmy Wales' Wikipedia comes close to
Britannica in terms of the accuracy of its
science entries, a *Nature* investigation finds.

By Jim Giles

One of the extraordinary stories of the Internet age is that of Wikipedia, a free online encyclopedia that anyone can edit. This radical and rapidly growing publication, which includes close to 4 million entries, is now a much-used resource. But it is also controversial: if anyone can edit entries, how do users know if Wikipedia is as accurate as established sources such as Encyclopaedia Britannica? [1]

Several recent cases have highlighted the potential problems. One article was revealed as falsely suggesting that a former assistant to US Senator Robert Kennedy may have been involved in his assassination. And podcasting pioneer [2] Adam Curry has been accused of editing the entry on podcasting to remove references to competitors' work. Curry says he merely thought he was making the entry more accurate.

However, an expert-led investigation carried out by *Nature*—the first to use peer review to compare Wikipedia and Britannica's coverage of science—suggests that such high-profile examples are the exception rather than the rule. [3]

The exercise revealed numerous errors in both encyclopedias, but among 42 entries tested, the difference in accuracy was not particularly great: the average science entry in Wikipedia contained around four inaccuracies; Britannica, about three. [4]

Considering how Wikipedia articles are written, that result might seem surprising. A solar physicist could, for example, work on the entry on the Sun, but would have the same status as a contributor without an academic background. Disputes about content are usually resolved by discussion among users.

But Jimmy Wales, co-founder of Wikipedia and president of the encyclopedia's parent organization, the Wikimedia Foundation of St Petersburg, Florida, says the finding shows the potential of Wikipedia. "I'm pleased," he says. "Our goal is to get to Britannica quality, or better."

Wikipedia is growing fast. The encyclopedia has added 3.7 million articles in 200 languages since it was founded in 2001. The English version has more than 45,000 registered users, and added about 1,500 new articles every day of October 2005. Wikipedia has become the 37th most visited website, according to Alexa, a web ranking service.

But critics have raised concerns about the site's increasing influence, questioning whether multiple, unpaid editors can match paid professionals for accuracy. Writing in the online magazine *TCS* last year, former Britannica editor Robert McHenry declared one Wikipedia entry—on U.S. founding father Alexander Hamilton—as "what might be expected of a high-school student." Opening up the editing process to all, regardless of expertise, means that reliability can never be ensured, he concluded.

Yet *Nature*'s investigation suggests that Britannica's advantage may not be great, at

Kurt Jansson (left), president of Wikimedia Deutschland, displays a list of 10,000 Wikipedia authors; Wikipedia's entry on global warming has been a source of contention for its contributors.

least when it comes to science entries. In the study, entries were chosen from the websites of Wikipedia and Encyclopedia Britannica on a broad range of scientific disciplines and sent to a relevant expert for peer review. Each reviewer examined the entry on a single subject from the two encyclopaedias; they were not told which article came from which encyclopedia. A total of 42 usable reviews were returned out of 50 sent out, and were then examined by *Nature*'s news team.

Only eight serious errors, such as misinterpretations of important concepts, were detected in the pairs of articles reviewed, four from each encyclopedia. But reviewers also found many factual errors, omissions or misleading statements: 162 and 123 in Wikipedia and Britannica, respectively. 10

Editors at Britannica would not discuss the findings, but say their own studies of Wikipedia have uncovered numerous flaws. "We have nothing against Wikipedia," says Tom Panelas, director of corporate communications at the company's headquarters in Chicago. "But it is not the case that errors creep in on an occa- 11

sional basis or that a couple of articles are poorly written. There are lots of articles in that condition. They need a good editor."

Several *Nature* reviewers agreed with Panelas' point on readability, commenting that the Wikipedia article they reviewed was poorly structured and confusing. This criticism is common among information scientists, who also point to other problems with article quality, such as undue prominence given to controversial scientific theories. But Michael Twidale, an information scientist at the University of Illinois at Urbana-Champaign, says that Wikipedia's strongest suit is the speed at which it can be updated, a factor not considered by *Nature*'s reviewers. 12

"People will find it shocking to see how many errors there are in Britannica," Twidale adds. "Print encyclopedias are often set up as the gold standards of information quality against which the failings of faster or cheaper resources can be compared. These findings remind us that we have an 18-carat standard, not a 24-carat one." 13

The most error-strewn article, that on Dmitry Mendeleev, co-creator of the periodic table, illustrates this. Michael Gordin, a science histo- 14 rian at Princeton University who wrote a 2004 book on Mendeleev, identified 19 errors in Wikipedia and 8 in Britannica. These range from minor mistakes, such as describing Mendeleev as the 14th child in his family when he was the 13th, to more significant inaccuracies. Wikipedia, for example, incorrectly describes how Mendeleev's work relates to that of British chemist John Dalton. "Who wrote this stuff?" asked another reviewer. "Do they bother to check with experts?"

But to improve Wikipedia, Wales is not so much interested in checking articles with experts as getting them to write the articles in the first place. 15

As well as comparing the two encyclopedias, *Nature* surveyed more than 1,000 *Nature* authors and found that although more than 70% had heard of Wikipedia and 17% of those consulted it on a weekly basis, less than 10% help to 16

> ## "Scientists' involvement would lead to a multiplier effect. Experts can help write specifics in a nuanced way."

update it. The steady trickle of scientists who have contributed to articles describe the experience as rewarding, if occasionally frustrating (see 'Challenges of being a Wikipedian,' below).

Greater involvement by scientists would lead to a "multiplier effect," says Wales. Most entries are edited by enthusiasts, and the addition of a researcher can boost article quality hugely. "Experts can help write specifics in a nuanced way," he says. 17

Wales also plans to introduce a 'stable' version of each entry. Once an article reaches a specific quality threshold it will be tagged as stable. Further edits will be made to a separate 'live' version that would replace the stable version when deemed to be a significant improvement. One method for determining that threshold, where users rate article quality, will be trialled early next year. ∎ 18

Challenges of Being a Wikipedian

Vaughan Bell, a neuropsychologist at the Institute of Psychiatry in London, UK, has reworked Wikipedia's entry on schizophrenia over the past two years. Around five others regularly contribute to the reworking, most of whom have not revealed whether they have academic backgrounds. Bell says that is not a problem, as disputes are settled through the discussion page linked to the entry, often by citing academic articles. "It's about the quality of what you do, not who you are," he explains.

While admitting it can be difficult settling arguments, Bell says he often learns something by doing so. One user posted a section on schizophrenia and violence that Bell considered little more than a "rant" about the need to lock up people with the illness. "But editing it did stimulate me to look up literature on schizophrenia and violence," he says. "Even people who are a pain in the arse can stimulate new thinking."

Others, particularly those who contribute to politically sensitive entries, have found the editing process more fraught. William Connolley, a climate researcher at the British Antarctic Survey in Cambridge, has fought for two years with climate-change sceptics over the entry on global warming. When Connolley was insulted by one of the sceptics and the editing became a 'revert war'— where editors repeatedly undo each others' changes—the matter was referred to the encyclopedia's administrators.

Two of Connolley's opponents were banned from editing any climate article for six months, but it was a bumpy process. The Wikipedia editors who oversaw the case took three months to reach a decision. They also punished Connolley for repeatedly changing the sceptics' edits, placing him on a six-month parole during which he is limited to one revert a day. Users who support Connolley have contested the decision.

"It takes a long time to deal with troublemakers," admits Jimmy Wales, the encyclopedia's co-founder. "Connolley has done such amazing work and has had to deal with a fair amount of nonsense."

Reflecting on What You Have Read

1 The *Encyclopaedia Britannica* is highly regarded for, among other things, providing accurate factual details in all of its entries. But when the editors of the encyclopaedia claim they have found "numerous flaws" in Wikipedia, they provide no evidence for their claim. Does this lack of detail reduce the credibility of their claim? Why or why not?

2 Giles claims that Wikipedia is approximately as accurate as the *Encyclopaedia Britannica*. But he mentions several serious criticisms of Wikipedia. What reasons do you see for including (or omitting) such criticisms?

3 Giles cites one authority who claims that Wikipedia should be judged not only by the factual accuracy of its entries but also by the speed with which inaccuracies can be corrected. Other authorities in the article mention other criteria that lead them to appreciate Wikipedia. What are these other criteria, and how are they similar to or different from the criteria you would use in assessing the value of a source of information found on the Internet? How valid do these criteria seem?

4 According to a survey of more than a thousand scholars who have published articles in *Nature*, only 17 percent consult Wikipedia regularly, and less than 10 percent help keep entries up to date. Do results of this survey make Wikipedia seem less credible? Why or why not?

5 At the end of his article, Giles mentions ways in which one of Wikipedia's cofounders plans to improve the accuracy of Wikipedia entries. Do these plans seem likely to produce the hoped-for improvements?

Thinking Ahead

The Internet's vast store of information and opinions about almost any topic is from sources that include personal blogs, Web sites created by individuals, and Web sites created by organizations. For example, both Yahoo! (http://health.yahoo.com/) and the National Center for Disease Control and Prevention (http://www.cdc.gov/) provide information on health-related topics. Examine the way a given topic is treated on two different sites and explain why one seems more accurate or credible than the other. Or read highly respected print sources of information about a particular topic and then compare information from those sources with information found on a blog related to the same topic.

Popcorn: Which Kernels Are King?
Consumer Reports

"Popcorn: Which Kernels Are King?" originally appeared in *Consumer Reports*, a magazine widely respected for giving impartial, highly informative reviews of a wide range of products—automobiles, toys, stocks and bonds, and so forth. But despite this reputation for impartiality, articles in *Consumer Reports* frequently express what sound like strong personal opinions, sometimes without providing any evidence for the opinions. For example, this article does not explain the basis for its claim that the popcorns' "'butter' flavor was unmistakably artificial." As you read this review, notice the personal opinions it expresses and decide how credible you find them.

Popcorn: Which Kernels Are King?

Popcorn is one of those rare snacks that's not only beloved (on average, Americans eat about a quart a week) but also healthful. It's whole grain, high in fiber, low in calories and fat, and bulky, so it may fill you up faster than other snacks. 1

Unfortunately, plain kernels popped without oil or butter can be tough, and taste bland and dry. The trick is to add enough fat and salt to make popcorn tasty but not so much that it becomes a nutritional no-no. 2

Our experts tried 11 microwavable popcorns, the kind bagged with oil and salt, that aim to strike that compromise. Some have about half the calories and less than one-fifth the fat of other popcorns. 3

What We Found

Most of the popcorns were crispy, crunchy, and nicely salted. They tasted quite similar, with only subtle differences in favor intensity and saltiness. However, their "butter" flavor was 4

Popcorn vs. chips vs. pretzels

'Buttery' popcorn	Lower-fat popcorn	Air-popped corn	Light tortilla chips	Potato chips
Calories 210	Calories 110	Calories 90	Calories 90	Calories 150
Total fat ....15 g	Total fat ....2 g	Total fat ....0 g	Total fat ....1 g	Total fat ....10 g
Fiber.................4 g	Fiber.................4 g	Fiber ....5 g	Fiber ....1 g	Fiber ....1 g
Sodium 420 mg	Sodium ....290 mg	Sodium ....0 mg	Sodium......105 mg	Sodium.....180 mg

Figures are for Jolly Time ButterLicious popcorn, Pop Secret 94% Fat Free popcorn, Orville Redenbacher Original popcorn kernels, Tostitos Light tortilla chips with Olestra, Lay's Classic potato chips, Terra vegetable chips, and Snyder's pretzel sticks. Serving sizes are about a half-bag for popcorn, about an ounce for others.

unmistakably artificial. They lacked a strong corn flavor and the intense toasted-grain character and tenderness that comes from corn popped in plenty of oil. The two lowest-rated products, Newman's Own 94% Fat Free Butter and Light Butter, also had an unexpected cheese-like flavor.

Nutrition of the tested popcorns varies 5 slightly from product to product. A half-bag of popped corn—a more sensible serving size than the 2 to 4 tablespoons of uncooked kernels that's cited on nutrition labels—contains 105 to 199 calories, 126 to 355 milligrams of sodium, and 1.8 to 6.6 grams of total fat. Many of the products provide 20 percent or more of the government's recommended daily amount of fiber: 25 grams.

All of the popcorns except Target's Market 6 Pantry claim to be free of trans fat, which raises the risk of heart disease. Officially, a product can have some trans fat—less than 0.5 gram per manufacturer's serving—and still be labeled trans fat free. When the modest servings listed on the packages were popped, all met their claim. Per half-bag, most popcorns were still under the limit. Jolly Time, however, had 0.5 gram of trans fat per half-bag; Market Pantry, 1.4 grams. Whatever the product, the words "partially hydrogenated oil" in the ingredients list indicate that it contains at least some trans fat.

Many manufacturers are replacing trans fat 7 with palm oil, which isn't a whole lot better for you. Palm oil is high in saturated fat, which raises the risk of heart disease. The Ratings list total fat and saturated fat. Per day, people consuming 2,000 calories should limit total fat to 65 grams and saturated fat to 20 grams.

How To Choose

Nine of the 11 popcorns tasted very good, and 8 there was little difference in flavor or texture. It makes sense to shop by price or nutrition, taking your particular needs into account:

To forgo fat. Try Orville Redenbacher's 9 Smart Pop Butter 94% Fat Free, Act II 94% Fat Free Butter, or Pop Secret Butter 94% Fat Free, which have no more than 2 grams of total fat per serving and minimal amounts of saturated fat.

If sodium is a concern. Choose Smart 10 Balance Light Butter, which has 126 milligrams per half-bag.

To save money. Consider Act II Light 11 Butter, which costs 26 cents per half-bag.

Vegetable chips		**Pretzel sticks**	
Calories	150	Calories	110
Total fat	9 g	Total fat	1 g
Fiber	3 g	Fiber	1 g
Sodium	50 mg	Sodium	300 mg

The cheapest product is Market Pantry, but its 1.4 grams of trans fat argue against choosing it.

To pop it yourself. Cooking kernels yourself in an air 12 popper, on the stove, or in a microwavable bowl is inexpensive and allows you to control the amount and type of fat (try peanut, corn, or canola oil) and sodium. We found that the Nordic Ware Corn Popper, a 12-cup bowl for microwave ovens, worked well. It costs about $10 and is widely sold in stores and online. You simply pour in kernels (with or without oil) and place the lid on top.

Never microwave kernels in a glass bowl, which could be shat- 13 tered by the sudden temperature change caused by the popcorn's steam. The Popcorn Board, a trade group, also warns against popping corn in plain paper bags, because they could catch fire or damage the oven.

If you like it sweet. Kettle corn is popped with sugar or 14 related flavorings (brown sugar or maple syrup, for instance). A lower-calorie, microwave kettle corn we tested, from Orville Redenbacher, had a strong flavor of the artificial sweetener sucralose. Consider making a "light" kettle corn yourself by adding small amounts of sugar, salt, and oil to kernels and popping them on the stove. ∎

1 Orville Redenbacher's Light Butter   **2** ACT II Light Butter   **3** Pop Secret Light Butter

Ratings microwave popcorn

Listed in order of quality.

Key number	Product	Cost	Calories	Per half-bag		Sodium (mg)	Buttery	Salty
				Total fat (g)	Saturated fat (g)			
	VERY GOOD							
1	**Orville Redenbacher's** Light Butter	37¢	135	5.1	2.3	211		•
2	**ACT II** Light Butter	26	136	4.6	2.1	270	•	•
3	**Pop Secret** Light Butter	36	120	4.5	3.5	300	•	•
4	**Market Pantry** Butter Light (Target)	11	146	4.0	.8	144		
5	**Smart Balance** Light Butter	42	147	5.5	1.8	126		•
6	**Orville Redenbacher's** Smart Pop Butter 94% Fat Free	37	111	1.9	.6	229		
7	**ACT II** 94% Fat Free Butter	25	108	1.8	.5	189		
8	**Pop Secret** Butter 94% Fat Free	35	110	2.0	.5	290		
9	**Jolly Time** Healthy Pop Butter 94% Fat Free	28	105	2.5	.5	210		
	GOOD							
10	**Newman's Own** 94% Fat Free Butter	39	156	2.1	0	355		
11	**Newman's Own** Light Butter	40	199	6.6	2.5	281		

Guide to the Ratings

Results are based on blind taste tests by our trained sensory panelists and reflect judgments of flavor and texture. **Cost** is based on the approximate retail price. Information on **calories, total fat, saturated fat,** and **sodium** is from the manufacturer. Only two products had 0.5 grams or more of trans fat per half-bag: Market Pantry had 1.4 grams; Jolly Time, 0.5. The popcorns had 3.5 grams to 7.5 grams of fiber per half-bag.

Reflecting on What You Have Read

1 *Consumer Reports'* review of different brands of popcorn also compares different types of popcorn with other snacks. Since this comparison does not directly answer the question in the title of the article, do you think it should have been included in the article? Why or why not?

2 If you were in the grocery store trying to decide which brand of popcorn to buy, what criteria would you use in making your decision? How would these criteria be similar to or different from the criteria used in the *Consumer Reports* article? What do these similarities and differences tell you about the audience for whom the *Consumer Reports* article was written?

3 The table of ratings included in the article makes a clear judgment about which popcorn is best. But the written text includes no such judgment. Instead, it concludes by judging different brands according to the needs of different groups of readers. Does this make sense? Why or why not?

4 In addition to information about the different brands of popcorn, the *Consumer Reports* article includes information about the dangers of palm oil, the amount of fat people should consume each day, and the best product to use if readers want to cook their own popcorn. What reasons do you see for including (or omitting) this sort of information?

5 Although "Popcorn: Which Kernels Are King?" and "Is America Ready to Get Smart?" (p. 366) are both reviews of products, only the review of the Smart car contains comments from people who have bought (or are considering buying) the product being reviewed. What reasons do you see for *Consumer Reports* omitting such comments? Would the review be more effective if it included this sort of comment?

Thinking Ahead

Think of a type of food or beverage people like to consume—a type of fast food, for example, or food supplements that claim to provide large amounts of protein or low amounts of carbohydrates. Especially look for products whose manufacturers claim their products have similar health benefits. Identify an audience that would need to know which product is actually best and show how one or more of these products meet (or fail to meet) standards that would be important to your audience.

You Call This Progress?
Seth Shostak

The preceding readings in this chapter evaluate a Web resource and a product. Writing for the "My Turn" column in *Newsweek*, Seth Shostak evaluates a social trend: the dramatic increase in people's use of e-mail. Shostak is an astronomer at the SETI (Search for Extraterrestrial Intelligence) Institute in California, a scientific research organization, and he writes frequently on such topics as astronomy, film, and technology. He is the host for a weekly radio program, *Are We Alone?*, on which he interviews authorities on a wide range of scientific topics. He also has a monthly radio show, *Skeptical Sunday*, on which he explains the faulty science underlying belief in such topics as UFOs and astrology. He is a reliable, credible source of information about many scientific subjects. As you read, consider whether Shostak's work as a scientist contributes to his credibility as a critic of e-mail.

You Call This Progress?
E-mail has become a steady drip of dubious prose, bad jokes and impatient requests.

By Seth Shostak

It's as ubiquitous as 1 winter damp. A pernicious miasma that brings rot and ruin to society's delicate underpinnings. I speak of e-mail, the greatest threat to civilization since lead dinnerware addled the brains of the Roman aristocracy.

A technical byproduct of the Internet, e-mail 2 lets 10 million Americans pound out correspondence faster than you can say QWERTY. One twitch of the finger is all it takes to dispatch missives to the next continent or the next cubicle at light speed. The result is a flood of what is loosely called communication, a tsunami of bytes that is threatening to drown white-collar workers everywhere. Masquerading as a better way to put everyone in touch, e-mail has become an incessant distraction, a nonstop obligation and a sure source of stress and anxiety. I expect that a public statement by the surgeon general is in the offing.

Mind you, e-mail started out cute and 3 cuddly, an inoffensive spinoff from a government defense project. The technically inclined used it to send personal messages to colleagues without the need for a stamp or a wait. Only a small group of folks—mostly at universities—were plugged in to this select network. The amount of traffic was manageable. E-mail was something to be checked every week or so. But technology marches on. Today access to the Internet is widespread, as common and accessible as a cheap motel. Everyone's wired, and everyone has something to say.

Unfortunately, this is not polite correspondence, the gentle art of letter writing in electronic form. E-mail is aggressive. It has a built-in, insistent arrogance. Because it arrives more or less instantaneously, the assumption is that you will deal with it quickly. "Quickly" might mean minutes, or possibly hours. Certainly not days. Failure to respond directly usually produces a second missive sporting the mildly critical plaint, "Didn't you get my last e-mail?" This imperative for the immediate makes me yearn for old-style written communication, in which a week might lapse between inquiry and response. Questions and discussion could be considered in depth. A reply could be considered (or mentally shelved, depending on circumstance). Today, however, all is knee-jerk reaction.

In addition, there is the dismaying fact that electronically generated mail, despite being easy to edit, is usually prose at its worst. Of every 10 e-mails I read, nine suffer from major spelling faults, convoluted grammar and a stunning lack of logical organization. For years I assumed this was an inevitable byproduct of the low student test scores so regularly lamented in newspaper editorials. Johnny can't read, so it's not surprising that he can't write either. But now I believe that the reason for all this unimpressive prose is something else: e-mail has made correspondents of folks who would otherwise never compose a text. It encourages messaging because it is relatively anonymous. The shy, the introverted and the socially inept can all hunker down before a glowing computer and whisper to the world. This is not the telephone, with its brutally personal, audible contact. It's not the post, for which an actual sheet of paper, touched by the writer and displaying his imperfect calligraphic

skills, will end up under the nose of the recipient. E-mails are surreptitiously thrown over an electronic transom in the dead of night, packaged in plain manila envelopes.

Still, it is not these esthetic debilities that make e-mail such a threat. Rather, it's the unstoppable proliferation. Like the brooms unleashed by the sorcerer's apprentice, e-mails are beginning to overwhelm those who use them. Electronic correspondence is not one to one. It is one to many, and that's bad news on the receiving end. The ease with which copies of any correspondence can be dispensed to the world ensures that I am "kept informed" of my co-workers' every move. Such bureaucratic banter was once held in check by the technical limitations of carbon paper. Now my colleagues just punch a plastic mouse to ensure my exposure to their thoughts, their plans and the endless missives that supposedly prove that they're doing their jobs.

Because of e-mail's many-tentacled reach, its practitioners hardly care whether I'm around or not. I'm just another address in a list. So the deluge of digital correspondence continues irrespective of whether I'm sitting in my cubicle doing the boss's business or lying on the Côte d'Azur squeezing sand through my toes. Either way the e-mail, like a horde of motivated Mongolians, just keeps a-comin'. Vacations have lost their allure, and I hesitate to leave town. Consider: if I disappear for two weeks of rest and recreation, I can be sure of confronting screenfuls of e-mail upon my return. It's enough to make a grown man groan. The alternative is to take a laptop computer along, in the desperate hope of keeping up with e-mail's steady drip, drip, drip. Needless to say, there's something unholy about answering e-mails from your holiday suite. A friend recently told me that he can't afford to die: the e-mail would pile up and nobody could handle it.

Today I will receive 50 electronic messages. Of that number, at least half require a reply. (Many of the others consist of jokes, irrelevant bulletins and important announcements about secret cookie recipes. I actually like getting such junk e-mails as they allow the pleasure of a quick delete without guilt.) If I spend five minutes considering and composing a response to each correspondence, then two hours of my day are busied with e-mail, even if I don't initiate a single one. Since the 8 number of Internet users is doubling about once a year, I expect that by the start of the new millennium, I—and millions like me—will be doing nothing but writing e-mails. The collapse of commerce and polite society will quickly follow.

I'm as much in favor of technology as the next guy. Personally, I think the Luddites should have welcomed the steam looms. But if you insist on telling me that e-mail is an advance, do me a favor and use the phone. ■ 9

Reflecting on What You Have Read

1 What are Shostak's main criticisms of e-mail?

2 Given his criteria and evidence, do you agree with Shostak's criticisms?

3 Assess Shostak's evaluation of e-mail. Do his criteria seem appropriate? What other criteria might he have considered? How does your experience support or challenge Shostak's claims?

4 Compare the overall visual appearance of Shostak's essay with that of "Popcorn: Which Kernels Are King?" (p. 352). Think of the different situations in which each piece was intended to be read. How might those situations justify the different visual formats of the two pieces?

Thinking Ahead

Consider trends you are aware of, especially trends that affect you directly. How would you evaluate the changes those trends represent? Do they constitute "progress"? What criteria would you use to evaluate those trends?

Breakfast at Manory's

Patrick Vitarius

While an undergraduate at Rensselaer Polytechnic Institute, Patrick Vitarius wrote the following restaurant review for the college newspaper, *The Polytechnic*. Patrick grew up in the city (Troy, NY) where Rensselaer is located, and he was concerned that many of his classmates failed to recognize some of the attractive features of his hometown. This review was part of a year-long series of articles explaining interesting things to do in Troy for relatively little money. After graduating from Rensselaer, Patrick taught for two years in the Peace Corps and is currently doing graduate work in physics. As you read this review, notice the ways in which Vitarius understands the knowledge and values of his readers.

Breakfast at Manory's

PATRICK VITARIUS

---

1 If there's one thing I've missed since I left home, it's breakfast.

2 See, I have the less-than-admirable habit of getting up at the last possible moment—typically, fifteen minutes after my first class of the morning starts. (I should take this opportunity to thank Professor Kapila for starting each class with a twenty minute review of the previous class; otherwise, I surely would not have passed Advanced Calculus.)

3 The unfortunate side effect to this sleeping (or rather, waking) schedule is that there is never time for breakfast. How I missed the salty sensation of sizzling bacon! How I longed for the tangy taste of tantalizing sausage! What I wouldn't have said or done for a single sniff of sumptuous egg! I had thought that that chapter of my life was over and done with upon the first droning sentences of my college courseload.

4 Then I discovered Manory's Restaurant, home of the all-day breakfast.

5 Have you ever had pancakes after dark? Have you ever dined over eggs and bacon as the sun set over the Hudson River? Have you ever danced with the devil in the pale moonlight? If your answer to either of the first two questions was "no," you must go to Manory's right away. If your answer to the third question was "yes," you should look in the Yellow Pages under "Help—Psychiatric" and call the first local number you come to.

Now, some of you may have 6 observed by now my tendency to single out a single reason to visit a downtown business—Music Shack only for their used CD bin, China Pagoda only for their lunch buffet, Aquilonia Comics and Cards only for their "three for a buck" boxes. I am about to do the same thing here. Because even though Manory's has a perfectly wonderful breakfast, lunch, dinner, and dessert menu, I am not even going to tell you about them. Oh, you act indignant. If you're so interested, you'll go there for yourself. I'm just going to talk about their all-day breakfast specials. Live with it.

The $3.09 breakfast special is, 7 if nothing else, aptly named—it is a breakfast, it is "special," and it costs three dollars and nine cents (plus tax and tip). This breakfast is comprised of two eggs (cooked any style), toast, coffee, and juice. Just the right size for the student watching his calories and his budget. As if such a student exists. The only students I know don't even know what a calorie is (chem majors excluded) and have no budget to speak of, unless change found in friends' cars can be called a budget.

The meal for us is the Big 8 Breakfast. This is a meal near and dear to my own heart. At $4.95, it comes in right under the mark—tax and a 15 percent tip put it un-

---

THINGS TO DO ON YOUR WAY TO MANORY'S (FROM THE RPI CAMPUS)

1. Play a fun variation on the road game "Padiddle": every time you see a green-roofed, ivy-covered building on campus, you get to hit your friend.
2. On your way past West Hall, pop in and look for the Rocks and Fossils Room. Neat horse skull.
3. Cross 8th Street, and race down the Fulton Footpath. Last one to the bottom buys everyone breakfast.
4. On your way down Fulton Street, stop in front of the Gurley Building. In your best Schwarzenegger accent, say "Hey, look at the Gurley Building."
5. At the intersection of Fulton and Fourth, make fun of all the high school punk gangstas hanging out in front of "Nite Owl News." Then, quickly, make a left onto Fourth. Run.
6. Stop at the corner of Fourth and Congress. You're there. Hurrah.

---

der six dollars. And what a well-spent six dollars it is. Again, two eggs cooked any style. With two sausage links. And a couple strips of bacon. And three (count 'em, three) huge pancakes, with butter and syrup. And coffee. And juice. No "one from Column A" breakfast, this. You get it all. The eggs are fresh off the grill. The bacon is thick, just the right crispness, and salty enough to disinfect gunshot wounds. The sausages are spicy and cooked to perfection. The pancakes are fluffy and sweet, and served with enough whipped butter and maple syrup (on the side, by default) to make a meal in themselves. The coffee is bad for you, so I never order it. I get water instead. (The water, incidentally, ain't bad.) And the juice? Well, I

wouldn't know. I've never gotten enough to actually taste it.

See, Manory's has got these 9 teeny little juice glasses. You know the ones I'm talking about. These things make shot glasses look like two-handed beer mugs. These glasses are not big enough to trap fireflies in, not even one at a time. If they made "Fight cancer, Fight harder" commercials with these glasses, the caption would say "Tick cancer off just a wee bit." Man, I've seen OJ defense theories that hold more water than these glasses would. I've seen people walk into emergency rooms with their thumbs stuck in these glasses.

Okay, I'm done ranting about 10 the size of the juice glasses. The rest of the meal more than makes up for this slight, if common flaw. Take my advice. Go to Manory's. Go there. Go now, no matter what time of day it is. After all, if I wanted more juice for my money, I'd buy a half gallon at the convenience store.

And If I did that, it wouldn't 11 come with all the rest.

Reflecting on What You Have Read

1 Did you find this restaurant review engaging? Why or why not? Cite examples from the text to support your answer.

2 Vitarius includes some background information in his review, including his tendency to sleep late and his fondness for breakfast. What reasons do you see for including this background information?

3 What was your reaction to the photographs that accompany this review? What details in these photos made you react in that way?

Thinking Ahead

This restaurant review contains a wealth of details that convey a distinct impression of a specific place. Remembering that *place* can refer to a variety of things—a ballpark, concert venue, chat room, or dormitory, for example—imagine a place you would consider evaluating. Think about that place from different perspectives, such as a first-time visitor, for example, or someone who uses a wheelchair. What details about the place impress you? How might those details add up to your overall evaluation of the place?

The New York Times

First published July 27, 2007, the following review of *The Simpsons Movie* appeared in the *New York Times*. A. O. Scott, one of the most widely read and respected reviewers in the *Times*, offers his evaluation as a long-time fan of *The Simpsons*. One of the most important functions of an evaluation is to help readers pay careful attention to details they might otherwise overlook. This is especially true in reviews of movies or other performances in which sounds, images, and actions compete for viewers' attention. But Scott provides relatively few such details. As you read Scott's review, notice the ways in which he assumes readers share his knowledge of and appreciation for *The Simpsons*.

We'll Always Have Springfield: The Simpsons Movie

A. O. SCOTT

1   I have long been of the opinion that the entire history of American popular culture—maybe even of Western civilization—amounts to little more than a long prelude to "The Simpsons." I don't think I'm alone in this belief. But it does not follow that "The Simpsons Movie" represents a creative peak toward which the show's 18 seasons and 400 episodes have been a long, slow climb. Let's keep things in perspective. "The Simpsons" is an inexhaustible repository of humor, invention and insight, an achievement without precedent or peer in the history of broadcast television, perhaps the purest distillation of our glories and failings as a nation ever conceived. "The Simpsons Movie" is, well, a movie.

2   Don't get me wrong. It's a very funny movie, loaded with dumb jokes that are often as funny as the clever ones, and full of the anarchic, generous, good-natured humor that is the show's enduring signature. From the very start, when Ralph Wiggum stands inside the 20th Century Fox logo and sings along with the company fanfare, to the last frames of the closing credits, "The Simpsons Movie" provides plenty of amusement for both casual fans and hard-core zealots. It is not better than the best episodes—it's no "22 Short Films About Springfield" or "Homer's Enemy" or "Krusty Gets Busted" or "Lisa the Vegetarian"—and it doesn't strain to be. (I'd put it at about the level of "Trash of the Titans," the 200th episode, with which it shares an environmental theme.)

3   Instead of trying to top "The Simpsons" or sum it all up, the film's director, David Silverman (whose association with the series

In a scene from "The Simpsons Movie," the Simpsons and other citizens of Springfield look up in fear as disaster seems to approach.

goes back to the days of "The Tracey Ullman Show"), and the writers (who among them have at least a century's worth of experience on the show) take advantage of the opportunity to go wider and longer. CinemaScope, the wide-screen format developed by Fox in the 1950s to combat the rise of television, turns out to be the ideal way to appreciate the small-screen, small-town paradise that is Springfield. In a variation on the show's opening sequence, we swoop through the town, seeing it from new angles and appreciating its history and beauty anew.

There are also crowd scenes 4 on a scale rarely attempted on television, spectacles that compensate somewhat for the skimpy screen time granted some of the secondary characters. Everyone has a little, thank goodness, but for my taste there was too much Flanders and not enough Krusty. Less Cletus, please, and more Groundskeeper Willie. And where were Patty and Selma? I will say that the "Itchy and Scratchy" movie at the beginning is pure genius, though.

At this point, the temptation 5 is strong to rifle through my notes and repeat my favorite jokes—to tell you about Bart's full frontal nudity and Homer and Marge's bedroom scene and the bomb-defusing robot and the many acts

A heartwarming account of father and son laboring together.

of auto-homage that made my inner Comic Book Guy exclaim, "Oh yeah, I remember that episode." Instead, I'll just spoil the plot: Homer does something really stupid. Also, Lisa develops a crush, Bart gets in trouble and Marge expresses concern and disapproval. Sorry.

Homer's main screw-up is not 6 necessarily more or less idiotic than anything he's done before. (All I'll say is that it involves a pig.) The consequences, though, are proportionate to what you might expect from a summer blockbuster action movie. That is, they involve Arnold Schwarzenegger, who has been elected president of the United States; the elite attack forces of the Environmental Protection Agency; and the near-destruction of Springfield. Also motorcycles.

The head of the E.P.A. is 7 voiced by the "Simpsons" stalwart Albert Brooks, but the movie is generally light on celebrity cameos and voice-overs, properly emphasizing the talents of the series regulars (Dan Castellaneta, Julie Kavner, Yeardley Smith and Nancy Cartwright as the family, with Hank Azaria and Harry Shearer filling out much of the non-Simpson Springfield phone directory). There is Green Day, performing an excellent revved-up version of Danny Elfman's theme song, but other than that the filmmakers stick to the solid core of family and town, and to the mixture of irreverence and sentiment that has underwritten the program's longevity.

One of the esoteric pursuits 8 that divert "Simpsons" devotees is what might be called the question of authorship. A movie may be the work of a single, imperial auteur, but a television comedy, more often than not, arises from the collective, at times antagonistic labor of a bunch of writers in a room. It is easy enough to identify the graphic style and populist sensibilities of Matt Groening, and to intuit the sharp, fuzzy humanism of James L. Brooks. But over the years dozens of writers have passed through the bungalows on the Fox lot where "The Simpsons" is written. Many have stuck around, come back after grazing elsewhere or left traces of their influence behind. They are, as a group, responsible for the show's variety and its consistency, for its high points and its occasional doldrums.

Quite a few storied figures of 9 "Simpsons" history turn up in the movie credits—the screenplay is attributed to Mr. Groening, Mr.

Homer Simpson and Bart Simpson make yet another narrow escape.

Brooks, Al Jean, Ian Maxtone-Graham, George Meyer, David Mirkin, Mike Reiss, Mike Scully, Matt Selman, John Swartzwelder and Jon Vitti, several of whom have served in the crucial and mysterious role of show runner—and this is a sign that the movie is more to its makers than a byproduct or an afterthought.

Except, of course, that it in- 10 evitably is. Ten or 15 years ago, "The Simpsons Movie," which has been contemplated for almost as long as the show has been on the air, might have felt riskier and wilder. But "The Simpsons," for all its mischief and iconoclasm, has become an institution, and that status has kept this film from taking too many chances. Why mess with the formula when you can extend the brand? Do I sound disappointed? I'm not, really. Or only a little. "The Simpsons Movie," in the end, is as good as an average episode of "The Simpsons." In other words, I'd be willing to watch it only—excuse me while I crunch some numbers here—20 or 30 more times.

Reflecting on What You Have Read

1 In his review of *The Simpsons Movie*, Scott frequently makes exaggerated claims. How seriously does he seem to expect readers to take these claims? Would his review have been better if he had not included these claims? Why or why not?

2 Scott claims that *The Simpsons Movie* is "not better than the best episodes" of *The Simpsons* television program. In support of his claim, Scott mentions several episodes in the series ("Krusty Gets Busted," for example), but he does not justify his claim by citing any details about those episodes or details from the movie. In not including such details, what assumptions does he appear to be making about his audience?

3 What are the criteria by which Scott is judging *The Simpsons Movie*? How clearly does he define those criteria? Should he have defined his criteria more fully? Why or why not?

4 Scott's review includes several still images taken from the movie. What reasons do you see for including those specific images? Since many of his readers had probably seen the movie by the time the review appeared, did Scott need to include any images at all?

Thinking Ahead

The Simpsons Movie was preceded by a long series of television episodes about the Simpsons. Think of the most recent movie in a series of movies (the James Bond movies, for example) or the most recent episode of a television program you watch regularly. How would you assess the quality of such a movie or episode? Does it meet (or exceed or fail to meet) the standards by which you judged previous movies or episodes?

Is America Ready to Get Smart?

McKenzie Funk

McKenzie Funk has written for a wide range of magazines, including *Skiing, Harper's, Mother Jones, Audubon,* and *Men's Journal,* as well as *Popular Science,* in which the following article appears. He is also a contributing editor for *National Geographic.* In 2004, he was a finalist for a National Magazine Award, and in 2007, he was a finalist for a Livingston Award, which honors excellent work by magazine writers under the age of thirty-five. Funk frequently draws on personal experiences in writing about such diverse topics as environmental change in China and Bolivia, Internet addiction, mountain biking, and the relation between mathematics and IQ. As you read the following review, notice the way he draws on his personal experience in presenting technical information about the Smart car.

FUTURE OF THE CAR: EFFICIENCY

Is America Ready to Get Smart?

They had one week, 1,500 miles and, oh, about $100 in gas money to answer the question.

By McKenzie Funk

DETROIT TO MARSHALL, MICHIGAN

2.21 gallons, $5.83, 48 miles per gallon

"How about y'all get in the back. Just put you and your entire car in the back, and I'll take you wherever you want to go."

—Chevy Tahoe driver in downtown Detroit

The Rouge, Henry Ford's 2,000-acre icon of American industry, a complex of steel furnaces and railroad tracks and twisting assembly lines just outside Detroit, makes trucks. It didn't always make trucks. Starting in 1917, it made anti-submarine boats, then it made tractors, and then it made cars: Model A's, V8s, Thunderbirds and four hallowed generations of Mustangs. In the 1930s it was the largest auto plant in the world, toured by queens, presidents and rival barons, and what it built, it built from scratch. It had 100,000 employees in 93 buildings who produced

ON THE ROAD The tiny Smart For Two will officially hit U.S. highways early next year.

THREE KEY FACTS

1 Since 1998, more than **770,000 two-seat Smart cars** have been sold in Europe.

2 The car **can get 60 mpg** and has crash-test ratings better than other small cars.

3 The revamped 2008 model—the first available in the U.S.—will have a **bigger engine and more horsepower.**

Left: ordering at Lou Mitchell's diner, on Route 66. Above: planning the route.

1,500 tons of iron and 500 tons of glass a day. A hunk of raw iron became a vehicle in 72 hours. The Rouge spit out a new car every 49 seconds.

But today the modernized Rouge spits out 2 only trucks—red F-150s, white F-150s, black F-150s—enough Ford trucks in three days to stretch bumper-to-bumper to downtown Detroit, nine miles away. Enough trucks in five months to stretch bumper-to-bumper to New York City. Enough trucks to meet what for so long has seemed an insatiable demand for the full-size, 200-plus-horsepower pickup, America's best-selling vehicle for 25 straight years and best-selling truck of all time. Enough trucks to make me and my girlfriend, Jenny, look like heretics when we pull into the Rouge-tour parking lot. No, worse than heretics—like Europeans.

The car we're driving is the Smart car, an 3 eight-foot-long product of France that gets upward of 40 miles per gallon to the F-150's 15 mpg. It has two seats and three cylinders and a 0.7-liter, 61-horsepower engine. It is shorter than a golf cart. It can park headfirst in a parallel spot. When we drive it, heads turn and cameraphones get pulled out, and other drivers, trying to figure out what it is, tailgate us so closely that we worry about accidents. Some signal us to roll down our window as we're going 75 on the freeway.

Sold in Europe for nearly a decade—770,000 4 cars in 36 countries and counting—the Smart is coming to U.S. shores in the most talked-about launch of 2008. Already a 44-city road show is kicking off. Drivers from New York to Miami to Seattle to Austin, Texas, will be able to see the Smart, sit in it, and take it for a spin. A Web reservation system is up and running. Go to *smartusa.com*, pay a refundable $99, and you're on the list to get one of the first American Smarts to roll off the line.

Jenny and I got our Smart—a gray-market 5 version imported from Europe and made street-legal here—the old-fashioned way: We rented it from a Budget franchise in the Chicago suburbs. We brought it to Detroit to begin a makeshift road show of our own, a 1,500-mile jaunt through the heartland in which we try to answer a simple question: Is America ready to embrace such an un-American ride?

Inside the Rouge, we join a tour with a pair 6 who are obviously spies from China, ill-disguised as tourists, and a couple of Orthodox Jewish teenagers in formal wear on an apparent first date. We watch a video about the plant's

FUTURE OF THE CAR: EFFICIENCY

"HMPH. NOT MUCH ROOM FOR HITCHHIKERS."

SIZE MATTERS
Sharing the road south of Memphis.

history, set to an original score by the Detroit Symphony Orchestra, and are shuttled into a planetarium-like room of swiveling chairs for a full-sensory "what it's like to become a Ford F-150" presentation. It involves crashing sounds, piped-in smells, and bursts of patriotic welding and smelting shown on innumerable wrap-around movie screens.

What goes unsaid is that F-150 sales have 7 been tanking of late, along with full-size SUV and pickup sales in general, a decline that economist Steven Szakaly of the Center for Automotive Research says is a fundamental "structural shift." As gas prices began to climb above $3 a gallon last July, Ford's truck-division sales fell by 44 percent. Domestic rival General Motors's fell by 28 percent. Ford ended the year with the worst losses in its 103-year history—$12.7 billion, more money than the Gross Domestic Product of 82 of the world's countries—and Chrysler announced plans to close four plants and cut 13,000 jobs after a $1.5-billion loss of its own. Both manufacturers' U.S. sales were overtaken by Toyota's. For the first time, the Big Three weren't the big three anymore.

After a display of the Rouge's environmental 8 rebirth—songbird habitat, revitalized wetlands, a 10-acre "living roof" that's the largest in the world—we watch F-150 shells flow through a four-mile-long assembly line. Robots use lasers to place windshields with perfect precision; United Auto Workers unionists in street clothes use mechanical arms to lift heavy parts. Everything is smooth, bright, orderly, laudable—and oddly anachronistic. As we get back into our tiny car, I can't shake the feeling that the factory of the future is pumping out what may be the vehicle of the past.

MARSHALL, MICHIGAN, TO WILMINGTON, ILLINOIS
7.89 gallons, $20.19, 37 miles per gallon

"Your car should make other people smile. It should make you smile. Anybody can sit in traffic in a Taurus, you know?"
—Ron Durchin, car collector and Budget franchise owner near Chicago

Interstate 94 through Michigan is broad and 9 straight, and before Jenny and I pull into the

SMALL BUT PROUD
From left: Jenny takes the wheel in downtown
Detroit; Smart owner Ron Durchin at his Illinois auto-body shop; quite a stretch in Detroit.

Shell station in Marshall, we've been cruising in sixth gear at a steady 85 miles an hour. The ride has been smooth, so much like that of a normal sedan that it's still a shock when I step out the Smart's driver-side door and am already at the back of the car. "Whoa, that looks like Urkel's car," says a long-haired gas-station attendant. "Geeks of the world, unite!" adds his co-worker. This guy—thin, wearing thick glasses, terminally awkward—is named Pete. He sells us two window-mounted plastic cup holders for $1.69 apiece (our European Smart lacks these, although it does have a huge ashtray; the second-generation model that's coming next year corrects the oversight) and then asks if he can sit in the Smart. Pete slides his long frame into the driver's seat and looks around, taking in the car's surprisingly spacious fishbowl interior. He messes with the gearshift and adjusts the mirror. He grasps the wheel with both hands. "Sweeeet," he squeaks. "Huh. I might have to get one myself."

Steve Urkel, the nerd-star of the 1990s sitcom 10 *Family Matters*, drove an Isetta, a BMW-built bubble car that was one of the most successful micros in post–World War II Europe. With three wheels and a windshield-cum-front-door, Urkel's car must have been the prop department's dream come true. As an example of a car that reflects its driver's personality, it's hard to match. Although the psychology of car buying is murky—in market surveys, owners can always come up with a "need" that explains their desire—certain vehicles are clearly meant to appeal more to the senses than to a sense of utility. Here in Marshall, we're witnessing a burst of geek emotion over the Smart, something that has everything to do with image and little to do with practicality. "I don't like the storage space," Pete says. "But . . . sweet."

A few hours down the road, Jenny and I make 11 a detour to meet Ron Durchin, a man infected with a similarly impractical love of the Smart and the owner of the only agency in the country that will rent you one. A tall, gregarious car freak whose father opened Chicago's first Budget franchise 38 years ago, he had invited us to his new 40,000-foot body shop, AutoWerks, the largest in the Midwest. There, inside a cavernous garage, he tells the story of his Smarts' arrival. After being converted for American roads by a California company, his six cars were stacked sideways

FUTURE OF THE CAR: EFFICIENCY

THE SMART'S INGENUITY IS THAT IT'S A NORMAL CAR. JUST SMALLER.

WHAT WOULD ELVIS DRIVE? Hunkered down at the Memphis-Graceland RV Park.

on a semi and trucked out here. The truck driver took twice as long as usual, because every time he stopped, people peppered him with questions. The Smarts were finally dropped off outside the Budget office in Skokie. "We probably had 500 people stop by that first day," Durchin says, "It got so bad that we had to lock them, because every time we went outside, someone was sitting down in one."

After import fees and conversion fees and 12 transportation fees, the Smarts cost Durchin about $26,000 each. (Those coming directly to the U.S. market will be significantly cheaper; Smart estimates a price point below $15,000 for the 2008 launch, with the *Wall Street Journal* reporting it at close to $11,000 for an entry-level model.) Durchin rents them for $60 a day. His Web site's hits have gone up from 40,000 to 105,000 a month since he began using the cars for advertising, and he hopes for similar things for AutoWerks after he fixes up one of the Smarts to look like a Mercedes that's been smashed in on both ends. Still, for him, the appeal of the Smarts isn't altogether rational. He's not making any money off them, and when the fleet came in, he borrowed one of the cars for two months just so he could commute in it.

He ticks off a quick list of what he likes about 13 the Smart mechanically—its zippiness off the line, the steel safety cell that surrounds passengers, the fact that he can get 65 miles a gallon (I'm getting around 40, but I have a lead foot). Yet it's obvious that what he really likes is the spectacle. "You can take it to a bar or restaurant and have fun just watching people's reactions," he says. "It's the car that comes with a social life." . . .

ST. LOUIS, MISSOURI, TO MEMPHIS, TENNESSEE
7.89 gallons, $18.38, 34 miles per gallon

"I don't know what all it's supposed to do, but if it starts talking, I'm gone."
—Marla, parking-lot security guard at Graceland's Rock 'n' Roll Café in Memphis

Far left: Bill Shea at his Gas Station Museum. Left: the Crossroads café in western Illinois.

In the St. Louis suburbs, Jenny and I peel off Route 66 and join up with the Great River Road, a winding, sometimes hilly highway that parallels the Mississippi and is the stuff that car tests are made of. In its current incarnation, the Smart is said to top out at 85 miles an hour—though I've pushed it faster—and we're often the speediest thing on the road. I figure that its strange looks will inspire any cop who pulls me over for speeding to ask questions rather than issue tickets.

The Smart is not designed to be a road-trip car, but it's certainly a highway car—a Mercedes, after all. A product of DaimlerChrysler, it was born of a joint venture between the Swatch watch company and Mercedes, and it has a pedigree to live up to. The four wheels are literally at the four corners of the car—making for a wheelbase of 71 inches, 22 inches shorter than a Porsche 911's—and we gun the Smart around turns, hugging the road. Its acceleration, panned by *Consumer Reports*, which tested a pokier diesel model, is noticeably weak only on uphills (though perhaps I've been numbed by the acceleration-proof 1989 Mitsubishi Montero that I normally drive). The main thing

14 is that Jenny and I don't feel small. The cockpit is roomier than my own SUV's, we're sitting upright and high off the ground, and we don't notice that the back half of our car is missing when we're looking ahead at the blur of fields and shortleaf forests.

15 Our biggest gripe is the transmission, which is fine in (clutchless) manual mode but hopelessly jerky in automatic. Perhaps more annoying is a mysterious power down—some strange Euro security feature—that's triggered when we leave the parked car unlocked for too long. More than once we've found ourselves sitting in the darkened car, locking and unlocking its doors and shifting through the gears as we try to get it going again. But all this is set for an overhaul in the second-generation Smart. The new American model will also come with a bigger, 71-horsepower engine, and it will have a top speed of 90 miles an hour. As if to prepare for the gluttonous U.S. market, it's also rumored to get worse gas mileage.

17 As we approach Memphis, high winds and a rainstorm hit, and the Smart is blown back and forth in a way that's reminiscent of my box of a Montero. I need to keep both hands on the wheel.

FUTURE OF THE CAR: EFFICIENCY

ROADSIDE ATTRACTIONS

The Smart was a spectacle on most of the trip, but among the bizarre landmarks of Route 66, it couldn't compete. Below: The son and great-grandson of Gas Station Museum owner Bill Shea eye the little car.

We take shelter at the Memphis-Graceland RV Park & Campground, where a Smart-size cabin is tucked away on the corner of Don't Be Cruel Lane, not far from Blue Suede Lane, Shook Up Lane and Hound Dog Way. The RV park has free Wi-Fi. A sign in the bathroom reads "Don't spit out tobacco in our washroom."

Elvis was a car lover, the owner of a pink 18 Cadillac, a 1966 Rolls-Royce and a pair of 250-horsepower Stutz Blackhawks. But the closest thing to a Smart that we see when we tour his Graceland car museum the next morning is a red MG that he drove in *Blue Hawaii*. He eventually gave it to his secretary. We've left the Smart in a parking lot outside the Rock 'n' Roll Café, and when we get back a security guard named Marla in a cap and heavy coat tells us it's been drawing a steady stream of curious tourists. A Hyundai Sonata driver, she seems afraid to touch the Smart and circles it warily. She asks the usual raft of questions. What is it? Is it electric? Is it a hybrid? What kind of mileage does it get? She's surprised to learn that its basic ingenuity is that it's a normal car. Just smaller.

MEMPHIS, TENNESSEE, TO HOULKA, MISSISSIPPI

4.10 gallons, $10, 38 miles per gallon

"I tell you what, I'm not saying nothing about it, that's a nice-looking car. But I wouldn't want to have a wreck in that thing."

—Billy Joe Logan, Houlka, Mississippi

South of Memphis, Highway 78 is nightmarish, a 19 three-lane artery clogged almost exclusively with semi trucks. Stuck among them, Jenny and I must look comical—or suicidal. As we creep forward, a toothless woman in a yellow J.B. Hunt hat leans out the window of a neighboring semi and yells down at us, "Hey, is that a prototype?" The wind and rain pick up, and we keep weaving between the giants.

"At least you're sitting high enough that you don't feel like a victim," Dan Hall, of the consultancy AutoPacific, says of the Smart. This is the kind of damning praise experts heap on the car, which will have to fight the perception that its size makes it unsafe. On its side is that rollovers, which are involved in a third of U.S. traffic deaths, are a symptom of trucks and SUVs, not of cars. And in statistics for single-vehicle crashes, small cars fare far better than pickups. Half of all road fatalities are from multiple-car accidents, however, and in these the laws of physics are straightforward: It's the little guy who takes the hit. The multiple-vehicle fatality rate for subcompact drivers is 94 deaths per million drivers, twice the average. The fatality rate for SUV drivers is 21 per million. [20]

The problem for the Smart is not the Smart itself, but that it's caught in the middle of America's SUV arms race, with everyone trying to be the safest on the road by being the biggest on the road—a sort of vehicular mutual assured destruction. If the country migrates to "crossover" SUVs on car platforms (and this is a growing trend), the Smart will become safer. Also, the IIHS's dire statistics—already skewed by the fact that young, fast, dangerous drivers are more often in subcompacts than large SUVs—don't account for the fact that not all subcompacts are equal; the Smart is no Chevy Aveo or Hyundai Accent. In Europe's NCAP crash tests, the first-generation Smart got three out of five stars, better than the Ford Escort hatchback. The 2008 model will keep the "tridion safety cell," a roll cage of a cockpit [21] that spreads impacts over the whole of the car, and will have four airbags and standard electronic stability control, a skid-prevention mechanism that the IIHS says can reduce the risk of fatal single-vehicle crashes by 50 percent. As for the antilock brakes, I use them to great effect when a cop in Oxford, Mississippi, waves us down. Turns out he just wants to ask about the car. . . .

MONTGOMERY TO DOTHAN, ALABAMA
3.12 gallons, $7.75, 38 miles per gallon

"You should put a great big handle on the top. Then if you break down, you can just pick it up and carry it with you."
—Donnie Mock, regular at the BBQ House in Troy, Alabama

We've picked the final stop of our road trip, Dothan, almost solely because of its Continental Drive-In theater, which operates four screens year-round below the starry Alabama sky. We're almost there when we spot a bar and restaurant called the BBQ House on a lonely stretch of Highway 231 and decide to stop in for some ribs. Parked outside are full-size trucks—an F-350, a Silverado—and parked inside are full-size people. Paul weighs 350 pounds, Donnie weighs 330, Chester is 6′ 3″ and stands rather than sits due to a "broke knee." [22]

At first their comments are polite but unenthusiastic, even a little snide—"Not much room for luggage," "I wouldn't want to get in a wreck in it," "Truckers must want to squash you like a bug"—but one of the regulars, Ron, seems to take the Smart seriously. "Well, I'll be damned," he says. "I need one of those just to get back and forth from my house." He makes his living delivering oversize signs around the country, and for that there's only one tool: his '07 Dodge Ram with the 6.7-liter Cummins turbodiesel. [23]

For his nightly 30-mile commute between his home and the BBQ House, he falls back on his hunting vehicle, a gas-guzzling Ford 4x4. The Smart is looking mighty appealing.

24 After Paul asks if he can put his Chihuahua, Chico, in the Smart, Chester decides to sit down in our "little buggy." He emerges impressed. "I tell you what," he says, "if I can get in there with my knee, anybody can get in there." He tells us that the last time he went to the drive-in was with a girl named Jackie Eddins in 1962, just before he joined the Air Force. "These cars will sell," he says. "We need these. We need a whole bunch of these." It's this reaction that must be Smart's dearest hope—that people will look at it not as a fashion statement, but as a simple solution to a problem.

25 At the drive-in, images of Jude Law and Cameron Diaz fill the windshield, and our rapture is interrupted only by the periodic automatic shutdown of the radio. The car is smart enough to let you turn on the radio without a key in the ignition but not smart enough to know that you might want to listen to a whole movie.

26 I'm checking us out of Dothan's Best Western the next morning when a maid named Freda taps me on the shoulder. "Is that your car?" she asks. "Lord, that's the ugliest little car I have ever seen in my entire life. Nobody in their right mind would buy a little car like that." It's a rental, I say. She asks why I'm in Dothan, and I explain that Jenny and I wanted to go to the drive-in. Freda laments that most of the other drive-ins have closed. "It's probably because of all the baby-making that went on there." I assure her that's not a problem in the Smart. "It's still weird-looking," she says. "It looks like it's been chopped off at both ends." A maintenance man has been listening in from across the lobby, and finally he interjects: "I'll bet it gets real good gas mileage, though." I tell him I've been getting 40 miles a gallon, and Freda pauses long enough to take another look at the Smart.

27 "What other colors does it come in?" she asks. ■

Reflecting on What You Have Read

1 In his review of the Smart car, Funk quotes a number of people who criticize or make fun of the car. Many of these criticisms appear just underneath a main heading, a position that calls readers' attention to these negative comments. What reasons do you see for including such comments? Would it make sense to omit them or at least put them in places that would call less attention to them? Why or why not?

2 What are the criteria by which Funk judges the Smart car? At what points does Funk make these criteria explicit? At what points are they implicit? Would Funk's evaluation be better if he had made all these criteria explicit or had highlighted them like he did the criticisms of the Smart car?

3 Funk begins his article by giving some background information about Ford Motor Company and about the large number of pickup trucks Ford currently makes. What reasons do you see for including (or excluding) this information?

4 As do many car reviews, Funk's article contains some technical information about the Smart car—its horsepower, wheel base, and gasoline mileage. But he includes much more information about the people he meets and the sights he sees on his road trip. Since his article appears in a magazine (*Popular Science*) where articles often contain a good bit of technical information, should he have included more technical information? Why or why not?

5 Funk concludes his evaluation of the Smart car with a brief story about a person who initially had a very negative opinion of the car. Would it have been more appropriate if the author had concluded by briefly summarizing what he learned about the car and expressing his own opinion? Why or why not?

6 Funk's review includes photographs of the Smart car in a number of different settings. Do you think all these photos are necessary? Would it make sense to eliminate all or some of these photos? Why or why not?

7 When Funk wrote this review, the Smart Car had just been introduced to the United States. In what ways have recent evaluations of the car confirmed, modified, or contradicted Funk's evaluation of the car?

Thinking Ahead

The Smart car was introduced into the United States at a time when dramatic increases in the price of gasoline created a need for more fuel-efficient cars. Think of other products invented to meet the needs of large groups of people. These products may be tangible (cars or household items, for example) or intangible (weight-loss programs, for example). Choose one such product and evaluate it using criteria that might be especially important to people who are considering buying the product.

Ground Zero at RPI: A Great New Venue in the Northeast
Zane Van Dusen

Zane Van Dusen is a recent graduate of Rensselaer Polytechnic Institute (RPI) with a dual degree in computer science and electronic media arts and communication. While attending RPI, Zane was in charge of Ground Zero, a student-run performing arts venue, where he organized many concerts and events featuring local and touring musicians. During his senior year at college, Zane helped develop a musical instrument designed for people with cerebral palsy. Currently, Zane works as a software developer and musician in New York City.

Ground Zero at RPI: A Great New Venue in the Northeast

When one thinks of places with great music scenes, a tech school in the middle of the capital region doesn't usually come to mind. Many people assume that these institutes completely lack a music scene since their student bodies have become known for their fondness for video games and frat parties. However, at Rensselaer Polytechnic Institute (Troy, NY), one group of students has produced its own music scene through the creation of its own concert venue known as "Ground Zero" (GZ). 1

Fig. 1. Brooklyn-based band, Japanther, rocks out at RPI's Ground Zero (Piette).

In 1999, a group of RPI students renovated an old computer lab located in the basement of one of RPI's residence halls. Within a matter of months, they had turned the space into a legitimate concert venue. The venue was opened in 2000 under the name "Ground Zero" because the founders worked with the intention of creating "a site of some cultural impact to the RPI community."[1] 2

[1]Ground Zero's official Web site: http://www.gzbasement.net

Fig. 2. A typical Ground Zero crowd enjoys a performance by Skarmy of Darkness (Newman).

Ever since its inception, GZ   3
has been a place for RPI students and residents of Troy to see and showcase a wide variety of musical talent. Despite the venue's former use and modest size, Ground Zero is a great venue with high-quality equipment, good acoustics, moderate financial benefits, and great open-minded audiences. Any band looking for a new place to play in the Northeast should definitely check out Ground Zero.

Top of the Line Equipment

Ground Zero prides itself on its high-quality audio equipment and experienced   4
personnel. The venue was formed without any funding from RPI; however, over the years, through generous donations, it was able to acquire a surprisingly sophisticated sound system. In fact, the bulk of GZ's equipment is the industry standard for live sound. And not only is GZ's equipment high quality (see table), but it is also extremely versatile. With last year's addition of a 16-channel snake cable running from the mixing board to the stage, GZ has been able to accommodate almost any kind of musical setup.

One example of the sound   5
system's versatility is the performance by the band Battles, in the fall of 2004. Battles' live show consists of three guitars, a five-piece drum set, two keyboards, a beat-boxer, and a sequencer. Not

Fig. 3. Battles' complicated setup is not a problem for Ground Zero's sophisticated and accommodating sound system (personal photograph).

only were they able to fit all the members and equipment on stage, but the show sounded great and was easily one of Ground Zero's most popular events (even though it was on a Thursday!).

The only real issue with Ground Zero's equipment is its wear and tear. The equipment has been slightly damaged over the years due to so many different kinds of musical performances. While everything is in working condition, most of the speakers produce a slight hiss when they are in use. However, this is a common problem at many venues, and the actual noise is barely audible when a band is playing at a decent level. Overall, GZ has an excellent and versatile sound system.

However, the quality of a venue's equipment is almost meaningless unless there are qualified personnel to operate it, and Ground Zero is not in short supply. In fact, much of

Ground Zero's Audio Setup

Equipment	Brand/Product	Description
Mixing Board	Soundcraft Spirit FX16	16-channel mixer. Industry standard for live sound.[2]
Snake Cable/Box	EWI PSPX	A high quality professional 16-Channel (XLR) Snake.[3]
Speaker Heads (2)	Samson db500a Active Monitors	500-watt active speakers designed for professional live sound.[4]
Stage Monitors (2)	JBL EON15 G2	One of the most widely used speakers for live sound.[5]
Direct Inputs (3)	Whirlwind IMP2	The industry standard for converting line level input to mic level.[6]

Ground Zero's current audio setup is surprisingly professional and extremely versatile.

[2] http://www.soundcraft.com/product_sheet.asp?product_id=22
[3] http://tandjsound.com/main/Products/Pro_audio/Snakes/prod_chord_Snakes_ewi_01.htm
[4] http://www.samsontech.com/products/productpage.cfm?prodId=1644&brandID=2
[5] http://www.jblpro.com/eong2/eon15g2.htm
[6] http://www.whirlwindusa.com/dirbox.html

the staff at Ground Zero consists of students pursuing degrees in music production "with the know-how to produce *good* sound" (Plesniak 10). The staff also has plenty of experience producing live sound from the venue's biweekly "open mic" nights. At "open mics," the staff gains experience working with a wide variety of musical setups, from acoustic singer-songwriters to heavy metal bands. Any style of music will sound great at Ground Zero.

A Room with Good Sound

While the concert space may have started as a computer lab, the students of   8
Ground Zero have managed to transform the room into an acoustically acceptable venue with only a few minor problems. Rooms that are considered to have good acoustics are those that reflect very little sound, so that the audio mix does not get muddy. Ground Zero does a good job absorbing sound, despite its concrete foundation. Concrete is notoriously bad at absorbing sound, and on average reflects about 97 percent of all sound ("Sound"). To fix this problem, Ground Zero's thick concrete floor is completely covered with a foam mat, which is capable of absorbing over 70 percent of all sound. On the other hand, GZ's walls have been left untreated since they are so thin that the concrete is not able to reflect sound very well. However, this can sometimes lead to another sound problem: leakage.

Artists Who Have Recently Played at Ground Zero
• Always the Runner
• Battles
• Bobby Birdman
• The Dead Science
• Death By 1000 Cuts
• Japanther
• The Kiss Ups
• Parts & Labor
• Skarmy of Darkness
• Talibam!
• The Unit Breed
• Y.A.C.H.T.
• Brad Yoder

Ground Zero's thin walls may keep sound   9
manageable inside the room; however, outside the concert space performers in the basement can sometimes be heard from as far as two floors away. This can potentially lead to noise complaints and a strict limit on the volume level of shows. Luckily, RPI has granted Ground Zero the entire floor above the venue for housing its staff members. This is a huge benefit, since Ground Zero's staff will probably not have any noise complaints since they usually run these concerts. Overall, the staff of Ground Zero have done a great job making the venue an acoustically sound space. According to Ian Vanek, from the band Japanther (who used their own equipment instead of GZ's sound system), "the room sounds great, and the kids are top notch."

"All performers are received with ample applause and open arms by the Ground Zero community."

—Sarah Toner (*The Polytechnic*)

A Great Crowd

One of Ground Zero's finest qualities is its open-minded and adventurous audiences.   10
Over the years, GZ has developed a moderately sized regular audience, who are willing to see just about anything at the venue. On average, a typical GZ concert consists of thirty to forty of these "regulars" and up to thirty newcomers (with a maximum capacity of seventy people). The regulars are the heart of every GZ event, with their undying enthusiasm and respect for any type of self-expression, from rock bands, like Japanther and Skarmy of Darkness, to experimental artists, like Battles and Bobby Birdman. In fact, GZ's audiences are so enthusiastic that any artist can expect to sell a good amount of merchandise to the audience.

However, money is not what makes a GZ audience special. What makes it unique is   11
the venue's degree of intimacy. Unlike most venues, where a band disappears behind a curtain after their performance, GZ encourages its performers to stay after their performance and "hang out" with the audience. Most artists find these "hang outs" to be very special since they offer much more than endless flattery from die-hard fans. In fact, many artists who have played at GZ have noted that they felt like they were spending time with people who are just like them. By the end of the night, most artists have exchanged tips, stories, or contact information with people they met in the audience. GZ's unique and intimate environment keeps its crowds interested and excited. The enthusiasm of these crowds is what keeps Ground Zero alive both in spirit and in finances.

Fig. 4. Ground Zero's audiences are just as willing to sit as they are to stand, depending on the performer's genre (personal photograph).

Financial Convenience

While GZ may not have a lot of money to pay its performers, the staff have tried their   12
hardest to make performances at the venue worthwhile. Since Ground Zero receives absolutely
no funding from the university, its budget for touring bands is minimal. GZ usually puts on its
events for $100–$200 (which is covered by the club's own money and a $3 admission), which
all goes to the touring band. This may not be a lot, especially for bands embarking on long
tours; however, GZ does offer performers free housing for the night in the RPI dorms. On
average, a deal like this can save a band with four members from spending $100 on a hotel
room (Orbitz). It also provides increased security for the band's equipment, since they are
allowed to keep instruments in the venue's two locking storage rooms.

Another financial advantage of the club is its central location. Troy is a relatively easy   13
stop to make on any tour of the Northeast. Troy is located two and a half hours from both
Boston and New York City, and can easily be reached from I-87 or I-90. It's even more
convenient for those planning college tours in the Northeast. RPI is only about an hour
away from both Bard and Vassar Colleges, and only half an hour from Skidmore College.
While Ground Zero may not be able to offer a lot of actual money, the other financial
benefits may make the trip to this top-notch venue worthwhile.

How Ground Zero Ranks

Only four years after its creation, Ground Zero was ranked as the number four music hot   14
spot in the Capital District, in a recent article in the
Polytechnic. In the article, Ground Zero outranked
large professional venues like Saratoga Winners,
Valentine's, and Revolution Hall. Ground Zero's
professional equipment, good acoustics, financial
advantages, and great audiences make it a real
competitor in the upstate New York music scene. Any
artists planning a tour of the Northeast should
definitely contact Ground Zero. Bands interested in
playing at Ground Zero should send an e-mail to
vanduz@rpi.edu, with links to song files and an
estimate of how much money they will need to make
the trip worthwhile.

The *Polytechnic*'s Top Ten Music Hot Spots
10. Saratoga Winners
9. The Larkin
8. Mother's Wine Emporium
7. Valentine's
6. Revolution Hall
5. Battle of the Bands
4. Ground Zero
3. The Glenville Spot
2. UPAC Concerts
1. Northern Lights

Works Cited

"dB500a Active Loudspeaker." *Samson Audio*. Samson Technologies. Web. 29 Mar. 2008.

Newman, Jesse. *Skarmy of Darkness Crowd*. 13 Oct, 2006. Ground Zero. GZ: Underground
     Arts and Culture at RPI. Web. 31 Mar. 2008.

"Orbitz: Discount Hotels, Resorts, Motels, Lodging." *Orbitz*. Orbitz Worldwide, 2008. Web.
     2 Apr. 2008.

Piette, Caitlinn. *Japanther*. 2 Oct. 2004. Ground Zero. GZ: Underground Arts and Culture at
     RPI. Web. 31 Mar. 2008.

Plesniak, Adam. "Top Ten Music Hot Spots" *Polytechnic* 8 Sep. 2004: 10+. Print.

"PSPX Series." *EWI Snakes*. T & J Sound, 2008. Web. 31 Mar. 2008.

"Sound Absorption." *Acoustics 101*. Acoustical Surfaces, 2008. Web. 2 Apr. 2008.

"Spirit FX16." *Soundcraft*. Harman International Industries, 2008. Web. 31 Mar. 2008.

Van Dusen, Zane. Battles. Personal photograph. 11 Nov. 2004. JPEG file.

Van Dusen, Zane. Ground Zero audience. Personal photograph. 13 Oct. 2006. JPEG file.

Reflecting on What You Have Read

1 Zane begins his review of Ground Zero by admitting that his school, Rensselaer Polytechnic Institute (RPI), might not seem to offer a good venue for a touring band to perform. Why do you think that it makes sense (or doesn't make sense) to begin with this admission?

2 Zane's review includes a lot of technical information about equipment found at Ground Zero. How interesting or informative do you find this information? What reasons do you see for including (or omitting) such information?

3 What are the criteria by which you judge a place to hear music and dance? How are your criteria similar to or different from the criteria Zane uses? To the extent that your criteria are different from those Zane uses, what do these differences tell you about Zane's assumptions about his audience?

4 Zane includes information about how Ground Zero ranks among other music venues near his school. But this ranking appeared in his school's student newspaper, the *Polytechnic*. Does this ranking seem as valid or credible as a ranking that might appear in a local commercial newspaper? Why or why not?

4 Zane includes several very different photographs taken at Ground Zero. In including these photographs, what assumptions does Zane appear to be making about his audience? Since most of his review includes so much technical information, would it make sense to omit these pictures altogether?

Thinking Ahead

Identify a business (a restaurant, a store, a music venue) that friends, family, or colleagues might not know about but that you think is especially good. Write an evaluation that would help readers see the business's good qualities. Or identify a business that people you know think is especially good or bad, and write an evaluation that shows why they need to reconsider their opinion of that business.

Guide to Writing an Evaluation

▷ GUIDE TO WRITING AN EVALUATION

The remainder of this chapter will guide you through the process of writing an evaluation that readers can use in making a decision or that will influence readers' estimation of a particular topic. The first step is covered in Getting Started—selecting a topic, analyzing your audience, and identifying the specific purpose(s) you hope to achieve by writing your evaluation. The next section, Creating a Draft, will introduce you to strategies (illustrated by evaluations in Reading to Write) that can help you explore your topic, write an introduction that will engage readers' interest, create an appropriate voice, organize your work, conclude your report effectively, design your report and integrate visual elements, and create a review draft. Finally, the section Reviewing and Revising will guide you in assessing your work carefully and using that assessment to revise your evaluation.

As you work through the assignment for this chapter, you can read a little bit about how undergraduate student Zane Van Dusen wrote his evaluation of Ground Zero, a music venue on his college campus. In the Student Q & A box on page 389, you will find the first of several brief conversations that Zane had with the authors of this text.

▷ Assignment

Write an evaluation of a product, service, performance, trend, or organization that a specific person or group needs or wants to have evaluated. The topic you choose should be one that affects your readers and that you are competent to evaluate. In carrying out this evaluation, identify and define criteria—that is, standards that your topic does or does not meet—that seem appropriate given your topic and audience. Then look closely at the subject of your evaluation, identifying specific details that clearly relate to the criteria you are using. Your evaluation should assert a clear judgment without oversimplifying.

Your instructor may have specific requirements about how long the evaluation should be, what sort of topic you should write about, whether you should prepare the evaluation as a print or online document (or as an oral presentation), and whether you should include or exclude any particular visual elements or use a particular documentation style to cite sources. Be sure you understand those requirements before you start working on the assignment.

GETTING STARTED

To get started on this assignment, it might help to think of topics about which you personally want to make a strong value judgment because they meet (or fail to meet) your own standards—your sense of what is good or bad, fair or unfair, right or wrong. But eventually, you will have to select a topic about which you can help others make an informed value judgment. Consequently, the next section of this chapter will help you select an appropriate topic and become very clear about your audience and purpose.

Selecting a Topic

As you begin working on this assignment, think of topics that will allow you to do the following.

▶ Help readers make some sort of choice, ranging from the mundane (whether to see a particular movie) to the more far reaching (deciding on a career)

▶ Draw on both personal experience and secondary sources

▶ Make a fair judgment, considering both pro and con

An evaluation is, quite simply, a judgment about a given topic, an argument showing that something is good or bad, fair or unfair, desirable or undesirable, or better or worse than something else. See page 343 for a list of some more specific purposes writers often try to achieve in writing an evaluation. If your topic does not allow you to accomplish one or more of these purposes, you should consider writing on a different topic.

Coming Up with Ideas for a Topic

If you're not sure where to begin, you might identify good topics by reading the suggestions in the Thinking Ahead passages that follow each of the evaluations in Reading to Write. Or you might consider some of the kinds of topics about which people often make value judgments.

▶ Products

▶ Entertainment (movies, performers, restaurants, clubs, sports teams)

▶ Regulations or policies in school, businesses, social organizations

▶ Trends in society

▶ Programs (training programs, student orientations)

▶ Jobs or careers

You might also get some ideas for topics by engaging in the following activities.

Brainstorm ideas for topics. Writing as quickly as you can, list things (events, policies, products) to which you have a strong positive or negative reaction. Complete sentences such as the following:

One thing I really like/dislike is _____.

The best/worst thing I can think of is _____.

Another thing I like/dislike is _____ .

Another good/bad thing I can think of is _____ .

For now, don't worry about which possibility is best (or worst). Just write as fast as you can, getting down as many ideas as possible.

Review what you have written with a small group or the entire class. Which topics strike them as something readers might need to have evaluated? See if classmates can think of related topics. Don't feel you have to accept their suggestions; just see if any sound like good possibilities.

Select a topic that seems like it might have potential and then brainstorm about that topic. Writing as quickly as you can, answer the following questions.

What experiences have I had with this topic?

What did I observe?

What aspects of the topic struck me as significantly good or bad—and why?

What criteria am I (explicitly or implicitly) using to make my evaluation?

How has this topic affected other people?

How have they reacted to it?

Where or how might I get additional information about it?

If you can answer at least some of these questions, you probably have a topic with good potential. If not, you may need to go back and engage in some of the activities listed above.

Assessing Your Choice of a Topic

Once you have identified a topic you might like to evaluate, you need to assess your choice, making sure that you can find plenty of information about it and that you have identified readers who will want or need to read an evaluation of that topic. The following activities, done either with a small group or the entire class, should help you do this.

Summarize what you have written and share with a group. Ask the group to help you think of audiences who might want or need to read an evaluation of your topic. As is true with your choice of topic, your choice of an audience may change. But if you and your classmates can't think of someone who would need to read an evaluation on your topic, you should consider writing about something else.

Think further about your own experience. Write down as much as you can remember about specific times you have used or been affected by the subject of your evaluation. What experiences did you have? What made it seem good or bad?

Talk with others who have had experiences with your topic. If you are evaluating a product or service, find out what they noticed when they used it. If you are writing about a policy, find out how they were affected by it. Were their experiences positive or negative? What made them so?

Do some reading. Do a preliminary search in your library's databases or the Internet. See whether others have evaluated your topic. Also look for background information (for example, product specifications) from people who created a product or service or initiated a particular policy. (Remember, of course, that information on the Internet is not always reliable or complete.) Don't try to read everything carefully at this point. Just read enough to confirm that your proposed topic is interesting and worthwhile and that there is plenty of credible material available on it.

Look for visual information—images, charts, graphs, and so forth—that helps you understand the positive or negative points of the topic you are evaluating.

Conduct a brief reality check after doing a fair amount of reading, talking, and listening. Are you finding plenty of interesting material? Have you identified an audience that actually needs or wants to know what you have to say about the topic? Do you see a compelling reason why the audience will want to read about this topic at this particular time? If you can't answer yes to at least two of these questions, consider changing your topic or your audience. Do this now, not the night before the assignment is due.

 **Student Q & A**   **Selecting a Topic**

Writing Now: What other topics did you consider writing about? Why did you decide on Ground Zero?

Zane Van Dusen: I thought about doing a movie review or an evaluation of some sort of technology—speakers or receivers, maybe. But I've been doing a lot of work with Ground Zero and wanted to be able to show touring bands that it's a good venue for indie rock music. ■

Understanding Your Audience and Purpose

So far, you have probably been thinking about your topic from your own perspective, using criteria that seem important to you and recording your own impressions of the subject (movie, product, plan, idea) you want to evaluate. Now you need to start thinking about the readers you hope to reach and the purposes you hope to accomplish in writing for them.

If you want your audience to take your evaluation seriously, you need to understand that audience as fully as possible. And you need to think carefully about the purpose(s) you hope to accomplish. As you work on your evaluation, your understanding of your audience and your specific purpose(s) may change. But at this point, you should be as clear and specific as you can, so you should write out answers to the following questions, and then revise your answers as necessary.

Guidelines for Analyzing Your Audience and Identifying Purpose

Audience knowledge, needs, and attitudes

- What do readers already know about your topic? What have they heard or read concerning your topic? What sort of personal experiences have they had with it? Have their experiences been positive or negative? Have others' comments been positive or negative?

- Why would readers need to read an evaluation on this topic? For example, are they considering spending some money on it? Are they trying to choose from among several alternative products, services, or courses of action?

- What biases or preconceptions do readers have concerning your topic?

- Are readers aware of any recent events that might prompt them to read your evaluation? If so, what are they?

Audience expectations for content

- What questions are readers likely to want to have answered?

- What criteria are readers likely to find important?

- What kinds of information will readers see as credible?

Audience expectations for layout or format

- Are there any visual features (for example, photographs, charts, or bulleted lists) that readers are likely to expect or appreciate?

- What sort of layout will readers expect? For example, should you use one column or two? Do you need to cite sources? To use pull quotes or tables?

For more information about layout, see Chapter 9, pages 526–38.

Purpose

- In addition to conveying your value judgment, what else do you hope to accomplish by writing your evaluation? For example, do you want to persuade readers to accept or reject the subject you are evaluating? Articulate a feeling or belief that readers may have but have not explored in any detail? Give readers a new perspective on a familiar topic, perhaps challenging their preconceptions or showing them more good (or bad) qualities than they had previously recognized? Give readers a sound basis for making a decision?

- What sort of voice do you want readers to hear when they read your evaluation? What image do you want to convey of yourself?

⊳ Go to **bedfordstmartins.com/ writingnow** to download these questions from Chapter 6 > Worksheets.

To answer these questions about audience and purpose, you should talk with one or more members of your audience, asking them what they already know, mentioning some of the experiences you have had with your topic, and noting whether they have had similar experiences. Also, draw on your knowledge of yourself, asking such questions as these: If I were in my audience's place, what criteria would matter to me? What questions would I want to have answered? Then use what you are learning about your audience and topic to decide on the purpose(s) you hope to accomplish by writing your evaluation.

As you work on the evaluation, your understanding of your audience and purpose may change. You may, for example, get a clearer sense of the criteria your audience values or their reasons for wanting to read an evaluation of your topic. Similarly, you may want to revise your ideas about the sort of format that is appropriate. Consequently, you may want to revise your responses to the Guidelines for Analyzing Audience and Identifying Purpose as you work on the evaluation. But for now, be as clear and specific as possible.

Student Analysis of Audience and Purpose

Zane Van Dusen's evaluation of the music venue Ground Zero might be interesting to any indie rock band. But when he wrote his evaluation, he had one particular group in mind: an artist named Why? who tours with a band of four people. Why? is an established artist in the indie community, who receives enough show offers that he can pick and choose his tour dates.

Audience knowledge, needs, and attitudes

He has never heard of Ground Zero (GZ), and he has never played in the area. However, he does have experience with student-run concerts at various colleges in the United States. He knows a lot about live sound systems and acoustics from previous tours, and he also knows that many small clubs' sound systems are not compatible with some of his less common musical equipment (samplers, turntables, etc.).

He is always looking for new places to play, so he would need to read this evaluation in order to decide if GZ is a worthwhile location for him to perform during his upcoming tour. On this tour, he wants to play shows that are geographically close to each other.

He has never performed in this area and may not want to play here since he has developed a substantial fan base in other nearby cities, like New York, Boston, and Poughkeepsie. Also, if he's like other musicians who have performed at Rensselaer, he may assume that technological universities don't have good live music venues.

He is currently planning an East Coast tour. This will be his first tour with a full band and therefore will be more expensive than previous tours.

Audience expectations for content

Criteria

- Money (the amount he will receive for performing and from merchandise sales)
- Proximity to other concert venues on his tour
- High-quality equipment (high-wattage PA speakers that sound good, equally good stage monitors, and a system that can accommodate his band's requirements)

- Good acoustics (sound that travels well throughout the room and doesn't get too loud or "muddy")
- Large audiences that are receptive to new music

Questions

- What bands/artists have played at GZ in the past?
- What kind of equipment does GZ use for its sound system, and will it meet his band's technical requirements?
- What have other comparable bands thought of GZ?
- What do reviews in local publications say about GZ?
- How large and receptive an audience is he likely to have?
- How much money will he make if he performs at GZ?
- How close is Troy to major cities in the Northeast?

Audience expectations for layout or format

He will be looking for photos from previous concerts at GZ and detailed charts about GZ's musical equipment.

He will mainly be looking for charts and inset boxes that will let him easily find the information he is looking for.

Purpose

I want to inform my audience (a small indie rock band) about Ground Zero and show them why GZ would be a good venue for them to visit during one of their tours.

I want to sound very positive about Ground Zero, but I don't want to sound like I'm "selling" it. Also, I want to sound like someone who completely understands the things (technical requirements, fans) that will matter most to a touring indie band.

{ Student
Q & A } 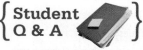 **Analyzing Audience and Purpose**

Writing Now: You seem to have a very good sense of your audience. How did you come to such a detailed understanding?

Zane Van Dusen: I had been booking concerts at Ground Zero for about six months when I wrote this evaluation. Therefore, I had learned from experience what most bands wanted to know about new venues. In addition, I had contacted the band I was trying to convince with this paper, and I asked what information they needed to seriously consider a new venue. ∎

CREATING A DRAFT

Even before you began analyzing your audience and identifying your purpose(s) for writing your evaluation, there's a good chance you had made at least a tentative value judgment about the subject for your evaluation. The word *tentative* here is very important. You should remain open to the possibility you will modify that judgment or change it completely. But whether or not you change your views of your topic, you need to develop your initial ideas into a coherent, thoughtful evaluation that someone else will want or need to read. The next few sections of this chapter outline a variety of verbal and visual strategies that will help you do this, taking you through the processes of exploring your topic, engaging your audience, and so forth. As in other chapters in this book, you will be working with strategies that appear in readings found in Reading to Write. The following discussions, along with the strategies in the how-to charts, will help you see how specific passages reflect strategies that you can apply to your own writing. You can always add to these lists of strategies by analyzing other evaluations you find interesting and credible.

Exploring Your Topic

To make and justify an evaluation, you will need to explore your topic thoroughly, gathering information your audience will see as credible and reflecting on that information in order to formulate your thesis, the basic value judgment you want to make.

Gathering Information

The information you gather may come from your own experiences, especially from observing your topic carefully. It may also come from a variety of secondary sources that, depending on your topic, may include background information (a manufacturer's product specifications, for example) and interviews with other people who have had experience with your topic.

Draw on personal experiences. Observe carefully. Most of the evaluations you write will rely heavily on your own observations of the subject you are evaluating. Especially if you feel strongly about your topic, you will need to be systematic in making these observations, being especially careful that you do not let your feelings cause you to overlook or downplay aspects of your topic that might challenge your feelings.

Use secondary sources. Even if you base most of your evaluation on your own experiences with your topic, you should look for ways to supplement your experiences, trying to find other perspectives or gather background information about your topic.

The following chart illustrates strategies for drawing on personal experiences as well as using secondary sources.

How to Gather Information

STRATEGIES	EXAMPLES FROM READINGS
Observe or work with the subject you are evaluating on several different occasions and in different circumstances. Each time notice what happens and whether the subject lives up to what you hope or expect.	In "You Call This Progress?" (p. 356), the criticism of e-mail is based not on a single, isolated experience but on numerous experiences, all of which reinforce the writer's view that e-mail does not constitute progress.
Look for alternative perspectives. It's rare that something is completely good or completely bad. You'll gain credibility with most readers when you acknowledge both pros and cons.	 In "Internet Encyclopedias Go Head to Head" (p. 347), Jim Giles presents opinions of experts who have widely differing opinions of Wikipedia. And although his evaluation of Wikipedia is basically favorable, Giles also acknowledges that Wikipedia has some weaknesses.
Take a historical perspective. What led up to the creation of your topic? How has it evolved?	In "Is America Ready to Get Smart?" (p. 366) Funk recounts some of the changes in the automobile industry, among them the fact that Toyota now sells more vehicles than do the "big three" U.S. automakers—Ford, General Motors, and Chrysler. Then Funk implies that his subject, the Smart car, may represent the future of the auto industry.
Read background material. This material could include other people's evaluations or comments on your subject, advertising and promotional items, and print or Web-based technical specifications. Look especially for photographs that reflect your attitude toward your topic and for statistical data that can be represented in a chart or table.	For "Popcorn: Which Kernels Are King?" (p. 352), the author gathered specific information about such things as cost and nutritional information for each brand of popcorn evaluated. For "Ground Zero at RPI" (p. 377), Zane Van Dusen found some of the history about how Ground Zero came into being. He also found information about the technical specifications for the equipment at Ground Zero.

Keep track of information. As you begin drafting, it can be very frustrating to find that you remember only part of an important quotation or that you aren't sure where you found an interesting statistic. To avoid this frustration, you should do two things. First, keep detailed notes of any personal experiences you want to include in your evaluation. Refer to the notes you made while selecting a topic (p. 387). Jot down responses to questions such as the following.

▶ What did I see or hear?

▶ What did people do or say?

▶ What was the setting?

Second, create a working bibliography. In a notebook or separate computer file, keep complete bibliographic information for each source you read. Record the author's name, the title of the piece (article, book, Web site), pages, publisher, dates, and any other information required to locate the piece. Later on, you will need all this information in order to create a formal list of the sources you're using, so noting all this information now will save you time at that stage. Also note the main point of each source and how it relates to the issue you are discussing. It can be especially useful to list the main questions the source poses and summarize the answers it gives.

For advice on taking notes and creating a working bibliography, see Chapter 12.

 **Student Q & A**   **Using Secondary Sources**

Writing Now: You included a good bit of technical information in your evaluation. How did you come up with that information?

Zane Van Dusen: Acquiring the technical information for this evaluation was pretty easy because most manufacturers of sound equipment are very forthcoming with their technical specifications, since those are extremely important to buyers. I first looked through any manuals that came with Ground Zero's equipment. Then I filled in the gaps by searching for the equipment in online music stores, which post a lot of detailed information about their products. ∎

Reflecting on Information

After you have read several secondary sources and observed your subject on several occasions, you should begin reflecting on what you are learning about your topic, trying to articulate and justify the value judgments you want to make. But before you begin this work, reread the way you answered questions about audience and purpose in the list on page 390. Are there some questions that aren't answered very well? For example, do you understand the criteria by which your readers want to judge your topic? Do you need more information about your readers' experiences with your topic? At this point, finish completing your responses to the best of your ability. Also review the notes you took for your working bibliography. Underline or mark key facts or reasons. After doing this, don't try to write a formal essay right away; don't even worry about paragraphing or organization. Just set aside twenty to thirty minutes and write as rapidly as you can in response to the following prompts, making and justifying your value judgments.

One way in which I think this subject is so good/bad is _____.

I think this because _____.

Without stopping to look back at the information you gathered, elaborate on that statement as much as you can.

Another way in which I think this subject is so good/bad is _____.

Continue to elaborate as much as possible from memory.

I think this because _____.

Another way _____.

Keep making and justifying your value judgments until you have used up your allotted time.

After completing this reflective work, read or show what you have written to other students (either to a small group or to the entire class). Describe your intended audience and then ask your classmates to answer the following questions.

▶ Do any of my value judgments seem likely to be especially credible or important to my audience? (If so, one of these points may become the thesis of your evaluation, or several of your points may become the topic sentences of paragraphs.)

▶ Can you think of additional questions my audience might want to have answered?

▶ Can you think of other types of information I might use to elaborate on the value judgments I am trying to make?

▶ Can you think of places where some sort of visual (a photograph or a chart, for example) might make my evaluation more informative or credible?

Formulating a Thesis

After discussing your work with your classmates, complete the following sentence:

▶ The basic point I want to make is _____.

This sentence will become your tentative thesis, the principal claim you think you will want to make in your evaluation. As you continue to develop your topic, you may want to revise this thesis. But it will serve as the starting point from which you can look for ways to make your value judgment as clear and reasonable as possible.

Developing Your Ideas

Once you have a tentative thesis, you need to develop your ideas in ways that will justify your evaluation of your topic. To do this, begin by reviewing the work you did to answer the questions above, where you listed and briefly explained the valve judgments you thought you would make in your evaluation. Decide whether you need to eliminate or modify some points or add others. Then develop these ideas by identifying and defining criteria, elaborating on your claims, and if appropriate, training judges to make reliable evaluations.

　　Identify and define criteria.　One key to the success of your evaluation will be your ability to identify clear, appropriate criteria, the standards by which you will judge your topic. As you clarify your criteria, you will almost certainly find that you need to gather more information to show how your topic does or does not meet each criterion. Here are some strategies you can use in identifying and defining your criteria.

How to Identify and Define Criteria

STRATEGIES	EXAMPLES FROM READINGS
Begin by thinking about your own values. If you are reviewing a movie, for example, ask yourself what matters most to you in a movie and what distinguishes a really good movie from a mediocre one. Realistic special effects? A plot that takes surprising twists? Witty dialogue?	 In identifying criteria by which he would evaluate Ground Zero (p. 377), Zane Van Dusen knew he could draw on his own experience in working with indie rock bands.
Consider your readers' perspective. What qualities are likely to matter to your readers? How are those qualities similar to or different from the qualities that are important to you?	The author of "Popcorn: Which Kernels Are King?" (p. 352) could assume that his or her evaluation would be read by people who like popcorn but are concerned about their health and weight. Thus it makes sense that the author talks about such matters as sodium or fat content of the brands of popcorn evaluated.
Define ambiguous terms by identifying the specific qualities that distinguish between good and bad examples of what you are evaluating. Ambiguous terms have different meanings for different readers. One way to define such terms is to point out contrasts that indicate exactly what distinguishes an excellent product, social trend, or idea from one that is not quite so good. (For more on pointing out contrasts, see Chapter 4, p. 231.)	 Jim Giles identifies two different levels of accuracy in "Internet Encyclopedias Go Head to Head" (p. 347): "minor mistakes" and "significant inaccuracies." He explains that minor mistakes consist of "factual errors, omissions, or misleading statements" (e.g., Wikipedia identified the scientist Mendeleev as the fourteenth rather than the thirteenth child in his family); the significant mistakes consist of "misinterpretations of important concepts" (e.g., incorrectly explaining how Mendeleev's work relates to that of another scientist).

{ **Student Q & A** }  **Identifying Criteria**

Writing Now: How did you choose the criteria you mentioned in your evaluation? How did you know that those were the right criteria?

Zane Van Dusen: As I mentioned previously, I chose my criteria based on the things that other bands had asked me about in the past. Once I compiled a list of what I thought were the key criteria, I presented them to the band that I was trying to book and asked them "Would you be willing to play at our venue, if we meet your expectations for the following criteria?" ■

{ **Exercise** } **Defining Criteria**

As you begin to develop your ideas, it may be helpful to write a list of the criteria you plan to use in evaluating your topic. Explain those criteria to some classmates; then ask them to identify any terms that could have different meanings for different people. Ask them whether your criteria seem appropriate given your topic and audience.

If you have questions about whether you need to define a particular word or phrase, ask members of your audience how they would define it. If different people in your intended audience give you the same definition, you probably do not need to include a definition in your evaluation. ■

Elaborate on your claims. Unless your readers are predisposed to accept your evaluation uncritically, they will probably want you to elaborate on your claims. Now that you have a clear idea about the criteria on which you will base your evaluation, look back at the notes you made while gathering material. Use the strategies explained on page 394. Also try the following.

How to Elaborate

STRATEGIES	EXAMPLES FROM READINGS
Identify specific ways in which your topic meets or fails to meet each of your criteria.	In his review of Ground Zero (p. 377), Zane Van Dusen mentions several examples of "top of the line equipment" found at that venue.
Note comparisons and contrasts. When you compare and contrast, you answer such questions as these: Is the topic as good as something else? Better than something else? Worse? In some ways better and some ways worse?	 In his review of *The Simpsons Movie* (p. 362), A. O. Scott compares the movie to episodes of the TV series.

STRATEGIES	EXAMPLES FROM READINGS
Elaborate on claims, especially when your readers may be skeptical of or need reassurance about those claims.	In "Ground Zero at RPI," Zane claims that visiting musicians find that Ground Zero crowds are "just like them." Since Zane's audience includes the leader of an indie band whose music might not be to everyone's taste, he elaborates on his claim: "By the end of the night, most artists have exchanged tips, stories, and/or contact information with people they met from the audience."
Explain how different groups might use or be affected by your topic.	 In explaining how readers might choose from among the various brands of popcorn, "Popcorn: Which Kernels Are King?" (p. 352) notes, for example, that people who are concerned about fat content of popcorn should buy one brand, whereas people who are concerned about salt should consider a different brand.
Mention ways different people react to your topic.	In "Is America Ready to Get Smart?" (p. 366), McKenzie Funk cites reactions from a wide variety of people, ranging from a diner in a ribs joint ("Not much room for luggage"), to the owner of a car rental agency ("It got so bad we had to lock them [the Smart cars on his lot], because every time we went outside, someone was sitting down in one") to a filling station attendant ("Huh. I might have to get one myself").
Acknowledge exceptions to the points you want to make.	 In "Breakfast at Manory's" (p. 359), Patrick Vitarius notes that the "Big Breakfast" is not ideal in every respect. Although most portions are generous, the juice is served in glasses that "make shot glasses look like two-handed beer mugs." Vitarius believes the rest of the meal makes up for this flaw.

Test your evaluations. If you are evaluating a product or service, you may want to supplement your personal observations by gathering information from a group of judges who can make independent, unbiased judgments. You probably will also need to provide them with some guidance in making their evaluations. For example, in rating the quality of pizzas from several restaurants, you might want to determine whether the sauce is too sweet or too salty. In that case, you would have judges taste several samples of sauce until they could agree on what seemed an acceptable level of sweetness or saltiness. Then, if possible, you should conduct a blind taste test, having judges taste and rate samples of your subject or product without knowing the names or brands of each product or how other judges rate the product.

When you conduct tests, keep careful notes in response to the following questions.

▶ Whom did you choose as judges?

▶ Why did you choose these people? What makes you think they will give you honest, unbiased information?

▶ What instructions will you have them follow in making their judgments?

▶ How often do they agree with each other?

Testing often results in some sort of numerical data (the number of people, for example, who found a product easy or difficult to use). Record your data carefully, and determine the kind of chart, graph, or table that will represent that data most clearly and accurately in your written evaluation. To be fair, your test must use the product or service under the conditions for which it is intended. If a software program is designed to be used with a computer with a lot of memory, for example, do not test the program on an old computer with insufficient memory. If you cannot replicate the conditions for which the product or service was designed, you should find another topic or try to develop your evaluation in another way.

For more information on creating charts, tables, and graphs, see Chapter 9.

Engaging Your Audience: Writing an Introduction

Since people routinely make value judgments about almost every aspect of their lives—movies, restaurants, entertainers, products, people, policies, laws, and so on—how do you get people to pay attention to and take your evaluations seriously? The answer has two parts. You must establish a relationship with your readers, helping them see how your specific topic relates to a value judgment they are concerned with. You will also need to establish a conflict (problem, question, uncertainty, dissonance), especially one that can be resolved by reading your evaluation.

Relating to Readers

The evaluations in the Reading to Write section display a variety of strategies for relating to readers. Here are six strategies that will help you relate to or develop common ground with your readers.

How to Relate to Readers

STRATEGIES	EXAMPLES FROM READINGS
Create an image readers can recognize or appreciate. You can do this with visual images that encourage a strong emotional reaction or with verbal pictures created with specific details that readily conjure up images in readers' minds.	 The first pages of "We'll Always Have Springfield" (p. 362) and "Ground Zero at RPI" (p. 377) feature images that would be immediately recognizable to, respectively, any fan of the Simpsons or member of an indie rock group.
Refer to an experience your readers probably share. Mention shared experiences that might prompt readers to read or see or buy or visit the thing you are evaluating.	"Breakfast at Manory's" (p. 359) begins by mentioning a tendency (sleeping late) that many of the author's readers, fellow college students, probably share. This experience creates a problem, the lack of a full, satisfying breakfast, which might make readers receptive to what the writer has to say about the restaurant.
Make an assertion your readers will probably agree with.	 "Popcorn: Which Kernels Are King?" (p. 352) begins with claims that most people who like popcorn would agree with. Not only is it "healthful," it is also "whole grain, high in fiber, low in calories and fat, and bulky, so it may fill you up faster than other snacks."
Mention a question or problem that is probably on your readers' minds. Specifically, mention a question or problem that might be answered or solved by the subject you are evaluating.	After acknowledging that Wikipedia is very popular, Jim Giles (p. 347) goes on to point out a controversy his readers are probably aware of—whether entries in Wikipedia are as accurate as respected print encyclopedia entries.
Provide background information that will help readers understand the basis for your judgment.	 To help readers appreciate the potential impact of the Smart car, McKenzie Funk (p. 366) gives a brief history of a Ford manufacturing plant, showing how American automobile manufacturing has declined in recent years.
Use a layout or format that your readers will expect and appreciate.	Readers of *Consumer Reports* expect to find detailed information laid out in tables and graphs, as is the case in "Popcorn: Which Kernels Are King?" Tables allow detailed comparisons among products being reviewed.

Creating Conflict

In addition to letting readers see how your topic relates to what they know, care about, or need, you should create a conflict that will motivate them to read your evaluation. Here are three strategies for doing this.

How to Create Conflict

STRATEGIES	EXAMPLES FROM READINGS
Suggest a disparity between what readers might expect or assume and what is true. One way to do this is to mention a strongly positive (or negative) impression and then consider whether that impression is valid.	In "Ground Zero at RPI" (p. 377), Zane Van Dusen acknowledges that readers might not expect a technological university to have a strong music scene. Then he asserts that a music venue at his university contradicts this expectation.
Mention conflicting points of view.	Jim Giles (p. 347) begins his review of Wikipedia by mentioning two incidents that have caused some people to doubt the accuracy of Wikipedia entries; he then goes on to cite a study, conducted by the highly regarded journal for which he is writing, that illustrates how reliable Wikipedia entries are.
Anticipate a disagreement with readers.	A. O. Scott begins his review (p. 362) by saying that *The Simpsons Movie* "is, well, a movie" rather than the "creative peak" toward which televised episodes of *The Simpsons* has been moving. In the very next paragraph, Scott acknowledges that some readers may feel he has too little regard for the movie: "Don't get me wrong. It's a very funny movie," filled with the sort of jokes *Simpsons* fans have come to appreciate.

{ **Exercise** } **Engaging the Audience**

Look on the Web, in magazines, and in books to find an evaluation in which the first few paragraphs do a good job of engaging readers' interest. Be prepared to show this evaluation to your classmates and explain your answers to the following questions. What assumptions does the writer appear to be making about readers' knowledge, needs, and attitudes? What aspects of the beginning of the evaluation would appeal to a person with the knowledge, needs, and attitudes you have identified? ■

Creating an Appropriate Voice

The evaluative articles in Reading to Write reflect a wide range of voices—personalities, attitudes, even the literal sounds of someone speaking. It's easy, for example, to imagine where a listener would hear the exasperation in Seth Shostak's voice if he were reading "You Call This Progress?" (p. 356) aloud. But he also conveys the impression of someone with a sense of humor talking to a good friend. By contrast, the voice in "Popcorn: Which Kernels Are King?" (p. 352) sounds relatively impersonal; there is no indication of who wrote this article, and the author or authors appear to be expressing the opinions of "highly trained judges" rather than giving their own opinions.

One way writers create voice is by carefully selecting the pronouns they use. The first-person pronouns *I* and *we* and the second-person pronoun *you* can suggest a relatively informal relationship between reader and writer. Third-person pronouns (*he, she, it, they*) often suggest a more formal, academic stance. In addition to their selection of pronouns, the authors of the evaluative pieces in this chapter also create their distinctive voices by using one or more of the strategies listed here.

How to Create an Appropriate Voice

STRATEGIES	EXAMPLES FROM READINGS
Choose words and a level of formality that your audience will find appealing and appropriate. For most academic and professional audiences, more formal language is appropriate and ensures that your readers will understand your meaning.	A. O. Scott, in "We'll Always Have Springfield" (p. 362), refers to a mistake someone has made using the informal term *screw-up*. Scott also uses contractions and directly addresses readers ("Don't get me wrong") so that he sounds as though he is having a conversation with another *Simpsons* fan. Jim Giles ("Internet Encyclopedias Go Head to Head," p. 347), by contrast, never uses contractions and never addresses readers directly. Giles cites an error by commenting that one Wikipedia entry "was revealed as falsely suggesting" that something was true. His word choices are formal and academic in ways one would expect of a writer for the scientific journal *Nature*.
Make comparisons that imply or reinforce the attitudes you want to convey.	Seth Shostak indicates his low opinion of e-mail in "You Call This Progress?" (p. 356) with this remark: "Today access to the Internet is widespread, as common and accessible as a cheap motel."

continued on next page ▶

How to Create an Appropriate Voice (continued)

STRATEGIES	EXAMPLES FROM READINGS
Decide whose value judgments you should express. If you think your readers will be especially interested in personal judgments about your topic, specifically refer to your own judgments or observations. If not, consider including value judgments others have arrived at, either by summarizing, paraphrasing, or quoting those judgments.	It's clear that Patrick Vitarius ("Breakfast at Manory's," p. 359) and A. O. Scott ("We'll Always Have Springfield") are giving their own opinions. The review of microwavable popcorns ("Popcorn: Which Kernels Are King?" p. 352) presents the conclusions of a group of anonymous judges, and the author of "Internet Encyclopedias Go Head to Head" never asserts the author's personal opinions; instead he reports opinions of authorities in the field.
Consider exaggerating. But be careful with this. Make sure you are exaggerating in order to reflect your extreme enthusiasm rather than expecting your readers to take what you say literally.	Presumably Scott does not expect readers to take him seriously when he begins his review of *The Simpsons Movie* by claiming that "the entire history of American popular culture—maybe even of Western civilization—amounts to little more than a long prelude to *The Simpsons*." He's simply overstating his enthusiasm in ways that will allow him to be a little critical of the movie without leading *Simpsons* fans to dismiss him as someone who just doesn't appreciate the show.

For more advice on using exaggeration to good effect, see Chapter 2, page 75.

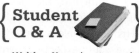 **Student Q & A**   **Creating an Appropriate Voice**

Writing Now: In your original analysis of audience and purpose, you said you wanted to sound positive without sounding like you are "selling" Ground Zero. You also said you wanted to make sure your audience saw you as someone who understood things that matter to a touring band. How would you describe your voice now that you have completed a draft of your evaluation?

Zane Van Dusen: At this point, I would describe my voice as an odd mix of professional and casual tone. I chose this type of voice because I wanted the band to feel like I knew what I was doing (since their livelihood depended on it), but that I did not take myself too seriously, because I wanted them to feel like this was a *fun* place to play. ■

{ **Exercise** } **Creating an Appropriate Voice**

Think carefully about the voice you want to convey in your evaluation. Keep in mind that as you think about voice, you may discover a need to change the substance of your evaluation. For example, if you have come to be enthusiastic about your topic, you may need to gather additional information that will justify that enthusiasm. You might also get some ideas for the voice you want to create by engaging in the following activities.

- Review, and if necessary revise, your audience analysis and statement of purpose.

- List some of the words and phrases you hope readers would use to describe the voice in your evaluation. Do you want your voice to sound personal or impersonal? Formal or informal? Serious? Sarcastic? Friendly? Knowledgeable? Enthusiastic? Reserved? Excited? Calm and reflective?

- Check with a classmate or your instructor to see whether the voice you hope to create makes sense given what your context analysis says about your audience and purposes.

- Using what you learn from your classmate or instructor, revise the list of words that describe the voice you want to create.

- Ask someone (a classmate, your instructor, or a friend) to read a section of your draft aloud, and listen to the sound of his or her voice. Can you hear the attitude you want to create in the sound of this reader's voice? If you can, good. If you can't, look closely at your draft to see what words and phrases you need to change in order to create the voice you want.

- Ask someone to read your introductory paragraph(s) (aloud or silently), and then list the words he or she would use to describe the voice you have created. Does this reader's list match yours? On the basis of what this reader tells you, decide whether you need to revise either your conception of the voice you want to create or your introduction. Or do you need to revise both? ▪

Organizing

When people read evaluations, they usually want answers to two basic questions: What is the writer's judgment? (That is, is the subject good or bad, fair or unfair, desirable or undesirable, and so forth.) What basis does the writer have for making that judgment? Consequently, one good way to organize an evaluation is to assert your opinion in a thesis or topic sentence and then follow up with relevant detail. There are, however, several other strategies you can use—either separately or in combination—to organize your evaluation in ways that let readers find answers to their questions.

For other organizational strategies, see Chapter 4, pages 238–39.

{ **Exercise** } **Organization**

Bring to class a copy of an evaluation that is very well organized. Be prepared to show your instructor and classmates the strategies the writer used in organizing his or her evaluation. ▪

How to Organize

STRATEGIES	EXAMPLES FROM READINGS
Group information around criteria.	Each heading in "Ground Zero at RPI" (p. 378) mentions a criterion ("Top of the Line Equipment") that seems certain to matter to a touring rock band. The text that follows each heading shows how Ground Zero meets each of the author's criteria.
Follow a chronological sequence.	In "Is America Ready to Get Smart?" (p. 366), McKenzie Funk takes readers along with him as he travels from one town to another, occasionally describing what he sees at some of the stops he makes.
Move from good news to bad news or from problem to solution.	In assessing the safety of the Smart car, Funk notes that it is relatively unlikely to roll over and that at least in "single-vehicle crashes, small cars fare far better than pickups." However, he acknowledges that "half of all road fatalities are from multiple-car accidents, . . . and in these . . . it's the little guy who takes the hit."
Expand your title or use a subtitle.	The title of Zane Van Dusen's evaluation, "Ground Zero at RPI," is intriguing but ambiguous. To clarify this title and give his audience a reason for reading the rest of the essay, Van Dusen adds the subtitle "A Great New Venue in the Northeast."
Use visuals to highlight key pieces of information.	As is typical of articles in *Consumer Reports*, "Popcorn: Which Kernels Are King?" (p. 354) concludes with a chart that lets readers see the data underlying *Consumer Reports*' rating of various brands of popcorn.

Concluding

Since the basic goal of an evaluation is to express and justify a judgment about your topic, one good way to conclude is simply to reiterate your judgment, much as A. O. Scott does at the end of "We'll Always Have Springfield" (p. 364). He admits that he is a little "disappointed" in the movie but would still be willing to watch it "only . . . twenty or thirty more times." There are, however, several other strategies you can use in concluding your evaluation.

How to Conclude

STRATEGIES	EXAMPLES FROM READINGS
Make a recommendation.	At the end of "Breakfast at Manory's" (p. 361), Patrick Vitarius urges readers, "Go to Manory's. Go there. Go now, no matter what time of day it is."
Indicate future developments that will improve (or harm) your topic.	After assessing the strengths and weaknesses of Wikipedia entries (p. 350), Jim Giles mentions ways in which the founder of Wikipedia intends to improve the accuracy of the entries on all topics.
Indicate how readers can get additional information about the subject being evaluated.	Zane Van Dusen concludes his review of Ground Zero (p. 382) by telling readers how they can answer a very pragmatic question: How much money can a band expect to make by playing at Ground Zero?
Qualify the value judgments you have made previously.	At the end of strong criticism of e-mail ("You Call This Progress?" p. 358), Seth Shostak acknowledges, "I'm as much in favor of technology as the next guy." But he does suggest that if people want to tell him that e-mail is an advance in communication technology, they should "do me a favor and use the phone."

continued on next page ▶

How to Conclude (continued)

STRATEGIES	EXAMPLES FROM READINGS
Tell a brief story that will convey your attitude toward your topic.	 As McKenzie Funk (p. 375) is checking out of a motel, a maid (Freda) sees the Smart car and comments, "'Lord, that's the ugliest little car I have ever seen in my entire life. Nobody in their right mind would buy a little car like that.'" A motel maintenance man overhears the conversation and remarks, "'I'll bet it gets real good gas mileage, though.'" When Funk tells the maintenance man that the car gets 40 miles per gallon, "Freda pauses long enough to take another look at the Smart. 'What other colors does it come in?' she asks."

Designing Your Evaluation and Integrating Visual Information

As you have seen from the selections in Reading to Write, evaluations may include a variety of visual elements, ranging from photographs to inset boxes to (in the case of online evaluations) video clips. But especially in reviews of products, one important kind of visual is a chart or table. When you choose (or create) a chart or table, you need to make sure it does the following:

▶ Presents data that answer the questions readers are most interested in

▶ Enables readers to make comparisons

▶ Shows clear relationships, usually the ways in which one product is better than others

▶ Includes the criteria and types of details readers are most interested in

You can find general guidelines on layout and the use of visuals in any type of writing in Chapter 9.

If the table includes the opinions of judges, those opinions should be stated as succinctly as possible.

To see how these guidelines apply to a specific table, see Reading Visuals in Evaluations, pages 344–45.

As you consider how best to design your evaluation, look again at your analysis of your audience and purpose. What sort of page or screen layout might make sense given your assignment, topic, audience, and purpose(s)?

Finally, remember to use visuals effectively and make sure that all visual elements in your evaluation are helpful to and appropriate for your intended readers. Be certain each visual is clearly labeled, is connected to your argument, and has a clear reason for being included in your evaluation. Don't use visuals just for the sake of making your work look unique.

{ **Student**
  Q & A } **Designing and Integrating**
              Visual Information

Writing Now: On the first page of your evaluation, you include two photographs taken at Ground Zero. Why did you choose those photographs?

Zane Van Dusen: I wanted the reader to instantly get a feeling for what the venue was like, and what kind of concerts we booked. The first photo is of Japanther, who are fairly well known in the indie-rock music scene and have a similarly sized fan base to that of my audience. The second photo depicts a really excited crowd having a good time at a Ground Zero event, which is very important to my audience. ■

Creating a Review Draft

As a result of the work you have done thus far, you should now have a clear understanding of the good and bad points of the subject you are evaluating. You should also be ready to write a review draft of your evaluation. After completing this draft, you will need to assess it carefully not only by critiquing it yourself but also by getting others' perspectives. This means that you will subject the review draft to a final review (from one or more of your classmates or from your instructor). Then you will use this assessment to make revisions in content, organization, style, and format.

In preparation for writing the review draft, look back at what you have said about your audience and purpose. Has your understanding of audience and purpose changed? If so, revise what you have said about audience and purpose and keep that in mind as you decide what to say and how to say it in the review draft. Also, look back at what you wrote when you were reflecting on information you had gathered. Do you need to modify any of the value judgments expressed there? Are there any places where you need to add information that would make your judgments clearer or answer questions the audience is likely to ask?

As you work on your review draft, think carefully about your introduction and conclusion. Does the introductory material establish the voice you want to create? Does it seem likely to engage the intended audience? Does the conclusion reinforce the basic value judgment you want to convey? Do your introduction and conclusion still seem appropriate for your audience and topic? If not, modify them by using one or more of the strategies identified in this chapter.

In addition, take some pains to make the organization clear. It might help to write an informal outline indicating the main points about how your subject does or does not meet your criteria. You should also organize your evaluation by using the strategies described on page 406.

REVIEWING AND REVISING

Once you have made your review draft as complete and polished as you can, you need to have it reviewed by one or more people who understand the principles (analyzing audience, engaging readers, and so on) that you have been working with in this chapter. Choose people who will give you an honest, careful review. Then you will use this review to guide a revision of your review draft before you turn in your work for grading.

Getting a Final Review

Give the reviewer a copy of your draft, one he or she can make notes on. Also give the reviewer a copy of your statement of audience and purpose. If necessary, revise that statement before giving it to the reviewer. Ask the reviewer to adopt the perspective of the audience you have described, and then use the following checklist in commenting on your work.

Checklist for
Final Review

1. What is the overall judgment I am making about my topic? That is, am I saying that my topic is good or bad? Does it meet or fail to meet some standard? Is it better or worse than something else? Is it good in some respects and less good in others?

2. In my statement analyzing my audience and purpose, please highlight any statements that give you a good sense of the knowledge, needs, and attitudes of my intended audience. Then highlight statements that help you understand exactly what purpose(s) I am hoping to achieve. If necessary, point out ways my purpose(s) could be made clearer. (For examples of purposes that evaluations are often intended to accomplish, see page 343.) Please indicate any statements that need to be clarified.

3. In what specific passages of my draft have I developed my topic thoroughly? Where have I have used criteria that are clear and appropriate for my audience? What are some passages in which I give specific details that relate to my criteria and answer readers' questions? What are some passages where I mention different perspectives (positive and negative) on the thing I am evaluating? In which passages could I make my evaluation clearer or more useful to readers? What are some strategies I might use to do this? (See pp. 397–400.)

4. What portions of my introduction seem likely to engage the interest of my intended audience? What are some strategies (explained on pp. 401 and 402) that might make the introduction more engaging?

5. How would you describe the voice I have created? At what points does that voice seem appropriate, given my intended audience and topic? What strategies (explained on pp. 403–04) might help me make the voice clearer or more appropriate?

6. What are some words and phrases that provide a clear organization for my evaluation? What strategies (explained on p. 406) might I use to make the organization of my evaluation clearer?

7. How does the conclusion reinforce or extend the value judgment I am trying to convey in my evaluation? What strategies (explained on pp. 407–08) might I use to make my conclusion more effective?

8. If the evaluation includes photographs, tables, or other visual elements, what does this material contribute to the clarity and usefulness of my evaluation? Do I need to add or revise captions for photographs or legends for charts or graphs? Are there any places in the draft where I need to add visual information? If so, what kinds of visuals should I add?

▷ Go to
bedfordstmartins.com/
writingnow to download these
questions from Chapter 6 >
Worksheets.

If possible, ask the reviewer to talk with you about your review draft as well as make notes on it. Listen to what your reviewer says but also to the way he or she says it. Does the reviewer sound annoyed? Convinced? Skeptical? Try to find out as much as you can about why your reviewer has these reactions. Also watch your reviewer's facial expressions and body language. If he or she shows a reaction, try to find out what the reaction is to and why (for example: "I noticed that you were frowning when you read that second paragraph. Can you tell me about that reaction?").

Since reasonable people often differ in their evaluations of the same subject, it is possible that your reviewer will disagree with one or more points you make. If this happens, be careful not to argue with the reviewer. Instead, try to find out why he or she disagrees with you. Once you have a good idea of the concerns or objections, you might respond to what he or she has said, asking the reviewer how clear and reasonable your responses are.

Revising Your Evaluation

Up to this point, you have listened to your reviewer's comments without arguing or making judgments about the validity of those comments. But once you have a good idea of your reviewer's response, it is time to go back through your notes on those comments. Bearing in mind your intended audience and purpose, decide which comments are most valid. Then revise your evaluation as necessary, using strategies referred to in the Checklist for Final Review.

After resolving all the issues that need attention, proofread carefully and correct any typographical or formatting errors. Then submit this final draft to your instructor.

▷ TAKING STOCK OF WHERE YOU ARE

Once the instructor has returned the final draft of your work, think back over all the comments you received—from classmates as well as the instructor—and write out answers to the following questions. (You might want to keep these in a journal or in a special section of a notebook.)

[**Questions for Assessing Your Growth as a Writer**]

1. What appears to be my greatest area of strength?
2. Where am I having the greatest difficulty?
3. What am I learning about the process of writing?
4. What am I learning about giving and receiving feedback on writing?
5. What have I learned from writing an evaluation that I can use in my next assignment for this course, for another course, or for work?

The responses that follow are Zane Van Dusen's answers to these questions for the evaluation he wrote about a campus music venue (p. 377).

▷ Go to bedfordstmartins.com/writingnow to download these question from Chapter 6 > Worksheets.

1. I think that my greatest strength in this piece was my knowledge and understanding of the audience. I understood exactly what my audience wanted to know and how they expected to see it.

2. The biggest difficulty I had with this assignment was finding and maintaining an appropriate voice. I did not want the reader to feel like they were reading a technical report, but I also wanted the reader to take me seriously.

3. I learned that writing involves a lot of research, not just about the topic, but also about the audience and potential competitors/opponents. To successfully persuade someone to agree with your evaluation, you have to know the reasons why they might be skeptical. Therefore, even though your first instinct might be to simply sing the praises of the thing you are trying to promote, it is much more important to be able to respond to potential criticisms or doubts people might have.

4. It is really important to take note of any feedback you receive, no matter what your initial response is. Sometimes you get so caught up in a certain mindset that you won't notice things that may seem obvious to others. Some of the best suggestions I received for this evaluation were ideas that I didn't like at first.

5. I learned that having a clear understanding of who your audience is, and what they want to know, is essential to writing any document. It plays a major role in deciding what information to include, what voice to use, and how to convey certain information. I can use this every day at my work, when I write technical documents for people with varying degrees of experience with technology.

7 ▷

Proposals

In some respects, proposals are very similar to other types of writing you have done for this book. In writing a proposal, you will probably have to report some information, take a position on an issue, or evaluate something (a policy, an organization, a social trend). The unique thing about proposals, however, is that you are not writing primarily to inform your audience or express an opinion. Your goal in writing a proposal is to push readers to make some change, to implement your ideas.

Proposals can take several forms. Most often, proposals are written, but they are also presented orally. They may be accompanied by pictures, charts, or, in the case of oral or Web presentations, videos. Whatever form they take, proposals appear in a number of different settings. City councils or school boards, for example, routinely hear—and often invite—proposals to improve some aspect of city services or educational programs. Corporations often issue requests for proposals, inviting consultants or even divisions within the corporation to propose ways to improve a product or meet a request from a client. In college, courses in engineering or psychology sometimes invite students to propose ways to test products or carry out experiments. In music courses, students may write a proposal for a concert program. Courses in science writing often ask students to write a proposal for obtaining a research grant. And in addition to proposals written for their courses, students often propose ways to improve some aspect of campus life, either an academic program or a service intended to meet students' extracurricular needs.

In all these cases, proposal writers have one basic goal: to solve a problem experienced in their personal, social, academic, or business lives. When people think about solving problems—at school, at work, or in society—it is easy to go to extremes, ranging from a wild optimism, in which it seems possible to change anything, to an extreme pessimism, in which any effort to make change seems futile. Both extremes are right, and both extremes are wrong. Occasionally, there really are simple solutions to problems, and all you have to do to bring about change is to point out an answer that seems obvious to you. There are also problems so complicated that they are insoluble—especially during the relatively short time you will have to work on your assignment for this chapter. Yet things do get done, changes are made, and students manage to have some influence on what goes on around them. And that is the goal of your work in this chapter: proposing and explaining a course of action that will make a difference at your school, on your job, in an organization you belong to, or in the community in which you live.

▷ READING PROPOSALS

In the following section, you will find proposals on a wide variety of topics ranging from sleep deprivation for teenagers to global warming. Following each proposal, you will find questions that pertain specifically to the proposal you have just read. In addition to these specific questions, there are several basic questions you should ask in reading any proposal.

Questions for Reading Proposals

▶ **Who is the intended audience?** Consider the language, visuals, and information included (and excluded) from the proposal. What does the writer appear to be assuming about the following?

- Readers' background knowledge of the subject
- The biases or preconceptions readers have concerning the subject
- The questions members of the audience want to have answered

▶ **What specific purpose(s) is the writer trying to accomplish?** In addition to achieving the basic goal of getting the audience to accept and implement a course of action, is the writer trying to accomplish a more specific purpose, such as one or more of the following?

- Make readers feel strongly about the need for change or about a proposed course of action
- Help them see exactly how to implement a suggested change
- Reassure them that a difficult situation can actually be remedied

▶ **How informative is the proposal?**

- What questions does the proposal answer?
- Are these the kinds of questions the intended audience would want to have answered? Are they the kinds of questions *you* would want to have answered?
- Are there significant questions that the proposal does not answer?

▶ **How credible is the proposal?**

- Are the facts accurate and up to date?
- Does the writer understand what is causing the problem the proposal is intended to solve?

- Does the proposed course of action seem realistic? Is it likely that the proposed action will actually solve the problem? Can the proposal be implemented with the resources readers have access to?

- Is information drawn from sources readers are likely to trust?

- If it's likely that there are multiple perspectives on the topic, are those perspectives presented fairly? Are any perspectives left out?

- If there are alternative solutions, has the writer mentioned them and either explained why they are not suitable or incorporated the best elements of these alternatives into his or her own proposal?

▶ **How well organized is the proposal?**

- Can readers find the information they are looking for?

- Can readers readily identify the main idea, or thesis, of the proposal?

- Can readers identify the main point of each paragraph? Of each visual?

- Does the proposal seem to "flow," giving readers a clear sense of how a particular sentence or paragraph leads to the next?

▶ **What sort of voice would readers hear in the proposal?**

- What attitudes, values, or emotions are suggested in the text? Does the writer seem fair? Alarmed? Calm and reasonable? Angry? Biased? Sympathetic toward the audience or toward the people or organizations mentioned in the proposal?

- Does the writer appear to have the experience and knowledge needed to speak authoritatively on the subject?

{ For Collaboration }   **Reading Proposals**

Scan the editorials section of a newspaper, looking for editorials, op-ed pieces, or letters to the editor that recommend a course of action or propose a solution to an important public issue. Bring a copy of one of these pieces to class, and be prepared to discuss the ways it addresses one or more of the questions above. ■

A proposal can contain a variety of visual elements, including photographs, bulleted lists, and graphs. Whatever form the visuals take, they serve one basic purpose: to make information accessible, either by making it easy for readers to find the information they are looking for or by highlighting the key features of a problem or a proposed solution. Here are important questions to ask when reading or analyzing the visual elements in a proposal.

For further discussion of emotional, logical, and ethical appeals, see pages 326–30.

▶ If headings are used, do they give a clear idea of the information that will appear in the text?

▶ If sidebars (inset boxes of text) or pull quotes (highlighted quotations from the text) are used, what purposes do they serve? Do they contain information intended to appeal to readers' emotions? Or do they help make information accessible?

▶ Are there variations in the size and style of type? If so, what functions do these variations serve?

▶ If there are photographs or drawings, do they help convey the attitudes expressed in the written text? Or do they serve to make information accessible? In either case, what details are included (or excluded), and how do these details contribute to the proposal? (For more questions to ask when analyzing photographs, see Chapter 8.)

For more information on the effective uses of visual elements, see Chapter 9.

To see how these questions can guide an analysis of the visual elements in one proposal, consider the following pages from "Homeroom Zombies" (p. 421). These pages originally appeared in *Newsweek*, and they include many visual elements: photos, a table, and subheadings.

{ **Exercise** } ▶ Go to bedfordstmartins.com/writingnow to Chapter 7 > Visuals.

For practice analyzing the visual information in another proposal, see the visual exercises online. ∎

Layout Large boldface type in subtitle draws attention to a key point: Students need more sleep than they are getting.

Photograph Emphasizes sleeping student by putting him in the foreground; includes only enough other detail to suggest the student is in a classroom.

Photograph Angles in the picture—the student's arm and back—reinforce a sense of tension or conflict between what the student is doing and what he should be doing.

Photograph The case of soft drinks takes up over half of the photograph, emphasizing how much caffeine students are probably consuming.

Caption Prominent caption "Dozing Off" highlights problem.

Caption Expresses the point of the table.

Table Provides quick explanation of the problem, showing the difference between how much sleep students need and how much they actually get.

Table Source line gives credit for information presented in the table.

Headings Boldface type highlights steps readers could take to solve the problem.

Health for Life

Homeroom Zombies

Teens need at least nine hours of sleep a night, though few get that much and early school start times don't help. Here's what parents can do.

BY LAWRENCE EPSTEIN, M.D., AND STEVEN MARDON

AS THE SCHOOL YEAR KICKS off, parents are once again struggling to cajole and, if need be, drag their exhausted teens out of bed. Later, teachers get a close-up view of sleep deprivation's effects, as bleary students zone out and even doze off in class. "I've learned never to dim the lights, even to show a video," says Lauren Boyle, a history teacher at Waltham High School in Massachusetts. "If I do, there are days when a third of the class falls asleep."

That image may make you laugh, but lack of sleep is no joke. Adolescents who don't get enough rest have more learning, health, behavior and mood problems than students who get at least nine hours a night. In some cases, teens may be incorrectly diagnosed with ADHD when sleep deprivation is actually the source of their symptoms. Perpetual lack of sleep is tied to diabetes, heart disease, obesity, depression and a shortened life span in adults, underscoring the importance of establishing good sleep habits early in life. Lack of sleep can be especially deadly for teens; car accidents are the leading cause of death among adolescents, and safety experts believe drowsy driving is a major factor.

Unfortunately, few adolescents get the sleep they need. In one recent study, researchers at Case Western Reserve University found that more than half of students slept seven hours or less, and almost one in five got less than six hours. In a survey of middle-and high-school students, University of Colorado researchers found that 82 percent said they woke up tired and unrefreshed, and more than half had trouble concentrating during the day at least once a week.

Blame multitasking for some of this. Many students are juggling after-school activities, homework and part-time jobs. Even when they manage to fulfill these obligations by a reasonable hour, the Internet, videogames, phone calls and text messages to friends often keep them awake deep into the night. (On average, 12th graders have four major electronic devices in their bedrooms.) Taking caffeinated soda and energy drinks late in the day and going to late-night parties on weekends add to sleep debt.

Biology also works against adolescents' sleep. The body's internal clock, which controls when a person starts to feel tired, shifts after puberty, making it hard for most teens to fall asleep befor... Class usually begins before 8:15 a... many high schools starting as ear... a.m. To get to school on time, m... have to get up by 6:30 a.m., guar... they'll be sleep-deprived during t... Teens often sleep much later o... ends to catch up, making it ev... to fall asleep on Sunday night a... up Monday morning. Playing ... on weekends also doesn't help t... alert when they need it most: du... week at school.

Since the 1990s, middle a... schools in more t... dozen states have ... mented with late... start times. The ... have been enco... more sleep, incre... tendance, better grades and fewe... accidents. For example, ninth... daily attendance rose from 83 p... 87 percent and overall grades slightly when Minneapolis high... moved the start time from 7:15... a.m. And car crashes involving te... ers fell 16 percent when high s... Fayette County, Ky., switched t... school start time from 7:30 to 8... But most schools still start early... teens have their work cut out for... they want to get enough sleep.

Despite all these obstacles,...

DOZING OFF: Drowsy kids may have trouble staying awake in class

---

CUT CAFFEINE: Adolescents should limit their intake of coffee, tea and some soda

...can play a huge role in helping adolescents get the right amount of sleep. Here are some tips:

Educate your kids about sleep. Teens need to understand that their bodies require at least nine hours of sleep a day in order for them to do their best in school and enjoy their social lives. Explain that even a brief spell of short sleep raises their chances of feeling irritable and anxious, and experiencing minor ills such as headaches and stomach problems.

Keep a regular sleep/wake schedule. This conditions the body to expect to go to bed and get up at the same time every day. Teens should have a regular bedtime on school nights and should avoid staying up more than an hour later on weekends.

Develop a pre-sleep routine. This sets the stage for sleep. Wind down with nonstrenuous activities such as reading, listening to relaxing music or taking a shower. Avoid bright light in the evening, which signals the brain to stay alert. That includes TVs and computer screens.

Monitor late-night activities. Keep TV and videogames in the family room, not the bedroom. Teens are less likely to stay up late if these entertainment options are less accessible. Moving these activities out of the bedroom also gives parents a more realistic picture of when their kids really go to sleep.

Limit caffeine intake. Sleep-deprived teens increasingly rely on coffee, soda and caffeinated energy drinks to stay awake during the day. High caffeine intake can make it harder to fall asleep, perpetuating a cycle of bad sleep and daytime fatigue. Adolescents should drink no more than two caffeinated drinks a day and none after 5 p.m. They should also steer clear of stimulant medication as "study aids"; these do not take the place of sleep.

Adopt a healthy lifestyle. Teens who exer-cise regularly, maintain a healthy diet and avoid alcohol tend to fall asleep faster and stay asleep longer than those who don't. (The same is true for adults.) Teens who smoke or use chewing tobacco should quit for many reasons, but getting better sleep is an additional motivation. Nicotine is a stimulant that can disturb sleep.

Take naps. Buildup of some sleep debt is inevitable—given most schools' yawn-inducing start times and the obstacles to falling asleep at 11. Teens who routinely get much less sleep than they need can make up for some of the difference with a nap after school. To prevent nighttime sleep disruption, teens shouldn't nap longer than 60 minutes or in the evening after dinner.

Set rules. Forbidding teens to drive after 11 p.m. (when they're most likely to nod off) won't win Mom and Dad any popularity contests, but it can save lives.

Be alert for sleep disorders. Teens may suffer from the same disorders that prevent adults from getting a decent night's sleep. These include obstructive sleep apnea (a nighttime breathing disorder), narcolepsy and restless-legs syndrome.

Provide a good example. If parents are staying up late and battling sleep deprivation with gallons of coffee, why should teens follow their advice to get a good night's sleep?

Above all, don't give up. Boyle, the teacher in Massachusetts, talks one-on-one with students who repeatedly fall asleep in class about the importance of sleep and calls parents if the problem continues. "These aren't bad kids," she says. "Often, they're highly motivated, spending hours on homework and also working to save money for college. If you talk to them, you can have a big impact."

EPSTEIN, former president of the American Academy of Sleep Medicine, is an instructor at Harvard Medical School and the medical director for Sleep HealthCenters in Boston. MARDON is a medical writer. They are the authors of "The Harvard Medical School Guide to a Good Night's Sleep" (McGraw Hill, 2006). For more information on sleep, go to health.harvard.edu/newsweek.

Haven't Slept a Wink

Teenagers tend to sleep later than preadolescents, and like adults, they don't get enough sleep on the weekdays. How sleep patterns change with age:

Age	Natural bedtime*	Hours of sleep: recommended	actual†
0-1 yrs.	7-8 p.m.	14-15 hrs.**	12.8 all days**
1-2	7-8	12-14**	11.8**
3-6	7-8	11-13**	10.3**
7-11	8-9	10-11	9.4
12-17	10:30-11:30	8.5-9.5	7.6 weekdays / 8.9 weekends
18-54	10-12	7-8.5	6.8 weekdays / 7.4 weekends
55-84	8-10	7-8.5	6.9 weekdays / 7.5 weekends

*REFERS TO BEDTIME IN THE NATURAL SLEEP/WAKE CYCLE. ACTUAL BEDTIMES WILL VARY. **BASED ON NATL. SLEEP FOUNDATION (NSF) SURVEYS, 2003-2006. †INCLUDES DAY AND NIGHTTIME SLEEP. SOURCES: NSF; DR. JUDITH OWENS, HASBRO CHILDREN'S HOSPITAL.

GEORGE RUHE – BLOOMBERG NEWS-LANDOV

▷ READING TO WRITE

In the following section of this chapter, you will find proposals taken from many of the same sources as readings from other chapters: op-ed pages of newspapers, books, and periodicals (some are from magazines intended for a wide range of readers, while one is from a journal intended for people who share a specific interest).

In all cases, proposals have to respond to one basic question: What should be done in order to solve a problem, achieve a particular goal, or improve a troublesome situation? In many cases, proposals have to address several other questions: Who has to do what in order to implement a proposed solution? Why is one proposed solution better than others? And sometimes proposals need to address more basic questions: Why does anything need to be done? What's wrong with the way things are now?

Answers to these questions appear in the readings you will find in the next pages of this chapter. Each reading is followed by passages titled Reflecting on What You Have Read and Thinking Ahead. The questions in "Reflecting" will help you not only assess the content of the proposal but also recognize strategies and techniques you can use in writing your own proposal. The Thinking Ahead prompts will suggest ways to decide on a topic for your proposal.

{ For Collaboration }   **Analyzing Proposals**

Choose one of the proposals in Reading to Write. Working with one or more classmates, list the questions this proposal answers, as well as the questions it does not answer. In light of these questions and answers, decide what assumptions the proposal makes about what the intended audience knows, needs, or cares about. ■

    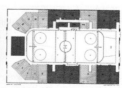

HEALTH FOR LIFE SLEEPY **TEENS**, QUIRKY **KIDS** AND HEALTHY **PREGNANCIES**

Newsweek

What Kind of **Decider** Would She Be?
By Jonathan Darman

Homeroom Zombies
Lawrence Epstein and Steven Mardon

Lawrence Epstein is a doctor and instructor at Harvard Medical School and also the medical director for Sleep HealthCenters in Boston, where he specializes in sleep medicine. Steven Mardon is a freelance writer who writes frequently on health topics. In addition to authoring many articles and books, he has a career as a country singer and songwriter. Together, Epstein and Mardon are coauthors of *The Harvard Medical School Guide to a Good Night's Sleep* (2007). Their book offers a plan to improve sleep and avoid common sleep issues. The following essay focusing on sleep deprivation in teenagers appeared in *Newsweek* in a special section, "Health for Life." As you read, notice the kinds of evidence the proposal cites to show that teenagers' lack of sleep is a serious problem.

Homeroom Zombies

Teens need at least nine hours of sleep a night, though few get that much and early school start times don't help. Here's what parents can do.

By Lawrence Epstein, MD, and Steven Mardon

As the school year kicks off, parents are once again struggling to cajole and, if need be, drag their exhausted teens out of bed. Later, teachers get a close-up view of sleep deprivation's effects, as bleary students zone out and even doze off in class. "I've learned never to dim the lights, even to show a video," says Lauren Boyle, a history teacher at Waltham High School in Massachusetts. "If I do, there are days when a third of the class falls asleep."

That image may make you laugh, but lack of 2 sleep is no joke. Adolescents who don't get enough rest have more learning, health, behavior and mood problems than students who get at least nine hours a night. In some cases, teens may be incorrectly diagnosed with ADHD when

DOZING OFF: Drowsy kids may have trouble staying awake in class.

sleep deprivation is actually the source of their symptoms. Perpetual lack of sleep is tied to diabetes, heart disease, obesity, depression and a shortened life span in adults, underscoring the importance of establishing good sleep habits early in life. Lack of sleep can be especially deadly for teens; car accidents are the leading cause of death among adolescents, and safety experts believe drowsy driving is a major factor.

Unfortunately, few adolescents get the sleep 3 they need. In one recent study, researchers at Case Western Reserve University found that more than half of students slept seven hours or less, and almost one in five got less than six hours. In a survey of middle- and high-school students, University of Colorado researchers found that 82 percent said they woke up tired and unrefreshed, and more than half had trouble concentrating during the day at least once a week.

Blame multitasking for some of this. Many 4 students are juggling after-school activities, homework and part-time jobs. Even when they manage to fulfill these obligations by a reasonable hour, television, the Internet, videogames, phone calls and text messages to friends often keep them awake deep into the night. (On average, 12th graders have four major electronic devices in their bedrooms.) Taking caffeinated soda and energy drinks late in the day and going to late-night parties on weekends add to sleep debt.

Biology also works against adolescents' 5 sleep. The body's internal clock, which controls when a person starts to feel tired, shifts after puberty, making it hard for most teens to fall asleep before 11 p.m. Class usually begins before 8:15 a.m., with many high schools starting as early as 7:15 a.m. To get to school on time, most teens have to get up by 6:30 a.m., guaranteeing they'll be sleep-deprived during the week. Teens often sleep much later on weekends to catch up, making it even harder to fall asleep on Sunday night and wake up Monday morning. Playing catch-up on weekends also doesn't help teens stay alert when they need it most: during the week at school.

Since the 1990s, middle and high schools in 6 more than two dozen states have experimented with later school start times. The results have been encouraging: more sleep, increased attendance, better grades and fewer driving accidents. For example, ninth graders' daily attendance rose from 83 percent to 87 percent and overall grades went up slightly when Minneapolis high schools moved the start time from 7:15 to 8:40 a.m. And car crashes involving teen drivers fell 15 percent when high schools in Fayette County, Ky., switched the high-school start time from 7:30 to 8:30 a.m. But most schools still start early, meaning teens have their work cut out for them if they want to get enough sleep.

Despite all these obstacles, parents can play 7 a huge role in helping adolescents get the right amount of sleep. Here are some tips:

Educate your kids about sleep. Teens 8 need to understand that their bodies require at least nine hours of sleep a day in order for them to do their best in school and enjoy their social lives. Explain that even a brief spell of short sleep raises their chances of feeling irritable and anxious, and experiencing minor ills such as headaches and stomach problems.

Keep a regular sleep/wake schedule. 9 This conditions the body to expect to go to bed and get up at the same time every day. Teens should have a regular bedtime on school nights and should avoid staying up more than an hour later on weekends.

Develop a pre-sleep routine. This sets the 10 stage for sleep. Wind down with nonstrenuous activities such as reading, listening to relaxing music or taking a shower. Avoid bright light in

CUT CAFFEINE: Adolescents should limit their intake of coffee, tea and some soda.

the evening, which signals the brain to stay alert. That includes TVs and computer screens.

Monitor late-night activities. Keep TV 11 and videogames in the family room, not the bedroom. Teens are less likely to stay up late if these entertainment options are less accessible. Moving these activities out of the bedroom also gives parents a more realistic picture of when their kids really go to sleep.

Limit caffeine intake. Sleep-deprived 12 teens increasingly rely on coffee, soda and caffeinated energy drinks to stay awake during the day. High caffeine intake can make it harder to fall asleep, perpetuating a cycle of bad sleep and daytime fatigue. Adolescents should drink no more than two caffeinated drinks a day and none after 5 p.m. They should also steer clear of stimulant medication as "study aids"; these do not take the place of sleep.

Adopt a healthy lifestyle. Teens who exer- 13 cise regularly, maintain a healthy diet and avoid

Haven't Slept a Wink

Teenagers tend to sleep later than preadolescents, and like adults, they don't get enough sleep on the weekdays. How sleep patterns change with age:

Age	Natural bedtime*	Hours of sleep: recommended	actual†
0–1 yrs.	7–8 p.m.	14–15 hrs.**	12.8 all days**
1–2	7–8	12–14**	11.8**
3–6	7–8	11–13**	10.3**
7–11	8–9	10–11	9.4
12–17	10:30–11:30	8.5–9.5	7.6 weekdays 8.9 weekends
18–54	10–12	7–8.5	6.8 weekdays 7.4 weekends
55–84	8–10	7–8.5	6.9 weekdays 7.5 weekends

*REFERS TO BEDTIME IN THE NATURAL SLEEP-WAKE CYCLE. ACTUAL BEDTIMES WILL VARY.
†BASED ON NATL. SLEEP FOUNDATION (NSF) SURVEYS, 2003–2006. **INCLUDES DAY AND NIGHTTIME SLEEP. SOURCES: NSF; DR. JUDITH OWENS, HASBRO CHILDREN'S HOSPITAL.

alcohol tend to fall asleep faster and stay asleep longer than those who don't. (The same is true for adults.) Teens who smoke or use chewing tobacco should quit for many reasons, but getting better sleep is an additional motivation. Nicotine is a stimulant that can disturb sleep.

Take naps. Buildup of some sleep debt is inevitable—given most schools' yawn-inducing start times and the obstacles to falling asleep at 11. Teens who routinely get much less sleep than they need can make up for some of the difference with a nap after school. To prevent nighttime sleep disruption, teens shouldn't nap longer than 60 minutes or in the evening after dinner. 14

Set rules. Forbidding teens to drive after 11 p.m. (when they're most likely to nod off) won't win Mom and Dad any popularity contests, but it can save lives. 15

Be alert for sleep disorders. Teens may suffer from the same disorders that prevent adults from getting a decent night's sleep. These include obstructive sleep apnea (a nighttime breathing disorder), narcolepsy and restless-legs syndrome. 16

Provide a good example. If parents are staying up late and battling sleep deprivation with gallons of coffee, why should teens follow their advice to get a good night's sleep? 17

Above all, don't give up. Boyle, the teacher in Massachusetts, talks one-on-one with students who repeatedly fall asleep in class about the importance of sleep and calls parents if the problem continues. "These aren't bad kids," she says. "Often, they're highly motivated, spending hours on homework and also working to save money for college. If you talk to them, you can have a big impact." ■ 18

Reflecting on What You Have Read

1 According to this article, lack of sleep can have a number of long-term consequences such as depression or diabetes. But both the first paragraph and the first visual point to a relatively short-term consequence: teenagers sleeping in class. What reasons do you see for beginning with such a short-term consequence, especially when long-term consequences are much more severe?

2 The title of this proposal uses the term *zombies* to refer to students who sleep in class. Considering the connotations of the term *zombie*, what reasons do you see for (or against) using this term?

3 Although there is some evidence that justifies beginning high school classes at 8:30 a.m. or later, apparently few schools have made this change. What reasons might schools have for not changing? Think of your own high school: What obstacles might school administrators have faced if they began high school later? How well does this proposal help readers see how to overcome these obstacles? Should the article have provided this help?

4 This article recommends several ways parents can help their teenagers get enough sleep. Choose any one recommendation and, considering your own experience and that of your high school friends, explain how feasible this recommendation is.

5 The proposal concludes on an optimistic note: "If you [adults] talk to them, you can have a big impact." Do you think this optimism is justified? Why or why not?

6 The table on page 423 presents information not only about how much sleep children and teenagers need, but also about how much sleep adults of all ages need. Does this information seem necessary or appropriate for this article? Why or why not?

Thinking Ahead

Think of a problem that affects high school or college students you know. How serious is this problem? What are the causes of this problem, and what, if anything, is being done to solve it? According to people (researchers, teachers, administrators) who are concerned about this problem, what else should be done in order to solve it? Consider the strengths and limitations of other people's proposed solutions, and then devise your own solution. Be sure to show how to overcome obstacles that interfere with putting your proposal into practice.

Leave No Child Inside
Richard Louv

Richard Louv is the author of many books about family, nature, and community, including *Last Child in the Woods: Saving Our Children from Nature-Deficit Disorder* (2005). He also directs a nonprofit organization dedicated to the movement to reconnect children with nature. In the following essay, he acknowledges that for some people, thinking about environmental issues is frightening, causing feelings of despair and hopelessness. Louv argues that fears and limits on outdoor play have distanced young people from nature. Adapting the language of the education bill No Child Left Behind, he proposes a new "Leave No Child Inside" campaign to get children back into nature. As you read, notice ways in which this proposal is specifically addressed to readers of *Sierra* magazine, a publication of the Sierra Club, which has the mission "to explore, enjoy, and protect the wild places of the earth."

Leave No Child Inside
The remedy for environmental despair is as close as the front door.

By Richard Louv

Arno Chrispeels, a high school science 1 teacher in Poway, California, recently asked his students to list the messages they hear most often about the environment. The students offered a few positive statements about the beauty of nature, but the dominant themes were fear, death, and loss:

> "Humans are a bad environment for other humans."

> "You will see the earth reach its end."

> "The environment will die."

> "If you go out [in nature], there has to be a parent because you can't protect yourself." And so on.

Earlier that month, Chrispeels had invited a 2 biology professor from the University of California at San Diego to speak about overpopulation. "He basically told them that we've run out of time. The kids' eyes froze over," Chrispeels says. They'd heard that message before.

In many of the interviews I've been doing 3 with young people in recent years, I hear the same hopelessness. "When I think about the destruction of the environment, it's too painful," a 17-year-old student told me. "So I don't think about it."

In an era when politicians routinely ignore the 4 challenges of climate change and other environmental threats, such a reaction is understandable. Yet if our goal is to save the natural world, despair will not get us there. Moreover, many of the kids we are scaring about nature have had precious few opportunities to directly experience its joys and mysteries. As naturalist Robert Michael Pyle writes, "What is the extinction of a condor to a child who has never seen a wren?"

David Sobel, codirector of the Center for 5
Place-Based Education at the Antioch New
England Institute, was one of the first to ring
the alarm about this phenomenon. He described the growth of "ecophobia," a debilitating fear for the future of the planet. "Between
the end of morning recess and the beginning of
lunch," Sobel writes, "schoolchildren will learn
that more than 10,000 acres of rainforest will
be cut down." Then they'll be told that "by
recycling their *Weekly Readers* and milk
cartons, they can help save the planet" and
grow up to be responsible stewards of the earth.
Or will they?

Children learn about rainforests, writes Sobel 6
in *Beyond Ecophobia: Reclaiming the Heart in
Nature Education*, but usually not about their
own region's forests or "even just the meadow
outside the classroom door." While young
people do need to know about ecological deteri-
oration, Sobel found that emphasizing gloom
and doom too early "ends up distancing children from, rather than connecting them with,
the natural world. The natural world is being
abused, and they just don't want to have to deal
with it." Emotionally, they turn off.

Indoctrination in ecophobia begins early; a 7
new genre of well-intentioned but dismal children's books has appeared, so that bedtime
readings are often tales of ecological collapse.
The next day at play, children are increasingly
unlikely to experience the balancing joy and
wonder of nature.

Over the past 15 years, I have interviewed 8
families across the country about the changes
in their lives, including their relationship to
nature. With few exceptions, even in rural
areas, parents say the same thing: Most children aren't playing outside anymore, not in the
woods or fields or canyons. A fifth-grader in San
Diego described his world succinctly: "I like to
play indoors better 'cause that's where all the
electrical outlets are."

When asked why their kids resist going 9
outside, parents point to diminishing access
to natural areas, competition with electronic
entertainment, longer school hours, increased
homework, and other time pressures. Most frequently, though, they (as well as school officials)
cite fear—of traffic, of being sued, and, above
all, of strangers. Despite evidence that the number of child abductions has been falling for
years (and most of those that do occur are not
by strangers), many parents and kids now
firmly believe that a bogeyman—if not the
Blair Witch—lurks on every street corner and
wooded lot.

One antidote to the fear of "stranger danger" 10
is to start thinking in terms of comparative risk.

Yes, there are hazards outside the home. But, in most cases, they pale in comparison to those of raising young people under what amounts to protective house arrest. Kids growing up indoors may suffer fewer broken bones and skinned knees, but pediatricians now report an increase in children with repetitive stress injuries, which can last for decades. Too many limits on outdoor play may also put children at risk of diabetes: A third of U.S. children and teens—25 million kids—are either overweight or nearly so. That's the highest number ever recorded, according to the National Health and Nutrition Examination Survey.

By not getting outdoors, science is demon- 11 strating, kids are missing out on the enormously positive impact of direct nature experiences on their cognitive development, creativity, and emotional health. Environmental psychologists report, for example, that greenery in or around the home helps reduce stress and maintain children's mental well-being. A study by researchers at the Human-Environment Research Laboratory at the University of Illinois at Urbana-Champaign revealed that children as young as five show a significant reduction in the symptoms of attention deficit disorder when they engage with nature. Other studies show that kids who play in natural settings are more cooperative and more likely to create their own games than those who play on flat turf or asphalt playgrounds.

Students in schools that use outdoor class- 12 rooms also do better academically across the board, from social studies to standardized test scores. A 2005 study conducted by an independent research group, funded by the Sierra Club and released by the California Department of Education, found that kids in outdoor classrooms improved their science scores by 27 percent. Rather than canceling recess and field trips, as many school districts are doing, the

"When I sat down in nature, I found myself reconnected, my insides and outsides."

evidence suggests that students need *more* time learning outside the classroom.

Beyond leaving no child behind, we need a 13 "Leave No Child Inside" campaign to reconnect kids with the restorative, challenging, primal qualities of nature. Such a movement is now being born. In the past year, nature-focused preschools and public high schools have been established, and major environmental organizations as well as several state governments are substantially increasing their commitment to getting kids outside.

But getting children out in the woods is not 14 necessarily enough to counteract ecophobia, the dread of losing those woods. Dealing with such hopelessness requires that we reconnect with the optimistic, assertive spirit that fueled earlier environmentalism. That doesn't mean we should hold back on reporting bad news to young people at an appropriate age, but we must dramatically widen the discussion. Bradley Smith, a dean at Western Washington University and former president of the Council of Environmental Deans and Directors, takes issue with the bleak views he hears expressed by students. "During the next forty years, we're going to have to do everything differently," he says. He doesn't mean that to be depressing news; far from it. From green architecture to organic farming to alternative energy, Smith foresees an array of exciting careers emerging as we build a new, greener civilization. That's the kind of message that will turn despair into creativity and hope—especially when accompanied by more time spent in nature.

As evidence, there's the second stack of student papers Chrispeels sent me. He'd challenged his students to spend a half hour in a natural setting and to write about it. That may not sound like much time, but for some of these 15

youngsters, it was an introduction to a new world. Among 100 essays, there wasn't a cynical or despairing one. Confronted by nature, the teenagers expressed awe and surprise.

"For the past few months, I've found myself unmotivated," wrote one young man. "I almost felt a disconnection from myself because I couldn't take the time to think. When I sat down in nature to write this weekend, I found myself reconnected, my insides and outsides." Another student noticed that "it wasn't boring at all being alone, and I saw more stars than I have probably ever seen in my entire life." 16

What these young people experienced, if in the smallest of tastes, was something they'll never get from a video game: a sense of the possibilities of the vast, unnoticed universe. It's up to those of us who were lucky enough to grow up in closer contact with nature to help kindle that spark. Just as the light can go out in children's eyes, it can quickly come back on again. ■ 17

Reflecting on What You Have Read

1 In "Leave No Child Inside," Louv begins by citing examples of the hopelessness many students feel where the environment is concerned. To what extent is this attitude shared by people you know? Do the examples Louv cites persuade you that these attitudes constitute a serious problem?

2 Louv argues that much of the information schools provide about the environment causes students to "turn off emotionally." Consider environmental information offered by your high school or college. What sort of impact has it had on you and people you know? In what ways did it succeed or fail in affecting your ideas and actions? How can you account for this success or failure?

3 Louv mentions a number of reasons parents do not encourage their children to spend more time out of doors. How valid do these reasons seem? How does Louv respond to them? And how persuasive do you find Louv's response?

4 Louv cites a number of ways students can benefit from spending time in natural settings (as opposed to city streets and playgrounds). What do these benefits tell you about the assumptions Louv is making about his audience?

5 Near the end of his proposal, Louv mentions that after spending a half hour in a natural setting, students came away with very positive attitudes toward spending time in nature. Do these students' reactions persuade you that spending time in nature will have significant effects on large numbers of students? Why or why not?

Thinking Ahead

Louv suggests that schools need to do a better job of engaging students with their natural environment, and he implies that setting up "outdoor classrooms" might be a way to do this. But he doesn't explain how to go about setting up such classrooms; nor does he suggest less radical ways in which schools might help students develop more positive attitudes toward their environment. What if your college wanted to help students become more engaged with their environment? How might it go about it? How might courses or existing programs be changed in order to accomplish this goal? How might your school go about instituting new programs?

AN
INCONVENIENT
TRUTH
THE PLANETARY EMERGENCY OF GLOBAL WARMING AND WHAT WE CAN DO ABOUT IT
AL GORE

from *An Inconvenient Truth*

Al Gore

Al Gore is the author of the bestselling book *An Inconvenient Truth* (2006), which was the companion to the award-winning documentary film of the same name. Since leaving public office in 2001, former vice president Gore has led a campaign to raise public awareness on global warming. He received the Nobel Peace Prize in 2007 for this work. The following excerpt from the last section of his book presents some of the steps individuals can take to address climate change and reduce emissions. As you read, notice the ways in which Gore tries to show that his recommendations are practical.

So here's what you personally can do to help solve the climate crisis:

When considering a problem as vast as global warming, it's easy to feel overwhelmed and powerless—skeptical that individual efforts can really have an impact. But we need to resist that response, because this crisis will get resolved only if we as individuals take responsibility for it. By educating ourselves and others, by doing our part to minimize our use and waste of resources, by becoming more politically active and demanding change—in these ways and many others, each of us can make a difference.

On the following pages you will find a range of practical steps anyone can take to reduce the stress our high-tech lives exert on the natural world. As we incorporate these suggestions into our lives, we may well find that not only are we contributing to a global solution, we are also making our lives better. In some cases, the returns are quantifiable: Using less electricity and fuel, for example, saves money. Further: more walking and biking improve our health; diets of locally grown produce bring enhanced taste and nutrition; breathing cleaner air is energizing and healing; and creating a world of restored natural balance ensures a future for our children and grandchildren.

One way to begin making a difference is to learn how the way we live our lives impacts our global environment. All of us contribute to climate change through the daily choices we make—from the energy we use at home to the cars and other vehicles we drive, from the products and services we consume to the trail of waste we leave behind. The average American is responsible for about 15,000 pounds of carbon dioxide emissions each year. This per capita number is greater than that of any other industrialized country. In fact, the United States—a country with 5% of the world's people—produces nearly 25% of the world's total greenhouse-gas emissions.

To calculate your impact on the climate in terms of the total amount of greenhouse gases you produce, visit **www.climatecrisis.net**. There, with the help of an interactive energy meter, you can calculate what your individual impact—your "carbon footprint"—currently is. This tool will also help you evaluate which areas of your life produce the most emissions. Armed with this information, you can begin to take effective action and work toward living a carbon-neutral life.

Consume less, conserve more

Reduce emissions by consuming less and conserving wisely

In America, we have grown used to an environment of plenty, with an enormous variety of consumer products always available and constant enticement to buy "more," "new," and "improved." This consumer culture has become so intrinsic to our worldview that we've lost sight of the huge toll we are taking on the world around us. By cultivating a new awareness of how our shopping and lifestyle choices impact the environment and directly cause carbon emissions, we can begin to make positive changes to reduce our negative effects. Here are some specific ideas on how we can achieve this.

Consume less

Energy is consumed in the manufacturing and transport of everything you buy, which means there are fossil-fuel emissions at every stage of production. A good way to reduce the amount of energy you use is simply to buy less. Before making a purchase, ask yourself if you really need it. Can you make do with what you already have? Can you borrow or rent? Can you find the item secondhand? More and more Americans are beginning to simplify their lives and choose to reduce consumption.

▶ **For ideas on how to pare down, visit www.newdream.org**

Buy things that last

"Reduce, reuse, and recycle" has become the motto of a growing movement dedicated to producing less waste and reducing emissions by buying less, choosing durable items over disposable ones, repairing rather than discarding, and passing on items that are no longer needed to someone who can make use of them.

▶ **For more information about the three Rs, visit www.epa.gov/msw/reduce.htm**

▶ **To learn how to find a new home for something you no longer need, visit www.freecycle.org**

Pre-cycle—reduce waste before you buy

Discarded packaging materials make up about one-third of the waste clogging our landfills. Vast amounts of natural resources and fossil fuels are consumed each year to produce the paper, plastic, aluminum, glass, and Styrofoam that hold and wrap our purchases. Obviously, some degree of packaging is necessary to transport and protect the products we need, but all too often manufacturers add extraneous wrappers over wrappers and layers of unnecessary plastic. You can let companies know your objection to such excess by boycotting their products. Give preference to those products that use recycled packaging,

"There is nothing we can do about climate change. It's already too late."

This is the worst misconception of all. If "denial ain't just a river in Egypt," despair ain't just a tire in the trunk. There are lots of things we can do—but we need to start now. We can't ignore the causes and impacts of climate change any longer. We need to reduce our use of fossil fuels, through a combination of government initiatives, industry innovation, and individual action. Dozens of things you can do are outlined in this resource guide.

or that don't use excess packaging. When possible, buy in bulk and seek out things that come in refillable glass bottles.

▶ **For more ideas about how to pre-cycle, visit www.environmentaldefense.org/article. cfm?contentid=2194**

Recycle

Most communities provide facilities for the collection and recycling of paper, glass, steel, aluminum, and plastic. While it does take energy to gather, haul, sort, clean, and reprocess these materials, recycling takes far less energy than does sending recyclables to landfills and creating new paper,

bottles, and cans from raw materials. It has been suggested that if 100,000 people who currently don't recycle began to do so, they would collectively reduce carbon emissions by 42,000 tons per year. As an added benefit, recycling reduces pollution and saves natural resources, including precious trees that absorb carbon dioxide. And in addition to the usual materials, some facilities are equipped to recycle motor oil, tires, coolant, and asphalt shingles, among other products.

▶ **To learn about where you can recycle just about anything in your area, visit www.earth911.org/master.asp?s=ls&a= recycle&cat=1 or www.epa.gov/epaoswer/ non-hw/muncpl/recycle.htm**

Don't waste paper

Paper manufacturing is the fourth-most energy-intensive industry, not to mention one of the most polluting and destructive to our forests. It takes an entire forest—more than 500,000 trees—to supply Americans with their Sunday newspapers each week. In addition to recycling your used paper, there are things you can do to reduce your overall paper consumption. Limit your use of paper towels and use cloth rags instead. Use cloth napkins instead of disposables. Use both sides of paper whenever possible. And stop unwanted junk mail.

▶ **For information about how to remove your name from mailing lists, visit www.newdream.org/junkmail or www. dmaconsumers.org/offmailinglist.html**

Bag your groceries and other purchases in a reusable tote

Americans go through 100 billion grocery bags every year. One estimate suggests that Americans use more than 12 million barrels of oil each year just to produce plastic grocery bags that end up in landfills after only one use and then take centuries to decompose. Paper bags are a problem too: To ensure that they are strong

315

enough to hold a full load, most are produced from virgin paper, which requires cutting down trees that absorb carbon dioxide. It is estimated that about 15 million trees are cut down annually to produce the 10 billion paper bags we go through each year in the United States. Make a point to carry a reusable bag with you when you shop, and then when you're asked, "Paper or plastic?" you can say, "Neither."

▶ To purchase reusable bags, learn more bag facts, and find about actions you can take, visit www.reusablebags.com

Compost

When organic waste materials, such as kitchen scraps and raked leaves, are disposed of in the general trash, they end up compacted deep in landfills. Without oxygen to aerate and assist in their natural decomposition, the organic matter ferments and gives off methane, which is the most potent of the greenhouse gases—23 times more potent than carbon dioxide in global-warming terms. Organic materials rotting in landfills account for about one-third of man-made methane emissions in the United States. By contrast, when organic waste is properly composted

in gardens, it produces rich nutrients that add energy and food to the soil—and of course also decreases the volume added to our landfills.

▶ For information about how to compost, visit www.epa.gov/compost/index.htm or www.mastercomposter.com

Carry your own refillable bottle for water or other beverages

Instead of buying single-use plastic bottles that require significant energy and resources to produce, buy a reusable container and fill it up yourself. In addition to the emissions created by producing the bottles themselves, imported water is especially energy inefficient because it has to be transported over long distances. If you're

MISCONCEPTION 6

"Antarctica's ice sheets are growing, so it must not be true that global warming is causing glaciers and sea ice to melt."

Some ice on Antarctica may be growing—though other areas of the continent are clearly melting and a new 2006 study shows that overall the ice is shrinking in Antarctica. Even if some of the ice is getting bigger, not shrinking, this doesn't change the fact that global warming is causing glaciers and sea ice to melt around the world. Globally, more than 85% of glaciers are shrinking. And in any case, localized impacts of climate change don't cancel out the global trends that scientists are observing.

Some people also mistakenly claim (in Michael Crichton's novel *State of Fear*, for instance) that Greenland's ice is growing. In fact, recent satellite data from NASA shows that Greenland's ice cap is shrinking every year, causing sea levels to rise. The loss of that ice doubled from 1996 to 2005. Greenland lost 50 cubic kilometers of ice in 2005 alone.

concerned about the taste or quality of your tap water, consider using an inexpensive water purifier or filter. Also consider buying large bottles of juice or soda and filling your own portable bottle daily. Using your own mug or thermos could also help reduce the 25 billion disposable cups Americans throw away each year.

▶ For more information about the benefits of using refillable beverage containers, visit www.grrn.org/beverage/refillables/index.html

Modify your diet to include less meat

Americans consume almost a quarter of all the beef produced in the world. Aside from health issues associated with eating lots of meat, a high-meat diet translates into a tremendous amount of carbon emissions. It takes far more fossil-fuel energy to produce and transport meat than to deliver equivalent amounts of protein from plant sources.

MISCONCEPTION 7

"Global warming is a good thing, because it will rid us of frigid winters and make plants grow more quickly."

This myth just doesn't seem to die. Because local impacts will vary, it's true that some specific places may experience more pleasant winter weather. But the negative impact of climate change vastly outweighs any local benefits. Take the oceans, for example. Changes to the oceans caused by global warming are already causing massive die-offs of coral reefs, which are crucial sources of food and shelter for creatures at every stage of the ocean food chain, all the way up to us. Melting ice sheets are causing sea levels to rise, and if big ice sheets melt into the ocean, many coastal cities around the world will flood and millions of people will become refugees. These are just some of the consequences of global warming. Other predicted impacts include prolonged periods of drought, more severe flooding, more intense storms, soil erosion, mass species extinction, and human health risks from new diseases. The small number of people who experience better weather may be doing it in a landscape that is nearly unrecognizable.

In addition, much of the world's deforestation is a result of clearing and burning to create more grazing land for livestock. This creates further damage by destroying trees that would otherwise absorb carbon dioxide. Fruits, vegetables, and grains, on the other hand, require 95% less raw materials to produce and, when combined properly, can provide a complete and nutritious diet. If more Americans shifted to a less meat-intensive diet, we could greatly reduce CO_2 emissions and also save vast quantities of water and other precious natural resources.

▶ For more information about cows and global warming, visit www.earthsave.org/globalwarming.htm and www.epa.gov/methane/rlep/faq.html

Buy local

In addition to the environmental impact that comes from manufacturing the product you are buying, the effects on CO_2 emissions from transporting those goods at each and every stage of production must also be calculated. It is estimated that the average meal travels well over 1,200 miles by truck, ship, and/or plane before it reaches your dining room table. Often it takes more calories of fossil-fuel energy to get the meal to the consumer than the meal itself provides in nutritional energy. It is much more carbon efficient to buy food that doesn't have to make such a long journey.

One way to address this is to eat foods that are grown or produced close to where you live. As much as possible, buy from local farmers' markets or from community-supported agriculture cooperatives. By the same token, it makes sense to design your diet as much as possible around foods currently in season in your area, rather than foods that need to be shipped from far-off places.

▶ To learn more about eating local and how to fight global warming with your knife and fork, visit www.climatebiz.com/sections/news_detail.cfm?NewsID=27338

Purchase offsets to neutralize your remaining emissions

So many things we do in our day-to-day lives—driving, cooking, heating our homes, working on our computers—result in greenhouse-gas emissions. It is virtually impossible to eliminate our personal contributions to the climate crisis through reducing emissions alone. You can, however, reduce your impact to the equivalent of zero emissions by purchasing carbon offsets.

When you purchase carbon offsets, you are funding a project that reduces greenhouse-gas emissions elsewhere by, for example, increasing energy efficiency, developing renewable energy, restoring forests, or sequestering carbon in soil.

▶ For more information and links to specific carbon offsetting organizations, visit www.NativeEnergy.com/climatecrisis

---

MISCONCEPTION 8

"The warming scientists are recording is just the effect of cities trapping heat, rather than anything to do with greenhouse gases."

People who want to deny global warming because it's easier than dealing with it try to argue that what scientists are really observing is just the "urban heat island" effect, meaning that cities tend to trap heat because of all the buildings and asphalt. This is simply wrong. Temperature measurements are generally taken in parks, which are actually cool areas within the urban heat islands. And long-term temperature records showing just rural areas are nearly identical to long-term records that include both rural areas and cities. Most scientific research shows that "urban heat islands" have a negligible effect on the overall warming of the planet.

Reflecting on What You Have Read

1 Gore begins his proposal by claiming that "this crisis will get resolved only if we as individuals take responsibility for it." What is your initial reaction to this claim? As you read the rest of the proposal, does your reaction change? Why or why not?

2 Gore mentions a number of ways daily activities (using plastic shopping bags, for example) can contribute to climate change. What are some of the facts that you found most surprising? To what extent did they persuade (or fail to persuade) you that you personally are contributing to climate change?

3 Gore recommends a number of steps individuals can take to help reduce climate change. Choose one that seems feasible and explain why you find it so feasible. Choose another recommendation that does not seem feasible. Why doesn't it seem feasible? What are some of the obstacles to implementing this change? Can you think of ways the recommendation could be modified to make it more feasible without diminishing its effectiveness?

4 Sidebars (inset boxes) in this reading highlight arguments against Gore's recommendations. What reasons do you see for highlighting these arguments? How persuasive (or unpersuasive) are Gore's responses to these arguments?

5 Questions and answers in the sidebars sound as though Gore is having a conversation with someone who is raising questions about his proposal. How would you characterize the tone of these questions? That is, if you heard someone raise these questions in a public meeting, how would they sound? How would you characterize the tone of Gore's responses? What reasons do you see for including these conversations? What reasons do you see for the tone they convey?

Thinking Ahead

Think about practices at school or at a job that waste a good bit of energy. How might these practices be modified or replaced by less wasteful practices? Who is in a position to approve or implement changes in these practices? How can you show that a change is feasible and that it would benefit your school or your employer?

Let Teenagers Try Adulthood

Leon Botstein

Leon Botstein is the president of Bard College in upstate New York and a professor of arts and humanities. He also serves as conductor and musical director of the American Symphony Orchestra at Lincoln Center in New York City. He is the author of many articles about art, music, and education, including *Jefferson's Children: Education and the Promise of American Culture* (1997), which argues for reform of high school education and a national early college system. The following op-ed piece also addresses the restructuring of high schools. It originally appeared in the *New York Times* in May 1999, following the shootings at Columbine High School in Littleton, Colorado, and during wide debate over the causes of school shootings. As you read his proposal, consider several questions. Does he persuade you that the problem he is addressing is serious? How practical does his proposal sound? If his proposal had been implemented in your high school, how might it have affected you or your friends?

Let Teenagers Try Adulthood

LEON BOTSTEIN

1   The national outpouring after the Littleton shootings has forced us to confront something we have suspected for a long time: the American high school is obsolete and should be abolished. In the last month, high school students present and past have come forward with stories about cliques and the artificial intensity of a world defined by insiders and outsiders, in which the insiders hold sway because of superficial definitions of good looks and attractiveness, popularity and sports prowess.

2   The team sports of high school dominate more than student culture. A community's loyalty to the high school system is often based on the extent to which varsity teams succeed. High school administrators and faculty members are often former coaches, and the coaches themselves are placed in a separate, untouchable category. The result is that the culture of the inside elite is not contested by the adults in the school. Individuality and dissent are discouraged.

3   But the rules of high school turn out not to be the rules of life. Often the high school outsider becomes the more successful and admired adult. The definitions of masculinity and femininity go through sufficient transformation to make the game of popularity in high school an embarrassment.

No other group of adults young or old is confined to an age-segregated environment, much like a gang in which individuals of the same age group define each other's world. In no workplace, not even in colleges or universities, is there such a narrow segmentation by chronology.

4   Given the poor quality of recruitment and training for high school teachers, it is no wonder that the curriculum and the enterprise of learning hold so little sway over young people. When puberty meets education and learning in modern America, the victory of puberty masquerading as popular culture and the tyranny of peer groups based on ludicrous values meet little resistance.

5   By the time those who graduate from high school go on to

college and realize what really is at stake in becoming an adult, too many opportunities have been lost and too much time has been wasted. Most thoughtful young people suffer the high school environment in silence and in their junior and senior years mark time waiting for college to begin. The Littleton killers, above and beyond the psychological demons that drove them to violence, felt trapped in the artificiality of the high school world and believed it to be real. They engineered their moment of undivided attention and importance in the absence of any confidence that life after high school could have a different meaning.

6 Adults should face the fact that they don't like adolescents and that they have used high school to isolate the pubescent and hormonally active adolescent away from both the picture-book idealized innocence of childhood and the more accountable world of adulthood. But the primary reason high school doesn't work anymore, if it ever did, is that young people mature substantially earlier in the late 20th century than they did when the high school was invented. For example, the age of first menstruation has dropped at least two years since the beginning of this century, and not surprisingly, the onset of sexual activity has dropped in proportion. An institution intended for children in transition now holds young adults back well beyond the developmental point for which high school was originally designed.

7 Furthermore, whatever constraints to the presumption of adulthood among young people may have existed decades ago have now fallen away. Information and images, as well as the real and virtual freedom of movement we associate with adulthood, are now accessible to every 15- and 16-year-old.

8 Secondary education must be rethought. Elementary school should begin at age 4 or 5 and end with the sixth grade. We should entirely abandon the concept of the middle school and junior high school. Beginning with the seventh grade, there should be four years of secondary education that we may call high school. Young people should graduate at 16 rather than 18.

9 They could then enter the real world, the world of work or national service, in which they would take a place of responsibility alongside older adults in mixed company. They could stay at home and attend junior college, or they could go away to college. For all the faults of college, at least the adults who dominate the world of colleges, the faculty, were selected precisely because they were exceptional and different, not because they were popular. Despite the often cavalier attitude toward teaching in college, at least physicists know their physics, mathematicians know and love their mathematics, and music is taught by musicians, not by graduates of education schools, where the disciplines are subordinated to the study of classroom management.

10 For those 16-year-olds who do not want to do any of the above, we might construct new kinds of institutions, each dedicated to one activity, from science to dance, to which adolescents could devote their energies while working together with professionals in those fields.

11 At 16, young Americans are prepared to be taken seriously and to develop the motivations and interests that will serve them well in adult life. They need to enter a world where they are not in a lunchroom with only their peers, estranged from other age groups and cut off from the game of life as it is really played. There is nothing utopian about this idea; it is immensely practical and efficient, and its implementation is long overdue. We need to face biological and cultural facts and not prolong the life of a flawed institution that is out of date.

Reflecting on What You Have Read

1 In this proposal, Botstein claims that shootings in a Colorado high school happened in part because students who did the shooting "felt trapped in the artificiality of the high school world." What is there in your own experience that leads you to agree (or disagree) with Botstein's assumption that the high school world is artificial? What reasons do you have for accepting (or rejecting) his claim that college or the workplace is less artificial than high school?

2 Botstein makes a number of claims without providing any specific evidence: In high school, "individuality and dissent are discouraged"; "adults . . . don't like adolescents"; and high school "now holds young adults back well beyond the developmental point for which high school was originally designed." To what extent do your own experiences help justify (or challenge) Botstein's claims? In what ways might Botstein be justified in omitting detailed evidence for his claims?

3 Consider the school district where you went to high school. In what ways and for what reasons might parents and teachers agree with Botstein's proposal? What questions or objections do you anticipate that parents and teachers in that school district would raise in response to Botstein's proposal?

4 If a school district were to implement Botstein's proposal, what would be the consequences for teachers? For students? For the community at large? If your school district had implemented Botstein's proposal while you were still in elementary school, how would you have been affected?

5 What reasons does Botstein give for claiming that his proposal is "immensely practical and efficient"? What bases do you have for accepting (or rejecting) those reasons?

Thinking Ahead

Even those people who do not agree with Botstein's proposal might be concerned about the quality of high school education. Consider your own experiences in high school. Are there courses you wish you had been able to take? Are there programs (Junior Achievement or college advisement, for example) you think should have been implemented or improved? Who is in a position to approve or implement some changes you would like to see made? What would it take to show your readers exactly why change is desirable and how a proposed change might be implemented?

Cameras in the Station House
Richard D. Emery

The following proposal by Richard Emery originally appeared in *Criminal Justice Ethics*, a journal published for both the general public and a specialized audience of criminal justice professionals and scholars. Emery, a civil rights lawyer in New York City, observes that accounts of confrontations between police and citizens are often confusing and contradictory. Citizens involved often claim police brutality, whereas the police officers often deny the claims or argue that force was necessary to subdue a suspect or protect the officers involved. In this proposal, Emery argues that, at least in some instances, videotaping could eliminate much of the confusion and uncertainty. As you read, notice ways in which Emery tries to respond to objections readers might raise.

Cameras in the Station House

By Richard D. Emery

Video cameras operating 24 hours a day in police precincts are the most important component of police oversight that is now missing in efforts to stem police brutality and abuse of authority. No other device or procedure can substitute for an instant replay of events that are alleged to constitute police misconduct. Only in this way can both the public and the accused police officers be more assured of a fair assessment of police actions. 1

Inevitably, every accusation of police misconduct includes ambiguous and confusing events. Police most often either deny that they abused a victim or claim that their physical actions were necessary as proper restraint of their accuser. Accusers invariably deny any improper conduct that warrants a physical restraint, let alone abuse. And invariably the interactions between police officers and people in custody are ambiguous, subject to interpretation and, at a minimum, confusing in the sequence of events that led to physical injuries. 2

The result is that subsequent testimony of witnesses is often nearly useless. Witnesses contradict each other and allow emotions to color the interpretation of events. These events in normal time happen very quickly, and the mind is a fundamentally flawed recorder. Most often the victim does not even know exactly what happened, let alone nearby witnesses who are not part of the action. Of course the police officers involved are so biased by the fear of accusation and punishment that their story quickly becomes totally unreliable. 3

Put simply, the best way to sort these complicated confrontations is the same way we look at instant replays in slow motion for basketball and football. Often, with multiple parties coming in close physical contact to one another, the only way that a true version of events can be gleaned is [by] painstakingly analyzing video tape. Certainly with a video tape more can be determined about who did what to whom than in any other after-the-fact 4 method. Thus the value of video tape in sorting out police/citizen confrontations cannot be overestimated. As we have learned repeatedly from events that were caught on video tape, far more can be determined in subsequent court proceedings than through witnesses whose memories are highly suspect even on day one, let alone months or even years after the event. And even recorded corroborative activity that will show who was in the area, the witnesses' vantage points, and who was with whom will be valuable in the event that the actual physical confrontation is not caught on tape.

The question then is, "[W]hat is the cost of 5 videotaping police activities?" The answer is: very little. Video cameras placed at locations in precinct houses that are not invasive of personal privacy—[not, for example] in locker rooms where personnel change or in the actual stalls of restrooms—do not trample expectations of privacy. In a public precinct, police officers who are public officials should not and cannot have any expectation of privacy. After all, their superior officers at a minimum, and more likely even the press and public, have general access to these areas in precinct houses. Certainly any police officer knows that any other fellow officer would have an obligation to report misconduct that he or she saw in a precinct, to which all fellow officers presumably have full access in any event. Therefore, no police officer can argue that expectations of privacy within a precinct predominate over the value of video recordings of alleged police misconduct.

Similarly, police officers should have video 6 cameras placed in police cars to record scenes of confrontation on the street or in the car itself. Certainly there can be no expectation of privacy that outweighs the value of a record of such confrontations that occur in the street or even in a police car where the interior can always be viewed from the outside anyway. Consequently, claims of expectations of privacy in these contexts are even slimmer.

Whether the same can be said for audio tape 7 is a somewhat closer question. It may well be that police officers have a right to audio privacy even in a police precinct or in a police cruiser. But the simple fact is that audio recordings are far less important than video recordings. I for one would certainly advocate that audio recordings should be made along with video recordings both in police precincts and in police cars, notwithstanding that the intrusion into police privacy is somewhat greater in the context of audio recordings.

It is for this reason that police departments 8 in Florida and California employ video cameras. We see them on television shows frequently and they are now commonplace as evidence in proceedings involving police chases, arrests, and precinct activities.

Of course the main value to video cameras is 9 to assure the public that what their police do is legitimate. In all likelihood, in most instances, false accusations of police misconduct can be quickly disposed of by virtue of a video tape vindicating the version of events of a police officer wrongly accused. In those cases where police officers abuse their authority, of course the video tape is crucial to hold officers accountable, especially when they are presumptively thought to be innocent.

Finally, there may in fact be some modest 10 deterrent effect on police officers if they do not become accustomed to constant video tape and ignore cameras as part of their everyday life. However, all too often, police officers are not deterred whatsoever by video cameras when they abuse their authority and physically mistreat citizens. Nonetheless, many officers who would cross the line if no cameras were watching may be restrained in the face of knowing that they will be caught red-handed.

In conclusion, it is hard to imagine a convincing argument that civil liberties expectations of privacy outweigh the value of video tape in what is essentially the recording of the public functions of police officers. Moreover, given the value and the accuracy of such video 11 tapes in these highly publicized and hotly contested controversies, the case for installation of video cameras to record almost every aspect of police life is compelling.

Given the urgency of controlling police violence and assuring the public that their police operate humanely and fairly, video tape is our best weapon as a salutary response to the current police brutality crisis. ■ 12

Reflecting on What You Have Read

1 In the second paragraph of this proposal, Emery makes some sweeping generalizations ("Inevitably . . ." "Police most often . . ." "Accusers invariably deny . . .") without providing factual support. Given his audience, readers of the journal *Criminal Justice Ethics*, should Emery have elaborated on his generalizations? Do you find these generalizations credible? Why or why not?

2 What objections does Emery anticipate? How well does he respond to these objections?

3 Do you agree with his claim, "it is important to hold [police] officers accountable"? Why or why not? Should he have made the same claim about the people they arrest? Why or why not?

4 In trying to show that his proposal is practical and appropriate, Emery suggests that videotaping police encounters with citizens is comparable to videotaping sporting events. What reasons do you see for accepting (or rejecting) this suggestion?

5 Do you believe that his proposal will bring the benefits Emery claims? Why or why not?

Thinking Ahead

As Emery's proposal suggests, some problems exist because participants in any given situation can have widely divergent impressions of what took place. Think of another problem that arises because of people's different impressions. Can you propose something that would reduce these differences? Also think of anecdotes (that is, complaints) you have heard from friends or family members about difficulties they have had because other people perceived the same events in different ways. What were the difficulties? What were the differences in perception? Does one of these anecdotes or complaints focus on a problem for which you might be able to propose a viable solution?

Ticket to the Top
Melanie Markham and Jonathan Quimby

The following proposal was written for a college writing course by Melanie Markham and Jonathan Quimby, both students at Rensselaer Polytechnic Institute (RPI). Melanie Markham is an electronic arts and communication major. Her hobbies include RPI hockey, music, and computer graphics. She is planning to pursue a career in graphic design. Jonathan Quimby majored in industrial and management engineering. His hobbies include basketball and cooking, and he was president of the Zeta Phi fraternity. Melanie and Jonathan wrote the following proposal to address a local issue—the difficulty in selecting and purchasing tickets at their campus arena for the school's very popular hockey games. As you read their proposal, especially notice the ways Melanie and Jonathan avoid criticizing their audience, even though they believe that their audience's current procedures are causing the problem they want to solve.

Ticket to the Top

The Houston Field House is a lively, exciting place to watch a hockey game, and 1
with good reason: hockey is the only Division I sport at RPI, and by far the most popular of the varsity sports. Despite having the largest arena in the ECAC Hockey League, the men's team still manages to pull in a sell-out at least once a year, and usually records over three thousand fans in the stands. With so many tickets being sold, many of them season tickets, the task of keeping track of the attendance and of which seats belong to which ticket-holders is a daunting operation indeed. The box office staff currently needs to count tickets by hand in order to keep track of the attendance at each game, and before the start of each season the staff needs to sort hundreds of season ticket applications to fit the seats together. This particular aspect is especially difficult when it comes to the non-student side of the arena; on this side, season tickets are renewed each year, and the staff thus needs to manage each new application, each fan who wishes to change seats, and each application which was not renewed—and then somehow make sure no two fans end up in the same seat.

This job could be made much easier and more efficient if a new, more electronic 2
system was implemented. Such a system would use electronic seating charts and databases to store information about who has purchased tickets and would also require buying handheld barcode scanners to scan tickets for entry to the Field House. Ticket-holders and the box office staff alike would enjoy the benefits of a system like this.

Problem

The current system is more complicated than it needs to be for everyone involved. When fans buy season tickets in the hockey line, they select their seats on a huge paper diagram, one for each section of the arena. These diagrams are basically a large grid, with the rows and columns labeled with row letters and seat numbers. However, these labels are small and it is hard to see which labels go with which rows and columns, so it is difficult to select tickets. Once customers choose their seats, their names are written in the boxes corresponding to those seats, and once they pay, the process is complete. Because this is all done on paper, there is no practical way for receipts to be offered, so when this is combined with the difficulty of choosing seats in the first place, it is all too easy to not know or to forget which seats you have purchased. This is especially true for fans buying tickets in large groups who want to be able to report back to the group which seats have been purchased. Without a receipt, it is also possible to encounter disputes when picking up tickets, since season tickets are picked up at a later date. If a set of tickets ends up filed under the wrong name or otherwise is misplaced, it can be very hard to tell who should receive the tickets.

3

Fig. 1. Counting tickets for this many hockey fans is no easy task, but bar code scanners could make it easy (Markham).

Hand in hand with these problems come difficulties for the box office staff as well. Using the large paper diagrams is unnecessarily cumbersome and unwieldy, and it also makes it difficult to keep track of who has which seats (Fig. 1). Because everything is done by hand on paper, keeping track of all the information is very complicated, and it is impossible to prevent the small errors such as a ticket being filed under the wrong name. Then the same paper-intensive system which spawns these errors in the first place makes them difficult to

4

resolve. In addition, the Houston Field House staff must hand-count the tickets for each game in order to record the attendance; this figure is usually above three thousand tickets and on some occasions runs upwards of five thousand. The arena also faces a possible financial loss due to the possibilities of fraud, as it is conceivable that someone could enter the game by using a ticket for a different game or a ticket that has already been used.

Solution

We propose a more electronic system for handling hockey tickets at RPI. This system   5
would make the process easier and more efficient for both the ticket-holders and the box office staff by improving the procedures for purchasing and using tickets. The changes to the method for buying tickets would come in two main parts: an improved seating chart and an electronic database to store ticket information. The Houston Field House's Web site currently includes a chart diagramming the seats in the arena (RPI Houston Field House). This seating map is a great starting point for the new system, as it allows fans to see where the various sections are located and choose which section they would like to sit in. There is also a feature that allows fans to click on a section to see a photograph of the view from those seats; there are two photographs per section. This is a very helpful feature and should definitely be maintained. However, the current chart does not allow fans to see clearly where individual seats are located within a section; for example, viewing the chart does not make it clear which end of a row has the lower-numbered seats or what letter a given row is labeled with (Fig. 2). Consequently, we feel it would also be helpful to have a larger version of the chart available. This chart could be designed so that a label to the side of the chart would identify row and seat numbers as the viewer held his or her cursor over a seat. This would allow fans to get a feel for which seats they would like to purchase within a section in addition to which section of the arena they prefer.

The more complex part of the new system for purchasing tickets is the electronic   6
database that would store ticket information. This would be similar to the software libraries use to keep track of which titles, authors, and subjects are represented in their collections. The software for the Houston Field House would need to store certain information for each seat—most notably the name of the person who had purchased it, and possibly also the method of payment and the other seats which were purchased in the same group. This database would then be searchable by seat or by name of ticket-holder.

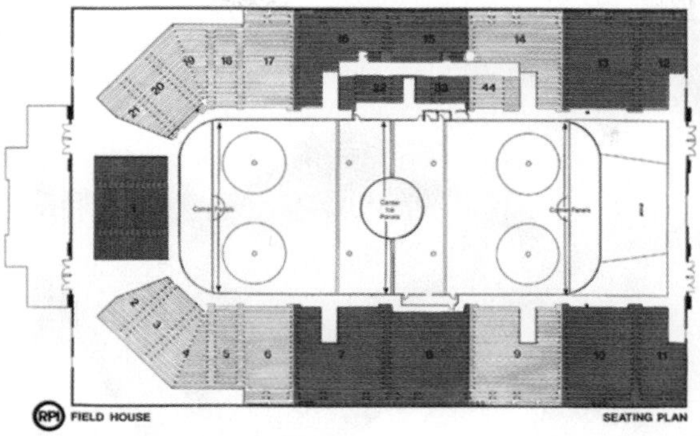

Fig. 2. The current seating chart for the Houston Field House allows fans to get a good feel for which section they prefer, but there is room for improvement ("Seating Chart").

This would allow for easy look-up of which tickets customers should receive if they felt there was a dispute, or of which customer should receive a certain ticket if it was found to be misfiled. From a programming standpoint, such a database would be quite simple to implement. The program would match each seat number to the other information about the seat and would only require a few functions to add, remove, access, and edit this information. This could even be performed as freelance work by an RPI Computer Science or Information Technology major; RPI students would almost certainly be willing and able to implement this system at a much lower cost than hiring an outside company would involve.

The second major facet of the new system would come into play with regard to using tickets and would involve implementing the use of barcode scanners to scan tickets for entry to games (Fig. 3). This could be accomplished through Ticketmaster's AccessManager system, allowing the Houston Field House to maintain their relationship with Ticketmaster. This system enables the ticket-takers to scan a barcode on each ticket as each fan enters the building, and the scanners verify that each ticket is authentic. The system also provides for constant monitoring of the attendance and also offers the ability to generate reports of attendance patterns, the times fans are entering the building, the number of season tickets as compared to individual game tickets, and other such factors ("AccessManager").

Fig. 3. Ticketmaster's scanning system offers many benefits (Topping).

Precedents

Many venues currently employ the use of features such as the Ticketmaster company,   8
barcode scanners, and electronic seating charts. As of right now, RPI uses Ticketmaster as
their main ticket provider. RPI has been using Ticketmaster's services for many years and
has a very good working relationship with them. Ticketmaster has proven that they are a
reliable company that can generate the tickets needed. Currently, hundreds of professional,
minor, and collegiate sports teams use Ticketmaster's services. Such collegiate hockey
teams include North Dakota, University of Maine, and University of Massachusetts at
Lowell, all of which have large hockey programs ("College Hockey").

Ticketmaster also provides its partners with the option to use barcode scanners to   9
track attendance figures. RPI has already shown much interest in purchasing these barcode
scanners. They are very handy and easy to operate, making the ticket checking process
smooth and efficient. Large professional sports teams also use these scanners. If the
Boston Red Sox, Philadelphia Eagles, and Colorado Avalanche can use these scanners with
their maximum capacity crowds, then RPI will definitely find them useful as well.

RPI also uses an online seating chart that currently needs to be updated. Many   10
professional and collegiate sports teams have on their Web site a way to find your seat
and check the view as if you were looking at the game. The Boston Celtics, New Jersey
Devils, and many more use this feature on their Web sites ("Seats 3D," "Seats View").

Questions and Obstacles

One factor that could create an obstacle to a new system is the financial aspect. 11
While price is a major consideration for a small venue such as the Houston Field House, we
feel the cost of this system would be very reasonable. In 2000 Tom Stockham, executive
vice president of Ticketmaster-Online CitySearch, explained that the barcode scanners
would cost around $100 each (Tedeschi). For a small venue which would not need many
scanners, this would result in a very reasonable price. The Houston Field House could
purchase two scanners for each entrance for under $1,000. Currently, there is an estimated
$5,000 in the budget which could be used for changes to the ticketing system; this cost
would stay well under that figure.

Where season tickets are concerned, the "hockey line" tradition for purchasing 12
them is a major part of RPI hockey. Students do not want to see the end of the hockey
line; therefore we find it beneficial that this new system could easily be integrated with
the hockey line. Two or three computer stations would need to be set up temporarily in
the Student Union where the hockey line is formed; the box office staff could then
access the software to update the database as fans choose and purchase tickets. Thus
the paper diagrams could be eliminated, and in addition the line would likely move
faster. This new system would therefore likely improve hockey line—quite the opposite
of ending the tradition.

Alternatives

We find this solution to be the best choice for the RPI hockey program; the 13
possible alternative solutions are all less practical. For example, a swipe card system
for season tickets could be implemented via the Ticket Track system (*Ticket Track
System*). This would entail each season ticket-holder receiving a credit-card-sized
swipe card which would be swiped for entry to each game. Although this idea would
be more technologically innovative and would also eliminate the problems of lost and
stolen tickets, we ultimately feel it would not be feasible. The main reason for this
is the cost of the equipment needed; the price seems likely to fall beyond the Houston
Field House's budget. Also, this alternative would not allow the Field House to
maintain its current satisfactory relationship with Ticketmaster. Finally, this
alternative would raise many additional obstacles such as the questions of how
individual game tickets (non-season tickets) would be handled. These factors lead us

to believe that the barcode scanning system would be a much more practical solution than swipe cards.

Another alternative we considered was the possibility of using the electronic seating chart to purchase tickets. In this alternative, a customer viewing the seating chart on the Web site would be able to click on seats to be taken to a screen to purchase those seats. As we began to consider this feature, logistical problems became apparent: for example, how would a customer click on and select more than one seat at a time? In addition, this feature is also not available through Ticketmaster, and we believe a program which allowed the Houston Field House to continue its affiliation with Ticketmaster would be beneficial. We thus decided that a simpler seating chart would be more feasible.

Benefits

This solution will engender numerous benefits for the box office staff and for the fans. The new seating chart will retain the benefits of the current chart by allowing fans to see which section they might prefer and to see what sort of view they can expect from those seats. It will also expand upon these benefits by allowing fans a more extensive opportunity to select individual rows and seats within the preferred section.

By looking at this chart while ordering tickets, fans could be sure they are actually selecting the tickets they wanted, whereas with the current paper diagrams it is much harder to identify which seats are which. Once seats are selected, the information can be entered in the electronic database, and thus the program could easily print a receipt for the customer. This would enable fans to keep track of which seats they have purchased, something which would be especially useful to those who are buying tickets for a large group such as a fraternity. Replacing the current paper diagrams with the electronic database would also be beneficial for the box office staff; they would not have to wait for the diagrams to become available and would not have to manage huge sheets of paper with names handwritten on them. The staff and fans alike would also enjoy the other major benefit of the system: It would practically put an end to disputes. When a customer purchased a ticket or group of tickets, the information would be entered in the database; thus, it would be fast and easy to retrieve the information and confirm that the customer was receiving all of the correct tickets. This would be

14

15

16

especially helpful in the case of season tickets, which are picked up at a later date than when they are purchased.

The barcode scanners would also introduce many benefits at the games themselves. First, scanning the tickets would get fans in the door faster than manually checking the tickets. Also, as ticket-takers manually check tickets, in an effort to get fans inside the arena quickly they often merely glance at the tickets as they tear them. Consequently, it is conceivable that somebody could use a ticket for a different game to get inside. Barcode scanners would eliminate this concern, as they would not accept any tickets for other games or events. They would also not accept any ticket that had already been scanned, which would remove the concern that a person could leave the game with multiple ticket stubs and then distribute the stubs to friends who could then enter the game without purchasing a ticket.

The Houston Field House has recently started to count the attendance at games by counting the number of tickets torn. Currently, the only way to do this is for the staff to hand-count every ticket stub (Conroy). Barcode scanners would put an end to this; at the end of the night they would easily display the number of tickets that had been scanned, thus eliminating a great deal of tedious work for the staff. As an additional advantage, if the arena begins using barcode scanners, fans can then use Ticketmaster's TicketFast system, which allows them to purchase tickets online and print them at home (*TicketFast*). Fans have expressed interest in being able to print tickets at home, and would most likely find the opportunity extremely convenient and worthwhile (Fig. 4).

This new program would not only put an end to this sort of unnecessarily monotonous work for the staff, it might also save money. Although in all

Fig. 4. Ticketmaster's TicketFast system allows fans to print tickets from their home computers ("Sample Ticketfast").

likelihood very few, if any, people are abusing the system by using incorrect tickets or using tickets more than once, these exploitations are possible. If they occur, the Houston Field House loses money. Barcode scanners would put a stopper in this possible leak and ensure that every person in the arena was paying for his or her ticket. In addition to this financial benefit, the system might even spark an increase in revenue. With the multitude of benefits for the fans, it might cause an increase in ticket sales. When Stanford University implemented a new ticket system for its basketball program it reduced the amount of time fans had to wait to get into the game. Consequently, the program saw an increase in attendance (Foster). If a similar result occurred at RPI, the program would make more money.

RPI is a technologically savvy school with many advancements to brag about.   20 However, the hockey ticket system is not one of them. If this new system is implemented, the school will benefit. Ticket sales will likely increase and in turn so will the revenue. With a new coaching staff and new renovations to the Houston Field House, the time is right for one more change that will benefit the program.

Works Cited

"AccessManager." *Ticketmaster Client Centre*. Ticketmaster, 2006. Web. 11 Dec. 2006.

"College Hockey." *TicketFast*. Ticketmaster, 2006. Web. 4 Dec. 2006.

Conroy, Dorothy. Personal interview. 21 Nov. 2006.

Foster, Christine. "It's All in the Cards." *Stanford Magazine*. Stanford Alumni Association, May/June 2000. Web. 18 Nov. 2006.

Markham, Nicholas R. *Big Red Freakout Fans*. 11 Feb. 2006. *RPIhockey.net*. Web. 4 Dec. 2006.

Pearson, Norris. Personal interview. 21 Nov. 2006.

"Sample TicketFast Ticket." *TicketFast*. Ticketmaster, 2006. Web. 4 Dec. 2006.

"Seat View Finder." *New Jersey Devils*. National Hockey League, 2006. Web. 9 Dec. 2006.

"Seating Chart." *RPI Houston Field House*. Rensselaer Polytechnic Institute, n.d. Web. 4 Dec. 2006.

"Seats 3D." *Boston Celtics*. NBA Media Ventures, 2006. Web. 9 Dec. 2006.

Tedeschi, Bob. "Ticketmaster Will Permit Home Printing of Tickets." *New York Times*. New York Times, 25 Jan. 2000. Web. 4 Dec. 2006.

Ticket Track System. The BeanMaster Corporation, 2002. Web. 18 Nov. 2006.

Topping, Jeff. *Ticket Scanner*. 28 Oct. 2004. *New York Times*. Web. 9 Dec. 2006.

Reflecting on What You Have Read

1 Melanie and Jonathan began working on this proposal because they were having difficulty getting good seats at Houston Field House, the venue for their school's hockey games. But they begin their proposal not by talking about their own concerns, but rather by identifying difficulties felt by the Field House staff. Would you recommend that they come right out and explain the difficulties they were having? Why or why not?

2 At what points do Melanie and Jonathan show they understand the current system for assigning seats at hockey games? How successful are they at showing how their proposal fits in with and improves on the current system?

3 At what points do Melanie and Jonathan show that their system is feasible? Are there points at which it seems they might have overlooked some difficulty in implementing their proposed solution? Are there points at which you think they should have gone into more detail about who needs to do what in order to implement their solution?

4 After explaining what they think needs to be done, Melanie and Jonathan explain why they have rejected two alternatives. What reasons do they give for rejecting these proposals? How persuasive do these reasons seem?

5 At the end of their proposal, Melanie and Jonathan say that their proposal would have many benefits for the Field House staff as well as for fans. Given what Melanie and Jonathan have said previously, does it seem reasonable to think that their proposal would actually bring these benefits?

6 In the conclusion to their proposal, Melanie and Jonathan spend relatively little time explaining ways their proposal will benefit fans. They concentrate on ways their proposal will benefit the Field House. Should they have spent more time explaining benefits to fans? Why or why not?

Thinking Ahead

Consider some of your school's programs (curricular or extracurricular) that affect large numbers of students. What kinds of problems do these programs create? Are there some ways in which these programs might be improved? Are there some existing programs that should be replaced with new programs? Can you show that these programs present serious problems for significant numbers of students? Will you be able to develop the expertise that will let you recommend a plausible solution to one of these problems?

Guide to Writing a Proposal

▷ GUIDE TO WRITING A PROPOSAL

The remainder of this chapter will guide you through the process of creating a proposal that can significantly improve some aspect of an organization or a community to which you belong. The first step is covered in Getting Started—selecting a topic (in this case, a problem with a viable solution) and understanding your audience and purpose. Then you will work on Creating a Draft, using many of the strategies or techniques illustrated in proposals included in Reading to Write. These strategies can help you explore your topic, write an introduction that will engage readers' interest, create an appropriate voice, organize your work, conclude your proposal effectively, and design your proposal and integrate visual elements. Finally, in Reviewing and Revising you will receive guidance in creating a review draft, assessing your work carefully, and using that assessment to revise your proposal.

As you work through the assignment for this chapter, you can read a little bit about how undergraduates Melanie Markham and Jonathan Quimby wrote their proposal. In the Student Q & A box on page 459, you will find the first of several brief conversations that Melanie and Jonathan had with the authors of this text.

▷ Assignment

Write a proposal that will remedy a problem or substantially improve some aspect of your school, your job, an organization you belong to, or the community where you live. You should address your proposal to a specific individual or small group of individuals who are in a position to approve and/or implement the course of action you recommend. Your instructor may have specific requirements about how long the proposal should be, what sort of subject you should write about, whether you should prepare the proposal as a print or online document (or as an oral presentation), and whether you should include or exclude any particular visual elements or use a particular documentation style to cite sources. Be sure you understand those requirements before you start working on the assignment.

GETTING STARTED

Almost all proposals entail helping people solve a problem that matters to them. There are plenty of problems that need solving and, therefore, plenty of potential topics for your proposal. But, as you might expect, some problems may not be solvable, at least not within the time and length limits of this assignment. The next several pages will help you select a topic for your proposal, analyze your audience, and identify the purpose(s) you hope to achieve in writing your proposal.

Selecting a Topic

Most of the readings for this chapter deal with enormously complex problems that affect huge numbers of people. But do not let the scope of these problems mislead you. Even if you are prepared to devote the rest of your life to, say, understanding and reducing global climate change, you should choose a much more limited topic for this assignment. How limited? Your topic should be one that allows you to do the following.

► Talk frequently with people involved in the problem and its solution

► Draw on your own experiences

► Develop some expertise that will put your experiences and ideas in a broader context (for example, by doing background reading, interviewing or surveying groups of people, or finding out how others have tried to solve the same problem)

► Devise a practical solution that others will actually be willing to adopt

And as you are thinking about possible topics, you should consider three other pieces of advice.

Choose a problem that matters. This should be a problem whose solution would make life better, not just for yourself but for others as well.

Think twice about trying to solve long-term problems. For example, there are probably complex reasons why no one has solved parking problems on your campus. To make any headway on solving this problem, you would have to learn a lot about campus politics, academic finance, and, possibly, civil engineering. You would also need a huge amount of good luck. Where luck is concerned, you should accept it when it comes. But don't count on it.

Think of a specific, willing audience. If you cannot find a specific individual who would be willing to consider implementing your proposed solution, find another problem to solve.

Coming Up with Ideas for a Topic

To identify a workable, interesting topic for your proposal, read back over the suggestions in the Thinking Ahead passages that follow each of the proposals in Reading to Write. You might also get some ideas for topics by engaging in the following activities.

Brainstorm ideas for topics. Writing as quickly as you can, list every problem you can think of that might have some potential as a topic for your proposal. It may help to complete the following sentences.

One problem that really annoys me about life on campus (in an organization, at work) is _____ .

Another is _____ .

One thing I'd like to see changed is _____ .

Another is _____ .

For the moment, don't try to elaborate on any of these ideas or worry about how good they sound; just list as many potential topics as possible.

Review what you have written with a small group or the entire class. Notice the potential topics that strike them as especially interesting. See if they can suggest related topics. Don't feel you have to accept their suggestions; just see if any sound like good possibilities.

Select a topic that seems like it might have potential and then make some notes about that topic. Write your answers to these questions.

What do I already know about this topic?

How does this topic affect me or people I care about?

What are some questions I might like to answer concerning this topic?

Who might be in a position to implement a solution to this problem?

If you can answer at least some of these questions, you probably have a topic with good potential. If not, you may need to go back and engage in some of the activities listed above.

Assessing Your Choice of a Topic

Once you have identified a topic that seems promising, you need to assess your topic, making sure the topic is one that matters to others, that your topic can be implemented by someone with whom you can discuss your solution, and that you can actually formulate a practical solution in the time you have available to work on this assignment. To do this, work with a small group or the entire class and try the following activities, making notes about what you learn.

Summarize what you have written and share with a group. Ask classmates to help you think of audiences who might be willing and able to implement a solution you come up with. As is true with your choice of topic, your choice of an audience may change. It is especially likely that the person you initially thought might be able to implement your solution is not the right audience. It may be, for example, that the audience you really need to address is that person's supervisor. But for now, make your best guess as to who your audience might be.

Think further about your own experience. Have you had any personal experience with the problem? Think about specific incidents in which you have been involved. What did you observe about ways you (and others) were affected by the problem? What have you observed about others' efforts to solve the problem? Try to be specific here: Who did what, when, how, why?

Talk with others who may know something about the problem or previous efforts to solve it. Are they aware of the problem? Can they tell you any good stories about how the problem affects them or how others attempted to solve it?

Do some reading. Look for published materials by doing a preliminary search in your library's databases (such as LexisNexis, Readers' Guide Abstracts, or Wilson Select) and on the Internet. Especially look for information that will either help you show how serious the problem is or give you some good ideas about how to solve it. Also look for such unpublished materials as memos, handbooks, bylaws, or statements of policy related to your topic.

Look for visual information—images, charts, graphs, and so forth—that might help persuade readers that the problem you are trying to solve is, in fact, a serious problem.

Conduct a brief reality check. After doing a fair amount of reading, talking, and listening, does it seem likely that you will be able to develop the expertise that will let you propose a credible solution? Have you identified an audience that actually needs or wants to solve the problem you are concerned about? Do you see a compelling reason why the audience will want to read your proposal at this particular time? If you can't answer yes to at least two of these questions, consider changing your topic or your audience. Do this now, not the night before the assignment is due.

Student Q & A **Selecting a Topic**

Writing Now: Why did you choose to write a proposal about the Houston Field House system for helping hockey fans select their season tickets?

Melanie Markham and Jonathan Quimby: We began thinking of this topic for two main reasons. We liked the idea of a proposal for something on campus because we wanted to be able to talk with the people who could make these changes and hopefully influence them with our proposal. We also liked the idea of something related to the hockey team because RPI hockey is very important to us and something we're quite knowledgeable about. The old adage "write what you know" is certainly applicable here; we wanted to choose a topic we were familiar with so we would have a better understanding of our audience. ■

For Collaboration **Identifying a Primary Audience**

Working with a small group or the entire class, think of a situation at your school that needs to be changed. List some of the reasons a change is necessary and the steps to take in making the change. Then identify a possible audience, a person who would be in a position to approve a change. Decide what objections or questions they would be likely to raise and ways you might respond to those questions or objections. ■

Understanding Your Audience and Purpose

If you are trying to solve a problem that really matters, it is almost certain that you will have to appeal to at least two different (but sometimes overlapping) groups.

▶ Your primary audience, the person or group in a position to implement or approve your proposal

▶ Various other stakeholders, especially the people who will actually have to do the work of carrying out your proposal or who otherwise will be directly affected by the solution you propose

Consequently, your proposal is likely to have at least two different purposes: to persuade decision makers and, at a minimum, to avoid annoying or alienating other stakeholders. For example, you want to make sure your proposal does not needlessly complicate the work of people who will have to implement your suggestions.

Given the importance of understanding your audience and purpose, and given the fact that you have begun gathering a good bit of information about your topic, you should be ready to start answering questions about the audience's knowledge, needs, and attitudes as well as their expectations for content and layout or format. You should also answer questions about the purpose(s) you hope to accomplish by writing your proposal. As you work on your proposal, your understanding of your audience and your specific purpose(s) may change. But at this point, you should be as clear and specific as you can, so you should write out answers to the following questions, and then revise your answers as necessary.

[
Guidelines for Analyzing Your Audience and Identifying Purpose
]

Audience knowledge, needs, and attitudes

- What do your readers already know about the problem you are trying to solve? Are they aware that a problem exists? Do they know if there have been previous efforts to solve this problem? If so, what do they know about why those efforts did not solve the problem?
- Do readers think the problem is serious enough to justify trying to solve it?
- Are readers optimistic about solving the problem, or are they skeptical?
- Why would readers need to read a proposal on your topic? For example, would it benefit them—or people and organizations they care about?
- Are readers aware of any recent events that might prompt them to read your proposal? If so, what are they?

Audience expectations for content

- What questions are your readers likely to want to have answered?
- What kinds of objections or counterarguments are they likely to raise?
- What kinds of information will they see as credible responses to their questions, counterarguments, and objections?

▶ Go to bedfordstmartins.com/ writingnow to download these questions from Chapter 7 > Worksheets.

Audience expectations for layout or format

- Are there any visual features (for example, photographs, tables, bulleted lists) your readers are likely to expect or appreciate?

- What sort of layout will readers expect? For example, should you use one column or two? Do you need to include a list of works cited? To use pull quotes or inset boxes?

For more information about layout, see Chapter 9, pages 526–38.

Purpose(s)

- In addition to persuading readers to implement your solution, what else do you hope to accomplish in writing your proposal? (See the list of purposes on p. 416.)

- What is the basic impression you want to convey? That there is a serious problem and something needs to be done? That if your audience implements your proposal, they will benefit in ways they don't currently understand? That solving the problem is both feasible and desirable?

- What sort of voice do you want readers to hear when they read your proposal? What image do you want to convey of yourself?

Student Q & A   **Analyzing Audience**

Writing Now: How did you determine who you should address your proposal to?

Melanie Markham and Jonathan Quimby: Because we are quite familiar with RPI hockey, we knew the logical person to address would be either Norris Pearson, the field house manager, or Ken Ralph, the athletic director at the time. Because we were acquainted with both individuals, we were able to e-mail Mr. Ralph and briefly explain our proposal and ask who in the athletic department we should be contacting. Mr. Ralph replied that although he would be happy to meet with us if it would help, Mr. Pearson was the one who would be able to make changes to the system, so we addressed our proposal to Mr. Pearson. ■

As with any assignment, you should think about the audience for your proposal as concretely as possible. Talk with members of your primary audience and with any key stakeholders you can identify. You may go back to the people you discussed the problem with as you selected your topic. Try to become friendly with them, and work to create a favorable impression. Find out what they know, think, or feel about the situation with which you are concerned. Also find out how your proposal might relate to other things they value. You might begin by briefly describing a situation you've been noticing lately. Then follow up with questions such as these. Have you heard or read anything about this? What was your reaction to what you heard or read? Do you know of anyone who is trying to remedy this situation? If so, how successful have these other remedies been? If they have failed, why or how have they failed?

As you do this, listen not only to what people say but also how they say it. Do members of your audience seem hostile? Doubtful that the problem can be solved? Indifferent? Or do they come across as supportive? Enthusiastic? Eager to help? Your answers to these questions will help you decide how much work you will have to do to engage and maintain your audience's interest. Also put yourself in your readers' place. Use what you are learning about your readers to answer such questions as the following. If I were in my readers' place, how would I react to the recommendations in the proposal? What questions would I want answered? What objections would I raise, and why?

In answering the preceding questions about your audience, you may get a strong sense of your purpose(s) in writing your proposal. If your readers are hostile or anxious, part of your purpose may be to reassure them that you want to help and that you are not going to threaten their interests. If your audience is eager to help, then part of your purpose may simply be to show that you have a good way to accomplish what you both desire. If your audience seems indifferent, part of your goal may be to dramatize the problem, thereby helping readers see why a solution is so important.

Here's how Melanie Markham and Jonathan Quimby analyzed their audience and purpose for their proposal "Ticket to the Top" (p. 444).

Student Analysis of Audience and Purpose

Our audience is Norris Pearson, the manager of the Houston Field House (HFH), where all our hockey games are played. We met with Mr. Pearson and Dorothy Conroy, the box office supervisor at the HFH, to discuss our proposal.

Audience knowledge, needs, and attitudes

Mr. Pearson knows all the details of the current system as well as the reasons behind it better than we could, so there might be problems and obstacles that we had not foreseen. Despite knowing how the current system works, the Houston Field House (HFH) staff might not know what it is like from a student's perspective.

The HFH, like any organization, aims to please customers, especially since customer satisfaction is directly related to revenue. Therefore, if a new system helps customers and might increase ticket sales, this could offset the cost of the system. The HFH wants to do whatever will make the most money, however, so expensive new systems might not be possible.

The Field House currently uses Ticketmaster, and Mr. Pearson is very happy with the company. Also, because the HFH does not bring in as much revenue as most Ticketmaster venues, they are very grateful to Ticketmaster for continuing the partnership. Therefore, they are very inclined to continue using Ticketmaster rather than another company or an in-house system.

Attendance is a big issue; the Field House and the school as a whole would like to get as many people as possible watching the games. If we can show that a system we propose will please customers, therefore selling more tickets and making more money, the staff may find it worthwhile. Audience needs are closely related to values; cost is the biggest concern. If a system is too expensive there is simply no way the Houston Field House will be able to use it.

Audience expectations for content

Mr. Pearson had quite a few questions for us regarding the details of our solution—how it works with the hockey line [the current system for buying season hockey tickets], how much it would cost, where the scanners would be, and so on.

One major obstacle Mr. Pearson saw was the cost of a scanner system. He mentioned a figure of $5,000 as the maximum amount that could be squeezed from the budget for something like this.

Mr. Pearson and Ms. Conroy will want to see examples of other schools and venues with similar systems. They asked us if we would be willing to help find some examples of similar systems that the Houston Field House could use in talks with Ticketmaster as examples of the sort of system they would like to implement. (Of course, we said we would be happy to help in this respect!)

Audience expectations for layout or format

Our audience doesn't have any particular expectations for visuals, but we will include several. The drawing of the current seating chart seemed important to help show how our plan would improve on the current plan.

We will include a Works Cited list, following MLA style, to represent interviews and other sources. Our readers may want to check some sources for themselves.

Purpose(s)

We are trying to make a difference for the students and anyone who is interested in RPI hockey. Besides showing the advantages of the changes, we are recommending, we want to show our audience that the changes are practical.

We want to show that we have listened to our audience's concerns and that the possible problems would not make the solution impossible. We are especially trying to show that the solution could work with Ticketmaster, since this seems important to our audience.

We want to create a voice that is both knowledgeable and personable. The proposal is serious and based on research, but we don't want to sound like we were attacking the current system.

CREATING A DRAFT

If you have chosen to solve a problem that matters a great deal to you, there is a good chance you already have some notions about what the problem is and how it should be solved. Those ideas can be a good beginning point, but the key word here is *beginning*. As you think carefully about the problem and solution, it is possible— and in most cases desirable—that your ideas will change. At the very least, you should remain open to that possibility. But whether or not you change your views of your topic, you need to develop your initial ideas into a coherent, thoughtful proposal that someone else will seriously consider implementing. The next few sections of this chapter list and give examples of a variety of verbal and visual strategies that will help you do this, taking you through the processes of exploring your topic, engaging your audience, and so forth. As in other chapters in this book, you will be working with strategies that appear in readings found in Reading to Write. The following discussions, along with the strategies and examples lists, will help you see how specific passages reflect strategies that you can apply to your own writing. You can always add to these lists of strategies by analyzing other proposals you find interesting and credible.

Exploring Your Topic

Sometimes problems and their solutions appear to be obvious. And in a few instances this may be true. But if the problem and solution really were that obvious, chances are the problem would have been solved before you began working on your proposal. Consequently, you will need to make sure you understand your topic thoroughly. This will entail gathering information (especially to make sure you have identified a significant problem that has not already been solved), reflecting on that information in ways that will help you understand the problem you are trying to solve, and then formulating your thesis and developing your ideas.

Gathering Information

Proposals often arise from a personal experience that the writer witnessed or was involved in, an experience that demonstrates why the problem needs to be remedied. Consequently, you may want to begin exploring your topic by relying in part on your own experience. But you should also consult secondary sources and talk with others who have either been affected by the problem or have attempted to solve it.

Draw on personal experiences. In working on your proposal, you should feel free to draw on personal experiences—either your own or those of someone you know or care about. For example, undergraduate students Melanie Markham and Jonathan Quimby wrote "Ticket to the Top" (p. 444) because they were both frustrated at the difficulties they had experienced in getting good seats for their school's hockey season. And "Leave No Child Inside" (p. 426) begins with the difficulty

{ **Student**
Q & A }  **Using Personal Experiences**

Writing Now: You didn't go into much detail about some of your own frustrations with the ticket system. Why not?

Melanie Markham and Jonathan Quimby: There were two main reasons for not going into much detail in this area. First, we thought spending a lot of time on this area might make the proposal seem overly critical of the current system. We did not want it to seem like a laundry list of everything that was wrong with the system. Instead, we wanted to show that while the current system was good, there were some aspects of it that had room for improvement. Also, we thought that making the problems too personal by mentioning our frustrations with the system might not be beneficial. We thought that if we spent too much time mentioning problems just the two of us had experienced, readers might wonder if these problems were really typical and if other students had the same problems. So we decided that not going into much detail on an individual's problems would make the proposal seem more universal, something that applied to every student who buys tickets. ■

experienced by a science teacher when he was trying to get students to think about their environment. But none of the proposals in Reading to Write talk exclusively about the writer's own concerns and experiences. There is a reason for this: When people focus narrowly on their personal experiences, it is easy for readers to dismiss the problem as the concern of a single individual, especially if that individual appears to be too emotionally involved. This is not to say that you should always avoid using the pronoun *I* in your proposal. Indeed, if it helps you to begin by identifying a problem that affects you personally, by all means do so. In fact, you might want to keep notes about all the times and all the ways you have been affected by the problem. And the pronoun *I* might eventually appear in your proposal. For example, Richard Louv uses this pronoun several times in "Leave No Child Inside." But he does so in talking about what he has learned from extensive interviews with "families across the country." By doing this, he establishes himself as an authority who bases his views not on his own experience in raising children but on the experiences of numerous others who do have this experience. Thus Louv's work establishes the main point you need to bear in mind when making a proposal: You want to make it clear that the problem you are concerned with is something that affects a lot of people and that it causes enough difficulty for enough people that readers will take the problem seriously.

Use secondary sources. If the problem you are trying to solve is significant or widespread, it is likely that other people will have described the problem and suggested ways to solve it. Consequently, you need to make sure you understand what others have said, either about the problem itself or about ways to solve the problem.

How to Use Secondary Sources

STRATEGIES	EXAMPLES FROM READINGS
Look for statistics. These should demonstrate that the problem is real or that a solution is possible.	 To show that students need to spend less time indoors, Richard Louv (p. 426) mentions a study showing that students who are in "outdoor classrooms improved their science scores by 27 percent." He also mentions results of another study that show "children as young as five show a significant reduction in the symptoms of attention deficit disorder when they engage with nature."
Identify efforts currently being made to solve the problem.	In the excerpt from *An Inconvenient Truth* (p. 431), Al Gore identifies a number of private and governmental organizations that are currently working to solve specific aspects of the "climate crisis."
Identify factors that may be contributing to the problem.	**Haven't Slept a Wink** [table] In "Homeroom Zombies" (p. 421), Lawrence Epstein and Steven Mardon cite studies showing that teenagers do not get enough sleep in part because they are "multitasking," engaging in too many school and out-of-school activities, and in part because their biological clocks make it difficult for them to get to sleep at a reasonable time in the evening.

Keep track of information. As you begin drafting, it can be very frustrating to find that you remember only part of an important quotation or that you aren't sure where you found an interesting statistic. To avoid this frustration, you should do two things. First, keep detailed notes of any personal experiences you want to include in your proposal. Jot down responses to questions such as the following.

- What did I see or hear?
- What did people do or say?
- What was the setting?

Second, create a working bibliography. In a notebook or separate computer file, keep complete bibliographic information for each source you read or for each person you interview. Record the author's (or interview subject's) name, the title of the source (article, book, Web site), and all the information required to locate the piece if you need to come back to it (the URL of the Web site and the date you accessed it, for example, or date and page numbers of the magazine article). Also note the main point of each source and how it relates to the issue you are discussing. It can be especially useful to list the main questions the source poses and summarize the answers it gives. You need not record all this information according to the precise guidelines of the documentation style you're using, but noting all this information will save you time later.

For advice on taking notes and creating a working bibliography, see Chapter 12.

Reflecting on Information

After you have read several secondary sources and observed your subject on several occasions, you should begin reflecting on what you are learning about the nature of the problem you hope to solve and about possible solutions. Exactly what is the problem? What has been done by others who have tried to solve it? To what extent have those efforts succeeded or failed? As you work on your proposal, your answers to these questions will probably change. But you should begin thinking about these questions even at this early stage of your work.

Before you begin this reflection, you should take a close look at the audience analysis and statement of purpose you wrote when you answered the questions on pages 460–61. Are these some questions that aren't answered very well? For example, are you lacking information about your readers' knowledge, needs, and attitudes? Do you have a good sense of what your readers will expect in terms of content, both verbal and visual? At this point, finish completing your responses to the best of your ability. Also review any notes you have taken for your working bibliography. Underline or mark key facts or reasons.

After reviewing your audience analysis and your notes, set aside ten to fifteen minutes and write as rapidly as you can (without interruption), completing the following sentences.

One reason I think there's a problem is _____ .

Another reason I think there's a problem is _____ .

Another reason is _____ .

Then spend another ten to fifteen minutes writing as rapidly as you can (without interruption), completing the following sentences.

One step to take in solving the problem is _____ .

Another step is _____ .

Another step is _____ .

Keep on describing the problem and speculating about a solution until you have used up your allotted time.

Once you have completed this work, read or show what you have written to other students (perhaps in a small group or perhaps to the entire class). Ask your classmates to help you answer the following questions.

▶ What are the points at which I have made the problem very clear and important?

▶ What are the points at which I have identified steps people might take to solve the problem?

▶ What are the points at which I need to describe the problem more fully or elaborate on the solution I'm considering proposing?

▶ Can you think of points at which some sort of visual (a photograph, for example, or a chart) might help me make the problem's seriousness more apparent or my solution clearer?

Formulating a Thesis

In contrast with the writing you have done for other assignments in this book, you will probably have two theses for your proposal, one saying what the problem is and another saying how you plan to solve it. So after discussing the preceding work with your classmates, complete the following sentences.

The basic problem is _____ .

The main thing we can do to solve this problem is _____ .

These sentences will become your tentative theses, the principal claims you think you will want to make in your proposal. As you continue to develop your proposal, you may want to revise those claims still further. But they will serve as starting points from which you can develop your ideas, making your proposal as clear and reasonable as possible.

Developing Your Ideas

Once you have some initial ideas about what the problem is and how it can be solved, you need to develop your ideas more fully. Begin this process by reviewing the work you did responding to the questions on page 467, where you explained why you think there is a problem and how it might be solved. Then develop your ideas by showing that a problem exists, defining the problem, and proposing a solution that is both feasible and desirable.

Show that a problem exists. In some situations, readers may already know that the problem exists and may have sent out a request for proposal (RFP) to solve the problem. Frequently, however, readers may be unaware of the problem or may even be reluctant to admit that a problem exists. In such cases, you will have to persuade readers that a problem exists and needs to be solved. The proposals in Reading to Write suggest several effective strategies for doing this.

How to Show That a Problem Exists

STRATEGIES	EXAMPLES FROM READINGS
Identify a difficulty felt by someone or that is something readers know and care about. Not all difficulties and problems are equal; the problems that matter most to readers are those that affect the people, institutions, animals, or objects that readers know and care about.	In "Homeroom Zombies" (p. 421), Lawrence Epstein and Steven Mardon mention difficulties felt by parents ("struggling to cajole and, if need be, drag their exhausted teens out of bed") and teachers (students who go to sleep the moment classroom lights are dimmed for a movie).
Describe a need that is not currently being met. The more readers care about the need that is not currently being met, the more likely they are to think that the problem you're addressing is significant.	"Cameras in the Station House" (p. 441) begins by citing the need for a "fair assessment" of the actions of police officers.
Mention negative consequences of the current situation.	In criticizing the current system of requiring all children to complete twelve years of schooling, Leon Botstein ("Let Teenagers Try Adulthood," p. 438) argues, "by the time those who graduate from high school go on to college and realize what really is at stake in becoming an adult, too many opportunities have been lost and too much time has been wasted."
Point out a gap between what readers originally intended to do and what they actually did.	 In "Leave No Child Inside" (p. 427), Richard Louv notes that "a genre of well-intentioned" textbooks has set out to make students more concerned about their environment. But these textbooks succeeded chiefly in overwhelming students and creating "ecophobia."
Acknowledge existing efforts to solve the problem, and show why they are inadequate. If the problem is significant, others have probably tried to solve it, and their solutions, although flawed, also have strengths. If you can acknowledge those strengths, you may avoid putting readers on the defensive. You might also learn something that you can build on in proposing your own solution.	In "Ticket to the Top" (p. 444), Melanie Markham and Jonathan Quimby acknowledge that "[the current] seating map [used in selecting tickets to hockey games] is a great starting point for the new system." Then they point out that, in its current form, the seating chart does not allow students to see the exact location of tickets they are buying.

continued on next page ▶

How to Show That a Problem Exists (continued)

STRATEGIES	EXAMPLES FROM READINGS
Provide readers with a way to determine how and whether they may be contributing to the problem.	Although most readers are likely to assume that their actions have relatively little influence on climate change, Al Gore (p. 431) points out that "the average American is responsible for about 15,000 pounds of carbon dioxide emissions each year." He also refers readers to a Web site that will help them determine their individual "carbon footprint."

To further explore what you already know, believe, or feel about the topic you have chosen for your proposal, use some of the strategies in the chart above to list additional information that makes you believe there is a serious problem. Show your list to a classmate or a friend. Ask this person to help you identify statements that seem factual or documentable, eliminate statements that sound like rumor or whining, and identify new sources of information.

Then write a paragraph explaining what the problem is, and identify a specific individual who has the authority to implement your solution. Discuss this paragraph with your classmates and instructor. Get their responses to the following questions.

▶ Have I identified a problem that is serious to people other than myself?

▶ Is it a problem for which I can probably come up with a plausible solution in the time I have to work on this assignment?

▶ If I can come up with a good solution, can I also identify someone who would be willing and able to implement it?

If you answered no to any of these questions, you probably should consider a different topic for your proposal (see p. 457). But if the answer to each of these questions is yes, you can continue gathering information to show that the problem is serious, that it has severe consequences, and that a solution to the problem would provide significant benefits. To do this, talk further with the people who are affected by the problem, especially people with whom readers are likely to sympathize. Also talk with a range of people to make sure the problem is not limited to just one or two people. And look for articles demonstrating that the problem occurs elsewhere.

As you read and talk with people, make notes in response to the following questions.

▶ What difficulties are these people encountering?

▶ What needs are not being met?

▶ What evidence demonstrates that these difficulties or needs are significant?

▶ Is the problem caused by a conflict between two groups of people? Between what someone claims is the case and what actually is the case? Between what someone intended to do and what he or she actually did do?

▶ Have there been previous efforts to solve the problem? Why didn't those solutions work?

For advice on conducting interviews and taking notes, see Chapter 11.

Define the problem. People may realize that something is wrong, but they may be unsure—or mistaken—about exactly what the problem is. Consequently, it is usually necessary to articulate the problem carefully. A good problem statement will identify the cause of the problem and imply what needs to be done to solve it.

Use the strategies in the following chart to write out a problem statement. Then show this statement to others, including your instructor, your classmates, and various stakeholders. Ask them to tell you whether you have identified a fundamental cause of the situation, a cause that could actually be remedied. Be willing to revise your problem statement as you gain additional information and insight from others.

How to Define the Problem

STRATEGIES	EXAMPLES FROM READINGS
Identify the cause of the difficulty people are having. For example: Does the difficulty exist because someone lacks needed information? Because a policy is inherently flawed? Because someone is trying to make life difficult for someone else? Does it exist because people are not aware of possible solutions or of the consequences of their actions? Each of these questions (and this list is by no means exhaustive) implies a different cause, and each cause implies a different solution.	 In "Cameras in the Station House" (p. 441), Richard Emery points out that in confrontations between police and accused persons, "events in normal time happen very quickly, and the mind is a fundamentally flawed recorder."
State the problem as something that can be acted on. Indicate, explicitly or implicitly, what people need to do, stop doing, or do differently.	Emery's definition of the problem implies a relatively straightforward course of action: We need to identify a means of obtaining a less biased record of events.

Think of solutions. Throughout the process of gathering information and defining the problem, you have probably been thinking about possible solutions. Now is the time to focus on solutions in earnest. Brainstorm for ten minutes and list every solution you can think of. Don't worry about how good the solutions seem right now. You will think more about that as you go along.

Get a classmate or friend to help you think of other possible solutions. Consider as many different solutions as you can, even far-fetched solutions that might contain an idea that could develop into something useful. Keep a list of all the solutions that occur to you. Add to this list as you think of new possibilities.

Also do some quick reading. Survey your library's databases and search the Internet to see if others have attempted to solve this problem. Skim the materials you find. In addition, review your notes about your personal experiences with the problem (pp. 464–65) and other secondary sources you have already gathered (pp. 465–66). Can you see ways to benefit from others' successes or failures? (Remember: You don't want to reinvent the wheel.)

Review all the solutions you have thought or read about and choose the solution that seems best for a reality check. Write a two- to three-paragraph explanation of how you intend to solve the problem. Finally, get feedback by asking a classmate or your instructor to read these paragraphs and tell you where you need to add explanations or anticipate questions and objections.

Demonstrate feasibility. One of the easiest ways for a hostile audience to criticize a proposal is to point out that its writer has not shown how to implement the proposed solution and, therefore, has not demonstrated the feasibility of the proposal. Often, this criticism is justified: The writer has failed to anticipate exactly what would be involved in implementing the solution—the financial costs, for example, or the amount of time and energy required. In such cases, the audience's response is likely to be something like, "Don't give me any grand-sounding, half-baked ideas. Show me that what you're proposing can actually be implemented." To avoid this sort of response, consider using the following strategies for demonstrating feasibility.

How to Demonstrate Feasibility

STRATEGIES

Explain the logistics involved in implementing your solution. Readers will require varying amounts of detail. Those who are unfamiliar with a solution will need a lot of detail about implementation, whereas readers with a good idea of how to implement the solution will only need to know exactly what you are proposing. If you are uncertain as to how detailed you should be, discuss your proposed solution with your readers and find out where they have questions about what to do or how to do it.

EXAMPLES FROM READINGS

In explaining their proposal to implement a new system for selecting seats for hockey games, Melanie Markham and Jonathan Quimby (p. 444) explain how their proposal would incorporate elements of the existing system. Then they describe the database work their system would require and identify people who could perform that work at a reasonable cost.

STRATEGIES	EXAMPLES FROM READINGS
Identify precedents that suggest your proposal will work. Solving a problem involves change, which for many people implies risk. To reduce this sense of risk, mention ways people in other situations have succeeded in solving similar problems. You might recommend modifying what others have done, so that their solution fits the specific situation with which you are concerned.	In proposing the installation of video cameras in police station houses, Richard Emery (p. 441) notes that videotape replays have been used successfully in athletic events and by police departments in Florida and California.
Anticipate and respond to questions and objections readers are likely to raise. Audience members may be hostile or they may simply want to make sure your solution is well thought out. When presenting your proposal—orally or in writing—anticipate and respond to their questions and objections before they have a chance to raise them.	In recommending that video cameras be installed in police stations, Emery anticipates that readers may object that this would invade officers' privacy. Emery responds that the cameras be placed only where others—fellow officers, their superiors, and the press—might reasonably expect to have access. The cameras would not be placed in locker rooms or restroom stalls.

Demonstrate desirability. Most audiences need to be persuaded that a proposal is attractive as well as feasible. To enhance the appeal of your proposal, try the following strategies.

How to Demonstrate Desirability

STRATEGIES	EXAMPLES FROM READINGS
Identify plausible alternatives and explain why they are less attractive than your solution. You don't need to discuss every possible alternative—just those readers are likely to know and find attractive.	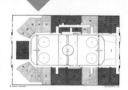 In "Ticket to the Top" (p. 450), Melanie Markham and Jonathan Quimby acknowledge that the field house at their university could provide students with an "electronic seating chart" to use in selecting hockey tickets. But they point out that this is not compatible with other technology that the field house relies on.
Point out ways your proposed solution will benefit readers. Readers often ask, in effect, "What's in this for me?" or "How will this benefit someone or something I care about?" The more persuasively you answer these questions, the more likely readers are to accept and implement your solution.	In "Cameras in the Station House" (p. 442), Richard Emery concludes by suggesting that these cameras would assure citizens that "what their police do is legitimate" and may restrain the actions of those police who would "cross the line" in their treatment of prisoners.

Engaging Your Audience: Writing an Introduction

If you hope for readers to accept—or even pay attention to—your proposal, you have to be sure they recognize the existence and seriousness of the problem. Sometimes this is relatively simple. Anyone who has read accounts of police brutality is likely to recognize that the situation can be serious, even if it is relatively infrequent or more apparent in some cities than in others. Consequently, in writing "Cameras in the Station House" (p. 441), Richard Emery is able to take the problem as a given and begin his proposal in the first sentences of his essay. More typically, however, you will have to find some way to engage your readers. You will probably have to provide background information that will show not only how a problematic situation relates to them or to people they care about, but also how this situation entails a conflict that matters to them. This may be a conflict between two groups, between what is currently happening and what should or could happen, or between what readers currently know and what they need to know or understand. The amount of background information you will need, of course, depends heavily on your readers' understanding of and attitudes toward the situation you are concerned with.

Relating to Readers

The proposals in the Reading to Write section display a variety of strategies for making sure readers see how a topic relates to them. Here are three strategies that will help your writing relate to your readers.

How to Relate to Readers

STRATEGIES	EXAMPLES FROM READINGS
Mention an experience readers are likely to share.	"Homeroom Zombies" (p. 421) begins by citing experiences parents and teachers of teenagers almost certainly share: waking teenagers in time to get to school and keeping them awake once they get there.
Mention a feeling readers are likely to share.	At the beginning of the excerpt from *An Inconvenient Truth* (p. 431), Al Gore acknowledges that "when considering a problem as vast as global warming, it's easy to feel overwhelmed and powerless—skeptical that individual efforts can really have an impact."

STRATEGIES	EXAMPLES FROM READINGS
Refer to an event—current or past—readers are likely to have heard about or remember.	**The New York Times** Even years after the school shootings in Littleton, Colorado, Leon Botstein (p. 438) can assume that his primary audience of adults will remember those shootings, especially since they seem to have begun a trend that continues even today.

{ Student Q & A } Engaging an Audience

Writing Now: In your first paragraph, you referred to the size of crowds at Houston Field House (HFH). Why did you include that information?

Melanie Markham and Jonathan Quimby: Because so many students are very interested in hockey, it is important to have an efficient system for ticket sales and ticket-taking. We also wanted to acknowledge everything the HFH is doing well so the proposal would not seem critical. By mentioning the many fans who attend games, we wanted to show that the Field House must be doing a good job already because many people want to be there. Mentioning the large numbers of fans (and showing them in the accompanying visual) also demonstrates the need for efficiency in the system. ■

{ Exercise } Writing an Introduction

Review—and, if necessary, revise—your audience analysis and statement of purpose, being especially careful to describe your readers' knowledge, needs, and attitudes. Then, using the strategies for relating to readers and establishing conflict, write one or more introductory paragraphs that will engage your intended audience. You might want to try more than one approach. Bring your draft introduction to class, along with your audience analysis and statement of purpose. Ask several classmates to comment on whether it includes enough details—and the right kind of details—to make your audience appreciate the severity of the problem and see how the problem relates to them or to people they care about. ■

Creating Conflict

To create conflict that will motivate readers to read your proposal, try using one or more of the strategies for showing that a problem exists (pp. 469–70). You might also consider using one or more of the following strategies.

How to Create Conflict

STRATEGIES	EXAMPLES FROM READINGS
Challenge existing attitudes about the problem, causes of the problem, or possible solutions.	 After acknowledging that the problem of climate change can leave individuals feeling overwhelmed, powerless, and skeptical, Al Gore (p. 431) asserts, "But we need to resist that response, because this crisis will get resolved only if we as individuals take responsibility for it."
Provide background information that explains the severity of the problem.	In "Homeroom Zombies" (p. 422), Lawrence Epstein and Steven Mardon point out that continual failure to get enough sleep can eventually lead to "diabetes, heart disease, obesity, depression, and a shortened life span in adults."
Provide information—verbal and/or visual—that conflicts with readers' values.	 Most readers of the magazine in which "Leave No Child Inside" (p. 426) appeared are environmentalists who are likely to be concerned to hear that young people are reluctant to think about threats to the environment because, as one student said, "it's too painful." "Homeroom Zombies" begins with a picture of a student sleeping at what appears to be a school desk. Even people who themselves have taken an occasional nap in school will acknowledge that this is not a good idea.
Point out that current efforts are creating difficulties, especially difficulties for the readers of your proposal. This can be particularly effective when you can show that the current situation is not inevitable, that alternatives to current efforts are well proven and readily available.	In "Ticket to the Top" (p. 444), Melanie Markham and Jonathan Quimby refer to the difficulties Field House staff must overcome in the current system of managing applications for season hockey tickets and keeping track of attendance at hockey games.

Creating an Appropriate Voice

As a rule, the voice in your proposal should be characterized by appeals to logic—that is, through the use of strategies mentioned earlier, you should show that a problem exists and that your proposed solution is feasible and desirable. However, there may be times when you want to sound more personal, addressing readers directly and allowing some of your emotions to come through. If you do decide to create a personal voice, be sure to avoid attacking your audience. Instead, show appreciation for useful things they have accomplished or difficulties they may be facing. Also, do not whine or complain about grievances you personally have experienced. Instead, focus on situations that affect a number of people, especially people your readers care about. And, of course, make sure that a personal voice is appropriate, given your audience, purpose, and topic.

For more on using logical appeals, see Chapter 5, page 327.

 **{ Exercise }** **Creating an Appropriate Voice**

Think about the impression you want your proposal to leave on your readers. To clarify and perhaps revise the voice of your proposal, review your audience analysis and statement of purpose. (Revise this material if you need to.) Then try some of the following activities.

- List some of the words and phrases you hope readers would use to describe the voice in your proposal. When you have done this, show your audience analysis, your statement of purpose, and the list of words and phrases to someone else (a classmate or your instructor). Ask this person to tell you whether the voice you hope to create makes sense, given what your analysis says about your intended audience and purpose.

- Using what you learn from your classmate or instructor, revise the list of words that describe the voice you want to create.

- Write a paragraph or two of any segment of your proposal—the introduction, for example, or the part in which you show that there really is a problem.

- Ask someone (a classmate, your instructor, or a friend) to read this passage aloud, and listen to the sound of his or her voice. Can you hear the attitude you want to create in the sound of this reader's voice? If you can, good. If you can't, look closely at your draft to see what words and phrases you need to change in order to create the voice you want. ■

{ Student Q & A } **Creating an Appropriate Voice**

Writing Now: How would you describe the voice you were trying to create? Why did you choose to create that particular voice?

Melanie Markham and Jonathan Quimby: As we said in our statement of purpose, we attempted to create a voice that was both knowledgeable and personable. We wanted to be sure our proposal was serious, as well as making it clear that we had done our research. However, we also wanted the voice to be personable because we wanted it to be easy and interesting to read. Using a more personable voice also helped our proposal to seem nonthreatening; we did not want to seem as if we were attacking the current system. ■

The following chart presents some strategies for creating an appropriate voice.

How to Create an Appropriate Voice

STRATEGIES	EXAMPLES FROM READINGS
Use personal pronouns such as *you*, *we*, and *our*. But be careful. As a rule, you should not use *you* as the subject of a sentence in which you refer to an objectionable action or attitude.	 In the excerpt from *An Inconvenient Truth* (p. 431), Al Gore mentions an attitude with which he disagrees: skepticism about an individual's having an impact on the environment. But the word *you* never appears in that context. Instead, he writes, "*it's* easy to feel overwhelmed and powerless—skeptical that individual efforts can really have an impact." Then he talks about what *we* need to do in responding to the crisis. When he implies a criticism of readers, he expresses it in terms of *our*. He refers, for example, to "*our* use and waste of resources."
Let facts speak for you. Include details that will have as much emotional impact for your readers as they do for you. But again, be careful. If you select only details that reflect your attitudes and ignore details that might contradict your views, you will lose credibility.	In expressing his concern about young people's attitudes toward the environment, Richard Louv (p. 426) cites comments made by students ("The environment will die") that will concern his audience as much as they do him.
Use emotional language that reflects your readers' values as much as it does your own.	 Lawrence Epstein and Steven Mardon (p. 421) occasionally use emotionally loaded terms: parents have to *cajole* or *drag* their children out of bed on school mornings. Failure to get enough sleep "can be *deadly*." These terms reflect Epstein and Mardon's own attitudes, but they also refer to attitudes and values shared by many parents of teenagers.
Let others—especially if they are authorities—express your feelings.	Clearly, Louv feels strongly that children receive too many messages of "gloom and doom" about the environment. But he leaves it to David Sobel (codirector of environmental education at a prestigious school) to express an alarming conse-quence of these messages: When children hear only such messages, "emotionally, they turn off."

Organizing

In organizing your proposal, you can rely on many of the strategies described elsewhere in this book, asserting a clear thesis, for example, or beginning paragraphs
with topic sentences. In proposals, it is especially important to get directly to the
point in answering two questions: Exactly what is the problem, and what do you
propose to do about it? Several other strategies for organizing a proposal are illustrated in the following chart.

How to Organize

STRATEGIES	EXAMPLES FROM READINGS
"Chunk" information. Group related facts together and separate them from other groups of facts. Especially group facts around questions that are likely to be important to your readers.	In "Cameras in the Station House" (p. 441), Richard Emery assumes that his readers are likely to ask the following questions: What do you propose? What's causing the problem? Are there any precedents for what you're proposing? What costs will the solution entail? What are the benefits of your proposed solution? Consequently, Emery opens with a recommendation for handling conflicting accounts of police brutality. Then he presents several chunks of information: descriptions of conflicts that cause the problem (paras. 2–3), precedents that help justify the solution proposed (para. 4), responses to possible questions or objections (paras. 5–8), and benefits of the proposal (paras. 9–10).
Consider using headings to let readers find the specific set of facts they are concerned with. Not all proposals include headings. But those that do frequently use one of two basic types of headings: (1) headings that identify steps readers need to take in solving the problems, or (2) headings that correspond to the topics explained in the section on developing your ideas: problem, solution, precedents, alternatives, questions and objections, and benefits.	 Al Gore (p. 431) uses headings that identify the steps readers can take. One heading, for example, advises readers to "Pre-cycle—reduce waste before you buy." Melanie Markham and Jonathan Quimby (p. 444) use the second type of heading, to label the parts of their proposal: "Problem," "Solution," and so on.
Establish a pattern in the way you present ideas and sequence information.	In explaining his solution to the climate change problem, Gore usually presents a brief bit of background about each recommendation he makes. Then he presents the recommendation and mentions a Web site where readers can find out more about how to implement the recommendation.

Concluding

Readers looking primarily for information in a report or an evaluation may not always read the conclusion. For instance, in reading a report, readers may just look for key pieces of information they need; in reading an evaluation, they may just read until they can tell whether they are interested in the specific topic or item being evaluated. But with proposals, readers are likely to look closely at the concluding paragraphs, if only to get a sense of the "bottom line" or "what's in it for me." In your proposal, the conclusion is your last shot at persuading readers to do what you want. So make it a good shot.

The kind of conclusion you write will depend on the needs and values of your readers. The proposals in Reading to Write employ a variety of strategies that you may consider as you conclude your own proposal.

How to Conclude

STRATEGIES	EXAMPLES FROM READINGS
Reiterate your basic argument, and restate your recommendation. Especially if your proposal is lengthy or complicated, it can help if you summarize your proposal, making sure the basic outline of your ideas is fresh in your readers' minds.	The next-to-last paragraph of "Cameras in the Station House" (p. 443) repeats the two basic assumptions underlying the proposal: (1) that placing video cameras in police stations and other public places is not an invasion of police officers' or others' privacy, and (2) that video cameras provide a more reliable, accurate record than do eyewitness accounts. The final paragraph restates the recommendation that video cameras be installed in police stations because "video tape is our best weapon as a salutary response to the current police brutality crisis."
Point out ways your proposal will benefit the audience, thereby ending on a strong, positive note. But be realistic. Do not promise benefits unless you have strong reasons for believing that those benefits will actually materialize. If you promise more than your proposal can deliver, readers will be skeptical of your entire proposal—and of any subsequent proposal you may make.	 In concluding "Ticket to the Top" (p. 450), Melanie Markham and Jonathan Quimby point out that adopting their proposed ticket system would benefit Field House staff in several ways. It would reduce paperwork, resolve disputes about seating assignments, and reduce the amount of time staff have to spend checking on tickets when fans enter the Field House.

STRATEGIES	EXAMPLES FROM READINGS
Show how your proposal will help others achieve their goals.	In concluding "Leave No Child Inside" (p. 429), Richard Louv suggests that programs like the one he has described can give children "a sense of the possibilities of the vast, unnoticed universe," an experience he assumes readers have had and would like to provide for the current generation of children.

{ Exercise } **Concluding**

Review the solution you wrote about in response to the prompts on page 467, noting all the ways you have revised it. Using a strategy identified above (or a different strategy from a proposal you have analyzed), write a conclusion for your proposal. Share this conclusion with your instructor or some classmates who have previously read your ideas about how to solve the problem you're concerned with. Ask your classmates to identify the strategy or strategies you have used and tell you whether the conclusion seems persuasive and appropriate, given what you have said about your audience. ■

Designing Your Proposal and Integrating Visual Information

As you have seen in several of the readings for this chapter ("Homeroom Zombies," for example), proposals may include any of the visual elements used in other types of writing—headings, graphs, bulleted lists, sidebars (inset boxes), and pull quotes. In planning your proposal, consider whether visual elements might be useful in presenting your ideas effectively to the audience you are addressing. These elements are not always necessary, nor are they always appropriate. But for some audiences and situations, they can be highly effective.

Chapter 5 includes a section on designing a position paper (pp. 333–34) that includes specific strategies that apply well to integrating visuals in a proposal. Also, review the questions related to reading visual information in proposals (p. 418).

Then look back over the selections in Reading to Write, and identify types of visual features that you might put to effective use in your proposal. As you think about the design of your proposal, check with your instructor about the kinds of visual elements that may be appropriate for your assignment. Keeping your instructor's comments in mind, identify the visual features you want your proposal to have and revise your draft to make sure it incorporates those features.

{ Student Q & A }   **Choosing and Integrating Visual Information**

Writing Now: Where and how did you find the visuals you used in your proposal?

Melanie Markham and Jonathan Quimby: Most of the visuals came either from Houston Field House's Web site or Ticketmaster's Web site, so we found them as we were researching for our proposal. When it came time to choose visuals, we were easily able to find the images we needed on those sites. One visual, the photo taken in the Field House that shows all the fans at a hockey game, comes from the Web site Melanie's family runs, *rpihockey.net*. ■

Creating a Review Draft

It is now time to bring together all the work you have done thus far on your proposal. You should be ready to write a review draft that meets the goals set out in the assignment for this chapter. This draft should clearly identify the problem, present a practical solution, point out the benefits of the solution, and persuade readers to make the changes you propose. After completing the review draft, you will need a few more days to finish working on your proposal. During this time, you will assess your writing carefully, not only by critiquing your draft yourself but also by getting others' perspectives on your work. Then you will use what you learn from these assessments to make any needed revisions in the content, organization, style, and format of your proposal.

In preparation for writing your review draft, look back at what you have said about your audience and purpose. Has your sense of audience and purpose changed? For example, have you learned something new about your audience's values, or have you found information that might influence the voice you want to create or the type of appeal you want to make? If so, revise what you have said about your audience and purpose and keep that in mind as you decide what to say and how to say it in the review draft. Also, look back at what you wrote when you were reflecting on information you had gathered. Ask yourself whether you need to change your statement of the problem, be more explicit about how to carry out the solution you propose, or explain why you reject alternative solutions. Notice points at which you will want to add, modify, or delete some aspect of either the problem or the solution.

As you work on your review draft, examine the introduction and conclusion. Do these sections establish the voice you want to create? Does the introduction seem likely to engage the intended audience? Is the conclusion convincing? Will it persuade readers that your proposal should be implemented—or at least considered seriously? Revise these sections as needed, using the strategies discussed in this chapter. In addition, take some pains to make the structure clear. To do this, it might help to write an informal outline indicating the main reasons you think there is a problem and the main steps that should be taken in order to solve it. You should also use strategies found on page 479 to organize your proposal, especially by chunking information, using headings, and establishing a pattern in the ways you present ideas and sequence information.

REVIEWING AND REVISING

Once you have made your review draft as complete and polished as you can, you need to have it reviewed by one or more people who understand the principles (analyzing audience, engaging readers, and so on) that you have been working with in this chapter. Then you will use this review to guide a revision of your review draft before you turn your work in for grading.

Getting a Final Review

Give the reviewer a copy of your draft, one he or she can make notes on. Also give the reviewer a copy of your statement of audience and purpose. If necessary, revise that statement before giving it to the reviewer. Ask the reviewer to adopt the perspective of the audience you have described, and then use the following checklist in commenting on your work.

1. In my statement of audience and purpose, please highlight any statements that give you a good sense of the knowledge, needs, and attitudes of my intended audience. Also highlight statements that help you understand exactly what purpose(s) I am hoping to achieve. Please indicate any statements that need to be clarified.

2. Given what I say in my statement of audience and purpose, how likely does it seem that my arguments will be persuasive to the audience I am trying to reach?

3. In what specific passages have I developed my topic thoroughly and credibly, especially by showing that a problem exists, defining the problem, thinking of solutions, and demonstrating the feasibility and desirability of my solution? What are some strategies (explained on pp. 469–70, 471, 472–73, and 476) I might use to make my proposal clearer and more compelling?

4. What portions of my introduction seem likely to engage the interest of my intended audience? Which strategies (explained on pp. 474–75) might help make the introduction more engaging?

5. How would you describe the voice I have created? At what points does that voice seem appropriate, given my intended audience and the subject matter of my proposal? What strategies (explained on p. 478) might help me make the voice clearer or more appropriate?

[**Checklist for Final Review**]

▶ Go to
bedfordstmartins.com/
writingnow to download these
questions from Chapter 7 >
Worksheets.

6. In what passages is the organization clear, either because I have used strategies explained on page 479 or because I have used topic sentences or transition words? What are places where I need to make the organization clearer?

7. How does the conclusion help make my proposal more attractive to my intended audience? What strategies (explained on p. 480) might I use to make my conclusion more effective?

8. If the proposal includes photographs or other visual elements, how do they help establish the importance of the problem or the nature of the solution? Do I need to add or revise any captions?

If possible, ask the reviewer to talk with you about your review draft as well as make notes on it. In particular, ask the reviewer to pose questions and raise objections to what you have written. Be careful not to argue with your reviewer, especially when he or she poses questions or disagrees with points you have made. When this happens, try to find out why the reviewer has questions or objections and make notes about what they are.

Revising Your Proposal

Up to this point, you have listened to your reviewer's comments without explaining, arguing, or making judgments about the validity of those comments. Once you have a good idea of how your reviewer responds to your proposal, however, you should go back through your notes on his or her comments. Bearing in mind your intended audience and purpose, decide which comments are most valid. Then use the strategies referred to in the Checklist for Final Review to revise your proposal.

After resolving all the issues that need attention, proofread carefully and correct any typographical or formatting errors. Then submit this final draft to your instructor.

▷ TAKING STOCK OF WHERE YOU ARE

Although you will find differences among the writing assignments in this book, there are also some important similarities. For example, you always have to analyze the intended audience, write an introduction that will engage that particular audience, and so forth. Consequently, there should be a cumulative quality to the writing assignments you do from this book. Each assignment should teach you strategies that can help you grow as a writer and improve your work on subsequent assignments. But this will only happen if you make a conscious effort to assess your development as a writer as you go along.

After your instructor has returned the final draft of your work, think back over all the comments you received—from classmates as well as your instructor—and write out answers to the following questions. (You might want to keep these in a journal or a special section of a notebook.)

1. What appears to be my greatest area of strength?
2. Where am I having the greatest difficulty?
3. What am I learning about the process of writing?
4. What am I learning about giving and receiving feedback on writing?
5. What have I learned from writing the proposal that I can use in my next assignment for this course, for another course, or for work?

Questions for Assessing Your Growth as a Writer

▶ Go to bedfordstmartins.com/writingnow to download these questions from Chapter 7 > Worksheets.

The responses that follow are Melanie Markham and Jonathan Quimby's answers to these questions for the proposal they wrote about improving the hockey ticket sales system on their campus (p. 444).

1. Being able to identify the audience. Having purchased season tickets for many years, we are very accustomed to the process from a student's point of view. However, our meeting with our audience helped us to get a very good understanding of what they wanted and needed as well as helping us identify the potential problems they would see with our solution. Seeing both sides in this way helped us to find a solution that would make things easier for students but would also be workable for the Field House.

2. Our greatest difficulty during the process of writing was in refining our original ideas into a workable solution. Originally we had many grandiose ideas, such as the swipe card system. We had to give up some ideas based on financial concerns. We also decided that our final solution should be able to stay with the Ticketmaster company since the Field House was very interested in doing so. Also, editing can be a problem. We needed a few people to look over the writing because it was hard to see mistakes or see it from a different point of view.

3. That writing is not just sitting down and starting to write. There is a lot of preparation that goes along with creating a good paper. We also learned a lot about covering every detail and answering every question. Our audience's questions during our meeting showed that they were very interested in what we had to say and that they would put serious thought into our ideas. This helped us realize that we needed to be thorough in our writing and address every possible concern.

4. It is very important to get different points of view because, as always, two eyes are better than one, and the person reviewing your writing may pick up things you never saw. Also we're now able to be much more specific about the reasons for feedback we give about writing. Instead of saying a certain wording would "sound better," we can explain exactly how the wording affects the reader's perception and the conveyance of information. In terms of receiving feedback, a better understanding of these reasons also allows us to use feedback more efficiently. Understanding the reasons for the feedback usually allows you to see right away why potential changes might be better.

5. The ideas about audience analysis have been especially useful. Also, we see how getting good feedback on our writing can help in lots of situations.

[PART TWO]

Strategies for Design and Research ▷

8 ▷

Reading and Writing about Visual Images

As you know from your own experience and from working with the readings in this book, visual information can take many different forms, ranging from photographs or paintings to charts, graphs, page layout, and the size and shape of type. Throughout this book you'll find suggestions for how to read (that is, to analyze and evaluate) all of these types of visual elements of a text. But for now, we want to concentrate on visual images—photographs, drawings, paintings, videos. As is the case with reading written texts, the way you read a specific image depends in part on your reasons for reading the image and the goals someone (an artist, an advertiser, a journalist) hoped to accomplish by creating it. But nonetheless, there are several basic strategies you can use in analyzing images in very different media. This chapter introduces you to some of these strategies and then shows you how students used those strategies in analyzing several very different types of images— a movie poster, a painting, and a televised public service ad. Although we won't talk specifically about sculpture, much of what we have to say about paintings and other images applies to sculptures as well.

▷ STRATEGIES FOR READING VISUAL IMAGES

No matter what kind of image you are looking at, it is always useful to do the following as you try to analyze and interpret that image.

- ▶ Notice your first reaction.
- ▶ Identify the audience for whom the image seems intended.
- ▶ Look closely at details.

▶ Notice the composition.

▶ Put the image in context.

Although the following strategies for reading images are presented in an orderly list, you probably will not use them in that way. It can be helpful to start with the first strategy in the list, noting your first impressions. But it is likely that as you start looking closely at an image, you will find yourself moving back and forth from one strategy to another.

Noticing Your First Reaction or Impression

First impressions can be misleading, but often they are valid responses. In almost every case, they are a good place to begin your analysis of an image, especially if you consider questions such as the following.

▶ What emotions or reactions does the image evoke?

▶ How does the image make you feel?

▶ Does the image seem to be making a point or expressing an idea?

Identifying the Audience

Think about the background knowledge a likely viewer or audience of this image will have.

▶ **Who is this image likely to appeal to? What sort of background knowledge, attitudes, assumptions, or values would someone need in order to appreciate (or critique) the image?** You can always assume that ads are designed to appeal to a particular group of people who have some common interests, needs, and values. Works of art—paintings, sculptures, or photographs—are less likely to be created with a specific audience in mind. But especially when you look at an unfamiliar artwork, you will recognize that it is likely to be most appealing to people who have a certain amount of background knowledge or share certain attitudes.

Looking Closely at Details

Imagine that you are using a camera and can focus in on specific parts of the image.

▶ **What details do you notice? Are there details that you would expect to find but do not? If people are depicted, what do you notice about their facial expressions, gestures, posture, or clothing?**

▶ **What colors do you notice, and what emotions or reactions do they evoke?** "Warm" colors such as orange or red typically evoke strong emotional reactions; "cool" colors such as blue can have a calming effect; dark colors can have a wide variety of associations, ranging from elegance (tuxedos, for example, are usually black) to formality, mystery, threat, or despair.

▶ **What is your viewing angle?** If you get the feeling that you are looking up at the object or person being represented in an image, that object or person may seem especially powerful or important. If you get the feeling that you are looking down, the object may seem relatively weak or unimportant. If you are looking at the object "eye to eye," this can suggest that you and the object are on the same footing, both literally and figuratively.

Noticing the Composition

Think about the composition of the image, that is, the people or objects that are shown, and how they are related to each other.

▶ **Are the people or objects in the image close to each other or distant? Are they similar to or different from each other? What is the setting in which they are located?** Things are likely to seem relatively important or powerful if they are larger than others, if they are located in the upper half of a picture, or if they appear closer to the viewer. The opposite is often true for things that are relatively small, located in the lower half of a picture, or in the background. People or objects located closer to each other than to other people or objects are likely to seem closely related to each other. The setting can also influence your reactions. (It's no coincidence, for example, that luxury cars are often shown in front of an expensive home or in an exotic location.)

▶ **What kinds of lines and shapes do you notice?** Diagonal lines can suggest movement or threat; jagged lines often create tension or anxiety. Shapes that appear ready to collide, collapse, or crush other shapes can also create tension, anxiety, or threat. Curved or straight lines can seem soothing or calming; straight lines can suggest stability.

Putting the Image in Context

Thinking about the context of an image means considering the setting you found it in, what you know about images of this kind, and other background information.

▶ **Where is the image located?** In a museum? Someone's home? A park or playground? Is it included in a magazine or newspaper? Online? In a book? Is it accompanied by written or spoken text that might help explain its significance? Paintings, sculpture, or photographs in a museum can seem relatively remote, protected, and valuable. They may be accompanied by short statements about the artist, but their meaning may not seem readily understandable unless you know something about the history and theory of art. Also, chances are that the museum is the only place you will find the original, there are guards and signs telling you not to touch or even take pictures of the artwork, and you probably couldn't afford it even if it was for sale.

By contrast, pieces of sculpture in a park or playground are likely to be more accessible and viewer friendly; children (and pigeons) are likely to be perched on them. Pictures in a newspaper, magazine, or online are usually even more accessible: You can cut them out or print them and frame them or, if you know how to use software such as PhotoShop, you can manipulate them in any way you choose. Further, it is relatively easy to understand these pictures, since they usually appear with written text dealing with the same subject matter.

▶ **What does the image remind you of? How is it similar to or different from other images of the same type?** To understand anything (an artwork, a movie, a comment, a gesture), people have to relate it to what they already know, comparing and contrasting it with other things in their experience. Even if an image seems unfamiliar or puzzling, and even if you have never taken a course in art or photography, you never approach an image as a blank slate; you always have some sort of knowledge that you can draw on.

▶ **What is the historical, social, and intellectual context?** Some visual images have an enduring quality. A painting, for example, may be as interesting and powerful today as it was when it was created hundreds of years ago. But, as is the case with all images, that painting is an effort to give meaning to events or personal experiences that were important to a particular artist (or group of artists) in a particular society at a particular time in history. Even if you have to do a bit of background reading, your understanding of the image will be richer if you know something about when, where, and why it was created.

▷ EXAMPLES OF STUDENT VISUAL ANALYSES

In the following pages, you will see how three students responded to the following assignment.

> Analyze a visually interesting image such as a painting, a piece of sculpture, or a poster. Be sure to choose an image that has a lot of meaning for you and that you think other college students would find engaging. In analyzing the image, assume that you are writing for an audience of college students who have seen and been impressed by the image but do not understand how the visual details work together to create an effect on viewers. You may use secondary sources if they help you better understand certain details of the image. But focus primarily on your response and the details of the image that prompted that response. Be sure to use MLA documentation guidelines when citing the source of the image and in acknowledging any secondary sources you have drawn upon.

See Chapter 13 for complete advice on MLA documentation.

In their work for this assignment, the three students chose to analyze a famous painting, two movie posters, and a public service ad intended to warn parents about the dangers of underage drinking. To help you understand the process of analyzing and writing about a visual image, the next several pages show you how one student analyzed a painting by using the strategies listed on pages 490–91. Then you will see the essay in which she presented results of her analysis. Following that essay, you will find essays in which two other students analyzed the posters and the public service ad.

The first analysis comes from undergraduate Jenna Gatsch, a dual major in biology and psychology, who is writing about a famous painting, *Nighthawks*, by Edward Hopper. In preparation for writing her essay, Jenna made the following notes based on the questions listed in the Strategies for Reading Visual Images on pages 489–90.

Nighthawks, Edward Hopper.

Student Analysis of a Visual Image

Noticing your first reaction or impression

What emotions or reactions does the image evoke?

> It creates a sense of loneliness. People are in a diner, but they are keeping to themselves, not socializing.

How does the image make you feel?

> It makes me sort of sad but also curious. Who are these people, and what brought them to this place? What are they thinking, since each seems lost in their own thoughts?

Does the image seem to be making a point or expressing an idea?

> Maybe it's saying something about how lonely people can be in a large city.

Identifying the audience

Who is this image likely to appeal to? What sort of background knowledge, attitudes, assumptions, or values would someone need in order to appreciate (or critique) the image?

> This painting likely appeals to people who enjoy art and not necessarily a pretty landscape or some other purely attractive piece. These people would like art that must be interpreted and is not necessarily happy. They would need to have some knowledge of human characteristics/mannerisms—for example, how the hunched backs and hats make

the people at the diner seem closed in, as though they want to be left alone and not talk to anyone. They are likely to appreciate things that seem mysterious or that make them feel curious. I looked for some background information about nighthawks, so it would help if people knew about nighthawks or were willing to find out.

Looking closely at details

Imagine that you are using a camera and can focus in on specific parts of the image. What details do you notice? Are there details that you would expect to find but do not? If people are depicted, what do you notice about their facial expressions, gestures, posture, or clothing?

Customers in the diner look absorbed in their own thoughts—they don't seem to welcome outsiders, as shown by their body language. Shoulders are hunched, and each diner is keeping to their own personal space. None of them show any sense of being intimate with the others. The man and woman sitting close to each other, simply based on proximity, are likely a couple, but based on body language do not seem to be intimate. There is no touching or other signal to indicate closeness, nor is there any eye contact. The man on the left seems the most mysterious and alone because he is shown from the back with only a slight hint of face visible. He appears the most singled out and therefore the loneliest of all.

What colors do you notice, and what emotions or reactions do they evoke?

The men's suits are dark. Shadows and the overall darkness of night seem to contribute to the aloneness, as well as sadness and mystery. The woman's dress is red, like she might have been to a party. The interior of the diner is bright, like a completely different world from dark city streets—more like the people are alone in their "cage" in the diner that has no doors to the outside. The difference in color between the two men at the bar and the employee seem to hint at their different roles in the painting. The men at the bar are wearing dark colors and do not seem to welcome any interaction with other people. The man working at the diner is wearing white and has no choice but to interact.

What is your viewing angle?

Viewing angle is straight on. Makes you feel like you are looking at people who could be your equals. Maybe they're not all that different from you. Because the view is outside looking in, this seems to enhance the curiosity about the people who are inside.

Noticing the composition

What people or objects are shown, and how are they related to each other? Are they close to each other or distant? Are they similar to or different from each other? What is the setting in which they are located?

People are close physically but not emotionally. Everything in the picture—like the Phillies cigar sign above the diner—is really large. The people are very small, almost like they are insignificant or vulnerable.

What kinds of lines and shapes do you notice?

Lines in this painting are predominantly straight. The straightness indicates the stability of the diner and the city around it. It is always there, and the diner is always open for people like these nighthawks who need to go somewhere this late at night. Because of perspective, the ceiling of the diner seems to be slanted down, maybe like it's pressing down on people in the diner.

Putting the visual image in context

Where is the image located?

The painting is located in a museum (The Art Institute of Chicago). This makes it more rare and prestigious, adding to the mystique of it. It is an important piece of work that can be enjoyed by people in a controlled setting from a certain distance.

What does the image remind you of? How is it similar to or different from other images of the same type?

It reminds me of movies from a long time ago where men are sitting alone at the bar with a hat on. I'm not sure what movie I'm picturing, but it was in black and white. It also reminds me of going to a diner in the middle of the night, which I have done before. None of my experiences were so lonely, however.

What is the historical, social, and intellectual context?

The painting was done in the 1940s, during World War II and just a couple of years after the Great Depression ended.

Using these notes as a starting point, Jenna wrote the following analysis of *Nighthawks*.

Gatsch 1

Jenna Gatsch
Professor Appel
English 2960
12 March 2008

The Emotion of *Nighthawks*

Introduction describes the people shown and how they are related.

Edward Hopper's painting *Nighthawks* shows four people in a diner late at night while the rest of the city sleeps around them. Three of these people are customers seated at the counter of the diner. One customer is seated by himself and has his back to the viewer. The other two customers are a man and woman who appear to be a couple and are facing the viewer. The fourth person, a waiter, is behind the counter, leaning over as if he is putting something under the counter while looking up as though he is talking to the couple.

Describes the emotions evoked.

Usually this scene would seem very ordinary. But Hopper makes the people seem very lonely, even though they are seated relatively close to each other, and he makes the whole picture—the people, the diner, and the streets around it—seem more sinister than the viewer might expect.

Gives background knowledge the viewer might need.

A "nighthawk," like a night owl, is a person who is awake and active late at night. Both owls and hawks are predatory birds, but the connotation of *hawk* is more intense. Nighthawks belong to the family Caprimulgidae, meaning "goatsucker." According to ancient Greek legend, these birds would come out at night and drink milk from the teats of goats. While this tale is not true, it indicates one reason the birds have always been viewed as more sinister than the common owls ("Goatsuckers").

Describes the dark colors and the emotions they evoke.

Additionally, nighthawks are adept at camouflaging themselves. Their coloring is typically a mixture of black, brown, and grey, enabling them to blend in with branches during the day and blend in with the darkness at night ("Common Nighthawk"). For these reasons, Hopper seems to imply that these people are much more than simply "night owls" and possibly might share in some of the sinister qualities with which nighthawks are associated.

Explains the location in the painting and other details of the setting.

The setting of the painting is important in conveying a feeling of loneliness. The city appears deserted except for those in the diner; no one is walking around or driving on the streets (Fig. 1). The buildings around the diner are dark as are the streets, with all of the light in the painting

Gatsch 2

Fig. 1. *Nighthawks* by Edward Hopper, 1942.

coming from inside the diner. The storefront across the street and the advertisement above the diner both indicate that during the day, people are active here. But at night the area is dark and deserted. The intense darkness of the painting is interrupted only by the light coming from the diner. This creates shadows, which also contribute to the creepy and lonely feeling of the setting. The bright interior of the diner separates it from the different world of darkness outside, making it seem even more like the people are alone. Because there are no doors to the outside, the diner appears to be a glass cage with no way out. This indicates that the people inside are the most important part of the painting while the darkness serves as a backdrop.

A closer analysis of the "nighthawks" lends even more support to the lonely and sinister feeling of the painting. All of the customers in the diner look absorbed in their own thoughts and do not appear to welcome outsiders, as shown by their body language. Their hunched appearances are reminiscent of a perched bird, linking them to the title of the painting, and each is keeping to his or her own personal space. The man and woman are sitting close to each other, and simply based on proximity, they are likely a couple. But based on body language, they do not seem to be intimate. There is no touching or other signal to indicate closeness, nor is there any eye contact. Little detail is shown of the customers' facial features. However, the faces of the man and woman,

Considers specific details.

Alludes to details that seem to be missing.

Notices nonverbal language.

Makes comparison between picture and other things the writer knows.

which are shown most fully, bear a strong resemblance to the nighthawks to which they are being compared. The noses of the man and woman look beak-like and are very prominent on their faces. Their eyes are also obscured, making them look less human and more like frightening creatures. In addition, the hats the men are wearing make them seem more anonymous and sinister by further obscuring their facial features. The man on the left seems the most mysterious and alone because he is shown from the back, with only a slight hint of face visible.

Indicates the historical period.

All of the men's clothes, which are typical of the time period, are darker in color, emphasizing the dark and lonely tone. The colors also keep them from standing out and, rather, help them to blend in with the night tones. The woman's red dress and red hair give the impression that she planned to do something more exciting with her night but ended up in this desolate situation. Her attempt to look passionate in this setting contributes to her loneliness.

Contrasts the people in the painting.

The waiter is apart from the rest in many ways. He is not a "nighthawk" like the rest, but rather is there to work. His facial features are much more human-like than the others. Contrary to the rest, he is wearing bright white. He cannot be alone and aloof because it is his job to interact with others. The difference in colors differentiates their roles in the situation.

Gives a further supporting point about historical period.

A final method of understanding the meaning behind *Nighthawks* is looking at it in historical context. It was painted in 1942, soon after the bombing at Pearl Harbor and not so long after the Great Depression. Hopper may have been trying to convey either his or society's mood at that time. War in itself is sinister and evil, involving the killing of numerous innocent people. Hopper may have been personifying this evil in his characters. Additionally, loneliness is a common emotion when facing a time of such confusion and loss. However, the theme of loneliness can be understood throughout time periods, not just in the 1940s during World War II. There will always be either personal or societal events that can make a person identify with the *Nighthawks*.

Through the use of details such as setting, characters, and light versus dark, Hopper created lonely and sinister feelings to which even contemporary audiences can relate.

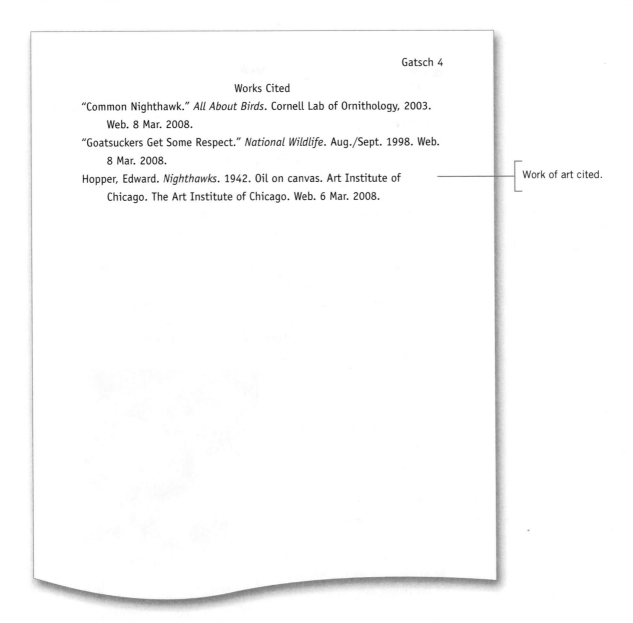

Gatsch 4

Works Cited

"Common Nighthawk." *All About Birds*. Cornell Lab of Ornithology, 2003.
Web. 8 Mar. 2008.

"Goatsuckers Get Some Respect." *National Wildlife*. Aug./Sept. 1998. Web.
8 Mar. 2008.

Hopper, Edward. *Nighthawks*. 1942. Oil on canvas. Art Institute of
Chicago. The Art Institute of Chicago. Web. 6 Mar. 2008.

Work of art cited.

The second visual analysis comes from Kyle Okaly. He is a communication major and a great fan of Spider-Man movies, so he wrote a visual analysis of two Spider-Man movie posters, one for the first Spider-Man movie and one for the third. He located copies of these online via the movies' Web site and incorporates them here following MLA style for working with images.

Okaly 1

Kyle Okaly

Professor Chang

English 2960

12 March 2008

The Two Sides of Spider-Man:

A Visual Analysis of Movie Posters

Superman—who stands for "truth, justice, and the American way"— is one of the most famous and popular superheroes of all time. His superpowers make him nearly invincible, and he's a classic example of a stereotypical superhero. Spider-Man, by contrast, is a much less "super" hero on many levels. His superpowers are much less miraculous, and he is, as a result, much more vulnerable. Unlike Superman, he started his superhero career as a troubled teenager and has been constantly plagued by self-doubt, inadequacies, and personal tragedies. Because he was one of the first superheroes to face these problems, however, he became a much more complex character than those who came before him.

This complexity appears in two of the posters that were used in advertising two Spider-Man movies: the first is a poster for the original 2002 movie, *Spider-Man* (see Fig. 1), and the second is from the 2007 film *Spider-Man 3*. The 2002 *Spider-Man* poster depicts a heroic scene. The sun, which appears to be shining in from the left side of the image, reflects intensely off of the windows Spider-Man is climbing as well as Spider-Man himself, giving the majority of

Fig. 1. Poster for *Spider-Man*, 2002 (Spider-Man).

Annotations in the left margin:

Introduction gives background information to help viewers understand the poster.

Addresses question, what point or idea is the image expressing?

Okaly 2

the image an evocative yellow glow that blends well with the bright red and blue in his costume. In contrast, the 2007 *Spider-Man 3* poster (see Fig. 2) creates a dismal scene. The poster is basically black and white, with slight hues of blue both on his costume and in the sky.

> Describes colors and the emotions they evoke.

Similar differences also appear in Spider-Man's body language in the two posters. The first poster shows him poised and alert. Every joint of his arms, from his shoulders to his fingers, is bent or twisted—almost awkwardly—to the point that it seems as if he's suppressing some huge amount of energy. His crawling position and jutting elbows make it seem as if this energy might explode at any moment in the form of a lightning-fast leap that you might expect from an actual spider. His position in the second poster, however, is the absolute opposite (see Fig. 2). His head is hanging low in despair, and he seems utterly lacking in energy. His arms and head are hanging loosely, and his legs are curled up below him rather than supporting his body upright. While the first image shows Spider-Man's energy and physical potential, the second shows an exhausted and vulnerable side of Spider-Man that many superheroes never display.

> Gives details about figure's body language.

> Compares images, listing differences.

In addition to the vastly different body positions exhibited in each poster, Spider-Man is portrayed in two vastly different environments. The original *Spider-Man* poster portrays a standard superhero scene: the hero is exhibiting one of his super powers in a bright scene with a lot of motion. (Since it's a still image, there can be no actual movement, but the assumption is that Spider-

> Analyzes setting in both posters.

Fig. 2. Poster for *Spider-Man 3*, 2007 (Spider-Man 3).

Okaly 3

Man is crawling forward and the cars in the background are all moving.)
The *Spider-Man 3* poster sharply opposes this standard scene by portraying
a dejected hero crouching in the rain. There's no movement (aside from
the depressing rainfall). Nothing but the cloudy sky, a very small ledge on
which Spider-Man is perched, and Spider-Man himself is visible. In
contrast to his eye contact and alert state in the older poster, he seems
indifferent to his surroundings, including the deluge of rain pouring down
upon him. The first poster clearly emphasizes his superpowers and
courage, but the second emphasizes his fallibility, a quality we rarely see
in other action heroes.

The classic idea of a superhero is someone with absolute dedication
toward helping others, unshakable confidence, and nothing else to do—
ever. Spider-Man, by contrast, was one of the first superheroes who had
problems of his own, both before and after becoming a hero. His personal
relationships and self-doubt often hinder his ability to work effectively,
and he's often responsible for the deaths of close friends and relatives.
The *Spider-Man* poster reminds us that Spider-Man has superpowers, but
the *Spider-Man 3* poster reminds us that he has weaknesses—a fact that
distinguishes him as a more complex and realistic character than many
superheroes who came before him. This additional layer of realism allows
fans to relate to Spider-Man on a deeper level than they are able to with
most other superheroes, and this ability to connect with fans is one of
the reasons he is among the most popular superheroes in existence today.

Conclusion contrasts the images with similar images.

Okaly 4

Works Cited

Spider-Man. 2002. *Sony Pictures*. Web. 7 Mar. 2008.

Spider-Man 3. 2007. *Sony Pictures*. Web. 7 Mar. 2008.

The third visual analysis, written by engineering major Michelle Pelersi, concerns a public service television ad created by the Ad Council, a not-for-profit group that organizes and distributes campaigns from advertising agencies that volunteer to create public service ads dealing with social issues. This particular ad is intended to make viewers (especially parents) aware of the increasing number of children who begin drinking before they even become teenagers.

Pelersi 1

Michelle Pelersi
Professor Noonan
English 2960
12 March 2008

"Brandon": A Prospective Alcoholic

Teenagers have been drinking underage for decades, without letting the rise in the legal drinking age slow them down. Consequently, many parents and adults assume high school graduates and undergraduate college students party with alcohol. Most parents, however, do not assume or expect that teenagers ending middle school and starting high school might be partying with alcohol. Yet, "underage" no longer pertains to teenagers sixteen and above as it once did. Now children as young as ten or eleven are starting to experiment and abuse alcohol. Since most parents want to believe their child would never drink so young, an organization of advertising professionals, the Ad Council, has created a series of public service announcements to target and warn parents their children could be experimenting with alcohol and putting themselves at risk. The advertisement specifically targets parents who believe that many common assumptions about underage drinking still hold true.

The setting of the ad is an Alcoholics Anonymous (A.A.) meeting with people sitting in a circle. The camera perspective in the beginning of the ad is an aerial view of the room. This perspective enables the audience to view the group members who are of different ages, races, genders, and classes (Fig. 1). Every group member appears to be a typical adult, dressed modestly, average height, and healthy. Having typical, middle class adults in this setting makes it possible for the majority of viewers to relate to the advertisement. All members are adult except for Brandon. Brandon is a shaggy blond-haired boy about eight years old wearing a collared shirt who is just starting to get his adult teeth. There are no other children at the meeting. Brandon starts off by saying, in an innocent boy's voice, "My name's Brandon and in nine years, I'll be an alcoholic." Brandon's appearance and voice make him stick out in the scene, therefore drawing all the attention.

Introduction answers question about the social context.

Describes the setting.

Information about perspective explains the viewing angle in one part of ad.

Describes appearance of people.

Reports dialogue and explains significance of those words.

Pelersi 2

Fig. 1. Wide shot of people at the meeting in "Brandon"
("Brandon").

As Brandon speaks, camera perspectives shift, making it possible for
the viewer to see the body language and expressions of the men and
women at the meeting. Once Brandon begins telling his story, the camera
scans the room from left to right and zooms in from above on the group.
Members uncross their legs and lean in toward Brandon, listening intently
and giving him their undivided attention.

> Analyzes body language.

Many of the men and women have sympathetic expressions, which
change to shock as Brandon progresses. At one point, the older man
sitting next to Brandon looks away from the boy toward another member
of the group. His eyes clearly show he is in disbelief.

Many adults do not realize children can experience problems with
alcohol. The effect of having Brandon tell his story, compared to
another adult, is profound. Brandon's naïve expression shows he does
not completely understand the effect of his story on his life. However,
there are shocked reactions written across every other face because the
adults understand. The camera perspective switches back to Brandon
and focuses on him as he finishes his story. He makes eye contact with
the whole group while he speaks to convey the seriousness of the
subject matter.

> Addresses things that are
> surprising or unexpected.

> Describes how people
> react to one another.

Describes setting.

At first glance, it is evident that the setting lacks carpet, plush furniture, and internal lighting, which suggests a serious mood. This ad does not have vibrant colors or a cozy feeling, but as the video progresses, the setting, lighting, and body language create a safe-feeling environment. The room is large with everyone sitting in a circle of chairs in the center of the room. There are floor-to-ceiling windows in the background with light-colored, sheer drapes. The outside light illuminates the room through the large windows. There are potted plants placed around the room and a large bulletin board with many colorful flyers posted on it. The group members are sitting in wooden chairs as opposed to metal folding chairs, which help to warm the environment. The safe environment encourages openness, sharing, and understanding between the group members. The comforting, safe feeling of this setting makes Brandon's story all the more disturbing, since the likelihood of his becoming an alcoholic is not safe or comforting.

Analyzes setting further and the effect it has on viewers.

Alcohol abuse has affected millions of people both directly and indirectly. As a viewer, the first emotions evoked are sympathy and empathy. Brandon's story makes the subject matter personal by making the audience realize how alcohol abuse can affect even very young people. Through the use of color, camera perspectives, setting, and emotions, the overall message and effect of the ad is conveyed to the viewer. All these elements combined work together to bring to light the untruth of common assumptions about underage drinking in order to leave a lasting impact on the audience, specifically parents.

Pelersi 4

Work Cited

"Brandon." *Underage Drinking Prevention*. 19 Jan. 2006. Ad Council. Web.
6 Mar. 2008.

▷ IMAGES FOR ANALYSIS AND REFLECTION

In this chapter, you've read ways three undergraduates (Jenna, Kyle, and Michelle) analyzed three different types of visual images: a well-known painting (*Nighthawks*), movie posters (images of Spider-Man), and a televised public service announcement ("Brandon") warning parents that even very young children may be in danger of becoming alcoholics. The next twelve pages present a number of additional images in several different media: photography, magazine layouts, posters, advertisements, video games, and paintings. You can use concepts from this chapter to analyze and respond to these images, either in a class discussion or in a written text.

If you want additional images to analyze, you might consider images you've encountered in your own experience, drawing on the same media (advertisements, video games, and so on) as the images on the following pages. In deciding on an image to analyze, make sure you choose one (or perhaps a pair of images) that you find meaningful and that is rich with the sort of detail you saw in the images Jenna, Kyle, and Michelle analyzed. If you write about a pair of images, consider writing about images that present widely differing views of the same subject (as in the two images representing Uncle Sam on pp. 508 and 509 and the two images of Thanksgiving dinner on p. 515) or that show how a similar attitude exists in widely differing situations (as in posters from *March of the Penguins* and *Arctic Tale*, on p. 511).

Uncle Sam Images
James Montgomery Flagg and anonymous

Here are two images of Uncle Sam, the iconic figure often used to represent the United States. The first of these images appeared on a magazine cover in 1916, the year in which the United States entered World War I, taking the side of England and France, who had been at war with Germany for several years. The World War I era was a time of strong patriotism and confidence in U.S. military might. This image was so widely admired that, according to the Library of Congress, four million copies were printed during World War I, and the image was used in recruiting posters during World War II.

The second image appeared on the Internet after passage of the Patriot Act, a piece of legislation prompted by the terrorist attacks of September 11, 2001. This act increased the ability of law enforcement agencies to search information (telephone records, e-mails, financial records) that previously would have been private unless a court had given a law enforcement agency permission to collect this information. As you compare these two images, consider this question: What are the differences between ways Uncle Sam is depicted in each, especially differences in color and facial expressions? What attitudes are implied in each depiction? Consider ways in which the text within each image relates to the way Uncle Sam is depicted.

Fleeing a Dust Storm
Arthur Rothstein

During the 1930s, prairie states in the central part of the United States (northern Texas, Oklahoma, Kansas, New Mexico, and Colorado) experienced several years of extreme drought, made worse by years of farming that killed off most of the grasses that helped keep moisture in prairie soil. Deprived of this moisture, much of that soil turned to dust, which strong winds turned into an environmental disaster that came to be called the Dust Bowl. Many farmers in the region migrated to the western United States. Others had to remain where they were, surviving the dust storms as best they could. This photograph depicts one Oklahoma farmer, Arthur Coble, walking with his two sons toward the only shelter they had. How does this picture help you understand the plight of the Coble family and others living in the Dust Bowl? As you consider this question, notice details about the shelter and about the people's clothing and posture. Also use whatever you know about farms to consider what is missing from this picture of the Coble farm.

Arctic Tale AND *March of the Penguins*

Several years ago, the cover of *Newsweek* magazine posed this question: "Do animals have feelings?" Since then *Newsweek*'s question has been answered in a variety of sources, notably the films *March of the Penguins* and *Arctic Tale*. The two posters show two different creatures in essentially the same situation, nurturing their young. Before you look closely at the posters, think of what you already know about polar bears and penguins, whether from watching the movies or from other sources. Then especially notice body language, lines, and picture composition as you consider how these two images answer *Newsweek*'s question.

For more on composition, see page 491.

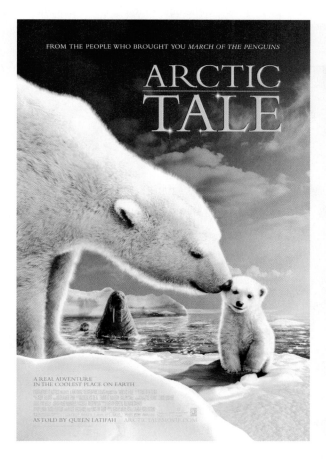

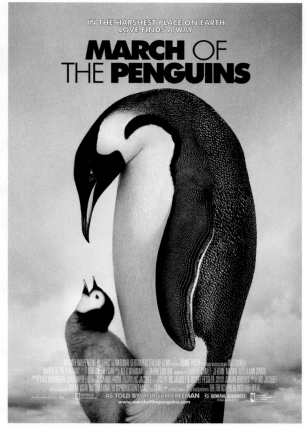

"Generous Nation" Public Service Ad
Ad Council

This ad is part of a campaign, "Generous Nation," designed to provide inspiration and motivation for all Americans to get involved in philanthropy by turning almost givers into givers—people willing to donate their time, their money, or whatever it takes—to help their fellow Americans. The ad makes no reference to specific charities, focusing instead on the image of one person seated on a park bench. Consider several aspects of the picture: the body language and clothing of the figure, the details of the physical setting, the viewing angle, and the details that are not included in the picture. What is the overall effect of this image? What reasons do you see for using this image as a way to encourage people to become involved in philanthropy? Given what you see in the picture, what reasons do you see for including this ad as part of a campaign titled "Generous Nation"? This black and white image was created to appear in newspapers.

New York Times Magazine, The Money Issue
Catherine Gilmore-Barnes and Christoph Niemann

When we think of addiction, we tend to think of alcohol, nicotine, illegal drugs, or perhaps gambling. However, it would seem that many Americans are also addicted to debt. Americans currently owe more than one trillion dollars in credit card debt—and that's in addition to whatever they owe on their houses and cars. Individually, the average American has about nine thousand dollars in credit card debt, which carries an average interest rate of 18 percent. Apparently, this debt is also a habit many people are unwilling or unable to break.

The dangers of this habit are described in a special edition of the *New York Times Magazine,* The Money Issue, which featured this cover. Although excessive borrowing is a personal habit, most of the cover is occupied by a very impersonal image. What reasons do you see for using such an impersonal image? What are the distinctive details of the word *debt*? What details do you notice in the lower portion of the cover? And what attitudes are conveyed by the way this image is composed?

For more about composition, see page 491.

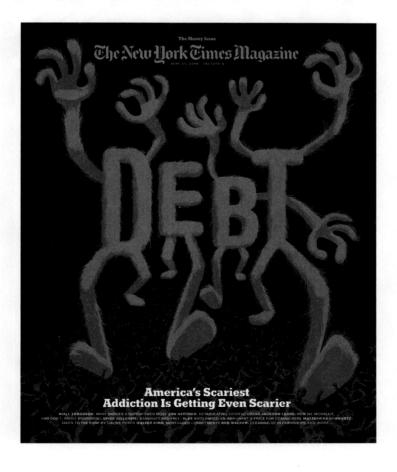

Big Money and Politics: Who Gets Hurt?
Time

This *Time* magazine cover appeared just after Congress had passed a bill that was princi-pally devoted to the funding of public education but that also included substantial tax breaks for wealthy donors to both Democratic and Republican members of Congress. In an article related to this cover ("How the Little Guy Gets Crunched"), *Time* authors Donald L. Barlett and James B. Steele point out that the bill "is typical among the growing litany of examples of how Washington extends favorable treatment to one set of citizens at the expense of another. It's a process that frequently causes serious, sometimes fatal economic harm to unwary individuals and businesses that are in the way." In examining this visual, notice how the composition of the magazine cover reflects Barlett and Steele's attitudes toward their subject matter.

Freedom from Want AND *Thanksgiving*
Norman Rockwell and John Currin

If Uncle Sam is one of the figures most associated with American democracy, Norman Rockwell is one of the painters most associated with idealized images of daily life in America. His painting *Freedom from Want* is one of a series of paintings, created during World War II, depicting the "four freedoms" identified by President Franklin D. Roosevelt in a speech he made just after the bombing of Pearl Harbor. Rockwell's depiction of Thanksgiving dinner differs sharply from that painted in 2003 by the provocative contemporary artist John Currin. Focus on either Currin's or Rockwell's depiction of Thanksgiving dinner, especially noticing people's body language, dress, and facial expression, as well as the objects and settings in which people are located. To help identify significant details in the picture you have chosen, you may find it useful to notice ways in which each picture differs from the other. Once you have carefully examined the painting you chose, respond to these questions: What attitude is the artist expressing toward Thanksgiving dinner? What are the visual details that convey this attitude?

Trail Runner
Four Wheeler

This page appeared in 1996 as part of a spread in *Four Wheeler* magazine, a publication intended for people who like the excitement of driving specially modified four-wheel trucks in extreme off-road conditions, in this case the desert near Moab, Utah. This page begins an article that goes into detail about how the four wheeler depicted was customized to be a high-performance off-road vehicle. What reasons do you see for including this image at the beginning of the article in *Four Wheeler*? How would you predict a reader of *Four Wheeler* might react to this picture? How do you imagine an environmentalist is likely to react to this image? What is there in the central image that might provoke either of these reactions? As you reflect on one or two of these questions, consider the use of color, line, and viewing angle, as well as distinctive features of the car, the setting, and the driver.

For more about considering a viewing angle, see page 491.

A 1994 Toyota 4Runner with 5.29:1s and ARB Air Lockers

By Greg Grasmehr

TRAIL RUNNER

JULY 1996

Muhammad Ali Stands over Fallen Challenger Sonny Liston, 1965
John Rooney

In the 1960s Sonny Liston was one of the most feared heavyweight boxers in the world, having defeated the previous champion, Floyd Patterson, by knocking him out during the first round of their championship fight. In his first fight against Muhammad Ali (then known as Cassius Clay), Liston suffered a technical knockout when he had to withdraw because of a shoulder injury. Prior to the second fight, Ali taunted Liston, calling him, among other things, an "ugly bear," and predicting he would win by a knockout. In this photograph, Ali is standing over Liston (in the dark trunks), who appears to be knocked out. But since no one in the audience had seen a knockout punch, some questioned whether Ali had actually knocked Liston out or whether Liston had taken a dive, perhaps because he owed money to organized crime and had bet against himself. As you look at this photograph, notice the details that indicate Ali's attitude toward Liston and that justify Ali's confidence that he could easily defeat Liston. Especially notice body language and the use of angles and slanted lines.

For help analyzing angles in visuals, see page 491.

Pollution and Progress in China
Yutian, Hebei Province
Peter Parks

For centuries, China's economy has been largely based on agriculture and, more recently, on government-controlled light industry. In recent years, however, China has allowed private industry to grow and encouraged foreign investment. These developments have helped China become the fastest growing economy in the world, one that ranks behind only Japan and the United States. A key source of China's growth has been development of heavy industry, especially the manufacture of automobiles and petrochemicals. This industry is proving to be a mixed blessing; it increases the country's wealth but also produces such terrible pollution that the English newspaper the *Guardian* published an article with this headline: "Dust, Waste, and Dirty Water: The Deadly Price of China's Miracle." Included was this image of cyclists riding through a factory's cloud of pollution. As you examine this photograph, notice visual details—especially composition and the use of color—that give insight into ways economic development appears to be affecting the lives of ordinary Chinese citizens.

For advice on analyzing color, see page 547 in Chapter 9.

Grand Theft Auto IV
Rockstar Games

With the release of *Grand Theft Auto* in 1997, the Scottish company Rockstar North began a series of video games that, in its first decade, sold over seventy million copies. In each game in the series, players are asked to adopt the character of a criminal, usually one with a vague but deeply troubled background, in a big city. For example, one character explains his background this way: "During the war we did some bad things. And bad things happened to us. I was very young. And very angry." Although proud of his abilities, this character acknowledges, "A creature that could do these things doesn't have a soul." How are these characteristics—especially anger and lack of soul—reflected in this picture of one of the characters from *Grand Theft Auto IV*? How does the context in which the picture appears influence your reaction to this character?

9 ▷

Designing Pages and Screens

This chapter provides a quick guide to basic design concepts that will help you create both print and online documents that work for your purposes. The design and visual elements of a text always affect the way the readers interpret the message. If the design is applied appropriately and the visuals are well chosen, they will be helpful in fulfilling your objectives as a writer. However, if the design is inappropriate or the visuals are chosen haphazardly, they may interfere with your ability to reach those objectives.

This chapter is not divided into separate sections about designing print and online documents. The concepts that will help you arrange words and images effectively on a sheet of paper also apply to arranging words and images for Web text. When there are certain strategies or options that work better for Web design, this chapter will point them out. In each of the following sections, you will see annotated models that demonstrate the concepts and provide simple instructions for how to incorporate the various features or elements.

▷ Go to
bedfordstmartins.com/
writingnow for advice and
tutorials on design.

▶ Understanding design principles: basic concepts that provide guidance in planning the appearance of a text

▶ Establishing layout: the arrangement of words and images on a piece of paper or a computer screen

▶ Integrating images: pictorial representations

▶ Creating tables, charts, and graphs: graphical forms for presenting data

▶ Adding color: a visual aspect that draws attention but that should be used with caution and care

▶ Choosing typefaces and fonts: the different shapes and sizes of letters and other characters

Bring any magazine to class. With a small group of classmates, look through the magazines and choose one article or advertisement that has a lot of visuals. See if you can figure out what the creator of that article or ad wanted the visual elements to convey about the subject. What do the visuals say about the author's view of the readers of that particular magazine? See if you can identify differences in the readership of the various magazines on the basis of the visual elements. Hint: You might start with ads for automobiles—these are often quite different depending on readership. ■

▷ UNDERSTANDING DESIGN PRINCIPLES

This section covers five essential principles of design that are important for creating effective documents.

- ▶ Alignment
- ▶ Chunking
- ▶ Contrast
- ▶ Consistency
- ▶ Tension

In addition to annotated models (pp. 523–24), you will find brief definitions of each of the principles and suggestions for how to incorporate them into your texts.

Alignment

Professional document designers typically use grid lines to help them align the elements on a page effectively. You can use the "layout" view's rulers at the top and side of your computer screen to help you align the visual elements in your documents. There are several important points to remember about alignment.

Align similar elements. Generally, all the like elements on a page should be aligned with one another. For example, in a document with several lists, even though the lists might contain different types of information, they should be aligned because they are all lists.

Avoid having too many vertical "lines" in your document. In any document, the reader's mind's eye can draw vertical lines at each indentation, and too many indentations will lead to confusion.

Use of Design Principles in Packaging

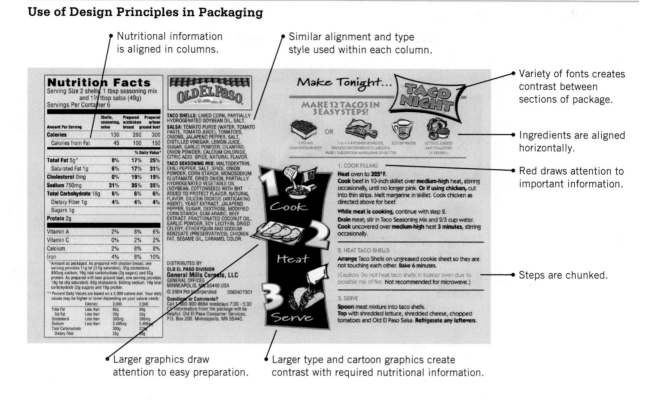

Nutritional information is aligned in columns.

Similar alignment and type style used within each column.

Variety of fonts creates contrast between sections of package.

Ingredients are aligned horizontally.

Red draws attention to important information.

Steps are chunked.

Larger graphics draw attention to easy preparation.

Larger type and cartoon graphics create contrast with required nutritional information.

Do not ignore the alignment of any graphic elements. Photos, tables, charts, and so forth need to be aligned, not just randomly placed. After you have determined why the graphic is necessary and how it supports or clarifies the reader's understanding, then you should visually link the graphic to the words it supports by aligning it (vertically or horizontally) with those words.

Chunking

Chunking, or clustering, means arranging parts of the text that go together—the words, sentences, lists, paragraphs, graphic elements, and so forth that are related to one another and in some way distinct from other parts of the text—and visually separating them from other parts of the text. Chunking makes it easier for readers to see the logical structure of your text and find the information they need. There are three easy ways to create visual chunks.

▶ Insert a heading before each chunk of information.

▶ Use indentation to group related items, such as items in a list.

▶ Use white space (blank lines or vertical space) to separate chunks of information.

Use of Design Principles in a Web Site

Images are aligned vertically.

Repeated image frames page.

Red type indicates which page is being viewed.

Subheadings create chunks of information.

Gray type creates contrast with text.

Text is aligned in a single column.

When designing a Web text, be sure that your chunks of information are fairly short. Although research suggests that readers are becoming more tolerant of pages that go beyond one screen, they still prefer to read short paragraphs and lists.

Contrast

The variations in appearance that are used to create contrast can increase readability and accessibility while adding visual interest to a text. There are many ways to create contrast in a document. The following suggestions describe some of the most common (and easiest) ones.

Use color to add emphasis in either the background or the type (or both). A colored background (or screen) emphasizes the text it anchors. Notice, however, that it is easiest to read black type on a background that is a light color. Both in print and on screen, readers have less eye strain reading dark type on a light background. One of the advantages of online documents is that you can easily try an almost endless variety of color combinations.

For more on typefaces and fonts, see page 551.

Choose dramatically different typefaces. Use distinct fonts (typefaces in differing styles, sizes, or colors) to place more or less emphasis on an element of your text.

Systematically vary the amount of space between, around, or within chunks. Adding white space around an element adds emphasis and creates contrast.

Combine large and small graphics on the same page or in the same document. You may also want to vary the size of the graphics in your text, depending on the purpose they serve.

Consistency

Consistency does not mean that every print page or Web page should be identical, but that every page should be reminiscent of the other pages. That is, the basics of alignment, typeface, color choices, and so forth should be the same or similar on each page.

Format all pages in such a way that they all look like parts of the same document. A consistent, connected look using repetition creates a sense of coherence for readers.

When designing a Web text, you may want to make the home page simpler than subsequent pages "deeper" in the site. A home page is essentially analogous to either a magazine cover or a table of contents. In the first case, the home page tries to attract readers' attention and invite them into the site, just as the cover art on many magazines engages readers with blurbs and headlines describing articles in the issue. In the second case, the home page tries to direct readers to the information they want or need.

Tension

This principle is important for creating a sense of how well various elements on a page get along. Tension also describes the feeling invoked in readers when they see a well-designed print or online document. Do the elements on the page work well together, or do they compete for attention? Do they create a particular mood? Here are some ideas to help you think about how to create tension.

Keep in mind that anything unexpected creates tension. Strong contrasts, unusual colors, unexpected shapes, large amounts of white space, and strange photographs or drawings are just a few of the features that can create tension on a page or screen.

Use graphic elements that incorporate diagonal lines. Examine the photographs or drawings you plan to use and trace or imagine the lines the elements in these images create. Diagonal lines remind us of motion. However, the odd thing about diagonal lines in images is that they can create a frightening kind of tension when they are positioned so that they appear to fall on something or someone, but if they are positioned to lean away from something or someone, they give an entirely different feel to the page. Diagonal lines that lean away give a sense of opening up (think of flowers blooming) or of progress (think of a line graph that goes up and to the right or an airplane taking off).

Incorporate photographs or drawings that face into the page. The amount and kind of tension this creates will depend on the graphic element and its position on the page and the kind of text you are designing. In general terms, photographs of people who face off the page will be seen as distant, unfriendly, unhappy, or separate. Photographs of people who face into the text or toward a facing page (as in a magazine spread) will seem friendly, optimistic, inclusive, and natural.

▷ ESTABLISHING LAYOUT

Layout refers to the options you have in designing the look of a print or online document. Today's word processing and desktop publishing software provide writers with numerous options for creating complex layouts. With so many options, how do you know what is most appropriate? There is no one correct answer because what is appropriate will depend on the audience and purpose of the text you are creating. However, whether you are designing a report, a brochure, or a Web site, you want to generate a consistent layout that will guide your work for the entire document.

In general, most of the elements of layout can be created or modified by using the menus and tools in various software programs. This section presents a number of suggestions for making decisions about these elements, beginning with basic elements such as margins and indentations and moving on to more sophisticated aspects such as pull quotes and text wrapping.

{ Exercise } **Analyzing Layout**

Pick up a popular magazine that has a lot of photographs, such as *People* or *Ebony*. Take a look at where the photographs are positioned on each page, and note especially which way the people face. Can you see any pattern? How do you react to the photos? What causes that reaction? ■

Margins

Most instructors require one-inch margins for academic work, and word processing software usually sets default margins of one inch or a bit more. (You should check your settings and the requirements of your course.) But there are times when other margins are used to meet specific purposes.

Identify the reason for changing the margins. Are you trying to cram a lot of information onto one or two pages? (This may make the page too busy and

Layout Elements in a Student Essay

Consistent margins are used on all sides.

Text wraps around photograph and caption.

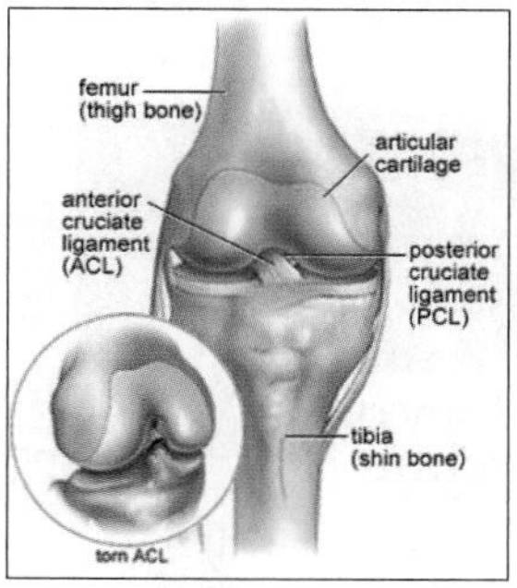

Text is double spaced.

Bold heading adds emphasis.

Heading appears in the form of a question.

femur
(thigh bone)

articular
cartilage

anterior
cruciate
ligament
(ACL)

posterior
cruciate
ligament
(PCL)

tibia
(shin bone)

torn ACL

Fig. 2. Diagram of the ACL (What Is the ACL?).

especially among high school and college players. As the number of women competing in sports continues to increase, understanding the causes of this common injury will enable us to help these athletes reduce their risk.

What Is the ACL?

The anterior cruciate ligament, ACL for short, is a ligament in the knee to which much of the stress of physical activity is transmitted. The knee depends so much on the ACL that it is one of the most vulnerable parts of the human body. When people run or walk, the knee bears the entire weight of the body, continually flexing and absorbing the shock of every step. Central to all this activity and stress is the ACL, which runs through the knee to form a cross connecting the thigh bone (femur) with the shin bone (tibia) (Wilkinson 68). (See Fig. 2.) The ACL keeps the femur aligned with the tibia when the knee is bent and prevents the tibia from sliding forward too much (Hawaleshka). It also stabilizes the knee while an athlete is running and changing directions. When an ACL tear occurs, the knee gives out and becomes unstable. This instability does not go away until the injury is treated through surgery and rehabilitation. Even after all this, athletes with torn ACLs may have problems with recurrent instability, further joint damage, and early arthritis.

3

When Are ACL Injuries Most Common?

ACL injuries can happen at almost any time, but the majority of ACL injuries are non-contact, resulting from "planting" on one foot or making lateral movements such as changing direction suddenly. Other movements, such as straight-knee landings and one-step stopping

4

Text is left justified.

First line of each paragraph is indented five spaces.

Blank line used above heading.

See page 211 to review the layout of Margaret Tomeo's essay.

unreadable.) Are you trying to accommodate letterhead, graphics, or other formatting needs? Are you trying to meet a page requirement for an assignment by increasing the margins? (Most instructors will not approve.)

Decide how much white space is appropriate. Including appropriate amounts of white space around the visual and textual elements of the document can make the material stand out and attract attention. Conversely too much white space could dwarf the text and make it seem insignificant.

For example, when producing a résumé, you might use smaller margins at the top or bottom to give yourself more room (so you can keep the résumé to one page). When producing a document that will be bound or hole-punched, you should make the left margin wider to accommodate the binding.

For an example of a student essay following MLA style for margins, see Chapter 13.

Layout Elements in a Magazine Article

Magazine uses multiple columns.

Key facts summarized in bar graphs.

See pages 176–180 for the full text of this article.

Color and photographs draw attention to important information.

Visual elements aligned in wide column.

Bulleted list used.

Important statistics presented in large font.

{ For Collaboration }   Considering Paper

With several of your classmates, make a list of all the situations you can think of where the paper used—for a school project, flyer, mailing, newspaper, or magazine—was not a standard size. How did the audience, circumstances, or purposes justify an atypical paper size? ■

Indentation

There are three primary instances where you need to be concerned about indentation: at the beginning of paragraphs, at headings, and in lists. There are no hard-and-fast rules about this, but the following discussion offers guidelines that can help you decide how much to indent.

Layout Elements in a Web Page

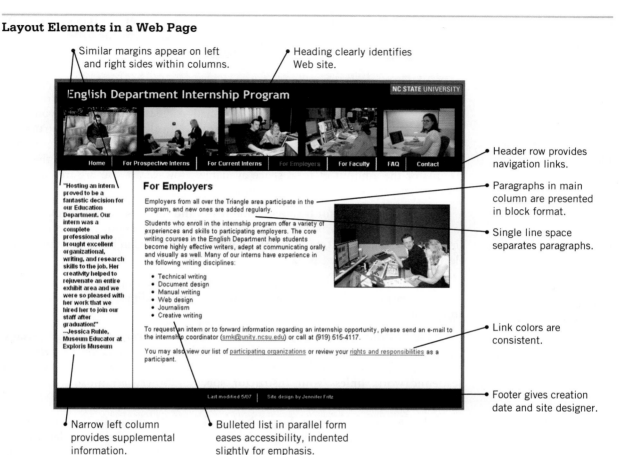

Similar margins appear on left and right sides within columns.

Heading clearly identifies Web site.

Header row provides navigation links.

Paragraphs in main column are presented in block format.

Single line space separates paragraphs.

Link colors are consistent.

Footer gives creation date and site designer.

Narrow left column provides supplemental information.

Bulleted list in parallel form eases accessibility, indented slightly for emphasis.

Indent the first line of every paragraph. Unless you are writing a block-style document, the length of the indentation should be three to five character spaces. If your instructor requires MLA or APA documentation style, the standard indentation is five spaces or one-half inch.

Do not indent each paragraph if you are writing a block-style document. Most business letters and memos, and many electronic documents, use block-style indentation. Use an extra line space (extra blank space between the lines) to indicate that a new paragraph is starting. Because of the double space between paragraphs, block-style documents are usually single spaced.

Plan standard indentations for all other elements. Headings, lists, graphs, charts, tables, and bibliographic entries all should have consistent indentation. Think of the entire document and make sure that you do not have too many different indentations (see the section on alignment on p. 522).

See Chapter 13 for more about formatting works cited lists and reference lists.

Use hanging indents when you create a works cited or references list. Type the first line at the left margin and indent any additional lines one half-inch.

Spacing

Spacing refers to the amount of space between lines of typed words. The most common spacing options are single, one and one-half, and double. The choice you make for spacing will probably be determined by some outside source—the instructions from a teacher or supervisor, the conventions of a document type (for instance, MLA-style and APA-style research essays should be double spaced), or the constraints of the amount of total space available. However, if you are free to make choices, here are some general guidelines.

Use single spacing for business documents and for most online texts. Letters, memos, and other short (one- or two-page) business documents are generally single spaced. Add an extra blank space between paragraphs in block-style print and electronic documents (see p. 529).

Use one and one-half spacing for longer documents. In particular, use one and one-half spacing for texts with minimal interruption (headings, charts, photographs, and so forth) of word-heavy passages.

Reserve double spacing for drafts, including final drafts of academic essays. Double spacing is commonly used for draft documents, where you or a reviewer may need room to write comments or revision ideas. Double-space your essays for academic work, unless your instructor specifies otherwise; most style guides require it.

Add more space between lines when working with especially large type sizes. Many software applications allow you to set a specific amount of space (called *leading*) between lines of text. Doing a search using "leading" as your search term should take you to the correct information in your software's Help system.

Page Numbers

Page numbers can typically be added to a document in one of three ways: through the creation of a header or footer, by using the software Insert menu, or by clicking on a page number icon. Your instructor or course will likely have specific formatting requirements for page numbers. For essays written in either MLA or APA style, put the page number in the upper right-hand corner, one inch from the right edge and one-half inch from the top edge, as part of the header. (See Chapter 13 for a sample MLA student essay.) If you have flexibility in numbering, the following advice will help you choose an appropriate style.

Always include page numbers on printed documents. This is a good habit to develop; you will never be wrong to include them. Page numbers are rarely used in Web texts, however.

Choose the style of your page numbers. The page number can be as simple as the numeral itself (most common), can have the abbreviation "p." in front of the numeral, or can be surrounded by dashes (- 3 -). The version with dashes is most commonly used in centered page numbers.

Choose the position of your page numbers. Depending on the purpose for your document, you might place page numbers in the following positions.

- Centered at the top or bottom of the page
- The upper or lower right-hand corner
- In the upper or lower outside corner (if the pages of the document will be printed front and back)

Be consistent about page number position throughout your document. If you are unsure where to put the page number, check with the person who will review your document (your instructor or supervisor).

Headings

Headings are guideposts that help readers find the information they want or need in documents as short as a brochure and as long as an encyclopedia. Headings highlight the organization of your text and are particularly important in Web sites, where readers tend to look at headings as they surf. There are several things to consider when creating headings.

Look for concise, informative wording for headings. Headings should be concise, but should capture the core of what is covered in a section. Try to create headings that describe the section (for examples, look at the headings in this chapter). Some assignments and courses will require specific headings such as *Abstract* or *Conclusion*; check with your instructor or look at other documents created for the discipline.

Make your headings grammatically parallel whenever possible. For example, if you use nouns or noun phrases, use all nouns or noun phrases consistently throughout the document. If you use questions or complete sentences, make sure that all your headings are either questions or complete sentences.

Choose an appropriate typeface. Sans serif typefaces (see p. 552) are often used for headings in print documents because they attract attention.

Determine where to position the heading, and position each level consistently. There are a lot of options for positioning headings, but the most common position for your first heading (the title) is centered. Secondary headings can appear in four positions.

- Flush left
- Indented the same amount as your paragraph indentation
- Outdented (hanging out into the margin)
- Run-in (continuous with the text)

In essays using APA style, headings should be centered (with all major words capitalized). Headings are not required in MLA-style essays; check to see whether your instructor has preferences for their use.

Choosing the Number of Levels for Your Headings

The documentation style you are using may determine the number of levels of headings that you have. MLA-style documentation, commonly required in English and many other humanities courses, does not advocate headings within a paper. On the other hand, APA style, used in many social science classes, allows five levels of headings. When in doubt, consult your instructor.

One easy way to think of the levels is to compare them to the parts of an outline. Here is an excerpt from a formal outline.

How I Spent My Summer Vacation

  I. July
     A. Summer school
        1. Algebra
           a. Homework
           b. Tests
        2. Geography
           a. Maps
           b. Movies
  II. August
     A. Family trip (with appropriate subheadings)
     B. Swimming (with appropriate subheadings)

In this example, the items with uppercase Roman numerals would be level 1 headings, and the uppercase letters would be level 2 headings. If you were to write a lengthy, detailed report, you might add a third level of headings for the items with Arabic numerals (1 and 2 in this example). It is unlikely that you would go into enough detail for a fourth level of headings; if you did, the items identified with lowercase letters would form those headings.

Notice that in this outline, each level includes two items. When you decide to add a level of headings, make sure to have at least two items at that level. If you can think of only one heading for a particular level, there is not enough complexity in your topic to divide it into subtopics.

Each level should look distinctive enough that readers get a sense of where they are in the hierarchy of your document. The most common ways to create these distinctions are through type size and placement, but you can also use bold, underlining, or italics to make headings distinct from one another.

{ Exercise } **Considering Heading Style**

Outdented headings hang over into the left margin. You will often see out-dented headings in magazine articles and textbooks. Run-in headings are on the same line as the text that they introduce. Look at some of the headings in this book and explain why a particular type of heading was used in each instance. ■

Make sure the heading is closer to the text that follows it than to the text that precedes it. A simple way to make sure the heading is positioned appropriately is to double-space before a heading and single-space after it.

Decide how many levels to use. For the most part, the kinds of documents you write in school will not need more than two levels of headings beyond the title—one level for major headings and one level for subheadings. See the box on page 532 for more information about levels.

Justification

Justification is a term that describes how a document is aligned on its left and right edges. Your software program gives several options. You can create text that is left, right, fully, or center justified.

Use left-justified text for most of your writing projects. In left-justified text, all the words line up on the left side of the page, but the right side is "ragged."

Reserve right-justified text for special uses such as posters, flyers, and brochures. Right-justified text is the opposite of left-justified text: All the words line up on the right side, but the left side is ragged. Right-justified text is not used often because it is hard to read. You will most often see it in advertising, in magazine titles, and on the Web.

Avoid using fully justified text. Fully justified text has the words lined up evenly on both margins. Most books are fully justified (as is most of the text in this book), as are many documents written in columns, such as newspapers, magazines, and newsletters. The danger in fully justified text is that distracting rivers of white space often appear between the words or sometimes there are big gaps in lines of text—especially if the document contains a significant number of lengthy words or line length is short.

{ Exercise } **Considering Justification**

Collect some examples of left-, right-, fully, and center-justified texts. See if you can figure out why each text was printed with that type of justification. Do you agree with the author's or designer's decision? Why or why not? ■

Reserve center-justified text for very short texts. Titles, headings, and cover pages, as well as documents such as formal invitations, advertisements, and posters, are all good candidates for center-justified text.

Lists

Of the several types of lists that you will often see in documents, numbered lists and bulleted lists are two of the most common. Lists are very useful for bringing readers' attention to a series of steps or items. Lists are also used a great deal in Web texts because they are easier to scan than paragraphs. In the slides, posters, or other visual aids you create for oral presentations, they help the audience focus on key points.

For more about visual elements for oral presentations, see Chapter 18.

Use bulleted lists as a clear, concise way to present information that is not necessarily sequential but is related. Lists are often preferable to paragraphs in some texts because the items in a list are relatively brief and easy for the reader to scan.

For most bulleted lists, use your software's default symbol for the bullets. However, there are situations when a character other than a round bullet can be a useful cue for your readers. For example, you might use the following symbols.

- A checkmark (✔) for items in a checklist
- An empty box (□) that readers could check off themselves
- A pointing hand (☞) or arrow (→) to make a set of instructions more obvious

Reserve numbered lists for items where the order is critical. For example, you would want to use numbered lists where the sequence is important, as when writing for the following situations.

- The steps in a set of instructions
- A key that matches labels to images (such as a parts diagram or a campus map)
- A list of maps or figures for a book or some other lengthy document

Align lists to indent the same amount as the paragraph indent. You may also align the list with the left margin.

Be consistent with the format for wrapping text in lists.

- When the text hangs under the bullet (as in this example), the words in subsequent lines of the item line up with the bullet.

For information about creating and formatting lists of works cited or references, see Chapter 13.

- When the text hangs under the previous line of text (as in this example), the first words of each line in the item line up under one another. Aligning the text this way makes the bullet symbol more obvious and separates each item more distinctly.

{ For Collaboration } **Analyzing Lists**

Find a document that has some type of bulleted list and bring it to class. Try to find a list that uses a symbol other than the standard bullet. With two or three of your classmates, compare the symbols that are used to identify the items in the lists and answer the following questions.

- How many different symbols did you find?
- Do you think the symbols are appropriate for the audience and purpose of the document? What makes each symbol appropriate or inappropriate?
- Would a numbered list have been more appropriate? Why or why not?
- Does everyone in the group know how to create a bulleted list using each of those symbols? If not, ask the ones who do to share their knowledge with the rest of the group.
- If the text for any of the items runs to a second line, how is that text aligned? What effect does this alignment achieve? ■

Line Length

When lines of type are too long or too short, readers have trouble reading. Line length refers not only to the actual measured length of a line of type but also to the number of characters (letters, numbers, punctuation marks, symbols) and blank spaces that appear on that line. Thinking of line length in terms of numbers of characters is useful because different-sized fonts will allow for different numbers of characters in the same amount of physical space. For example, a line length that works well for a 12-point typeface does not work as well for a font that is larger or smaller.

For more about typefaces and fonts, see page 551.

Create lines that are between 40 and 70 characters long for printed texts. Count the spaces between the words, too. Use your software program's Word Count feature to count the spaces and characters for you.

Create lines that are between 40 and 55 characters long for online documents. Shorter line length on screen will make your column of text easier to read.

Headers and Footers

Headers (sometimes called running heads) and footers are small spaces at the top and bottom of a page in a printed document that may contain the page number (see p. 530), the title or author of the document, and/or the date the document was produced. The primary function of headers and footers is to remind readers where they are in a document or to give them reference points for returning to information.

Insert headers or footers early in the production of your document. In some software programs, the space for the header and footer is reserved regardless of whether you choose to enter anything into that space. In other programs, adding a header or footer decreases the amount of space available on the page.

- In MLA style, create headers on each page that include your last name and the page number.
- In APA style, create headers on each page that include a shortened title and the page number.

Outside of academic work, omit the header or footer on the first page. Most software programs make it easy to set "first page different" or "omit header/footer this/first page."

In online documents, use headers and footers consistently. Headers typically appear in the form of a navigation bar. Because the header appears the same on all screens in an online document, it can serve to unify all the Web pages in your site visually. When used as a navigation bar, the header also enables readers to find different parts of the site easily. Unlike print documents, where readers typically look at the first page before moving into subsequent pages, online documents can be entered at any point. A unifying header can enable readers to find the home page and other important segments of the document.

Online footers also may be used to provide navigation (for example, providing links to Home) and to provide information about the editor or sponsor of the page, date of publication, and so on.

To see an example of a Web site with a header and footer, see page 529.

For an example of a student essay following MLA style for headers, see Chapter 13.

Columns

With your word processor you can create many of the types of columns you see in newspapers, magazines, newsletters, brochures, Web sites, and tables. Your software program likely offers you the opportunity to create text in one of two types of columns, most commonly called newspaper and parallel columns.

Use newspaper columns for any print document that mimics a newspaper, newsletter, or magazine article. In newspaper columns (see image on p. 712 in Chapter 16), text begins at the top of the first column and continues to the end of the page, then moves to the top of the second column on that same page. These columns should divide the available space on the page into columns of equal width. Be careful not to crowd too many onto the page. The more columns you have, the shorter each line of text will be, possibly making the text harder to read (see the discussion of line length on p. 535). Do not use newspaper columns in Web texts as they increase the chance that your reader will need to scroll up and down the page.

Use parallel columns to present information that is read across the page. Parallel columns are similar to tables or charts, where the information on the left has a relationship to the information on the right. Use parallel columns in Web texts, especially in directories or other information lists. The information that appears in each column should help you determine the width of the columns.

You may need to use your software's Table feature to create parallel columns. If so, simply create a table with the number of columns you want. To make it look like columns, you then delete the lines (or borders) that separate the cells of the table. Making borderless tables is also a way to create columns in Web texts.

Pull Quotes and Sidebars

Although pull quotes and sidebars are rarely used in academic papers, for this course you may want to break up dense passages of text by positioning some information outside the standard paragraph structure.

Pull quotes are short segments from the main text—usually no more than a sentence or two—that are particularly important or intriguing. These segments are highlighted as a way of engaging the readers' attention. You have seen pull quotes (sometimes referred to as callouts) in many of the readings in this book (for example, see "Seeing Is Not Believing" on p. 182). There are two standard ways to present a pull quote.

Use a large type size. Use the same typeface as the body text or a different typeface and then separate it from the rest of the text with a solid line above and below it.

Use your word processing program to create pull quotes. Create a text box and then type the quote inside the box, again using a larger type size than the body text. You may put a border around the text box or simply wrap the text around it.

Incorporate sidebars to set off nonessential information. Sidebars contain nonessential information that appears peripherally to the main text. There are several sidebars, for example, in the complete version of "The Record Industry's Slow Fade," which begins on page 176.

Integrate paragraphs, bulleted lists, images, or other graphics into your sidebar.

Position your sidebar effectively and separate it from the main text. You can do this with a single line, put it inside a text box, or just wrap the text around it.

Text Wrapping

One way to incorporate visuals and other elements in your document is to format the text so that it wraps around or appears close to the visual element—a photograph, a drawing, a pull quote, or even another article. Many software programs allow you to wrap text easily. Just make sure that wrapping the text does not result in a column that is too narrow (a line length that is too short) or that makes it too hard for the reader to follow your train of thought.

When you wrap text around a visual, your software will give you options about how you want the text to be formatted around the visual.

▶ **Square** means that a straight margin will form between the text and the image. Most wrapped text is set this way.

▶ **In line** means that the image is between the lines of the text.

▶ **Tight** means that the words flow around the shape of the image.

▶ **In front** means that the words are superimposed on the image.

▶ **In back** means that the image covers some of the words. This is rarely used because it obliterates the words and thus disrupts the meaning.

Links

Links are highlighted words and phrases, buttons, tabs, or other visual cues that connect elements in an online document and improve its accessibility. Links enable readers to make choices about what they read and the order in which they read the pieces of a text. You should plan links carefully to provide obvious cues to readers. Internal links connect readers to other parts of the same site. External links connect readers to pages in other sites.

Make sure that readers can get back to their prior position easily. Although readers may use the Back button to return to previous pages, thoughtful Web-page designers also provide return links—buttons that say "Return to home" or "Return to top." With external links, readers will have to rely on the Back button to return to the original site unless you create links that automatically open in a new window.

Create text links that are concise but meaningful. You can use a single word or a simple phrase, but do not use a lengthy sentence for a link. Pick out a key word or phrase in the sentence to use as the link to decrease the interference with reading for those readers who choose not to follow each link.

You can also create links by using icons, buttons, or other images. If you use images, consider adding captions so that readers (or the screen readers used by visually impaired readers) know what the image will link them to.

▷ INTEGRATING IMAGES

There are times when words alone cannot describe an object with sufficient clarity or present an object in its most appealing or useful light. Images—or pictorial representations—are the photographs, drawings, cartoons, and schematic drawings that show what something is actually like.

Not so long ago, it was fairly difficult to include photographs or drawings in papers and reports. Writers could cut them out and paste them onto their pages and then photocopy the result, or they could hire a graphic artist or a printer to incorporate visuals in their work. Today, scanners, computer drawing programs, and vast libraries of clip art (drawings and other images that can be "clipped"—cut and pasted—for free or for a fee) enable anyone to include a tremendous variety of images. However, just because you can do it doesn't mean you should; and just because you can do it doesn't mean you can do it right.

As you make your plans to include an image (photo, drawing, diagram, map, or clip art) in your print or online document, review the suggestions below that will help you integrate images appropriately. These suggestions fall into four general categories.

- ▶ Choosing images
- ▶ Preparing images
- ▶ Positioning images
- ▶ Using images ethically

Web Site with Integrated Images

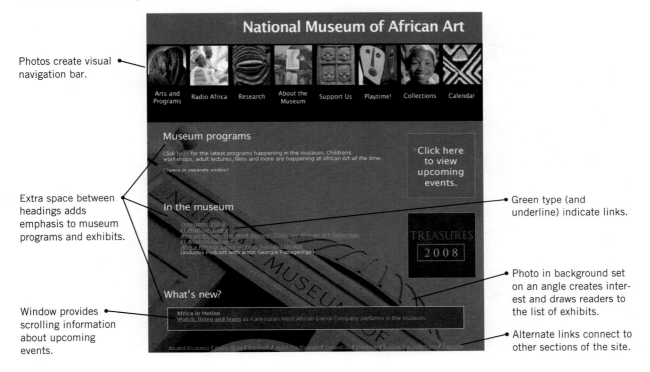

Photos create visual navigation bar.

Extra space between headings adds emphasis to museum programs and exhibits.

Window provides scrolling information about upcoming events.

Green type (and underline) indicate links.

Photo in background set on an angle creates interest and draws readers to the list of exhibits.

Alternate links connect to other sections of the site.

Choosing Images

You have a lot of choices when it comes to images, but you need to make some decisions before you begin to create or search for those images.

Decide what type of image you need. Photographs add realism and personality; drawings and diagrams can simplify complex artifacts or processes; maps can add perspective and precision.

Search for images (including clip art) on the Internet through design sites and at photo archives. The term *clip art* refers to copyright-free or royalty-free drawings and photographs that are widely available online or integrated in many software programs. Note, however, that if you choose images that are copyrighted, you will need to contact the author or publisher of the site to request permission to reuse the images in any text that will be posted online.

Make sure the image has a clear purpose. For example, you can use images to engage the reader, make information more accessible, or contribute to the voice you are trying to create. Use images that have relevance to your subject.

Magazine Article with Integrated Images

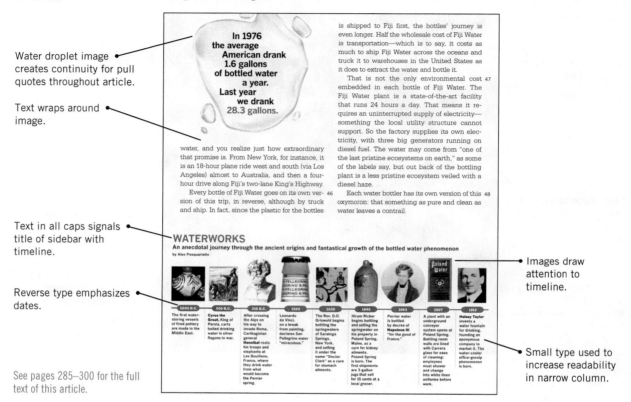

Water droplet image creates continuity for pull quotes throughout article.

Text wraps around image.

Text in all caps signals title of sidebar with timeline.

Reverse type emphasizes dates.

See pages 285–300 for the full text of this article.

Images draw attention to timeline.

Small type used to increase readability in narrow column.

When choosing graphics of any kind for online use, consider the length of time it will take for a reader to load the graphic. Large and complex graphics may be visually appealing, but they may also discourage readers from looking at your site. Avoid large graphics, especially at the top of a Web page, when designing online documents. To be on the safe side, limit yourself so that any given page of your site—including images—is no more than 50 kilobytes total.

Preparing Images

Once you have chosen your image or images, you need to make further decisions about how they will look on your page or screen. Computer programs that are fairly easy to use allow you to modify images, but you need to be sure that you don't distort the image or the *meaning* of the image. The section below on using images ethically (pp. 542–43) provides guidelines to help you.

Use your word processing program to import and paste images into your texts. If you work on a PC, you can copy and paste the image directly into your text by highlighting the image you find online, right-clicking on it, selecting Copy, positioning your cursor in your document, and right-clicking again to select Paste. You can also save a picture as an image file by right-clicking on the image and selecting Save Picture As. To place the image in your text in Microsoft Word, for example, position your cursor in the correct place in the document and use the Insert menu, choosing Picture and selecting From File.

If you work on a Mac, you can insert a saved image by using the Insert menu, or you can drag the online image from your Web browser to the location in your text where you want to add it.

Use software tools such as the freeware program PrintKey or other programs such as Pearl Crescent and Snagit to create screen shots and manipulate images that you download. Image editing programs such as Microsoft Paint or Adobe Photoshop allow users to crop, flip, resize, and edit details in images.

Check sites such as Flickr for images that are free for reuse. Flickr includes many images that have been posted under a Creative Commons license. Images with the Creative Commons tag are offered by photographers as "free for certain uses" as long as you follow the listed terms and give appropriate credit.

Use a scanner to capture images from print sources. Many campus computer labs offer access to scanners.

Decide whether the image should be presented in color or black and white. A color image may not print or photocopy well in black and white. You need to be sure that the image is clear and will reproduce well in the required format.

Resize the image if necessary. The image should be big enough for the reader to see and understand it clearly. Be sure you don't inadvertently distort the shape of the drawing as you resize it. In most applications, when you click on an image you can move the mouse to different positions on the image to get symbols that indicate alterations to the figure. As you move the mouse to a corner, you will see a box with arrows in the upper left and lower right corners. As you move the mouse diagonally in line with those arrows, you make the image larger or smaller without any distortion.

Decide whether the image would be more effective if it were cropped. What happens to the meaning of the image if you delete some of the information? How does that affect the message that the image conveys? (See pp. 542–43 for more on editing images ethically.)

Add an appropriate caption or label. In nonacademic texts, add a caption unless a visual or image is self-explanatory or your reference to the image in the text explains it thoroughly.

When using MLA style, include a caption and position the image as close as you can to the reference in your text. Number figures consecutively within the document. Under the image, include the label "Fig." (for Figure) and the number for the image, followed by a description and source information in a caption. The label and caption should appear directly below the image.

When using APA style, include identifying numbers and captions for any figures. Number figures consecutively within the document. Spell out the word "Figure" in your reference to the figure within the text and in the label for the visual. Include source information in the caption. Place the number, title, and caption below the image, flush left.

Be sure to include labels for diagrams and keys for maps. Cite source information in the label or key in the same way you would for other visuals.

Add a reference to the image within the text in an academic document. You must mention any image you include within an academic text to make clear the connection between the image and the text. Integrating the reference to a visual carefully allows you to emphasize the point your image is making or supporting in your text.

Positioning Images

The placement of your images within your text can make a big difference to the effectiveness of those images. Although it is impossible to give you precise directions about where to place images, keep the following concepts in mind and experiment with different positions. Your software should allow you to move images easily.

Determine the appropriate placement for the image on the page or screen. Typically, the image should be near the text that refers to it or near the text that it supports.

Follow basic design principles when integrating images. Refer to the sections on alignment (p. 522), tension (p. 525), and text wrapping (p. 537) as you plan the position of your images.

Using Images Ethically

Though it is easy to copy images into your work, doing so ethically, giving credit where appropriate, builds your credibility with readers. As you incorporate images into your texts, make sure that you follow these guidelines.

Use images ethically. Do not distort an important fact or truth when you modify an image. For example, imagine you are creating a brochure for a summer recreation program, and you have a series of photographs of participants from prior years. However, the photographs all show white teenagers, and you need to show that teenagers of all races are welcome in this program. Adding color to the skin tones or pasting in photos of teenagers of color who had not participated would be distorting the truth and would therefore be unethical. One solution to this problem would be to take some new photos that show the actual diversity of the program participants. Or, if you are making the brochure after the program has ended, you might choose to use the photos you have, cropping them in interesting ways to emphasize the activities over the participants.

Give credit to the originator of the graphic. Just as you would cite the source for quotes, paraphrases, and summarized ideas, you need to cite the source for any visual images used in your text. Include this information in the caption. In some nonacademic texts, the source information may be the only caption. If you generated the image yourself—for example, a photograph you shot yourself—be sure to include this information.

Make sure you have obtained permission to use the image. If the image was created by someone else, make sure that it is legal to copy it before you use it. Many Web sites provide free artwork, but others will tell you that the material is not to be copied. If you are using someone else's graphic in a text that will be published—in print or online—you must get written permission from the owner of that graphic. Many people do not realize that material published on the Internet is protected by the same copyright laws that protect material published on paper. If you are using the graphic for an assignment that will not be posted on the Web, you may be permitted to use it under the "fair use" exception, which allows use of material for some educational purposes.

For an example of a student essay that includes captions in MLA style, see Chapter 13.

For advice on citing photographs and other images, see Chapter 13.

▷ CREATING TABLES, CHARTS, AND GRAPHS

Computers have made the creation of tables, charts, and graphs so easy that you will most likely be expected to use them in many situations throughout your academic and professional careers. There are many instances when the information that you need to convey to readers is too complex to be written in paragraph form or even in lists. You need to determine which graphic form will answer the kinds of questions readers will have about your topic. This section describes several of the most common types of graphic representations of information.

Tables

Tables are used to make large amounts of information accessible to readers. They also demonstrate relationships among the individual pieces of information, usually by placing the information in categories described by the columns and rows of the tables.

Most word processing software makes it easy to create tables, typically providing several different ways to do it. You can use menus—often there is a "Table" menu that will allow you to either draw or insert a table—or icons on one of the toolbars to create a table. While there are numerous options for the numbers of columns and rows, borders, shading, internal margins, and other formatting attributes, a basic table that is a simple, easy-to-read grid will be sufficient for most situations. There are only a few decisions that have to be made as you create a table.

Choosing Effective Tables, Charts, and Graphs

Text tables organize complex textual information in an accessible format.

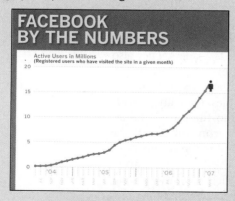

Is It a Cold or the Flu?

Symptoms	Cold	Flu
Fever	Rare	Usual; high (100°F to 102°F; occasionally higher, especially in young children); lasts 3 to 4 days
Headache	Rare	Common
General Aches, Pains	Slight	Usual; often severe

Data tables organize complex numerical information in an accessible format.

Age	Natural bedtime*	Hours of sleep: recommended	Hours of sleep: actual†
0–1 yrs.	7–8 p.m.	14–15 hrs.**	12.8 all days**
1–2	7–8	12–14**	11.8**
3–6	7–8	11–13**	10.3**
7–11	8–9	10–11	9.4
12–17	10:30–11:30	8.5–9.5	7.6 weekdays 8.9 weekends
18–54	10–12	7–8.5	6.8 weekdays 7.4 weekends
55–84	8–10	7–8.5	6.9 weekdays 7.5 weekends

*REFERS TO BEDTIME IN THE NATURAL SLEEP-WAKE CYCLE. ACTUAL BEDTIMES WILL VARY.
†BASED ON NATL. SLEEP FOUNDATION (NSF) SURVEYS, 2003–2006. **INCLUDES DAY AND
NIGHTTIME SLEEP. SOURCES: NSF; DR. JUDITH OWENS, HASBRO CHILDREN'S HOSPITAL.

Pie charts provide a quick picture of relationships.

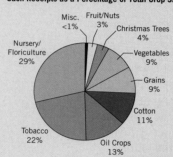

Cash Receipts as a Percentage of Total Crop Sales—2004

Misc. <1%
Fruit/Nuts 3%
Christmas Trees 4%
Nursery/Floriculture 29%
Vegetables 9%
Grains 9%
Cotton 11%
Tobacco 22%
Oil Crops 13%

Bar graphs compare numerical data.

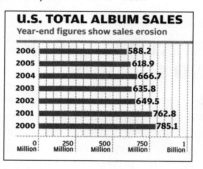

U.S. TOTAL ALBUM SALES
Year-end figures show sales erosion

Year	Sales
2006	588.2
2005	618.9
2004	666.7
2003	635.8
2002	649.5
2001	762.8
2000	785.1

0 Million — 250 Million — 500 Million — 750 Million — 1 Billion

Line graphs represent change over time.

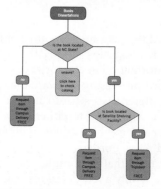

FACEBOOK BY THE NUMBERS

Active Users in Millions
(Registered users who have visited the site in a given month)

'04   '05   '06   '07

Flow charts show steps in a process.

How to Obtain Books or Dissertations from the Library

Books Dissertations

Is the book located at NC State?

no

unsure? click here to check catalog

yes

Request item through Campus Delivery FREE

Is book located at Satellite Shelving Facility?

no

yes

Request item through Campus Delivery FREE

Request item through Tripsaver FREE

Organizational charts represent personnel relationships.

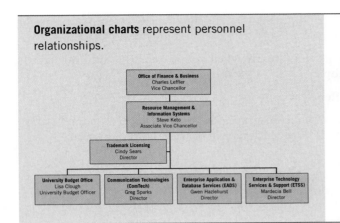

Maps represent geographical locations.

Determine the number of columns you need. It is easy to change the number of rows as you work on the table, but it is best to plan the number of columns ahead of time.

Determine the width of each column. Your software will automatically make all columns the same width, but you are likely to want to revise the width to meet the needs of the content of each column. Most software will allow you to resize columns by using the mouse to select the line between two columns and moving it left or right. Be aware that it will automatically resize the other columns as you do this, so start with the column on the right side of the page and work to the left.

Choose headings for the top row of the table. Headings should be concise, but informative. If the table will continue beyond the first page, you can set the heading to repeat at the top of each new page. You may want to format your table so that the text in the heading row is emphasized, perhaps by using bold type, a different size type, or a different typeface.

Text tables present sentences or paragraphs in parallel rows and columns. Because Western readers read from left to right, tables pull the reader across the column to see the related information.

Data tables present information, usually in columns, that is complex and detailed. Data tables can present numerical information, textual information, or a combination of data represented in words and numbers.

Charts and Graphs

There are many kinds of charts and graphs, and your computer probably has software to help you create a lot of them. Like tables, charts and graphs are visual tools that enable you to present a great deal of information in a succinct way. There are several basic rules that apply to all types of charts and graphs.

Keep it simple. Charts and graphs that are cluttered with too many lines or too many labels are hard to read and may confuse the audience.

Use colors and symbols consistently when you are creating multiple charts and graphs on the same topic.

Choose colors that offer clear contrast.

Choose the right type of chart or graph for your purpose. The information in this chapter will help you decide which type of chart or graph you need.

{ For Collaboration }   **Creating Tables, Charts, and Graphs**

Assume that you work for a local nonprofit organization with the following income and expenses for 2008:

Income	Expenses
Government grants: $375,000	Program services: $741,935
Fees: $273,467	Administrative costs: $88,500
Contributions: $114,763	Miscellaneous: $5,230
Special events: $58,450	
Product sales: $12,468	
Total income: $834,148	Total expenses: $835,665

As directors of the organization, you are responsible for bringing in more money and must present the past year's financial information to two groups of people, as described in the following scenarios.

- Within the community is a core group of consistent contributors who give the same amount each year, even though the cost of running the organization continues to go up. You must convince these contributors to give additional funds during your presentation at the annual fundraising banquet. You need to create graphic representations of financial data that will convince the contributors of the need for additional funds and that will reassure them that the money they gave in the past has been spent wisely.

- Your organization is eligible to apply for a new grant from a federal agency. You have to write a proposal explaining why your organization needs the money and demonstrating that it is fiscally responsible. There is a strict page limitation, so you must present financial information concisely but in enough detail to make a strong case.

Working with one or two classmates, sketch out the visuals (by hand or using a computer) that you would create for the presentation and the proposal. Be prepared to justify your choice of visuals based on the audience and your purposes for each situation. ■

Use pie charts to give a quick picture of how some "pie," or whole, is divided. This type of chart is usually used when there are a relatively small number of "pieces" and the important thing is the relationship among those pieces rather than their actual size. Your software program should have several design options for creating labels, using color, and so on for each type of chart.

For examples of charts and graphs, see pages 544–45.

Use bar graphs to show the relationship among quantities. Bar graphs usually present slightly more precise information than pie charts (and less precise information than tables). You will need to label both axes on your bar graph, and you may also need to create a key. Note that the labels on the graph axes indicate the primary information (criteria being measured, such as time, quantity, and so forth); the labels in the key indicate the secondary information (items being compared).

Use line graphs to show change over time. Line graphs are commonly used in business, primarily to demonstrate increases (or decreases) in sales, customers, clients, or prices. A line graph with multiple lines allows the reader to compare two or more sets of data over time.

Use flow charts to show steps in a process. Flow charts take the reader from start to finish, often providing options along the way to help with decision making. Flow charts are commonly used for industrial processes, but they can also be used to describe processes such as using definite and indefinite articles, finding materials in a library, or enacting legislation.

Use organizational charts to describe organizational structure. Organizational charts ensure that all participants understand the roles, responsibilities, and relationships of people, departments, or other divisions within an organization.

Use maps to show geographic locations. Maps can provide information about geography, topography, demographics, locations, distances, and so forth.

▷ ADDING COLOR

This section offers advice about using color for print and online documents. It will help you figure out the answers to three important questions.

▶ When (in what documents) should I use color?

▶ Where should I position color?

▶ What color(s) should I choose?

Using Color Effectively

With increasingly easy access to inexpensive color printers, many writers have begun to incorporate color into documents that were formerly produced only in black and white. Color makes pages (print or electronic) more interesting, but do

Article that Demonstrates Effective Use of Color

Color photograph draws attention.

Contrasting color makes names stand out.

Blue, yellow, and red are basic colors. They are used to attract the reader's attention throughout this article.

Red type pulls the reader's eye to the quote.

See the full article beginning on page 91.

Zuckerberg's college-kid style reinforces the doubts of those who see the decision to keep Facebook independent as a lapse in judgment. In less than two years, the two reigning Web 2.0 titans have sold out to major corporations: MySpace accepted $580 million to join News Corp., and YouTube took $1.5 billion from Google. Surely any smart entrepreneur would jump at a chance to piggyback on those deals.

Looming over the Facebook talk is the specter of Friendster, the first significant social-networking site. It reportedly turned down a chance to sell out to Google in 2002 for $30 million, which if paid in stock, would be worth about $1 billion today. Now Friendster is struggling in the Web-o-sphere, having been swiftly eclipsed by the next generation of sites. The same thing could happen to Facebook. New social-networking sites are popping up every day. Cisco bought Five Across, which sells a software platform for social networking to corporate clients. Microsoft is beta-testing a site named Wallop. Even Reuters is planning to launch its own online face book, targeting fund managers and traders.

So is Zuckerberg being greedy—holding out for a bigger money buyout? If so, will that come back to haunt him? If not, what exactly is his game plan?

Zuckerberg's answer is that he's playing a different kind of game. "I'm here to build something for the long term," he says. "Anything else is a distraction." He and his compatriots at the helm of the company—cofounder and VP of engineering Dustin Moskovitz, 22, his roommate at Harvard, and chief technology officer Adam D'Angelo, 23, whom he met in prep school—are true believers. Their faith: that the openness, collaboration, and sharing of information epitomized by social networking can make the world work better. You might think they

DUSTIN MOSKOVITZ
Cofounder

LOCKDOWN

MATT COHLER
VP of strategy

MARK ZUCKERBERG
Founder and CEO

"I'm here to build something for the long term. Anything else is a distraction."
—MARK ZUCKERBERG

YOUTH PATROL
Zuckerberg's brain trust is populated mostly by twenty-somethings. Here, he shares a moment with Moskovitz, 22, and Cohler—an old hand at 30.

not add color just to get people to look at a page. When readers look at that page and see color, they should see something that they need or want to know. Here is a short list of some text elements and kinds of documents that make the best use of color.

▶ Use color to draw attention to titles, headings, and subheadings.

▶ Place blocks of color along a top or side margin to help readers find chapters or sections more easily.

▶ Make photographs, drawings, charts, and graphs more meaningful, easier to read, and more conspicuous by presenting them in color.

▶ Ensure that readers do not overlook vital information, such as warnings, by adding color.

▶ Use unexpected colors to draw extra attention to any element on the page.

Web Page that Demonstrates Effective Use of Color

Red type used for page title; blue for subtitle.

Rainbow symbolizes hope, provides vibrant colors.

Image of house is enlivened with colored windows.

Navigation uses colors from rainbow.

Bricks suggest strength, stability.

Link to site designer in obvious contrast with internal links.

The Women's Center of Wake County

Helping Women from Surviving to Thriving

Home | Services | About Us | Products | Donate | News | Links

How To Help | Our Wish List | Wacky Ball | Dappled Path Studio | website by

▶ **Join Abbeygail's Email List**

Privacy by ☒ SafeSubscribe℠
For Email Marketing you can trust

128 E. Hargett Street, Suite 10, Raleigh, NC 27601
Phone: (919) 829-3711, FAX: (919) 829-9960
© 2006 The Women's Center of Wake County.
The javascript on this site is safe; if Internet Explorer beeps a warning, choose 'allow blocked content'.
Home | Services | About Us | Products | Donate | News | Links

Using Color for Type

Although color is distinctive, no color will contrast as well as black when printed against a white background. Therefore, keep a few things in mind when using color for type.

When using color to emphasize a few words within the text, make those words bold. This will make the letters thicker, adding contrast and making them more noticeable.

Remember that not all colors are equally legible (see type samples on p. 550). In general, darker colors are easier to read than lighter colors because they give more contrast.

Maintain sufficient contrast between the type and the background. As people grow older, their visual acuity diminishes. As with type size, think about the age of your audience when considering contrast.

Minimize the amount of text that is printed or presented in a light color on a dark background (reversed). Even though white on black is a strong contrast, it is much harder to read than black on white.

Color Contrast for Legibility

Can you read this line easily?	Can you read this line easily?
Can you read this line easily?	Can you read this line easily?
Can you read this line easily?	Can you read this line easily?
Can you read this line easily?	

Positioning Color

Color makes a strong visual statement. On an otherwise black and white page, the reader's eye will go to an element that is in color no matter what color you choose. Because of color's strength, you need to position it wisely.

Use color sparingly, and keep the number of colors to a minimum. Use color for headings, bullets, boxes, images, and graphics.

Reserve color for the most important elements on the page. When color is used for trivial details, readers may not find the important information.

Use color consistently. For example, use the same color for all subheadings to connect them visually. When color is used inconsistently, it can confuse the readers.

Choosing Color

Although there are no hard-and-fast rules about what colors to choose for every purpose, there are some general guidelines for choosing colors that work well together, that do not work well in certain situations, and that carry conventional or cultural meanings.

When using only one or two colors, make sure that they will work in all situations where you want them. For most print documents for academic work, you will be limited to one or perhaps two colors. Be sure to check with your instructor for specific guidelines.

When using more than several colors, choose a combination of strong, dark colors and light colors. You may want to use multiple colors within the same color family—for example, lighter and darker shades of green for a nature preserve brochure. Combining strong, dark colors with lighter, more subtle ones gives contrast that will add interest and provides a palette of colors for various uses (pale tints for background images, darker shades for headings and graphics that need emphasis, contrasting colors for pie charts, and so on).

Get feedback from others. Let others look at the colors you have chosen and the way you are planning to use them. Make sure these readers find the colors comfortable and appropriate. Since different people "see" colors differently, make sure that the people you ask to check your color choices belong to or represent your intended audience.

Check the final product before turning it in or distributing it. Color combinations that look good in a Web text may not look the same when printed. Colors used in electronic texts may not look the same on other browsers or operating systems, so try to check several before posting your pages to the Web.

If you use color for a print document that has to be duplicated, the cost will increase dramatically. Before adding color to such a document, find out how much it will cost to print or photocopy, and make sure that you (or whoever is paying) can afford it.

{ Exercise } **Analyzing Colors**

Look at the images on pages 523, 524, 539, and 549 to see what you think of the colors. Do they make sense? How do they make you feel? Can you think of any reason why the authors or designers might have chosen those colors? ■

▷ CHOOSING TYPEFACES AND FONTS

Typefaces are families of characters—letters, numbers, and symbols. A typeface, such as Times Roman, might be available with different options for emphasis—italic or bold. A font is a set of type in a particular size and style, such as 11-point Times Roman. You might consider three important aspects of typefaces and fonts—style, size, and emphasis—to help you make decisions when designing your print or online documents.

Following are some general rules about choosing a type style. Keep in mind, however, that you should always follow any specific guidelines that your instructor or supervisor provides.

Web Invitation with Multiple Typefaces

Standard type set in unique color and placement emphasizes wordplay.

Less formal sans serif font presents basic information.

Event name set in large font with eye-catching design.

Decorative font attracts attention, complements tone established by image.

Painting emphasizes the nature of the event, an art auction.

Color and increased size stress important information.

Centered text and serif font mimics formal printed invitation.

Italics indicate title of painting.

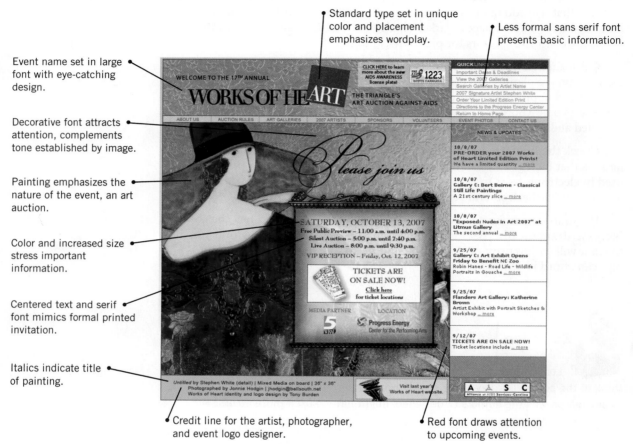

Credit line for the artist, photographer, and event logo designer.

Red font draws attention to upcoming events.

Type Style

Although there are several ways to categorize styles of type, one of the most useful is to identify whether the typeface is serif or sans serif. The *serif* is the little "tail" that is readily visible in the letter T—notice the tails that come down from the crossbar at the top and that extend on each side of the bottom. It's easiest to see if you compare it to an uppercase T from a typeface that is sans (or "without") serif. A sans serif T is made with just two straight lines. Three additional type categories that you should know about are script, handwriting, and decorative, each of which can be serif or sans serif.

Choose an easy-to-read typeface for body text in printed documents. Some readers find serif typefaces easier and less fatiguing to read in large chunks.

In printed documents using more than one typeface, use sans serif typefaces for headings and captions. Long lines in some sans serif typefaces are harder to read on paper.

For more information about headings, see page 531.

Do not mix too many typefaces in one document. One serif and one sans serif should be sufficient.

Use script and handwriting typefaces sparingly. These typefaces are often difficult to read, so limit their use to special purposes. Script and handwriting typefaces are most often used in personal or display documents—invitations, announcements, flyers, posters, brochures, advertisements, and so forth.

Limit your use of decorative typefaces. They're fun and distinctive—and often hard to read in large blocks. Like script typefaces, decorative ones are most often used for display—for headings or signposts or attention-getters—or for informal, personal documents.

For Web documents, choose a common sans serif typeface. Using Helvetica, Arial, or default styles will ensure that your text will be legible on a variety of browsers. Some typefaces, such as Verdana, have been created specifically for use on the Web.

Size

The bigger the type, the more emphasis the words will get; conversely, the smaller the type, the less attention the words will get. Type size is traditionally measured in fractions of an inch called points.

In general, use 10-, 11-, or 12-point type for body copy in printed texts.

You may use a larger font for major text headings. When using font size to differentiate among headings, you need to increase or decrease by at least two points for the difference to be noticeable.

Emphasis

Be careful not to use too many forms of emphasis in any one document or on any one page (print or electronic). The purpose of emphasis is to engage readers' attention, to draw them to particular words, phrases, or sections that are important. If you put in too many different kinds of emphasis, your readers will become confused and will not know what to look at.

Serif and Sans Serif Typefaces

Serif	Sans Serif
Courier	Arial
Palatino	**Chicago**
Garamond	Verdana
Times Roman	Helvetica

Script, Handwriting, and Decorative Typefaces

Script	Handwriting	Decorative
Freestyle Script	**Sand**	*Vivaldi*
French Script	Bradley Hand	**Broadway**
Edwardian Script	Kidprint	ALGERIAN

Use italics to give words emphasis by setting them off from other words in a sentence. Italics are also used to set off titles, to set off terms being highlighted as terms, and to designate words from a foreign language.

Use bold to draw readers' eyes to a specific word or phrase, to make that word or phrase jump out on the page. Bold can be very helpful when it is important for readers to be able to scan a page of text and find key words, such as items that are defined in a glossary.

Use italics and bold, individually or together, to create effective headings. You should use these forms of emphasis consistently and sparingly, however.

Print words in a different color to add strong emphasis. You probably noticed the word color written in red as soon as you turned to this page. However, it is important to use color carefully and consistently (see p. 547).

Use <u>underlining</u> as a substitute for italic type—for example, when a text is handwritten. However, underlining tends to make the text difficult to read, so use italics if available. In the past, underlining was used to indicate titles in documenting sources, and some disciplines and instructors still prefer it. With the current widespread use of personal computers, underlining is gradually disappearing as a means of identifying titles, but check with your instructor to make sure you understand the requirements for your particular course. Today, underlining is most often used in low-level headings and online to indicate a link.

Save the use of all UPPERCASE, or caps (short for "capital letters"), for one- or two-word headings. Uppercase text is difficult to read because words that are written in all uppercase have fairly similar shapes. In contrast, the distinctive shapes of lowercase words actually help the reader read.

Another way to add emphasis is to use SMALL CAPS. These are uppercase letter forms, but they are smaller than the regular caps in any particular font. A combination of caps and small caps is a style most often used in headings.

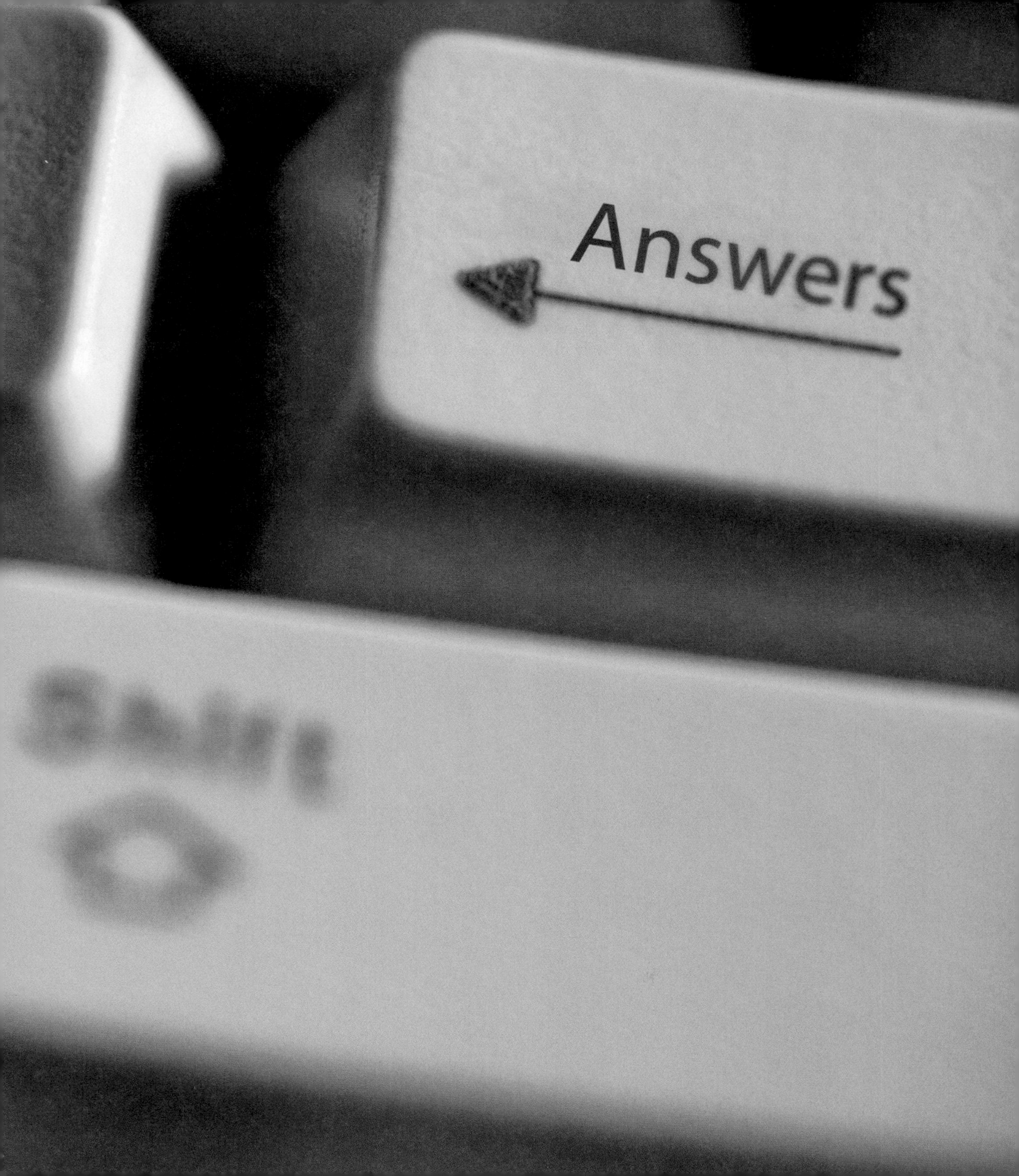
Answers

Starting Research and Finding Sources

It is likely that you will need to do at least some research for many of the assignments in this textbook, but the type of research and the sources that you use will vary depending on the type of text you are creating and your audience and purpose. You have probably already written research papers or conducted research projects, and you may know a great deal about using the library and the Internet to find information. Whether you're an experienced researcher or a novice, this chapter will give an overview of the resources that are likely to be available at your school, as well as some suggestions about using them effectively. The chapters that follow will explore specific research skills and strategies, some of which are introduced in this chapter.

▷ STARTING YOUR RESEARCH

When a college instructor assigns you a research project, regardless of the discipline or topic, you can count on certain basic requirements. For example, you will be expected to do the following.

▶ Write about a topic that bears scrutiny—usually a topic that others have investigated before.

▶ Conduct research to answer specific questions about the topic.

▶ Synthesize information that you find through library and Internet research (and sometimes through field research).

▶ Present your findings clearly so that others can see what you have learned.

▶ Attribute and properly cite your sources (discussed in Chapter 13).

If you have read any of the chapters in Part 1 of this book, you already have ideas about how to do some of these things. This chapter focuses on helping you manage your time, decide what type of information you need to gather, and search for that information using your library and the Internet.

Analyzing Your Research Assignment

Before you begin to gather information for a research project, read the assignment carefully (or talk to the instructor) so that you know what is expected. Be sure you have essential information about the required length of the final project, what form it should take (print or electronic), and when it is due. As with all assignments, you need to understand your audience and purpose, but for any assignment that requires a significant amount of research, you also need to think about the following questions.

For more advice on reading assignments, see Chapter 14.

▶ Does your instructor require a specific number of sources?

▶ Will you be expected to include (or avoid) certain types of sources?

▶ Are you expected to do field research?

▶ What kinds of visual elements should you include?

Knowing the answers to these key questions as you approach the assignment will save time—and trouble—later on in the research and writing process.

You usually will have a good deal of notice about when a research project is due—sometimes several months—so your instructor will expect you to "do your homework." That obviously means doing whatever research is required; but even more, it means that your final project should be written clearly, with appropriate transitions, a logical organization, an appropriate voice, and few (if any) grammatical or typographical errors. In most cases the instructor will want a research essay that is computer-generated or typed, and in many cases you will be expected to include appropriate visual elements, such as charts, graphs, photographs, maps, or other images. You may also be expected to know how to format your essay according to the instructor's specifications, including the use of a particular documentation style, certain typefaces and sizes, headings, margins, system of page numbering, and so on.

You can get a good idea of how much time to spend on the research assignment by checking the course syllabus and by asking yourself the following questions.

▶ **How detailed are the instructions?** Detailed instructions often indicate higher expectations for the final product, which should indicate a greater amount of time and effort on your part.

▶ **How much is the assignment worth in terms of the final grade?** A project that will count as 25 percent should demand more of your time than one that will count as 10 percent.

▶ **How long is the project supposed to be?** Instructors often give page or word-length guidelines. The longer the project, the more time you should spend on it.

▶ **How much other work is the instructor assigning at the same time?** If the instructor has given you lots of other out-of-class assignments that are due at the same time, that should help you budget your time on the research project.

▶ **How much advance notice did the instructor give?** If you had a good deal of advance notice (more than two weeks), you are probably expected to spend quite a bit of time on the research project.

Managing Your Time

Once you have a sense of how much time you should spend on this project, you need to determine how you will complete it within that time frame. One of the best ways to manage your time is to create a plan. You can use your calendar, a time line, or a simple checklist. The format doesn't matter, as long as you think carefully about all the things you have to do and allocate sufficient time for each task. The headings and subheadings in the Guide to Writing section of any of the chapters in Part 1 can help you think of items for your checklist, but you will need to add specific tasks and deadlines. You can modify the sample checklist on the next page depending on your assignment. On page 560 you will see how one student, Zane Van Dusen, modified the checklist for his research essay about recording music on analog tape.

On February 25, Zane's class started on a research essay assignment. After thinking of several different topics, he decided to write about the demise of analog tape as a recording medium for music. Zane transferred the steps from his checklist into his online calendar.

Read more about how Zane chose his topic below.

Choosing a Topic, Developing a Research Question, and Planning Your Research

Unless your instructor has assigned a topic, your first challenge will be to come up with a topic that you would like to investigate. If nothing comes to mind, try brainstorming a list of ideas or issues that you want to learn more about. For example, when Zane was assigned to write an evaluation, he started by brainstorming about his hobbies and extracurricular activities. He soon decided to do something specific pertaining to music. Here's how Zane described his search for a topic.

> I was browsing various newspapers' Web sites, looking for articles about music, since that is my main hobby. I found a lot of articles about the music industry, and the controversy over Internet piracy; however, I was really tired of that subject. Finally, I found a small article about Quantegy Inc. shutting down its analog tape factory. This article immediately sparked my interest because it mentioned many artists that I admire,

and because I do a lot of recording with both digital and analog technologies, and I often have to consider the pros and cons of both technologies. Also, I am a bit of an audiophile (I still collect and prefer vinyl records over CDs, when they are available); therefore, hearing that this could be the end of analog recording was extremely alarming to me.

Sample Research Project Checklist

Task	Finish by
Receive Assignment	
Analyze assignment; identify topic; analyze audience; clarify purpose	_____
Conduct Research	
Create a system for keeping track of sources; gather information	_____
Narrow topic; develop a research question; formulate a thesis	_____
Do additional research (if needed)	_____
Search for (or create) relevant visuals	_____
Create Draft	
Review notes; analyze any data gathered	_____
Develop ideas; create rough outline	_____
Draft introduction	_____
Organize and synthesize information	_____
Write a tentative conclusion	_____
Integrate visual information	_____
Complete a review draft	_____
Revise Draft	
Submit for feedback	_____
Revise draft based on feedback	_____
Compile list of works cited	_____
Format and edit revised draft; proofread	_____
Submit final draft	_____

As Zane's description of his topic search shows, using the Internet is a great way to get started. In addition to looking at specific Web sites, you could use a search engine to look for material on specific keywords (see more about using search engines beginning on page 578). Another brainstorming technique would be to look at a magazine, journal, or specialized radio or TV program for ideas. Here are some suggestions that might help you get started.

▶ For something related to science, you could
- go to http://www.npr.org and check out topics that had been covered recently on the program "Talk of the Nation/Science Friday";
- review article titles in a recent issue of a general-interest science magazine such as *Discover*;
- review titles for a recent episode of the public television program *Nova*.

Sample Research Project Schedule

FEBRUARY / MARCH

SUNDAY	MONDAY	TUESDAY	WEDNESDAY	THURSDAY	FRIDAY	SATURDAY
24	25 Receive assignment. Identify topic.	26 Analyze audience and purpose. Create research log. Google keywords to get started.	27 Submit topic and analysis of audience and purpose in class. Research online if time.	28 Research online if time.	29 Research online if time.	MAR 1 Library day—find a book. Narrow topic and formulate thesis.
2	3 Submit thesis in class. Review data gathered. Write intro and make outline if time.	4 Learn more about technical aspects of recording.	5	6 Start writing.	7 Look for visuals. Photos of equipment?	8 Finish review draft.
9 Finish review draft.	10 Peer review in class.	11 Revise based on peer review.	12	13 Compile works cited and proofread.	14 SUBMIT final draft.	15

> ▶ For a history, political science, or government course, you could
> - go to the home page of the History Channel (http://www.history.com) and review recent program titles;
> - go to a Web site such as http://www.historyguy.com and read through the list of portals, such as comics history, military history, and biofiles;
> - find a local, state, or government source of information—perhaps as simple as http://www.usa.gov—and scan for ideas.

For more on brainstorming topic ideas, see the advice on selecting a topic in Chapter 3, page 134.

> ▶ For just about any course, you could
> - find a textbook other than the one you are using in your class and review the topics in the table of contents;
> - go to a Web site such as Amazon.com and look at recent book titles in a specific category;
> - talk with friends, classmates, or family members about the requirements of the assignment.

Many topics that would make a good starting point for a college research project will require fine-tuning to bring them down to a manageable size that is appropriate for the assignment's audience and purpose and your time and length constraints.

Narrowing a Topic by Asking Questions

Think of your research as an attempt to answer some questions about that topic; specifically think about the questions that your audience wants you to answer and your purpose in presenting this information to that audience. For example, although Zane Van Dusen thought about his topic as "the demise of analog recording," he needed to formulate questions about it, such as these.

> ▶ What is analog recording?
>
> ▶ Why is analog recording no longer dominant?
>
> ▶ What are the pros and cons of analog?
>
> ▶ What is the history of analog recording?
>
> ▶ Why has digital recording surpassed analog as the recording technique of choice?
>
> ▶ If analog recording ceases to exist, why should we care?

Your research project will not necessarily answer each question you initially formulated about the topic. From an initial set of questions, you can focus on just one or two related questions. Let your understanding of your audience and purpose guide you in selecting the questions that will form the focus of your text.

Developing a Research Question and a Working Thesis

After selecting a general topic and thinking of several relevant questions, you will need to formulate a focused research question. As you begin to gather and explore sources of information on your topic, you may discover that there is a wealth of information on one aspect of your topic (one or more related questions), but not much on other aspects. If so, you will probably want to focus your research on an area where you can find a lot of sources, and this will also help you narrow your topic. In other cases, you may discover that you are more intrigued by one or more of your questions than by others. Whenever possible, choose a question that you *and your audience* care about—a personal interest will make the assignment more meaningful and help you do a better job.

As you refine and focus the research question, you will develop an answer to the question that becomes your working thesis. The purpose of your research paper is to gather sufficient credible evidence to support the thesis. Because the working thesis will evolve as you find sources that support or challenge it, you should be open to refocusing your work as you proceed.

Using a Research Question to Plan Research

While looking for ways to answer the questions you have formulated, you will probably need to use different types of research to locate the sources you need to support your thesis. The logical place to start any research project is on your library's Web site. The home page or portal to your library provides access to a wealth of information in a variety of formats and from a variety of sources. You are also likely to use Internet sources and—in some cases—you may even conduct original field research (see Chapter 11). The chart below lists several of the most common types of research that you might integrate into your project.

Common Types of Research

Library Research	Your library's online databases can help you find scholarly and popular journals, magazines, and newspapers; online catalogs describe hard-copy holdings such as books.
Internet Research	A search engine such as Google or Yahoo! can provide access to informative Web sites. (See pp. 578–83 for more on Internet searching.) Instructors often have guidelines about using materials from blogs and wikis (such as Wikipedia), so be sure to check before using them. Evaluate all Internet sources carefully for relevance and credibility. (See Chapter 12 for more on evaluating sources.)
Field Research	Interviews, surveys, and observations are the most common types of field research that you might be asked to use for college research projects. (See Chapter 11 for help using these research methods.)

As you plan your research, you also need to consider whether to include visuals in your project. To determine whether to use visuals, ask yourself the following questions.

For advice on creating visuals, see Chapter 9. For more on finding and working with visual sources, see page 584.

▶ Does your instructor require visual elements or value them highly?

▶ Does your topic lend itself to charts, graphs, or tables?

▶ Would you be able to answer the research questions more clearly or persuasively by adding photos, drawings, diagrams, or maps?

If you think ahead about the types of visual information you might want to incorporate, you can look for effective examples (or gather data to create your own) as you search for written information.

For advice on taking notes, see Chapter 12.

Regardless of the way you search for information, be sure to take notes to help keep track of what you have found and where you have found it.

Working with Different Kinds of Sources

To understand what kinds of sources to gather for your research project, you should first consider the different kinds of sources that are available. Some types of sources will be more appropriate for your project than others, and some will lend themselves more readily to one search method than another. In most cases, your instructor will be able to help you decide which types of sources will be most useful—and appropriate—for your research topic and assignment.

For advice on evaluating online sources, see Chapter 12.

Print and Online Sources

Web sites, blogs, and wikis contain a vast amount of material, and by working online you can often get quick access to some sources that also appear in print. Because of the way online sources are published, they can be easily and frequently updated, so some very current information is available online. But because material on the Internet is so easily edited or deleted, information online can change overnight. Therefore, it is important to make print copies of electronic materials you find, make a note of the date you retrieved the information from an online source, and keep accurate bibliographic information for online sources as you locate them.

For information on keeping track of sources, see page 585.

Print sources, on the other hand, are relatively stable, if not always as readily accessible as electronic ones. Although certain print sources may be available online—for example, in the form of databases, online books, or electronic versions of periodicals—many print sources are not found on the Internet. If your search focuses only on online sources, you may overlook a huge number of helpful, appropriate print sources.

Primary and Secondary Sources

The material that you gather during research can come from either *primary* or *secondary* sources. A primary source is a firsthand account or direct observation by an eyewitness or participant. Primary sources are important because they add credibility to your work. A secondary source is a summary, analysis, interpretation, or evaluation of information gathered from one or more primary sources.

In historical research, a primary source is material from the historical period under investigation—for instance, a photograph, a diary or letter, a newspaper article reporting on an event, or an audio recording of a meeting. A secondary source would be a historian's analysis of that period based on research into original material such as speeches, legal documents, and news accounts. In literature, a primary source is an original text—such as a novel, an essay, a poem, or a short story—whereas a secondary source would be a literary critique or interpretation of a primary text or texts. In the sciences, primary sources include original research results and findings, whereas secondary sources would be books or articles written about someone else's research results. Primary and secondary sources each have their own merits, but all sources need to be evaluated for bias and credibility (see Chapter 12).

Determining whether a Source Is Secondary

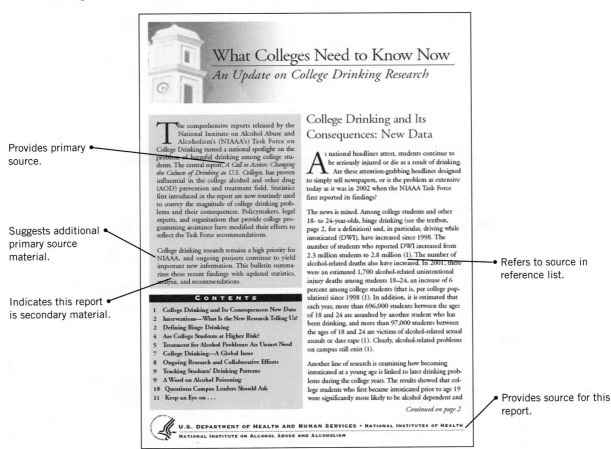

Provides primary source.

Suggests additional primary source material.

Indicates this report is secondary material.

Refers to source in reference list.

Provides source for this report.

Determining whether a Source Is Scholarly, Popular, or Trade

Criteria	Scholarly Journal	Popular Magazine	Trade Magazine/Journal
Example			
Content (Accuracy)	**In-depth**, primary account of **original** findings written by the researcher(s); very **specific** information, with the goal of scholarly communication.	**Secondary** discussion of someone else's research; may include personal narrative or **opinion; general** information, purpose is to entertain or inform.	Current **news, trends, and products** in a specific industry; practical information **for professionals** working in the field or industry.
Author (Authority)	Author's **credentials are provided**; usually a scholar or specialist with subject expertise.	Author is frequently a journalist paid to write articles, may or **may not have subject expertise.**	Author is usually a **professional in the field**, sometimes a journalist with subject expertise.
Audience (Coverage)	Scholars, researchers, and students.	General public; the interested non-specialist.	Professionals in the field; the interested non-specialist.
Language (Coverage)	**Specialized terminology** or jargon of the field; requires expertise in subject area.	Vocabulary in general usage; **easily understandable** to most readers.	**Specialized terminology** or jargon of the field, but **not as technical** as a scholarly journal.
Graphics (Coverage)	Graphs, charts, and tables; **very few advertisements** and photographs.	Graphs, charts, and tables; lots of **glossy advertisements and photographs.**	Photographs; **some graphics** and charts; **advertisements** targeted to professionals in the field.
Layout & Organization (Currency)	**Structured**; includes the article abstract, goals and objectives, methodology, results (evidence), discussion, conclusion, and bibliography.	**Informal;** may include non-standard formatting. **May not present supporting evidence** or a conclusion.	**Informal**; articles organized like a journal or a newsletter. Evidence drawn from **personal experience or common knowledge.**
Accountability (Objectivity)	Articles are **evaluated by peer-reviewers** or referees who are experts in the field; edited for **content, format, and style.**	Articles are **evaluated by editorial staff**, not experts in the field; edited for **format and style.**	Articles are evaluated by editorial staff who may be experts in the field, **not peer-reviewed**; edited for **format and style.**
References (Objectivity)	**Required.** Quotes and facts are verifiable.	**Rare.** Little, if any, information about source materials is given.	Occasional **brief** bibliographies, but not required.
Paging	Page numbers are consecutive throughout the volume.	Each issue begins with page 1.	Each issue begins with page 1.
Other Examples	Scholarly Journal *Annals of Mathematics, Journal of Abnormal Psychology, History of Education Quarterly*; almost anything with *Journal* in the title.	Popular Magazine *Sports Illustrated, National Geographic, Time, Newsweek, Ladies Home Journal, Cooking Light, Discover.*	Trade Magazine/Journal *Architectural Record, PC World, Restaurant Business, American Libraries, Psychology Today, School Band and Orchestra.*

If you were doing research on binge drinking among college students, secondary sources would be reports based on research studies, such as the National Institutes of Health Report, the first page of which is shown on page 565. For primary information, you might read the original studies cited in this report or conduct a survey of students on your own campus. If you were doing research on the strength of titanium, your secondary sources would be reports from various laboratories or manufacturers. Primary research would involve creating and conducting experiments to determine the strength of the metal.

Often, gathering information from previously published materials will be just the beginning of your research. Many projects will involve going beyond primary and secondary sources that you find in the library or on the Internet and doing field research to investigate how people think or feel about a particular topic. When you are out in the field, the people you interview, survey, or observe become your primary sources.

For advice on conducting field research, see Chapter 11.

Scholarly, Popular, and Trade Sources

When conducting research, it is important to distinguish between sources that are journal articles and magazine articles. Journal articles are typically referred to as "scholarly," while magazine articles are usually considered "popular." A third category, "trade" magazines or journals, are written for professionals in a particular field but are not strictly research related. The value of scholarly, popular, and trade sources to your project will vary according to your audience and topic (as well as the credentials of the individual writer).

The table on page 566 from the North Carolina State University library offers additional criteria to consider when differentiating between journals and magazines. Note how each category is related to the five criteria for information evaluation: accuracy, authority, objectivity, currency, and coverage.

▷ SEARCHING FOR INFORMATION USING YOUR LIBRARY'S RESOURCES

Libraries have always been important repositories of information, but today's wired libraries are truly amazing. They not only house significantly greater stores of information than libraries could in the pre-digital age but in many cases allow you to access an array of textual and visual resources without even leaving your room. As long as you can use the Internet to connect to your library's home page, you can find your way to catalogs, databases, image galleries, interlibrary loan forms, and much more. Most libraries have classes, tours, electronic tutorials, and printed handouts that describe the resources and services available at the library itself and through the Internet. If you have not already done so, take time now to learn about what your library has to offer.

One of the crucial things to think about as you begin your research is the difference between *discovery* and *access*. Some research tools will help you discover relevant materials—a card catalog, some databases, most online search engines—but will not give you direct access to those materials. That is, you may find a title, an author, an abstract, or a summary, but you may not be able to view the entire article from the search tool. However, the information you have found will be sufficient for you to see if your library has the book or article, and thus you will know if you can access the material—either online, in the library's stacks, or in the library's microforms (microfilm or microfiche) collection. Most books are accessible only in the physical library, and many journals and magazines have only recent material available online. If you discover relevant articles written prior to about 1970, you may need to go to the library to read the articles in the stacks or on microfiche or microfilm.

The information presented in this chapter cannot substitute for a tour of your school's library, but it will give you general information about using library resources. Consider whether you are in a position to take advantage of all the available resources by answering the following questions.

► Do you know how to use the library's online catalog?

► Are you familiar with the electronic indexes and databases at the library?

► Do you know how to access the library's online catalog and electronic databases from your own computer or from computers on campus?

► Do you know how to find books and periodicals at the library?

Social Bookmarking Web Sites

When you are searching for material on the Internet, you can use online social bookmarking Web sites such as del.icio.us, ma.gnolia, furl, or clipmarks to keep track of useful sites that you find. These sites allow you to store your bookmarks online and are helpful because they allow you to create keywords called *tags* for sites that you want to bookmark. These tags allow you to organize the sites you find and to access them easily from any computer. The social networking aspect occurs when your tags match up with other users' tags, allowing you to connect to sites that like-minded individuals have found useful. For example, if you were researching green living trends, you might tag relevant sites as "green lifestyle." Bookmarking sites allow you to keep your list private or to share your links with others, making these sites particularly helpful for group projects. There are many social bookmarking sites on the Internet, so check for the features you need, such as the ability to create a shared account for a group project, before you set up your account.

▶ Are you familiar with the kinds of reference books that might help with your research, including indexes, bibliographies, and annotated bibliographies?

▶ Do you know what kinds of help the library's reference librarians can provide?

▶ Do you know the library's interlibrary loan policies?

Once you know all the types of resources you can access, the sheer number of options might appear overwhelming. Many libraries now allow students to create personal pages within the library's Web site, enabling them to keep track of the resources they find most useful. You may be able to create a customized page that displays links to specific databases, electronic journals, and other Web sites, including electronic reference books. Take advantage of such tools, the Bookmark or Favorites feature of your Web browser, or a social bookmarking Web site (see the box on p. 568) to eliminate some of the confusion that can arise from trying to remember which database you used previously or where you found a particular type of information. This section will describe many ways to search for information in the library.

Using the Library Catalog

One of the most familiar and useful tools available at the library is the catalog. A library catalog is a database containing descriptions of material housed in that particular library (or network of libraries), along with information on how to access that material. Most libraries now have their catalogs available online, though some libraries still maintain card catalogs. Although every library's catalog has a unique appearance, the pages depicted in the figures in this section demonstrate the type of information you will find within your library's catalog. Both online and card catalogs allow you to search for specific titles, authors, and subjects, but only online catalogs allow you to search by using keywords.

To get the most out of your search, try these strategies.

Search by title. Each source you find may lead to other sources. For example, you may have found an article in a journal that cites relevant information from a book. To see if your library has a copy of that book, you would search your library's catalog by the title.

Search by author. If an author has written a book or article on your research subject, the chances are good that he or she has written more than one work on that topic. Enter that author's name in the catalog search engine to see if there are any other sources that will help with your project.

Search by subject. Because libraries catalog their materials according to a list of standard subject headings (usually ones established by the Library of Congress), you can look for resources in an online catalog by typing in a short description of your topic. Most electronic catalogs will tell you the official subject heading that is most closely related to the subject you have entered. Or try typing in synonyms for your subject or asking a reference librarian for a list of all the official Library of

Library Catalog Subject Search Request

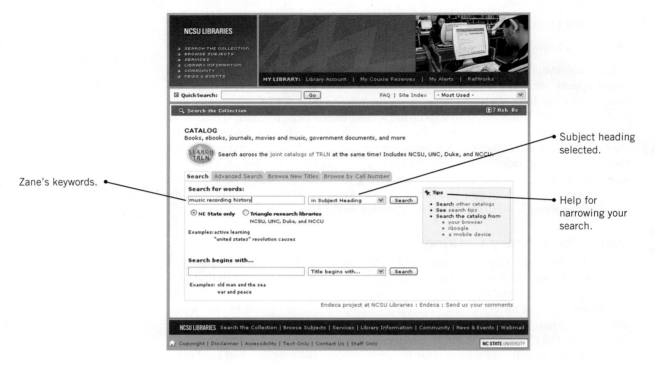

Zane's keywords.

Subject heading selected.

Help for narrowing your search.

Congress subject headings. Then you can browse for headings that seem relevant to your topic. The figures above and on page 571 show examples of the kind of search tools and results you will find using a subject search.

Search by keyword. Conduct a keyword search by typing in words that appear anywhere in the record for a source—the title, subject words, author's name, or, for some works, a summary or an abstract. A keyword search is less restrictive than a subject search because a single source can be located through many different keywords but would be assigned only one subject heading. Two or more keywords can be combined in one search to locate the most specific information—for example, the author's last name and a single word that describes your subject.

Analyze your search results. After entering your search terms and finding a list of entries, you can look at each item individually to see if it is likely to be useful. If the search brings up too many entries, try narrowing the search in some way—for example, by adding another search term, specifying only the most recent material, or focusing on a particular format.

Although the library catalog does not tell much about the contents of a book or periodical, it does give a lot of information that might help you decide whether a

For tips on adding search terms, see Searching Indexes and Databases, page 576.

For suggestions on identifying the most useful sources, see Sorting through Your Sources, page 583.

Library Catalog Subject Search Results

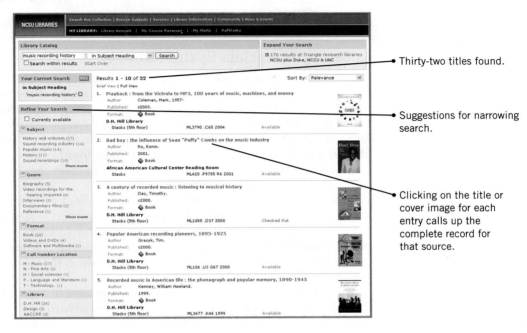

Thirty-two titles found.

Suggestions for narrowing search.

Clicking on the title or cover image for each entry calls up the complete record for that source.

Library Catalog Record for a Book

Click on author's name for other works by Coleman in the catalog.

Links to additional sources.

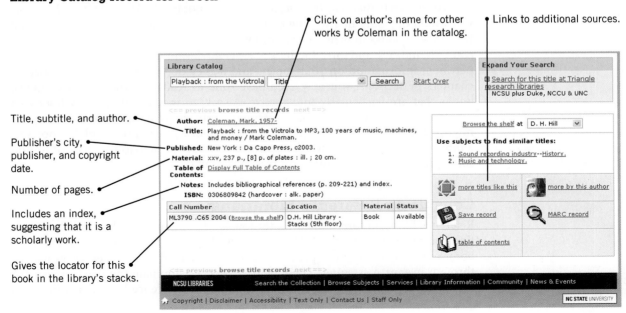

Title, subtitle, and author.

Publisher's city, publisher, and copyright date.

Number of pages.

Includes an index, suggesting that it is a scholarly work.

Gives the locator for this book in the library's stacks.

source is worth pursuing. The individual record for a source lists information that will help you determine whether a work might be appropriate for your topic—or at least worth looking at in the stacks.

Locating Materials in the Library

After analyzing your search results and deciding which books and other sources look the most promising, the next step is to skim a copy of the source. The online catalog entry will provide a link to materials that are available electronically or the basic information you need to locate books and other print material—namely, the location where the source is shelved (the specific library or collection within a library) and the call number. Books are grouped together by topic, so you should browse the shelves near books you have located to find other books that may also turn out to be relevant to your topic.

Most college libraries permit students to find books and many periodicals for themselves in the stacks, rather than requesting a particular work and waiting for a librarian to retrieve it. Within any library, you should look for a map, chart, or online guide detailing the general location of different call numbers (by floor or section) so that you don't have to wander aimlessly in the stacks looking for what you need.

You should also be careful not to wander aimlessly in a more figurative way: In these days of easy access to the Internet and other electronic resources, it is worth noting that books are often still the best source of information for college research projects. You might be tempted to think that you can find everything you need without getting up from the computer and venturing into the stacks. For some types of research, that may be true, but probably not for the kind of research project you would be doing in a writing class or most other college courses. You may not have to read books in their entirety, but you can certainly look through the tables of contents, indexes, and introductions of several relevant books to see if they contain pertinent information on your topic—and if they do, you can read those specific chapters or sections. You may even have time to read (or skim) a few complete books that are particularly informative. Also keep in mind that many books on scholarly topics are collections of essays or articles by different authors, so you might be able to find a lot of good sources all in one place. If the book has notes or a bibliography or works cited list, you will probably be able to use that list to find some promising leads for other sources to consult.

For ideas about using citations to find new sources, see the box on page 577.

Consulting Reference Librarians

Reference librarians are trained professionals whose primary job is to help people find the materials they need. Most libraries allow you to telephone the reference librarians, and many now provide online access to them—either by e-mail or through instant messaging. These helpful services eliminate the need to visit the library in person each time you have a question. Reference librarians can be an amazingly helpful resource at any stage of the research process. For example, you can ask questions such as these.

▶ Where can I find information on my topic?

▶ What databases might have articles about this topic?

▶ Where could I find statistics (or quotations or facts) about this topic?

▶ How do I do a search in [specific database]?

▶ Where could I find a drawing (or diagram, photograph, map, and so forth) of a particular item?

▶ I've already tried several resources to search for my topic. Can you think of any other sources I should try?

▶ I'm having trouble connecting to the library catalog, a different library's catalog, or a database. Can you help me?

▶ What journal does the abbreviation in this database listing represent?

▶ How do I get a book or article through interlibrary loan?

A reference librarian can also help you locate other library resources that you may not have considered.

▶ **Government documents.** Many reports produced by federal, state, and local government agencies, especially older reports, are available in print or on microfiche in libraries. Many more are now readily available on the Internet, and you can link to them through a variety of databases.

▶ **Audiovisual materials.** These collections often include audio recordings, films, videotapes, DVDs, slides, and so forth. Such collections could be particularly helpful if you need visuals for a Web project or for an oral presentation.

▶ **Special collections.** Many libraries have collections of rare books and other documents or artifacts of particular local interest. These collections are not generally open to the public, but a reference librarian can get you access to them.

▶ **Vertical files.** These are collections of pamphlets, brochures, and annual reports from a variety of organizations, companies, and agencies.

Using Reference Books

Although many people have come to rely on electronic resources, you may be able to obtain some information more easily by looking through reference books, such as encyclopedias, disciplinary guides, or bibliographies. Check with a reference librarian to determine the availability of these resources.

▶ **Encyclopedias.** Specialized encyclopedias devoted to a particular subject area (for example, the *Encyclopedia of Philosophy*) give a more thorough introduction to and summary of a topic than general encyclopedias (such as the *Encyclopaedia Britannica*). Look for specialized encyclopedias rather than general ones.

▶ **Disciplinary guides.** These guides provide lists of reference tools—books, journals, bibliographies, electronic databases, and so forth—for specific subject areas or disciplines. To find a relevant disciplinary guide, consult a general guide such as Robert Balay's *Guide to Reference Books*.

▶ **Specialized reference works.** Your library will have many biographical dictionaries and indexes, almanacs, yearbooks, atlases, and other reference works that offer information in depth on particular topics. These resources can be useful to find background information, to narrow your topic, or to find keywords for a search. Check with a reference librarian to determine which specialized reference works are available in the field that relates to your topic.

▶ **Bibliographies.** Bibliographies are useful lists of published research—journal articles, books, research reports, Web sites, and so forth—on particular topics. An annotated bibliography is a reference tool that lists sources of information relating to a specific topic and provides a summary of each source's contents and relevance. To find a specific bibliography, add the term "bibliography" or "annotated bibliography" to your keyword search or ask a reference librarian for help.

Using reference tools such as these may give you a faster start on your research than an electronic search because the book's editors and compilers will already have made informed decisions about what to include and exclude. Also, since not all reference books have been published online, some material may be available only in print. Other reference sources may be available electronically, either on the Internet or on CD-ROM, but your library may not have access. A reference librarian can tell you about resources appropriate to your topic that are not available electronically, are not available at your library, or are simply easier to search in print than in electronic form.

Using Indexes and Databases

The term *index* usually refers to a guide to articles in periodicals or in book collections or to material related to a specialized subject. The term *database* is used more generally to describe a searchable collection of reference material, either in print or electronic form. (In some cases, *index* and *database* are used interchangeably to refer to such a collection.) The indexes and databases in a research library *may* connect the reader to full-text, downloadable, and printable articles; to abstracts or summaries of material; or to a listing of author, title, and publication information. In other words, they *may* give you access, but it is possible that they will only help you discover relevant materials and you will have to take additional steps to find and read the book or article.

When you start to search for material, keep in mind the type of information you are seeking so that you can choose the appropriate index or database. For example, do you need to cite scholarly research that reflects expert opinion, or could you use less academic material from the popular press? Alternatively, do you need articles from specialized trade journals and newsletters directed to insiders in a particular field? Many indexes or databases link to only one of these types of sources, so you need to be aware of the differences and then decide which indexes or databases will be the most useful for your particular research.

For more on the differences among popular, trade, and scholarly publications, see page 566.

Choosing Indexes and Databases

Indexes and databases all have limitations—you are unlikely to find all the information you need in one place. Most indexes and databases that you can access through the library are organized by subject area (discipline), so first you should figure out what subject area is most likely to yield information on your topic. You may need to do some brainstorming or talk with a reference librarian to get ideas. For many topics, you may want to look in the indexes and databases for more than one subject area. For example, in writing a paper about child abuse, you might check specialized indexes and databases on psychology, sociology, social work, and maybe even criminal justice. (Some database services cover several different subject areas.)

Keep in mind that there are hundreds of indexes and databases, but it's unlikely that more than a few will be helpful on any given topic. Unless you stay focused, you might waste a lot of time searching in the wrong subject area. Your library will probably offer the option of choosing databases and indexes from an alphabetical list or by subject area. Unless you know exactly what database or index you need, try starting with a broad subject area and gradually narrowing to the appropriate databases or indexes. For example, the North Carolina State University library lists nearly one hundred disciplinary categories for its electronic databases, including the following.

Agriculture	Linguistics
Business & Management	Music
Criminology	Natural Resources
Environmental Science	Physiology
Film Studies	Textile Engineering
History	Veterinary Medicine
Industrial Design	

Choosing any category will bring up a list of electronic resources available under that category (some libraries break down each broad category into subcategories), with links to each source so that you can investigate it further. At some libraries, you can link directly from the category list to the different resources under that subject area—journals, reference books, electronic texts, and so on—without first linking to a specific index or database.

If you have trouble determining which subject areas are relevant to your topic, ask your instructor or a reference librarian for ideas—or for the title of a particular journal that might be useful. Most indexes and databases provide a list of the journals they include; once you have a title, you can choose a database or index that includes the publication you are looking for and assume that you will find other relevant journals there as well. When linking directly to a list of journals from the library's subject category list (rather than first linking to a specific database or index), you can take the same approach—namely, checking the list to see what other journals are included under that subject area.

Finally, be sure to check to see how far back the material covered in the database goes. Some journals do not publish older material electronically. The lack of old material may not be relevant if you're writing a paper on the latest AIDS research, but many other topics will warrant a search into earlier sources—for example, looking at the original coverage of Ronald Reagan's acting career or discovering the origin of a newspaper comic strip. You may be able to use print versions of indexes, many of which have been published for decades, to look for older sources.

Searching Indexes and Databases

Once you've chosen one or more indexes or databases—or linked to a particular journal—you are ready to conduct a search. Most indexes and databases allow you to search by author, title, keyword, or subject heading. Keep in mind that not all electronic databases use the same Library of Congress subject headings employed by library catalogs (see p. 569), so you may need to search for synonyms when conducting a subject search. With some electronic databases, you can use Advanced Search techniques similar to the following ones that you may be familiar with from Internet search engines.

▶ **AND limits your search.** If you connect two words or phrases with AND, the search will find only items that include both search terms (music AND recording).

▶ **OR expands your search.** Adding OR to a search will give you all items that include either one of your terms (music OR recording).

▶ **NOT limits your search.** If you put NOT in front of a term, you exclude any results that contain that term (music NOT radio).

▶ **Quotation marks limit your search.** Putting quotation marks around two or more words will return only results that include those exact words in that exact order ("music recording history").

For information on using the Advanced Search feature of search engines, see page 581.

If all goes well, your search will result in a list of sources relevant to your topic. If the database provides a full-text version of articles, you can skim through each one online to see if it is definitely useful. To avoid wasting paper and ink, time, and

{ **For Collaboration** }   **Citation Indexes**

Read over the box Using Citations and Citation Indexes on the next page. With a small group of classmates, talk about what it means if an original article you find has been cited frequently in a citation index. How would this affect your opinion of the article? ∎

Using Citations and Citation Indexes

Use citations to your advantage by following these strategies.

▶ When reading an article, make note of any statements or quotations that seem particularly relevant to your topic and then check to see if the author has included a reference to the source.

▶ Use the sources listed at the end of every scholarly article (and in some trade and popular press articles as well). This list points you to the original material cited in the article. Often, you can find several additional sources for your topic just by reading one relevant article carefully.

▶ Use a citation index, a specialized index that lists published articles that have been cited in other articles, to find other useful sources. For example, if you have found a useful article, you can check a citation index to find more recently published articles that include references to the useful article. Many of them will likely be on the same topic—and some may prove useful to you as well. Before beginning a search, check with a reference librarian or view the list of journals included in a particular citation index to make sure you are using one that includes the original article you found.

Database Search Using Academic Search Premier

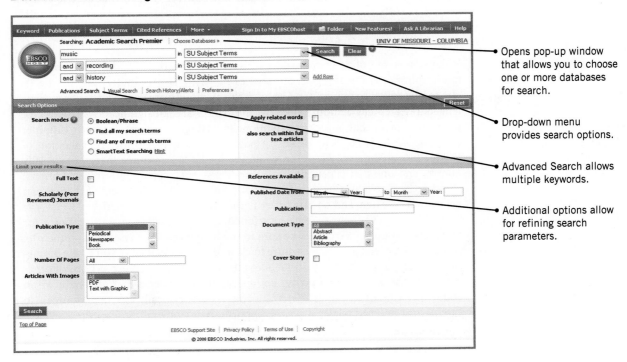

money (if your school or library charges printing fees), try to read as much as possible online, and print only the material you really need.

If the database provides only an abstract or a citation for a source, you may not be able to tell if it will be helpful. Check the library's catalog to see if you have easy access to the print version. If the library does not own the book, subscribe to that periodical, or have the issue in which the article appears, you might want to request it through interlibrary loan.

Once you have at least one really good, in-depth source on your topic, you have one more way to search for additional information that could be the most useful of all. The box on page 577 explains how to use citations—both within and to a source—to locate other relevant sources on your topic.

▷ SEARCHING FOR INFORMATION ON THE INTERNET

One of the crucial things to keep in mind when searching for information on the Internet is the previously discussed difference between *discovery* and *access*. The Internet can be extremely helpful with the process of discovery. For example, you can use Google Scholar to help you locate material that may be relevant to your topic. However, in most instances, Google Scholar cannot get you access to the actual article that you need to read and reference as a source. To gain that access, you will

Wikipedia

Wikipedia is an online encyclopedia with millions of articles and discussions on a nearly infinite variety of topics. The articles are written by volunteers, and most articles can be edited by any reader. Although the credibility of Wikipedia has been challenged, research has demonstrated that the articles are not significantly less credible than the articles that appear in traditionally written encyclopedias. (See "Internet Encyclopedias Go Head to Head" on page 347 of Chapter 6 for an evaluation of Wikipedia's credibility.) However, while Wikipedia is a resource that is universally known, and one that is gaining in respect, it has not attained universal credibility. Check to be sure that your instructor allows you to use Wikipedia entries before you begin your research, and be sure to verify the sources cited in the article.

Wikipedia, like any general encyclopedia, is best used as a starting point for research. If you use Wikipedia, be sure to use all the available resources on the site. After you have read an article, be sure to click on the tab that takes you to the discussion section so you can learn about alternate perspectives, see the reactions of other readers to the article, and uncover any questions or concerns that may have arisen about the content of the article. Wikipedia articles typically cite their sources, so careful or concerned readers have the opportunity to look up those sources.

need to make a note of the publication title and date, article title, and author, and then use that information to access the article through your library. Some libraries have a link to Google Scholar on their Web sites, so that you can start your search with Google Scholar from inside your library, limiting the search to your library's holdings and accessing the article with a simple click. Or you can use Scholar Preferences on Google Scholar to limit the search to your school's library.

Although specialized search engines like Google Scholar cannot guarantee access to all materials, search engines do provide access to a vast array of information on virtually any topic you can imagine. Unfortunately, not all Internet sources are necessarily reliable—in fact, you need to be extra cautious when evaluating the credibility and determining the viewpoint (and possible bias) of material located on the Internet. Chapter 12 offers detailed suggestions for assessing the accuracy and perspective of content you find in books and periodicals and on Web sites. However, before we consider these important issues, it will be useful to look at some good ways to go about searching for information on the Internet.

Using Search Tools

Search engines are not all the same—and they're constantly reinventing themselves as companies buy one another, develop partnerships to use someone else's search technology, or tinker with the design and philosophy of their own sites.

A search engine relies on automated searching software that "crawls" through the Internet and adds Web pages to its database. It then ranks and organizes these pages within its search results on the basis of a particular set of criteria or mathematical instructions. However, no search engine can truly search the entire Internet. Many sites, such as the Web sites of scholarly journals or many professional organizations, have limited access to paid subscribers or members. Other sites are not linked to or by any other pages. These sites make up what has been referred to as the deep, hidden, or invisible Web. Because your library has subscriptions and memberships to many of these sites, you will want to be sure to search through your library's portal in addition to searching with Internet search engines.

The search methodologies and ranking systems of the many different search engines vary and are constantly changing. That's why different search engines yield such different results. Therefore, you should not rely on just one search tool; try a few and see which one works best for your particular research needs.

The mark of a good search tool is getting relevant results within the first page or two, so that you do not have to scroll through hundreds (or even thousands) of hits to find the information you need. Choose a search tool that provides enough good results; theoretically, the more Web pages and other kinds of files a search engine indexes, the better your chances of finding appropriate hits. Another consideration is the quality of the searching experience—how the site looks, how easy it is to use, and what kinds of filters or preferences it offers, such as being able to limit your search by geographical region, language, or date. The box on page 580 lists some popular search tools.

Popular Search Engines and Search Sites

Search Engines	
AlltheWeb	**www.alltheweb.com** Multimedia search engine with image, audio, and advanced searches.
AltaVista	**www.altavista.com** Very complete search engine with a news page and various multimedia searches, including images, audio, and video. Also has a link to Babel Fish for translation.
Ask.com	**www.ask.com** Site allows keyword and question searches for images, news, and city and product searches, among others.
Google	**www.google.com** World's largest search engine—more than 200 million searches a day. Search by subject, keyword, or image, or choose from a wide variety of categories and options such as Google Scholar and Google Maps. Advanced Search options available. Google News "aggregates" or collects links to multiple sources on a wide range of news.
Windows Live Search	**www.live.com** In addition to standard Web search, search for images, news, maps, and classifieds.

Search Sites	
About.com	Content site owned by the *New York Times*. About.com has an internal-only search engine that examines content on thousands of topics compiled by freelance experts in each field.
AOL	**www.aol.com** Search function of this site is powered by Google search engine.
Lycos	**www.lycos.com** Features topic searches as well as keyword or phrase searches. Leading Spanish and Portuguese language site. Powered by Ask.com.
MSN	**www.msn.com** Search function of this site is powered by Windows Live Search.
Yahoo!	**www.yahoo.com** Comprehensive, multimedia search site. Search by subject, field of interest, or keyword.

Metasearch Sites	
Dogpile	**www.dogpile.com** Metasearch site powered by About.com, Ask.com, Google, Windows Live Search, Yahoo!, and other search engines.
HotBot	**www.hotbot.com** Powered by Ask.com and MSN.
Ixquick	**www.ixquick.com** Multimedia, metasearch site with strong privacy policy. Features searches in many different languages.
Search.com	**www.search.com** Search multimedia, or by categories such as reference, directory, downloads, and many more. Advanced Search features.
WebCrawler	**www.webcrawler.com** Metasearch site uses Ask.com, Google, Windows Live Search, Yahoo!, and others. Search for images, audio, video, news, and local information.

Google

What's the best search engine? That's hard to say. But when this book was written, Google was by far the Web's most popular search engine, handling nearly 65 percent of all searches—through both its own site and the partner sites that license its search technology.

Google is also the largest search engine in terms of the number of Web pages it indexes (several billion), as well as a variety of other kinds of files (such as images, videos, maps, and more). In fact, Google is now so popular that the word *Google* as a verb has become a synonym for "search the Web."

Google may be the Web's dominant search engine, but you should not think it's the only option. In fact, Google's unparalleled popularity has forced its competitors to redesign their sites and refocus their search technology, so it is worth experimenting to see what else is out there.

Using Advanced Search Options

To give you an example of how to use some of the Advanced Search options on a typical search engine, let's take a look at how one student began her search for an assignment where her instructor had asked that students include at least four academic sources in their research. The student decided to write her research paper on the relationship between violence and video games. She began her search with Google Scholar, typing in the keywords "violence" and "video games."

Since this search returned thousands of responses, the student decided to try using the Advanced Scholar Search to get a more focused result. But first she scanned through the first few pages to get help with narrowing her topic. She noticed that many of the entries specifically mentioned the link between violent video games and aggression, and several of them specifically talked about the effect on males. She wondered what would happen if she decided to look at the effect on females. She further narrowed the search by focusing on adolescents (or teens), eliminating "education" as a topic, limiting her search to recent (2000–2008) material, and choosing a specific subject area. This resulted in just 141 entries, which is a reasonable number to scan.

Some search sites suggest either related searches or categories that draw on subject directories to narrow a search automatically. For example, WiseNut's WiseGuide section presents a list of related categories that can help whittle down extremely long lists of sources. When even these results need further refining in order to be useful, you need to think of a way to make the topic even narrower. By adding words and phrases to the original string of search terms, you can then search only within the results already obtained. To narrow your list further, scan the first few hits to find additional phrases to add to your search terms. A good goal is a short list of thirty to fifty potential sources, a size that you could reasonably look at without wasting too much time. And narrowing search results in this way will help you to focus on a topic that is much more specific.

Google Scholar Keyword Search Results

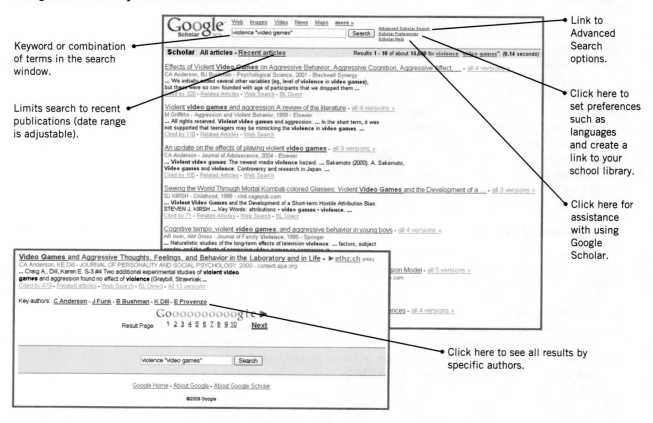

Keyword or combination of terms in the search window.

Limits search to recent publications (date range is adjustable).

Link to Advanced Search options.

Click here to set preferences such as languages and create a link to your school library.

Click here for assistance with using Google Scholar.

Click here to see all results by specific authors.

{ Exercise } **Advanced Search**

Conduct a search, using any search engine of your choice, that would help you locate material to answer the following research question:

In 2007, Hollywood writers, members of the Writers Guild of America, went on strike. How did that strike affect subsequent production of movies and television programs in the United States?

Print out the first page of your search, and then (in class) meet with two or three of your classmates to discuss the following questions: Which search engines did you use? How different are the results from different search engines? What keywords did you use? How could you improve your results? Which items look most likely to lead to useful information? Why? Which sources can be immediately eliminated? Why? ■

Google Scholar Advanced Search Screen

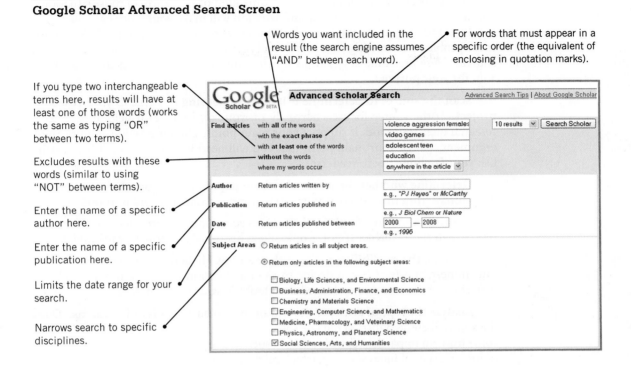

Words you want included in the result (the search engine assumes "AND" between each word).

For words that must appear in a specific order (the equivalent of enclosing in quotation marks).

If you type two interchangeable terms here, results will have at least one of those words (works the same as typing "OR" between two terms).

Excludes results with these words (similar to using "NOT" between terms).

Enter the name of a specific author here.

Enter the name of a specific publication here.

Limits the date range for your search.

Narrows search to specific disciplines.

▷ SORTING THROUGH YOUR SOURCES

Once you have used the library and Internet to find potential sources, you need to make decisions about which ones to pursue. This section provides advice on making those decisions while keeping audience and purpose in mind. It also offers suggestions for thinking about visuals. Remember, while choosing sources you need to keep track of bibliographic information so that you can find the sources again and also create a list of works cited. Many instructors call this list of potential sources a working bibliography; it is always subject to revision because you are constantly working on it.

For more information on in-text citations and lists of works cited, see Chapter 13.

Making Decisions about Sources

As you begin to look through your sources, think carefully about how many you will need. When working on an assignment for school, your instructor will probably give you an idea of how many sources to incorporate into the final project, as well as what types of visuals to include. When doing research for some other purpose—for a job, a community organization, an extracurricular activity, or a personal project—you will not have the same kind of guidance. In those situations, you will need to decide how much information will make your work credible.

If you have access to the Internet and a variety of databases, you will likely have more problems narrowing your search and sorting through the results than finding sources. Here are some suggestions for determining which sources are most relevant for your purposes.

Scan the source to determine if it adds something of value to your research project. Is the source focused narrowly on your topic? Does it help answer your research question? Does it support your main point? Does it provide an important argument against your main point that you will need to refute? Does it help establish your credibility with readers?

Determine whether the material is from popular, trade, or scholarly sources. Are sources from this category appropriate for your audience and purpose?

Consider the date of publication. Does your topic require a focus on the most recent material available? If not, would older, historical material be preferable?

Evaluate the credibility of the author and publisher. Are your sources accurate, honest, and fair? If you decide to use information from a source you are not sure about, have you acknowledged that doubt in your research paper?

Analyze the type of evidence the author uses to back up his or her claims. Does the source include statistical data or some other type of research data? Does the data come from an impartial, reputable source such as a university (as opposed to a corporation or a special interest group, which might present biased or incomplete information)? Does the author quote recognized experts or provide reasonable examples?

For more on recognizing perspective, see Chapter 12.

Identify the perspective of the source. Have you figured out what perspective each source represents to ensure that your research project examines multiple points of view?

Choose sources from more than one medium. Have you incorporated a mix of reference materials: books; magazine, newspaper, and journal articles; Web sites; and so forth?

Thinking about Visual Sources

For more information on layout and design elements, see Chapter 9.

As you research your topic, you may realize that visual information will help make your argument or support your thesis better. If you are citing statistics, you may want to create or adapt a table. If you are analyzing how something has changed over time, you may want to create a bar or line graph. If you need to show what something or someone looks like, a drawing or photograph will probably be most effective. One of the best ways to determine what visuals you need is to look closely at the visual elements incorporated into the sources you are selecting. How do those authors and publishers use visuals to convey information? Do you have data or ideas that could be presented in a similar way? Remember also to analyze key sources for their use of visual elements such as headings, color, and so forth. You may want to use those sources as models for your own project.

Most search engines allow you to search for images, so if you need a photograph, drawing, map, diagram, or other image, you may be able to find what you need on the Internet. If you are producing a text that will be submitted to your instructor, your classmates, and no one else, you may be able to use any image you find on the Internet. But if your work will be posted on a course Web site or disseminated to anyone beyond the classroom, you may need to ask for permission to use the image. And in any case, you will need to give credit to the owner of the image. Be sure to keep a record of where any images come from so that you can properly credit the owner.

For more advice on crediting visual sources, see Chapter 13.

For more on asking permission to use visual material, see Chapter 9, page 543.

Preparing a Working Bibliography

Research involves synthesizing a lot of facts, ideas, and opinions before coming to conclusions of your own about a topic. To synthesize means to bring different parts together into a whole. Your research will lack credibility if you don't find out what other people have said, written, or done that is relevant to your topic—but your project will lack coherence if you don't figure out how to unify these concepts and voices.

No matter what you are writing about, you cannot expect to remember everything you read or see during your research. You have to take notes about important facts, ideas, and visual elements. Specifically, you will look for memorable statements you can quote, key concepts you can paraphrase, complex information you can summarize, and data you can present graphically. The success of your project—whether it is a research project, oral presentation, annotated bibliography, or one of the writing genres covered in Part 1 of this book—will depend on your ability to find good sources and take accurate notes. Sources must be documented properly—both in the text and in a bibliography (often called either works cited or references). The information you need to gather will depend on the documentation style your instructor requires, so make sure to find out whether you are expected to use MLA, APA, CSE, Chicago, or another style for your research.

For suggestions on what type of notes to take, when to take them, and how to organize and synthesize your information, see Chapter 12.

For advice on MLA and APA documentation styles, see Chapter 13.

You will be most successful at taking notes if you create an organized system for gathering information—either on paper or in your computer. The system can be as simple as a file of index cards or as complex as a computer database. (A notebook without removable pages is not a good choice because at some point you will want to sort through your notes and rearrange them.) Whatever format you choose, it will be helpful to use the checklist on the next page to remind you to record bibliographic information from different types of sources.

Once you have established a system for recording bibliographic information, you are ready to start looking through your sources and taking notes. Below the checklist are a few tips that will make your efforts more efficient and productive.

Checklist for Bibliographic Information

	Books or Parts of Books	Journals, Magazines, and Newspapers (print or electronic)	Online Sources
Author	✓	✓	✓
Editor	✓		
Title (and subtitle)	✓	✓	✓
Periodical title		✓	
Chapter title	✓		
Site name			✓
Place of publication	✓		
Publisher	✓		
Page numbers	✓	✓	✓ (if available)
Date of publication	✓	✓	✓
Volume number		✓	
Name of sponsoring institution or organization			✓
Medium of publication	✓	✓	✓
Date of your access		✓ (if electronic access)	✓
Call number	✓		
Electronic address (URL)		✓ (if electronic access)	✓
Other information (if relevant and available)	translator, edition, volume	translator, issue	paragraph numbers

Skim through the article, book, or Web site before you start to take notes. Doing research is time consuming, and you don't want to waste time making notes about an article that turns out to be irrelevant or inappropriate.

Write down all the bibliographic information as soon as you decide that a source will be useful. Add this information to your working bibliography and be sure to include the specific page numbers where information came from in your notes.

Print or copy pages with pertinent visual elements if you cannot describe the visuals succinctly or summarize the data they present. By printing or copying pages and marking each with the source, you can easily sort through the images when you are ready to create or integrate a visual for your paper.

Continuing Your Research

As you conduct research—in the library, on the Internet, or in the field—you may find that your research needs have changed. For example, you may discover that the kind of information you need is unavailable or that your research question has changed. You may realize that it would take too long to meet the time frame of a school assignment or that your topic is too broad for a single research project. You may come across some new information that sends you back to the library, onto the Web, or into the field in pursuit of verification, contradiction, or another point of view. You may decide that only field research will produce the kind of information you need, in which case you will find help in Chapter 11. Regardless of the kind of research you conduct and the number of times you feel compelled to search for more information, however, at some point you will need to just start writing.

How will you know when to start writing? Only you can make that decision. If you created a time line before beginning the project, you will have allocated a certain amount of time for your research and a deadline for beginning to write. Do your best to stick with that plan, but be aware that you may need to make minor changes.

For advice on managing your time and creating a plan, see page 559.

11

Conducting Field Research

In some situations, it will be important to bolster your library or Internet research with field research. Internet and library research often involve looking at information from secondary sources—material created by people who were not witnesses to the events they describe. Field research, on the other hand, requires you to conduct firsthand research using primary sources involving people or situations connected to your research topic. You may need to do field research if you want data that does not yet exist in another form—information about a hot issue on your campus or the habits of its current students, for example, or about local people or practices in a community today.

This chapter presents guidelines to help you conduct the type of primary field research you may be asked to do for an English class. You will find information here about three common methods of gathering primary research data: interviews, observations, and surveys.

▷ CONDUCTING INTERVIEWS

Interviews can be extremely useful sources of information and opinions, especially in the early stages of an investigation. You can use interviews to accomplish the following tasks.

▶ Gather new information on a topic, based on a person's firsthand experience or expertise

▶ Identify varying opinions or perspectives on a topic

▶ Gather interesting and relevant quotes to add to your project

See excerpts from an article that incorporates information from interviews on page 594. See the full article beginning on page 28.

▶ Gather anecdotal evidence to support your position on a topic

▶ Get suggestions and advice on additional sources of information to pursue

Setting Up the Interview

You will have to make a number of decisions before you can conduct the interview.

Decide who would be the most appropriate person or people to interview. This choice will depend on your audience and purpose. For a research report on a disease, such as mononucleosis, you might want to interview a doctor who is an expert in diagnosing and treating the disease as well as a patient who has had it. For a project on an environmental issue, such as the effects of recycling programs on a particular community, you might want to interview a town official, an environmental activist, and a local resident. You also need to decide how many people to interview. Is the topic extremely controversial? If the answer is yes, you cannot simply present one point of view—you will need to interview at least two people who have differing perspectives. Even for a profile, you will probably want to interview not only the person being profiled but also some of that person's friends, colleagues, and family members who can offer additional insight into your subject's life or work.

Figure out how you are going to approach each person you want to interview. Do you already know this person? If not, do you know someone who does and who would be willing to make the initial contact for you? Do you think this person would be willing to talk to you? Keep in mind that most people—even busy professionals— are happy to talk about themselves and their work and are often enthusiastic about helping students (as long as those students sound motivated and polite). Before you contact each person to schedule the interview, be sure to think about exactly what you want to say and how you want to say it. You might even consider preparing a script requesting an interview, but be sure to rehearse it so that you do not have to read it awkwardly over the phone. (See the box on Requesting an Interview on page 591 for tips on what to include in your script.)

Decide whether you will be able to conduct the interview in a face-to-face setting. You will get the most information from this type of interview because people communicate a great deal through facial expressions, gestures, and body language; thus you can more fully "read" a person's responses when you are talking face to face. You can also learn a lot by observing a person's home or office (if the interview takes place there), and then you can add descriptive, personality-revealing details of setting. If such a meeting is impossible or impractical, consider conducting the interview over the telephone. You can still establish rapport with your interviewee and can learn a lot from his or her tone of voice, general attitude toward you and the topic, and the pauses in the conversation. If all else fails, you can conduct the interview by e-mail, sending questions that the interviewee will respond to in a reply message, or by using instant messaging. Recognize, however, that with an electronic interview you will lose a great deal of the richness of human communication.

Requesting an Interview

It is often helpful to prepare exactly what you are going to say before you contact a potential interview subject. If you use a script for requesting an interview, try to include the following types of information.

▶ Your name and why you are calling ("Hi, my name is Dan George, and I'm writing a research report on campus safety for my English class at North Carolina State University.")

▶ Any connection you have to this person and what you want from him or her ("My instructor, Professor Fetzer, suggested that you might be willing to talk to me about the new call-box system that has been installed on campus this year.")

▶ A specific suggestion about how long the interview will take ("I would like to talk with you for about thirty minutes.")

▶ A few alternative dates and times, as well as a suggestion for where the interview might take place ("I could meet with you at your office any time next Tuesday or Thursday morning or after 3:00 p.m. next Wednesday.")

▶ A specific request for an appointment ("Would you be able to meet with me at one of those times next week?")

▶ A sincere thank-you at the end, and a repetition of the date, time, and meeting place that you have both agreed on ("Thank you for your help with my project. I look forward to talking with you at 4 o'clock next Wednesday afternoon at your office.")

Preparing for the Interview

Before you go to the interview, you will want to do some preparation. Be sure to build in ample time to set up, prepare for, conduct, and analyze your interview. Contact your interviewee well in advance of the actual date when you want to conduct the interview. This allows for the possibility of a last-minute cancellation or postponement. You will also need to allow time in your schedule for follow-up phone calls or e-mails if you find that you need to clarify a point or ask another question. Other preparations include the following.

Prepare a list of questions that elicit meaningful answers. This list should be relevant to your topic and appropriate for the person you are interviewing. Avoid writing questions in such a way that you tell the person what you want (or expect) to hear.

Avoid questions that can be answered by a simple yes or no or with a brief factual response. Ask open-ended questions that inspire answers full of details, opinions, anecdotes, and analysis. Try asking the interviewee to describe, explain, or simply tell you about something.

Practice your interview questions with a friend or family member so that you feel comfortable. Audio- or video-record yourself asking the questions and then play back the recording to hear how you sound (or look).

Decide whether you are going to record the interview or just take notes. If you record the interview, take notes as a backup because recording devices can malfunction, and some people can be hard to understand on the recording. If you use a recording device, be sure to get the permission of the person you are interviewing, even if you are recording a phone interview.

Consider taking one or more photographs of the interview. Depending on the type of research project, you may want to add the visual impact of a well-chosen photo—either of the interviewee or of a setting or object that is important to that person. Again, be sure to ask permission before taking any photographs.

The day before the interview, call or e-mail to confirm the appointment. If you have decided to take photographs or tape-record the interview, now is the time to ask permission. If the person says no, be gracious and agreeable.

Make sure that all equipment is in working order. If you are recording the interview, be sure your recorder is working properly and that you have extra batteries. Also make sure to have good note-taking equipment—a pad, notebook, or laptop computer, as well as several sharpened pencils or working pens. If you plan to take photographs, make sure that your camera works.

{ **Exercise** } **Interview Questions**

Why are the following questions inappropriate for an interview? Rewrite them in a way that requests the same type of information while eliciting a meaningful response.

- Whose bright idea was it to have the clock tower chime all night long?
- Don't you agree that the dorms need to be renovated?
- Why doesn't someone solve the parking problem on campus?
- Doesn't it bother you that your medical research involves killing innocent animals?

Now read the next group of interview questions. Rewrite these questions so they are phrased to solicit more detailed, informative answers instead of one-word answers.

- Do you like your job?
- Was it hard to be a working mother during the 1960s?
- Was your first job out of college meaningful?
- Did you find the transition from a small town to a big city difficult? ∎

Effective Interviews

With one or two classmates, make a list of all the different types of interviews (or articles based on interviews) that you have read, seen, or heard. Are some of them more informative or revealing than others? Why? Which interviews seem like credible reporting, and which ones seem like publicity puff pieces? ■

Conducting the Interview

Everyone has his or her own style of conducting an interview, but here are a few tips that can help you in any interview situation.

On the day of the interview, arrive on time, dressed appropriately, with all the equipment and writing tools you need. If you have to wait, be patient. If the person originally gave you permission to record the interview or take photographs, ask again before turning on the tape recorder or taking out your camera.

During the interview, speak slowly and clearly and try to establish friendly eye contact. Resist the temptation to look down at your notes the whole time.

Write down not only what the interviewee says but also descriptive details. Notes about his or her appearance, voice, body language, gestures, or setting might enliven your report.

Remember that your list of prepared questions is just a starting point. Be flexible, and allow the interview to move in a new direction if necessary (without going completely off course).

Keep within the time limits you agreed on in your initial request for an interview. If you run out of time and the person does not invite you to stay longer, ask if you may call or e-mail in a few days to complete the interview.

Ask for permission to call or e-mail if any additional questions arise. You may find in the writing of your report that you need to contact the interview subject again to clarify a particular point.

Say a sincere thank-you before you leave. If you make a positive impression, your interview subject will likely be receptive to any follow-up queries that you might have.

Writing Up the Interview

Once the interview is over, it is easy to relax and think that the hard part is done. However, while the interview is still fresh in your mind, it is important to take several additional steps.

Using Data

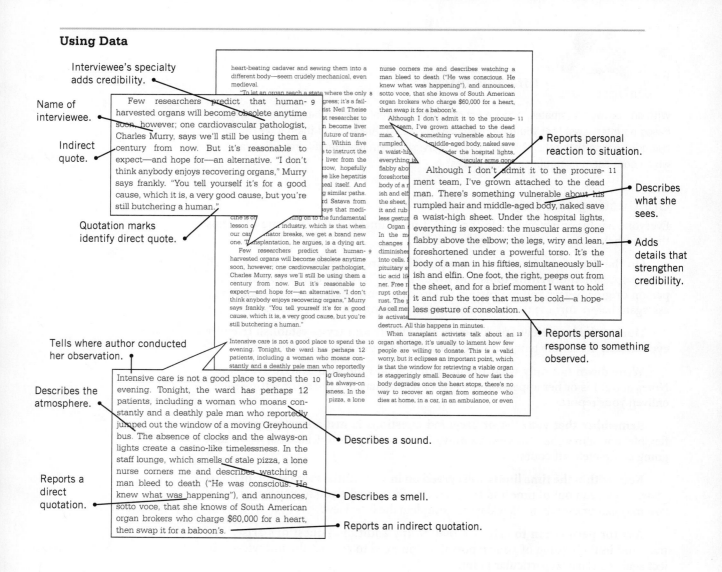

Interviewee's specialty adds credibility.

Name of interviewee.

Indirect quote.

Quotation marks identify direct quote.

Tells where author conducted her observation.

Describes the atmosphere.

Reports a direct quotation.

Reports personal reaction to situation.

Describes what she sees.

Adds details that strengthen credibility.

Reports personal response to something observed.

Describes a sound.

Describes a smell.

Reports an indirect quotation.

heart-beating cadaver and sewing them into a different body—seem crudely mechanical, even medieval.

"To let an organ reach a state where the only progress; it's a fail- 8 list Neil Theise st researcher to n become liver future of trans- n. Within five to instruct the liver from the row, hopefully se like hepatitis eal itself. And g similar paths. d Satava from ays that medi- ng on to the fundamental lesson of industry, which is that when our capitator breaks, we get a brand new one. Transplantation, he argues, is a dying art.

Few researchers predict that human- 9 harvested organs will become obsolete anytime soon, however; one cardiovascular pathologist, Charles Murry, says we'll still be using them a century from now. But it's reasonable to expect—and hope for—an alternative. "I don't think anybody enjoys recovering organs," Murry says frankly. "You tell yourself it's for a good cause, which it is, a very good cause, but you're still butchering a human."

Intensive care is not a good place to spend the 10 evening. Tonight, the ward has perhaps 12 patients, including a woman who moans constantly and a deathly pale man who reportedly jumped out the window of a moving Greyhound bus. The absence of clocks and the always-on lights create a casino-like timelessness. In the staff lounge, which smells of stale pizza, a lone nurse corners me and describes watching a man bleed to death ("He was conscious. He knew what was happening"), and announces, sotto voce, that she knows of South American organ brokers who charge $60,000 for a heart, then swap it for a baboon's.

nurse corners me and describes watching a man bleed to death ("He was conscious. He knew what was happening"), and announces, sotto voce, that she knows of South American organ brokers who charge $60,000 for a heart, then swap it for a baboon's.

Although I don't admit it to the procure- 11 ment team, I've grown attached to the dead man. something vulnerable about his rumpled middle-aged body, naked save a waist-hi der the hospital lights, everything is uscular arms gone flabby abo foreshorte body of a r ish and elf the sheet, it and rub less gestur

Organ In the m changes diminishes into cells. pituitary s tic acid lik ner. Free r rupt other rust. The p As cell me is activate destruct. All this happens in minutes.

When transplant activists talk about an 13 organ shortage, it's usually to lament how few people are willing to donate. This is a valid worry, but it eclipses an important point, which is that the window for retrieving a viable organ is staggeringly small. Because of how fast the body degrades once the heart stops, there's no way to recover an organ from someone who dies at home, in a car, in an ambulance, or even

Although I don't admit it to the procure- 11 ment team, I've grown attached to the dead man. There's something vulnerable about his rumpled hair and middle-aged body, naked save a waist-high sheet. Under the hospital lights, everything is exposed: the muscular arms gone flabby above the elbow; the legs, wiry and lean, foreshortened under a powerful torso. It's the body of a man in his fifties, simultaneously bullish and elfin. One foot, the right, peeps out from the sheet, and for a brief moment I want to hold it and rub the toes that must be cold—a hopeless gesture of consolation.

See the full article beginning on page 28.

Write up your notes as soon as possible. If you do this within an hour or two, you will remember a lot of details that would otherwise become fuzzy.

Write down your own thoughts about the interview in addition to fleshing out your notes about what the interviewee said. For example, did the person seem knowledgeable and insightful? Did he or she demonstrate any strong opinions or reactions to your questions or to the general topic? Did the person say or do anything to indicate a particular bias? If so, does that bias seem strong enough to affect his or her credibility as a source for your research project, or is the bias something you could simply point out in your project?

Reflect on what you learned during the interview, and write down your response to what the interviewee said. Looking back at the interview, do you think you asked the right questions? Did you stick too rigidly to your script? Is there a point you should have pursued more aggressively or a fact you still don't understand? If so, consider calling or e-mailing with a follow-up question.

Send a thank-you note after the interview, particularly if it took place at the person's home or lasted a long time. In your note, offer to send copies of any photographs you took (or perhaps even your finished research project).

Integrate Data Effectively

Information that you gather through your research, whether interviews, observations, surveys, or other forms of research, must be integrated into your written text. The example on page 594 shows how one author used interviews along with observation to gather data about organ transplants, which she then integrated into a report of her personal experience. Notice how she identifies the sources of her information, uses both direct and indirect quotes, and includes lots of detail about what she saw and heard—and even what she could smell. She also reports on her personal reaction to the environment and the people she interviewed and observed.

▷ MAKING OBSERVATIONS

Before reading this chapter, you probably already knew that interviews and surveys are frequently used as research strategies, but you may not have realized that it is also possible to conduct research by simply observing the behaviors of others. In fact, observations can be a useful way to accomplish the following research tasks.

► See how people behave in their natural environment

► Collect data without influencing the participants

► Gather anecdotal evidence (see box on p. 596) that will make your research report more realistic

► Generate questions and ideas that can be investigated further through interviews and surveys

► Verify the information gained through interviews or surveys

► Collect data without relying on the interpretation, memory, accuracy, or honesty of interviewees or survey participants

► Gain a great deal of information about specific groups or situations, often in a short amount of time

See an excerpt from an article that incorporates information from observations on page 594. See the full article beginning on page 28.

Anecdotal Evidence

An *anecdote* is a little story; thus, anecdotal evidence uses a story or stories to prove a point. Often anecdotal evidence comes from your own experience, but it can also come from observations. An anecdote makes a great opening paragraph because a story is a good hook to get the reader interested in your topic. You can also intersperse anecdotes throughout a report to support specific points. A memorable anecdote may even work well as a conclusion. The following is an example of an anecdote that you might use in an opening for a research paper about Lyme disease.

> The recurring low-grade fever that had plagued me for three months indicated that something was wrong. But despite repeated trips to the doctor, the fever's cause remained a mystery. I was surprised when a new doctor suggested that I get tested for Lyme disease. Even more surprising is that my eventual diagnosis was just one of twenty new confirmed cases of the disease this month in our county.

Although some researchers and reporters make their observations fairly quickly, other researchers, such as anthropologists, conduct very detailed, long-term observations of groups of people. For example, many researchers visit remote parts of the world to live with and observe aboriginal peoples and then report on their observations. Many issues of *National Geographic* contain reports based largely on observation. This type of study is done with the permission of the people being observed and may involve years of field research. It also requires years of training.

However, it is possible to conduct some types of observation in a short amount of time, without any formal training, and often without asking for permission. For example, if you are researching the number of people who try to drive the wrong way down a poorly marked one-way street, you can stand on the corner of the street and keep track of how many people make the attempt during a certain period without asking anyone's permission to do so. But if you want to observe the number of people who order salads in a particular fast-food restaurant at lunchtime, you will need to ask the manager for permission to sit at a table and take notes.

In another type of observational research, you might want to watch a specific person or group of people over an extended period. For example, you might be interested in writing a report on students' attentiveness in large lecture courses at your college. To do this, you would need permission to attend several different lecture courses. Then you would sit quietly and observe the students, lecturer, and classroom (or lecture hall) setting, taking notes about your observations of details such as those in the example on the next page.

In your report, you might present a chart or table summarizing some of this information. You might also want to make sketches to show how certain physical and environmental features affect students' attentiveness.

Observation Notes

Course: American History 101

Number of Students: 43

Classroom description: Large auditorium. Professor lectures from a "stage" with students seated in rising rows of chairs, a third of which are empty. Lighting is dim and room is overheated. Good acoustics.

Technology: PowerPoint slides displayed on a large dropdown screen. A white board had a notice that the reading assignment for the next session had been changed. The notice stayed up throughout the class period.

Student behavior:

- took notes actively |||| |||| |||| |||
- read from laptop |||
- texted messages on their cell phones |||| ||
- dozed or slept ||
- appeared to listen but didn't take notes ||||
- arrived late ||
- left early and didn't return |
- asked questions   0
- stayed after class to speak to professor |||

Professor's behavior: Lectured throughout with no time for discussion or Q & A. Used slides effectively, but otherwise read from a prepared lecture with little deviation from it.

General impression: Most students seemed to be paying attention, but there was little engagement between them and their instructor except at the end of class when a few students went up to talk to the professor about an upcoming assignment.

Planning the Observation

As with any research project, the most important steps are in the planning stage. Your first step is to figure out what you want to accomplish by conducting an observation. What research question(s) do you hope to answer? What will you need to

For more advice on formulating
a research question, see
Chapter 10, page 562.

observe to get your answer(s)? How much time will be required? You then need to decide exactly what you want to focus on. For example, an observation for a report on food preferences might involve sitting in a fast-food restaurant for several hours and keeping track of the kinds of food people order. Do you want to answer questions about the number of people who order salads? French fries? Diet versus regular soft drinks? If so, you would need some kind of chart to keep track of all the orders; and because most fast-food restaurants offer a lot of variety, you would probably need to group your observations into broad categories. These categories would vary according to the research questions. For example, if you were interested only in salads versus burgers, you could have three categories: Salads, Burgers, Other. During the observation, you would record the total number of people who order anything so that you could say, "X percent of all customers ordered . . ." or "X out of Y customers ordered . . . ."

Once you have established the focus of your observation, you will need to make decisions about the following.

Select an appropriate site for your observation. If you choose a public site (such as a city park), you probably will not have to ask permission. If the site you choose is private (such as a shopping mall or store), you must get permission from an authority to conduct the observation. When asking, be sure to say who you are, what you plan to observe and why, when you want to conduct the observation, and how long you will be there.

Make a visit to the site beforehand to get a sense of the available space. Will you be able to sit down and use a table to take notes? How obvious will you be to those you are observing? Is there adequate lighting for note taking, or should you bring a pen light (for example, at a theater)? If you plan to plug in a piece of equipment, are there electrical outlets?

Decide how you will record your observations. Depending on the site, you might use a laptop computer, an audio or video recorder, a notebook, or preformatted data charts to log in your observations. If you want to videotape, photograph, or electronically record someone's words and actions, you must get that person's permission.

Conducting the Observation

Once you have a plan in place, you are ready to begin your observation. Here are some suggestions for getting the most out of gathering data through observation.

Arrive early with all your tools and equipment. Make sure that you have everything you need with you and that your equipment is in working order (pens, sharpened pencils, notebook or pad, camera, tape recorder, and so on).

If the site is private, immediately announce yourself to the person who gave you permission, and restate your project and purpose. If the person who originally granted you permission is not there, give that person's name and title to the person who is on site, explaining that your original contact approved your observation.

Find a position where you can observe without interfering with other people. Try to be unobtrusive—it may help to think of yourself as a spy or plainclothes detective trying to blend into the scene.

Take notes on everything you see or hear. Put quotation marks around any direct quotes so you can remember later which words are your own and which ones are someone else's. Take notes about the people, place, and actions you observe (making sketches or taking photographs if you plan to include visuals) and your own thoughts and feelings.

Reviewing Your Observational Notes

As with interviews, you want to gather your thoughts about your observation as soon as possible after you have completed your observation. Review your notes carefully as follows.

Read through your notes and add any other ideas that occur to you. Now is the time to flesh out your observations by writing down your thoughts about what the observation revealed, as well as additional details about the people, setting, and actions—things you may have been too busy to record as they were happening.

Clarify what you meant by any abbreviations that you may have used to speed up your note taking. Do this as soon as possible—preferably within an hour or two of the observation—while your memory is still fresh.

Decide if you need to conduct additional observations. If your observation did not adequately answer your research question, you may need to conduct one or more additional observations. Think carefully about what you still need. Should you return to the same place at a different time or day, or would it be better to try a different site? Do you need to collect more of the same type of information, or should you focus on a slightly different research question?

Analyzing and Presenting the Data

You will probably have gathered a great deal of information. Don't feel overwhelmed; use your research question to guide your analysis. What did you see that might help answer your question(s)? Use the following suggestions to help you figure out what to do with all the data.

Read through your notes carefully to find any patterns. Use a highlighter or colored pen to mark patterns or particular observations that provide evidence to support the claims you plan to make in your report. Pay attention to the exceptions—the information you gathered that does not fit the pattern—to see if it sheds an interesting light on the topic. For example, if in fact you observed that more men than women ordered cheeseburgers, you might want to take a look at the women who did order cheeseburgers: Did they have any characteristics in common?

If you conducted observations at more than one site, check to see if the data from the different sites were consistent. If not, can you draw any conclusions about the differences? For example, if you conducted observations at several fast-food restaurants, you might have observed significant variations in the physical settings, types of food ordered, hours of operation, or employee-customer interactions. In analyzing the data, you might suggest possible causes or effects of these differences. Here are some other questions to consider as you analyze your data.

► What did I observe that I expected to see?

► What did I observe that surprised me?

► Did I observe anything that upset or angered me?

► How did my observation support or amplify what I learned through my other research (including interviews and surveys)?

► Did my observation contradict any of my other sources?

► As a result of my observation, do I need to conduct additional research?

Think about how to incorporate your observational research into your project. Observational research can be used as the centerpiece of your research, as support for aspect of your argument, or for detail. How you plan to use it will dictate the form it takes in your paper. Will you present the data as anecdotal evidence or in a more formal way? How will you use this data in conjunction with the information you gathered from other sources? Will the results of your observation provide backup for your other research or represent a major element of your project?

▷ CONDUCTING SURVEYS

Surveys (sometimes called questionnaires) typically consist of a series of questions that can be asked and answered in writing, in person, or over the phone. Surveys are used all the time by marketing consultants who want information about the public's response to new products and services. Those surveys are scientifically designed and conducted, and they lead to quantitative results—the kind that are often trumpeted in ads with claims such as "Four out of five dentists surveyed recommend product X." (See the box on page 601 for a discussion of the differences between quantitative and qualitative data.) A survey that you conduct for this course will probably not allow you to make generalizations about large groups of people because you will not have the time or the resources to develop a scientifically valid survey that collects a large number of responses. However, the answers to the questions in a simple survey can help you generate information for localized populations about topics such as the following.

► The prevalence of a particular practice ("How many people in this class have e-mailed the instructor about an assignment?")

▶ Varying points of view ("What do people in this dorm think of the food in the dining hall?")

▶ Preferences for particular products ("What brand of running shoes are preferred by men between the ages of eighteen and twenty-five?")

▶ The beliefs of a particular group with regard to a particular topic ("Is the electoral college an appropriate mechanism for electing the president of the United States?")

▶ The feelings of a particular group ("How do first-year students feel about being away from home?")

Quantitative and Qualitative Data

Quantitative data is any data that can be reported in numbers. Quantitative data that answers these questions may be helpful in your research.

▶ How many? ("Nine out of ten participants in the study showed improvement on this medication.")

▶ How much? ("Thirty percent of the precipitation fell as sleet before turning to rain.")

▶ How likely? ("Forty percent of all marriages in the United States are likely to end in divorce.")

Quantitative data deals in generalizations; it clusters facts together and counts them. Most people have a lot of confidence in quantitative data, which typically comes from surveys or experiments.

Qualitative data is descriptive and specific. It can give a more vivid picture of how people think, feel, or behave than quantitative data. Consider these statements that use qualitative data.

▶ "Every Friday, employees were allowed to wear casual clothes to work, which may have contributed to more casual behavior, such as less formality in meetings, no strict adherence to specified break times, and more personal conversations in the hallways."

▶ "Aleksandr R. Luria, a Soviet psychologist, found that illiterate peasants gave colors metaphorical names such as 'liver' or 'apple' instead of brown or red."

▶ "Cuna women wear intricate beaded bracelets on their arms and legs, bright shirts with elaborately appliquéd designs, and gold hoops in their noses."

While qualitative data is not generalizable, it can add the type of detail that makes writing more interesting or more believable. Qualitative data typically comes from interviews, open-ended survey questions, and observations.

{ Exercise } **Sources Using Surveys**

Look through newspapers and popular magazines such as *Time* for examples of information derived from a survey. How was this material incorporated into the article? Did the inclusion of this material help to make the writer's main point more compelling? Why or why not? ■

See the box on page 605 for closed and open-ended question options for surveys.

If you were going to write a report on the type of food that college students purchase at fast-food restaurants, you might create a survey such as the following to gather primary data (see page 564 in Chapter 10 for more on primary data). The student creating this survey used the online tool SurveyMonkey to organize and distribute her survey.

Sample Survey Created Using SurveyMonkey

Fast Food Preferences	Exit this survey >>

1. Questions

Thank you for agreeing to participate in this survey of fast food preferences. Please submit your responses to me by March 1. I appreciate your help!

1. At a fast-food restaurant, I am likely to order (check all that apply):

☐ hamburger   ☐ diet soda

☐ chicken nuggets   ☐ salad

☐ regular soda   ☐ French fries

☐ cheeseburger   ☐ chicken sandwich

☐ taco   ☐ milkshake

Other (please specify)

[   ]

2. Using the following scale, rate the different reasons you eat fast food.

	1 = very important	2 = somewhat important	3 = not at all important
convenience	○	○	○
low cost	○	○	○
taste	○	○	○
variety of offerings	○	○	○
familiarity with menu	○	○	○
fast service	○	○	○
drive-through access	○	○	○

3. Which fast food restaurants do you go to the most?

[   ]

4. Describe a typical meal that you would order at a fast food restaurant.

[   ]

5. Are there any menu items that you would like to see added to the typical fast food menu? Please describe.

[   ]

6. Why do you eat off campus?

[   ]

[Done >>]

Planning the Survey

As with interviews, there are many steps you have to take and decisions you have to make before you can conduct your research.

Figure out the characteristics of the people you want to survey. These characteristics will vary according to your audience and purpose. For a report requested by the Dean of Advising on the reasons students drop out of your college, you will need to find people who have dropped out. For a workshop for instructors on the advantages and disadvantages of lecture-based courses versus discussion-based courses, you will need to survey students who have taken both types of courses. There may be other considerations, too: Are you writing about a topic that has a particular geographical limitation? Are you writing about a topic that has a gender, race, or age limitation?

Decide how many people need to complete the survey. For statistically significant studies, there are scientific ways to determine the number of participants (respondents) needed. However, for your purposes, you will probably be able to survey a relatively small population as a representative sample. For the purposes of a writing course, you can probably get credible information if you survey at least twenty-five participants.

Decide whether the participants can remain anonymous. If you are asking questions about a sensitive topic (such as sexuality, weight, drug or alcohol use, depression, or domestic violence), you will get a more honest response if you can guarantee that you will not reveal the identity of any participants. To do so, you must come up with a way to gather, store, and code the survey data so that no one can possibly know any of the respondents' names. Keep in mind that even if the respondents remain anonymous, you may still want them to identify their age, gender, race, ethnicity, or other characteristics. Also keep in mind that, theoretically, surveys conducted in person or over the phone can be anonymous in the sense that names and other identifying information will not be connected to the data. As a practical matter, however, participants usually will not feel that their survey responses are truly anonymous if, for example, they are your own classmates or relatives.

Decide whether you want to conduct the survey in writing, in person, or over the phone. Each method has advantages and disadvantages. One advantage of a written survey is that participants usually answer more honestly when they are not speaking directly with the researcher. However, you may have a better chance of getting people to answer the survey (and not forget to submit their responses to you) if you sit down with them in person or ask your questions over the phone. Another option is to create a Web-based survey that participants can view and submit online. Check with your instructor to see if your school has a free Web-based application for creating a survey.

Determine how to find and convince people to participate. Do any of your friends or relatives have the appropriate characteristics? Do you belong to a group that would allow you to survey its members? Would classmates or students who live in your dorm be suitable respondents? Once you've identified a target group for your survey, you will need to tell prospective participants why you need this information and what you plan to do with it. For a survey that you will mail or e-mail, write a cover letter supplying this information, asking people to complete the survey and giving them a deadline or due date. You might also want to assure them that the survey is brief and will not take too much of their time.

Develop a system for respondents to return surveys. Include postage-paid, self-addressed envelopes for the return of completed print surveys. If you ask respondents to complete a questionnaire online, you have the added benefit of cutting and pasting material from individual surveys into your analysis. If you can guarantee their anonymity, include that information in the cover letter or message.

Calculate how much time you can expect the participants to spend responding to the survey. This will help you decide how many questions you need to write. Many people are willing to take a few minutes to complete a survey, but very few will respond if they think it will take more than fifteen or twenty minutes.

Writing the Survey Questions

Writing a survey that elicits useful responses is challenging. It is usually a good idea to ask both closed and open-ended questions, as described in the box on page 605. In addition, the following suggestions will help you as you write your survey.

Avoid asking two questions at the same time. Asking a question such as "Do you think you eat a healthy diet and get enough exercise?" will cause a problem because respondents might have a different answer for each part or neglect to answer one part.

Avoid asking leading questions. If your question gives a hint about what you think the answer might be, your respondents may tell you what they think you want to hear. For example, if you ask whether they eat "junk food," the word "junk" has a negative connotation, so even if they do eat junk food, they may not admit it.

Ask questions in a neutral and nonjudgmental way. Avoid emotionally loaded terms that might indicate your own feelings about what is the correct answer.

Ask key questions in two different ways—in different parts of the survey— and then check to see if the participant answered both versions consistently. For example, suppose you wanted to find out about students' eating habits. You might ask a series of questions about the types of food they eat regularly. In one section of the survey, you might have checklist questions such as the first item in the sample survey on page 602. Then, in a later section of the survey, you might ask an open-ended question such as question 4 on the sample survey and compare the two answers to see if the respondent answered consistently. Keep in mind that when you write two versions of the same question, you need to make sure that you really are teasing out inconsistencies. For example, if you worded the open-ended question to ask people to describe a typical meal that they eat off campus, you would be introducing a new, confounding element—because students might eat off-campus meals at a variety of places other than fast-food restaurants.

Closed and Open-Ended Questions

Closed questions ask participants to choose an answer from a set of fixed choices. Common types of closed questions include the following.

▶ Multiple-choice questions

▶ Checklist questions ("Put a checkmark next to the modes of communication that you use most frequently.")

▶ Ranking questions ("Using this scale, rank how often you engage in the following list of leisure activities. 1 = never, 2 = rarely, 3 = sometimes, 4 = often, 5 = very often")

▶ *True/false* and *yes/no* questions

Open-ended questions ask participants to explain or describe something in their own words or to provide a specific factual response. Typically, open-ended questions require a short answer. Here are some examples.

▶ "How old were you when you first tried alcohol?"

▶ "List the different ways in which you practice a green lifestyle."

▶ "What qualities were most important to you in deciding which car to buy?"

Closed questions are easiest for participants to answer and for you to analyze, but if a respondent is frustrated by the choices, misinterprets the question, or rushes through the survey, you may not get accurate or nuanced answers. Open-ended questions often elicit more thoughtful responses and can provide information that you never considered when you designed the survey. When designing a survey, it is usually best to include both closed and open-ended questions.

Keep your questions fairly simple. Make sure they do not require expertise beyond participants' level. For example, asking how many calories they consume in a fast-food meal would be problematic because most people know too little about the caloric content of foods to give a correct answer.

Avoid questions that are vague, ambiguous, or open to different interpretations. For example, if you want respondents to indicate how often they engage in a certain activity, such as eating at a fast-food restaurant, it would be better to provide a range of specific numbers of visits per week or month rather than subjective choices such as often, sometimes, and rarely.

Phrase questions carefully to avoid sexist language or unwarranted assumptions. Don't introduce any biases about respondents' gender, race, ethnicity, marital status, sexual orientation, and so on.

Think about the survey's design. Use a typeface and layout that are attractive and legible; include ample white space. Be sure respondents have enough space to write out the responses to open-ended questions.

For more on typefaces and layout, see Chapter 9.

Testing the Survey

Whether you plan to conduct your survey in writing or on the phone, once you have drafted all your questions you should test the survey with friends or family members who will not be participating.

▶ Ask testers to identify any confusing or difficult questions.

▶ Make sure that the time needed to complete the survey is realistic and easily achievable (usually no more than twenty minutes).

▶ Consider whether the test survey results indicate a problem with particular questions—for example, leading, biased, or easily misinterpreted questions.

▶ Revise any questions that have caused or revealed problems.

Conducting the Survey

After revising problematic questions, you are ready to conduct the survey. Regardless of your distribution method, make sure to ask participants to complete the survey and return it to you by a specific date.

▶ **Distribute the survey in person.** For example, you might hand it out in the dining hall. If you choose to distribute the survey in person, be sure you have a mechanism for collecting surveys, such as a collection box or a return envelope.

▶ **Mail it to participants.** You will get the best response rate with mailed surveys if you include a stamped, self-addressed return envelope.

▶ **Distribute the survey electronically via e-mail or by using a Web site.** In addition to using e-mail, there are many free, easy-to-use survey Web sites that you can use with tools for distributing and collating your survey.

Analyzing and Presenting the Results

Your method of analysis and presentation will vary depending on the type of data you gathered.

For multiple-choice, checklist, and ranking questions, simply tally the results. Count how many participants gave each possible answer. For the checklist question about fast food on page 602, you would count the number of people who reported that they order hamburgers, salads, and so on. For yes/no and true/false questions, just count the total number of each answer. A computer application such as Excel can help you add up the data, calculate percentages, and so on.

Refer to the quantitative data—the things you have counted—in percentages or in actual numbers. Put the data results in numbers that your reader will understand. You might say "Fifty percent of all participants order hamburgers or cheeseburgers in fast-food restaurants, whereas only 8 percent order salads" or "Only 2 out of 25 participants reported ordering salads in fast-food restaurants."

Break down data more specifically if you note significant differences based on specific criteria. Trends may emerge that you had not asked about but that are relevant. For example, if you asked participants to give their gender, age, or other characteristics, you might be able to say something like "Only women order salads."

For open-ended questions, read all the responses to see how many types of answers were given. Create a list of all the different types of responses and then record the number of times each response occurs. It is often helpful to cluster the answers into categories. For example, if you asked twenty-five students "Why do you eat off campus?" you might organize the answers around these recurring categories.

1. better food
2. shorter lines
3. takes less time
4. can eat anytime

5. costs less
6. better variety
7. to eat with friends
8. fresher salads

9. quieter
10. less crowded

You could cluster these responses further into categories such as *Quality of food* (#1, 6, 8), *Convenience* (#2, 3, 4), and *Environment* (#9, 10). You may find that some of the responses do not fit neatly into any recurring category (for example, "to eat with friends"). While you should note this information, it may be statistically insignificant or too off track to use in your final analysis.

If you cluster the data from open-ended questions, you can quantify it and present it the same way you present other quantitative data. For example, using the data from the question above, you can calculate the percentage of respondents who eat off campus for convenience.

Incorporate the survey results into your research project. Determine whether you will present the data visually—for example, in pie charts or bar graphs. (If you used a spreadsheet, you can also have it generate graphic elements based on that data.) Most important, you must come up with a way to summarize your results, making generalizations and drawing conclusions about what the survey revealed. You must present not only the data but also your interpretation of that data in relationship to your topic and research questions. Use quotes from open-ended questions to add credibility and detail to your report. If relevant, explain how your survey results compare or contrast with the information you found in other sources.

For advice on presenting data visually, see Chapter 9.

Decide what to do with incomplete and invalid surveys. It is likely that you will not be able to use every returned survey. Some participants might not take the survey seriously—for example, they may write an implausible or flippant response to an open-ended question. Other participants might not complete the entire survey. Use your judgment to decide whether to include these results. If a participant made inappropriate responses, you will probably decide to discard that survey. However, if the participant simply failed to respond to certain questions, you can still use the data provided. When you write up your research, include information about the total number of surveys and how many were not fully completed.

12

Evaluating Sources and Taking Notes

In the not-too-distant past, people got most of their information from newspapers, radio, and just three major television networks. Computers were used solely for word and data processing, and everyday objects such as cereal boxes included only minimal information about their contents. Times have changed, and so have our sources of information. These days, hundreds of television stations provide news, entertainment, and information around the clock; the Internet offers access to millions of information sites around the world; and cereal boxes sometimes present footnoted articles about topics such as nutrition and high blood pressure. Everywhere you look, you are bombarded by information. What does this bombardment mean?

On the one hand, it means you have access to a great many more sources of information than people of any generation ever had before. On the other hand, it means you cannot get away from a constant stream of information, often on topics that are of no interest to you. The availability of so much material also means that even though you can easily find information on any topic, you may have a hard time sorting through and evaluating everything you find.

For advice on finding sources, see Chapter 10.

Once you have used the library and Internet to find potential sources for your project, and perhaps done field research as well, you will need to start making decisions about which sources to pursue more seriously. This chapter will provide advice on evaluating your sources, and it will also provide suggestions for taking notes and integrating source material into your paper.

▷ EVALUATING THE APPROPRIATENESS OF SOURCES

Regardless of how interesting or timely a source may be, it must be appropriate for your project. To make sure each source fits your research topic, think about your purpose, audience, and research question.

Considering Purpose and Audience

As you look at your sources, think about your overall reason for writing. For example, if you are writing to persuade people to act on a proposal, you will need sources that will convince readers of the thoroughness of your understanding of the problem and the feasibility of your proposed solution. You would therefore want sources (1) that the audience recognizes and believes and (2) that reflect different perspectives on the proposal to show that you have taken various approaches into consideration. On the other hand, if you are writing to evaluate (support or oppose) a proposal, your focus might be more factual or statistical. You might include excerpts from the proposal itself or compare the proposal to similar ones in an effort to help readers understand your position.

Also keep in mind who your audience is and what sources your readers will consider most credible and persuasive. If you are writing for an academic audience (such as one of your college instructors), you would probably include scholarly works and journal articles. If you are writing for specialists in a particular field (such as auto mechanics or graphic designers), you may need to seek out journals that target that specific field. If you are writing for enthusiasts of a particular sport or hobby (such as golfers or bird watchers), you should look for magazines or Web sites that focus on that activity.

Imagine, for instance, a research project on proposed revisions to gun control laws in your state. Your sources might vary considerably, depending on whether your audience consists of members of Students Against Drunk Driving, the National Rifle Association, your state legislators, or a municipal police force.

Using Your Research Question to Find Relevant Sources

If you are writing a research paper, focus on the question that the main point of your paper will answer. Use the following guidelines to help you zero in on the sources that are most relevant to your research question.

For help in framing your research question, see Chapter 10, pages 559–64.

Keep in mind the specific question your research is about. As you skim potential sources, ask yourself if the source helps you answer the research question. Does it support your main point? Are there quotations you might include to support your main point? Does it provide an important argument against your main point that you will need to refute? Does it help establish your credibility with readers?

For more on primary and secondary sources, see Chapter 10, pages 564–67.

Determine whether you have found the right kinds of sources. Most research projects require a mix of primary and secondary sources. Many assignments require you to use scholarly sources written by authorities, as opposed to popular sources written by journalists for a general audience. It is also a good idea to use sources from several media (Web sites, magazines, newspapers, books, scholarly journals, and so forth). If all your sources are from only one kind of media, chances are you have overlooked important sources elsewhere.

Decide how important the publication date of your sources is. How current is the source? Some fields or topics require the most recent material available. But in other fields, such as history, older sources may be appropriate. For online sources, be sure to check the publication date or the latest update. Internet sources that regularly list the dates when content is updated are generally the most reliable.

Find sources that disagree as well as agree with you. As you evaluate sources, make sure to cover more than one side of an issue. Papers that take a position should include sources that bolster your position, sources that disagree with you, and your own rebuttal to those who disagree.

Look for sources with visuals that help achieve your purpose. Consider how your sources use visuals to convey information. Do the visuals enhance what the authors are saying? Do you have data or ideas that you could present in a similar way? For example, if you are citing lots of statistics, you may want to create or adapt a table.

For more advice on creating visual representations of information, see Chapter 9.

For more advice on citing visual sources, see Chapter 13.

▷ EVALUATING THE TRUSTWORTHINESS OF SOURCES

The sources you choose must not only be appropriate for your research, they must also be trustworthy—accurate, honest, and fair. To determine that your sources are credible, you need to carefully evaluate all print and online sources. You can determine the trustworthiness of a source by taking a close look at both the author and the publisher.

Considering the Author

A careful assessment of an author's credibility will point you to sources with expertise and authority. The author of a print source is usually easy to identify, but individual authors are not always listed on Web sources. If you are not certain who the author is, consider the publisher of the source instead (see p. 613).

Examine the author's credentials and/or experience. You can often find background about the author in an "About the Author" section or link. If the source does not include this information, conduct a Web search using the author's name. If you find that the author is frequently cited by others in scholarly journals or is listed in a biographical database, you can be relatively certain that the source is knowledgeable.

Review the types of evidence the author uses and the opinions the author expresses. As you evaluate each source, ask whether the main thesis is backed up by solid evidence. Does the author name his or her sources, and if so, are they recognized experts? If statistics are included, can you determine that they are accurate and used fairly? Or does the author use statistics selectively to prove a point, overlooking data that might weaken the argument? Use the Web to check sources online and to verify names, quotes, and statistics.

Evaluating Articles

Look at the title of the publication or journal. Is it scholarly or popular?

Identify the publisher of the journal or periodical. Does background information tell you about the source?

What is the date of publication? How important is currency for your research project?

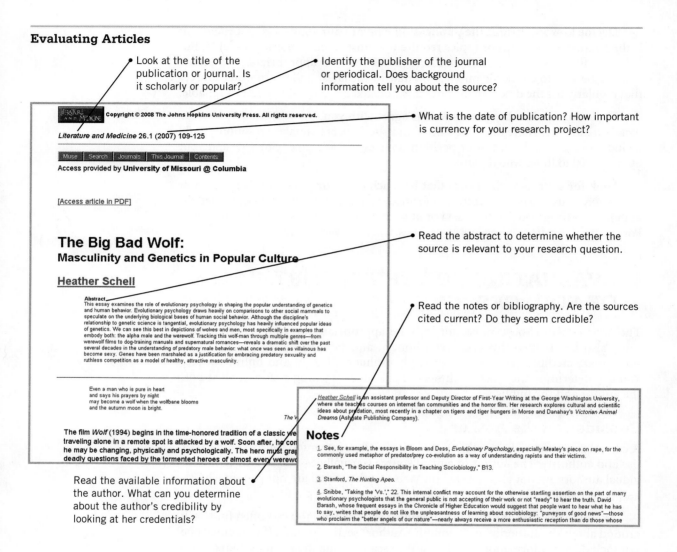

Copyright © 2008 The Johns Hopkins University Press. All rights reserved.

Literature and Medicine 26.1 (2007) 109-125

Muse | Search | Journals | This Journal | Contents

Access provided by **University of Missouri @ Columbia**

[Access article in PDF]

The Big Bad Wolf:
Masculinity and Genetics in Popular Culture

Heather Schell

Abstract
This essay examines the role of evolutionary psychology in shaping the popular understanding of genetics and human behavior. Evolutionary psychology draws heavily on comparisons to other social mammals to speculate on the underlying biological bases of human social behavior. Although the discipline's relationship to genetic science is tangential, evolutionary psychology has heavily influenced popular ideas of genetics. We can see this best in depictions of wolves and men, most specifically in examples that embody both: the alpha male and the werewolf. Tracking this wolf-man through multiple genres—from werewolf films to dog-training manuals and supernatural romances—reveals a dramatic shift over the past several decades in the understanding of predatory male behavior: what once was seen as villainous has become sexy. Genes have been marshaled as a justification for embracing predatory sexuality and ruthless competition as a model of healthy, attractive masculinity.

Even a man who is pure in heart
and says his prayers by night
may become a wolf when the wolfbane blooms
and the autumn moon is bright.

The W

The film *Wolf* (1994) begins in the time-honored tradition of a classic we
traveling alone in a remote spot is attacked by a wolf. Soon after, he con
he may be changing, physically and psychologically. The hero must grap
deadly questions faced by the tormented heroes of almost every werewolf

Heather Schell is an assistant professor and Deputy Director of First-Year Writing at the George Washington University, where she teaches courses on internet fan communities and the horror film. Her research explores cultural and scientific ideas about predation, most recently in a chapter on tigers and tiger hungers in Morse and Danahay's *Victorian Animal Dreams* (Ashgate Publishing Company).

Notes

1. See, for example, the essays in Bloom and Dess, *Evolutionary Psychology*, especially Mealey's piece on rape, for the commonly used metaphor of predator/prey co-evolution as a way of understanding rapists and their victims.

2. Barash, "The Social Responsibility in Teaching Sociobiology," B13.

3. Stanford, *The Hunting Apes*.

4. Snibbe, "Taking the 'Vs.'," 22. This internal conflict may account for the otherwise startling assertion on the part of many evolutionary psychologists that the general public is not accepting of their work or not "ready" to hear the truth. David Barash, whose frequent essays in the Chronicle of Higher Education would suggest that people want to hear what he has to say, writes that people do not like the unpleasantness of learning about sociobiology: "purveyors of good news"—those who proclaim the "better angels of our nature"—nearly always receive a more enthusiastic reception than do those whose

Read the abstract to determine whether the source is relevant to your research question.

Read the notes or bibliography. Are the sources cited current? Do they seem credible?

Read the available information about the author. What can you determine about the author's credibility by looking at her credentials?

Evaluate the author's stance. In the most effective arguments, authors present more than one perspective. Be cautious of sources that do not take possible objections into account. Be wary of those who contradict themselves or who simply dismiss those who disagree with them. Also check to see if the author is associated with a particular interest group that might be influencing the content.

Determine the author's perspective or bias. An author's credentials or experience may reveal his or her point of view or bias. Consider how this bias affects the writer's opinion, though you may still want to use sources you disagree with as an opposing viewpoint. For example, for a project on gun control, you might include sources written by the president of the National Rifle Association, by a senator fighting for tougher handgun laws, and by the parent of a child who was killed in a drive-by shooting.

Considering the Publisher

Consider carefully what you know about the publisher or sponsor of a source. Doing so will help you determine which sources are most appropriate to your research project.

Identify the publisher. The publisher is listed on the copyright page in books and on the masthead in magazines, newspapers, and journals. Examining the domain in the URL for Web sources will tell you about the kind of group sponsoring the site: governmental (.gov), educational (.edu), commercial (.com), or nonprofit organization (.org). Many Web sources include a link offering more information about the sponsor of the site.

Identify the reputation and motivation of the publisher. Is the publisher one whose name you recognize or about whom you can locate information? Is the publisher associated with a special interest group? Are there political or religious views that it promotes? Is it selling something? Be wary of bias in blogs and wikis that are often open to the writing of anyone, or nearly anyone, who chooses to contribute, often without any oversight.

Consider the perspective or bias of the publisher. It may be fine to use sources that have a definite bias as long as you and your readers are aware of what the bias is. For example, if you are researching cold treatments, you may include information from commercial (.com) Web sites sponsored by pharmaceutical companies. However, you would not want to rely solely on them, because they are in the business of promoting their products. A government (.gov) site, sponsored by an agency such as the U.S. Department of Health and Human Services, discussing the pros and cons of cold remedies would be a less biased source.

Be sure to record any important information that you learn about the background of the publisher or author in your notes. For example, "author was a member of Phi Beta Kappa" or "the Discovery Guides Web site is sponsored by advertisers."

▷ TAKING NOTES

As you find and evaluate sources, you will find it useful to keep track of them in a *working bibliography*, a list of the sources you may eventually use in your research project. Keeping an annotated bibliography—where you record your personal responses and comments on the sources you find—will help you recall later what each source is about.

For more on creating a working bibliography, see Chapter 10, pages 585.

When you decide that some sources will be especially helpful, you also need to take notes so that you have a record of important facts, ideas, and visual elements. When taking notes, record the information listed on page 615.

Evaluating Web Sources

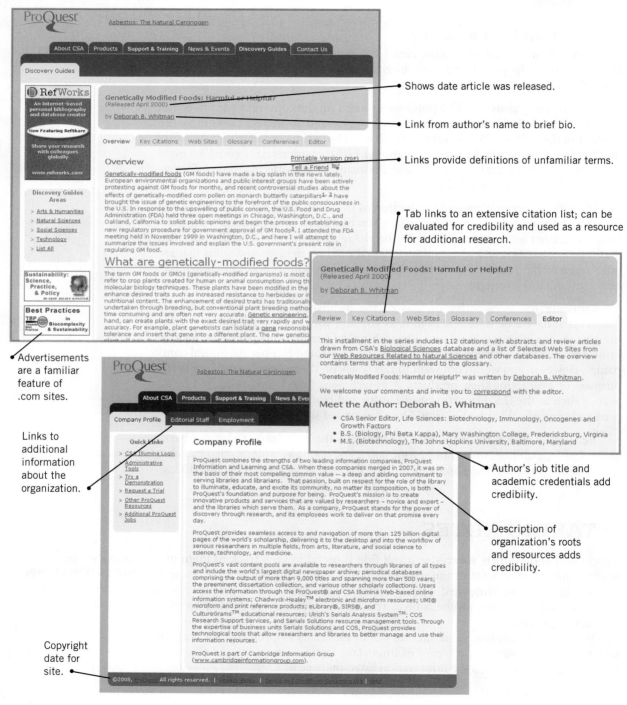

▶ **Subject heading.** A brief subject heading on each note will help you organize your notes by subtopics later.

▶ **Source information.** Always include all the information you will need to cite the source fully, including the author's name or the title (or a shortened form of the title) and the page(s) on which you found the material. For online sources, record the paragraph or other section information. (You can record complete bibliographic information on the source in a working bibliography.)

▶ **Type of note.** To avoid inadvertent plagiarism, indicate whether the note is a quotation, paraphrase, summary, or some other kind of information. Carefully record quotations as they appear in the original source and be sure to summarize and paraphrase in your own words.

You may not remember all the major points of a source later on, so be sure your notes are complete. Double-check notes for accuracy, especially for quotes, statistics, and factual information.

As you take notes, be on the lookout for memorable statements that you can quote, key concepts that you can paraphrase, complex information that you will have to summarize, and data that you can best present graphically.

Quoting

Save quotations for situations where an author has said something so clearly or so memorable that you cannot imagine any other way to say it. If you find a memorable quotation that asks a question you are going to answer in your project, quoting it may be a good way to engage the reader right away. If you find a solid quotation that supports your conclusions, quoting it may be a dramatic way to end your project.

When you find a direct quotation that you might want to use, here are some guidelines for writing it down accurately.

▶ Copy it down word for word and include the exact punctuation.

▶ Make sure to enclose it in quotation marks and indicate the source and page number(s) for print sources or date retrieved for electronic sources.

▶ Double-check your notes against the original source to make sure you wrote the quotation exactly as it appears. Label your note as a quotation.

▶ If the author misspelled a word or made a grammatical error, add the Latin word *sic* (meaning "thus") in brackets directly after the error to show that it was the writer's mistake and not yours.

▶ If you want to use only part of a quotation, use ellipsis points (. . .) to indicate where you omitted words or whole sentences within the original passage.

▶ Use brackets to introduce changes or new words to the quotation.

▶ If you shorten a quotation, carefully reread the original text to make sure you have not taken the quotation out of context or changed the author's meaning by omitting parts of the passage.

For advice on organizing research notes, see page 621.

For more advice on avoiding plagiarism, see page 623.

▶ Go to **bedfordstmartins.com/ writingnow** to Chapter 12 > Worksheets for help with your working bibliography.

For MLA and APA guidelines on information to include for sources you cite, see Chapter 13.

For more advice on using brackets and ellipses, see p. 622.

Student Zane Van Dusen recorded the following quote in his notes.

Quotation Note

Subject heading. ● ——————— Digital—pros and cons

Source. ● ——————— Gendron, "Analog Recording Tries to Survive a Digital World," p. 14

Signal phrase indicates ● ———— Steve Albini, recording engineer and studio owner: "Digital doesn't allow for a
who is being quoted. permanent master. The storage media changes and becomes inevitably obsolescent,
frozen in time with that day's technology. As someone who's paid to make
recordings, I'd be irresponsible to make something that wasn't permanent and
Quotation marks around ● ———— playable in the future."
exact quote.

Type of note. ● ——————— Quotation

To read Zane's complete essay,
see page 651 in Chapter 13.

Paraphrasing

When you paraphrase, you state someone else's ideas in your own words without changing the meaning or adding your own opinion. Paraphrases are typically about the same length as the original text. Paraphrasing is useful when you want to make sure that readers understand what someone else has to say, but the author's original wording is not necessary or, perhaps, not appropriate. For example, if the author of your source material is writing for an academic journal and you are writing for a school newspaper, you would probably want to use different language and a different style. By paraphrasing the original, you could relate all the author's key points and details in a way that your readers would understand. Here's one way to paraphrase.

▶ Make a list or highlight the writer's key points in order with any details that support each of those points.

▶ Write each key point in your own words.

▶ Write a paraphrase that contains all of the key points of the entire passage in your own words.

Here is a simple example showing text from a toothpaste package that shows how you might use these instructions to create a paraphrase.

Original text

Crest has been shown to be an effective decay-preventive dentifrice that can be of significant value when used as directed in a conscientiously applied program of oral hygiene and regular professional care.

—Council on Scientific Affairs—American
Dental Association, Crest package

List of key points

- According to the American Dental Association, Crest may prevent tooth decay.
- It works only if users take good care of their teeth by brushing daily and seeing their dentists regularly.

Paraphrase

The American Dental Association says that using Crest toothpaste can prevent cavities if users take good care of their teeth by brushing daily and getting dental checkups regularly.

Following is a paraphrase of a longer passage from the same newspaper article on the analog tape Zane Van Dusen quoted above. First, Zane created a bulleted list of key points in the passage before including a paraphrase in his notes on the pros and cons of digital recording.

Original text

Artists and hobbyists alike can record on a hard drive, edit on a computer and store material on optical discs. Conversely, analog methods call for tape at every turn, from original recordings to backup copies going on reel-to-reels. Digital also makes retrieval a cinch by permitting users access to a given song in seconds; analog requires the fast forwarding or reversing of a tape. And while performing editing tasks on digital recordings boils down to a few mouse clicks and keyboard strokes, analog can involve complicated splicing techniques.

—Bob Gendron, "Analog Recording Tries
to Survive a Digital World"

List of key points

- You don't need any professional experience to learn how to use a computer to digitally record and edit music.
- Tape is needed at every stage of the analog recording process.
- It is slow and cumbersome to find a song using analog tape, whereas digital allows you to find a given track quickly and easily with the click of a button.
- Where digital editing is done easily on the computer, analog editing is difficult because of the physical act of tape splicing that must occur.

Next, Zane paraphrased this passage as follows.

Paraphrase Note

Subject heading. ●————————— Digital—pros and cons

Source. ●————————— Gendron, "Analog Recording Tries to Survive a Digital World," p. 14

Paraphrase roughly the ●————————— Unlike analog, you don't need any professional experience to learn how to digitally
same length as the original. record and edit music. No reel-to-reel tape or hard-to-find equipment is needed
beyond a computer and the proper software. And while it is slow and cumbersome
to find a song using the reel-to-reel tape required by analog recording techniques,
digital recording software allows you to find music tracks quickly and easily with
the click of a button. The same computer software allows the user to make edits
with ease. Analog editing is difficult because of the physical act of tape splicing
that must occur.

Type of note. ●————————— Paraphrase

To see this paragraph in Zane's essay, see page 655.

Sometimes writers are tempted to simply "translate" the author's words and phrases into their own synonyms while maintaining the basic sentence structure of the original, but this is not appropriate or acceptable. It also often leads to awkward sentences that are stylistically incompatible with the author's own writing. The following is an unacceptable paraphrase of the text about the benefits of digital recording. Phrasing that is too close to the original is highlighted.

Unacceptable Paraphrase

Professionals and nonprofessionals alike can make and edit digital recordings on a computer. On the other hand, analog recording techniques require that you use tape for everything, from the first recording to reel-to-reel backup copies. Digital is also easier because it allows users access to a song in a few seconds, while analog makes you fast-forward or reverse the tape to find music tracks. Digital editing is as quick as clicking a mouse or typing on your keyboard, while for analog you have to use complicated splicing to make your edits.

When you paraphrase, you are still presenting someone else's ideas even though you are rephrasing them. So, just as with a direct quotation, keep track of the source and page number(s) or date retrieved for Internet sources so you can acknowledge the source fully in your paper (see the paraphrase note on page 618). If you need to include some of the author's words within the paraphrase, enclose them in quotation marks. If you present another writer's ideas as your own without acknowledgment, even if they are paraphrased, or if you offer a paraphrase that is too close to the original, even if you credit the source, you are guilty of plagiarism—stealing someone else's words or ideas. If you are unsure of what constitutes a paraphrase that is too close to the original, check with your instructor.

Summarizing

Unlike a paraphrase, which relates all of an author's main points in about the same amount of text, a summary presents an abbreviated version of a passage or whole work. When you summarize, you want the readers to understand basic ideas, but you don't think they need a lot of detail. Follow these steps to create a note that summarizes a passage.

▶ Read the passage carefully once or twice.

▶ Record the source information, indicating the page number(s) for print sources or date retrieved for electronic sources.

▶ Highlight or jot down the key points and supporting details you might want to include in your project.

▶ Write a sentence or paragraph in your own words that emphasizes the key points, eliminating any extraneous details and shortening the text.

▶ If it suits your purposes, you can present your summary visually using bulleted points or in a chart or other type of figure.

▶ Include a subject label with the note or visual and mark it as a summary.

You can also summarize by taking statistics or other data that are presented as text and putting them in a table, chart, graph, bulleted list, or other visual element. Depending on your topic and the specific type of data you want to convey, a visual summary can be an effective and concise way to present a lot of information.

To summarize the whole newspaper article, Zane might instead use a visual to show the pros and cons of digital and analog recording. He created a table summarizing the main points in the article. (For comparison, the points that are summarized from the original passage shown on page 617 are highlighted.)

For samples and advice on creating graphs and tables, see Chapter 9.

Because a summary is a presentation of someone else's ideas, you must cite that original source in your work, both in the text of your essay and in your list of works cited. When you create a visual summary, especially if your note becomes a visual you use in your final draft, be sure to acknowledge the source of the data.

On the next page you will find summaries of the Gendron passage shown on page 617.

Summary Note

Subject heading. •────────── Digital—pros and cons

Source. •────────── Gendron, "Analog Recording Tries to Survive a Digital World," p. 14

Digital recording offers some clear benefits over analog, most notably the fact that anyone with access to a computer and the correct software can quickly and easily record, edit, and store music recordings.

Summary covers main •─────── points of original in brief.

Summary

Summary in Table Form

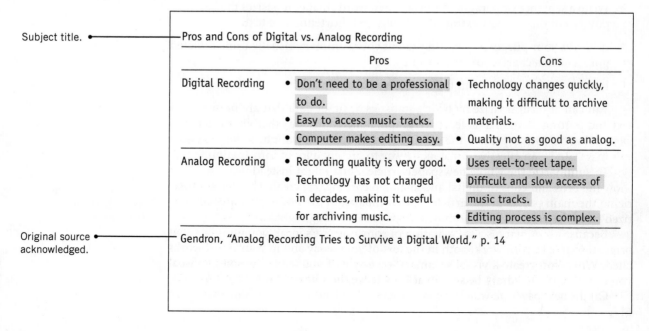

Subject title. •────────── Pros and Cons of Digital vs. Analog Recording

	Pros	Cons
Digital Recording	• Don't need to be a professional to do. • Easy to access music tracks. • Computer makes editing easy.	• Technology changes quickly, making it difficult to archive materials. • Quality not as good as analog.
Analog Recording	• Recording quality is very good. • Technology has not changed in decades, making it useful for archiving music.	• Uses reel-to-reel tape. • Difficult and slow access of music tracks. • Editing process is complex.

Original source •────── Gendron, "Analog Recording Tries to Survive a Digital World," p. 14
acknowledged.

▷ SYNTHESIZING YOUR RESEARCH

Research involves synthesizing a lot of facts, ideas, and opinions before coming to some conclusions of your own about a topic. To synthesize means to bring different parts together into a whole. Your research will lack credibility if you don't find out what other people have said, written, or done that is relevant to your topic—but your project will lack coherence if you don't figure out how to work these different concepts and voices into a unified piece of writing.

A common mistake when writing any type of research project is to simply summarize each source and string those summaries together. While this is acceptable for some genres, such as an annotated bibliography, it does not produce a coherent, synthesized research essay. In this section you will find suggestions for how to synthesize by reviewing, sorting, and ordering your notes along with advice on integrating source material.

Reviewing Your Notes

Begin by reading through your research notes carefully. As you read, flag or highlight particular points that you are sure you want to include in your own text. Keep in mind your audience and purpose, and let those factors influence your decision about what is important. For example, do you have information that will help you establish common ground with your readers? Do you have information that will answer questions your readers have about your topic? Do you have facts that will provide credible evidence for an argument or a position?

Sort and Order Your Notes

One of the biggest challenges in writing is figuring out how to organize the information. The chapters in Part 1 of this textbook give you suggestions based on the particular conventions of each genre. Regardless of genre, keep in mind that you need to create a coherent, logical movement from one category or type of information to the next. Use your research notes to help determine the order of your essay.

Begin by reading through your highlighted notes to see what themes or patterns emerge. Next, group your notes around the subject headings on them and by any new categories that occur in your reading of your notes. Keep in mind that one source might provide information for several different categories.

After you have grouped your notes by category, you are ready to determine the order of your project. One strategy is to start with something that is familiar to your reader and then move to things that are less familiar. Your analysis of the intended audience will give you the best ideas about where to start, but after that it's up to you to determine what logically comes next. You might consider whether this is a topic where chronological order is important. Can you organize information based on level of severity or relevance? Do you need to build to a climax, or should you start with the most important information?

Once you have determined the order, arrange your notes in that order. If you are keeping your notes on index cards, physically arrange them in order. If you are keeping your notes electronically, cut and paste to rearrange. You may want to make copies of some notes that fit in more than one category so that you can put a copy in each position in your arrangement.

Integrating Source Materials

After you are done ordering your notes, you will be ready to synthesize your research into your paper. Your research question, audience, purpose, and organized notes will determine how best to integrate sources into your research paper.

Integrating quotations, paraphrases, and summaries into your writing requires you to follow certain conventions to make the material fit your own material smoothly and clearly. Use the following guidelines to incorporate your research notes seamlessly into your paper.

Include a signal phrase. The signal phrase gives the author's name or provides other information about the source when introducing source material.

Signal phrase before a quote

Gastwirt believes that analog tape is "a much more musical medium."

Signal phrase after a quote

"Analog music, like the tone from a violin string, is a single smooth wave," explains Roy Furchgott.

Signal phrase in the middle of a paraphrase

When audiophiles talk about "warmth," they are referring to what Gendron describes as the imperfections that distinguish analog from digital.

Mark any omissions with ellipsis points. There will be times when you need to omit words from a quotation to make it more concise or to make it fit the structure of your own sentence, but you must let your reader know that you have left something out and the edited quotation must be grammatically correct.

"What we've lost . . . are the records that sound so good that you get lost in them" (Gomes B1).

Indicate any added letters or words by enclosing them in square brackets. If you need to insert a word to make the quotation fit the structure of your sentence or to clarify the material, be sure to signal that change with brackets.

Smith and McBride estimate "that as few as 5% of albums are recorded and mixed using [analog] audio tape."

Use block form for long quotations. When using MLA style, quotations over four lines are indented ten spaces on every line. When using APA style, long quotation are indented five to seven spaces on every line. Block quotations begin on a new line and are introduced by a phrase or sentence followed by a colon.

Block quotation in MLA style

> Producer Steve Albini agrees, explaining his reliance on analog as follows:
> Digital doesn't allow for a permanent master. The storage media changes and becomes inevitably obsolescent, frozen in time with that day's technology. As someone who's paid to make recordings, I'd be irresponsible to make something that wasn't permanent and playable in the future. (qtd. in Gendron 14)

Be careful not to overuse quotations. Paraphrase and summarize passages from different sources as needed, reserving quotations for those instances when you have trouble thinking of a better or different way to say something important.

Integrate visuals so that they contribute to your objectives. As you know from the chapters in Part 1, visuals can help you engage your audience, create an appropriate voice, and so forth. A critical factor in making sure that the visuals perform their task is that they are placed appropriately and referenced within the text. Position visuals as close as possible to the point in your text where you mention them, sizing them so that they are clear and readable.

For more information about using and modifying visuals, see Chapter 9.

▷ AVOIDING PLAGIARISM

Presenting another person's words or ideas as your own is considered plagiarism. Plagiarism is improper—and often illegal, whether it is intentional or not. Plagiarism occurs when a writer, speaker, or artist "borrows" (steals) someone else's words, ideas, or images without giving credit to the original creator. In most schools, plagiarism is a serious academic offense; students who plagiarize are subject to disciplinary action—they may fail a course, be suspended, or even be expelled. The following tips will help you avoid plagiarism.

Take notes carefully. When you copy the exact wording of a source, put those words within quotation marks. When you paraphrase or summarize, include a notation that will remind you whether your note is a paraphrase or a summary. Also keep track of the full reference information for each source so that you can give proper credit.

Acknowledge your sources. Give credit to the source for any specific words (quotations), general ideas (paraphrases and summaries), or elements (charts, graphs, and so on) that you use in your paper.

Give credit to visual sources. Copyright law protects visual elements just as it protects verbal passages. You can use visuals in a printed paper as long as you give credit to the source, just as if you were quoting someone's words. However, if the assignment will appear on a Web site or if you plan to publish your work (in print or electronic form), you may need to get permission from the source.

For advice on crediting the sources of visual elements, see Chapter 9, page 543.

Provide source information for anything that is not common knowledge. If an idea or fact is common knowledge (for example, "the earth rotates around the sun" or "the Declaration of Independence was written in 1776"), you do not have to provide a reference or citation. If you are unsure whether certain information needs to be credited to a source, check with your instructor.

To combat the rise in plagiarism, a number of Internet-based services now make it easier for instructors and other readers to detect plagiarized work. For example, a service might compare the text of a specific student paper to millions of documents held in a database. Instructors can also use search engines such as Google to check suspicious passages or phrases in their students' work, especially if they think a student has plagiarized a source available online.

Copying an essay or even a phrase or idea from another writer is never a good idea, even if that writer has willingly provided such a service for a fee and even if you are in a hurry. The time you spend trying to avoid doing work—and avoid getting caught—would be much better spent developing your own ideas and doing your own research and writing. If you feel overwhelmed by an assignment or a deadline, talk to the instructor rather than resort to cheating.

13 ▷

Documenting Sources: MLA and APA Style

This chapter offers a brief guide to two of the most widely used systems of documentation, MLA (Modern Language Association) and APA (American Psychological Association). This guide will help you create in-text citations and a bibliographic list of the works you have cited so that your readers will be able to identify where the information is from and refer to the original if they choose to do so. At the end of this chapter you will find a student research paper that demonstrates the effective use of sources and the MLA style of documentation.

Chapter 12 emphasized the researcher's need to rely on work that has been done by others. As the writer of a research paper, you need to document any sources you have used in preparing your paper. Proper documentation provides the information that will enable readers who may want to do further reading and investigation to find your sources. Just as important, proper citation of your sources will help you avoid the possibility of plagiarism. You can do this by providing in-text citations and reference lists. The nuts and bolts of citing sources in the text and formatting the entries in your list of references will vary depending on your academic discipline. Check with your instructor or academic department to find out what documentation style your assignment requires. The table on page 628 lists the most commonly used documentation style manuals used by different academic disciplines.

For more on avoiding plagiarism, see Chapter 12, pages 623–24.

For the purposes of a first-year writing class, you probably will not be required to master all the conventions for academic work in a particular discipline. But once you have chosen a major field of study, you should know that disciplinary style manuals offer scholars and writers important editorial and formatting information in addition to documentation guidelines. Such information typically includes topics as diverse as the types of research being published in the discipline, preferred formats for tables and graphs, acceptable units of measurement, conventions for pronoun usage, and more.

Commonly Used Documentation Style Manuals

Discipline	Style Manual
English and General Humanities	*MLA Handbook for Writers of Research Papers*, 7th ed. (New York: MLA, 2009)
History and Some Humanities	*The Chicago Manual of Style*, 15th ed. (Chicago: U of Chicago P, 2003)
Psychology, Social Sciences, and Nursing	*Publication Manual of the American Psychological Association*, 5th ed. (Washington: APA, 2001)
Biology and Natural Sciences	*Scientific Style and Format: The CSE Manual for Authors, Editors, and Publishers*, 7th ed. (Reston: Council of Science Editors, 2006)
Chemistry	*The ACS Style Guide: Effective Communication of Scientific Information*, 3rd ed. (Washington: American Chemical Society, 2006)
Law	*The Bluebook: A Uniform System of Citation*. Comp. editors of Columbia Law Review et al., 18th ed. (Cambridge: Harvard Law Review, 2005)

Formal conventions for citing material from electronic sources evolve rapidly, so it is a good idea to check online for updates to the print version of the style guide you are consulting. Sometimes you will not be able to find instructions for the exact type of source that you want to use, so you will have to improvise. In those cases, refer to the generic description of the way the information should be organized that is typically introduced in each section of the appropriate style guide, and then pick the closest thing you can find as a model. Always use your sense of what your audience will need to know as a guide in determining what information to include.

▶ Go to **bedfordstmartins.com/ writingnow** to Chapter 13 > Links for documentation advice in a variety of disciplines.

▷ USING MLA STYLE

MLA style is used in books, journal articles, and electronic materials produced by scholars and students in English and the general humanities. The MLA system for citing sources requires documentation within the text for all materials you quote, paraphrase, or summarize. MLA style also requires that you include all of the works that you have cited in a list of works cited at the end of your project.

For a detailed discussion of quoting, paraphrasing, and summarizing, see Chapter 12, pages 613–20.

For more advice on documenting sources according to MLA style, see the *MLA Handbook for Writers of Research Papers*, 7th ed. (New York: MLA, 2009). For more information on MLA style, you can also consult the MLA's Web site (www.mla.org).

Directory to MLA Style

In-Text Citations

Works Cited

Books

Periodicals

Electronic Sources

Other Sources

MLA In-Text Citations

MLA style suggests that you include the author's last name and the page number for the referenced information in the sentence where the work is cited. The basic format is the same whether you are quoting directly, paraphrasing, summarizing, or referring to the original source. For example:

> One of the key principles of visual design is alignment (Williams 14).

If you include the author's name in the sentence, you can simply put the page number in the parentheses:

> Williams says that one of the key principles of visual design is alignment (14).

As in these examples, in-text citations usually consist of signal phrases and parenthetical references. A signal phrase introduces the cited material, indicating that something has been taken from a source and may include the author's name. A parenthetical reference is placed after the material you are citing and includes page numbers and, sometimes, other information to direct the reader to more information in the works cited list.

Generally, it is best to keep parenthetical references brief and as close to the material cited as possible. For any sources you cite, the choice between placing an author's name in parentheses and indicating it in a signal phrase is yours. Always think about what you have already told the members of your audience and what they will want to know or may need to be reminded of. Note that you do not put the word *page* or the abbreviation *p.* in front of the page number in MLA style.

The following examples of in-text citations will help you see how to refer to different kinds of works and how to avoid confusing your readers when you cite more than one work by an author, works by two different authors with the same last name, and so on.

1. Work with one author

> Beowulf's disposition has been called "strange and not entirely safe" (Ker 166).

> Ker calls Beowulf's disposition "strange and not entirely safe" (166).

2. Work with more than one author

List all last names in a signal phrase or include the names in a parenthetical reference: (Gross and McDowell 162).

> According to Gross and McDowell, Eliot sees poetry as striving to attain the emotional heights of music: "To Eliot 'the music of poetry' means a great deal more than melodious verse, achieved through smooth textures and verbal tone color" (162).

3. Two or more works by the same author

Provide enough information so that the reader knows which work is being cited, including the title of the work in a signal phrase or in the parenthetical reference.

On the contrary, Gordon tells us that Sartre and Fanon were both "acutely aware of the simultaneous fluidity and rigidity of institutional power" (*Fanon and the Crisis* 25).

To include both the author and the title in parentheses, put a comma after the author's name, then insert the title of the work (if it's short) or a shortened version of the title.

4. Work by a corporate author

Give the group's or corporation's name either in the signal phrase or in the parenthetical reference.

The National Center for Health Statistics points out that measuring the longevity of a population is easier than assessing overall health status (1).

5. Works by two or more authors with the same last name

Add the initial of the first name to distinguish between authors with the same last name.

Van Gogh's works "lacked the elegant sinuosity of the line that informs even Gauguin's most 'primitive' figures" (B. Collins 75).

6. Work with an unknown author

Cite the title of the document if the author is unknown. Titles of books are italicized; titles of articles are put in quotation marks.

One local newspaper argues that "sometimes it takes just one generous-minded individual to get the ball rolling" ("A $20 Million Investment" 4).

7. Indirect source (source quoted in another source)

Begin with the abbreviation "qtd. in" (for "quoted in"), followed by the author and page number for the source where you found the quotation.

Expressing the anger of many teachers, a school principal complained, "We teach to the test. We'd be idiots not to. But school, real education, is not just about taking tests" (qtd. in Ivins and Dubose 91).

8. Electronic or nonprint source

Treat material from the Internet in the same way as printed material. If you do not know the author, include the title of the document. If the document has numbered paragraphs instead of stable page numbers, include those numbers with a comma after the author's name and the abbreviation "par." If the source has no numbered pages or paragraphs, omit the number.

Shakespeare's Globe Theatre "was actually the first to be built specifically for an existing acting company and financed by the company itself" (Gurr).

9. Multivolume work

In the parenthetical reference, put the volume number after the author's name. Separate it from the page number with a colon and one space.

> During World War I, Eleanor Roosevelt "organized the Red Cross Canteen, and with Addie Daniels organized the Navy Red Cross. She knitted and distributed free wool to the Navy League, entertained troops in and out of Washington's Union Station, and made coffee and sandwiches" (Cook 1: 215).

10. Two or more works in the same reference

Put the author and page information in the citation in the same order as the works appear on the works cited page. Separate the citations with a semicolon.

> Poetry's emotive effects can be traced to the way its syntax creates feelings apart from meaning, much like the arrangement of tones to produce a certain abstract emotion (Gross 82; Snodgrass 1).

11. Entire work or one-page source

Include the author's name in a signal phrase rather than in a parenthetical reference.

> Malcolm Gladwell suggests that we can understand how and why cultural changes occur by thinking about these changes as social epidemics.

12. Work in an anthology

Include the name of the author of the anthologized work and the page number(s). Do not refer to the name of the editor or compiler of the anthology in an in-text citation.

> Oliver uses vivid sensory details, notably color: "I make coffee and walk from window to window, lifting the shades, watching the pink, tangerine, apricot, lavender light dart and sail along the eastern horizon" (219).

13. Work without page numbers

If a work has no page numbers, include only the author's name.

> Pissarro's innovation of dividing colors can be seen in *The Garden of Les Mathurins at Pontoise*, "where the sunlit path is made up of brushstrokes of pink, blue, white and yellow ochre" (MacDuffee).

14. Literary work

Literary works, especially those that are well known, often come in many different editions. First put the page number(s) from the edition you used, followed by a semicolon, then give other information that would help readers find the passage in any edition. For a novel, indicate the page number, followed by a semicolon, then the section or chapter.

> When the undead finally appear in Stoker's *Dracula*, they lure human prey with voices that
> are "diabolically sweet" (37; ch. 16).

For a play, indicate the page number, followed by a semicolon, and the act and scene. For a verse play, you need only cite the act, scene, and line numbers.

> Thomasina tells her tutor that "if there is an equation for a curve like a bell, there must
> be an equation for one like a bluebell" (Stoppard 327; act 1, sc. 3).

For a poem, cite the section (if there is one) followed by a period and the line(s); page numbers are not required. If you cite only line numbers for a poem, use the word "line(s)" in the first citation; for subsequent citations, just cite the number.

> The use of repetition reinforces the "silent and endless" suffering in Whitman's "Hours
> Continuing Long" (line 21).

15. Sacred text

To cite a sacred text such as the Bible or the Qur'an, give the title of the edition, the title of the book, and the chapter and verse separated by periods. Use abbreviations for books of the Bible included in parenthetical references.

> She was fond of reminding him that "a foolish son is a sorrow to his mother" (*New
> American Standard Bible*, Prov. 10.1).

MLA List of Works Cited

At the end of a research paper, the author needs to include a list of all of the sources that are cited within that paper. In MLA style, this reference list is called *Works Cited*. The information in the list contains all of the relevant publication information that will enable readers to locate specific books, journals, Web sites, and other original sources that they are interested in reading.

For most documentation styles, you will need the same general information to complete an entry in any reference list or bibliography. However, the form and order of that information will vary. Throughout this section are visual "essential" guides that show four different types of entries that are typically found in an MLA-style works cited list: books, articles from periodicals, works from Web sites, and articles from online periodicals. The annotations explain the information presented, including sequence of elements, punctuation, and acceptable or required abbreviations.

MLA no longer requires the use of underlining but instead recognizes that most writers are able to produce italics in their word processing programs. MLA entries now include the medium of publication (for example, "Print," "CD-ROM"), the medium consulted ("Web"), or other relevant medium ("Television," "Performance"). The sample works cited entries that follow observe these guidelines.

For a complete sample of a student works cited page written using MLA style, see page 656.

Books

1. Book by one author

Wright, Esmond. *Fabric of Freedom: 1763-1800*. New York: Hill and Wang, 1961. Print.

2. Book by two or three authors

Hales, Steven D., and Rex Welshon. *Nietzsche's Perspectivism*. Urbana: U of Illinois P, 2000. Print.

Porter, Lewis, Michael Ullman, and Ed Hazell. *Jazz: From Its Origins to the Present*. Englewood Cliffs: Prentice Hall, 1993. Print.

3. Book by four or more authors

When a book has four or more authors, the *MLA Handbook* gives you a choice. You can list just the first author's name followed by "et al." (meaning "and others"), or you can list all authors as they are listed on the title page of the book. Some people believe that it is more appropriate to list all the authors so that all who contributed to the book are given credit for their work. You may want to check with your instructor if you have a book with four or more authors.

Grand, Gale, Rick Tramonto, Julia Moskin, and Marty Tiersky. *American Brasserie*. New York: Macmillan, 1997. Print.

Grand, Gale, et al. *American Brasserie*. New York: Macmillan, 1997. Print.

4. Book by an unknown author

If the author is unknown, alphabetize the work by its title.

Art Meets Science and Spirituality. London: Academy Editions, 1990. Print.

5. Book by a corporate or group author

American Heart Association. *To Your Health! A Guide to Heart-Smart Living*. New York: Clarkson Potter, 2001. Print.

6. Translation

List a translated book by its original author. Insert the abbreviation "Trans." (for "Translated by") after the title, and then insert the first and last name of the translator. Then add the publication information and end with the medium.

Alighieri, Dante. *The Inferno of Dante*. Trans. Robert Pinsky. New York: Farrar, 1994. Print.

7. Book by an author and an editor

List an edited book by its original author. Insert the abbreviation "Ed." (for "Edited by") after the title, then insert the first and last name of the editor, and end with the medium.

Warhol, Andy. *The Andy Warhol Diaries*. Ed. Pat Hackett. New York: Warner, 1989. Print.

8. Anthology or collection with an editor

List an edited collection or anthology by the first editor's last name; after all of the editors' names, insert a comma and "ed." or "eds." (for "editor" or "editors").

> Keller, Michael, ed. *Reading Popular Culture: An Anthology for Writers*. Dubuque:
>
>   Kendall/Hunt, 2002. Print.

9. Book in a series

After the title of the book, include the publication information (city, publisher, year) and the medium ("Print"). Then provide the title of the series (with no quotation marks or italics) followed by the number of the book within the series. Include "Ser." if the word *Series* is part of the title.

> Larkin, Bruce D. *War Stories*. New York: Lang, 2001. Print. Conflict and Consciousness:
>
>   Studies in War, Peace, and Social Thought 10.

10. Multivolume work

If you use one volume of a multivolume work, after the title, give the volume number, the publication information, and the medium. End with the total number of volumes.

> Cook, Blanche Wiesen. *Eleanor Roosevelt*. Vol. 1. New York: Viking, 1999. Print. 2 vols.

If you use two or more volumes, give the total number of volumes after the title and end with the medium.

> Cook, Blanche Wiesen. *Eleanor Roosevelt*. 2 vols. New York: Viking, 1999. Print.

11. Work in an anthology or a collection

List the author of the work, then the title of the work in quotation marks. After the title of the anthology or collection, identify the editor(s). Then list the publication information and include the pages on which the selection you are citing appears. End with the medium.

> Oliver, Mary. "Dust." *The Best American Essays 2001*. Ed. Kathleen Norris and Robert
>
>   Atwan. Boston: Houghton, 2001. 218-20. Print.

12. Edition other than the first

> Smith, Charles D. *Palestine and the Arab-Israeli Conflict*. 4th ed. Boston: Bedford, 2001.
>
>   Print.

13. Entry in a reference book

List the author's name if it is given; otherwise, begin with the entry's title in quotation marks. Then follow with the title of the reference book in italics, the editors (if any), the publication information, and the medium. For a well-known reference work, after the title of the book simply list the edition, the year of publication, and

The Essentials of Citing Books—MLA Style

To cite a book in MLA style, include the following elements.

1 **Author,** last name first.

2 **Title,** italicized with first word and all major words capitalized.

3 **Place of publication,** followed with colon (include abbreviation for the country when omission could be confusing).

4 **Publisher,** shortened (for example, *Oxford UP* for *Oxford University Press*).

5 **Year of publication.**

6 **Medium.**

Works cited entry for a book.

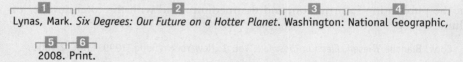

Lynas, Mark. *Six Degrees: Our Future on a Hotter Planet*. Washington: National Geographic,

    5 **6**
    2008. Print.

❓ FAQs

I found the copyright page but can't locate the year of publication. Where should I look for this information? Look for *Copyright* and/or the symbol © followed by the year of publication on the copyright page (see example). Placement varies, though usually you will find this information in the top half of the page. If more than one date is given, use only the most recent date.

Do I need to include all of the places of publication if more than one is listed? No. Use only the first one listed.

For more on citing books using MLA style, see page 634. Instructions on how to cite other types of sources using MLA style can be found on pages 638–50.

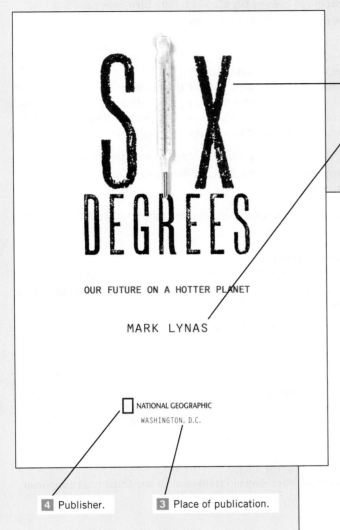

2 Title.

1 Author.

5 Year of publication, also known as the copyright date.

Published by the National Geographic Society,
by arrangement with HarperCollins Publishers Ltd.
Copyright © 2008 Mark Lynas

All rights reserved. Reproduction of the whole or any part of the
contents without written permission from the publisher is prohibited.

ISBN 978-1-4262-0213-1

Library of Congress Cataloging-in-Publication Data

Lynas, Mark, 1973-
    Six degrees : our future on a hotter planet / by Mark Lynas.
    p. cm.
    ISBN 978-1-4262-0213-1 (hardcover : alk. paper)
    1. Global warming--Environmental aspects. 2. Human beings--
Effect of climate on. 3. Climatic changes--Social aspects. I.
Title.
QC981.8.G56L983 2008
551.6--dc22

                                                2007030864

Founded in 1888, the National Geographic Society is one of the largest nonprofit
scientific and educational organizations in the world. It reaches more than 285 million people each month through its official journal, NATIONAL GEOGRAPHIC,
and its four other magazines; the National Geographic Channel; television documen-
taries; radio programs; films; books; videos and DVDs; maps; and interactive media.
National Geographic has funded more than 8,000 scientific research projects and
supports an education program combating geographic illiteracy.

For more information, please call 1-800-NGS LINE (647-5463)
or write to the following address:

National Geographic Society
1145 17th Street N.W
Washington, D.C. 20036-4688 U.S.A.

Visit us online at www.nationalgeographic.com/books

For information about special discounts for bulk purchases, please contact
National Geographic Books Special Sales: ngspecsales@ngs.org

For rights or permissions inquiries, please contact National Geographic Books
Subsidiary Rights: ngbookrights@ngs.org

Printed in U.S.A. on 100 percent post–consumer waste recycled paper.

Interior design: Cameron Zotter

4 Publisher.

3 Place of publication.

the medium. If the reference book alphabetizes entries, no volume or page numbers are needed.

> "Cinderella." *Encyclopedia of Folklore and Literature*. Ed. Mary Ellen Brown and Bruce A. Rosenberg. Santa Barbara: ABC-CLIO, 1998. Print.

> "Natural Selection." *Merriam-Webster's Collegiate Dictionary*. 11th ed. 2003. Print.

14. Introduction, preface, foreword, or afterword

List the author of the introduction or other part of the book and the name of that part, followed by the title of the book and the author or editor of the book (preceded by the word "By" or "Ed."). Then follow with the publication information, including the inclusive page numbers, and end with the medium.

> Holman, Bob. Foreword. *Burning Down the House: Selected Poems from the Nuyorican Poets Café's National Poetry Slam Champions*. By Roger Bonair-Agard et al. New York: Soft Skull, 2000. xv-xvii. Print.

> Keynes, Sir Geoffrey. Introduction. *Songs of Innocence and Experience*. By William Blake. Oxford: Oxford UP, 1989. 7-15. Print.

15. Multiple works by the same author

List the works in alphabetical order by title. (Titles are alphabetized letter by letter.) Put the author's name as the first item in the first work. After that, use three hyphens followed by a period in place of the author's name.

> Angelou, Maya. *And Still I Rise*. New York: Random, 1978. Print.

> ---. *A Song Flung Up to Heaven*. New York: Random, 2002. Print.

16. Title within a title

When a book title includes the title of another book, the title within the title is not italicized.

> Kinnamon, Keneth, ed. *New Essays on* Native Son. Cambridge: Cambridge UP, 1990. Print.

17. Sacred text

> *Bhagavad-Gita: The Song of God*. Trans. Swami Prabhavananda and Christopher Isherwood. New York: Signet, 2002. Print.

Periodicals

18. Article in a journal

MLA does not distinguish between journals paginated by volume and those paginated by issue. Include the issue number (if any) in all cases. Separate the volume number from the issue number with a period. Follow with the year in parentheses, a colon, and the page numbers. End with the medium.

> Basney, Lionel. "Teacher: Eleven Notes." *American Scholar* 71.1 (2002): 75-88. Print.

Godwin-Jones, Bob. "Blogs and Wikis: Environments for Online Collaboration." *Language Learning and Technology* 7.2 (2003): 12-16. Print.

19. Article in a magazine

Wilson, Ann Lloyd. "Architecture for Art's Sake." *Atlantic Monthly* June 2001: 85-88. Print.

Cagle, Jess. "The Women Who Run Hollywood." *Time* 29 July 2002: 52-57. Print.

20. Article in a newspaper

Estes, Andrea, and Scott Allen. "Secret Talks Stall in Big Dig Suit." *Boston Globe* 30 June 2007: A1+. Print.

21. Unsigned or anonymous article

"Producers Give Thanks for a Windfall of Family Films." *New York Times* 1 Dec. 2003, late ed.: E5. Print.

22. Review

List the reviewer's name and the title of the review. Then add the abbreviation "Rev." (for "Review") and the word "of" followed by the title and a comma, then the word "by" and the creator of the work being reviewed. Provide publication information for the review, not for the work reviewed.

Meadows, Susannah. "Son of a Sort of Goddess." Rev. of *The Impressionist*, by Hari Kunzru. *New York Times Book Review* 12 May 2002: 27. Print.

23. Editorial

"Volunteer Opportunity." Editorial. *Boston Globe* 30 Sept. 2002: A18. Print.

24. Letter to the editor

If the letter has a title, insert it in quotation marks after the author's name. If there is no title, simply give the designation "Letter" following the author's name.

Pieper, Bill. "Life as Film." Letter. *New Yorker* 5 May 2008: 5. Print.

Electronic Sources

25. Entire Web site

If you can determine the name of the person or organization that created the site, begin your entry with that name; otherwise begin with the title of the site, italicized. If there is no title, write a description such as "Home page." Do not italicize the description. Follow the title with the name of the organization or sponsor of the site, or "N.p." if not available. (The sponsor's name usually appears at the bottom of the site's home page.) Then add the date of electronic publication or of the latest update (or "n.d." if not available), the medium consulted ("Web"), and the date you accessed the site. MLA no longer requires a

The Essentials of Citing Articles from Periodicals—MLA Style

To cite an article from a periodical in MLA style, include the following elements.

1 Author, last name first.

2 Title, in quotation marks with major words capitalized.

3 Name of periodical, italicized with major words capitalized.

4 Date of publication.

5 Page number (or inclusive if more than one page).

6 Medium.

Works cited entry for an article from a periodical.

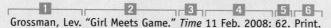

Grossman, Lev. "Girl Meets Game." *Time* 11 Feb. 2008: 62. Print.

❓ FAQs

When do I include the volume and issue number and where do I find it? Look for this information in the periodical's table of contents or *masthead,* the listing of the editors, subscription information, and other key information about the publisher located at the front of most periodicals. You do not need to include this information for weekly or monthly magazines. Include it only for scholarly journals.

How do I cite the date of publication? For scholarly journals, include the year of publication in parentheses following the volume and issue numbers. For magazines and other non-scholarly periodicals, do not use parentheses to enclose the date. For those published monthly, give the month and year after the name of the periodical. For daily, weekly, or bi-weekly periodicals, give the day, month, and year (in that order) after the name. Abbreviate months except for May, June, and July.

How do I format inclusive page numbers? Page numbers appear after the date of publication. For sources that appear on consecutive pages, include the page range separated by a hyphen (for example, *42–45*). For numbers over 99, include only the last two digits of the second number (*150–53*) unless the range enters the next hundred (*199–202*). If your source does not appear on consecutive pages, you need only include the first number followed by a plus sign (*45+*). For newspaper articles, include the section if given (for example, *L1*).

For more on citing periodical articles using MLA style, see page 638. Instructions on how to cite other types of sources using MLA style can be found on pages 634–38 and 639–50.

1 Author.

2 Title of article.

3 Name of periodical.

4 Date of publication.

5 Page number.

6 Volume and issue numbers (use only for scholarly journals).

URL, but if you do include a URL, put it after the period after the date of access, enclose it in angle brackets, and put a period after the closing bracket.

> Lesser, Zachary. Home page. U Penn, 2006. Web. 27 Jan. 2009.

> Kiernan, Kevin, ed. *A Guide to Electronic Beowulf*. U of Kentucky, 2003. Web. 15 Apr. 2009.

> *The Nature Conservancy*. The Nature Conservancy, 2008. Web 8 June 2008.

26. Work from a Web site

Include all of the following elements if they are available, separated by periods: the author of the work; the title of the work in quotation marks; the name of the Web site, italicized; the name of the publisher or sponsor of the Web site (use "N.p." if none is available) followed by a comma and the date of publication or latest update (use "n.d." if not available); the medium consulted ("Web"); and the date you accessed the site.

> Breuer, János. "Bartók and the Third Reich." *Hungarian Quarterly*. Hungary Network, 1995. Web. 30 Aug. 2008.

> Renan, Ernest. "Poetry of the Celtic Races I." *Bartleby.com*. Bartleby.com, 2001. Web. 15 June 2008.

27. Article in an online periodical

If the work also appeared in print, give the same information as for a print periodical. Include the name of the database (if any), then follow with the medium ("Web") and the date of access. (If there are no page numbers for the online article, use "n. pag." instead.)

> Jewett, Thomas. "Terrorism in Early America: The U.S. Wages War against the Barbary States to End International Blackmail and Terrorism." *Early America Review* 4.1 (2002): n. pag. Web. 30 Jan. 2002.

28. Article in an online magazine or newspaper

List the author, the title of the article in quotation marks, the name of the magazine or newspaper in italics, the publisher or sponsor of the Web site, the date of the article, medium consulted ("Web"), and the date of access.

> Park, Alice. "Could the Spinach Scare Happen Again?" *Time*. Time, 21 Sept. 2006. Web. 31 Jan. 2008.

> Swett, Nancy. "Wealthy Schools Shun Fair-Aid Meet." *New York Times*. New York Times, 23 Nov. 2003. Web. 26 July 2007.

29. Online book

> Gatto, John Taylor. *The Underground History of American Education*. New York: Odysseus, 2003. *The Odysseus Group*. Web. 8 Sept. 2008.

30. Online government document

List the name of the government and the name of the agency that issued the document. Then list the title of the document, italicized, followed by the sponsor of the site, the date of publication or latest update, the medium ("Web"), and the date of access.

> United States. Census Bureau. *State & County QuickFacts: Bucks County, Pennsylvania*. U.S. Census Bureau, 24 Sept. 2002. Web. 10 Oct. 2004.

31. Material accessed through an online database or subscription service

First list the publication information using the appropriate model (books, periodicals, etc.). Then list the name of the database, italicized, the medium consulted ("Web"), and the date of access. MLA no longer requires the name of the subscription service you used or the library or the location where you accessed the material.

> Cutler, Maggie. "Whodunit—the Media?" *Nation* 26 Mar. 2001: 18-20. *Academic OneFile*. Web. 25 July 2004.

> Sipe, Thomas Owen. "Beethoven, Shakespeare, and the 'Appassionata.'" *Beethoven Forum* 4.1 (1995): 73-97. *RILM*. Web. 24 Sept. 2004.

32. Material published on CD-ROM, magnetic tape, or diskette

For material published on CD-ROM, cite the medium after the publication information.

> *The North American Bird Reference Guide*. Seattle: Multimedia, 2004. CD-ROM.

For material accessed in a database or periodical published on CD-ROM or other media, cite the material as you would for a print source and then add the medium ("CD-ROM," "Diskette"); the title of the database (if any), italicized; the name of the vendor; and the publication date of the database.

> Bushman, Brad J., and Joanne Cantor. "Media Ratings for Violence and Sex: Implications for Policymakers and Parents." *American Psychologist* 58.2 (2003): 130-41. CD-ROM. *PsycARTICLES*. Ovid. Sept. 2003.

33. E-mail message

> Burns, Monica. "Re: Penn State Main Campus." Message to the author. 15 Sept. 2004. E-mail.

34. Instant message

> Betro, Elizabeth. Conversation about Picasso. 24 Apr. 2002. Instant message.

35. Online posting

> Oosthoek, K. "New Jersey's Environments: History and Policy." *H-Environment*. H-Net Online, 7 Oct. 2002. Web. 10 Oct. 2004.

The Essentials of Citing Web Sources—MLA Style

To cite a Web source in MLA style, include the following elements.

1 Author, last name first.

2 Name of work, in quotation marks.

3 Name of Web site, italicized.

4 Sponsoring organization.

5 Date of publication or latest update.

6 Medium.

7 Date of access, day followed by abbreviated month.

Works cited entry from a short work from a Web site.

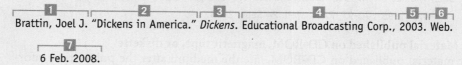

Brattin, Joel J. "Dickens in America." *Dickens.* Educational Broadcasting Corp., 2003. Web.

6 Feb. 2008.

❷ FAQs

How do I cite a source with no clear author? If you cannot identify the author, begin your citation with the name of the work.

How do I identify the name of the work? Carefully check the first page of the article or Web site for a title. If you cannot identify a clear title, begin your citation with the name of the Web site.

My source has no publisher listed or date of publication. If you cannot determine the sponsor or publisher, include "N.p." in your citation. When no date of publication is available, use "n.d." instead.

My source has a very long URL. Do I need to include the entire URL? MLA no longer requires a URL because readers are more likely to find resources on the Web by searching for titles and authors' names than by typing in long, complex URLs. If you do include a URL, put it after the period after the date of access, enclose it in angle brackets, and put a period after the closing bracket. Whenever a URL will not fit on one line, break it only after a slash; do not add a hyphen at the break.

For more on citing Web sources using MLA style, see page 639. Instructions on how to cite other types of sources using MLA style can be found on pages 634–39 and 648–50.

3 Name of Web site.

2 Name of work.

1 Author.

4 Sponsoring organization.

5 Date of publication or latest update.

The Essentials of Citing Articles from Databases—MLA Style

To cite an article from a database in MLA style, include the following elements.

1 Author, last name first.

2 Title of article, in quotation marks.

3 Name of periodical, italicized, delete leading *A*, *An*, or *The*.

4 Volume and issue number, separated by a period.

5 Date of publication, in parentheses.

6 Page numbers, inclusive.

7 Name of database, italicized.

8 Medium.

9 Date of access, day followed by abbreviated month and year.

Works cited entry for an article in a database.

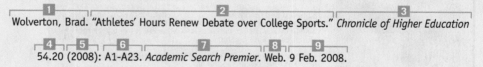

Wolverton, Brad. "Athletes' Hours Renew Debate over College Sports." *Chronicle of Higher Education*
54.20 (2008): A1-A23. *Academic Search Premier*. Web. 9 Feb. 2008.

❓FAQs

I located an article using my library's subscription database service. How do I cite this information? When you conduct an online library search, you will be linked to databases both directly and via subscription services like *EBSCO Host* and *InfoTrac*. Distinguishing between the subscription service and the database can be confusing, and you will need to look carefully to find this information. You need only cite the name of the database, not the subscription service or the name and location of the library you used.

How do I cite page numbers for an article that does not appear on consecutive pages? If an article skips pages, include just the first number followed by a plus sign (*21+*).

How much of the URL do I need to include? MLA does not require a URL because some URLs are unstable, are too long and complex, or because readers may not share access to the same subscription services. Be sure to include enough information about your source to enable readers to locate it by searching on the title, authors, and other relevant information using common search engines or database services.

For more on citing articles from a database using MLA style, see page 643. Instructions on how to cite other types of sources using MLA style can be found on pages 634–50.

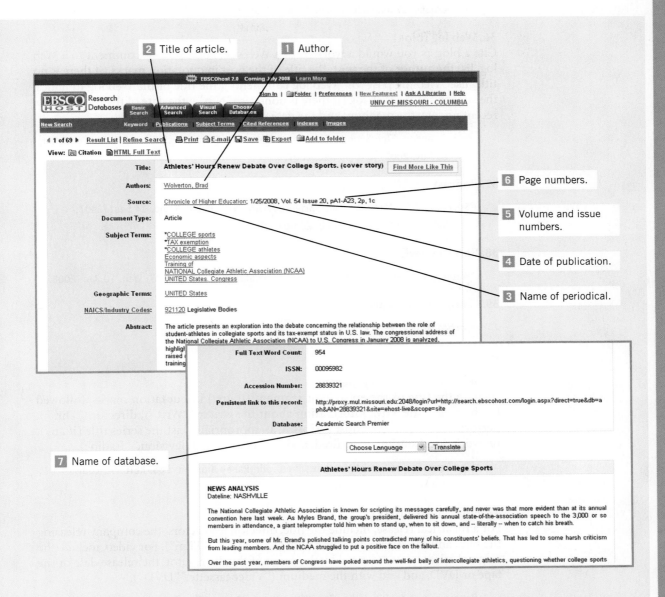

2 Title of article.

1 Author.

6 Page numbers.

5 Volume and issue numbers.

4 Date of publication.

3 Name of periodical.

7 Name of database.

Langly, Ringo. "Minimum Wage Going Up—What Good Will It Do?" *Soc.politics*. Google
Groups, 17 July 2004. Web. 27 July 2004.

36. Web log (blog)

Cite a blog as you would a work from a Web site. For a post or comment to a Web
log, list the author of the post; the title of the post in quotation marks (if there is no
title, use "Web log post" or "Web log comment"); the title of the Web log in italics;
the sponsor of the Web log (if there is none, use "N.p."); the date of the post or most
recent update; the medium; and the date of access.

Kelm, Brandon, "Too Soon to Give Up on Embryonic Stem Cells." *Wired Science*. CondéNet,
20 Nov. 2007. Web. 15 Dec. 2007.

37. Podcast

"Steven Pinker." Narr. Joe Palca. *Science Friday*. Natl. Public Radio. 14 Sept. 2007.
National Public Radio. Web. 20 Nov. 2007.

38. Entry in a wiki

"Water Resources." *Wikipedia*. Wikimedia Foundation, 24 Aug. 2007. Web. 10 Jan. 2008.

39. Computer software

Practica Musica. Vers. 4. Kirkland, WA: Ars Nova, 1999. CD-ROM.

Other Sources

40. Television or radio program

Include the title of the episode or segment (if any) in quotation marks, followed
by the series title. Give information about the writer ("Writ."), director ("Dir."),
performers ("Perf."), or host ("Host"), as appropriate. List the series title (if any),
network, local station, date aired, and the medium ("Television," "Radio").

"The Jesus Factor." *Frontline*. Writ., Prod., Dir. Raney Aronson. PBS. KETC, St. Louis.
29 Apr. 2004. Television.

41. Film, video, or DVD

For a theatrical release, include the title, director, lead actors, the company releasing
the film, and the release date. End with the medium ("Film"). For video, include the
original release date followed by the name of the distributor, the release date of the
tape or DVD, and end with the medium ("Videocassette," "DVD").

Bonnie and Clyde. Dir. Arthur Penn. Perf. Warren Beatty, Faye Dunaway. 1967. Warner,
1999. DVD.

Pollock. Dir. Ed Harris. Perf. Ed Harris, Marcia Gay Harden. Sony Picture Classics, 2000.
Film.

42. Music or sound recording

Beethoven, Ludwig van. *String Quartets: Op. 127, 130, 131, 132, 133, 135*. Perf. Alban
Berg Quartet. EMI, 1997. LP.

43. Cartoon or comic strip

Roberts, Victoria. Cartoon. *New Yorker* 8 Mar. 2003: 44. Print.

44. Advertisement

Secret. Advertisement. *Cosmopolitan* Sept. 2002: 248. Print.

45. Interview

Blackburn, Simon. "The Seven Deadly Sins: Envy." *Talk of the Nation*. Natl. Public Radio.
WBEZ, Chicago. 4 Sept. 2003. Radio.

Graves, Denise. Personal interview. 27 Apr. 2004.

46. Survey

Moravian College Food Services Questionnaire. Survey by the author. 2 Feb. 2004.

47. Lecture

Kress, Gunter. "Gains and Losses: New Forms of Texts, Knowledge, and Learning." Conf.
on Coll. Composition and Communication. Hyatt, San Antonio. 26 Mar. 2004.
Lecture.

48. Performance

Chamber Dance Project: Dancers and Musicians. Chor. Ann Carlson, Adam Hougland, and
Stanton Welch. Dir. Diane Coburn Bruning, Stanley L. Corfam, and Stacy Caddell.
Perf. Chris Bandy et al. Kaye Playhouse, New York. 6 June 2002. Performance.

49. Work of art or photograph

List the artist or photographer; the title of the work, italicized; the date the work was
created; the medium of composition (for example, "Oil on canvas," "Bronze," "Photograph"); the name of the museum or other institution; and the city. To cite a photograph or artwork that you have not seen in person, omit the medium of composition
and location of the artwork and include the publication information for the source
where the reproduction appears, ending with the number of the page, slide, plate, or
figure, and the medium of reproduction ("Print"). For a work viewed online, omit
the medium of composition but include the location of the artwork; then add the
title of the Web site, the medium consulted ("Web"), and the date of access.

Becker, Otto. *Custer's Last Fight*. 1896. *On the Rez*. Ian Frazier. New York: Picador, 2001.
120. Print.

Millais, John. *Ophelia*. 1851-52. Tate Gallery. London. *The Artchive*. Web. 27 July 2004.

Noland, Kenneth. *Turnsole*. 1961. Polymer paint on canvas. Museum of Mod. Art, New York.

50. Unpublished doctoral dissertation

Bauer, George. "Perpetual Displacements as a Creative and Critical Strategy of Inquiry into Sites of Meaning." Diss. Texas Tech U, 2002. Print.

51. Published doctoral dissertation

Jones, Anna Maria. *Problem Novels/Perverse Readers: Late-Victorian Fiction and the Perilous Pleasures of Identification*. Diss. U of Notre Dame, 2001. Ann Arbor: UMI, 2001. ATT 3028783. Print.

52. Government document

United States. Federal Bureau of Investigation. *United States Government Interagency Domestic Terrorism Concept of Operations Plan*. Washington: Federal Emergency Management Agency, 2001. Print.

For advice on citing online government documents, see page 643.

53. Pamphlet

American Cancer Society. *Making Strides against Breast Cancer*. New York: American Cancer Society, 2002. Print.

54. Personal letter

List the writer of the letter, followed by "Letter to" the recipient, the date, and the form of the material ("MS" for manuscript or handwritten letter, "TS" for typescript). For an unpublished letter, add the name and location of the library, museum, or private collection housing the letter.

Antoinette, Meghan. Letter to the author. 13 Feb. 2004. MS.

Wyatt, Liza. Letter to Dr. Claire Polin. 30 May 1972. MS. Claire Polin Archives, Harrington Park, NJ.

▷ SAMPLE RESEARCH ESSAY, MLA STYLE

The following pages show a sample research essay. Zane Van Dusen followed MLA guidelines for formatting his essay and for documenting sources. The annotations in the margins point out how various kinds of sources are integrated into the work and documented according to MLA style. Note that the essay is shown in reduced format to allow for these annotations.

Van Dusen 1

Zane Van Dusen

Professor Odell

English 101

9 December 2007

Analog Recording in Peril

When Jeff Tweedy and his band Wilco entered their Chicago recording studio in January 2005, they were shocked to find a complete lack of the analog audio tape that the band was accustomed to using for their recordings. Mr. Tweedy "was under the impression that there was a shortage of tape in Chicago," but was dismayed to learn that this shortage was not limited to the city (qtd. in Smith and McBride A1). In fact, just a few weeks earlier Quantegy Inc., the last producer of high-quality analog tape, declared bankruptcy and shut down its factory in Opelika, Alabama, making analog tape a rare and precious commodity.

While digital recording techniques are now the mainstay of the recording industry, analog reel-to-reel tape recording technology has historically dominated the industry (Fig. 1). Despite analog's superior sound and archival quality, over the last decade its dominance has been completely overturned by the ascendancy of the new and cheaper recording medium of digital recording. The demise and possible extinction of analog recording represents a loss to recording engineers, musicians, archivists, and casual listeners alike.

While Quantegy's shutdown may have been sudden, it did not come as a total surprise. Analog purists and producers like Steve Albini (who has worked with bands such as Nirvana and The Pixies) had

Fig. 1. Reel-to-reel analog tape (PunchStock).

Anecdote draws readers in.

Indirect source of a quotation identified by *qtd. in.*

Clear reference to figure.

Thesis statement.

Figure number and title included with illustrations.

Well-known bands give context and credibility to source.

Van Dusen 2

Clear transition to section on the history of analog.

"been expecting the news for about a year" (qtd. in Gendron). What is more surprising is how in one short decade an inferior recording mechanism has rendered the predominant recording mechanism for almost 60 years virtually obsolete.

Centered headings not standard MLA, but can be used with instructor approval.

A Brief Analog Recording History

The age of analog recording began just after World War II. In 1948, the Ampex Corporation released the first American tape recorder, the Ampex Model 200. This new technology caught on quickly, popularized by Bing Crosby and singers of the day

Parenthetical reference directs reader to figure.

(Fig. 2) and the American Broadcast Corporation (Schoenherr). Analog

Summarized material acknowledged.

tape soon dominated the recording industry and was used almost exclusively from the 1950s until the mid 1980s, when digital recording first became possible (Coleman 164).

Well-chosen visual with caption and source information.

Clear topic sentences used throughout.

In 1987, Digital Audio Tape (DAT) was introduced, taking the professional recording industry by storm. Producers found DATs to be extremely helpful because of their relatively low cost, large storage capabilities, and convenient size.

Fig. 2. Tenor David Hughes trying new reel-to-reel tape recorder in 1953 (Miller).

Many amateur producers stopped using tapes all together and began recording straight to their hard drives using programs like ProTools. Due to digital's immense popularity, it was able to replace analog as the standard for the recording industry in only a couple of years.

Signal phrase introduces quotation.

Smith and McBride estimate "that as few as 5% of albums are recorded

Added word inserted in brackets.

and mixed using [analog] audio tape" (A1). This virtually complete changeover in the recording industry technology occurred despite a

Transition to section on the benefits of analog.

strong consensus that analog sound quality was in fact better than digital.

Van Dusen 3

The Benefits of Analog Recording

While digital recording techniques may be cheaper and easier than analog, the superior sound and archival quality of analog make its demise all the more surprising. Gendron contends that many audiophiles "swear their allegiance to analog tape, prized for its warm, natural presence and archival superiority." Many analog purists, like producers Steve Albini and Joe Gastwirt (Grateful Dead), are so loyal that they refuse to work in any other medium. Gastwirt believes that analog tape is "a much more musical medium." He declares that its warmth acts like an instrument that "actually does something to the music" (qtd. in Smith and McBride A1).

So, what is this "warmth" that so many audio purists praise? When audiophiles talk about "warmth," they are referring to what Gendron describes as the imperfections that distinguish analog from digital. The presence of this natural distortion is clear if you compare any recording made before 1981 to a digital recording. Modern digital audio recorders record sounds at or above CD quality. However, many feel that the sound is a little *too* perfect. According to Timothy Powell, owner of Metro Mobile Recording, digital recording is analogous to "a news photographer taking a picture of someone's face, warts and all . . . [while] analog is akin to a colorized fashion picture--it has a certain sheen and smoothness" (qtd. in Gendron).

Furthermore, while digital recordings may sound cleaner than analog, digital sound is not necessarily more accurate. In fact, the way that digital sound is processed makes it less faithful to the original sounds. Digital recorders do not capture the actual sound waves; instead they use a process known as stair-stepping. In this process, the recorder takes "snapshots'" of the analog signal at a certain rate, approximating but not capturing the entire sound wave ("Is the Sound"). This leads to distortions in the original sound, especially when the sound wave moves faster than the sample rate.

Figure 3 illustrates the difference between digital and analog recording. Here the "stair-stepping" process of digital recording is illustrated by the green rectangles and the sound wave captured by

---

Topic sentence introduces first benefit of analog.

Question for topic sentence adds variety and interest.

Signal phrase used in center of a paraphrase with quoted word set in quotation marks.

Ellipsis points indicate text removed from the quotation.

Citation for paraphrased material uses shortened version of article title.

Figure referenced and explained clearly.

Van Dusen 4

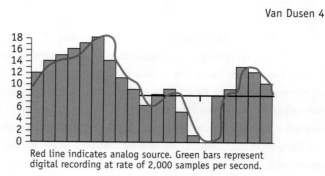

Red line indicates analog source. Green bars represent digital recording at rate of 2,000 samples per second.

Fig. 3. Digital recording of an analog source (Brain).

analog is shown in red. Notice the points in the recording where digital sampling fails to capture the sound wave as precisely as analog does. As Roy Furchgott explains, "analog music, like the tone from a violin string, is a single smooth wave; digital music is made of samples from points on that wave and later reconstructed" (H1). This process affects the quality of the recording and removes the natural warmth of an analog tape.

The other major argument for continuing to work solely in analog is its archival reliability. Analog tape technology has remained virtually unchanged since its inception after World War II. Therefore every analog tape ever made is still playable today. This allows any analog recording to theoretically last forever. By contrast, digital recording methods are constantly evolving and this constant change leads to the incompatibility of the original storage medium. Producer Steve Albini agrees, explaining his reliance on analog as follows:

> Digital doesn't allow for a permanent master. The storage media changes and becomes inevitably obsolescent, frozen in time with that day's technology. As someone who's paid to make recordings, I'd be irresponsible to make something that wasn't permanent and playable in the future. (qtd. in Gendron)

However, while analog is still very important and functional from a sonic and archival standpoint, the industry has opted to use digital because of its low cost and ease of use.

Annotations (left margin):

Signal phrase identifies source; page number included after quote.

Topic sentence introduces second reason for analog's superiority.

Signal phrase prepares readers for the quotation that follows.

Long quotation indented and cited without quotation marks.

Source at end in parentheses.

Van Dusen 5

Unlike analog, you don't need any professional experience to learn how to digitally record and edit music. No reel-to-reel tape or hard-to-find equipment is needed beyond a computer and the proper software. And while it is slow and cumbersome to find a song using the reel-to-reel tape required by analog recording techniques, digital recording software allows you to find music tracks quickly and easily with the click of a button. This same computer software allows the user to make edits with ease. Analog editing is difficult because of the physical act of tape splicing that must occur (Gendron).

Digital recording is also considered by some to be a better medium for archiving recordings. Despite the archival reliability of analog, analog tapes degrade over time. Each subsequent copy leads to a lessening of the tape's quality, a diminishment that Sam Brylawski of the Library of Congress likens to making carbon paper copies: "each generation or layer under your master was a little fainter . . . [with] a little more noise, a little more background hiss" ("Analog Tape"). Conversely, digital recordings do not degrade over time and, furthermore, add virtually no excess noise to the recordings.

The Future of Analog

So, what's in store for the future of analog recording? Analog die-hards are optimistic that the medium will continue and are hopeful that new suppliers will step in to fill the void left by the closing down of analog tape supplier Quantegy. In the meantime, audiophiles like Jeff Tweedy will be forced to find alternative supplies of analog tape such as stockpiling or recording over archived reels. Such stop-gap measures will not, however, do much to stop the medium from fading into history. Young listeners are sadly not aware of the sound quality that is being lost. "What we've lost with this new era of massive compression and low fidelity," according to veteran studio owner Skip Saylor, "are the records that sound so good that you get lost in them" (qtd. in Gomes B1). The special sound and archival qualities of analog tape are in real danger of extinction, lost to the cheaper, faster efficiency of digital tape.

Inclusion of opposing viewpoints strengthens argument.

Paraphrased material cited.

Source's affiliation with the Library of Congress establishes credibility.

In-text citation for radio broadcast found on the Web.

Conclusion begins with a question.

References to anecdote mentioned in first paragraph.

Colorful quote from newspaper article leaves strong impression.

Restates thesis.

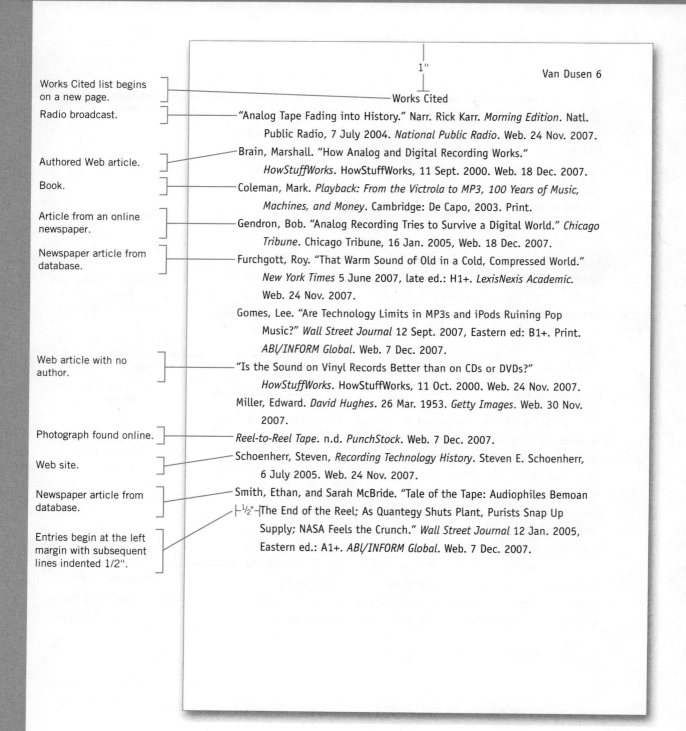

Van Dusen 6

Works Cited list begins on a new page.

Works Cited

Radio broadcast.

"Analog Tape Fading into History." Narr. Rick Karr. *Morning Edition*. Natl.
    Public Radio, 7 July 2004. *National Public Radio*. Web. 24 Nov. 2007.

Authored Web article.

Brain, Marshall. "How Analog and Digital Recording Works."
    HowStuffWorks. HowStuffWorks, 11 Sept. 2000. Web. 18 Dec. 2007.

Book.

Coleman, Mark. *Playback: From the Victrola to MP3, 100 Years of Music,
    Machines, and Money*. Cambridge: De Capo, 2003. Print.

Article from an online newspaper.

Gendron, Bob. "Analog Recording Tries to Survive a Digital World." *Chicago
    Tribune*. Chicago Tribune, 16 Jan. 2005, Web. 18 Dec. 2007.

Newspaper article from database.

Furchgott, Roy. "That Warm Sound of Old in a Cold, Compressed World."
    New York Times 5 June 2007, late ed.: H1+. *LexisNexis Academic*.
    Web. 24 Nov. 2007.

Gomes, Lee. "Are Technology Limits in MP3s and iPods Ruining Pop
    Music?" *Wall Street Journal* 12 Sept. 2007, Eastern ed: B1+. Print.
    ABI/INFORM Global. Web. 7 Dec. 2007.

Web article with no author.

"Is the Sound on Vinyl Records Better than on CDs or DVDs?"
    HowStuffWorks. HowStuffWorks, 11 Oct. 2000. Web. 24 Nov. 2007.

Miller, Edward. *David Hughes*. 26 Mar. 1953. *Getty Images*. Web. 30 Nov.
    2007.

Photograph found online.

Reel-to-Reel Tape. n.d. *PunchStock*. Web. 7 Dec. 2007.

Web site.

Schoenherr, Steven, *Recording Technology History*. Steven E. Schoenherr,
    6 July 2005. Web. 24 Nov. 2007.

Newspaper article from database.

Smith, Ethan, and Sarah McBride. "Tale of the Tape: Audiophiles Bemoan

Entries begin at the left margin with subsequent lines indented 1/2".

⊢ ½" ⊣ The End of the Reel; As Quantegy Shuts Plant, Purists Snap Up
    Supply; NASA Feels the Crunch." *Wall Street Journal* 12 Jan. 2005,
    Eastern ed.: A1+. *ABI/INFORM Global*. Web. 7 Dec. 2007.

▷ USING APA STYLE

APA style is typically used for research papers in the social sciences. It is used in books, journal articles, and electronic materials produced by scholars in a variety of fields, including psychology, sociology, and technical communication, as well as by students taking courses in these fields. The following pages describe the APA system for citing

Directory to APA Style

In-Text Citations

List of References

Books

Periodicals

Electronic Sources

Other Sources

▶ Go to
**bedfordstmartins.com/
writingnow** to download
Chapter 13 > Links for more
documentation help.

sources within the text of an essay as well as the format for listing the sources cited at the end of the essay. In APA style, this list is called *References*.

For more information on APA style, refer to the *Publication Manual of the American Psychological Association*, 5th ed. (Washington: APA, 2001). For up-to-date advice on documenting electronic sources, consult the *APA Style Guide to Electronic References* (2007) (www.apastyle.org/elecref.html).

APA In-Text Citations

The key elements in APA style for in-text citations are author and date. Writers using APA style include the author's last name and the publication date for the referenced information in the sentence where the work is cited. The name may be used in a signal phrase followed by the year in parentheses, or both name and year can be placed in parentheses at the end of the sentence if the name does not appear earlier. For example:

> Williams (1994) observed that one of the key principles of visual design is alignment.

> One of the key principles of visual design is alignment (Williams, 1994).

For a detailed discussion of
quoting, paraphrasing, and
summarizing, see Chapter 12,
pages 613–20.

If you are paraphrasing, as in the previous examples, you are not required to include the page number in parentheses (although you may do so if you think it will be helpful to the reader). If you are quoting, however, you do need to include it. Note that APA style requires a "p." in front of the page number. When using a signal phrase in a sentence with a quotation, put the page number after the quotation. Notice, too, that APA style requires you to use a verb in either the past tense (such as *observed* or *explained*) or the present perfect tense (*has observed, have explained*) in the signal phrase.

For more on signal phrases,
see page 630.

> Williams (1994) observed that one of the key principles of visual design is alignment, which "creates a clean, sophisticated, fresh look" (p. 14).

> One of the key principles of visual design is alignment, which "creates a clean, sophisticated, fresh look" (Williams, 1994, p. 14).

The following examples of in-text citations illustrate how to cite various types of works in APA style. They will help you avoid confusing the reader when you cite a single source more than once, when you cite more than one work by an author, and so on.

1. Work with one author

> Claxton (1994) pointed out that "the 1960s and 1970s sparked attempts to relate birth order to differences in attitudes and opinions, creativity, job selection, personality, sex-role identity, socialization, and psychiatric problems" (p. 477).

2. Work with two authors

> Ceci and Williams (1997) found a "high correlation between general intelligence and years of schooling" (p. 1052).

When both authors' names appear in parentheses instead of in a signal phrase, use an ampersand instead of the word *and* to join the two names.

> Schooling has been called "primarily a marker for intelligence" (Ceci & Williams, 1997, p. 1052).

3. Work with three to five authors

The first time you cite a work with three to five authors, list all authors by last name only, in the order listed in the publication.

> Tucker, McHale, and Crouter (2001) noted that "younger siblings whose parents have lower education levels rely on older siblings for support with schoolwork" (p. 327).

If you refer to the same text a second time, include only the last name of the first author, followed by "et al." (Latin for "and others").

> Tucker et al. (2001) observed . . .

4. Work with six or more authors

Cite only the first author's name, followed by "et al." in either a signal phrase or a parenthetical reference.

> As Gilbert et al. (2007) noted, "Striving to avoid inferiority was a significant predictor of psychopathologies" (p. 633).

> According to one report, "striving to avoid inferiority was a significant predictor of psychopathologies" (Gilbert et al., 2007, p. 633).

5. Work with an unknown author

Include the title of the work or the first few words of the title, either in parentheses or in a signal phrase. Titles of books should be italicized; titles of articles and short works are placed inside quotation marks.

> People succumb to shock from a variety of causes, including massive infections called sepsis ("Treating Shock," 2004).

6. Work with a group author

If the group name is long, use the full name in a signal phrase or parenthetical reference the first time you cite the source. If the group is known by a familiar abbreviation, include the abbreviation in brackets after the full name. In subsequent references to the source, use the abbreviation alone.

> FIRST CITATION (Environmental Protection Agency [EPA], 2004)

> SECOND CITATION (EPA, 2004)

7. Web site or electronic document

To cite a whole Web site, give the URL in a parenthetical reference (www.globalwarming .org) in the text and do not include the Web site on the references page. To cite a specific Web document or electronic document, include the same information as for a print document (name and date). If an electronic source's date of publication is unknown, use "n.d." ("no date"). If there is no author, either include the document title in a signal phrase or use a shortened version of the title in parentheses.

> According to the World Health Organization's Web site, there is no significant threat to the public in China from new outbreaks of SARS ("China," 2004).

If page numbers are unavailable, use paragraph numbers to document quotations.

> Through the use of brain imaging, Tapert, G. Brown, Baratta, and S. Brown (2003) have demonstrated that "craving can influence treatment of substance use disorders, but is difficult to measure objectively" (para. 1).

8. Two or more works in the same reference

Present the works in the parenthetical reference in the same order that they appear in the references list, separated by semicolons.

> The confluence hypothesis expanded the idea that firstborns had a higher IQ due to extended contact with their parents to include the effect that their relative position to their younger siblings and family size had on their intelligence (Ernst & Angst, 1983; Zajonc, 1975).

9. Two or more works by the same author

When your references list includes two or more works by the same author, the date will provide the information needed to identify the source. However, if the references list contains two or more works by the same author published in the same year, you need to distinguish among them. List them in alphabetical order (by title) within that year, adding the lowercase letter "a" after the date for the first source entry, "b" for the second entry published in the same year, "c" for the third entry published in the same year, and so on. In the parenthetical reference, be sure to include the lowercase letter that identifies the appropriate source.

> According to Hawking (2002a), the concept of an expanding universe was not seriously theorized before the twentieth century.

10. Works by two or more authors with the same surname

Use the authors' initials along with their last names for each citation.

> S. Johnson (2004) described with fascination the results of his own MRI scan.

> One author described with fascination the results of his own MRI scan (S. Johnson, 2001).

11. E-mail or personal communication

Include the initials and last name of the author of the communication, and give as exact a date as possible. Do not include personal communications in the list of references.

> D. W. George (personal communication, December 19, 2007) listed fourteen different billing errors that had occurred since the first of the year.

12. Indirect source

To use information from a source that was cited in another source (a secondary source), cite the original source in a signal phrase. Include the secondary source in the list of references and, in the in-text citation, include it after the words *as cited in*.

> In an earlier report, Gellman describes "the first known acquisition of a nonconventional weapon other than cyanide by al Qaeda" (as cited in Shafer, 2004, para. 6).

APA List of References

In APA style, the list of all sources cited in a research paper is called *References*. The information in the list contains all the relevant publication information that will enable readers to locate specific books, journals, Web sites, and other sources that they are interested in reading. This list is organized alphabetically by authors' last names. If a work has no author, it is alphabetized by the title.

No matter what you use, usually you will need the same general information to create an entry in a list of references. However, the form and order of that information will vary. Throughout this section are visual "essential" guides that show annotated APA-style references for four different types of entries: books, articles from periodicals, works from a Web site, and articles from a database. These guides explain the way the information must be presented, including the sequence of elements, punctuation, and acceptable or required abbreviations. One of the most common errors that students make when using APA style is in the capitalization of titles. In APA style, only the first word, proper nouns, and the first word following a colon are capitalized in the titles of books and articles. All important words are capitalized in the titles of journals. In the following section, you will see sample entries for a variety of other types of sources in APA style.

Books

1. Book by a single author

> Stewart, L. (1992). *Changemakers: A Jungian perspective on sibling position and the family atmosphere*. New York: Routledge.

2. Book by two or more authors

> Pollock, D. C., & Van Reken, R. E. (2001). *Third culture kids: The experience of growing up among worlds*. Yarmouth, ME: Intercultural Press.

The Essentials of Citing Books—APA Style

To cite a book in APA style, include the following elements.

1 Author, last name followed by initial(s) for first name.

2 Year of publication, in parentheses.

3 Title, italicized, with capitals for first word in title and subtitle.

4 Place of publication, followed with colon (include abbreviation for the state or country when omission could be confusing).

5 Publisher, without words like *Inc.* and *Publisher.*

List of references entry for a book.

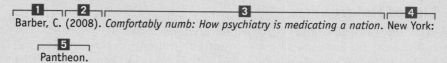

Barber, C. (2008). *Comfortably numb: How psychiatry is medicating a nation.* New York:

Pantheon.

❷ FAQs

The book I am citing lists more than one copyright date. Do I need to cite all of them? No. Include only the most recent date.

How do I handle a source with more than one place of publication? If more than one place of publication is included, use only the first one listed.

For more on citing books using APA style, see page 661. Instructions on how to cite other types of sources using APA style can be found on pages 661–75.

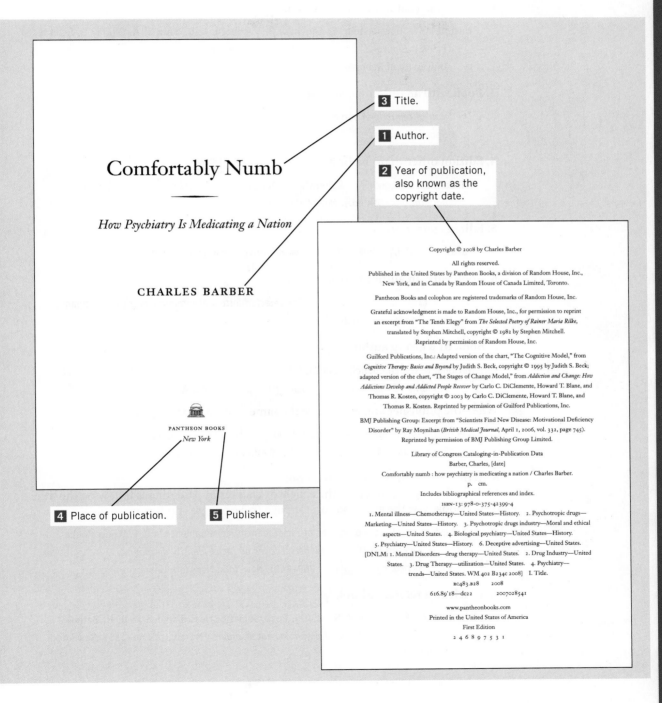

3 Title.

1 Author.

2 Year of publication, also known as the copyright date.

Comfortably Numb

How Psychiatry Is Medicating a Nation

CHARLES BARBER

PANTHEON BOOKS
New York

4 Place of publication.

5 Publisher.

Copyright © 2008 by Charles Barber

All rights reserved.

Published in the United States by Pantheon Books, a division of Random House, Inc.,
New York, and in Canada by Random House of Canada Limited, Toronto.

Pantheon Books and colophon are registered trademarks of Random House, Inc.

Grateful acknowledgment is made to Random House, Inc., for permission to reprint
an excerpt from "The Tenth Elegy" from *The Selected Poetry of Rainer Maria Rilke*,
translated by Stephen Mitchell, copyright © 1982 by Stephen Mitchell.
Reprinted by permission of Random House, Inc.

Guilford Publications, Inc.: Adapted version of the chart, "The Cognitive Model," from
Cognitive Therapy: Basics and Beyond by Judith S. Beck, copyright © 1995 by Judith S. Beck;
adapted version of the chart, "The Stages of Change Model," from *Addiction and Change: How
Addictions Develop and Addicted People Recover* by Carlo C. DiClemente, Howard T. Blane, and
Thomas R. Kosten, copyright © 2003 by Carlo C. DiClemente, Howard T. Blane, and
Thomas R. Kosten. Reprinted by permission of Guilford Publications, Inc.

BMJ Publishing Group: Excerpt from "Scientists Find New Disease: Motivational Deficiency
Disorder" by Ray Moynihan (*British Medical Journal*, April 1, 2006, vol. 332, page 745).
Reprinted by permission of BMJ Publishing Group Limited.

Library of Congress Cataloging-in-Publication Data
Barber, Charles, [date]
Comfortably numb : how psychiatry is medicating a nation / Charles Barber.
p.   cm.
Includes bibliographical references and index.
ISBN-13: 978-0-375-42399-4
1. Mental illness—Chemotherapy—United States—History.   2. Psychotropic drugs—
Marketing—United States—History.   3. Psychotropic drugs industry—Moral and ethical
aspects—United States.   4. Biological psychiatry—United States—History.
5. Psychiatry—United States—History.   6. Deceptive advertising—United States.
[DNLM: 1. Mental Disorders—drug therapy—United States.   2. Drug Industry—United
States.   3. Drug Therapy—utilization—United States.   4. Psychiatry—
trends—United States. WM 402 B234c 2008]   I. Title.
RC483.B28   2008
616.89'18—dc22   2007028541

www.pantheonbooks.com
Printed in the United States of America
First Edition
2 4 6 8 9 7 5 3 1

For a book with more than six authors, list the first six authors and abbreviate the rest as "et al." (Latin for "and others").

> Huston, A. C., Downerstein, E., Fairchild, H., Feshbach, N. D., Katz, P. A., Murray, J. P., et al. (1992). *Big world, small screen: The role of television in American society*. Lincoln: University of Nebraska Press.

3. Book with an unknown author

> *The Spanish republic--A survey of two years of progress*. (1933). London: Eyre & Spottiswoode.

4. Edition other than the first

> Randall, D., Burggren, W., & French, K. (2002). *Animal physiology: Mechanisms and adaptations* (5th ed.). New York: W. H. Freeman.

5. Edited collection

> Gates, H. L. (Ed.) (2002). *Classic slave narratives*. New York: Signet.

6. Book with an author and an editor

> Woolf, V. (1989). *Congenial spirits: The selected letters of Virginia Woolf* (J. Trautmann, Ed.). London: Hogarth.

7. Book by a group author

> National Research Council. (2002). *Effectiveness and impact of corporate average fuel economy (CAFE) standards*. Washington, DC: National Academy Press.

When the publisher and author are the same, use "Author" as publisher.

> American Psychological Association. (2001). *Publication manual of the American Psychological Association* (5th ed.). Washington, DC: Author.

8. Article or chapter in an edited book
Include the page numbers of the article or chapter in parentheses following the title of the book. Use the abbreviation for page (p.) or pages (pp.).

> Adams, M. (2001). Core processes of racial identity development. In C. L. Wijeyesinghe & B. W. Jackson III (Eds.), *New perspectives on racial identity development: A theoretical and practical anthology* (pp. 209–242). New York: New York University Press.

9. Article in a reference book

> Resick, P. A., & Calhoun, K. S. (2001). Posttraumatic stress disorder. In D. H. Barlow (Ed.), *Clinical handbook of psychological disorders* (3rd ed., pp. 60–113). New York: Guilford Press.

10. Multivolume work

Give the number of the volume you cite after the title or the total number of volumes if you are citing all volumes, in parentheses.

> Katz, S. H. (2003). *The encyclopedia of food and culture* (Vol. 2). New York: Scribner.

If you cite a volume with a separate title, use the title of the volume, followed by a colon, the abbreviation "Vol.," and the volume number. Then include the title of the multivolume work.

> Johnston, L. D., O'Malley, P. M., & Bachman, J. G. (2003). *College students and adults ages 19–40: Vol. 2. Monitoring the future: National survey results on drug use, 1975–2002.* Bethesda, MD: National Institute on Drug Abuse.

11. Translation

> Freud, S. (1999). *The interpretation of dreams* (J. Crick, Trans.). Oxford: Oxford University Press. (Original work published 1900)

12. Multiple works by the same author

List two or more works by the same author by year of publication with the earliest first, beginning with the author's name each time. When you use works by the same author published in the same year, alphabetize them by title within that year, adding the lowercase letter "a" after the date for the first entry, "b" for the second entry published in the same year, and so on.

> Gould, S. J. (2002a). *I have landed: The end of a beginning in natural history.* New York: Harmony Books.

> Gould, S. J. (2002b). *The structure of evolutionary theory.* Cambridge, MA: Belknap Press of Harvard University Press.

> Gould, S. J. (2003). *Triumph and tragedy in Mudville: A lifelong passion for baseball.* New York: Norton.

Periodicals

The APA no longer distinguishes between journals paginated by volume and those paginated by issue. Therefore, for journal articles always include the volume number and the issue number (if available).

13. Article in a journal

> Dingfelder, S. (2003). Tibeten Buddhism and research psychology: A match made in nirvana? *Monitor on Psychology, 34*(11), 46.

> Underwood, R. L., & Klein, N. M. (2002). Packaging as brand communication: Effects of product pictures on consumer responses to the package and brand. *Journal of Marketing Theory & Practice, 10*(4), 58–69.

The Essentials of Citing Articles from Periodicals—APA Style

To cite an article from a periodical in APA style, include the following elements.

1 **Author,** last name followed by initials for first and middle names.

2 **Date of publication,** in parentheses.

3 **Title of article,** with no italics, underlining, or quotation marks; capitals for first word in title (and subtitle, where included).

4 **Name of periodical,** italicized with major words capitalized.

5 **Volume number,** italicized; **issue number,** in parentheses.

6 **Page numbers,** inclusive.

List of references entry for an article from a periodical.

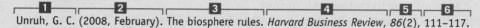

Unruh, G. C. (2008, February). The biosphere rules. *Harvard Business Review, 86*(2), 111–117.

❓ FAQs

I found a volume number but not an issue number. Where should I look for this information? Issue numbers can be found alongside the volume information in the table of contents or *masthead*, a listing of the editors, subscription information, and other key information about the publisher located in the front of most periodicals. However, some journals do not include issue numbers. When that is the case, you need only include the volume number.

When do I include the year of publication and when do I need a more specific date? If your source is a journal, use only the year. For magazines and other periodicals, use the year, month, and day (if given).

How do I cite page numbers that are not consecutive? Include all page numbers for articles that appear in different parts of a periodical. For example, *101–104, 120.*

For more on citing periodical articles using APA style, see page 665. Instructions on how to cite other types of sources using APA style can be found on pages 661–65 and 668–75.

BEST PRACTICE

3 Title of article.

1 Author.

The Biosphere Rules

Nature employs production processes that are surprisingly efficient, environmentally sound – and widely imitable.

by Gregory C. Unruh

SUSTAINABILITY – WHICH NATURAL SCIENTISTS define as the capacity of healthy ecosystems to continue functioning indefinitely – has become a clarion call for business. Consider General Electric's ambitious Ecomagination project, Coca-Cola's efforts to protect water quality, Wal-Mart's attempt to reduce packaging waste, and Nike's removal of toxic chemicals from its shoes. These and other laudable efforts are steps on a road described by the aluminum giant Alcan in its 2002 corporate sustainability report: "Sustainability is not a destination. It is a continuing journey of learning and change."

Unfortunately, Alcan had it wrong. At best, the view of sustainability as an endless journey of incremental steps does a disservice to managers seeking to square economy with ecology sooner rather than later. At worst, it serves as an excuse for

Paul Wearing

hbr.org | **February 2008** | Harvard Business Review **111**

🎓 **Harvard Business Review**

EDITOR AND MANAGING DIRECTOR
Thomas A. Stewart

DEPUTY EDITOR AND ASSISTANT MANAGING DIRECTOR
Karen Dillon

EDITORIAL DIRECTOR
Sarah Cliffe

ART DIRECTOR
Karen Player

SENIOR EDITORS
David Champion *(Paris)*
Diane Coutu
Bronwyn Fryer
Paul Hemp
Julia Kirby
Lew McCreary
Gardiner Morse
M. Ellen Peebles
Steven Prokesch
Anand P. Raman

ASSOCIATE EDITORS
Roberta A. Fusaro
Andrew O'Connell

CONSULTING EDITOR
Bernard Avishai

MANUSCRIPT EDITORS
Christina Bortz
Lisa Burrell
Steven DeMaio
Susan Donovan
Andrea Ovans
Martha Lee Spaulding

BUSINESS DEVELOPMENT EDITOR
John T. Landry

EDITORIAL RESEARCH MANAGER
Kassandra Duane

EDITORIAL COORDINATOR
Rasika Welankiwar

STAFF ASSISTANT
Christine C. Jack

SENIOR PRODUCTION MANAGER
Dana Lissy

EDITORIAL PRODUCTION MANAGER
Christine Wilder

SENIOR ASSOCIATE ART DIRECTOR
Chandra Tallman

SENIOR DESIGNER
Jill Manca

DESIGNER
Lindsay A. Sweeney

EDITORIAL PRODUCTION COORDINATOR
Josette Akresh-Gonzales

COMMUNICATIONS DIRECTOR
Cathy Olofson

COMMUNICATIONS ASSOCIATE
Siobhan C. Ford

CONTRIBUTING STAFF
Lilith Z.C. Fondulas
Amy L. Halliday
Annie Noonan
Eileen Roche
Kristin Murphy Romano
Debbie White

A NOTE TO READERS
The views expressed in articles are the authors' and not necessarily those of *Harvard Business Review*, Harvard Business School, or Harvard University. Authors may have consulting or other business relationships with the companies they discuss.

SUBMISSIONS
We encourage prospective authors to follow HBR's "Guidelines for Authors" before submitting manuscripts. To obtain a copy, please go to our website at www.hbr.org; write to The Editor, *Harvard Business Review*, 60 Harvard Way, Boston, MA 02163; or send e-mail to hbr_editorial@hbsp.harvard.edu. Unsolicited manuscripts will be returned only if accompanied by a self-addressed stamped envelope.

EDITORIAL OFFICES
60 Harvard Way, Boston, MA 02163
617-783-7410; fax: 617-783-7493
www.hbr.org

Volume 86, Number 2
February 2008
Printed in the U.S.A.

2 Date of publication.

6 Page number.

4 Name of periodical.

5 Volume and issue numbers.

14. Article with more than six authors

If an article has more than six authors, list the first six names followed by "et al." (the abbreviation for "and others").

> Dorhenwind, B. P., Lerav, I., Shrout, P. E., Schwartz, S., Nevah, G., Link, B. G., et al.
> (1992). Socioeconomic status and psychiatric disorders: The causation selection
> issue. *Science, 255*(5054), 946–952.

15. Article in a magazine

> Lemonick, M. (2003, December 1). Is Alzheimer's in the family? *Time,* 86–87.

16. Article in a newspaper

Page numbers for newspaper articles should include the abbreviation "p." or "pp." If the article appears on discontinuous pages, list all the page numbers, separated by commas.

> Duenwald, M. (2002, September 17). Students find another staple of campus life: Stress.
> *The New York Times,* pp. F5, F10.

17. Article with an unknown author

Alphabetize by the first important word in the title.

> Setting the stage. (2003, December). *Scientific American, 289*(6), 32.

18. Editorial

> Deregulation's weakness (2002, September 30). [Editorial]. *The Washington Post,*
> p. A18.

19. Letter to the editor

> Datnow, A., & Hubbard, L. (2002, March/April). Getting it right. [Letter to the editor].
> *Psychology Today, 35*(2), 6–7.

20. Review

> Shenk, J. W. (2003, May/June). Think different. [Review of the book *Saying yes: In
> defense of drug use*]. *Mother Jones,* 81–82.

Electronic Sources

21. Document from a Web site

To cite a whole Web site, give the URL in a parenthetical reference in text and do not include the Web site on the references page. To cite a specific document, include the author, publication date (if known), title of the document, title of the site, and "Retrieved from" followed by the URL. Include the retrieval date only if there is no publication date or if the information is likely to change.

Devlin, K. (2003, December 1). John von Neumann: The father of the modern computer. *MAA Online*. Retrieved from http://www.maa.org/devlin/devlin_12_03.html

22. Article from an online periodical

List the author, date, title, and publication information as for a print document (including the volume and issue numbers for all journal articles). If the article has a DOI ("digital object identifier"), include it after the publication information and do not list the URL. If the article does not have a DOI, include the URL for the article or the periodical's home page (if the article is available only by subscription). List the retrieval date only if the information is likely to differ from the print version.

Behncke, L. (2004, March). Mental skills training for sports: A brief review. *Athletic Insight, 6*(1). Retrieved from http://www.athleticinsight.com/Vol6Iss1/MentalSkillsReview.htm

Fitzmaurice, J., & Comegys, C. (2006). Materialism and social consumption. *Journal of Marketing Theory & Practice, 14*(4). doi: 10.2753/MTP1069-6679140403

If the material is based on a print source and is an exact duplicate of the print version, put the words "Electronic version" in square brackets after the article title. You do not need to include a retrieval date or a URL.

Rose, F. (2003, December). The second coming of Philip K. Dick [Electronic version]. *Wired, 11*(12), 198–209.

23. Article from an online newspaper

Give the URL for the newspaper site, not the exact source, if you access the article from a newspaper's searchable Web site.

Zakaria, T. (2004, April 28). Terrorist threat center tackles technology, privacy. *The Washington Post*. Retrieved from http://www.washingtonpost.com

24. Article or abstract from a database

List the author, date, title, and publication information as for a print document (including the volume and issue numbers for all journal articles). If the article has a DOI, include it after the publication information and do not list the database name. If the article does not have a DOI, list the database name and document number (if available).

Holden, C. (2007, March 7). Nuclear hazard has a new face. *Science, 315*(5816), 1199. Retrieved from Academic OneFile (A160713258).

Toplak, M. E., Liu, E., Macpherson, R., Toneatto, T., & Stanovich, K. E. (2007, April). The reasoning skills and thinking dispositions of problem gamblers: A dual-process taxonomy. *Journal of Behavioral Decision Making, 20*(2), 103–124. doi: 10.1002/bdm.544

The Essentials of Citing Web Sources—APA Style

To cite a Web source in APA style, include the following elements.

1 Author, last name followed by initials for first and middle names.

2 Date of publication or last update.

3 Name of work with no italics, underlining, or quotation marks; capitals for first word in title (and subtitle, where included).

4 Title of Web site.

5 URL, preceded by *Retrieved from.*

List of references entry for a Web source.

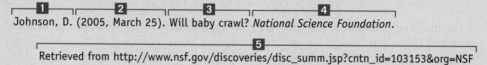

Johnson, D. (2005, March 25). Will baby crawl? *National Science Foundation.*

Retrieved from http://www.nsf.gov/discoveries/disc_summ.jsp?cntn_id=103153&org=NSF

❷ FAQs

Where do I find the date of publication? Oftentimes this information can be found at the bottom of the page, but not always. If an original publication date is included along with an update (as in the source above), use the latest update in your citation.

How do I cite a source with no publication date? Use the abbreviation "n.d." ("no date") if no publication date is provided.

How do I handle a source with no identifiable author? If there is no clear author, begin your citation with the name of the work.

For more on citing Web sources using APA style, see page 668. Instructions on how to cite other types of sources using APA style can be found on pages 661–68 and 674–75.

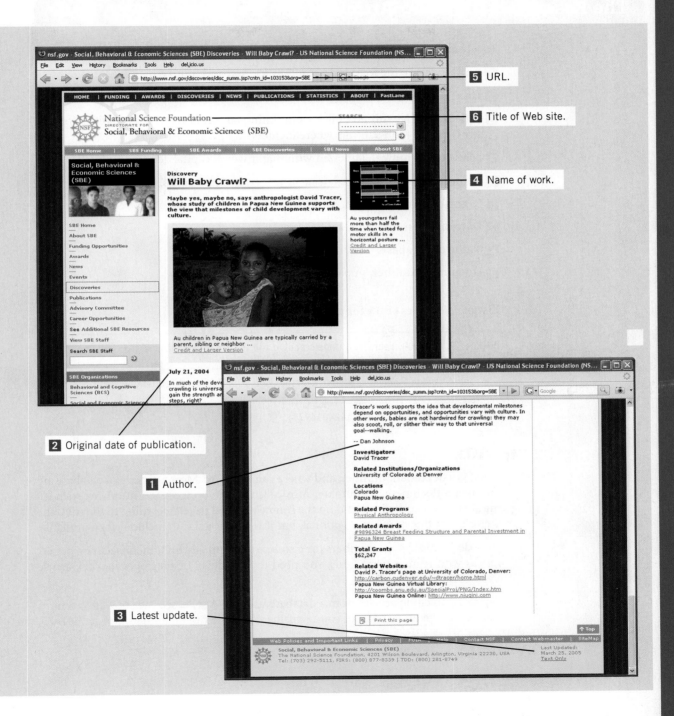

5 URL.

6 Title of Web site.

4 Name of work.

2 Original date of publication.

1 Author.

3 Latest update.

The Essentials of Citing Articles from Databases—APA Style

To cite an article from a database in APA style, include the following elements.

1 Author, last name followed by initials for first and middle names.

2 Date of publication, in parentheses.

3 Title of article with no italics, underlining, or quotation marks; capitals for first word in title (and subtitle, where included).

4 Name of periodical, italicized with major words capitalized.

5 Volume number, italicized; **issue number,** in parentheses.

6 Page numbers, inclusive.

7 Date of access, preceded by *Retrieved*.

8 Name of database.

9 Document number, in parentheses (if available).

List of references entry for an article from a database.

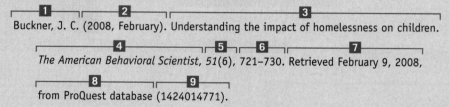

Buckner, J. C. (2008, February). Understanding the impact of homelessness on children.

The American Behavioral Scientist, 51(6), 721–730. Retrieved February 9, 2008,

from ProQuest database (1424014771).

❓ FAQs

What is a document number, and where can I find it? Most articles in a database are assigned a document ID number. Also called article or accession numbers, such ID numbers can usually be found on the source retrieval page. According to the APA, the inclusion of this number is optional, but it is always good to include when available.

How do I handle page numbers for a source that appears on nonconsecutive pages? Just as with regular periodicals, you need to include all of the pages that the article appears on, for example, *34, 73–75.*

For more on citing articles from a database using APA style, see page 669. Instructions on how to cite other types of sources using APA style can be found on pages 661–75.

8 Name of database.　　3 Title of article.　　4 Name of periodical.　　2 Date of publication.

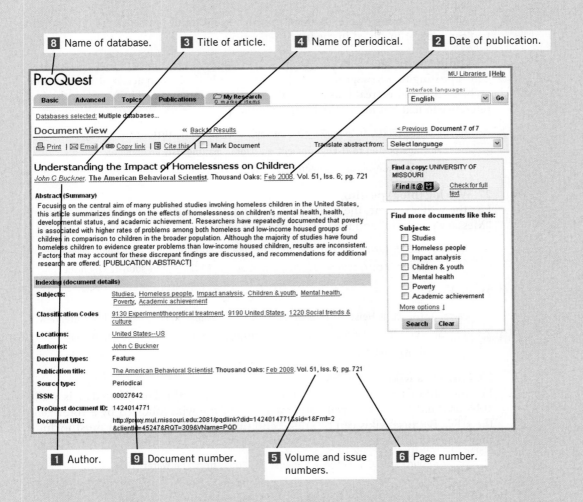

1 Author.　　9 Document number.　　5 Volume and issue numbers.　　6 Page number.

Tucker, C. J., McHale, S. M., & Crouter, A. C. (2001, June). Conditions of sibling support in adolescence. *Journal of Family Psychology, 15*(2), 254–271. Retrieved from PsycARTICLES database.

25. E-mail

As with other forms of personal communication, e-mail messages are cited in the text but are not included in the list of references.

26. Online posting

Cite a posting to a newsgroup or other forum only if you can access it in an online archive. Otherwise, treat it as personal communication and cite it in a parenthetical reference in text but not in the list of references.

Oosthoek, K. (2002, October 7). New Jersey's environments: History and policy. Message posted to H-Environment electronic mailing list, archived at http://www.h-net.org/~environ/

27. Web log (blog) posting

List the writer's name, the date of the posting, the title of the posting, followed by "Message posted to" and the URL of the Web log.

Keim, B. (2007, November 20). Too soon to give up on embryonic stem cells. Message posted to http://blog.wired.com/wiredscience/2007/11/too-soon-to-giv.html

28. Podcast

Palca, J. (Host), & Heist, A. (Producer). (2007, September 14). Steven Pinker [Interview]. *Science Friday*. Podcast retrieved from http://www.sciencefriday.com/program/archives/200709144

29. Entry in a wiki

List the author's name (if known), the title of the wiki, the date (if no date is available, use "n.d."), the retrieval date, the name of the wiki followed by a colon and the URL. Because wikis can be edited and updated at any time, you must include the retrieval date.

Water resources. (n.d.). Retrieved August 24, 2007, from The Water Wiki: http://water.wikia.com/wiki/Water_resources

30. Online government document

National Center for Infectious Diseases. (n.d.). *Viral hepatitis A*. Retrieved November 22, 2003, from http://www.cdc.gov/ncidod/diseases/hepatitis/a/index.htm

31. Computer software

Gray, P. (1999). Psychology 3e: Student activity CD-ROM [Computer software]. New York: Worth.

Other Sources

32. Television program

> Zuiker, A. E., & Donahue, A. (Writers), & Fink, K. (Director). (2002). Identity crisis
> [Television series episode]. In J. Berman (Producer), *CSI: Crime Scene Investigation*.
> New York: CBS Worldwide.

33. Film, video, or DVD

> Ball, C. J. (Producer), & Nolan, C. (Director). (2000). *Memento* [Motion picture]. United
> States: Columbia Tristar.

34. Music or sound recording

> Eminem. (2002). Cleanin out my closet. On *The Eminem show* [CD]. Santa Monica, CA:
> Interscope Records.

35. Interview

As with other types of personal communication, interviews are cited parenthetically within the text, but they are not listed in the references.

36. Photograph, table, figure, or graph

Include all of the information about the print or electronic source where you found the photograph, table, figure, or graph as a caption under the image where you insert it. The caption should resemble a references entry for the publication, beginning with a title (if any) and ending with a page number or reference marker for the location of the image. Do not include an entry for the photograph, table, figure, or graph on the references page.

37. Government document

> U.S. Senate. (2003). *Homeland security federal workforce act of 2003*. Washington, DC:
> U.S. Government Printing Office.

For advice on citing online government documents, see page 674.

38. Technical or research report

> Association of Certified Fraud Examiners. (1996). *Report to the nation on occupational
> fraud and abuse*. Austin, TX: Author.

39. Personal letter

As with other forms of personal communication, personal letters are cited in the text but are not included in the list of references.

▷ SAMPLE REFERENCES PAGE, APA STYLE

The following page shows Zane Van Dusen's works cited page from his research essay, "Analog Recording in Peril," presented as a list of references using APA style.

References begin new page with title centered.

Entries begin at the left margin with subsequent lines indented 1/2".

Newspaper article accessed online.

Newspaper article accessed through database.

Radio broadcast.

References

Brain, M. (2000, September 11). How analog and digital recording works. Retrieved December 18, 2007, from http://communication.howstuffworks.com/analog-digital3.htm

Coleman, M. (2003). *Playback: From the victrola to MP3, 100 years of music, machines, and money*. Cambridge: De Capo Press.

Gendron, B. (2005, January 16). Analog recording tries to survive a digital world. *Chicago Tribune*, p. 14. Retrieved December 18, 2007, from NewsBank database (CTR0501160455).

Is the sound on vinyl records better than on CDs or DVDs? (2000, October 11). How Stuff Works. Retrieved October 24, 2007, from <http://entertainment.howstuffworks.com/question487.htm>.

Furchgott, R. (2007, June 5). That warm sound of old in a cold, compressed world. *The New York Times*, p. H1, H3. Retrieved November 24, 2007, from *LexisNexis Academic*.

Gomes, L. (2007, September 12). Are technology limits in MP3s and iPods ruining pop music? *The Wall Street Journal*, p. B1, B8. Retrieved December 7, 2007, from *ABI/INFORM Global* (1334250291).

Karr, R. (Host) (2004, July 7). Analog tape fading into history [Radio series episode]. In *Morning Edition*. Retrieved December 18, 2007, from http://www.npr.org/templates/story/story.php?storyId=3178017

Schoenherr, S. (2005, July 6). Tape recording comes to America. Retrieved October 24, 2007, from http://history.sandiego.edu/GEN/recording/notes.html

Smith, E., & McBride, S. (2005, January 12). Tale of the tape: Audiophiles bemoan the end of the reel; as Quantegy shuts plant, purists snap up supply; NASA feels the crunch. *The Wall Street Journal*, p. A1. Retrieved December 18, 2007, from *ABI/INFORM Global* (777616901).

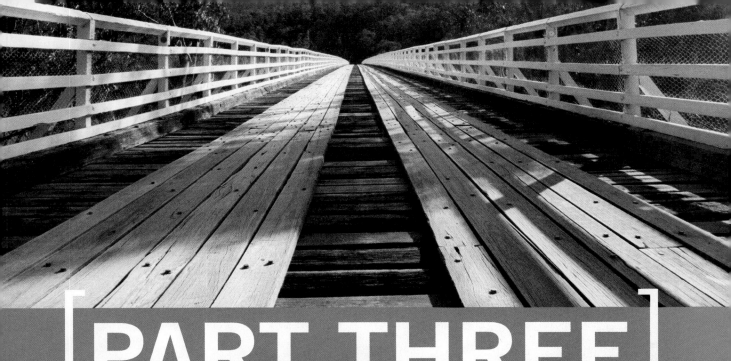

[PART THREE]

Strategies for Special Writing Situations ▷

Writing for Essay Exams

Essay exams are common in courses in nearly every academic discipline. Whether you write a response to an essay question at home or in class, the instructor's goal is to give you an opportunity to demonstrate what you have learned. In an essay exam, you not only describe or explain what you know about a topic but also expand on that knowledge. In other words, you have the opportunity to demonstrate that you can make connections, see distinctions, synthesize information, or reach conclusions. Although essay questions have many common characteristics regardless of the academic discipline, the criteria (standards) that are used to evaluate essays vary according to the discipline. Thus no single format or outline will work in every situation. In fact, you may find that the essay the instructor asks you to produce has many of the features of a report (Chapter 4), an evaluation (Chapter 6), or one of the other types of documents described in earlier chapters of this book. If you find that an essay you are assigned for another course is similar to one of the types of writing described in this book, you should review the appropriate chapter for more ideas on how to respond to that assignment.

Many of the strategies provided in this chapter for responding to essay exams can also be used for essay assignments in other courses. An essay assignment may be very similar to a take-home essay exam, so when you are asked to write an essay in another discipline, use the tools here to help you analyze the instructions, produce a draft, and review your work.

When the instructor asks you to respond to an essay question (whether in class or at home), he or she generally gives you instructions describing what is expected. This chapter shows you how to read those instructions carefully and use the information they contain to provide the kind of response that the instructor expects. The instructions for in-class essay exam questions are virtually identical to those for take-home essay exams. However, there is one important difference: In class, you will have a set amount of time in which to write. To help you make the most of your limited time, this chapter will suggest tips to help you use your time wisely to organize and draft your responses.

▷ RESPONDING TO ESSAY QUESTIONS IN CLASS

To prepare for an essay exam, you need to spend time focusing on the type of information that will enable you to respond fully and appropriately to the assigned essay questions. Although you may not know exactly what will be asked, you can do the following things ahead of time to improve your performance on the exam.

▶ **Learn as much as possible about what you will be expected to do.** Sample questions from previous exams can be helpful study aids if the instructor is willing to share them. Some instructors even provide sample student answers, which can provide useful tips about how to respond to exam questions.

▶ **Practice with sample questions.** Using sample questions from old exams or information about the questions that your instructor gives you ahead of time, practice your skills analyzing questions, writing a thesis sentence, drafting an outline, preparing a rough draft, and writing a full essay.

▶ **Time yourself.** When you practice, keep an eye on the clock to see how long each step takes. Practicing with sample questions can improve the speed with which you move through the initial stages so that you can spend more time writing and revising your essay.

Managing Your Time

One crucial thing to consider when you write in-class essay exams is the amount of time you are expected to spend on each essay. While in-class essays are not expected to be as polished as essays assigned ahead of time, you will still need to use your time wisely to create a well-organized and thoughtful response. Because you have a fixed amount of time to work on each essay, there will probably be limitations on your ability to do research, format your essay, and add visual elements. If the class meets in a computer classroom, you might have access to some formatting options, but you will probably be discouraged from spending much—if any—time on formatting (unless it's a technical writing course and the purpose of the exam is to demonstrate your ability to format).

Given the fixed amount of time for writing essays in class, you must budget your time carefully. Most instructors will indicate how much the question is worth (toward the total score of the exam), which gives an idea of how much time they expect you to spend answering it. For example, if you have three hours for the exam and one question is worth 20 percent of the grade, you should spend 20 percent of the time (approximately thirty-five minutes) writing your response. In thirty-five minutes, you would probably be expected to write a fairly coherent essay of at least five paragraphs.

Taking Notes

Use the first few minutes of in-class exam time to read the question slowly and make notes. It may help to underline important words in the question as you read. If you have thirty-five minutes to write an essay, use five to ten of those minutes to read, make notes, and plan your essay.

For advice on analyzing the important words in a question, see page 682.

▷ RESPONDING TO ESSAY QUESTIONS AT HOME

If you are asked to respond to an essay question outside of class, you usually will have a good deal of advance notice about when the take-home exam is due, so the instructor will expect you to produce a more detailed and polished response. That means doing whatever research is required; but more important, it means that your essay should be error free and written clearly in an appropriate voice with logical organization and transitions. In most cases the instructor will expect your essay to be typed and formatted according to his or her specifications, including the use of certain font types and sizes, margins, page numbering, and sometimes visual elements such as charts and graphs or headings.

For guidance with assignments that include significant amounts of research, see Chapter 10.

If the instructor hasn't already specified how much time to spend on your exam, ask yourself the following questions.

- ▶ **How detailed are the instructions?** Detailed instructions often indicate higher expectations for the final product, which implies a greater amount of time and effort on your part.

- ▶ **How much is the exam worth in terms of my final grade?** The class syllabus often lets you know how much each assignment is worth. An essay that will count as 25 percent of your final grade should demand more of your time than an essay that will count as 10 percent.

- ▶ **How long is the essay supposed to be?** Instructors often give page or word-length guidelines. The longer the essay, the more time you should spend on it.

- ▶ **How much advance notice did the instructor give?** If you were given more than two weeks' advance notice, you are probably expected to spend a good deal of time on the essay regardless of how much other work is assigned.

Don't put off the exam to the last minute. When you get the exam, be sure to read it right away—even if you will not be doing the work immediately. The instructor may have added certain requirements (such as incorporating charts and graphs, reading a particular text, or doing some research) that will take additional time before you begin to write the essay. Within the time frame that you have for completing the exam, be sure to allocate adequate time for organizing, researching, drafting, and revising your response.

▷ ANALYZING THE QUESTION

To be successful in responding to essay exam questions, think about the instructor you are writing for. What does he or she focus on? What topics come up in class discussions, assigned readings, homework, or other exam questions? Then pay close attention to the expectations built into the essay question in order to answer the question fully and appropriately. Expectations can be explicit (spelled out, obvious, clear) or implicit (implied, unspoken, understood), so be sure to read carefully. Many of the words used in the question contain important clues about how to respond, so think about each word as you read.

Finding and Understanding Explicit Cues

Some instructors will tell you very clearly what they expect you to write. Read carefully the following essay assignment for a sociology course. As you read, think about the instructor's expectations as indicated by the explicit cues in the assignment.

> Suppose you are writing a set of recommendations for the planners and curators of a museum exhibition and an accompanying catalog on Jamaican culture. Based on the materials presented in this course so far, choose five things that you would want to incorporate into your recommendations. State your five recommendations clearly, describe their implications, and explain why you think they are important.

Instructor asks for exactly five, no more, no less.

> Note: (1) While I do not have a specific set of recommendations in mind, I will be looking at your list in terms of whether it reflects an understanding of and engagement with all the class discussions and readings so far, including the assigned readings by Clifford, Marcus and Fischer, and Argun Appadurai. (2) While no specific detail about Jamaican culture is necessary for your essay, you may want to take into account certain characteristics it shares with many other cultures today, such as its diasporic nature.

Concentrate on those the instructor emphasized most.

Suggests especially important readings.

Important hint about what the instructor wants to see.

Finding and Understanding Implicit Cues

Many instructors are not nearly as explicit about what they expect as the sociology instructor whose essay assignment appears above, so you need to read carefully to find the implicit cues. You can often identify the instructor's expectations by looking for questioning words such as *who, what, when, where, why, which,* and *how.*

Each one of these questioning words signals a way to start thinking about the topic and about your essay. If you cannot find one, read the question over carefully and try to complete the following sentence.

The instructor wants to know _____.

When you complete the sentence, you will most likely use one of the questioning words.

Note the implicit cues for what the instructor wants to know in the following computer science essay exam question.

These days, some information about everyone is stored on a computer some-where. If you fill out forms online, send in warranty cards, answer question-naires, give out information on the phone or at the cash register, your personal information is collected somewhere. Do you think there should be a law to stop the accumulation of personal information in databases? Are there benefits to collecting this information?

> • Question implies a problem.
>
> • Question suggests the possibility of another point of view.

Here the instructor asks two questions that technically could be answered with a yes or a no. However, since the instructor has explicitly labeled it as an essay question, you know he is looking for a detailed response. An analysis of the ques-tion reveals that the instructor wants to know what kinds of problems might result from the collection of personal information in databases and what the benefits of such collection might be. The two questions represent two possible positions, and the instructor wants students to write about both. In answering this question, you would use your knowledge and understanding of class discus-sions and readings to establish your personal point of view and decide how best to respond.

Once you have located the questioning words in an assignment or exam ques-tion, you will have a good idea of what the instructor is looking for in your response. The table on page 684 provides suggestions for finding questioning words and using them to shape your essay.

In addition to identifying the questioning words, you should read your exam instructions very closely to locate and analyze the verbs that tell you how to approach the essay.

Analyzing the Verbs

Imperative verbs in instructions or questions tell you what the instructor wants you to do. An imperative verb is a word that commands or requests (*examine, argue, explain*). Many essay questions include several such verbs, so be sure to read each question completely and find all the verbs that tell you what to do. Consider, for

Finding and Using Questioning Words

Questioning Word	Suggestions for Shaping Your Essay	Examples
Who	*Who* questions ask you to describe a person or a group of people. Be sure your answer provides specific information about an individual or a group responsible for or connected to the topic in the question.	"Who were the key players in the Enron scandal?"
What	*What* questions want you to demonstrate that you can define and/or explain a topic or some aspect of a topic.	"In what ways did the American Revolution resemble the French Revolution?"
When	*When* questions may want you to show that you know the date or time of an event ("When did something happen?"). However, be careful because these could be questions that are looking for a consequence ("When X happens, what is the result?").	"When businesses ask employees to work virtually, what happens to the professional and personal lives of the workers?"
Where	*Where* questions are not very common. If you encounter one, you can be fairly certain that the instructor wants to know the location (geographical, temporal, sequential) of some event.	"Where in the report do you see evidence that contradicts the plaintiff's testimony?"
Why	*Why* questions call on you to explain or analyze a topic, often focusing on the causes of events (why something happened) or the thinking that supports your answer (why your response is valid).	"Why is there continuing controversy about the development of genetically modified food plants?"
Which	*Which* questions ask you to make a choice between two or more events, aspects, components, and so on. Read the rest of the question carefully; you are probably being asked to make a choice and then argue for your choice.	"Which sections of *Thus Spoke Zarathustra* condemn suffering as being necessary to an understanding of the meaning of life?"
How	*How* questions are closely related to *why* questions. Both require you to provide some kind of explanation or analysis. *How* questions may focus on causes, but they may also be testing your understanding of a process or sequence of events.	"How would you set out to modify your interpersonal style in order to develop and maintain truly supportive interpersonal relationships?"

example, the imperative verbs used in the following question from an essay exam for a zoology course.

<u>Study</u> two images below. The first is a low magnification of tissue from the nasal septum (the partition between the nostrils). The second is a higher magnification of the same tissue. <u>Write</u> a short essay <u>describing</u> the epithelium of this tissue, <u>using</u> the terminology you have learned from the online lesson and/or the reading assignment. <u>Describe</u> the epithelium as completely as possible, but only regarding aspects that are visible in these images.

• Asks you to analyze visual information.

• Read carefully to find hidden imperatives.

• Here the imperative verb is explicit, which re-inforces its importance.

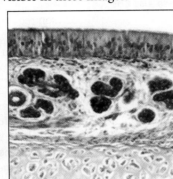

You will find imperative verbs in most essay exam questions. The table on pages 686–88 lists some of the most common of these verbs, along with suggestions for using the verbs to understand how to approach your answer to the question.

{ **Exercise** } **Analyzing Question Verbs**

Analyze the following essay questions for a geography course. Is the instructor explicit or implicit in what she wants? Consider in particular the use of imperative verbs. For each question, list the imperatives used. Then rewrite each question using questioning words without changing its meaning. Bring your revised question to class to compare with those of your classmates.

1. Critically examine Canadian migration policies and their role in the changing of Canadian society. Support your discussion with examples, statistics, and policy documents.

2. Is it likely that human numbers will stabilize at some point in the future? Discuss the conditions that can contribute to the solution of the population explosion.

3. It is argued that geopolitics gave way to geoeconomics. Explain the context and evolution of ideas about global security. ■

Common Imperative Verbs

Imperative Verb	What the Verb Suggests
Analyze	When you analyze something, you break it down into components or attributes and then put it back together with some kind of synthesis or conclusion. Analysis answers are generally quite detailed, and you will have to spend time planning your response. These questions generally tell you what to analyze and how to analyze it.
Argue (*see also* Critique)	An essay question that asks you to argue or state your opinion requires you to take a position and support it. The claim you are arguing must be backed up with evidence and reasoning. You might want to present opposing points of view and respond to that opposition.
Compare and Contrast	When you are asked to compare and/or contrast, you are expected to describe similarities and differences. Read the question carefully to see if the instructor wants you to describe both similarities and differences. If so, you can describe all the ways the things are similar and then describe all the ways they are different. Or, you could describe each thing fully and then summarize the similarities and differences in a conclusion.
Critique or Criticize (*see also* Argue)	A critique is a type of argument. When you are asked to critique, you must find the flaw (or flaws), state your claim about the flaw(s), and provide evidence to support your claim.
Define	Answers to essay-length definitions should provide the meaning for a word or phrase with complete sentences showing the instructor that you understand the term. You may want to include unique characteristics and also tell what something is not; for example, abstract art is art that is not a realistic representation of its subject. In some situations, it is important to show how the definition changes under different circumstances (time, place, culture, and so on).
Describe	Descriptions demonstrate that you understand what something "looks like." The something could be a physical object, a relationship, or a process such as a particular chemical reaction. When you write a description, you should explain the attributes of your subject, using terminology appropriate to the field. Descriptions often answer *how* questions.

For more advice on arguing, see Chapter 5.

Imperative Verb	What the Verb Suggests
Discuss	You need to read questions that ask you to *discuss* carefully to discover how the instructor wants you to talk about the topic. If the instructor does not give instructions on how to shape the discussion (for example, "discuss the *arguments* for a reduction in greenhouse gases"), you are probably free to write it as a comparison, a description, an explanation, or an analysis. If you are not certain how to organize your answer, try rewording the question to focus your response.
Evaluate (*see also* Argue)	When you are asked to evaluate, you are expected to examine a topic, issue, object, person, place, or process and determine its value. An evaluation should establish the criteria you use to make your judgment, make claims about the subject's positive and negative attributes, provide evidence to support those claims, and come to a conclusion about the worth of the subject.
Examine (*see also* Analyze)	In an essay question, *examine* means to look closely at a topic, as you would in an analysis.
Explain	An explanation requires you to demonstrate your understanding of a concept, process, or event. Using a definition may be a good way to start. Your answer should show that you understand a particular aspect of it such as its significance, behavior, effects, or causes. The wording of the question should give cues about what is expected; for example, it might ask you to explain *how* something works (which would be similar to a description) or to explain *why* something happened (which would be similar to an analysis).
Identify	Identifying an item or a list of items involves defining them and explaining their significance. If you are asked to identify terms that are commonly used in or specific to a particular academic discipline, you will need to show that you know what they mean and why they are important to that field.
Illustrate	When you see the verb *illustrate*, you are expected to describe something that exemplifies a general principle or concept. *Illustrate* is often used in conjunction with *define*. You might be asked to define a general concept (such as "class system") and then illustrate it with an example (such as the formal caste system of India or the less formal class system of Great Britain). Note that the word *illustrate* is unlikely to mean "include a visual"—although it could have that meaning if you are taking a course in design, art, architecture, or many of the sciences.

For more advice on evaluating, see Chapter 6.

continued on next page ▶

Common Imperative Verbs (continued)

Imperative Verb	What the Verb Suggests
Provide	When you see the word *provide*, be sure to read the rest of the question very carefully. The choice of this verb means that your instructor expects you to supply a particular type of information, but you will not know what it is you are supposed to supply without reading the question closely.
Refer	If the question includes the verb *refer*, the instructor expects you to use a specific text, event, or issue as evidence to support your answer. *Refer* will not be the primary focus of the question; rather, it will likely appear toward the end of the question.
Summarize	When you summarize, you touch briefly on the most important points about a topic. Plan your answer by making a list of everything you know about the topic, choosing aspects you think are most important, and writing a paragraph on each of them.
Support (*see also* Argue *and* Refer)	When you see the verb *support* in an essay question, the instructor wants you to provide evidence to back up any claims you are making. The evidence may be in the form of statistics, examples, personal experience, citations from course readings, or other sources appropriate to the course.
Synthesize	When an instructor asks you to synthesize, you are expected to blend material from different sources or different perspectives to create a meaningful whole. For example, you might be asked to synthesize the ideas presented in a series of readings on a particular topic. Your essay would be organized by the key ideas, not by the readings. If you are asked to synthesize, read the question carefully for cues about what the instructor wants you to synthesize and how he or she wants you to organize the information. The nouns used in the question are crucial in figuring out how to write an essay using synthesis.

For more advice on summarizing, see Chapter 12.

For more advice on support, see Chapter 7.

For more advice on synthesizing, see Chapter 12.

Examining the Nouns

While verbs give you suggestions about how to respond to an essay question, the nouns in a question can provide important cues about content to help you think about your essay. In the following example from an entomology exam, the nouns are underlined along with the adjectives that modify them.

> Because they have different types of sensory receptors, insects and humans may perceive the same environment very differently. What types of stimuli can humans detect more easily than insects, and what can insects detect that humans cannot?

This question requires students to demonstrate an understanding of the differences between the ways two species (insects and humans) perceive their environment. To organize your response, break the question down into a list of key points based on the nouns.

- ▶ The types of sensory receptors insects and humans have
- ▶ The ways insects and humans use their sensory receptors to perceive the environment
- ▶ The types of stimuli humans detect
- ▶ The types of stimuli insects detect

Your notes for each of these points, a simplified outline describing what you know about the sensory receptors of insects and humans, could form the basis for your response to the question.

As you make notes to guide you in answering an essay question, ask yourself the following questions.

- ▶ What words and phrases in the question are familiar?
- ▶ What was emphasized in class (or in readings) about those topics?
- ▶ What other topics were related to them?

When taking notes, be sure to think about how class discussions and readings might be used to support your answer. These notes will be especially important in planning a response to more complex questions, such as this one from a nursing education course.

> You are spending a clinical day in a homeless shelter. The nurse at the shelter explains that many homeless women come to the shelter from abusive relationships. The women have been abused as children (by parents) and as adults (by spouses, boyfriends). Many times they lack education, employment, and support systems. You learn that many of these women also lack education about HIV transmission and engage in intravenous drug use and unprotected sex. Using the Health Belief Model, describe why these women behave in this manner.

Imperative verb and a questioning word signal focus of essay.

This question is based on a scenario, a common technique in essay questions. Scenarios set a context for the question and the relevant response, but they also give cues about what the response should address. Often, students fail to read such questions carefully and end up writing lengthy responses that are inappropriate. Here, for example, they might erroneously write about the relationship between a history of abuse and homelessness, or between lack of education and unemployment. Be careful not to fall into the trap of writing about a scenario. Although the sample question includes a lot of information about homeless women, it is really only asking students to use a particular model to explain the reasons for two types of behavior: intravenous drug use and unprotected sex.

The nouns and noun phrases give cues about topics to include in your discussion. In this example, you would undoubtedly mention homeless women, abusive relationships, and education, but those topics would not be the focus of your essay. The final sentence of the instructions provides the focus. Always read through the whole question before you begin to make notes or write your essay.

Analyzing the Voice of the Question

In addition to verbs and nouns, be sure to notice the words that provide the question with its voice. The voice of the question is another cue to the kind of answer you should provide. Is the instructor's voice formal or informal? Does he or she use technical terminology or everyday language? The zoology question on page 685 includes technical words (*magnification, nasal septum, epithelium*) that indicate that you should use appropriate technical words in your response. The computer science question on page 683, however, is conversational: The instructor asks a series of questions directed to "you." Because his voice is informal, your essay can probably assume a similar voice (you can write, "I would . . ." or "I think . . ."). If the assignment has an informal voice, check with your instructor to make sure that you can respond with a similar informal voice.

▷ ORGANIZING YOUR ESSAY

After determining what information to include in your essay, you face the challenge of deciding how to organize that information. Again, the instructions themselves often give suggestions. Sometimes they are very clear and precise, as in this question from an English essay exam.

> Use the following quotation as the starting point for your discussion of a major theme in the works we have read.
>
> > "Let me hear no smooth talk of death from you, Odysseus, light of councils. Better, I say, to break sod as a farm hand for some poor country man, on iron rations, than lord it over all the exhausted dead."
>
> Suggested itinerary: First, discuss in two to five sentences the context of the quote for the work it comes from (who is talking to whom about what; what has just happened; what is about to happen). This is the only place in the answer where you need to give plot synopsis.

Next, discuss in three to ten sentences the general theme that the quote embodies. (Note: A statement of theme is a complete sentence/thought—for example, "death is final.") Be sure to define major terms/concepts.

Next, in one to two pages discuss how the work containing the quote develops this theme throughout; pay particular attention to any change or development that the work makes by its conclusions.

Finally, discuss how the other works we have read treat the same theme (about 1/4 to 1/2 page per work); spend more time on the works we spent more time on in class. (That is, if the quotation comes from the *Odyssey*, then discuss how *Medea* treats the same theme, and vice versa.)

The instructor's question provides a very detailed outline of how the essay response should be organized. He tells students what to write in each section, how much to include in each section, and what order to put the information in, and he even provides parenthetic definitions for terms such as *context* and clarification of potentially ambiguous instructions (see the final paragraph).

The students in this class were fortunate to have an instructor who provided so much information, but you should not expect your instructors to give this much help. More likely, the assignments or exam questions will be similar to this one from a management course on organizational behavior in a multicultural business context.

Compare and contrast the paths of Native Americans, African Americans, Latinos, Asian Pacific Americans, and white immigrants in their struggles to close the gap between the promise of democratic principles and actual American history and practice. What key views and differing attitudes on race and racial progress are currently held by members of these communities?

Imperative verbs.

Order of noun phrases suggests possible organization.

Questioning word.

The highlighted words tell what the assignment expects you to do, but they also give a cue about organization. The order of the question suggests that you begin your answer by first describing the similarities and differences, and then move on to describing current views and attitudes.

The words underlined here (the nouns and noun phrases) tell what kind of information to include, but they also suggest an organizational scheme: describe the paths of each group in the order suggested, compare and contrast them with one another, and then describe the current views and attitudes of each group—again, in the order suggested. Note that this would not be the only way to organize your essay, but it is acceptable because the question suggests it.

▷ DRAFTING YOUR ESSAY

Responding to an essay question has some benefits that more open assignments lack. For example, there is no need to spend time brainstorming to find a topic or thinking about a research question because the topic has been selected for you (or the instructor will provide a limited choice). Moreover, the context for your response has been identified (the audience and purpose are either known or have been given within the instructions).

Analyzing the question according to the strategies earlier in this chapter will give you ideas about the direction of your response as well as notes indicating key words or phrases that you will want to address in your answer. Using this information, draft a thesis sentence that states your main point. Then, using the cues in the question, create a brief outline that will guide the drafting of your essay. The outline also serves another purpose. If you run out of time completing the essay, your instructor can read the outline to see the other ideas you had planned to cover. An outline that demonstrates an understanding of the topic and a detailed plan for responding to the question may influence the instructor's review of your work.

Because you will not have much, if any, time to revise on a timed exam, careful planning before you start to write will result in a neater and better organized essay. Focus on the topic and stick to your outline. However, stop a few times and reread what you have written to make sure you are staying on track. Also, be sure to leave margins on both sides of the page so you can add details as you reread and review the essay. Write as neatly as you can so that the instructor does not have to struggle to decipher your handwriting.

If there is time and if it is appropriate, you may want to create a small chart or graph to illustrate an important point. Just don't spend so much time creating visual elements that you don't write enough to completely respond to the question.

▷ REVIEWING YOUR WORK

In a timed situation, keep an eye on the clock as you write so that you have time to do a final review of your work. There will be limited opportunity for revision, but you want to leave enough time at the end to proofread and fine-tune your answer. Pay particular attention to the following.

- ▶ Make sure that your answer responds to the question in full.

- ▶ Confirm that your essay includes a thesis statement.

- ▶ Fully develop and support each major point.

- ▶ Fix misspelled or inappropriate words.

- ▶ Make sure sentences are complete and grammatically correct.

- ▶ Be neat. Your answer should be legible with inserts and changes neatly marked.

As you review, you may see opportunities to add key words or phrases or respond more fully to the question. If you think you have left out any important details, use insertion marks to neatly make additions and corrections.

If essay exams cause you difficulty or undue stress, you may want to look for on-campus or electronic sources for assistance. Many schools have writing, learning, or counseling centers to help students feel more comfortable about taking tests. Furthermore, a great many Web sites are devoted to helping students do well on essay exams. For example, the University of Chicago Student Counseling and Resource Service Web site (http://counseling.uchicago.edu/resources/virtualpamphlets/) has links to many such sites under the heading *Test-Taking*.

▷ SAMPLE STUDENT ESSAY EXAMS

Throughout this chapter we have used real exam questions as examples, but you may also find it helpful to take a look at real student responses. In this section, you will see how two students responded to different types of exams. The first sample was written for a take-home exam with several short-answer essay questions; the second shows how another student responded to a longer in-class exam essay question.

Short-Answer Take-Home Exam

The question presented here was one of ten essay questions on a final exam in organizational communication. The student, Colleen Kanet, had to answer all ten questions, and each one was worth ten points. The final exam counted for 25 percent of the final grade. This was a take-home exam that the students were given one week in advance.

Organizational Communication Final Exam Question 1

Imagine that a company that has been structured according to the principles of scientific management for seventy-five years has decided that it should adopt a more modern approach to organizing. It turns to you as a consultant and asks how it can change the employee culture so that employees will be empowered to solve their own problems rather than always approaching a supervisor for decisions. Based on your understanding of organizational culture and communication, what recommendations would you offer this company to help it implement this change?

Imperative that hints that this question will describe a situation.

Scenario should be read carefully.

Last sentence provides assignment.

Colleen Kanet's Response

Since scientific management has been the structure of this organization for seventy-five years, it is important to take great care in assuring that this change will go as smoothly as possible. First of all, it is highly important to inform the organization of this change as early as possible. This will allow employees to get used to the idea. To make workers view the change positively, it is important to point out the advantages of the change. You could discuss how the change will benefit the organization as a whole (increase organization's reputation) and how it will affect employees individually (health benefits, job stability, increased technology to make jobs faster, easier, and more organized). It would also be wise to create training sessions to allow employees to have hands-on experience and understand how the new operation will work before it is actually implemented. It is also imperative to

Brief introduction also serves as a thesis statement.

Underlined passages are Colleen's recommendations.

Details explain why each recommendation is important and how to implement the change.

Conclusion. •————— make sure that employees have what they need to make a smooth transition, such as software or communication needs. Employees would be kept updated on ongoing changes. Further, it is essential that management makes sure that employees are committed to making this change and that they have all the skills and resources to do so. Using these methods will ensure a much smoother transition to the modern approach of organizing.

Colleen earned all ten points for her response because she gave several recommendations and explained the value of each recommendation. She gave enough detail to demonstrate that she understood the question and knew how to answer it without overwhelming the reader with irrelevant or superfluous information. Even though this response is only one paragraph, she gives an introduction and a conclusion that use words from the question to frame her response, and she uses transitions to move from one recommendation to the next (*first, also, further*) within the body of her answer.

In-Class Essay Exam

The question shown here was the first question out of four on a film history final exam, and the only essay portion. The other parts of the exam consisted of fill-in-the blank, multiple-choice, and short-answer questions. The essay question was worth forty out of one hundred points for the exam, and the exam itself was worth 30 percent of the final grade for the course. This exam was given during a three-hour final exam period. As discussed earlier, you can calculate how much time to spend on this exam based on its value. Since this question is worth 40 percent of the points for an exam, you would want to spend about 40 percent of the available time. In this case, that would mean 40 percent of three hours, which is about an hour and fifteen minutes.

The student whose response is shown here, Chris Hutton, first skimmed through the entire exam. He realized that he could answer the fill-in-the-blank and multiple-choice questions fairly quickly, so he did those parts first. Those two sections only took thirty minutes, so he still had plenty of time. Because he knew that he would really want to focus when working on the essay, he dealt with the short-answer questions next. The instructor had specifically said not to provide more than a couple of sentences for each of the ten short-answer questions, so Chris was able to complete them in just under an hour. This left him with just about ninety minutes to respond to the essay question and review his exam.

Some instructors will give you a choice of topics for essay questions, but Chris did not have such a choice. If you do have a choice, be sure to read each option carefully and select the one that you understand most clearly and know best. Once Chris started to focus on the essay question, he first went through looking for the important words that would suggest how he should approach the question, noticing that the instructor wanted a close reading (detailed discussion) with an emphasis on the story, a comparison to other films studied, and response to a numbered list of specific topics.

Chris took the time to draft a brief outline, following the points suggested in the question, and then drafted a thesis. His planning stage took about fifteen minutes, which left him with about an hour to draft his response, an additional five to ten minutes to review and proofread his draft, and a few more minutes to go back over all of his responses in the other sections to make sure he had answered all of the questions.

Film History Final Exam Question

Provide a close reading of *The Life of an American Fireman* (Edison Co., Edwin S. Porter, 1903). What kind of story does it tell, and how does it tell that story? Where else have we seen similar structural/formal or narrative elements found in this film? Is there anything unusual about the film?

In the course of your response, please discuss

1. editing,
2. the film's conception and presentation of time and space (including its use of sets/locations),
3. the point of view and camera work used throughout the film,
4. the way that the drama/tension of the story is conveyed.

You may also discuss anything else of interest.

- Imperative words *provide* and *discuss* signal how to approach essay.
- Questioning words explain what the instructor wants answer to provide.
- Asks for a comparison.
- An essay exam requires more than a yes or no answer.

- List gives specific areas to cover.

Chris Hutton's Response

The 1903 film *The Life of an American Fireman* by Edison Co. tells the story of a fire rescue, a popular genre of the time. The release of *Fire!* around 1900 is another example of this type of story. Both films are multi-shot narrative films with cuts on action aiding in the storytelling. *The Life of an American Fireman*, for instance, has the fire carriages enter from the right of the screen and exit the left side on a diagonal, only to cut to a shot where the carriages enter from the right. These shots begin statically, and then the carriages enter and the shot cuts away only after all carriages have left the screen. Continuity editing is taking a strong role in this film, still early in the development of continuity editing as a whole. This type of editing, these cuts on action, are using movement to make for "seamless" cuts and to pull the viewer through the film by force of narrative. This cutting on action also occurs in *Fire!* where a fireman carries a woman out a window seen from an interior shot and finishes in a juxtaposed exterior shot.

Yet *The Life of an American Fireman* is more than a duplicate of *Fire!* Though both tell the story in a linear manner initially, conceiving of each shot as a forward progression of time, *The Life of an American Fireman* drops this concept in its final shot. The film cuts from an interior fire rescue to a repeat of that same rescue from the exterior view. This sort of repetitious narrative element is more in line with George Méliès's 1902 film *A Trip to the Moon*, where the lunar landing is shown first from a distance and then again from the inner surface.

- Answers the question "what kind of story," and demonstrates awareness of the genre's history.
- Another film in same genre—one that becomes basis for many of the required comparisons.
- Response to "where else" question.
- Response to "how" question; begins discussion about editing.
- This is another way of saying "cuts on action," demonstrating awareness of appropriate terminology.
- Paragraph addresses the second required discussion point about time, and introduces another film for comparison.

Paragraph addresses the • "space" discussion point, as well as point of view and camera work. Two more films are used as comparison points.

Furthermore, *The Life of an American Fireman* begins with a fairly strong sense of space. Although its opening one-room shot is clearly painted besides a few props (theatrical set), the firehouse introduces movement as firemen frantically slide down the fire pole, entering the next shot where they mount carriages, ride off, and enter the next shot of the street, and so on, with one cut after another on action. During the entire sequence the frame is crowded with movement: dogs, horses, firemen, carriages, steam, and smoke. The rush to the fire ends on a panning camera movement far stronger than the meek attempts of the Porter film *The Great Train Robbery*.

Example of appropriate • terminology use.

This camera movement combined with the movement within this *mise-en-scene* [the way space is used in a particular scene] and the many exterior shots filmed on a diagonal (allowing for great depth as the carriages approach from background to foreground, in their rush through streets, much like the Lumiere's train in the 1895 *Arrival of a Train*) suggest great depth.

More examples in • support of the discussion of space, point of view, and camera work, as well as mention of sets and location.

Unfortunately, the static interior shots (central or almost symmetrical compositions from straight on the action—similar to a stage) without camera movements and minimal props (a bed and some wall hangings in the rescue scene) fight to reduce that depth much as the repetition of the rescue battles the otherwise contiguous editing. For instance, the interior rescue scene shows the room as if it were a stage with the window pane parallel to the plane of the lens or perpendicular to the camera. Without camera movement and devoid of any dynamic angles, only the movement of actors and smoke and the bare props bring depth or life to this scene. Much like the repetition of time with the final exterior shot, this interior shot is akin to Méliès's theatrical staging and absence of camera movement. Similarly, however, *Fire!*

Specific detail • demonstrates solid familiarity with the films.

also shot its interior scenes in a similar manner. In fact, other than a 90 degree difference in the bed and the presence of curtains, the interior rescue scene of *Fire!* was much the same.

This paragraph discusses • the final required point, tension.

The Life of an American Fireman creates tension with its cuts on action and its abundance of movement in the *mise-en-scene* (a staple of early cinema). It offers a continuous narrative except for one final interruption of continuity. This is the story of a fire rescue similar to other films of the time in staging and editing, such as *A Trip to the Moon* and *Fire!* Yet it stands out, with its continuity interruption and its diagonal movement compositions (evoking depth).

Introduction of a unique • characteristic.

Furthermore, it seems to play with editing, using irises in its opening dream sequence (similar to *View through a Telescope*) and with occasional fades and fire-like dissolves, such as the transition between the interior rescue and the repeated exterior view. This is a unique film while it is also consistent with films early in the development of continuity editing (circa 1900).

15 ▷

Writing Portfolios

A portfolio is a collection of work assembled to demonstrate the range, variety, and skill of an individual. Portfolios are used by artists, architects, photographers, fashion designers, and other professionals in the visual arts in a variety of situations, such as applying to graduate school, interviewing for a job, or making a presentation to a prospective client. Portfolios are also used by professional writers, such as journalists and technical writers, for the same purposes.

In academic settings, instructors often ask students to create portfolios of their work as a way of demonstrating what they have accomplished during a course, how they have developed as writers, and what they have learned about their own writing processes. If an instructor asks you to develop a writing portfolio, he or she will probably give you instructions on what it should contain and how it should be submitted (for example, as a hard copy in a binder or electronically as part of a Web portfolio). Regardless of the medium used to produce the portfolio, the material contained in it is essentially the same. This chapter offers background information about various types of portfolios, including information about audiences and purposes. It also presents guidelines for constructing a portfolio.

▷ PORTFOLIOS IN CONTEXT

As with any document, a writing portfolio exists within a context—for specific audiences and purposes. This chapter focuses on portfolios created in an academic context, but you should be aware that there are other contexts as well. The table on page 700 describes a variety of contexts where portfolios are used both in and out of the classroom. Later in the chapter (see p. 703) you will find more detailed suggestions for what to include in your portfolio.

The audience and purpose of an academic portfolio will largely dictate the types of materials that it contains. There are two primary audiences for an academic portfolio: the instructor and the student who creates the portfolio. As a student, you are your own audience in the sense that you can learn a great deal about how to improve your writing through the very act of assembling the portfolio materials. The portfolio's purpose will be to illustrate your development as a writer and demonstrate your competency in meeting the course requirements. Because a

▶ Go to
**bedfordstmartins.com/
writingnow** to Chapter 15 >
Examples to see sample
student Web portfolios.

great deal is riding on your performance in the portfolio, you need to take extra
care in gathering, selecting, and organizing the material you include.

The following table shows the audience and purpose for different types of writing
portfolios. In a composition course, you will likely be asked to prepare a process or
evaluation portfolio.

Variety of Portfolios

Type of Portfolio	Audience	Purpose	What to Include
Process	Instructor, self	• Demonstrates your learning in a particular course • Shows your strengths and weaknesses • Focuses on the process by which you learn and write	• Finished pieces • Notes, outlines, reflections, drafts, critiques, and other documents that demonstrate your process
Evaluation	Instructor	• Demonstrates your learning in a particular course • Emphasizes your strengths • Focuses on the products you have produced	• Finished pieces • May include descriptions of the context for each piece, reflections on your process, or other documents as required by your instructor
Best works, presentation	Instructor, employer	• Demonstrates your skill as a writer • Focuses on the best writing you have produced for a course or in the workplace • Often emphasizes writing relevant to a particular environment	• Finished pieces • May include a table of contents, an introduction, descriptions, and reflections
Exemption	Instructor, program director, program committee	• Demonstrates your skills as a writer • If sufficient writing skills are shown, you may be exempted from taking a required course	• Varies depending on the exemption requested, but typically includes finished pieces • May include a table of contents, an introduction, and descriptions
College experience	Instructors, administrators	• Demonstrates the full scope of your writing experiences and development • Shows best works over your entire college career	• Varies depending on the situation • Most likely includes your best work from a wide variety of courses

▷ CREATING YOUR PORTFOLIO

If you are creating the portfolio for a class, your instructor will probably tell you whether he or she wants it on paper or electronically. But outside the classroom, you have the opportunity to choose. Before you decide, you should think carefully about the audience and purposes of your portfolio. Ask yourself the following questions.

- ► Who will be reading your portfolio?

- ► Why will they read it?

- ► How will they gain access to it?

- ► Do you want something you can carry with you when you go on job interviews?

- ► Do you want something readers can link to from a business or personal Web site?

By answering these questions, you should be able to determine whether to create a paper or electronic portfolio.

Regardless of what kind of format you decide to use, there are three basic steps involved in creating a portfolio. First, you have to plan what to include; then you have to choose the materials outlined in your plan; and finally, you have to assemble those materials.

Planning Your Portfolio

No matter what you include, one thing is certain: You will not be able to create your portfolio overnight. A portfolio, by its very nature, is a collection that develops over time. Therefore, as soon as you know you need to create one, you should start thinking about how to keep track of appropriate material.

First, to make sure you understand exactly what you are expected to include, review any instructions you have been given. Some instructors may allow a great deal of freedom in choosing pieces to include (sometimes called an *open portfolio*), while others require everyone to follow a similar format and includes specific types of documents within the portfolio (sometimes called a *closed portfolio*). The following assignment is an example of a closed portfolio assignment.

Sample Writing Portfolio Assignment

For this course you will complete a report, a position paper, an evaluation, and a proposal. You will receive feedback from me on drafts of all of these assignments and from your peers on three of them. For your portfolio, choose any three of these assignments and revise them to include in your portfolio. For one of the assignments that was peer reviewed, include all your preliminary notes (such as brainstorming or other activities), your analysis of audience and purpose, all drafts, the notes from your peer reviewer, and the feedback I provided. For all three assignments, include

Explicitly lists what the portfolio should contain.

your response to the Taking Stock of Where You Are questions from the relevant textbook chapter. You should also include at least five pages of writing from any other course you are taking this semester. This work can be one five-page text (or slightly longer, but no more than eight pages) or a series of shorter assignments.

Identifies additional materials required by the instructor.

Create a cover page, a table of contents, and an introduction for your portfolio. In your introduction, explain the audience and purpose for each of the assignments and describe what you learned about writing from completing each assignment. For the material that is not from this course, explain why you chose it and what you might do to improve it if you had an opportunity to revise it. Put all materials in a report cover, folder, or thin three-ring binder. Use dividers to separate each assignment, and label the dividers with the type of assignment. Number all pages consecutively throughout the portfolio.

Gives formatting instructions.

Once you know what you need, make a checklist to keep track of what you have already completed and what is still needed. For example, see the following checklist as one student might have created it for the previous assignment.

Sample Checklist for a Writing Portfolio

☐ Assignment from this course (Position Paper and Taking Stock response)

☐ Assignment from this course (Proposal and Taking Stock response)

☐ Assignment from this course with all peripheral materials (Evaluation)

☐ Assignments from another course totaling at least five pages (Biology 101 lab report, 2 pages; World History 101 essay, 4 pages)

☐ Cover page

☐ Table of contents

☐ Introduction

☐ Binder

☐ Dividers

☐ Numbers on all pages

Second, develop a system for keeping copies of drafts, revision notes, peer-review responses, instructor responses, and final versions of every text you create that could potentially be included. If you are keeping an electronic portfolio, be sure to make backup versions of every document that you create.

Third, throughout the semester keep in mind the criteria your instructor provided for the portfolio. If you have to write descriptions for each entry, write them while the assignment is fresh in your mind. If you have to write reflections on each piece, begin this work as soon as you finish the piece, and add to it as you get feedback from classmates or the instructor. Completing the Taking Stock of Where You

Are questions at the end of each chapter in Part 1 for which you have completed an assignment will generate a wealth of information for writing a reflective essay.

Finally, if you are allowed to submit material from other courses, regularly analyze all your other writing assignments to see if they meet the criteria for the portfolio. As you find suitable materials, note them on your checklist. Be aware, however, that it's important to be flexible and choose the best materials, so keep an open mind about what to include.

Choosing Materials for a Writing Portfolio

Your instructor will probably provide guidelines for what to include in the portfolio. Here are some of the materials you may be asked to include, as well as questions to consider.

- ▶ **Assignments from this course.** Do you have a choice about which assignments to include? Is a specific number of pages required?

- ▶ **Drafts and revisions.** Should you include all drafts? Specific drafts? Can you do additional revision to your work before including it in the portfolio?

- ▶ **Peer reviews.** Should you include notes from classmates about your drafts? Do you need to demonstrate how you responded to those reviews?

- ▶ **In-class writing or homework.** Are you expected to include any of the less formal writing you did for this course? For example, should you include brainstorming lists or your analysis of audience and purpose for an assignment?

- ▶ **Reflective writing.** Are you expected to include material written specifically about your writing process in this course? Can you submit this as an introduction to the portfolio, or should there be a reflection for each piece?

- ▶ **An introduction.** Are you required to open your portfolio with some type of introduction? (See page 704 for suggestions on how to write the introduction.)

- ▶ **Descriptions of each piece.** Are you required to describe each piece? If so, include a brief description of the work itself, along with information about the intended audience and purpose as well as any details that will help the reader understand the text.

- ▶ **Materials from other situations.** Can you include documents written for other courses, an internship, or a job? How many such pieces can you include? Should you include all drafts or just the final version?

- ▶ **Table of contents.** Do you need to create a table of contents? If so, how should pages be labeled and numbered?

If the instructor has specified what to include, you may not have a lot of choices. However, if he or she has given you some freedom, you may have to think about what you have written that best meets the criteria established on the syllabus or assignment. For example, if the instructor for a first-year writing course wants to see your three best papers out of five written for the course using this textbook, you should reread all your papers, compare them to the features of the genre described in the appropriate chapter in Part 1, review any feedback you received, and determine how well you fulfilled the purpose of the assignment. Alternatively, the instructor might want to see papers that demonstrate how your writing has changed over the term, which suggests a chronological approach. In this case, be sure to include early drafts as well as final versions. If the instructor permits further revision, you might revise an earlier paper to show what you have learned.

Writing an Introduction for Your Portfolio

Most academic portfolios begin with some type of introductory document written specifically about the portfolio. This document can take many forms, and the instructor will probably give specific directions. Here are some of the types of information you may have to include in your introduction.

▶ **An overview of the contents.** Describe what the portfolio contains, identifying each item by title and genre. If the instructor has not requested individual descriptions for each piece, you might also mention each one's intended audience and purpose and other relevant information.

▶ **A rationale for your selections.** Explain what criteria you used in choosing the texts and what you want the reader to see or learn from reading each piece.

▶ **An evaluation of your work.** Describe the strengths and weaknesses of each piece and how it might be improved. (See Chapter 6 for more on writing an evaluation.)

▶ **A reflection on your development as a writer.** Reflect on what you have you learned, explaining how the texts in your portfolio demonstrate changes in your writing. Identify your strengths and weaknesses, discussing any areas that you still need to work on. (The questions in the Taking Stock of Where You Are sections in Part 1 of this textbook can provide the basis for reflective essays.)

The example on page 705 shows how a student created an introduction for her portfolio for a writing class.

The instructor may also require a brief description of the context for each piece. One paragraph that explains the audience and purpose for each text should be sufficient unless you are otherwise instructed. This description should occur in your introduction, as shown in the example, or immediately before the text. In portfolios created for the workplace, these descriptions are especially useful because they may be the only way the reader can learn about the purpose of the document and whether you achieved your goal in creating a particular text.

Assembling Your Portfolio

Some instructors give specific guidelines for assembling the portfolio, whereas others allow students to use their own judgment. Be sure you check the syllabus or

Sample Introduction for a Writing Portfolio

Beth Carson
April 28, 2008
Professor Borgese
ENG 111

Portfolio

This portfolio represents the best examples of my writing from my first-year composition course. I have included the following papers to demonstrate both my development as a writer and my ability to write for different purposes and audiences: a personal essay, a position paper, an evaluation paper, and a community-based writing project. One of the first writing critiques I received in this class urged me to remember that "thought is motion," and I have been working to develop stronger direction and to be more concise in my own writing ever since.

Lists contents, describes why the selections were chosen, and explains how class critiques have shaped her development as a writer.

Writing selections from my first-year composition course:

- *Personal Essay*—titled "Ties that Bind," this piece, based closely on my own experiences, is about the struggles, rewards, and frequent humor of being from a small town. The intended audience for this essay is fellow students who may not be from a small town.

- *Position Paper*—this essay, published in the school newspaper, argues that scholarships at our school should be granted on the basis of academic achievement and financial need only.

- *Evaluation*—a paper that assesses the effectiveness of using a car safety belt with children 12 and under. Sources include crash statistics, information provided by car manufacturers online, other online information, and articles.

- *Community Writing Project*—from a class assignment on writing for a community organization. Along with some other women in my class, I volunteer at a shelter for mothers and children who are homeless; this piece is a fund-raising pamphlet which I wrote the text for, which is currently being used by the shelter to solicit funding from individuals and corporations.

Describes each piece in detail.

assignment sheet for the instructor's requirements. If there are no instructions about organization, the following suggestions may be useful.

▶ **Create a cover or home page.** The cover page can be as simple as your name, the instructor's name, the course title and section, and the date. Or it can be a complex, highly visual representation of your work. However, avoid visuals that are irrelevant and may distract readers from the content.

▶ **Create a table of contents.** Tables of contents enable the reader to see quickly what is included and to easily access the material. Wait until the portfolio is complete before numbering pages and creating the table of contents.

▶ **Write an introduction.** If your instructor has not given specific instructions for the introduction, see Writing an Introduction for Your Portfolio (p. 704) for ideas.

▶ **Arrange the material logically.** Think carefully about the purpose of the portfolio. If the purpose is to show your development as a writer, start with your weaker papers and build to your best work. If the purpose is to show your achievement, your best work should come first.

▶ **Label each item.** To avoid confusion, create some type of label for every item in the portfolio, such as Final Draft: Report; Peer Review: Evaluation; or Audience and Purpose Statement: Proposal. It will be less confusing if you refer to the items by label instead of by title in the introduction, table of contents, and any other descriptive elements.

▶ **Cluster related materials.** If there are several items for one assignment (for example, an exploratory draft, a peer-review response sheet, and a final draft), assemble those items together in the order in which you created them.

▶ **Consider the presentation of the materials.** Make sure that your finished portfolio has a polished appearance that makes it easy for the reader to use.

The table on page 707 points out some specific organizational issues that you should be aware of that are associated with print and electronic portfolios.

Organizing Print and Electronic Portfolios

Organizational Feature	Print Portfolio	Electronic Portfolio
Cover page	Unless you have specific instructions, you can design the cover as a personal expression or representation of your work.	Create a home page with a navigation bar or menu that links the reader to each item in the portfolio. Subsequent pages should repeat those links or have a special link that returns the reader to the home page.
Table of contents	Create a numbering system that avoids confusion with the existing page numbers on your documents. For example, try putting the new numbers in a different position on the pages, using a different font, or printing the new numbers in color. Use this system consistently throughout the portfolio.	Your navigation bar or menu serves the function of a table of contents.
Introduction	This should be the first item after the table of contents.	The introduction may appear on your home page or as a separate page. If it is a separate page, it should be the first link on your navigation bar.
Labeling	Label each item clearly on the first page where it appears or on dividers that separate the items. Be sure to use the same labels in your table of contents.	The label will be a link to the item, but it should also appear on the page where the text appears so that the reader always knows where he or she is in the portfolio.
Clustering related materials	You may want to put a divider (with, for example, the label *Report* written on the tab) before each cluster.	Cluster related materials through a system of major and minor links, with the name of the assignment being the primary link and labels for any peripheral materials being secondary links.
Presentation	Think carefully about the container that you choose. Three-ring binders with sheet protectors create a very professional look. Multipocket folders, with a pocket for each item in the portfolio, also work well.	Consider page layout, heading style, and your background and font colors carefully to ensure that the texts in your portfolio are easy to read. (For more on design, see Chapter 9.)

16 ▷

Writing for the Community

Many colleges and universities are encouraging their students to become involved in community organizations. This involvement may happen through structured service-learning programs, student service organizations, or fraternities and sororities. No matter what the motivation for your involvement, your work within a community organization can be excellent preparation for the work you will do on co-op jobs and internships and in your career. This last statement may sound strange because the work you do for the community may have little or nothing to do with your intended career. But there's a good chance that you will have to do some writing for the organization, and the experience of writing for a community organization will be of great benefit to you. You may assume—as many undergraduates do—that you will have to do little or no writing for your career. But this assumption is wrong. Professionals in virtually every career, even science and engineering, have to do substantial amounts of writing, and learning to adapt your writing to the audiences and purposes of an organization will make it easier for you to adjust your writing for the workplace. This chapter focuses on writing that serves the needs of a community organization and includes guidelines and tips to help you find an organization to write for and produce the type of writing that will be beneficial to that organization.

Diverse as community organizations are, they tend to have several common traits. Most of them are understaffed and underfunded. Many organizations have documents that badly need to be revised, perhaps because they are out of date or because they were put together hurriedly by someone who was trying to accomplish several other tasks at the same time. These organizations can use your help. Common types of documents that you might be asked to help write include the following.

Action plans	Event invitations and programs
Annual reports	Informational flyers and posters
Brochures	Informational video scripts
Donor solicitation and thank-you letters	Newsletter articles

Op-ed essays
Presentations and speeches
Press releases
Procedures for staff to follow

Public service announcements
Research reports
Volunteer policies
Web pages

This chapter will present examples of some of the kinds of writing you may be asked to do for an organization in your community, and then it will answer questions students frequently ask when they perform this sort of work for the first time.

▷ WRITING SUCCESSFULLY FOR THE COMMUNITY

If you are asked to choose a community group to write for, make the choice carefully. Nothing is more crucial to your success than the choice of an organization with which to work. Do not automatically decide to work with the first organization that occurs to you or one that happens to be conveniently located. Instead, consider the following questions.

▶ Are the organization's goals and activities important to you?

▶ Are you willing to spend some time learning about the organization's background and the population it serves?

▶ Does your schedule permit you to spend time on-site?

▶ Do you have the skills and the temperament to work effectively in this organization?

If you answered yes to most of these questions, then the organization you are considering is probably a good fit for you. If you answered no to several of these questions, then you should probably look for a different organization.

As you will quickly learn, writing for an organization can be surprisingly complex and demanding. The writing you do will require an investment of time and energy. Make sure to work with an organization where you feel your investment will pay off for both you and the organization, even if the payoff for you is as intangible as a sense of having contributed to a cause you value.

When you work for any organization, your success as a writer—and, indeed, as a participant in that organization—depends largely on your understanding of the following points.

▶ **The organization has a distinct culture that influences much of what its members do.** This culture includes people's sense of the organization's mission, the way they work (including the way they write), their attitudes toward each other and the people the organization serves, and even the way they dress. You may or may not agree with this culture. But you cannot ignore it. And you cannot write well for the organization unless you understand its culture.

▶ **Your writing may not take the form of a conventional academic essay.** Page layout and a clear visual presentation that help the reader see—literally—the points you are making will be very important. At a minimum, you will need to use headings and lists. You will probably also use pictures, text or image boxes, pull quotes, and charts or graphs.

For more information on design, see Chapter 9.

▶ **You may be asked to write collaboratively.** That is, you are likely to work with your supervisor and other members of the organization as you plan, draft, and revise your work. Also, you may be writing just part of a larger document, so you will need to coordinate your style, content, and schedule with others.

▶ **Your writing may remain around the organization long after you have left.** Be aware that your work will probably have a relatively long shelf life.

▶ **Your writing will be read by many different audiences, some of whom may be affected by what you write.** If your work harms, angers, confuses, or inconveniences them, they will find ways to make their dissatisfaction known to you or your supervisor.

▶ **Your writing will have practical consequences.** People will rely on your writing to make a decision, settle an argument, carry out a procedure. They may react to it—and to you—in ways you may not be able to anticipate.

▶ **Your writing will become the basis for other people's conclusions about the organization and about you.** It may not be fair to judge a book/ organization/person by the cover/brochure/memo, but it happens all the time. Your readers will use your writing to determine the value of the organization you represent and your value as a member of that organization.

To show how these points apply to writing for community organizations, the following pages present samples of writing from a variety of community organizations.

{ **Exercise** } **Writing in Your Community**

Talk with students who volunteer for an organization in the community. Make a list of the kinds of writing they routinely have to do. Do you notice any connections between this list and some of the chapter titles in this book? ■

▷ SAMPLE WRITING FOR THE COMMUNITY

Although every organization will have its own guidelines, formats, and conventions for their documents, the samples shown in this chapter will give you an idea of the audiences and purposes for writing in the community.

Newsletter Article

Newsletters are commonly used by organizations to inform readers of key events associated with the group. They typically consist of brief articles and are sent at regular intervals to employees, supporters, or people who benefit from the services that the group provides. Design and format varies, ranging from inexpensively produced black and white photocopied sheets or glossy color versions sent by mail to electronic formats sent by e-mail.

The following newsletter article was written by a college student doing an internship for the Triangle Area Chapter of the American Red Cross, a local branch of the national organization devoted to providing disaster relief. Notice that the article starts out like a conventional newspaper story about a tornado, but the content shifts to focus on a volunteer's role in assisting the victims of the tornado.

Newsletter Article

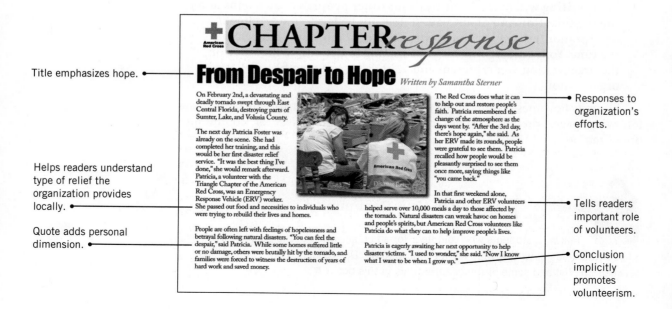

Title emphasizes hope.

Helps readers understand type of relief the organization provides locally.

Quote adds personal dimension.

Responses to organization's efforts.

Tells readers important role of volunteers.

Conclusion implicitly promotes volunteerism.

Event Materials

Flyers, posters, and invitations are special documents typically created for fund-raising or celebratory events. Flyers are typically produced on standard $8^1/2$" × 11" sheets that can be printed or photocopied easily. They may incorporate color, graphics, and other eye-catching visual features to accompany a minimal amount of text describing basic information about the event. Because of their standard size, flyers can also be sent out electronically, often accompanied by a request for the recipient to download, print, and post a copy. Posters are similar to flyers, but are larger and often have to be printed at a professional print or copy shop. Because of the larger format, they may contain more detailed visuals and information. Invitations can be produced in the form of a greeting card, a letter, a flyer or poster, or they can be posted on a Web site. (To see a sample invitation designed for the Web, see p. 552). Decisions about design and content are tailored based on the chosen format and are likely to be coordinated with other documents produced for the event.

For more information on design, see Chapter 9.

Brochure

Organizations produce brochures to highlight specific aspects of their mission, promote events, or educate people about the services that they provide. These brochures may be distributed to the organization's clients or used to solicit funds from prospective donors. Like newsletters, brochures can vary from simple photocopied documents to more elaborate, full-color, high-quality pieces.

The Center for International Understanding is an educational organization that focuses on helping North Carolina residents live and work with people from all over the globe. The brochure shown on pages 714 and 715 provides an overview of what the organization believes are the primary challenges affecting the state of North Carolina and explains how it is responding to those challenges. This brochure is printed and distributed by the organization and is also available as a downloadable PDF at the center's Web site (http://www.ciu.northcarolina.edu).

Research Report

Research reports may provide information resulting from analysis of the work of the organization, comparisons with other similar organizations, investigations of needs within the community, or many other relevant studies. The reports serve a variety of functions, but one of the primary goals is to demonstrate the importance of the organization's mission to current and prospective supporters. Reports can be printed and mailed to supporters or distributed at organizational events, or they may be produced electronically and either read online or downloaded by interested parties. Because research reports are typically lengthy and involved, they are usually produced through the efforts of a team of researchers, writers, and designers who make decisions about what type of content to include and how best to present that content.

For advice on writing reports, see Chapter 4.

Brochure

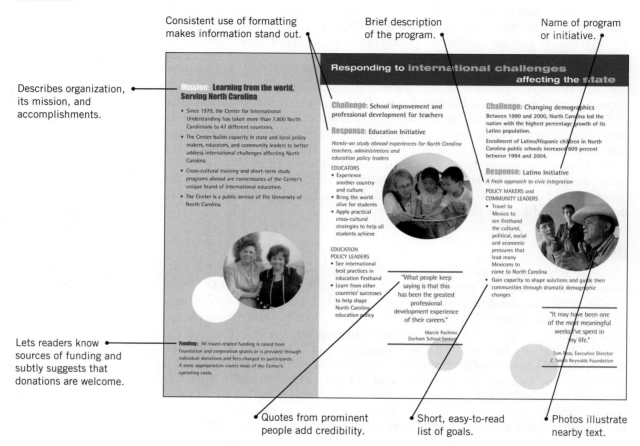

Consistent use of formatting makes information stand out.

Brief description of the program.

Name of program or initiative.

Describes organization, its mission, and accomplishments.

Lets readers know sources of funding and subtly suggests that donations are welcome.

Quotes from prominent people add credibility.

Short, easy-to-read list of goals.

Photos illustrate nearby text.

The North Carolina Arts Council is a division of the North Carolina Department of Cultural Resources. The mission of this government agency is to provide funding, assistance, and information for and about a wide variety of artistic endeavors throughout the state. To gain public support and funding, the agency undertook a major study of the role of the arts in North Carolina and produced a glossy, full-color, twenty-four–page report of its findings. The excerpt shown here (p. 716) presents research results that demonstrate that the arts are an important economic factor for the state, which makes this a fact-based argument for the continuation of support for the arts by governments, corporations, and individuals. This professionally produced report was made up of material from many different sources and was the result of a great deal of research. The research and presentation of the results, including the development of charts and graphs and writing summaries of the findings, are the types of work that could readily be done for an organization by students participating in internships or service-learning courses.

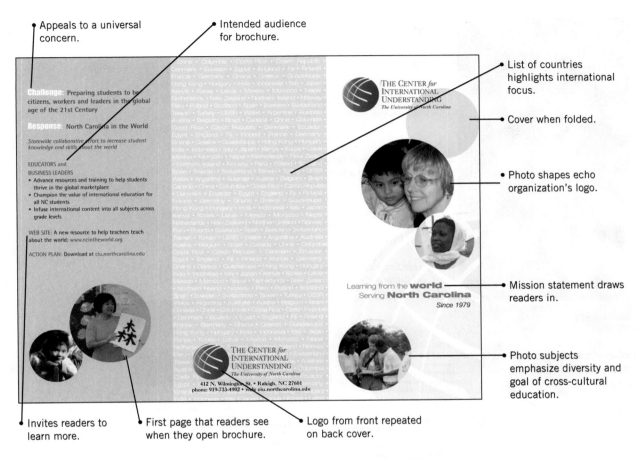

Appeals to a universal concern.

Intended audience for brochure.

List of countries highlights international focus.

Cover when folded.

Photo shapes echo organization's logo.

Mission statement draws readers in.

Photo subjects emphasize diversity and goal of cross-cultural education.

Invites readers to learn more.

First page that readers see when they open brochure.

Logo from front repeated on back cover.

▷ FREQUENTLY ASKED QUESTIONS ABOUT WRITING FOR THE COMMUNITY

When students begin writing for the community outside their classrooms, they often have questions. The next few pages present some of the most frequently asked questions, grouped by category, and accompanied by answers that reflect practical experience.

Finding an Appropriate Organization

How do I find an appropriate organization?
Begin by asking the instructor, who may already have contacts with organizations that need help. Also find out if your school has an office that coordinates

Research Report

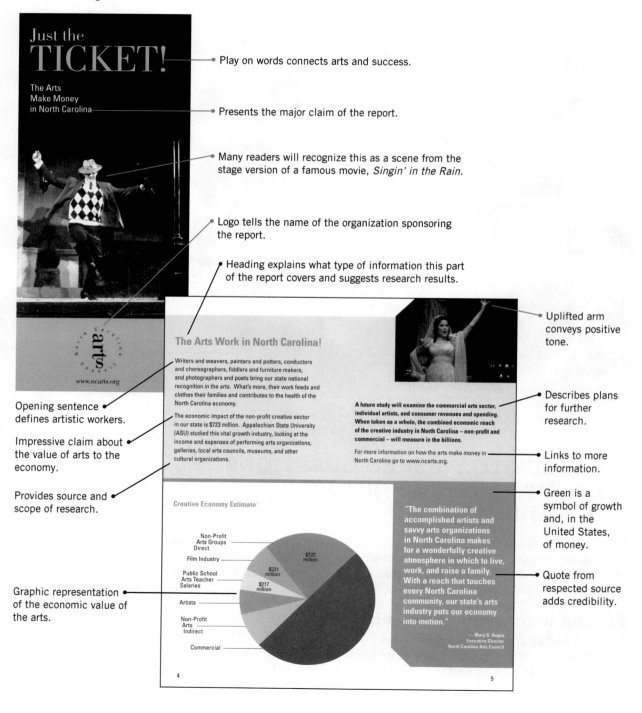

Play on words connects arts and success.

Presents the major claim of the report.

Many readers will recognize this as a scene from the stage version of a famous movie, *Singin' in the Rain.*

Logo tells the name of the organization sponsoring the report.

Heading explains what type of information this part of the report covers and suggests research results.

Uplifted arm conveys positive tone.

Describes plans for further research.

Links to more information.

Green is a symbol of growth and, in the United States, of money.

Quote from respected source adds credibility.

Opening sentence defines artistic workers.

Impressive claim about the value of arts to the economy.

Provides source and scope of research.

Graphic representation of the economic value of the arts.

The Arts Work in North Carolina!

Writers and weavers, painters and potters, conductors and choreographers, fiddlers and furniture makers, and photographers and poets bring our state national recognition in the arts. What's more, their work feeds and clothes their families and contributes to the health of the North Carolina economy.

The economic impact of the non-profit creative sector in our state is $723 million. Appalachian State University (ASU) studied this vital growth industry, looking at the income and expenses of performing arts organizations, galleries, local arts councils, museums, and other cultural organizations.

A future study will examine the commercial arts sector, individual artists, and consumer revenues and spending. When taken as a whole, the combined economic reach of the creative industry in North Carolina – non-profit and commercial – will measure in the billions.

For more information on how the arts make money in North Carolina go to www.ncarts.org.

Creative Economy Estimate

Non-Profit Arts Groups Direct
Film Industry
Public School Arts Teacher Salaries
Artists
Non-Profit Arts Indirect
Commercial

$723 million
$231 million
$217 million

"The combination of accomplished artists and savvy arts organizations in North Carolina makes for a wonderfully creative atmosphere in which to live, work, and raise a family. With a reach that touches every North Carolina community, our state's arts industry puts our economy into motion."

—Mary B. Regan
Executive Director
North Carolina Arts Council

www.ncarts.org

community-based internships or service projects. Other ways to find an organization include the following.

► **Look on the Internet for organizations that connect volunteers with non-profit organizations.** For example, volunteermatch.org lists volunteer opportunities by zip code nationwide.

► **Draw on your own experience.** Do you belong or have you belonged to a group that needs help in a specific area? Maybe writing a newsletter or updating a Web site?

► **Ask friends or family members about organizations they support.** In addition to local organizations, many national organizations such as Amnesty International, Habitat for Humanity, and the American Red Cross have local chapters that could use your help.

► **Think about what interests you.** Find an organization that supports your interests; for example, contact a museum if you are interested in art or a YMCA if you are interested in sports.

► **Listen to your classmates' ideas.** They may suggest an option you have overlooked or know of a project that could use the efforts of more than one student. If you decide to work with another student, check with your instructor to make sure that a collaborative project is appropriate.

How do I choose the right organization?

Choose an organization that will let you produce a document that your instructor considers appropriate for the course. Consider also the following.

► **Identify the requirements of the project.** Can you complete the project within the time allotted?

► **Consider the logistical issues.** Do you have a way to get there? Will the hours work with your class schedule?

► **Explore aspects of life outside your everyday experience, but be realistic.** If, for example, you have strong negative feelings about homeless people, you may not be able to overcome those feelings in a single project for a homeless shelter.

Getting Started

How do I make contact with the organization?

Before asking about doing some writing for a particular organization, make sure you know something about it. Skim through the organization's Web site, or stop by its main office and ask to see some brochures that describe the organization's mission, the clients it serves, and its main programs or activities. Whenever possible, use personal contacts. Find out if someone you know can prepare the way so that you can contact a person at the organization and say, "Mr./Ms./Dr. So-and-so suggested I contact you about the possibility of doing some writing for your organization." If that isn't possible, try one of the following.

► **Check the organization's Web site for name and contact information.** Try to find someone with a title like "Communications Director" or "Public/Press Relations Manager" that indicates an involvement with written documents.

► **Send an e-mail message to the organization.** Say something like, "I'm a student in a writing class at [your school], and I'd like to get some real-world writing experience. Is there anyone in your organization who might know whether there are some writing projects I could volunteer to do—an article for a newsletter, maybe, or a brochure?"

How do I get people in the organization to like and trust me?

The more people like and trust you, the more likely they are to help you find interesting writing projects and the more willing they are to guide you toward resources for carrying out those projects. Here are some ways to gain the trust and respect of the people in the organization.

► **Respect people's time.** Be on time for appointments and give lots of advance notice if you can't make it.

► **Meet deadlines.** If you have agreed to complete a certain piece of work by a certain date, get it done on time.

► **Show some interest in the work of the organization.** Pay attention to current events that may affect the organization. Ask people in the organization what they do and respond with interest and a smile.

► **Dress and act appropriately.** Pay attention to the way people in the organization dress and act and make a reasonable effort to fit in.

► **Never put things off until the last minute.** Don't procrastinate or expect people to have time or patience to deal with your last-minute crises.

How do I learn about the culture of the organization? And do I have to do this?

To create documents that the organization will be able to use, you have to understand the goals of the organization and the attitudes and values it wants to convey to the people it serves and the larger community. Learn as much as you can by doing the following.

► **Look on the Web site for a mission statement.** Read about the goals and objectives of the organization and try to discern the values that underlie its mission.

► **Ask other people in the organization to explain what they do.** Also ask how their work fits into the organization's overall goals. If you are working on a collaborative project, take advantage of the opportunities that project provides to talk to your coworkers about the organization.

► **Observe what goes on around you.** Notice how people in the organization dress, what they talk about, and how they treat each other and their clients.

▶ **Pay attention to the tone and message conveyed in documents that the organization publishes.** Previously published print and online materials are useful tools. Use them to guide you in your writing.

What if there's a conflict between the goals or activities of the organization and my personal values?

This question probably will not come up if you have chosen the organization carefully. But if it does, face it squarely and ethically. In deciding what to do, ask yourself the following questions.

▶ If I complete this assignment in the way people in the organization want me to, what effects will my work have?

▶ Are those effects likely to be consistent with my principles?

If the goals and tactics of the organization are in strong opposition to your own ethical principles, you should probably look for a different organization or at least for a different assignment within that organization.

Working on the Assignment

Where and/or how will I get my assignment?

Your assignment will come from someone in the organization. This person may give you very clear instructions ("I want a black and white brochure covering the following topics and based on your reading of the following materials and your interviews with the following people") or very little direction ("We could use a good human interest piece for our newsletter"). In the latter case, you may need to do some background reading and talk with two or three people, including your instructor, before coming back to your contact person with a more specific idea for the assignment. Once the assignment is fairly well set, make sure that everyone involved (instructor included) understands and agrees on the subject, purpose, audience, and format for the writing.

How much freedom will I have to shape my writing assignment?

Most organizations need so many different written documents that there will likely be a wide variety of projects from which to choose. In general, people will be most willing to let you take the initiative in deciding what to write if you can demonstrate the following characteristics.

▶ You understand the goals and needs of the organization.

▶ You have an idea that will help the organization meet those goals and/or satisfy those needs.

▶ You have a good chance of completing the project you propose.

▶ You have acted in ways that lead people to like and trust you (see p. 718).

How will I figure out what to say?

Use the strategies discussed in Chapters 2 to 7 to help develop your topic. Consider also drawing on one or more of the following sources of information.

- ▶ **Other materials the organization has produced** (Web pages, pamphlets, brochures, press releases, manuals, statements of policy)

- ▶ **Background readings** about subjects related to the organization's work

- ▶ **Interviews** with different groups of people: employees, volunteers, people who use the organization's services

Also, look at your topic from several perspectives and ask the following questions.

- ▶ What seems interesting, unusual, or potentially helpful about the information I am finding?

- ▶ What do readers need from the document? What questions are they likely to have? What aspects of the organization might they see as unique, helpful, or troubling?

- ▶ What does the organization hope to accomplish with what I am writing?

How will I know whether I'm on the right track—either with what I'm saying or with how I'm saying it?

Throughout your project, talk frequently with your contact person at the organization (and with your writing instructor if the project is for a course). To create the best possible work, follow these guidelines.

- ▶ In the early stages, summarize what you are learning, ask questions about the material, and seek ideas about other sources to consult or questions to ask.

- ▶ As you create a draft, request feedback from the contact person, from your instructor, and from your classmates. If possible, also have the draft reviewed by a member of the audience for whom it is intended.

- ▶ If you're working with a team, ask your coworkers to review early drafts or discuss your ideas with them before getting started.

- ▶ In the world outside the classroom, important documents may be revised many times before they are ready to be shown to the public. Allow time for revisions. There will surely be some.

Being Assessed

Who will assess my work?

If your writing project is part of a class assignment, it will be assessed by at least two people: the instructor and a representative of the organization with which you have been working. If you are volunteering on your own, one or more people in the organization will assess your work.

How much influence will each of these people have?

At a minimum, the instructor will probably want to know how well a representative from the organization thinks you have done on the assignment. Beyond that, the instructor will specify how much and what sort of weight to give the outside assessment.

What criteria will be used?

The organization's representative will likely focus on questions such as the following.

► Can we use this document?

► Does it accomplish the goal we had in mind for the audience we hoped to reach?

The instructor will focus on the following issues mentioned repeatedly throughout this book.

► Does the writing show a clear understanding of the context for the work?

► Given the word choice, content, organization, and visual appearance of the written product, is it likely to accomplish the intended purpose for the intended audience?

What if my instructor and the organization's representative disagree about the quality of my work?

Despite everyone's best efforts, people sometimes do disagree. What you should do when this happens depends in large measure on what people disagree about. For example, an organization may have a particular stylistic practice—such as avoiding the use of personal pronouns. Probably the instructor will understand if you explain this practice and show that you know how to use personal pronouns appropriately, even though you avoid them in the writing you do for the organization.

In other instances, people may disagree on what constitutes an acceptable piece of writing. For example, the organization's representative or your instructor may think your text needs one more round of revising and polishing. If that additional work is consistent with the needs and purposes of the organization—and the goals of your writing course—you should be prepared to do it.

{ **Exercise** } **Analyzing Writing for the Community**

Bring to class a brochure, annual report, or copy of a home page from a national or community organization that you are interested in. Be prepared to talk about the different types of writing utilized by the organization in this single document. Do you notice anything about the writing in the document that could benefit from improvement? ■

Writing in Online Environments

Although you may have been communicating online for years, take a moment to examine the ways you communicate and make sure they are appropriate for an academic environment. Many people instant message, text, and e-mail to keep in touch with friends and relatives and join groups to chat with people with similar interests. While you may also use these communication channels for course work, you may need to make some adjustments to what you say and how you say it. Just as a casual face-to-face conversation with a friend is different from a conversation with an instructor or a supervisor, your online communication with them should reflect a more formal context. Thus this chapter presents some guidelines for appropriate online communication in academic and workplace environments. Then it offers advice to keep in mind when responding to class discussion lists or forums, blogs, and wikis.

All these recommendations are a good place to start. You may find, however, that some professors will accept a more informal style of communication. For example, a discussion forum might be used for brainstorming, and thus grammar considerations might be suspended and the use of abbreviations and IM slang might be accepted. If in doubt about how you are expected to present yourself in your online communication in the context of a course assignment, ask the instructor. For all communication you initiate with professors, administrators, and staff, stick to the guidelines that follow.

▷ USING E-MAIL

Although using e-mail has become easy and commonplace today, in an academic context it is important to respect rules of conduct, grammar, and style. As the following pages explain and as the figure on page 726 illustrates, carefully prepared e-mails can ensure that you send and receive needed information and that you make a good impression on the recipient.

Netiquette

There are a lot of issues to consider when you use e-mail to respond to academic or workplace messages, not the least of which are basic rules commonly referred to as netiquette.

▶ Use uppercase letters (caps) only to emphasize one or two words; never type an entire message that way. Making all your text appear in all caps is the equivalent of shouting.

▶ Limit the use of italics for emphasis. They may not be visible on some e-mail programs, and they are difficult to read on the screen.

▶ Use concise paragraphs that make your point quickly.

▶ Use headings to break up sections if you must write a long message.

▶ Avoid sending angry messages. Conflicts can accelerate quickly via the medium of e-mail where tone is often hard to gauge. You are usually better off handling conflicts in person.

▶ Send only messages that people need. Although people commonly send jokes and games by e-mail, send them only to those you know will appreciate receiving them.

▶ Send copies of your messages only to people who need the information or have requested copies. Use the CC (carbon copy) feature to copy anyone who needs a copy of your message, reserving BCC (blind carbon copy) for people who will not need to be included on a "reply to all" response to your message.

▶ Limit each message to one or two clearly stated topics; you will get a better response that way.

▶ Be aware that most e-mail systems automatically include the original message in any reply that you send. If the recipient will not need a copy of the original message, delete it. However, don't reply with just "okay." The reader may not recall what you are saying okay to.

▶ Do not send mass mailings or copies of a message to everyone in your address book. This is the electronic equivalent of junk mail.

▶ Avoid multiple or lengthy attachments. Not everyone has a high-speed Internet connection, or if they do, their inbox might not allow messages with attachments over a certain size. You can use a program such as WinZip or Stuffit to both combine multiple items into one and compress files to make them smaller. But the best advice with large-sized or multiple attachments is to ask your recipient what he or she prefers. Also, ascertain what formats your recipients can open. If you are not sure, save your document in Rich Text Format (rtf) before attaching the file.

Privacy

One of the most important issues to consider when using e-mail is privacy. Be careful what you say in an e-mail message because you can never know who will see it. Once you press Send, you lose control of your text. The recipient can forward it to others, copy and paste it into another message, or copy it and use it in other documents. Furthermore, many organizations (particularly in the workplace) routinely monitor electronic messages that pass through their servers. In fact, messages should be considered permanent; copies can be retrieved even after they have been deleted. Follow this good advice: Don't ever write anything in an e-mail message that you wouldn't want your mother to read.

Grammatical Correctness

A friend may not care about punctuation, grammar, or capitalization, but an instructor, a colleague, or a supervisor may think you are sloppy or careless if you don't use standard English in your e-mail messages and postings. Many e-mail systems have a spell checker that will catch some, but not all, errors. If yours does not, create your message in word processing software with spelling and grammar checkers and then copy it into e-mail. Pay attention to the grammatical and typographical format of messages that you receive from others in your class or work group. Be prepared to modify your messages if the people you work with have higher standards of correctness than you are accustomed to.

Also be sure to notice how those you correspond with use abbreviations. It is common practice in informal online communication, especially in instant messaging, to abbreviate common phrases. For example, *by the way* becomes *btw, before* becomes *b4*, and *for what it's worth* becomes *fwiw*. However, these abbreviations are not acceptable in formal academic communication.

Proofreading

Before pressing the Send button, reread your e-mail message. In particular, make sure you have typed in the recipient's correct address. It is all too easy to send a message to the wrong person, especially if you are using addresses stored in an electronic address book. If your instructor and your best friend are both named Pat, you could easily make an embarrassing mistake.

Subject Lines

Include a subject line that is both specific and descriptive enough to convey the main topic of the message. Most people struggle to sort through spam and legitimate messages in their e-mail and will delete any that lack a subject line, especially if they don't know or aren't expecting mail from the sender. In the classroom or workplace, the subject line of an e-mail message is the equivalent of the subject line in a memo. For example, explicit subject lines such as "Visuals for evaluation assignment?" "Is this plagiarism?" and "Due date for evaluation?" make it very clear what the reader can expect in your message.

Sample of an Effective E-mail

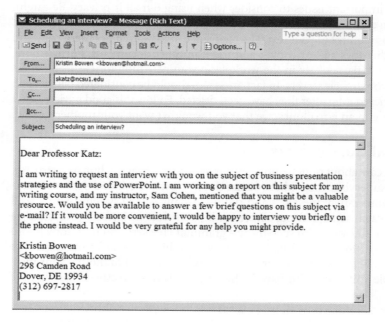

Greeting and Closing

Most e-mail systems automatically produce *To* and *From* headings. In this respect e-mails mimic memo format, which does not usually require a greeting ("Dear Alice,") or a closing ("Sincerely,"). However, you will not be wrong to include a greeting in formal e-mail. You should always put your name and contact information, including your e-mail address, at the bottom of your message because many e-mail programs will show your name but not your address in the "From" line.

▷ PARTICIPATING IN ONLINE DISCUSSIONS

Many instructors take advantage of new media to encourage conversation among their students beyond the typical classroom setting. In some cases, courses are taught entirely online and the only opportunity to discuss course content is through an electronic medium. In other cases, electronic media augment in-class discussion and out-of-class work. Be aware that if the instructor asks you to participate in an electronic forum, he or she may have specific guidelines for you to follow.

Discussion Lists and Forums

A discussion list enables you to post messages simultaneously to all the list's members. And as a member of a list, you receive all messages posted by other members.

Discussion lists are popular in many arenas outside of school, but they are also one way that instructors keep in touch with students and, sometimes, foster discussion. Instructors routinely use course discussion lists to send reminders to students or make minor changes to the schedule.

Discussion forums (sometimes called message boards) are similar to discussion lists, but they exist on Web sites. Whereas discussion list messages automatically come to your inbox, with a discussion board you have to visit the Web site to participate in the discussion. Discussion forums often display multiple topics (often called threads); you choose the topic you want to discuss. The messages on a discussion board are archived, or kept on file, so that you can read what everyone else has written before posting your own message.

As with discussion lists, instructors who use discussion forums often require (and sometimes grade) participation. Many instructors use either course discussion forums or lists to post questions or discussion topics and ask students to respond to the questions outside of class. Participation in these online discussions can also be helpful to students for generating ideas or getting feedback. Most of the guidelines regarding e-mail (pp. 724–26) apply equally to participation in discussion lists and forums. In addition, the following suggestions are useful.

> ▶ Take the time to compose a fully developed, coherent message that will initiate or contribute to the discussion. When you begin a discussion or respond to your instructor or classmates, you are not communicating in real time, so there's no excuse for sloppy writing or sloppy thinking.

> ▶ Feel free to ask follow-up questions or ask for clarification if you don't understand what someone else has written. This is the whole point of discussion—to add to everyone's understanding.

> ▶ Stay focused on the topic. Ask questions, add comments, explore tangential ideas, but make sure that everything you write is relevant to the discussion.

> ▶ Avoid posting questions with yes or no answers. Ask open-ended questions that will encourage other posters to think more broadly about the topic.

> ▶ Determine whether you need to reply to the whole group or just to the person who originated the message. An off-list reply may be more appropriate and could save you some embarrassment.

[Guidelines for
Participating in a
Discussion List or
Discussion Board]

▶ When you read a message you think is a flame—a message that is taken as rude or offensive—read it again. Take time and then respond with patience; this will establish your credibility and fairness.

▶ Never present someone else's thoughts or ideas as your own. If you are citing some type of research or external source for support of your ideas, tell readers what that source is. If appropriate, include a link to an Internet source so that readers can verify or examine your support. Be cautious about reposting someone else's copyrighted material; limit the number and extent of such quotes, and make sure to post the content in an environment in which it will be discussed and critiqued.

▶ Feel free to disagree, but do so respectfully. Avoid making personal attacks. Do not threaten anyone.

▶ Take the time to write a coherent, thoughtful message rather than multiple short messages.

▶ Do not send spam—unwelcome or excessive messages. Sending spam clogs up in-boxes and discussion space.

▶ Do not post jokes, chain letters, personality quizzes, and so forth. If you want to share something with the group that is off topic, create a new thread, or topic space, for that material.

Real-Time Discussions and Instant Messaging

Real-time discussions (chats) and instant messaging (IM) provide participants the opportunity to communicate synchronously: The communication takes place in real time. (Discussion lists and forums, in contrast, provide asynchronous communication.) Because chat and IM occur in real time, the pace of conversation is much faster than on a discussion list or discussion board. Chats take place in a virtual space (chat room), and many people can be invited to participate, so it may be difficult or impossible to keep up with all the messages being posted (streaming). However, the messages are typically archived, so you can go back to see what you missed. Instant messaging occurs between just two people.

Instructors may create one general chat room that can be used throughout the term to discuss any topic pertaining to the course, or they may create topic-specific chats to accompany particular readings or assignments, or they may have both generic and specific chats. Like discussion boards, chats are frequently used in online courses. However, chats enable the class to "meet" in the virtual space at an appointed day and time to discuss a particular topic. Again, in both traditional classroom and online courses, instructors may require or grade participation in the course chat.

Real-time discussions—whether between just two people or a whole group—can be useful for brainstorming and debating, especially at the early stages of an assignment or discussion. Real-time discussions may also be used by instructors for virtual office hours, and many libraries have IM options that allow students to get instant help from reference librarians.

All the guidelines for using e-mail (pp. 724–26), and all but the first guideline for discussion lists and discussion boards (pp. 727–28), apply to chats and IM. In addition, here are some unique guidelines for real-time discussions.

> ▶ Avoid writing long messages. Because the communication is happening in real time, the longer your message, the more you will miss of what others are saying and the longer you will interrupt the flow of conversation. Many programs may limit the number of characters foreach post.

> ▶ Learn the acronyms that are conventional for the particular group you are chatting with. For example, you might want to write *btw* instead of *by the way*, *lol* instead of *laugh out loud*. The group may even use shorthand such as *u* for *you*. However, be aware that most instructors do not accept such acronyms and shorthand in assignments and exams.

> ▶ Be patient with typographical errors—your own and those of others. When people communicate in real time, they type rapidly and are likely to make mistakes. If you cannot understand what has been written, ask a follow-up question or request clarification.

> ▶ Remember that if you write something and no one responds, you may repeat your message but should not complain about the lack of response. If you still get no response, frame your point or question in a different way, or move on to a different point.

> [**Guidelines for Participating in Real-Time Discussions or Instant Messaging**]

Writing in Blogs and Wikis

Blogs (short for "Web logs") and wikis (from the Hawaiian word *wiki*, which means rapid) are interactive media that have become more and more popular in classrooms over the past decade. Blogs and wikis have much in common with discussion forums, but with some distinct features.

A personal blog can function as an online diary or journal, or it can be dedicated to a particular topic, interest, event, or cause. Blogs incorporate text, images, audio and video files, and links to other blogs, Internet sites, or relevant information from other sources.

Blogs can be used for a wide variety of purposes in the classroom. For example, blogs may provide students with the following.

> ▶ A space to maintain a journal

> ▶ An opportunity to respond to assigned readings or ask questions about course content

▶ A place to brainstorm, try out ideas, or ask for feedback

▶ A place to post drafts for peer review

▶ A place where instructors can post assignments and students can respond

While blogs share some similarities with discussion lists or forums, there is one big difference: Blogs have the potential to be read by anyone with access to the Internet, and in most cases, if comments are allowed, anyone can comment. Remember that there is the possibility of a wider audience when posting to a blog.

Also, make sure you understand the course requirements for blogs that are created and used in your class. Will the writing you post be evaluated? If so, what are the criteria for evaluation? Is there a requirement for a specific number of posts to your own blog? Or comments to blogs of your classmates?

Like blogs, social networking spaces (such as Facebook) offer the opportunity to write in a public space, post visuals, and keep journals. And like blogs, these online spaces are accessible to almost anyone who can belong to the network. Information you share in blogs and these social networking sites could potentially be seen by anyone.

While blogs allow individuals to comment on writing posted by others, wikis allow individuals to work together to create content. A wiki is a type of content management system specifically designed to facilitate collaborative activities such as writing, revising, and editing. The most well-known wiki is Wikipedia, which was created in 2001 as an interactive online encyclopedia.

Read more about Wikipedia as a research source, on page 578.

The purpose of most wikis is to provide information by creating a reliable source. While some wikis are protected behind firewalls and thus unavailable to the public, most wikis can be accessed by anyone with a connection to the Internet. Wikis created for college courses may limit active participation (for example, editing rights) to students enrolled in the course, within a particular department, or registered at the college or university, but in most cases wikis are public and can be viewed by anyone. Thus you will want to think carefully about your writing in a wiki and about the people whom you want to read your work.

An important difference between writing in a wiki and other forms of online communication is the collaborative nature of the work. You and your classmates will all have access to the same files, the same resources, and the same versions of your document—and you will be able to access them wherever you are as long as you have a connection to the Internet. In a wiki, everyone with editing rights can modify the text, but those modifications can be viewed, changed, or reversed, and the history of all changes is readily available. Wikis also typically have a space where you can comment on a text, so you have the option of asking questions or making suggestions.

In general, blog posts or wiki contributions should follow the same rules as those for discussion lists and forums (pp. 727–28). The following are some additional issues to consider when writing in these environments.

▶ Create a memorable headline or title for your entry that clearly states the topic. While a blog is a personal space, you still want to attract readers and let them know what topics you are covering.

▶ Use links to show or connect with sources, but make sure those sources are relevant to the topic.

▶ Choose visuals with care, making sure that they contribute to the message.

▶ Take time to proofread and edit before posting.

There are other spaces online that your instructor may use, including MUVEs, or (multiuser virtual environments). One of the best-known MUVEs, Second Life, allows users to interact in a virtual world. As with all the other spaces for online communication, you will be wise to participate in any spaces or groups for a course or project with attention to the same netiquette rules as for other electronic media.

Making Oral Presentations

This is the kind of advice people often receive when they are about to deliver an oral presentation: "Stand up straight." "Make eye contact with your audience." "Don't talk in a monotone." "Don't be so nervous—try to relax." And it's good advice. But it is only part of what you need to know to make a good oral presentation. For a really effective oral presentation, the most important thing is to prepare carefully, using what you have learned from the other chapters in this book: analyze your audience, develop your topic thoroughly, compose an introduction that will engage your audience, and so on. Eye contact and good posture will not do you much good unless you are saying something that the audience realizes is worth listening to. Consequently, this chapter presents some guidelines for adapting what you have learned about writing to make effective oral presentations. It also provides examples from an actual presentation and concludes with frequently asked questions students often ask about *delivery*, such as overcoming nervousness, using visual aids, and being aware of body language and eye contact.

What you do in making a successful oral presentation depends in part on your personality, the subject you are addressing, and the circumstances in which you are speaking. For example, if you tend to use a lot of gestures when you talk informally with friends, you may find yourself doing the same thing when you make an oral presentation. However, there are several basic guidelines that can help you create and deliver a successful oral presentation regardless of individual personality traits, especially when you are addressing a relatively large group such as a class. In these situations, it is a good idea to do the following.

▶ **Create a compelling introduction.** Your introduction should be relatively brief—not more than a minute or two for an eight- to ten-minute presentation. Be sure to create common ground with your listeners and give them strong reasons for paying attention to what you have to say.

▶ **Forecast the main points you are going to make.** As soon as you have engaged the listeners' attention, provide them with a basic outline or road map that indicates the territory you will cover in your presentation.

733

▶ **Use visual aids to emphasize what you are getting at.** When appropriate, use overheads or slides to help the audience literally *see* what point you are making and how a given detail or example relates to your other points.

▶ **Elaborate on your visual aids.** Do not just read the words written on your slides, posters, or overheads. Supplement your visuals with details, examples, stories, or arguments that will convey your main point in a meaningful way.

▶ **Talk directly to your listeners.** Your oral presentation is not a written text that will be read by your audience, so as you plan what you're going to say, be sure to make it sound like talk. When you quote from or paraphrase outside sources, be sure to identify them, but do so concisely so as not to interrupt the flow of the presentation.

▶ **Finish strong.** Use the last thirty seconds or so to reiterate your main points in a memorable way, pose a question that will engage your listeners, or emphasize ways that the ideas you presented will affect your audience.

▷ CREATING A COMPELLING INTRODUCTION

The following opening is almost guaranteed to make you sound like a nervous beginner: "Umm, OK. The topic I'm going to talk about today is . . ." Instead, make use of strategies for engaging the audience's interest. Think about your topic from the listeners' perspective. Determine how your topic relates to what they know, care about, believe, or expect. Then look for something (a set of facts, an anecdote, a question, a situation) that will conflict with their knowledge, values, beliefs, or preferences. By including this type of element, you will likely capture their attention.

Throughout this section of this chapter, you will see examples from an oral presentation created by David Perry, a student in a college writing course. Early in the semester, the students were assigned to write a report on a topic of their own choosing. Later, they were asked to repurpose the report—to create an oral presentation based on the research that they had completed. As the first step in the assignment, students had to think of a specific audience and purpose for the presentation. David wrote his report about the danger of spending too much time in the hot sun, and here are his statements about the audience and purpose for the oral presentation.

Audience

My target audience members are parents with children still living in the house. These people live in the Northeast and are likely to be active in the outdoors year round. They have some knowledge of the dangers, but they do not know the difference between heat exhaustion and heat stroke.

First Slide: Introduction

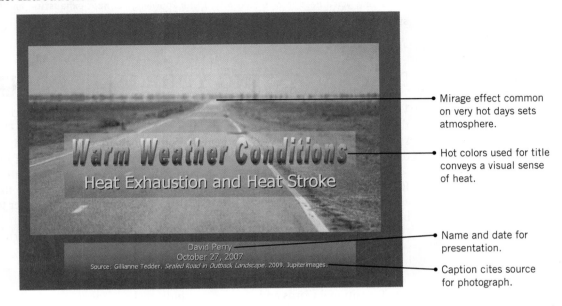

Mirage effect common on very hot days sets atmosphere.

Hot colors used for title conveys a visual sense of heat.

Name and date for presentation.

Caption cites source for photograph.

Purpose

My purpose is to make parents aware of the dangers that the hot sun can pose to both them and their children. Parents need to know what to look out for and how to prevent possibly life-threatening conditions for themselves and their children, who are often more susceptible to climate-related injuries.

To engage the interest of his audience, David chose to open his presentation with a visual that would evoke the intense heat of summer. David chose his introductory words carefully to go along with the opening visual, establishing common ground with his audience by referring to a story that had recently been in the news and then moving on to points that he knew would be of interest to his audience. In David's introductory remarks that follow, notice the words in bold, all of which tie directly back to his analysis of the presentation's audience and purpose. In addition to grabbing the audience's attention with a vivid story, David's introduction tells the audience what to expect from this presentation.

Introductory remarks

Seventeen-year-old Chris Stewart died a year before graduating from high school—another young man taken far before his time. But he wasn't killed by a terminal disease or a drunk driver: Chris was killed by the **hot sun** in an August football practice. It's important for

you and your kids to live a healthy lifestyle, and that means being **active outdoors**. To do this safely, you'll need to be armed with a firm knowledge of **heat exhaustion and heat stroke** and **how to prevent these conditions**.

▷ FORECASTING YOUR MAIN POINTS

When people read something you have written, they should be able to quickly get the gist of it by skimming or looking at headings and topic sentences. This reading strategy lets readers develop a general framework to which they can relate the details presented in the text. This sort of framework is also important in oral presentations because spoken words essentially disappear once you have uttered them. If listeners have a sense of the structure of what you are going to say, they will be able to relate specific details to this structure and, therefore, find it easier to remember them.

Any oral presentation should incorporate all of the following structural elements found in good writing.

▶ Thesis statements and topic sentences

▶ Transitional words and phrases that indicate how one point relates to the points that precede and follow it

▶ Forecasting phrases and sentences that announce the topics you are about to discuss

To give your audience a sense of your presentation's structure, it is often helpful to include a visual aid that presents an overview of the main points you will make. As a rule, you should present this overview early in the presentation, right after engaging the listeners' interest. In David's presentation, he showed this overview in his second slide, which clearly explains the topics that he will cover.

Notice that the following script that David wrote to accompany this slide supplements the information presented visually.

Script for second slide

It's important to understand what causes heat stroke and heat exhaustion, and then be able to recognize and treat both should they afflict your loved ones. In this presentation, I'll cover the causes, warning signs, and treatment of both heat exhaustion and heat stroke. Finally, we'll discuss simple methods to prevent both afflictions. Heat exhaustion and heat stroke progress differently but start the same way, and it's very easy to stop both from happening.

Not all speakers have to provide listeners with a forecast of their main points. In fact, this sort of structure rarely—if ever—appears in sermons, political speeches, graduation speeches, or comic monologues. But for most of the oral presentations

Second Slide: Forecasting Main Points

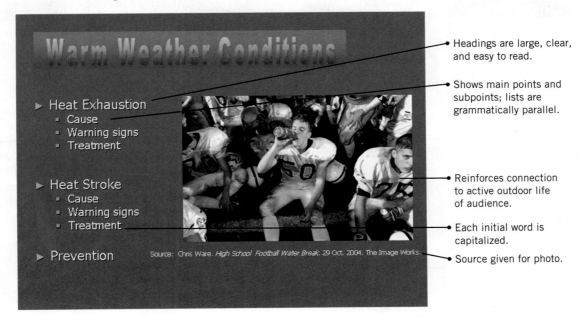

Headings are large, clear, and easy to read.

Shows main points and subpoints; lists are grammatically parallel.

Reinforces connection to active outdoor life of audience.

Each initial word is capitalized.

Source given for photo.

you will make, it's a good idea to provide listeners with a visual and verbal forecast of your main points. The effort to come up with concise, meaningful headings and sub-headings will help you understand exactly what you want to say. And as you improve your own understanding, you will improve that of your listeners as well.

▷ USING VISUAL AIDS

Your analysis of your audience, purpose, and the context of your presentation will help you determine what type of visual aid best emphasizes your main points.

Unless you are presenting in front of a small group, many visuals are best pro-jected onto a screen. This will allow your audience to see the image clearly. Visuals that lend themselves to this treatment (photographs, drawings, graphs, and so on) can be copied onto transparency film, shown via a document projector if copied on paper, or incorporated into presentation software to create a slide.

Many visual aids can also be reproduced as handouts, but giving handouts to your audience ahead of time is usually a distraction. The natural instinct of the audience will be to read ahead, which means they will not be listening to you. If you believe the members of your audience need to keep the material, create a handout that you can give them at the end of your presentation.

Visual Aids

Visual Aid	Example		When to Use
Props or models		For presentation on "How to Choose Running Shoes"	Use for demonstrations and when you want a tangible example. Because props or models tend to be small, they work best for small groups.
Photographs		For presentation on "The Growing Threat of Lyme Disease"	Use compelling images that convey a mood or depict people, objects, or events that you want to make a point about.
Drawings or diagrams		For presentation reporting on common ACL injuries in women athletes	Use to convey detailed information.
Maps		For presentation on "Preemption and the Iraq War"	Use to show geographic locations or to highlight spatial relationships. Depending on level of complexity, maps may need to be projected for legibility.
Screen shots		For presentation on "How to Use the Library's Databases"	Use to convey many different types of information, from tutorials on using the Web to images and illustrations captured from Web sources.

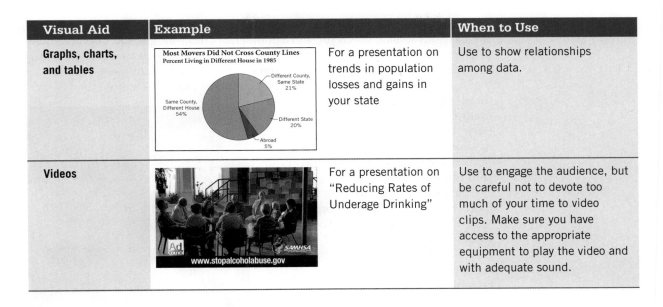

Visual Aid	Example		When to Use
Graphs, charts, and tables		For a presentation on trends in population losses and gains in your state	Use to show relationships among data.
Videos		For a presentation on "Reducing Rates of Underage Drinking"	Use to engage the audience, but be careful not to devote too much of your time to video clips. Make sure you have access to the appropriate equipment to play the video and with adequate sound.

Make sure you find out ahead of time what type of equipment you will have available to you. Depending on the venue and the needs of your presentation, you may need one or more of these types of equipment.

▶ Easel (to display photographs, drawings, charts, or other illustrations)

▶ Table (if required for demonstrations)

▶ Overhead projector for transparencies and screen (or blank wall)

▶ Document projector and screen (or blank wall)

▶ VCR/DVD/CD player

▶ Computer loaded with appropriate presentation software

▶ Internet connection (if you plan to project something from the Internet)

Computer-savvy students find that presentation software is especially attractive since it offers sophisticated design templates and visual effects. For example, you may have seen PowerPoint presentations in which pictures appear, text and graphics move, and one slide flows into another almost magically. Such visual effects can give your oral presentation a polished, professional look, but if they are used too frequently or if too many different effects are used, they will create a chaotic and unprofessional appearance. Special effects are not nearly as important as straightforward visual aids—slides or overhead transparencies—that help listeners see the structure of your message. No matter what type of equipment you use to project your visual aids, make them clear by following the suggestions in this chapter.

Regardless of the format that you use for the visual aids, remember to credit the source of any visuals. When you add a photograph, drawing, graphic, or other visual to slides, transparencies, or other documents to be projected, create a caption under the visual giving credit to the source. You can use a smaller font for the caption so that it does not detract from the primary focus of the page. (See any of David Perry's slides reproduced in this chapter for examples.) Check with the instructor to learn if you should also create a final page or slide of your presentation or separate printed sheet (handout) that lists all of your sources in detail.

On posters, you may want to include more information in your caption and then end with your source. For a document without a separate list of works cited such as a poster, the caption should include complete source information. For example, for a poster presentation on Lyme disease, you might have a photograph of a tick with the caption shown here.

If you create your own charts, graphs, or tables, you should give credit to the source of the information. In this case, your caption might say "Chart created with data from fda.gov."

This tick may harbor the infection that causes Lyme disease. Source: United States, Food and Drug Administration, Bureau of Ticks and Lyme Disease; *Ticks of the Species Ixodes;* 27 June 2007; *FDA Consumer Health Information;* Web; 26 Jan. 2007.

Guidelines for Making Slides or Overheads

▶ **Use large type.** Major headings should be in 40-point type or larger. Subpoints should be 24 to 30 points or larger.

▶ **Be concise.** Capture the gist of each main point in as few words as possible, without becoming so cryptic that your audience cannot figure out what you are saying.

▶ **Use brief bulleted or numbered points rather than long blocks of text.** Items in a list should be grammatically parallel.

▶ **Think about the room where you will be presenting.** Use a light background and dark type if your presentation will take place in a darkened room; use a dark background and light type if the room will be well lit.

▶ **Avoid choosing overly complex design templates that come with presentation software.** Work with designs that complement your subject and do not distract the audience.

▶ **Choose visuals that are easy to read when projected.** For graphs and other complex visuals, make labels and other text large enough for the audience to read.

▶ **Add information about sources for your visuals.** Source information can be in 12-point type.

▶ **Take into account the size of your audience.** For example, if you are presenting to a small group in a conference room, a poster or flip chart may be more appropriate than a projected presentation.

Elaborating on Visual Aids

Few things are more boring or ineffective than oral presentations in which speakers simply read the words that appear on their overheads or slides. Think of your visual aids simply as a way to present the framework of what you have to say. Your job as a speaker is to flesh out this framework, engaging your listeners' interest and creating an appropriate voice. In making an oral presentation, it is especially important to elaborate on your points with compelling, credible details—facts, examples, stories, statistics, or quotes. Many of the strategies discussed under Developing Your Ideas in Chapters 2 through 7 will be useful as you think of ways to elaborate on the main points of your oral presentation. Here are several suggestions that may be helpful.

▶ **Look for details that are likely to be meaningful to your listeners.** It is especially important when dealing with highly subjective or emotional subjects to choose details that make sense to your audience. For example, a presentation on why television is bad for kids might include statistics that link hours of viewing time to bad grades.

▶ **Choose details that relate clearly to your listeners' view of the world, either confirming or dramatically changing that view.** In David's presentation, he did not try to discourage his audience from valuing an active outdoor life. Rather, he focused on staying safe and healthy while enjoying the outdoors.

▶ **Create memorable conflicts or contrasts.** For one supporting point, David included a photograph of an ambulance to drive home the seriousness of heat stroke. This image was in sharp contrast with images of healthy, active people shown in other slides.

▶ **Present the opinion or experience of someone who is likely to have a high degree of credibility for your audience.** David incorporated two videos into his presentation at the points where he discussed the warning signs of heat exhaustion and of heat stroke. He believed the videos, depicting real athletes suffering from these afflictions, would offer evidence his audience would find credible.

▶ **Tell a story about someone whose experience typifies the subject you are discussing.** David began his presentation with a story about an athlete who had recently died from heat stroke.

When you have a wonderful anecdote or a powerful array of statistics, make sure your listeners can see how that information connects to a key point in your presentation.

Especially when inexperienced speakers know a lot about their subject, they often get so involved in presenting details that they and their listeners lose sight of the larger points. In some situations, usually when listeners are very familiar with the topic being discussed, they have little difficulty seeing the connection between a detail and the larger point. But you cannot always count on this. In terms of making the connection between details and key points, follow the guideline "When in doubt, spell it out."

▷ TALKING TO YOUR LISTENERS

No matter how anxious you feel about talking in front of a large group, try to give your listeners the feeling that you see them not as a terrifying sea of faces but as individuals who have some of the same feelings, values, interests, and needs that you have. In a conversational voice, talk to your audience as if you were talking one-on-one with individual listeners. This is not to say you should talk to all audiences as though you were conversing informally with your best friend. Obviously, some situations require you to be more formal. But in general, talk directly to—better yet, with—your listeners using the following guidelines.

▶ **Use personal pronouns with care.** Pronouns such as *I, we,* and *you* personalize your presentation and are almost always appropriate. However, be careful not to use *you* in a directive or critical sense; most audiences do not respond well to being told what to do.

▶ **Use conversational sentence fragments, but sparingly.** In informal conversations, people don't always speak in complete sentences. However, too many fragments make a presentation sound choppy, so use them only when you need to for emphasis.

▶ **Ask questions, but don't depend on the audience for answers.** To avoid long, uncomfortable periods of silence, ask a question listeners themselves might be prompted to ask and then provide a thoughtful answer.

{ Exercise } **Analyzing Oral Presentations**

   Observe a presentation (note that campus lectures are forms of presentation) and take notes. How does the speaker introduce the topic and use forecasting language to signal what is to come? How effective are the visuals used in the presentation? How does the speaker's voice (including tone, word choice, level of formality) affect your response to the presentation? How effective is the conclusion? Write a page or two analyzing the effectiveness of the presentation and bring your analysis to class to report your findings. ■

▷ FINISHING STRONG

This sort of conclusion is inappropriate and ineffective: "So . . . umm . . . that's about all I have to say." It certainly does not do justice to all the hard work you put into making your presentation engaging and informative. The chapters in Part 1 of this book include lists of strategies writers have used in concluding their work. Chances are that one or more of these strategies will be appropriate for your oral presentation. In particular, here are several strategies that are widely used in oral presentations.

▶ **Mention the implications of what you have just said.** Make sure listeners understand either the positive or the negative consequences of the situation you have described in your presentation.

▶ **Summarize your main arguments and conclude by restating your thesis.** Readers can always go back and review a written text. But in an oral presentation it is a good idea to remind listeners of the key points you have made and end by reiterating your thesis in a powerful or memorable way.

▶ **Frame your presentation.** In your conclusion, come back to something (a person, an idea, a set of statistics) with which you began your talk.

David used all of these strategies during his presentation's conclusion. To reinforce his final remarks, he used a slide that focused on how to prevent heat exhaustion and heat stroke. His concluding remarks elaborated on these points, reminding his audience of the crucial facts about heat exhaustion and heat stroke as he discussed in greater detail the various strategies for prevention. In closing, he referred back to the story that he opened his presentation with about the high school football player who had succumbed to heat stroke.

▷ FREQUENTLY ASKED QUESTIONS ABOUT DELIVERY

If you are saying something thoughtful and interesting, most audiences will forgive you if you sometimes fail to make eye contact or if your posture is less than perfect. But still, if you have invested time and effort in preparing thoroughly, you might as well do justice to all of your hard work by making a presentation that is as polished and effective as possible. Following are some of the most frequently asked questions about delivering a presentation.

Overcoming Nervousness

Making an oral presentation scares me to death. How do I get over being so nervous? You never get over being nervous—not if you are like most people. Even when the best public speakers stand in front of a group, they often have nervous reactions:

Their pulse rate may be high, their hands may be clammy, they may feel queasy. Rest assured that you are not alone in being nervous.

So other people get nervous too. How does knowing that help me?
You can begin conquering your anxiety by accepting the fact that you may be nervous. Indeed, being nervous does not mean that you are a bad speaker or that you are doomed to failure. If others can feel the same anxiety you do and still make effective oral presentations, so can you. Use the adrenaline to your advantage just as professionals do to avoid presentations that are listless, flat, and boring.

Okay, I'm resigned to being nervous. Isn't there anything else I can do about my nervousness?

▶ **As you are waiting for your turn to speak, practice breathing.** Take a deep breath and exhale slowly, counting silently as you do so. This will help your voice sound stronger and more confident (one reason people's voices sound weak or shaky is that they are taking quick, shallow breaths rather than breathing deeply). Deep breaths will also calm your nerves and give you something to think about other than how nervous you are.

▶ **While you are speaking, concentrate on what you are saying.** Anxiety can easily lead your mind in all sorts of irrelevant and harmful directions. Instead of letting your mind wander, focus on what you are saying. Remember your main points (your visual aids should help) and focus on making sure the listeners see how one main point leads to another.

▶ **Before—*long before*—the day of your presentation, rehearse.** Practice your presentation aloud until you get to the point where you can glance briefly at a visual aid and elaborate on it using quotes, statistics, facts, examples, or stories. Ideally, you should deliver the beginning and concluding sections without looking at any notes or slides. In this way, you will be able to make good eye contact with the audience and express your points clearly and emphatically. If possible, make a videotape of your rehearsal or practice in front of a friend. When viewing the video, consider such questions as these.

- Do the elaborations clearly relate to the phrases I have on my overheads or slides? (If not, change the elaboration, change the overhead or slide, or change both.)

- Are there places where I rush through key points? Do I pause to emphasize certain comments?

- Do my gestures help emphasize my key points, or am I making random, nervous movements?

Careful rehearsal won't eliminate all feelings of nervousness, but it will let you tell yourself that all you need to do when you stand up to speak is what you were doing all along in rehearsal.

Using Scripts and Visual Aids

In preparing my presentation, should I write out everything I am going to say and then read what I have written?
This is a point on which experienced speakers have different perspectives. See if one of the approaches from the authors of this textbook makes sense for you.

{ **Susan Katz** } When I was in high school, I did a lot of public speaking—but it was always the type where students competed in presenting a famous speech. In other words, I was almost always presenting something I had memorized, rarely something I had written myself. Perhaps that experience spoiled me. If I write out my presentation ahead of time, I feel I have to memorize the speech and present it word for word. I actually get more nervous, and the end result is often awkward and stilted. In the kind of public speaking I have done in my professional life—as an advertising executive and now as a college professor—I prefer to make presentations that sound more spontaneous. I never write out my whole presentation. But I very carefully write out my major and minor points. Actually, I write and rewrite those points until each one clearly and succinctly says exactly what I want to say. Then I practice each presentation aloud from beginning to end at least ten times (and sometimes many more than that). ■

{ **Lee Odell** } At this stage of my career, I do essentially what Susan does. But early on, I would write things out. I'd try to write them exactly the way I would say them if I were talking with an individual instead of addressing a large group. Then I'd practice reading what I had written until I could make my presentation sound as spontaneous as if I were working from notes. This might not have been the best way to do things, but I found that if I relied solely on notes, I would spend a lot of time worrying that I might forget to say something or that what I thought I had to say wasn't as good as I imagined it was. By writing things out, I could be confident that I actually had something worthwhile to say and that I wouldn't be likely to forget to say it while making my presentation. ■

Which should I use—overhead transparencies or presentation software slides?
Use the technology with which you are most comfortable. Overhead transparencies are a better choice if you are uncomfortable with PowerPoint software or projectors. The last thing you need is to worry about a technical glitch.

If you decide to use presentation software, be careful not to get carried away with the technology. *Keep things simple.* If you include a picture or chart, make sure it clearly relates to a point you want the listeners to remember. For more on using slides and overheads, see pages 737–42 of this chapter.

Being Aware of Body Language and Eye Contact

People say that I should stand up straight, keep my hands at my sides, and avoid moving around. How important is this?

It's fairly important. You don't want your body language (posture and gestures) to betray any nervousness. When people are nervous, they tend to gesture and move around abruptly. However, you probably can't—and shouldn't—stand completely still with your hands at your sides. As you do more presentations, you will find a style that suits your personality and ways of speaking. The main thing to remember is that you want to project a sense of confidence and enthusiasm.

▶ **Stand with your feet slightly apart, with most of your weight toward the balls of your feet.** Place one foot a few inches in front of the other. This gives you a stable base and suggests subtly enthusiasm toward your audience.

▶ **Stand straight with your chest up, your shoulders back, and your weight evenly distributed on both legs.** Make your body give the impression that you believe you are saying something important.

▶ **Keep your hands and body relatively still.** The key word here is *relatively*. It is perfectly all right to gesture, to shift your weight, even to move about a little. The important thing is to make sure that when you gesture or move, your actions emphasize the points you are making. Above all, don't move randomly.

▶ **Be especially careful with your hands.** Don't let them twitch. If you need something to do with them, consider holding some note cards in one hand, keeping them at a level where you can easily glance down and read them—but not so high that they cut off your view of your listeners. (If you do use note cards, make sure that the print is large and legible.)

How important is eye contact?

Eye contact is very important, at least in most Western cultures. In some Asian societies, it is considered rude to look people directly in the eye. But in Western cultures, your willingness to make eye contact with your audience indicates that you are honest and sincere.

How do I make eye contact with an entire group of people?

Start by looking somewhere toward the middle of the group, preferably with a relaxed expression on your face. As you talk, look toward individuals or small groups of individuals in different parts of the room. You shouldn't focus exclusively on one person or one part of the room, nor should you let your gaze swing mechanically back and forth across the group. Make a statement to one person or small group, and then shift your focus to another small group or individual. Think of eye contact as a form of nonverbal punctuation. When you come to a pause make eye contact with a different part of the audience. This will let listeners feel you are talking to them individually as well as collectively. It will also give you a way to emphasize key points.

But what if the room is dark because I am using presentation software such as PowerPoint? How can I make eye contact if I can't see clearly?

You might not be able to see your listeners, but they can see you. If you don't look in their direction, they will get the impression that you aren't very interested in communicating with them. Follow the procedures suggested above, even if you focus only on different areas of the room rather than on individual listeners.

▷ GROUP PRESENTATIONS

All of the advice in this chapter about structuring your presentation, creating and using visual aids, and delivering your presentation are just as valid for a group presentation as for an individual one. However, there are some additional considerations to think about when you are asked to make a group presentation.

- ▶ **Choose a leader.** Every group needs someone to keep all members focused on the task, to ensure that individuals are meeting their obligations, and to make sure that the final product is coherent.

- ▶ **Choose a topic and make an outline.** Brainstorm together to decide on a topic and then make an outline of all aspects of the topic that you want to cover.

- ▶ **Assign tasks.** Find out if anyone has expertise in creating visual aids, doing research, or writing scripts. Make a list of all the tasks that have to be done and decide who is going to do each task and when it should be done. You may want to assign a team member to modify the timeline shown in Chapter 10 (p. 560).

- ▶ **Talk to each other.** You can communicate in person, by phone, by e-mail, or through a discussion board—but be sure you communicate! If a group member is having trouble finishing his or her assigned task, you want to make sure you know about it well in advance and, as a group, figure out how to handle the problem.

- ▶ **Decide on your visual aids.** Will you use presentation software? Does everyone know how to use it? Choose one person to create a few samples of how the presentation might look and decide on one model. All slides don't need to be identical, but they should be coordinated in color and format.

- ▶ **Introduce one another during the presentation.** One person should introduce the group and the topic and forecast the main points that will be covered in the presentation. He or she should then introduce the next person. This transition can be short and simple, something like, "Now that I've given you an overview of our presentation on sustainable living, Jessica will provide you with additional details about earth-friendly products."

- ▶ **Take turns speaking.** Depending on the size of the group and the length of the presentation, you may each speak just once, or you may rotate among the group members. Make sure that each person has an opportunity to demonstrate his or her speaking abilities.

- ▶ **Practice your presentation together—several times!** The more you practice, the better you will look and sound. Make sure everyone in the group knows how to run any equipment and has a copy of the entire script, just in case.

Glossary of Visual and Rhetorical Terms

alignment in *layout* and *design*, the way in which text and *visual elements* are lined up on a page or screen. They might be lined up along the left margin (left-only justified), along the right margin (right-only justified), along both margins (fully justified), or in the center (centered or center-justified). See Chapter 9. See also *format*.

analogy strategy for developing a piece of writing in which the writer explains an unfamiliar thing by comparing it to a more familiar thing; useful for explaining complex ideas or objects. For example, "Hacker. Dropout. CEO." (Chapter 3) uses the analogy of Mark Zuckerberg's life as being like a movie script to emphasize that his life thus far has been "an adventure with unexpected, sometimes harrowing, moments that has turned out better than anyone might have predicted." See also *figure of speech*.

analyze, analysis to break a subject down into component parts in order to examine it in depth (analyze); a strategy for developing a piece of writing that examines the parts that make up a subject (analysis). See also *critical thinking*.

anecdote a short *narrative* (story or joke), usually based on personal experience, that provides support for a *claim*.

appeal a strategy used by writers for persuading readers or listeners to agree with the writers' opinion or *claim*. The three appeals most commonly used are ethical (*You should agree with me because I'm trustworthy*), logical (*You should agree with me because I'm reasonable*), and emotional (*You should agree with me because of how this makes you feel*). See Chapter 5.

argument the presentation of a *thesis* (*point of view*) regarding a particular issue, offering *reasons* and *evidence* in order to be persuasive. See Chapter 5.

assumption a belief or an opinion whose truth is taken for granted. Assumptions, which writers may state or imply and with which they may expect most or all readers to agree, affect both the writers' choices and the readers' reactions to the text. See also *critical thinking, reasons*.

audience the intended readers (viewers or listeners) of a written, visual, or auditory work. A primary audience includes those who will act or make decisions based on the information presented. A secondary audience includes those who will be affected by the information but will not directly act or make decisions based on it. See also *stakeholder*.

authority an expert who provides knowledge that lends credibility to a *claim*.

balance in *layout* and *design*, the principle by which text and *graphic elements* are evenly or harmoniously distributed on the page or screen. See Chapter 9. See also *format*.

banner a graphics-based Web advertising display space or unit; often referred to as a banner ad. Standard full-size banner is 468 pixels wide by 60 pixels tall.

bias a perspective based on a subjective or personal *point of view*, often without regard for opposing points of view. Bias can result in a lack of credibility for the writer.

blank space See *white space*.

blog an electronic journal or diary published online; short for "Web log." See Chapter 17.

bold, boldface a typographical highlighting technique whereby letters or lines are made heavier and darker than normal type to achieve emphasis through visual prominence. This is **boldface** type. See Chapter 9.

brainstorming an idea-generating technique that involves a writer compiling any and all ideas that come to mind concerning a subject without judging the value of the ideas. See also *exploratory writing, freewriting*.

bullet a marker or symbol used to denote a listed item. This is a standard bullet: •.

caption a short description or explanation of an *image* or other *visual element*, usually set alongside or underneath, that gives information about the image or element. See Chapter 9.

cause and effect a strategy for developing a piece of writing that focuses on why something happened or demonstrates the influence of one event on another. The effect is the consequence of the cause. When using this strategy, the writer must establish a chain of logic and *evidence* to show the relationship between the event and its cause or outcome. For example, "Stripped for Parts" (Chapter 2) describes the chemical changes (the effects) that occur within the human body in the first few moments after death (the cause).

chart a graphic element that helps readers compare and contrast data by means of a combination of columns and rows, images, and text. See also *graphics, line graph, pictogram, pie chart.*

chunking a way of clustering sections of text by visually separating those sections that go together (chunks) from other parts of the text; can be achieved by the use of *headings,* indentation, or *white space.* See Chapter 9. See also *balance, sidebar.*

claim a statement or proposition that serves as the foundation for an *argument;* also called an argumentative *thesis.*

classification a strategy for organizing information or ideas; can entail grouping related things into categories or dividing ideas, objects, or events into categories. For example, in the evaluation of "Ground Zero at RPI" (Chapter 6), the author evaluates the concert venue based on four main *criteria* (equipment, acoustics, audience, and convenience). Each of these categories is further divided into relevant subcategories, such as the topics of quality, versatility, personnel, or equipment. See also *division.*

color design element that draws a reader's eye; useful for adding emphasis and interest to a page or screen. See Chapter 9.

column the vertical space in a grid or table or items aligned in that vertical space. (The horizontal space in a grid or table is called a "row.") See Chapter 9.

common ground shared experiences, perspectives, interests, or goals that serve a writer and an audience as a platform for mutual understanding. Identifying common ground enables writers to produce texts that will engage readers. For example, Margaret Tomeo opens her report on ACL injuries (Chapter 4) with an anecdote that would engage her audience of women athletes.

comparison a strategy that highlights ways two or more things are similar (or different). Writers can use comparison to organize a text in a variety of ways:

Point by point: The writer moves back and forth between the items being compared. For example, in "Popcorn: Which Kernels Are King?" (Chapter 6), the article presents a point-by-point comparison between several different brands of popcorn, discussing details such as the amounts of fat and sodium, cost, cooking method, and so on.

Block structure: The writer discusses all the points related to one item and then all the points related to another item. For example, in "Ticket to the Top" (Chapter 7), the authors first describe all the problems with the current system for handling the sale of tickets to hockey games and then describe the benefits of a proposed new system.

Similarities: The writer focuses on features that the items have in common. For example, in "Internet Encyclopedias Go Head to Head" (Chapter 6), the author compares the accuracy of science articles in Wikipedia and the Encyclopedia Britannica by focusing on similarities in results of recent research.

Contrast: The writer focuses on dissimilarities between the items. See, for example, Sarah Vowell's comparison of her own reaction to her father's fondness for guns with that of her twin sister ("Shooting Dad," Chapter 2).

composition in *design,* the way in which an *image* is planned and organized to draw attention to certain areas or to evoke specific emotions in the viewer. See, for example, the analysis of the photographs in "Theatre Geek" (p. 51). See also *viewing angle.*

concession an acknowledgment of a valid point in a *counterargument,* often in order to establish the writer's *credibility* and strengthen other *claims.* For example, in "Drop in the Bucket" (Chapter 5), the author concedes that the need to rebuild New Orleans after Hurricane Katrina has led to some innovative approaches to housing. However, the author then continues by describing bureaucratic red tape and seemingly foolish decisions that bolster her primary *argument* that building efforts are insufficient to meet need. See also *refutation.*

conflict a sense of dissonance or disagreement, often created purposefully by the writer as a way to engage readers. For example, the title of "Shooting Dad" (Chapter 2) suggests conflict because it can be read two ways, with the word *shooting* serving as either a verb or an adjective. The opening sentences further the sense of conflict by using phrases such as *a house divided* and describing the author's home as a Civil War battleground.

consequence a result brought about by a cause or by particular conditions. See also *cause and effect.*

consistency in *design,* a way of making pages appear to belong to the same document by making every page conform to the same basic format or grid. See Chapter 9.

context the situation within which a text exists. Features of context include the *audience* for whom the text is written and designed and the writer's purposes in producing it. See also *rhetorical situation.*

contrast in *design*, the variations in appearance that enhance readability and add visual interest to a text; can be achieved by using different *colors, typefaces,* amounts of *white space, images,* and so forth. See Chapter 9 for more on visual contrast. See *comparison* for a discussion of contrast as a method of organizing a text.

counterargument a persuasive strategy by which a writer anticipates readers' objections and provides *evidence* to overcome those objections. By demonstrating fairness to counterarguments, a writer can establish *credibility*. See also *concession, refutation.*

credibility the degree to which a writer and his or her information can be believed or trusted, based on specific *evidence*. A credibility analysis involves investigating the veracity of the evidence used in an *argument*. See Chapter 5.

criteria standards used to evaluate an *argument*, product, service, statement, behavior, and so forth. Explicit criteria are stated outright; implicit criteria are suggested or stated indirectly. See Chapter 6.

critical thinking examining a text or an idea carefully to consider its *context*, its *credibility*, the amount and type of *evidence* in support of any *claim* it makes, and the validity of its *assumptions*. Critical thinking allows reasoned judgments about the text or idea. See also *analyze, argument, bias.*

critique an in-depth evaluation of a person's work or idea.

deductive reasoning assuming a general principle and then applying it to a particular case. For example, if you like Mexican food, you will be more likely to try a new Mexican restaurant because you can assume that you will find something appealing on the menu.

definition as a strategy for developing an essay, an explanation of a thing, concept, or word by listing one or more features particular to it that distinguish it from another. For example, "Seeing Is Not Believing" (Chapter 4) defines the term *digital watermark* by describing its characteristics and components. Conversely, a definition may explain what something is not: *An evergreen is a tree that does not lose its leaves in autumn.*

delivery the manner in which an oral presentation is made to the audience; includes type of presentation (memorized, extemporaneous, spontaneous, or scripted) and performance-related factors (pronunciation, enunciation, speed, pitch, and volume). See Chapter 18.

description a method of development that explains or illustrates a place, person, event, or thing so that readers can create a mental image of it. Descriptions use nouns, adjectives, and adverbs to name parts and provide distinctive details. For example, "Stripped for Parts" (Chapter 2) includes this vivid description: *His face is slack but flush, he breathes steadily, and his heart beats like a clock, despite the fact that his lungs have recently begun to leak fluid.*

design the way in which a text is visually arranged, both logically and aesthetically. Five essential principles of design are *alignment, chunking, contrast, consistency,* and *tension.* See Chapter 9.

discussion board See *discussion forum.*

discussion forum an electronic forum typically used in academic settings to encourage student participation. Also called "discussion board" or "message board." See Chapter 9.

discussion list an e-mail list with limited membership, typically used to send simultaneous messages to all members of a class or other group.

division a strategy for organizing information or ideas in which items or groups of items are placed into categories. See also *classification.*

evidence support that proves the validity of a *claim*; may include facts, authoritative opinions, data, quotations, paraphrased text, statistics, statements that enhance the writer's *credibility*, testimony, and so forth. See Chapter 5.

example a strategy for developing a piece of writing by giving instances to clarify something. "ACL: The Curse of Women Athletes" (Chapter 4) gives examples of ways a woman's leg structure differs from a man's to illustrate why women are more likely than men to suffer an ACL tear.

exploratory writing a *brainstorming* technique in which the writer refines ideas and plans what to include in a text.

figure of speech descriptive words or phrases used to emphasize the thing described, to create a vivid image in a reader's mind, or to make a difficult concept clearer. One common figure of speech is a simile, in which something is compared to something else using the word *like* or *as*. An example of a simile appears in "ACL: The Curse of Women Athletes" (Chapter 4), when the action of a woman's femur is compared to a guillotine cutting the ACL (paragraph 8). Another common figure of speech is a metaphor, in which something is said to be something else. An example of a metaphor appears in "SUVs Belong in Car Ads Only" (Chapter 5), in which sport utility vehicles are called "bullies of the highway" (paragraph 4). See also *analogy.*

font a set of type in a particular size and style. See Chapter 9. See also *typeface.*

forecasting term a word or phrase that appears near the beginning of a section of text and indicates the topic to be covered.

format the plan or design of a page or screen; includes the arrangement of textual elements and *visual elements* on the page or screen. See Chapter 9. See also *alignment, balance.*

freewriting a *brainstorming* technique that calls for the writer to concentrate on a single topic or issue, writing down every idea that comes to mind.

generalize to draw a conclusion about a group based on a sample of its members. If the sample size is large enough and if the members are truly representative of the group, a generalization can be a useful way to understand quantitative data; however, an unrepresentative sample or a sample that is too small can lead to mistaken assumptions about the characteristics of individual people, things, or ideas.

graphics *visual elements* used by the writer to present, enhance, or dramatize the message in print and electronic page design. Such elements include line drawings, bullets, photographs, charts, graphs, tables, icons, logos, banners, and the like. See Chapter 9.

heading a word or phrase used to guide readers to particular content in a text. See Chapter 9. See also *subheading.*

home page the introductory or core page of a Web site. See Chapter 9.

icon a symbol or an image that visually represents the ideas or activities to which it refers.

image in *design,* a graphic representation of a person, thing, idea, or action; in writing, a figure of speech. See Chapter 9.

inductive reasoning making a generalization based on specific instances. For example, after hearing a few songs from a new band, you may be able to make a decision about purchasing its CD.

inset box a section of text or *visual element,* often set off by lines or a box, inserted into the main text. For example, see "The Record Industry's Slow Fade" (Chapter 4). See also *chunking, sidebar, text wrap.*

italic a typographical highlighting technique that angles letters to the right to give visual emphasis. This is *italic* type.

layout the arrangement and design of text and *visual elements* in a print or electronic document. See Chapter 9.

leading See *line spacing.*

line graph a chart used to illustrate disparities in numerical data, with lines visually representing the numbers plotted on the chart. Best used to denote changes over time. See Chapter 9.

line spacing the amount of *white space,* or "leading," between lines of text. See Chapter 9.

link a highlighted word, phrase, or other visual cue on a Web page that brings the user to another area on the same Web page, another page on the same Web site, or a different Web site. Also called "hyperlink." See Chapter 9.

medium a written, auditory, or visual means of distributing information, such as a newspaper, magazine, Internet site, television, and so forth; the plural form is "media."

message board See *discussion forum.*

MUVE a computer-simulated environment in which individuals can interact with one another online through the use of "avatars," the graphic representation of a user; stands for "multi-user virtual environment." Second Life is a popular MUVE.

narrative information or a story presented with plot, setting, characterization, and sequence of events, often involving some type of conflict. Particularly useful in profiles, but often used in other texts to engage or maintain readers' interest. See Chapter 3.

navigation aid the element of a print or an electronic document that helps readers get from one place to another in the text or find specific information within the text; may include tables of contents, headers, footers, running heads, navigation bars, menus, links, indexes, and image maps. See Chapter 9.

objection a point in opposition to a writer's *claim.* See Chapter 5. See also *concession, refutation.*

objectivity perspective and reasoning based on facts rather than on personal beliefs or prejudices. See also *critical thinking, subjectivity.*

paraphrase a restatement that conveys the original meaning of the key points of an original text in roughly the same number of words; requires documentation. See Chapter 12.

perspective the way in which an individual relates to an *image*, object, or idea. For example, Ellen Goodman's experience has given her a negative perspective on SUVs (Chapter 5). See also *point of view*. For a definition of visual perspective, see *viewing angle*.

persuasion a strategy for developing a piece of writing that aims to influence another person, using *argument* and *evidence*, toward a particular *point of view*. See Chapter 5.

pictograph a visual, such as a chart or graph, that uses *icons* as elements to display information.

picture box a four-sided border used to contain an *image*.

pie chart a specialized graph, shaped like a circle or pie, that emphasizes an important relationship among percentages of like elements. See Chapter 9. See also *graphics*.

pixel one of the many tiny dots that make up a computer screen *image*; comes from the phrase "picture element."

plagiarism using someone else's ideas verbally and/or visually without giving credit to the original source.

point of view the position from which a writer evaluates a subject. See also *perspective*.

presentation software software, such as Microsoft Power-Point, that is used to prepare and present text- or graphics-based information to accompany oral presentations.

principle a fundamental or widely recognized rule: *Appropriate amounts of vitamins are essential for a healthy body.*

pull quote a short selection of relevant text that a writer copies from a source document and places near his or her original text to draw attention to an important point; usually visually distinguished by *font* size or other *typeface* treatment, position, or presentation (such as placing within an *inset box* or separating with *bold* lines). See Chapter 9.

purpose what the writer hopes to accomplish by producing a particular text for a particular *audience* in given circumstances. See also *context*.

qualifier wording that restricts the *claims* in an *argument*, decreasing the likelihood that the claims will be too extreme and thus protecting the writer's credibility. Common qualifiers include the words *some, many, may, possibly, often,* and *usually*: <u>Many</u> girls want to play football. Leaves are <u>usually</u> green. <u>Some</u> textbooks have companion Web sites.

qualitative data descriptive notes and observations about individual actions, events, or responses; typically drawn from interviews, open-ended survey questions, and observations. Cannot be used to prove theory but can add support, explore ideas, or generate questions; also adds the type of detail that makes writing more interesting or more believable. For example, "Stripped for Parts" (Chapter 2) relies on personal observation and interviews to describe aspects of organ donation. See Chapter 11.

quantitative data information that can be measured objectively in numbers or specific amounts. Can be persuasive, as most people are likely to trust such information. For example, see the statistical data in "What Decreased Crime?" (Chapter 5).

quotation a portion of text copied verbatim (without alteration); must appear within quotation marks, and the source must be acknowledged. See Chapter 12. See also *plagiarism*.

reasons information that supports an *argument* by linking *claims* and *evidence*. For example, Ellen Goodman makes the claim that SUVs belong in car ads only (Chapter 5). Her evidence includes the fact that SUVs cause thousands of deaths every year. The reason that connects the claim and the evidence is that SUVs make driving more dangerous for people in smaller vehicles. See also *warrant*.

rebuttal See *refutation*.

refutation a technique used to discredit an *argument* or a *counterargument* by demonstrating a failure in logic, *evidence*, or reasoning. In "What Decreased Crime?" (Chapter 5), the author presents the argument that the death penalty is not an effective deterrent to violent crime, but then uses evidence to refute that argument. See, for example, paragraphs 6 (objection and refutation), 7 (objection), or 8 and 9 (refutation). See also *concession*.

review draft an early version of a work that enables the writer to determine how effectively he or she has presented information; alternatively, the version of a text reviewed by someone other than the writer before completion.

rhetorical situation the context within which communication takes place, including the writer's *purpose, audience,* and the *circumstances* that give rise to the communication; a problematic situation that can be best resolved through discourse that will persuade individuals to change their beliefs, feelings, understandings, perspectives, or behaviors. See also *context*.

scenario a brief description of a hypothetical or real situation.

sidebar information, often set in a box, that appears alongside or surrounded by the main text on a page or screen. See Chapter 9. See also *chunking, inset box, text wrap.*

stakeholder an individual affected by the information contained in a work or text, either directly or indirectly; a person with some investment in the issue, situation, or person being discussed in a work or text. See also *audience.*

subheading a word or phrase, subordinate to a main *heading,* that identifies the content in a section of text.

subjectivity *perspective* and reasoning based on personal beliefs or views rather than objective facts. See also *critical thinking, objectivity.*

summary shortened or condensed version of material from a longer work; presents the main points of the original text but does not provide all the detail. See Chapter 12.

support See *evidence.*

tension a feeling invoked in readers by a well-designed print or electronic document; determined by the relationship among the text, the *visual elements,* and the *white space* on a given page. See Chapter 9. See also *design.*

text wrap text that flows (wraps) around a *visual element* on a page or screen. See Chapter 9.

thesis the central idea that states the writer's *point of view;* supporting a thesis with *evidence* is integral to a writer's *purpose.* For example, the following is the thesis sentence of "ACL: The Curse of Women Athletes" (Chapter 4): *As the number of women competing in sports continues to increase, understanding the causes of this common injury will enable us to help these athletes to reduce their risk.* See also *claim.*

tone the mood of expression or attitude conveyed by the writer. See also *voice.*

topic sentence a statement that briefly describes the point and the content of a paragraph, usually relating the paragraph to the work's *thesis.*

transition a word or phrase used to indicate relationships between ideas or phrases: *Stephanie saw Diana every time she visited the lab; consequently, Stephanie thought Diana spent most of her time in the lab. In fact, Diana also participated actively in her sorority.*

typeface a family of characters—including letters, numbers, and symbols. Typefaces are usually available in different styles (for example, *italic,* **bold**) and in different sizes (for example, 10-point or 12-point type). See Chapter 9. See also *font.*

viewing angle the vantage point from which an image is presented (for example, the angle from which a photograph is taken or the perspective from which a figure is drawn); can give more or less emphasis to the subject. See, for example, the analysis of the first page of "Hacker. Dropout. CEO." (Chapter 3). See also *composition.*

visual element a graphic feature that complements or enhances text-based information; examples include *color,* lines, photographs, line drawings, *charts, graphics, icons, inset boxes,* or *pull quotes.* See Chapter 9.

voice the aspect of a text that reflects a personality, a stance or set of attitudes, or even the literal sound of a person speaking. Related to *tone.* See Chapter 3.

warrant the underlying *assumption* or *principle* that connects claims and reasons. For example, Ellen Goodman makes the claim that SUVs belong in car ads only (Chapter 5). One of her reasons is that SUVs make driving more dangerous for people in smaller vehicles. The warrant that connects her claim and her reason is that limits should be placed on those things that endanger life. See also *claims, reasons.*

white space the area on a page or screen not occupied by text or *images,* such as margins and other blank space. Used to enhance visual *design* and readability, white space gives emphasis and helps to organize elements in a text. See Chapter 9. See also *balance, chunking.*

wiki an online content management system that allows for collaborative writing, editing, and revising. Wikipedia is the most well-known wiki. See Chapter 17.

(continuation of Acknowledgments from page iv)

Art

2 Collage Photography/Veer. 14 Flirt Photography/Veer. 19 Courtesy of David Perry. 21 Jacket design, Courtesy of Simon & Schuster Inc., published in 2001. Photo © David Levinthal. All rights reserved. 22 Courtesy of Tony Millionaire. 28 (top) Mike Ruiz / *Wired,* © Conde Nast Publications. 28 (bottom) *Wired,* © Conde Nast Publications. 29 Mike Lorrig. 31 Scientific Registry of Transplant Recipients, the Organ Procurement and Transplantation Network. 35 Photos by © Olivier Coret/In Visu/Corbis and © Hans Halberstadt/Corbis. 41 R. Kenton Nelson/*The New Yorker,* © Conde Nast Publications. 42 Chien-Chi Chang/Magnum Photos. 47 Entire book cover [Harper-Perennial rev. edition, 1988, 9780060915414] t/a "Total Eclipse"* from Teaching a Stone To Talk: Expeditions and Encounters by Annie Dillard. Copyright © 1982 by Annie Dillard. Reprinted by permission of HarperCollins Publishers. 52, 53, 54, 55 Courtesy of David Perry. 84 Uppercut/Veer. 89 Michael Elins/Corbis. 91 Used with permission of *Fast Company.* Copyright © 2008. All rights reserved. 91 Michael Elins/Corbis. 93, 95 Jonathan Sprague/Redux Pictures. 99 Jonathan Sprague/Redux Pictures. 105 Jacket cover from *Class Matters* by *The New York Times* and Bill Keller. Copyright © 2005 by Henry Holt and Company, LLC. Reprinted by permission of Henry Holt and Company, LLC. 106 Jim Wilson/*The New York Times/* Redux Pictures. 110 (top) Courtesy of *Wizard Magazine.* All rights reserved. 110 (bottom), 111 Tim Soter. 112 (top) Tim Soter. 112 (bottom) Courtesy of *Wizard Magazine.* All rights reserved. 113 Tim Soter. 117, 118 Naomi Harris. 120 www .danielmarquez.com. 127, 129 Photos courtesy Stephanie Guzik. 162 Image Source/Punchstock. 167 Justin Cederholm. 170, 171, 172 Karjean Levine. 176 Cover photo by Max Vadukul From *Rolling Stone,* June 28, 2007 © Rolling-Stone LLC 2007. All Rights Reserved. Reprinted by Permission. 177 Sales data courtesy Nielsen SoundScan. 177 Revenue figures courtesy IFPI. 177 (top left) © Disney Channel / Courtesy Everett Collection. 177 (top right) Frank Micelotta/ ImageDirect/Getty Images. 177 (bottom) WireImage/Getty Images. 179 BigChampagne / Store figures courtesy of Almighty Institute of Music Retail. 179 (top) Paul McConnell/Getty Images. 179 (bottom) Tim Graffam. 182 Courtesy of Bonnier Corporation. Reprinted with permission. 183 (top left) Courtesy of Worth1000.com. 183 (top right) Justin Cederholm. 183 (middle) Courtesy of Worth1000.com. 183 (middle right) Courtesy of Worth1000.com. 183 (middle right) Suthep Kritsanavarin/OnAsia. 183 (bottom left) Ensign John Gay/US Navy/Time Life Pictures/Getty Images. 183 (bottom middle) Courtesy of Worth1000.com. 183 (bottom right) Hany Farid. 186 (top left) Yann Layma/Getty Images. 186 (middle) AP/Wide World. 186 (bottom left) NASA. 186 (middle) NASA. 186, 187 Hany Farid. 190 (bottom left) Ken Light/Corbis. 190 (bottom middle) © Owen Franken/Corbis. 193 Reprinted with permission. *Discover* magazine, April 2004, Copyright © *Discover* Magazine. All rights reserved. 194, 195, 196, 199 © Jeff West Design. All Rights Reserved. 202 Peter De Seve / *The New Yorker.* © Conde Nast Publications. 203 Illustration by Steve Brodner. Originally published in *The New Yorker.* 211 AP Photo/Nick Wass/Wide World. 212 From "What is the ACL?" *ACL Solutions,* 2002, Medical Internet Solutions, 10 Mar. 2004 http://www.aclsolutions.com/theacl_1.php. 214 From "Stephen Pribut, "Runner's Knee," *Dr. Stephen M. Pribut's Sports Pages,* 22 Jan. 2004, 10 Mar. 2004 http://www.drpribut.com/sports/spknees.html. 248 dream stock/Canopy Photography/Veer. 253 Steve Sack/*Star Tribune* © 2002. 255 (top) © Globe Newspaper Company. 255 (bottom) Washington Post Writers Group. 258 Steve Sack/Star Tribune © 2002. 260 Courtesy of *Sierra Magazine.* Reprinted with permission. 261 Lori Eanes. 265 Courtesy of *Metropolis* Magazine. Reprinted with permission. 269 Book cover from *Freakonomics* by Steven D. Levitt and Stephen J. Dubner. Copyright © 2005 by Steven D. Levitt and Stephen J. Dubner. Reprinted by permission of HarperCollins Publishers. 274, 276 Courtesy of Regnery Publishing, Inc. Reprinted by permission. 285 Nigel Cox. 286, 287, 289, 290, 291, 294 Typography: Joe Zeff Design, Inc. 292 Nigel Cox. 294 (left

three images) The Granger Collection. 294 (fourth from left) Courtesy of Nestle Waters N.A. 294 (fifth from left) Gary Taxali. 294 (fourth from right) Brian Harris. 294 (third from right) Art Resource, NY. 294 (second from right) Brian Harris. 294 (right) Courtesy of Elkay Manufacturing Company. 295 Typography: Joe Zeff Design, Inc. 295 (left) James Baigrie/Getty Images. 295 (second from left) Courtesy of Nestle Waters N.A. 295 (third from left) Mediacolor/Alamy. 295 (fourth from left) Courtesy of Pepsi Corp. 295 (fifth from left) Courtesy of Coca-Cola Corp. 295 (third, fourth from right) Courtesy of Nestle Waters N.A. 295 (second from right) George Rose/Getty Images. 295 (right) Thinkstock/Jupiter Images. 296, 299 Typography: Joe Zeff Design, Inc. 340 Cat Gwynn/Corbis/Veer. 345 Courtesy of Consumers Union/Consumer Reports. 347 Reprinted by permission from Macmillan Publishers Ltd: *Nature* 438, 7070, 889–1050 (15 December 2005). © 2005. 348 AP Photo/Michael Probst/Wide World. 349 D. I. Franke/ Wikimedia FDN. 349 Courtesy of Wikimedia. 352, 353 Photos courtesy of Consumers Union/Consumer Reports. Copyright © 2007 by Consumers Union of U.S., Inc. 356 From *Newsweek,* January 19, 1999, © 1999 Newsweek, Inc. All rights reserved. 356 Courtesy Seth Shostak. 359, 360, 361 Patrick Vitarius. 362, 363, 364 © 20th Century Fox. All rights reserved/courtesy Everett Collection. 366 Courtesy of Bonnier Corporation. Reprinted with permission. 366 (left and center) McKenzie Funk. 366 (right) John B. Carnett/*Popular Science* Magazine. 367 (top left and bottom) McKenzie Funk. 367 (top right and center) John B. Carnett/*Popular Science* Magazine. 368 (left and right) John B. Carnett/*Popular Science* Magazine. 368 (center) McKenzie Funk. 369 John B. Carnett/*Popular Science* Magazine. 370 McKenzie Funk. 371 John B. Carnett/*Popular Science* Magazine. 372, 373 McKenzie Funk. 377 Photo by Caitlin Piette. 378 Photo by Jesse Newman. 378, 379 Photos by Zane Van Dusen. 414 © Richard M. Abarno/Corbis. 419 Reza Estakhrian/Getty Images. 419 George Ruhe/BLOOMBERG NEWS/Landov. 421 From *Newsweek,* September 17, 2007, © 2007 Newsweek, Inc. All rights reserved. Photo by Chip Somodevilla/Getty Images. 421 Reza Estakhrian/Getty Images. 423 George Ruhe/BLOOMBERG NEWS /Landov. 426 Courtesy of *Sierra Magazine.* Reprinted with permission. 427, 428 © Leigh Wells. 432 © Michael S. Yamashita/Corbis. 438 From *The New York Times,* July 14, 2008. © 2008. The New York Times. All rights reserved. Used by permission and protected by the Copyright Laws of the United States. The printing, copying, redistribution, or retransmission of the Material without express written permission is prohibited. 441 *Criminal Justice Ethics,* Volume 17, Number 1 [Winter/Spring 1998] Cover Page. Reprinted by permission of The Institute for Criminal Justice Ethics, 555 West 57th Street, Suite 607, New York, NY, 10019-1029. 445 Photographs copyright © 2006, Nicholas R. Markham. 448 Jeff Topping/*The New York Times*/Redux. 451 Courtesy of Ticketmaster.com. 488 Rainer Holz/Cusp Photography/Veer. 493, 497 Edward Hopper, Nighthawks, 1942, Oil on canvas, 84.1 x 152.4 cm, Friends of American Art Collection, 1942.51 Photograph by Robert Hashimoto. Reproduction, The Art Institute of Chicago. 500, 501 © Columbia/courtesy Everett Collection. 505 The Advertising Council, Inc. Reprinted with permission. 508 © Swim Ink 2, LLC/CORBIS. 509 Courtesy of worth1000.com. 510 Arthur Rothstein/Library of Congress/ Getty Images. 511 (right) © Warner Bros./Courtesy Everett Collection. 511 (left) Paramount Classics/Courtesy Everett Collection. 512 The Advertising Council, Inc. Reprinted with permission. 513 From *The New York Times,* June 11, 2006 © 2006. The New York Times. All Rights Reserved. Used by permission and protected by the Copyright Laws of the United States. The printing, copying, redistributing, or retransmission of the Material without express written permission is prohibited. 514 *Time,* Feb. 7, 2000/Getty Images. Illustration by Mark Hess 'Reprinted through the courtesy of the Editors of *Time* Magazine © 2009 Time Inc.' 515 (left) Printed by permission of the Norman Rockwell Family Agency Copyright ©1943 Norman Rockwell Family Entities. Photo by Norman Rockwell Art Collection Trust, Norman Rockwell Museum, Stockbridge, Massachu-

Index

Note: Numbers in **bold** refer to terms included in the Glossary of Visual and Rhetorical Terms.